Semi–Automatic Ontology Development:

Processes and Resources

Maria Teresa Pazienza
University of Roma Tor Vergata, Italy

Armando Stellato
University of Roma Tor Vergata, Italy

Information Science
REFERENCE

Managing Director:	Lindsay Johnston
Senior Editorial Director:	Heather Probst
Book Production Manager:	Sean Woznicki
Development Manager:	Joel Gamon
Development Editor:	Michael Killian
Acquisitions Editor:	Erika Gallagher
Typesetter:	Milan Vracarich, Jr.
Cover Design:	Nick Newcomer, Lisandro Gonzalez

Published in the United States of America by
Information Science Reference (an imprint of IGI Global)
701 E. Chocolate Avenue
Hershey PA 17033
Tel: 717-533-8845
Fax: 717-533-8661
E-mail: cust@igi-global.com
Web site: http://www.igi-global.com

Library of Congress Cataloging-in-Publication Data

Semi-automatic ontology development : processes and resources / Maria Teresa Pazienza and Armando Stellato, editors.
    p. cm.
  Includes bibliographical references and index.
  Summary: "This book includes state-of-the-art research results aimed at the automation of ontology development processes and the reuse of external resources becoming a reality, thus being of interest for a wide and diversified community of users"-- Provided by publisher.
  ISBN 978-1-4666-0188-8 (hardcover) -- ISBN 978-1-4666-0189-5 (ebook) -- ISBN 978-1-4666-0190-1 (print & perpetual access) 1. Semantic Web. 2. Ontologies (Information retrieval) 3. Semantic networks (Information theory) 4. Automatic data collection systems. 5. Knowledge acquisition (Expert systems) I. Pazienza, Maria Teresa. II. Stellato, Armando, 1975-
  TK5105.88815.S468 2012
  006.3'3--dc23
                        2011051816

British Cataloguing in Publication Data
A Cataloguing in Publication record for this book is available from the British Library.

All work contributed to this book is new, previously-unpublished material. The views expressed in this book are those of the authors, but not necessarily of the publisher.

Editorial Advisory Board

Table of Contents

Section 3
Relevant Resources Supporting Ontology Development

Detailed Table of Contents

Section 1
Knowledge Acquisition Systems

Elias Iosif, National Center for Scientific Research (NCSR) "Demokritos", Greece

Georgios Petasis, National Center for Scientific Research (NCSR) "Demokritos", Greece

Vangelis Karkaletsis, National Center for Scientific Research (NCSR) "Demokritos", Greece

The authors present an ontology based information extraction process, which operates in a bootstrapping framework. The novelty of this approach lies in its continuous semantics extraction from textual content in order to evolve the underlying ontology, while the evolved ontology enhances, in turn, the information extraction mechanism.

Davide Eynard, Politecnico di Milano, Italy

Matteo Matteucci, Politecnico di Milano, Italy

Fabio Marfia, Politecnico di Milano, Italy

In this chapter, the authors present a tool for the automatic discovery of basic ontologies—called seed ontologies—starting from a corpus of documents related to a specific domain of knowledge. These seed ontologies are not meant for direct use, but they can be used to bootstrap the knowledge acquisition process by providing a selection of relevant terms and fundamental relationships.

Andreea Diosteanu, Bucharest Academy of Economic Studies, Romania

Armando Stellato, University of Roma Tor Vergata, Italy

Andrea Turbati, University of Roma Tor Vergata, Italy

In this chapter, the authors present Service Oriented Data Acquisition (SODA), a service-deployable open-source platform for retrieving and dynamically aggregating information extraction and knowledge acquisition software components.

Section 2
Resource Adoption and Reuse to Build Ontologies and Semantic Repositories

Ivan Bedini, Alcatel-Lucent Bell Labs, Ireland

Benjamin Nguyen, University of Versailles, France

Christopher Matheus, Alcatel-Lucent Bell Labs, Ireland

Peter F. Patel-Schneider, Alcatel-Lucent Bell Labs, USA

Aidan Boran, Alcatel-Lucent Bell Labs, Ireland

In this chapter, the authors present a set of patterns that enable the automatic transformation from XML Schema into RDF and OWL, enabling the direct use of much XML data in the Semantic Web. The authors focus on a possible logical representation of the first language and present an implementation, including a comparison with related works.

Feten Baccar Ben Amar, University of Sfax, Tunisia

Bilel Gargouri, University of Sfax, Tunisia

Abdelmajid Ben Hamadou, University of Sfax, Tunisia

In this chapter, the authors propose an approach for generating domain ontologies from LMF standardized dictionaries (ISO-24613). It consists, firstly, of deriving the target ontology core systematically from the explicit information of the LMF dictionary structure. Secondly, it aims to enrich such a core, taking advantage of textual sources with guided semantic fields available in the definitions and the examples of lexical entries.

Christian M. Meyer, Technische Universität Darmstadt, Germany

Iryna Gurevych, Technische Universität Darmstadt, Germany

The main objective of this chapter is to introduce Wiktionary, which is a collaborative online dictionary encoding information about words, word senses, and relations between them, as a resource for ontology construction.

Mariana Damova, Ontotext AD, Bulgaria

Atanas Kiryakov, Ontotext AD, Bulgaria

Maurice Grinberg, Ontotext AD, Bulgaria & New Bulgarian University, Bulgaria

Michael K. Bergman, Structured Dynamics, USA

Frédérick Giasson, Structured Dynamics, USA

Kiril Simov, Ontotext AD, Bulgaria & Bulgarian Academy of Sciences, Bulgaria

The chapter introduces the process of design of two upper-level ontologies—PROTON and UMBEL— into reference ontologies and their integration in the so-called Reference Knowledge Stack (RKS). It is argued that RKS is an important step in the efforts of the Linked Open Data (LOD) project to transform the Web into a global data space with diverse real data, available for review and analysis.

Section 3
Relevant Resources Supporting Ontology Development

Chapter 8

Ernesto William De Luca, Berlin Institute of Technology, Germany

In this chapter, the author presents his approach to aggregating and maintaining Multilingual Linked Data. He describes Lexical Resources and Lexical Linked Data, presenting a hybridization research that ports the largest lexical resource, EuroWordNet, to the Linked Open Data cloud, interlinking it with other lexical resources.

Chapter 9

Silvana Hartmann, Technische Universität Darmstadt, Germany
György Szarvas, Technische Universität Darmstadt, Germany & Research Group on Artificial
    Intelligence, Hungarian Academy of Sciences, Hungary
Iryna Gurevych, Technische Universität Darmstadt, Germany

In this chapter, the authors address the extraction of multiword terminology, as multiword terms are very frequent in terminology, but typically poorly represented in standard lexical resources.

Chapter 10

Francesca Fallucchi, University of Rome – Guglielmo Marconi, Italy
Fabio Massimo Zanzotto, University of Rome – Tor Vergata, Italy

Capturing word meaning is one of the challenges of Natural Language Processing (NLP). Formal models of meaning such as ontologies are knowledge repositories used in a variety of applications. To be effectively used, these ontologies have to be large or, at least, adapted to specific domains. The authors' main goal is to contribute practically to the research on ontology learning models by covering different aspects of the task.

Preface

Exploitation of theoretical results in knowledge representation, language standardization by W3C and data publication initiatives such as Linked Open Data have definitively given concreteness to the field of ontology research. In light of these outcomes, ontology development has also found its way, benefiting from years of R&D on dedicated development tools.

However, while basic development and management technologies have reached a wide consensus in both academia and industry, those "more intelligent" aspects focused on how to automate these processes, how to reuse existing resources (from raw text to structured / linguistic resources) to improve existing knowledge, and how to properly interact with different kind of users, are failing to reach industry-standard. Despite interesting and promising results from the area of ontology learning, scientifically proven both on quality and performance of algorithms and on user perspective, there is a daily evidence that "ontologists" are not really exploiting these results, and support from robust and usable tools is quite far from being available.

The next quantum leap in ontology research should thus properly address these high-level aspects: resource reuse (linguistic resources, thesauri etc.), enrichment of contents, networking, support for collaboration between different experts (domain experts, ontologists, engineers, etc.) and knowledge acquisition from text.

This book aims to provide relevant theoretical frameworks and the latest empirical research findings in the ontology development and knowledge acquisition areas. It has been thought and written for researchers willing to find new scientific approaches on knowledge acquisition and management as well as for professionals who want to improve their understanding of these aspects.

The book is organized into three main topics: "Knowledge Acquisition Systems," "Resource Adoption and Reuse to Build Ontologies," and "Semantic Repositories and Relevant Resources Supporting Ontology Development," representing smoothly distinct aspects of Knowledge Acquisition and Evolution. For each of them, we present relevant contributions from researchers and practitioners in the area.

SECTION 1: KNOWLEDGE ACQUISITION SYSTEMS

The first part of this book presents some examples on the current state-of-the-art on systems for automatic knowledge acquisition and ontology development. Different aspects in the realization of such systems, covering methodologies, technological choices, workflow management, and interoperability are being considered under different perspectives and approaches in the first three chapters.

In Chapter 1, "Ontology based Information Extraction under a Bootstrapping Approach," Iosif, Petasis, and Vangelis present a system for acquiring ontological knowledge from multimedia content. The main contributions of their system lies in the combination of machine learning and reasoning approaches, and their bootstrapping framework, where the extraction mechanisms and the evolution of ontology can affect each other in a continuous loop of learn-extract-learn: new acquired data thus feeds the ontology which is evolved over time, and the new entries in the ontology are in turn fed to traditional a IE system, composed of Named Entity Recognizers and Classifiers (NERC) and co-reference processors. This synergic approach is a key feature for improving automatism in learning systems and for fine tuning them to a given domain by adaptively tailoring their behavior on the basis of the same data which represents that domain.

A similar approach to the previous one has been followed by Davide Eynard, Matteo Matteucci, and Fabio Marfia. In Chapter 2, "A modular Framework to Learn Seed Ontologies From Text," they describe their *Extraction* system which aims at producing seed ontologies starting from a corpus of documents relevant to their domain of interest. The ontologies are then used to bootstrap further knowledge acquisition processes by providing core terms and relations.

One characteristic of Extraction is its modularity, as it allows for dynamic pluggability of different and interchangeable methods/strategies for corpus indexing, term selection, hierarchy, and relationship discovery. The system also provides post-analysis viewing utilities, which can support the user even beyond the automatic synthesis performed by the system in a computer aided, though human-centered, process of ontology refinement.

A different perspective on the same task is offered in Chapter 3, "SODA: A Service Oriented Data Acquisition Framework," where Andreea Diosteanu, Armando Stellato, and Andrea Turbati completely focus on the architectural and managerial aspects of semi-automatic knowledge acquisition systems. By taking assessed architectures as a starting step and models for Unstructured Information Management which have reached industry-standard, the authors go beyond these results by proposing an Architecture (and an associated framework) for Computer-Aided Ontology Development (CODA). Former results for data acquisition from unstructured information are thus acknowledged and integrated in the overall architecture oriented to the development and acquisition of ontological data. By relying on these results and in their open interconnectivity, the authors finally present an open solution for rapid development and deployment of services for ontological knowledge acquisition.

SECTION 2: RESOURCE ADOPTION AND REUSE TO BUILD ONTOLOGIES AND SEMANTIC REPOSITORIES

The heterogeneity of available sources that can be processed to feed semantic repositories is not only limited to unstructured information access: the lack of explicit semantics in many data repositories (from databases to xml storages) makes them as unknown and unintelligible as any unstructured content. However, common sense and universally adopted patterns in modeling knowledge in existing data structures may lead to "guesses" which can be analyzed, tested, and verified.

In Chapter 4, "Mining XML Schemas to Extract Conceptual Knowledge," Ivan Bedini, Benjamin Nguyen, Christopher Matheus, Peter F. Patel-Schneider, and Aidan Boran present the result of their detailed analysis and classification work on patterns for automatic transformation of XML Schemas into RDF and OWL. The many variations in XML schema do not automatically (and univocally) imply given semantic patterns in ontology modeling, and an attempt to find such mappings between XML structures and RDF/OWL ends in the discovery of a n-to-n search space. Despite the discouraging premises, statistical expectances, cross-checking with available resources, and language analysis lay the constraints which may help to disambiguate this process, which seems to require more craft than analytical skills.

While XML may be seen as a less noble form of ontological data, where the semantics of data are implicit in the structure of the tags which has been thought by the author of the XMLSchema, there are also other resources where the semantics are more explicit. But it is their content which does not directly offer the same perspective on the information that is intended to be represented in a domain ontology. In those cases, semiautomatic processes for knowledge acquisition have to be highly informed about these different perspectives, and thus be able to extract, project, and eventually modify the information coming from the source to produce suitable ontologies/data.

In Chapter 5, "LMF Dictionary-Based Approach for Domain Ontology Generation," Feten Baccar Ben Amar, Bilel Gargouri, and Abdelmajid Ben Hamadou propose an approach for generating domain ontologies from Machine Readable Dictionaries and Lexicons written through the Lexical Markup Framework (LMF). The domain of the two worlds is different: ontologies are made of concepts, relations, and objects of the world, LMF dictionaries contain the words used to the describe these concepts, objects, and relations. Yet, both these domains may share a significant overlap on a common domain of discourse, and, after all, ontologies need natural language to be really shared by humans upon any sort of real-world interpretation dictated by common sense and common knowledge. With this principle in mind, the authors try to guide the development of ontologies through sets of evidence, common patterns, etc. provided by LMF lexicons and by defining a processing chain starting from the identification of the domain (and thus the cut to apply to the LMF dictionary), the selection of concepts, and the progressive enrichment of the ontology.

In Chapter 6, "OntoWiktionary: Constructing an Ontology from the Collaborative Online Dictionary Wiktionary," Christian Meyer and Iryna Gurevych describe their approach for constructing ontologies based on the extraction of terms from Wiktionary, a collaborative online dictionary encoding information about words, word senses, and relations between them. The collaborative nature of this resource, which closely recalls the Wikipedia approach (and comes in fact from the same Wikimedia Foundation that created Wikipedia), and the finer semantic organization of its entries with respect to its encyclopedic sibling, provides a fertile ground for building domain ontologies. In the same chapter, the authors report on the development of OntoWiktionary, an ontology which has been entirely derived by harvesting data from Wiktionary and by "ontologizing" this information.

The last frontier of "ontology development by reuse of existing resources" lies probably in the development of ontologies based on aggregation of other ontologies! or at least, that's what Mariana Damova, Atanas Kiryakov, Maurice Grinberg, Michael K. Bergman, Frédérick Giassonm, and Kiril Simov thought when they initiated their work (presented in Chapter 7, "Creation and Integration of Reference Ontologies for Efficient LOD Management") on the Reference Knowledge Stack (RKS). The RKS is thought of as a reference point for access to LOD data, where general upper ontologies with progressively more detailed levels of conceptualization are interconnected and made available to users, and where reasoning is made possible by means of reasonable views, a form of local pre-processing, matching, cleaning, and reasoning of given sections of the LOD (where "local" may still mean billions of triples). The chapter presents the methods (manual and semi-automatic) used in the creation of the RKS and provides examples illustrating advantages in the use of RKS for managing highly heterogeneous data and its usefulness in real life knowledge intense applications.

SECTION 3: RELEVANT RESOURCES SUPPORTING ONTOLOGY DEVELOPMENT

If resource reuse is an important aspect of ontology development, then there can be specialized resources addressing different aspects of the representation of knowledge that can be thought of as effectively reusable and interlinkable modules for domain ontologies. Proper representation of the linguistic aspects of information is one of these aspects which is often underestimated when one has to focus on the proper conceptualization for a given domain. So, why separate the two aspects: conceptualization and linguistic description, and provide rich and linguistically motivated resources, which can then be properly connected to entries in domain ontologies?

In Chapter 8, "Aggregation and Maintenance of Multilingual Linked Data," Ernesto William De Luca explores issues related to the aggregation and maintenance of Multilingual Linked Data, and how a proper linguistic characterization of ontologies may greatly support search and personalization in user-tailored systems.

Wikipedia is a semi-structured resource, as it features lot of free-text which is somewhat organized (there is a plethora of Wikipedia templates on how to write articles for specific themes, which bring explicit semantics at least to the structure of the article, and also help to disambiguate the terms inside it) and sometimes flanked by explicit semantic tags. As a consequence, elicitation of semantic content from its free-text is expected to be facilitated by the surrounding semantic context and the extracted information should be of high quality.

In Chapter 9, "Mining Multiword Terms from Wikipedia," Silvana Hartmann, György Szarvas, and Iryna Gurevych present their research work on the first necessary step for every automatic ontology development process: the extraction of terminology. In particular, they focus on the extraction of multiword terms, which are poorly represented in standard lexical resources, but which typically express explicit concepts on their own. The presented method thus benefits from the underlying semantic structure of Wikipedia and from the huge quantity of information which it provides as well.

The last chapter of this book, "Exploiting Transitivity in Probabilistic Models for Ontology Learning," by Francesca Fallucchi and Fabio Massimo Zanzotto, focuses on methods and techniques for incremental ontology learning: probabilistic methods to learn information for a specific domain by exploiting seed ontologies in more generic domains and solutions (supported by their development and integration inside a graphic ontology editing and knowledge acquisition tool) for putting "human feedback in the middle" of a statistical learning loop.

This book could not have been realized without the constant help and support of its Editorial Advisory Board, composed of an outstanding group of people who have greatly contributed to both the academia and industry in this field of research. Our thankful wishes thus go to Aldo Gangemi (Consiglio Nazionale delle Ricerche – CNR, Italy), Francesco Guerra (University of Modena and Reggio Emilia, Italy), Dickson Lukose (MIMOS, Malaysia), Diana Maynard (Sheffield University, UK), John McCrae (University of Bielefeld, Germany), Frederique Segond (Xerox Research Centere Europe, France), Michael Uschold (Semantic Arts, USA) and René Witte (Concordia University, Canada) for supporting this endeavor with their scientific reviewing and in many other ways. We would also like to send our kudos to the other people who kindly volunteered for supporting the review work: Éric Charton, Aaron Kaplan, Nikolaos Lagos, Marie-Jean Meurs, Alexandre Riazanov, Claude Roux, and Andrea Turbati.

We are grateful to the IGI Global Team for their support and assistance along the long path which leads to the publication of a new book.

Finally, a big "thank you" to the authors, who have contributed with their work and dedication, bringing interesting and novel approaches and ideas in this field of study. We thank you for your contribution to research.

Maria Teresa Pazienza
University of Roma Tor Vergata, Italy

Armando Stellato
University of Roma Tor Vergata, Italy

October, 2011

Section 1
Knowledge Acquisition Systems

Chapter 1
Ontology–Based Information Extraction under a Bootstrapping Approach

Elias Iosif
National Center for Scientific Research (NCSR) "Demokritos", Greece

Georgios Petasis
National Center for Scientific Research (NCSR) "Demokritos", Greece

Vangelis Karkaletsis
National Center for Scientific Research (NCSR) "Demokritos", Greece

ABSTRACT

The authors present an ontology-based information extraction process, which operates in a bootstrapping framework. The novelty of this approach lies in the continuous semantics extraction from textual content in order to evolve the underlying ontology, while the evolved ontology enhances in turn the information extraction mechanism. This process was implemented in the context of the R&D project BOEMIE[1]. The BOEMIE system was evaluated on the athletics domain.

INTRODUCTION

The task of Information Extraction (IE) from text has been the subject of significant research in the past two decades. Research was influenced by the Message Understanding Conferences (MUC) (DARPA, 1995, 1998), a series of evaluations of IE technology that helped to establish common evaluation measures. Robustness and fast adaptation to new domains are key issues in

IE systems. In the first MUC, IE was tackled as a full Natural Language Understanding (NLU) problem that required complete syntactic and semantic analysis, resulting in systems with limited computational efficiency. After the 3rd Message Understanding Conference in 1991, it became clear that IE systems differ significantly from traditional NLU systems. IE systems based on simple pattern matching techniques (Lehnert, 1991) were reported to achieve better results than systems that attempted to perform "deep" syntactic and semantic analysis (Hobbs, 1990). Also,

DOI: 10.4018/978-1-4666-0188-8.ch001

they were faster and easier to debug and adapt to new domains. Furthermore, several systems that employ machine learning techniques, e.g., Bikel (1997) and Soderland (1997), have been proved easier and faster to port to new domains, mainly compared to systems that use hand-crafted patterns and rules. Hybrid approaches that combine knowledge-based techniques with machine learning have been presented, in an attempt to exploit the advantages of both worlds (Mikheev, 1998).

Despite the advances introduced by the use of machine learning, portability to new thematic domains still remains an open issue. Many of the tasks performed by a traditional IE system have a strong dependency on knowledge about the thematic domain, which is very frequently scattered among the various tasks. Ontology-Based IE (OBIE) systems try to alleviate this problem through the use of ontologies, which provide the means to disassociate an IE system from the domain knowledge required for its operation. Making domain knowledge explicit through an ontology, not only enhances portability, but also provides new opportunities for IE systems, ranging from using the ontology for storing the extracted information to using reasoning for implementing various IE tasks.

The BOEMIE IE system, presented in this chapter, maintains the traditional Named Entity Recognition and Classification (NERC) and co-reference steps, whose results are used to populate an ontology, and substitutes all the template-related steps with reasoning over this ontology, driven by a set of inference rules stored explicitly, along with the ontology. In addition, the fact that domain knowledge is explicitly described by an ontology allows the adaptation of the system's behavior through changes in its ontology, usually in a synergistic approach where extracted information is used to enhance the ontology, which in return affects the performance of the IE system.

The chapter is organized as follows: In the next section, related work on OBIE is presented. In the third section, the BOEMIE approach is analyzed

and the modules performing information extraction and ontology evolution are described. The evaluation methodology and results are described in the fourth section. Finally, the fifth section discusses the presented approach and outlines interesting directions for further research.

RELATED WORK

Ontologies in OBIE systems provide the domain knowledge model required for the systems' operation. This model can be a rather poor one (e.g., a flat list of athlete names, location names, etc., the so-called gazetteer lists) or a rich one (e.g., a model built using an ontology language like OWL, which enables the representation of complex entities or events as well as the reasoning over them) enabling the categorization of IE systems according to the level of ontological knowledge they use. In order to classify OBIE systems we follow the classification proposed in Nedellec (2006), according to which four different levels of ontological knowledge can be exploited by an IE system.

The first level includes the domain entities (e.g., person, location) and their variations (synonyms, co-referents), as well as word classes (i.e., keywords/terms and their variations, specifiers/descriptors of entities). These are mainly used in the IE process for named entity recognition and classification, for named entity normalisation where the various forms of a name can be annotated with a value corresponding to their normalised form, as well as for co-reference resolution (e.g., that the phrases "she", "this athlete" co-refer to the person name "Tatiana Lebedeva"). In Ciravegna and Lavelli (2003) the domain model has a flat representation, where domain entities are manually annotated in order to train a machine learning approach. In Karkaletsis et al. (2004) a machine learning approach is also followed, but the entities are encoded in a domain ontology and the extraction process takes into consideration certain ontological constraints.

At a second level, domain entities or word classes are organized in conceptual hierarchies. For instance, an ontology for athletics may include a concept (class) "person" with sub-concepts for "athlete", "trainer", etc., whereas in WordNet (Fellbaum, 1998), word classes (synsets) are structured via the hypernym/hyponym relation into a hierarchy. Such conceptual hierarchies can be exploited by an IE system for generalizing/ specializing its extraction rules (either in a rule-based or a machine learning based system). In the case of the athletic domain, extraction rules for recognizing person names can be specialized in order to recognize those names that correspond to athletes exploiting some other features that are derived from the ontology. In Cimiano et al. (2005), generic hierarchical relationships are mined from web documents for NERC with respect to a given ontology. The relationships are discovered through the use of linguistic patterns that imply taxonomic relationships. In Basili et al. (2003) the exploited taxonomic relationships are not driven by generic linguistic patterns, but they are designed to capture specific events involving pairs of actors, which are encoded in the domain ontology.

The third level of ontological knowledge that can be exploited by IE systems concerns the concepts' properties and/or the relations between concepts. For example, the "athlete" concept can be defined by the "name" property filled by a string value, the property "age" filled by a numeric value, etc. These properties and relations guide the IE system in various processing stages, from named entity recognition to template relation extraction, independently of the techniques used. In Wang et al. (2005), a machine learning approach used regarding IE as a classification problem, where non-taxonomic relationships are used in order to annotate a training corpus. In Hahn et al. (2002), the extraction process is able to learn the conceptual type of an unknown entity through a series of hypotheses, which are constrained by

non-taxonomic relations. A different approach is proposed by Rosendfeld et al. (2005) where rule-based extraction is combined with statistical techniques and the non-taxonomic relations guide the development of rules.

The fourth level of ontological knowledge is the domain model itself. This knowledge is exploited at the final processing stage of IE, that of template filling. It is not enough to detect named entities inside the text, associate them with properties, and relate them with other named entities, according to the entity types (concepts), properties and relations types defined in the ontology. These extracted facts must be combined according to the domain model in order, for instance, to detect an athlete's instance and associate it with a sport in which the specific athlete participated. In Buitelaar et al. (2006, 2008), an IE approach is presented for domain-specific question answering using generic grammars as well as manually developed rules for the extraction of domain-specific entities and events. Discourse analysis is then employed in order to infer relations between the extracted events based on the event ordering, which takes into consideration the domain semantics. A more sophisticated and complete reasoning mechanism is used in Maedche et al. (2002) where the onto-logical scheme is described by rules in F-logic. This is an example in which reasoning enhances the extracted information by inferring relations between the extracted facts.

BOEMIE approach belongs also in this category of OBIE systems. All types of ontological relationships are taken into consideration through-out the extraction process. A reasoning mechanism, semantic interpretation, is employed, performing consistency checking and inference, according to the domain model. The results of semantic interpretation can evolve the ontology by inferring new conceptual instances (ontology population) and concepts (ontology enrichment). The phases of information extraction and semantic interpretation are combined into a bootstrapping approach, according to which the extraction process can evolve the ontology and subsequently the evolved ontology can improve the extraction mechanism.

The proposed BOEMIE system is closely related with two other systems, namely SOBA (Buitelaar, et al., 2006, 2008) and SMES (Maedche, et al., 2002). Their direct comparison is not feasible since they were tested over different domains. However, their similarities and differences can be outlined as follows. SOBA system follows a rule-based approach to populate the ontology. SMES incorporates machine learning methods over an annotated training corpus for bootstrapping purposes, while in BOEMIE both rule-based and machine learning techniques are applied. SMES and BOEMIE systems perform ontology evolution that is used during the information extraction process, following the bootstrapping way. Ontological knowledge is used for information extraction, while the latter enhances the former. In the case of SOBA, the domain knowledge is exploited through simple inference heuristics. These heuristics take advantage of the ordering of identified events. More sophisticated inference mechanisms are used in the case of SMES and BOEMIE systems. In the case of SMES system a logic-based language is used to infer relations among the extracted facts. The inference approach in the case of BOEMIE system has a greater ability for generalization, since it is applied during a higher extraction level.

Ontology evolution consists of two main stages: ontology population and ontology enrichment. Ontology population deals with the task of adding instances of known concepts and relations that hold between them, into an existing ontology, without modifying the ontological structure. In general, the process of ontology population builds upon the results of ontology-based information extraction, since the latter associates the extracted information to (or it is guided by) the ontological knowledge. A wide range of automatic methods have been applied, including lexico-syntactic patterns (Etzioni, et al., 2005), statistical and logic-based approaches (Craven, et al., 2000).

Many semi-automatic methods incorporate the participation of human experts who validate the intermediate system-generated results (Ciravegna, et al., 2002). In contrast to ontology population, ontology enrichment modifies the existing ontological structure by adding new concepts, relations and rules. This process is triggered in cases where the extracted information cannot be interpreted by the existing ontological knowledge, so new knowledge should be generated. The main steps of ontology enrichment can be outlined as follows: (a) candidate terms (and their synonyms) are identified, (b) clusters of candidate terms are validated for the creation of new concepts, (c) the linking of identified concepts via taxonomic and non-taxonomic relations is investigated, (d) logic-based rules are acquired that allow the derivation of new facts that are not explicitly encoded in the existing ontology. A wide diversity of features and methods is followed for the task of ontology enrichment including, syntactic analysis (Faure & Poibeau, 2002), clustering and formal concept analysis (Maedche & Staab, 2001), combinations of logical, linguistic, and template-driven methods (Shamsfar & Barforoush, 2002). A survey of state-of-the-art systems that incorporate ontology evolution can be found in Petasis et al. (2011).

THE BOEMIE APPROACH FOR IE

BOEMIE implements a bootstrapping approach to knowledge acquisition (Figure 1), which uses multimedia ontologies for fused extraction of semantics from multiple modalities, and feeds back the extracted information, aiming to automate the ontology evolution process. BOEMIE adopts a novel approach which separates the concepts into two types: "primitive" concepts that can be easily attributed to text segments, namely the Mid-Level Concepts (MLCs), and "composite" concepts, usually built on top of primitive ones. These "composite" concepts cannot be mapped

Figure 1. The BOEMIE bootstrapping approach

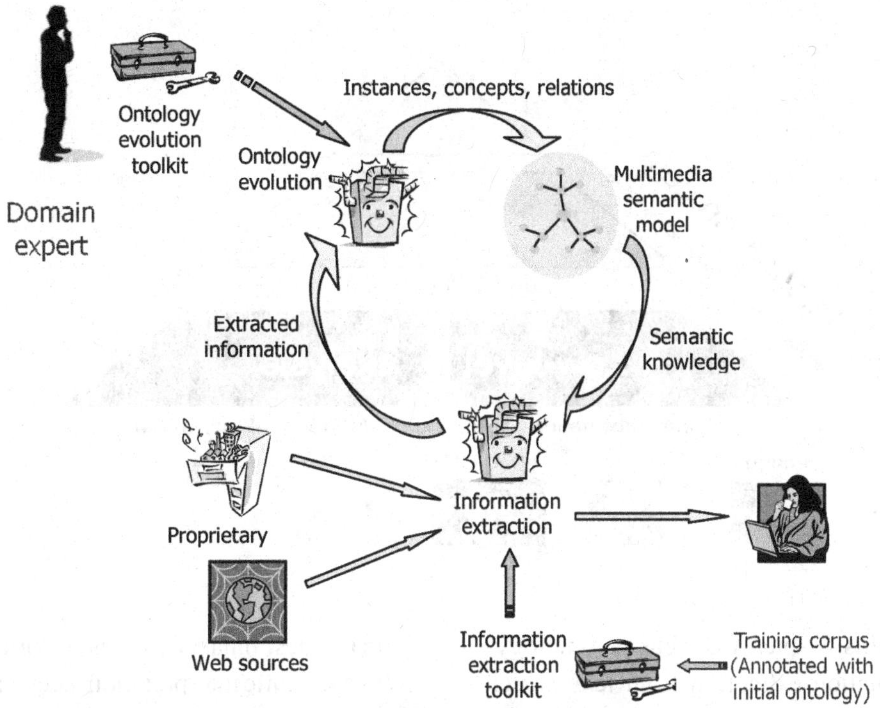

directly to a text segment and are known as High-Level Concepts (HLCs) within BOEMIE.

The general information extraction task in the framework of BOEMIE integrates numerous novel approaches exploiting different sources of information (modalities): video, video OCR, images, audio and text. The extraction architecture is layered in three different levels of abstraction, as is presented in Figure 2. In the lowest level, MLCs and relations among them are extracted from different modalities, following a distinct procedure for each modality. The middle level derives semantic interpretation for each individual modality using the corresponding extracted information, provided by the previous level (Castano, et al., 2008). Finally, the level of fusion combines interpretations for each single modality.

Once a multimedia document has been decomposed into single-modality elements and each element has been analysed and semantically in-terpreted separately, the various interpretations must be fused into one or more alternative explanations of the multimedia document as a whole. This process is performed at a third level, where the modality-specific HLC instances are fused in order to produce HLC instances that are not modality-specific. This extracted information is given to the ontology evolution services (see Figure 2) in the form of OWL ABoxes. These ABoxes typically include instances of MLCs, relations between them, HLCs, relations between them and possibly instances of the specific MLC "unknown" (when the low-level analysis could not classify a certain object).

Text-Based IE

The fusion of information acquired from different modalities can improve the performance of information extraction and ontology evolution compared to the use of information from a single

Figure 2. Semantic extraction from multimedia content

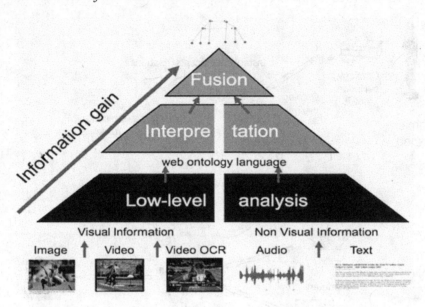

modality. In this chapter, we focus on ontology-driven information extraction from text, which is performed at the first two levels of Figure 1. At the first level, named entity recognition and relation extraction are performed in order to identify MLC instances and the relations between them. At the second level, the identified MLCs and their relations are processed by a reasoning mechanism, providing a semantic interpretation of them, deriving the HLCs. Consider for example, the sentence describing an athletic event:

At last night's IAAF World Athletics Tour meeting in **New York**, **Jamaica's Usain Bolt** *set a new World record for the* **men's 100m** *in a time of 9.72 seconds.*

The bold tokens, "New York", "Jamaica's", "Usain Bolt", "men's", and "100m", are recognized as named entities, being instances of the "City", "Country", "Name", "Gender", and "Sport" MLCs, respectively. During the process of relation extraction the following MLCs' relations are generated in the form of tuples: "(Usain Bolt, Jamaica)", "(Usain Bolt, men)", and "(100m, New York)". These binary relations are further exploited by the semantic interpretation mechanism in order to derive the following HLC instances: Athlete = (Name = "Usain Bolt", Gender = "men", Nationality = "Jamaica"), and Sport = (Name = "100m", City = "New York").

As noted, one of the main characteristics of the BOEMIE approach for information extraction is the bootstrapping process depicted in Figure 1. Since the extractions mechanisms are ontology-driven, any change during ontology evolution is reflected to the IE process. Ontology evolution in BOEMIE is performed in two stages: (a) ontology population adds to the ontology new instances of already known MLCs and HLCs, (b) ontology enrichment discovers and adds to the ontology new MLCs and HLCs, and relations between them. The proposed learning approach is able to identify new concepts, relations and rules as candidates for extending the existing ontology that drives the information extraction system. These candidate additions are formed through similarity-based clustering of the extracted information. The candidate additions are shown to a domain expert through a suitable interface, and the expert is provided with three functionalities: (a) accept, (b) revise, (c) reject them (Petasis, et al., 2011). At this point we should note that the manual workload is proportional to the amount of candidate additions. One can reduce this load by selecting a number of candidates that is tractable for manual inspection according to some qualitative criteria. During the iterative process of bootstrapping a document can be processed more than once. The bootstrapping iteration terminates if no additions are created or if the average amount of the new additions drops significantly.

In the following sub-sections, we describe the processes of named entity recognition, relation extraction and semantic interpretation, which compose the ontology-based information extraction mechanism. The techniques for ontology population and enrichment are also outlined.

Named Entity Recognition

The problem of named entity recognition can be formulated as the assignment of a label sequence given a sequence of observations. The words of a sentence can be regarded as the sequence of observations, and the labels as the categories of named entities to be predicted. Following the representation of Klinger and Tomanek (2007) and using the example of the third section the sequence of observations is:

At last night's IAAF World Athletics Tour meeting in **New York***,* **Jamaica's Usain Bolt** *set a new World record for the* **men's 100m** *in a time of 9.72 seconds.*

The goal of named entity recognition task is to predict a label sequence as follows

0 0 0 0 0 0 0 0 0 City City, Country Name Name 0 0 0 0 0 0 0 Gender Sport 0 0 0 0 0 0

Note that the labels denoted with "0" represent non-named entity mentions. Let the observation

be a discrete random variable, X, with every individual observation x ∈ X. Similarly, labeling can be regarded as a discrete random variable, Y, with every individual label y ∈ Y. In our example the random variables of observation and labeling take values from the finite sets {At, last, night's, . . .} and {0, City, Country, . . .}, respectively. Using this notation the task of named entity recognition is to estimate the probability of an observation sequence $\vec{x} = (x_1, \ldots, x_n)$ given a label sequence $\vec{y} = (y_1, \ldots, y_n)$, $p(\vec{x}, \vec{y})$.

According to the sequential formulation of the problem, we employed Conditional Random Fields (CRFs) (Lafferty, et al., 2001). CRFs have been proved to be a very effective framework for building probabilistic models to label sequential data. In contrast to other probabilistic models which model the dependencies between $\vec{x}$ and $\vec{y}$ as a joint probability, $p(\vec{x}, \vec{y})$, such as Hidden Markov Models (HMMs) (Rabiner, 1989), CRFs uses conditional probability $p(\vec{y} \mid \vec{x})$ to estimate $p(\vec{x}, \vec{y})$. The modeling of joint probabilities, $p(\vec{x}, \vec{y})$, suffers from high computational cost, so no dependency between the observations is assumed in order to tackle this complexity. In contrast, the dependencies between the observations are modeled by CRFs through the use of conditional probability $p(\vec{y} \mid \vec{x})$ (Klinger & Tomanek, 2007). The use of CRFs for building probabilistic models of sequential data has been employed in many natural language processing tasks, such as named entity recognition (McCallum & Li, 2003), part-of-speech tagging (Lafferty, et al., 2001), sentence splitting (Tomanek, et al., 2007), shallow parsing (Sha & Pereira, 2003). For this work we used a freely available implementation of CRF, CRF++ (http://crfpp. sourceforge.net/). CRF-based named entity recognition was shown to have sufficient performance. For example, for the CoNLL-2003 named entity extraction task for the English language, the system proposed in McCallum and Li (2003) achieved an F-Measure score equal to 84%, with respect to named entities such as person names, organization, locations, etc. In Settles (2004), CRF-based models were applied on a biomedical domain yielding F-Measure approximately equal to 70%. For the training of the CRF models, the named entities of a training corpus were identified by human experts. The training features include the token text and the corresponding part-of-speech tags.

Relation Extraction

We formalize the task of relation extraction as the extraction of $r = (s, ne_i, ne_j)$, where ne_i and ne_j are named entities that occur in sentence s, which are semantically related by relation r. Our approach for relation extraction has the following properties:

a. every relation *r* belongs to a set of relations, R, that are defined in accordance to the current ontology;
b. every relation *r* connects exactly two named entities, ne_i and ne_j;
c. the named entities of a relation are located within the boundaries of a sentence s.

For each mention of two named entities within a sentence, our approach detects if this mention constitutes a relation which is included in R. Detection of a possible relation is performed using a machine learning approach employing CRFs. During the training procedure, for each possible pair of named entities in every sentence, a feature vector is constructed given that the mentions of named entities have been labeled in the previous step of named entity recognition. The set of training features are presented in Table 1.

Although there are several research efforts in the area (e.g. Gumwon, 2005; Jiang & Zhai, 2007; Zhou, et al., 2005; Zhou & Zhang, 2007) feature selection for relation extraction using machine learning remains an open problem. The use of simpler features was often reported to give state-of-the-art results, while more complex features did not necessarily improve the performance (Jiang & Zhai, 2007). In our work, after experimentation we ended up with the features of Table 1. This feature set had low-cost and straightforward computational needs, achieving reasonable results. The first feature of Table 1 is a label which denotes the type of the semantic relation between the two named entities. For example, if the two related named entities refer to person name and person age, the label can have the form "PersonNameTo-Age." The second feature deals with the syntactic role of the related named entities and it has a binary value. More specifically, it is set according to the following rule: if the subject of the relation under consideration appears within a sentence before the object, then the value of this feature is

Table 1. Training features for relation extraction

Feature type	Description
Relation label	Label for $r = (s, ne_i, ne_j)$
Order	Syntactic role of ne_i and ne_j within s
Tokens	Number of tokens occurring between ne_i and ne_j within s
Nouns	Number of nouns occuring between ne_i and ne_j within s
Verbs	Number of verbs occurring between ne_i and ne_j within s
Adverbs	Number of adverbs occurring between ne_i and ne_j within s
Adjectives	Number of adjectives occurring between ne_i and ne_j within s
Pronouns	Number of pronouns occurring between ne_i and ne_j within s

set to "normal", otherwise it is set as "reversed". The third feature is used to encode the spatial proximity of the related named entities within a sentence. A relation between two named entities may exist out of the boundaries of a single sentence. However, in this study we restricted the identification and extraction of relations within single sentences to not add a computational cost to the relation extraction module by using co-reference resolution, which is necessary for extracting relations occurring in multiple sentences. The remaining features in Table 1 encode linguistic information and in particular they can serve as quantitative cues of this information since they are measures of several syntactic types occurring between the related named entities.

Semantic Interpretation

In BOEMIE we view semantic interpretation of a document as the process of finding High-Level Concepts (HLCs) from Middle-Level Concepts (MLCs) which have been extracted by the processes of named entity recognition and relation extraction. Abduction is used for this task, a type of reasoning, where the goal is to derive explanations (causes) for observations (effects). In the

framework of this work we regard as explanations the high-level semantics of a document, given the middle-level semantics, that is, we use the extracted MLCs in order to find HLCs (Espinosa et al., 2008). The reasoning process is guided by a set of rules (acquired automatically during ontology enrichment), which belong into two kinds of rules: deductive and abductive. Assuming a knowledge base, $\Sigma = (T, A)$ (i.e., an ontology), and a set of assertions Γ, (i.e., the assertions of the semantic interpretation of a document), abduction tries to derive all sets of assertions (interpretations) Δ such as, $\Sigma \cup \Delta \models \Gamma$, while the following conditions must be satisfied: (a) $\Sigma \cup \Delta$ is satisfiable, and (b) Δ is a minimal explanation for Γ, i.e., there exists no other explanation Δ' (not equivalent to Δ) that $\Sigma \cup \Delta' \models \Delta$ holds.

For example, assuming the following ontology Σ (containing both a "terminological component" – TBox, and a set of rules) (see Figure 3), and a document describing a pole vault event, whose analysis results Γ contain instances of the MLCs "Pole", "Human", "Bar" and a relation that the human is near the bar (see Figure 4).

The interpretation process splits the set of analysis assertions Γ into two subsets: (a) Γ_I (bona fide assertions): *{pole_i:Pole, human_i:Human,*

Figure 3. Ontology Σ

$$Jumper \sqsubseteq Human$$
$$Pole \sqsubseteq Sports\_Equipment$$
$$Bar \sqsubseteq Sports\_Equipment$$
$$Pole \sqcap Bar \sqsubseteq \bot$$
$$Pole \sqcap Jumper \sqsubseteq \bot$$
$$Jumper \sqcap Bar \sqsubseteq \bot$$
$$Jumping\_Event \sqsubseteq \exists_{\leq 1} hasParticipant.Jumper$$
$$Pole\_Vault \sqsubseteq Jumping\_Event \sqcap \exists hasPart.Pole \sqcap \exists hasPart.Bar$$
$$High\_Jump \sqsubseteq Jumping\_Event \sqcap \exists hasPart.Bar$$
$$near(Y,Z) \leftarrow Pole\_Vault(X), hasPart(X,Y), Bar(Y),$$
$$hasPart(X,W), Pole(W), hasParticipant(X,Z), Jumper(Z)$$
$$near(Y,Z) \leftarrow High\_Jump(X), hasPart(X,Y), Bar(Y),$$
$$hasParticipant(X,Z), Jumper(Z)$$

Figure 4. Analysis results Γ containing instances of the MLCs "pole", "human", "bar" and a relation that the human is near the bar

$$pole_1 : Pole$$
$$human_1 : Human$$
$$bar_1 : Bar$$
$$(bar_1, human_1) : near$$

$bar_1:Bar\}$, which are assumed to be true by default, and (b) Γ_2 (fiat assertions): $\{(bar_1, human_1:near)\}$, containing the assertions aimed to be explained. Since Γ_1 is always true, $\Sigma \cup \Delta \models \Gamma$ can be expressed as $\Sigma \cup \Gamma_1 \cup \Delta \models \Gamma_2$. Then, a query Q_1 is formed from each fiat assertion (Γ_2), such as $Q_1:= \{0 \mid near(bar_1, human_1)\}$. Executing the query, a set of possible interpretations is retrieved (see Figure 5).

Each interpretation is scored, according to a heuristic based on the number of hypothesized entities and the number of involved Γ_1 assertions used, and the best scoring interpretations are kept. For the example interpretations shown above, Δ_2 is the best scoring explanation, as Δ_1 has an excessive hypothesized entity (new_ind$_2$), and Δ_3 does not use the Pole instance from Γ_1. More details about interpretation through abduction can be found in Espinosa et al. (2008).

Ontology Evolution

As mentioned in the beginning of this section, ontology evolution plays a central role in the bootstrapping approach for information extraction, since the evolved ontology enhances the mechanism of information extraction. The two stages of ontology evolution, ontology population and ontology enrichment, are briefly described in the following paragraphs.

Ontology population is triggered when semantic interpretation derives one or more HLCs instances. Our ontology population approach is based on two axes: entity disambiguation and consistency maintenance. Entity disambiguation refers to the process of identifying instances that refer to the same real object or event. If an ontology is populated with an instance without checking if the real object or event represented by the instance already exists in the ontology (for example by an instance that has populated the ontology at an earlier population step), then redundant information will be inserted into the ontology. The second axe aims at maintaining the consistency of an ontology, as an inconsistent ontology cannot be used for reasoning. An inconsistent ontology can occur by the presence of redundant instances containing contradicting information.

The ontology population activity can be decomposed into the following tasks:

Figure 5. A set of possible interpretations

- $\Delta_1 = \{new\_ind_1 : Pole\_Vault, (new\_ind_1, bar_1) : hasPart, (new\_ind_1, new\_ind_2) : hasPart, new\_ind_2 : Pole, (new\_ind_1, human_1) : hasParticipant, human_1 : Jumper\}$
- $\Delta_2 = \{new\_ind_1 : Pole\_Vault, (new\_ind_1, bar_1) : hasPart, (new\_ind_1, pole_1) : hasPart,$
  $(new\_ind_1, human_1) : hasParticipant, human_1 : Jumper\}$
- $\Delta_3 = \{new\_ind_1 : High\_Jump, (new\_ind_1, bar_1) : hasPart, (new\_ind_1, human_1) : hasParticipant,$
  $human_1 : Jumper\}$

- Instance matching: The first task of the population activity is the identification of similar instances contained in the ontology. Assuming the semantic interpretation of a document, a similarity matrix is constructed: this similarity matrix contains a similarity measure of each incoming HLC instance (HLCi) with any other HLCi (of the same HLC) found in the ontology. Similarity between HLCis is calculated through matching techniques that work on the instance level, as provided by the ontology matching framework HMatch 2.0 (Castano, et al., 2008).

- Instance grouping: This task is responsible for grouping all the instances that represent the same real object or event, by exploiting the results of the instance matching task. Instance grouping employs clustering techniques operating on the similarity matrix returned by the instance matching task to decide which of these instances will be grouped together to form a group that represents the same real object or event.

- Validation: This task performs consistency checking, to detect possible inconsistencies due to the additions that will be performed to the ontology.

- Assimilation: The final task is responsible for performing the needed changes in the ontology (by creating all instances/relations in all ontological modules), in order to incorporate the instances that passed the phase of validation into the ontology.

For example assume that the semantic interpretation derived among others the following HLC instances: $Sport_i$ = (Sport $Name_i$ = "100m", Sport $City_i$ = "New York") and $Sport_j$ = (Sport $Name_j$ = "200m", Sport $City_j$ = "NewYork"), where the MLCs Sport Name and Sport City are included to the current ontology. These two instances are likely to be clustered to the same group in Step (b) of ontology population, since they are instances of the same HLC, which means that they were found to be quite similar in Step (a). So, the values of MLC instances Sport $Name_i$, Sport $Name_j$, Sport $City_i$ and Sport $City_j$ are candidates for being added to the ontology. An MLC instance value is added if it is proved to be new with respect the existing instance values of the corresponding MLC, i.e., no redundant information is added into the ontology. For example, if the processing of a number of documents yield more than once the value Sport Name = "100m", then this MLC instance value will be considered only once. A contradiction with respect to a certain MLC instance may arise due to erroneous named entity recognition and relation extraction. For example, for a sentence the system extracts a particular Sport Name instance, which is appeared to take two distinct and thus contradictory values. In such cases, the corresponding MLC instance is not taken into consideration. The candidate instances that are not found to contain redundant and contradicting information are furthermore validated for preserving the consistency of ontology. The consistency framework is implemented as a set of constraints, which are developed by the ontology designer, and they are encoded within the ontology as constraints over attribute values. An example of such constraint may be the fact that there is no realistic running sport with length greater than 42195m (the typical marathon length).

Ontology enrichment is performed in the following cases: (1) when semantic interpretation cannot find HLCs in the current ontology that interpret the extracted information, and (2) when the semantic extraction engine recognizes textual segments as potential MLC instances, which cannot be mapped to existing MLCs. These cases provide indications for the existence of new concepts and relations, which are candidate for being added to the ontology. In the first case, ontology enrichment includes the following steps:

a.   clustering techniques are applied for grouping the extracted information for which ontological information is missing, or commonalities can be identified in how instances are related to each other, or distinct ranges of values can be discriminated;

b. clustering results are used to propose new HLCs and/or relations;

c. proposed HLC can be optionally enhanced by consulting external resources, such as taxonomies;

d. a human expert approves the proposals and additionally is allowed to revise the definition of the proposals;

e. each proposal is validated to avoid inconsistencies;

f. the valid proposals are added to the ontology.

In the second case (proposal of new MLCs), only the last three steps are performed (d-f). For example, assume that two sets of MLCs have been identified, which ideally correspond to two similar sports (HLCs), let's say "Pole Vault" and "High Jump". Moreover, assume that the system does not have the necessary information (evidence) to map these set instances to the corresponding HLCs. As it was mentioned, in this case the process of ontology enrichment is triggered (steps a-f). Since the sets are very similar, are very likely to be clustered together in Step (a), forming this way a new HLC. In Step (d) this new HLC can be revised by a human expert. If the HLC pass this revision, as well as the validation of Step (e), it is added into the ontology.

EVALUATION

The BOEMIE corpus used for our experiments contains 3000 Web documents, retrieved from various sites of athletics associations like IAAF[2], EAA[3], and USATF[4], containing news, results and biographies. A pre-processing phase has been applied to this corpus including tokenization, sentence splitting, and part-of-speech tagging using the Ellogon[5] language engineering platform

(Petasis, et al., 2002). The corpus was then annotated manually with MLC and HLC instances, and relations. The annotations are used to train and evaluate the system modules for named entity recognition and relation extraction.

Named Entity Recognition and Relation Extraction

In this section, we present the evaluation results for the tasks of named entity recognition and relation extraction. Since our approach is ontology-driven the named entities correspond to ontological concepts and their relationships to ontological relations. We used the metrics of Precision (P), Recall (R) and F-Measure (F), defined as follows:

$$P = \frac{a}{b}, R = \frac{a}{c}, F = 2\frac{PR}{P+R},$$

where α are the total correct answers given by the system, b are the total answers produced by the system, and c are the total answers that exist in the gold standard. Before going into the overall evaluation of system performance it is important to illustrate how the proposed bootstrapping framework affects the mechanisms of named entity recognition and relation extraction. Recall that bootstrapping enables the addition of MLC instances to the ontology, which are used in the next cycle to improve the extraction performance. This effect is depicted in Figure 3, for a fraction of the experimental corpus.

The progress of ontology population is presented in the x-axis and is expressed by the number of MLC instances. Ontology population improves the performance of both named entity recognition and relation extraction mechanisms. This effect is significantly higher in named entity recognition. Also, it is interesting to note that for both tasks the improvement of performance tends to converge after the aggregation of few thousands of MLC instances. This can be considered as an indication

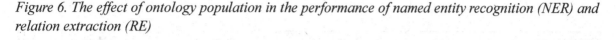

Figure 6. The effect of ontology population in the performance of named entity recognition (NER) and relation extraction (RE)

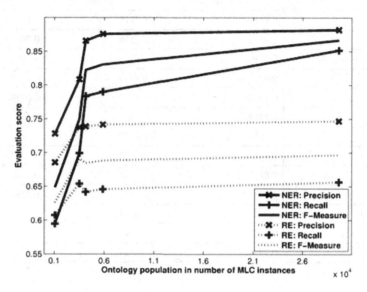

that we have adequate data for the reliable training of the extraction modules.

Whereas Figure 6 depicts how ontology population cycles affect the performance of the extraction tasks, in the next paragraphs we present the evaluation results after the completion of the bootstrapping procedure. That is, the evaluation was performed after the complete population of the ontology, using 10-fold cross validation.

As presented in Table 2, we observe that the results for the PersonName instances are among the highest ones. This fact is expected to have a positive contribution to the overall performance of the system, since the name of an athlete serves as a reference for many of the relations that are defined in the domain ontology. This contribution becomes more important if we consider that the name of an athlete can be regarded as the fundamental unit for Higher-Level Concepts (HLCs) such as Athlete, Sports Trial, etc. Also, for other entities which exist in the immediate context of PersonName, such as Performance and Ranking, we obtain good recognition results. This can be explained with respect to the algorithm used, CRF, which is appropriate for modeling sequential data.

In the experimental corpus, entities such as names, performances and rankings tend to occur in the same sequence. Thus, there are adequate sequential contextual features which enable a more efficient modeling within the framework of CRF. Of course there are documents where these entities are presented in a table format, a structure which cannot be efficiently exploited by CRF. This consideration can also explain the modest recognition results for the case of Date concept. In this case we observed that the date instances that are associated with athletic events tend to occur within documents in positions where no adequate contextual features exist. Overall scores show that named entity recognition process achieved fairly reliable results for all entities. Despite the fact that the above named entities cover the semantics of the underlying athletics domain, more than half of them can be considered as domain-generic ones (for example, age, city, country, date, gender, name, and nationality).

The evaluation results for the task of relation extraction are presented in Table 3. Regarding the relations that have PersonName as one of their arguments, the highest F-Measure score is

Table 2. Evaluation of named entity recognition

Named Entity	Precision	Recall	F-Measure
Age	0.8413	0.7519	0.7941
City	0.8340	0.7519	0.7908
Country	0.7739	0.6728	0.7198
Date	0.6022	0.4649	0.5247
Event Name	0.7648	0.7277	0.7458
Gender	0.8458	0.7959	0.8201
Name	0.8139	0.8327	0.8232
Nationality	0.8114	0.7788	0.7948
Performance	0.8165	0.8418	0.8290
Ranking	0.8334	0.8228	0.8281
Round Name	0.7745	0.6110	0.6831
Sport Name	0.7406	0.6988	0.7191
Stadium Name	0.7958	0.5627	0.6592

achieved for the relation PersonNameToNationality. This happens because it is common in the athletic literature to find a reference to an athlete's name in conjunction with his/her nationality. The mentions of name and nationality tend to occur in close proximity within sentences and this fact favors the CRF training. The lowest results are observed for relations that include EndDate, i.e., SportsNameToEndDate and SportsEventName-ToEndDate, while for the corresponding relations that have StartDate, SportsNameToStartDate and SportsEventNameToStartDate, the system performed well. This indicates that the extraction mechanism tends to relate with SportsName and SportsEventName only one date, which is considered to be the start date. Also, an extraction score equal to zero is observed for the Sports-NameToStadiumName relation. This can be explained by the fact that a lot of stadiums were named after an important person or geographic location, such as "Auf der Gugl" stadium, and by the fact that the stadium name may be mentioned once, usually at the beginning of an article, in an introductory paragraphs different than the ones describing sports and their participants or winners. A potential solution for this problem is to build a classifier that is able to discriminate person names and stadium names. Overall scores show that the relation extraction procedure obtained fairly good results for 9 out of the 14 relations. In general, the achieved Recall is lower than Precision. This can be attributed to the nature of the used corpus, which consists of unstructured text, i.e., web pages. Potentially, higher Recall can be achieved by exploiting more efficiently the structure of these pages.

Semantic Interpretation

Semantic interpretation exploits the results of named entity recognition and relation extraction in order to derive High-Level Concepts (HLC) through the abduction mechanism. This mechanism is dependent to the proposals made by the process of ontology evolution. In Figure 7 we present an example of how the evolution of ontology affects the generation of new HLC instances.

This example concerns a subset of the BOEMIE corpus and reflects the progress of ontology evolution in three distinct cycles. The number of cycles is presented in the x-axis, while the average number of extracted concept (MLC or HLC) in-

Table 3. Evaluation of relation extraction

Relation	Precision	Recall	F-Measure
PersonNameToNationality	0.82584	0.8009	0.8131
PersonNameToGender	0.6268	0.6019	0.6141
PersonNameToAge	0.7420	0.7714	0.7564
PersonNameToPerformance	0.7874	0.6711	0.7246
PersonNameToRanking	0.6409	0.5290	0.5796
SportsNameToCity	0.3884	0.2487	0.3032
SportsNameToStartDate	0.6202	0.5476	0.5816
SportsNameToEndDate	0	0	0
SportsNameToStadiumName	0	0	0
SportsRoundNameToDate	0.3619	0.3894	0.3751
SportsEventNameToCity	0.7121	0.6997	0.7058
SportsEventNameToCountry	0.7612	0.8244	0.7915
SportsEventNameToStartDate	0.7029	0.7469	0.7242
SportsEventNameToEndDate	0.0033	0.0033	0.0033

stances per document is shown in the y-axis. The first cycle is regarded as the initial state of the ontology, including in average 97 MLC instances and 80 HLC instances per document. Note that the latter correspond to the HLCs of Table 6. After the end of the first cycle, a new MLC ("PersonName") was discovered by the ontology evolution process and it was added to the ontology. During the second cycle, this addition caused the extraction of more MLC instances, 120, which correspond to the following MLCs: "Age", "Gender" and "Country." During the third cycle, the previously discovered MLCs were related to a new HLC, "Athlete", which was proposed by the

Figure 7. Ontology evolution in bootstrapping cycles

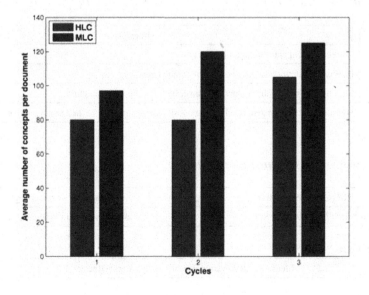

evolution process. That is, HLC "Athlete" consists of the following MLCs: "PersonName", "Age", "Gender" and "Country". Moreover, given the proposal of "Athlete", the mechanism of semantic interpretation managed to derive new HLC instances at the end of the third cycle, resulting to 105 instances per document. Next, we present the evaluation results after the completion of the bootstrapping procedure over the total derived HLC instances, with respect to the entire corpus. Since the derived HLCs are composed of relations between Mid-Level Concepts (MLC), we evaluate each system-generated HLC instance with respect to the MLC relations by which it is composed. As before, we used the human annotations as gold standard. A system-generated HLC instance is considered to be completely correct if (a) it includes exactly the same type and number of MLC relations, compared to the corresponding human annotation, (b) the two arguments for each MLC relation have the same type and value as the corresponding human annotation. In this framework we treat every MLC relation as an entry (or slot) and we use the following variable definitions (Karkaletsis, et al., 2000), which are the basic factors for the definition of evaluation metrics. Using the definitions of Table 4 the

evaluation metrics according to the MUC standards (Chinchor, et al., 2002; DARPA, 1995, 1998; Karkaletsis, et al., 2000), are defined in Table 5.

Precision and Recall reflect the accuracy and the completeness of the system-generated entries. Overgeneration expresses the tendency of the system to generate entries that are not present in the human annotations. The degree by which the system tends not to generate any entries that are included in the human annotations is given by Undergeneration metric. Substitution metric gives a rate of the Incorrect (INC) entries, while Error-per-Response metric makes an overall estimation of the total erroneous entries, i.e. INC, SPU, and MIS. F-Measure is the harmonic mean of Precision and Recall.

For the evaluation of semantic interpretation we followed two scenarios, which investigate the system from different perspectives:

Scenario 1: Interpretation using noise-free MLCs and MLC relations: the mechanism of semantic interpretation is fed with the correct MLCs and their relations, taken from the manual annotations. By this scenario we evaluate the semantic interpretation independently from the extraction modules, assuming that the preceding modules of named entity recognition and relation

Table 4. Variable definitions used in the evaluation metrics of semantic interpretation

Abbreviation	Description
COR	Correct: system entry matches human entry
INC	Incorrect: system entry does not match human entry
MIS	Missing: the system did not generate an entry to match a human entry
SPU	Spurious: the system generated an entry which is not included in the human annotation

Table 5. Metrics for evaluating semantic interpretation

Precision = COR / (COR+INC+SPU)	Recall = COR / (COR+INC+MIS)
Overgeneration = SPU / (COR+INC+SPU)	Undergeneration = MIS / (COR+INC+MIS)
Error-per-Response = (INC+SPU+MIS) / (COR+INC+SPU+MIS)	Substitution = INC / (COR+INC)
F-Measure = 2(Precision .Recall) / (Precision + Recall)	

Table 6. Evaluation of semantic interpretation. The metrics that correspond to human annotations (Scenario 1) and system annotations (Scenario 2) are denoted by "H" and "S", respectively.

Evaluation Metric	High Level Concepts (HLCs)				
	Athlete	Sports Trial	Sports Round	Sports Competition	Sports Event
Precision (H)	0.8008	0.7970	0.9114	0.8962	0.9606
Precision (S)	0.8100	0.7636	1	0.7922	0.8648
Recall (H)	0.6893	0.6250	0.7600	0.4645	0.4661
Recall (S)	0.5252	0.4751	0.2250	0.4445	0.3561
Undergeneration (H)	0.3074	0.2674	0.1723	0.4998	0.5218
Undergeneration (S)	0.4613	0.4124	0.7750	0.4893	0.6116
Overgeneration (H)	0.1954	0.0658	0.0073	0.0351	0.0145
Overgeneration (S)	0.1692	0.0558	0	0.0901	0.0569
Substitution (H)	0.0046	0.1467	0.0817	0.0710	0.0251
Substitution (S)	0.0249	0.1912	0	0.1293	0.0829
Error −per −Response (H)	0.4099	0.4056	0.2446	0.5437	0.5371
Error −per −Response (S)	0.5267	0.5407	0.7750	0.5768	0.6520
F −Measure (H)	0.7409	0.7006	0.8288	0.6119	0.6276
F −Measure (S)	0.6372	0.5858	0.3673	0.5695	0.5045

extraction have performed perfectly. This is done by considering the (correct) human annotations and we let the interpretation procedure to operate over this ideal input.

Scenario 2: Interpretation using system-extracted MLCs and relations between relations: the semantic interpretation is based on the MLCs and their relations that were extracted by the system during the preceding steps of named entity recognition and relation extraction, respectively. Now we provide an overall evaluation of the system.

The results of semantic interpretation for both scenarios are presented in Table 6.

As it was expected, the interpretation results that are based to the ideal input are higher compared to the case where the system-generated input was considered. This indicates that the semantic interpretation can perform well, reaching F-Measure greater than 0.60, as far as the MLCs and their relations are correctly extracted. On the other hand, the results for Scenario 2 suggest that the interpretation performance is strongly

dependent to the preceding steps of named entity recognition and relation extraction. Any erroneous extractions before semantic interpretation cannot be completely resolved by the reasoning mechanism. However, the overall performance of the system according to Scenario 2 is reasonably fair for 4 out of the 5 HLCs.

CONCLUSION

We presented an ontology based information extraction system which operates under a bootstrapping approach. For the task of information extraction we applied a combination of machine learning and reasoning approaches for extracting instances of mid- and high-level concepts. Considering the information extraction as an ontology-driven process, we showed how the information extraction modules are tightly connected with the ontology, and how the extraction mechanisms and the evolution of ontology can affect each other through the bootstrapping framework. The ontology evolution involves a population step where new MLC instances are added to the ontology, and an enrichment step where new, unseen HLCs, MLCs and relations are identified.

One of the main goals of this work was to show how these incremental ontological changes can be used to improve the extraction performance. For evaluation we proposed two different perspectives. The first one considered the performance of the components which were responsible for the tasks of named entity recognition, relation extraction and semantic interpretation. The second one focused on the overall system performance.

The evaluation results for the case of named entity recognition and relation extraction shows that the use of CRF is appropriate for building probabilistic models for sequential data, which is the case for the BOEMIE corpus. The use of CRFs raises the need of selecting training data with rich feature space to build more accurate models. The evaluation of semantic interpretation proved that the use of reasoning techniques over the extracted mid-level concepts can lead to reasonably derivation of high-level concepts, which cannot be directly attributed to textual fragments.

We also evaluated the overall system performance according to two different scenarios, with noise-free and system-generated input. It was shown that the final result of the system, which is the extraction of high-level concepts, is strongly dependent to the modules that extract low-level information. Finally, the major experimental finding of this work was the evaluation of the bootstrapping approach. We observed that ontology evolution is able to enhance the extraction performance, which in turn enables the extraction of more concepts for the further evolution of the ontology. Finally, we estimate that the proposed approach for information extraction according to a bootstrapping process can serve as generic paradigm that is applicable for other ontology-based information extraction systems.

It is important to note that the experimental corpus deals with a specific domain. However, the functionalities of named entity recognition and relation extraction can be ported to any domain with minor modifications, since the used features rely on generic linguistic information. The major limitation for domain portability is posed by the rules that are used for semantic interpretation. The experience that we acquired during the development of the presented system provides many directions for future work. Obviously, there are many feature space parameters which can be investigated for the training of CRF models. Furthermore, the reduction of manual effort regarding the development of rules for the task of semantic interpretation is an interesting direction. Finally, it is important to study in more depth the proposed bootstrapping approach by experimenting in diverse thematic domains.

ACKNOWLEDGMENT

This work has been supported by the BOEMIE Project, FP6-027538, 6th EU Framework Programme. We would like to thank our colleagues from Hamburg University of Technology and University of Milano, for the productive cooperation we had in relevant tasks to this work.

REFERENCES

Basili, R., Moschitti, A., Pazienza, M. T., & Zanzotto, F. (2003). Personalizing web publishing via information extraction. *IEEE Intelligent Systems and Their Applications*, *18*(1), 62–70. doi:10.1109/MIS.2003.1179195

Bikel, D., Miller, S., Schwartz, R., & Weischedel, R. (1997). Nymble: A high-performance learning name finder. In *Proceedings of the Fifth Conference on Applied Natural Language Processing*, (pp. 194-201). San Francisco, CA: Morgan Kaufmann.

Buitelaar, P., Cimiano, P., Frank, A., Hartung, M., & Racioppa, S. (2008). Ontology-based information extraction and integration from heterogeneous data sources. *International Journal of Human-Computer Studies*, *66*(11), 759–788. doi:10.1016/j.ijhcs.2008.07.007

Buitelaar, P., Cimiano, P., Racioppa, S., & Siegel, M. (2006). Ontology-based information extraction with soba. In *Proceedings of the International Conference on Language Resources and Evaluation*, (pp. 2321–2324). ACM Press.

Castano, S., Peraldi, I., Ferrara, A., Karkaletsis, V., Kaya, A., & Moller, R. (2009). Multimedia interpretation for dynamic ontology evolution. *Journal of Logic and Computation*, *19*(5), 859–897. doi:10.1093/logcom/exn049

Chinchor, N., Hirschman, L., & Lewis, D. D. (2002). Evaluating message understanding systems: An analysis of the third message understanding conference. *Computational Linguistics*, *19*, 409–449.

Cimiano, P., Ladwig, G., & Staab, S. (2005). Gimme the context: Context driven automatic semantic annotation with C-Pankow. In *Proceedings of the 14th International Conference on World Wide Web*, (pp. 332–341). IEEE Press.

Ciravegna, F., Dingli, A., & Petrelli, D. (2002). Document annotation via adaptive information extraction. In *Proceedings of the 25th Annual International ACM SIGIR Conference on Research and Development in Information Retrieval*. ACM Press.

Ciravegna, F., & Lavelli, A. (2003). Learning Pinocchio: Adaptive information extraction for real world applications. *Natural Language Engineering*, *1*(1), 1–21.

Craven, M., DiPasquo, D., Freitag, D., McCallum, A., Mitchell, T., Nigam, K., & Slattery, S. (2000). Learning to construct knowledge bases from the world wide web. *Artificial Intelligence*, *118*, 69–113. doi:10.1016/S0004-3702(00)00004-7

DARPA. (1995). Defense advanced research project agency. In *Proceedings of the 6th Message Understanding Conference*. DARPA Press.

DARPA. (1998). Defense advanced research project agency. In *Proceedings of the 7th Message Understanding Conference*. DARPA Press.

Espinosa, S., Kaya, A., Melzer, S., & Moller, R. (2008). On ontology based abduction for text interpretation. In *Proceedings of 9th International Conference on Intelligent Text Processing and Computational Linguistics (CICLing 2008)*, (pp. 194-205). Springer.

Etzioni, O., Kok, S., Soderland, S., Cagarella, M., Popescu, A. M., & Weld, D. S. (2005). Unsupervised named-entity extraction from the web: An experimental Study. *Artificial Intelligence*, *165*, 91–134. doi:10.1016/j.artint.2005.03.001

Faure, D., & Poibeau, T. (2000). First experiments of using semantic knowledge learned by ASIUM for information extraction task using INTEX. In *Proceedings of the ECAI Workshop on Ontology Learning*. ECAI Press.

Fellbaum, C. (1998). *WordNet: An electronic lexical database*. Cambridge, MA: MIT Press.

Gumwon, H. (2005). Relation extraction using support vector machine. In *Proceedings of the 2nd International Joint Conference on Natural Language Processing*, (pp. 366–377). IEEE Press.

Hahn, U., Romacker, M., & Schulz, S. (2002). Creating knowledge repositories from biomedical repots: Medsyndikate text mining system. In *Proceedings of the PSB*, (pp. 338–349). PSB Press.

Hobbs, J. R., Stickel, M., Appelt, D., & Martin, P. (1990). *Interpretation as abduction. Technical Note 499*. SRI International.

Jiang, J., & Zhai, C. (2007). A systematic exploration of the feature space for relation extraction. In *Proceedings of the North American Chapter of the Association for Computational Linguistics-Human Language Technologies Conference*. ACLHLT Press.

Karkaletsis, V., Farmakiotou, D., Androutsopoulos, I., Koutsiasa, J., Paliouras, G., & Spyropoulos, C. D. (2000). *Information extraction from Greek texts in the MITOS information management system. NCSR Technical Report*. Athens, Greece: NCSR.

Karkaletsis, V., Spyropoulos, C., Grover, C., Pazienza, M., Coch, J., & Souflis, D. (2004). A platform for cross-lingual, domain and user adaptive web information extraction. In *Proceedings of the European Conference in Artificial Intelligence*, (pp. 725–729). EAI Press.

Klinger, R., & Tomanek, K. (2007). *Classical probabilistic models and conditional random fields*. Technical Report TR07-2-013. Dortmund, Germany: Dortmund University of Technology.

Lafferty, J., McCallum, A., & Pereira, F. (2001). Conditional random fields: Probabilistic models for segmenting and labeling sequence data. In *Proceedings of the 18th International Conference on Machine Learning*, (pp. 282–289). IEEE Press.

Lehnert, W. C., Fisher, D., Riloff, E., & Williams, R. (1991). Description of the CIRCUS system as used for MUC-3. In *Proceedings of the Third Message Understanding Conference*. Boston, MA: Morgan Kaufmann.

Maedche, A., Neumann, G., & Staab, S. (2002). Bootstrapping an ontology-based information extraction system. In Szczepaniak, P. S., Segovia, J., Kacprzyk, J., & Zadeh, L. A. (Eds.), *Intelligent Exploration of the Web Series - Studies in Fuzziness and Soft Computing*. Berlin, Germany: Physica.

Maedche, A., & Staab, S. (2001). Ontology learning for the semantic web. *IEEE Journal on Intelligent Systems, 16*(2), 72–79. doi:10.1109/5254.920602

McCallum, A., & Li, W. (2003). Early results for named entity recognition with conditional random fields, feature induction and web-enhanced lexicons. In *Proceedings of the Seventh Conference on Natural Language Learning (CONLL) at HLT-NAACL*, (pp. 188-191). NAACL Press.

McCallum, A., & Li, W. (2003). Early results for named entity recognition with conditional random fields, feature induction and web-enhanced lexicons. In *Proceedings of the 7th Conference on Natural Language Learning at HLT-NAACL*, (pp. 188–191). NAACL Press.

Mikheev, A., Grover, C., & Moens, A. (1998). *Description of the LTG system used for MUC-7*. Retrieved from http://muc.saic.com/proceedings/muc_7_toc.html.

Nedellec, C., & Nazarenko, A. (2006). *Ontologies and information extraction*. Retrieved from http://arxiv.org/abs/cs/0609137.

Petasis, G., Karkaletsis, V., Paliouras, G., Androutsopoulos, I., & Spyropoulos, C. D. (2002). Ellogon: A new text engineering platform. In *Proceedings of the 3rd International Conference on Language Resources and Evaluation (LREC 2002)*, (vol 1), (pp. 72-78). Canary Islands, Spain: LREC Press.

Petasis, G., Karkaletsis, V., Paliouras, G., Krithara, A., & Zavitsanos, E. (2011). Ontology population and enrichment: State of the art. In Paliouras, G., Spyropoulos, C., & Tsatsaronis, G. (Eds.), *Knowledge-Driven Multimedia Information Extraction and Ontology Evolution*. Berlin, Germany: Springer Verlag. doi:10.1007/978-3-642-20795-2_6

Rabiner, L. R. (1989). A tutorial on hidden Markov models and selected applications in speech recognition. *Proceedings of the IEEE*, *77*(2), 257–286. doi:10.1109/5.18626

Rosendfeld, B., Feldman, R., & Fresko, M. (2005). Teg-a hybrid approach to information extraction. *Knowledge and Information Systems*, *9*(1), 1–18.

Settles, B. (2004). Biomedical named entity recognition using conditional random fields and rich feature sets. In *Proceedings of the International Joint Workshop on Natural Language Processing in Biomedicine and its Applications*, (pp. 104-107). IEEE Press.

Sha, F., & Pereira, F. (2003). Shallow parsing with conditional random fields. In *Proceedings of HLT-NAACL*, (pp. 134–141). NAACL Press.

Shamsfar, M., & Barforoush, A. A. (2002). An introduction to HASTI: An ontology learning system. In *Proceedings of 6th Conference on Artificial Intelligence and Soft Computing*. IEEE Press.

Soderland, S. (1997). *Learning text analysis rules for domain-specific natural language processing*. PhD Thesis. Amherst, MA: University of Massachusetts.

Tomanek, K., Wermter, J., & Hahn, U. (2007). Sentence and token splitting based on conditional random fields. In *Proceedings of the 10th Conference of the Pacific Association for Computational Linguistics*, (pp. 49–57). PACL Press.

Wang, T., Bontcheva, K., Li, Y., & Cunningham, H. (2005). *Ontology-based information extraction (obie) v 2*. Berlin, Germany: Semantically Enabled Knowledge Technologies.

Zhou, G., Su, J., Zhang, J., & Zhang, M. (2005). Exploring various knowledge in relation extraction. In *Proceedings of the 43rd Annual Meeting on Association for Computational Linguistics*, (pp. 427–434). ACL Press.

Zhou, G., & Zhang, M. (2007). Extracting relation information from text documents by exploring various types of knowledge. *Information Processing & Management*, *43*(4), 969–982. doi:10.1016/j.ipm.2006.09.012

ENDNOTES

[1] http://www.boemie.org/
[2] http://www.iaaf.org
[3] http://www.european-athletics.org
[4] http://www.usatf.org
[5] http://www.ellogon.org/

Chapter 2
A Modular Framework to Learn Seed Ontologies from Text

Davide Eynard
Politecnico di Milano, Italy

Matteo Matteucci
Politecnico di Milano, Italy

Fabio Marfia
Politecnico di Milano, Italy

ABSTRACT

Ontologies are the basic block of modern knowledge-based systems; however, the effort and expertise required to develop them often prevents their widespread adoption. In this chapter, the authors present a tool for the automatic discovery of basic ontologies—they call them seed ontologies—starting from a corpus of documents related to a specific domain of knowledge. These seed ontologies are not meant for direct use, but they can be used to bootstrap the knowledge acquisition process by providing a selection of relevant terms and fundamental relationships. The tool is modular and it allows the integration of different methods/strategies in the indexing of the corpus, selection of relevant terms, discovery of hierarchies, and other relationships among terms. Like any induction process, ontology learning from text is prone to errors, so the authors do not expect a 100% correct ontology; according to their evaluation the result is closer to 80%, but this should be enough for a domain expert to complete the work with limited effort and in a short time.

INTRODUCTION

In the last years, there has been a considerable increase in research on knowledge-based systems, especially in the context of the Semantic Web. However these systems, as they aim at something more than just supplying trivial functionalities, suffer in their development process of the so-called *knowledge acquisition bottleneck*: creating large, usable, expandable and valid representations of semantics about a specific domain of interest, i.e., ontologies, represents the most time-consuming task of the whole project.

DOI: 10.4018/978-1-4666-0188-8.ch002

One of the main reasons for this knowledge acquisition bottleneck is that these formal representations, representing semantics previously unknown to machines, need to be manually annotated by domain experts. In this ontology building process, two different kinds of expertise are usually required: the knowledge of the domain that has to be described, and the ability to encode the ontology in a machine interpretable, i.e., computational, format. Unfortunately, satisfying both of these requirements is, in most cases, not trivial (if not impossible). On the one hand, domain knowledge might be very specific and known only to a small community of practice usually not in the realm of ontology writers; on the other hand, the encoding process does not only depend on standards and tools, but also on the specific context in which this knowledge has to be used.

Easing this task means either making semantic technologies more accessible to domain experts or providing ontology experts with structured information about a domain. The work presented in this chapter is mainly focused on the second approach and it aims at providing an alternative to the manual generation of ontologies through the automatic extraction of candidate concepts and relationships from a set of documents. The generated seed ontology is just an initial and approximate representation of the domain knowledge, and it obviously needs to be further modified and expanded, but it considerably reduces the time required for the overall formalization of the domain knowledge from scratch.

There is already plenty of information available on the Internet (and in other more reliable digital libraries) which could be used to teach a machine about virtually any domain of knowledge. This information is stored as collections of Web pages, large document corpora, databases, and so on. These repositories, however, cannot be directly consumed by a machine as they contain no structured information according to any standard model for knowledge representation. In this scenario,

the main challenge we are interested in is the so-called *Ontology Learning from Text*. Free text is a valuable source of unstructured knowledge, and this requires researchers to adopt original heuristics in order to extract structured semantics from it. These heuristics often return inaccurate results, and have to be modified and validated by experts of the domain, but they can be exploited to bootstrap the whole ontology learning process.

Our work aims at providing a modular, semi-automatic framework that allows its users to apply different heuristics, (possibly) combine them, and finally measure their accuracy. The framework splits the process of ontology learning from text in well-defined steps and relies on different techniques at each stage. This provides some additional benefits to the whole process; for instance, it allows the use of the system with different combinations of algorithms, or to access any useful information generated at intermediate stages. The outcome of this work is a tool called Extraction, which allows the identification of main concepts and their basic relationships from a corpus of free text documents about a specific domain of knowledge.

This chapter has two purposes. On the one hand, we want to describe our modular architecture for the semi-automatic extraction of ontologies from text. This part should be especially useful for anyone trying to develop a similar system, as we provide insights into the building process and show the main issues we had to face, together with the choices we made to solve them. On the other hand, we review existing approaches for the extraction of relationships between terms, we evaluate them in the context of our framework, and we introduce a novel approach aimed at identifying new types of relationships, Action and Affection, which are distinct from classical subsumption.

The chapter is organized as follows: in the Background section we introduce the main concepts that characterize our work and describe the current state of the art about ontology learning from text. In the following section we suggest our design for a modular framework for ontology learning. This framework splits the whole process in steps, allowing users to customize them by applying their own metrics and to inspect the partial results returned by the system. Then the implementation of the framework is described, together with the description of the algorithms we decided to implement. In the following section we show the results of some experiments we ran by using Extraction, and finally we draw our conclusions about this project and suggest ideas for possible future work.

BACKGROUND

Ontology learning from text, in its most general meaning, is that branch of Information Retrieval that tries to generate formal and structured repositories of semantic information using, as its source, a corpus of unstructured text (typically dealing with a specific domain of knowledge). This process can be supervised by a human expert or use any sort of structured data as an additional source. In the former case, we talk about *assisted* or *semi-automatic learning*; in the latter, we refer to *oracle guided learning*; if the algorithm makes no use of structured sources or human help, it is considered an *automatic learner*. As an orthogonal definition, when the objective of the algorithm is the expansion of a pre-built ontology we usually talk about *bootstrapping* instead of *learning*.

Ontology learning is typically composed of different steps. Roughly, they can be grouped into two main families: acquisition of concepts (i.e., relevant terms extraction, name filtering, synonym identification, and concept identification) and acquisition of relations (i.e., hierarchies of concepts, other types of relations, and hierarchies of relations). As our experiments are mainly focused on different approaches for the acquisition of relations between concepts, we introduce these techniques in the following subsections.

Machine Readable Dictionaries and Hearst Patterns

Early work on extracting taxonomies from Machine Readable Dictionaries (MRDs) goes back to the early '80s (Amsler, 1981; Calzolari, 1984). The main idea is to exploit the regularities of dictionary entries to find a suitable hypernym for a given word. An important advantage of using dictionary definitions to build a taxonomy is that dictionaries separate different senses of words, allowing a machine to learn taxonomic relations between *concepts*, rather than between *terms*. In many cases, the head of the first noun appearing in the dictionary definition is actually a hypernym. We can consider, for example, the following definitions quoted by Dolan et al. (1993):

- *Spring*: "the season between winter and summer and in which leaves and flowers appear";
- *Nectar*: "the sweet liquid collected by bees from flowers";
- *Aster*: "a garden flower with a bright yellow center."

Of course, there are also some exceptions to the above rule. For instance, the hypernym can be preceded by an expression such as "a kind of," "a sort of," or "a type of." Some examples taken from Alshawi (1987) follow:

- *Hornbeam*: "a type of tree with a hard wood, sometimes used in hedges";
- *Roller coaster*: "a kind of small railway with sharp slopes and curves."

The above problem is easily solved by keeping an exception list with words such as "kind," "sort," "type" and taking the head of the noun following the preposition "of" as the searched term.

In general, approaches deriving taxonomic relations from MRDs are quite accurate. Dolan, for instance, mentions that 87% of the hypernym relations they extract are correct. Calzolari cites a precision of more than 90%, while Alshawi mentions a precision of 77%. These methods are quite accurate due to the fact that dictionary entries show a regular structure. We see, however, two main drawbacks in using a dictionary-based approach in ontology learning: the former is related to the fact that the acquired knowledge heavily depends on the stylistic (however regular) behaviour of the authors in writing dictionary entries. The latter is that in ontology learning we are mostly interested in acquiring domain-specific knowledge, while dictionaries are usually domain independent resources.

A different approach, that tries to exploit regularities in natural text and can therefore be employed to extract knowledge from domain-specific corpora, is the one suggested by Marti A. Hearst (1992) in her seminal work titled *Automatic Acquisition of Hyponyms from a Large Text Corpora*. The simple ideas contained in this work have heavily influenced many of the following approaches to ontology learning. The so-called *Hearst patterns* are a pre-defined collection of patterns indicating hyponymy relations in a text for a specific language. An example of such a pattern is:

"such NP_0 as NP_1, ..., NP_{n-1} (and|or) other NP_n"

where *NP* stands for an English noun phrase. If this pattern is matched in a text, according to Hearst we can derive that, for every *i* from *1* to *n*, NP_i is a hyponym of NP_0. The other patterns suggested by Hearst are the following ones:

- **NP** such as **NP$^+$** (and|or) **NP**
- such **NP** as **NP$^+$** (and|or) **NP**
- **NP$^+$** or other **NP**
- **NP$^+$** and other **NP**
- **NP** including **NP$^+$** (and|or) **NP**
- **NP** especially **NP$^+$** (and|or) **NP**

Here **NP$^+$** refers to a comma-separated list of NPs, possibly composed of a single element. As mentioned by Hearst, the value of such lexico-syntactic patterns is that they are quite accurate and can be easily identified. Working on a set of textual documents from the New York Times, Hearst showed that, out of 106 extracted relations whose hyponym and hypernym appeared in Word-Net, 61 were correct with respect to WordNet (i.e., 57.55% accuracy). The drawback of the patterns is however that they rarely appear and most of the words related through an *is-a* relation do not appear in Hearst-style patterns. Thus, one needs to process large corpora to find enough of these patterns. For this reason, more recently several researchers have attempted to look for these patterns using online search engines, i.e. considering the Web as a huge document repository (Markert, 2003; Pasca, 2004; Etzioni, 2004).

Distributional Similarity

A large number of methods for ontology learning from text are based on the same conceptual approach, called Distributional Similarity. This approach is based on the *distributional hypothesis* (Firth, 1957; Harris, 1968), according to which words found in similar contexts tend to be semantically similar. Different empirical investigations corroborate the validity of this hypothesis. Miller and Charles (Miller, 1991), for example, showed with several experiments that humans determine the semantic similarity of words on the basis of the similarity of the contexts they are used in. Grefenstette (Grefenstette, 1994) further showed that similarity in vector space correlates well with semantic relatedness of words. From a technological point of view, context similarity is analyzed by calculating the co-occurrence of words in the same sentence, paragraph, document, or other types of context. The more the distribution of two words in these contexts is similar, the more the words themselves are expected to be semantically similar.

In this family of approaches, concepts are extracted from a collection of documents and then organized using some representation that is based on their distributional similarity. Then, different methods can be used to identify relationships between neighbors. ASIUM (Faure, 1998), for example, is a software for the generation of concept hierarchies that uses as a context both the verb of the sentence where a concept appears and the syntactical function (i.e., subject, object, or other complements) of the concept itself. This tool leaves relation discovery to the user, by showing her similar words and allowing her to specify their hierarchical organization.

Caraballo (1999) presents an approach to build a hierarchy from a set of concepts extracted from a corpus of articles from the Wall Street Journal, with the parser described in (Caraballo & Charniak, 1998). The described model uses as a context the paragraph in which the terms appear and looks for Hearst patterns in the text to generate the hierarchy.

A different approach is the one called *Learning by Googling*: Hearst patterns can not only be found within document corpora, but they can also be searched on the Web. PANKOW (Cimiano, 2004), for instance, is a software that looks for Hearst patterns on Google and, according to the number of results returned by the engine, decides whether a subsumption relation between two concepts can be confirmed or not. A peculiarity of PANKOW is that it employs a variation of the classical Hearst patterns, using the plural form for classes of concepts (i.e. <CONCEPT>s such as <INSTANCE>). This choice is corroborated by Ritter (2009), who found that different patterns are characterized by a high precision only when their class name is identified as a plural by a POS tagger.

An alternative model is the one presented by Fionn Murtagh (2005, 2007). This is a Distributional Similarity approach that relies on Correspondence Analysis (a multivariate statistical technique developed by J.-P. Benzécri in the '60s to calculate the semantic similarity between concepts (Benzécri, 1976). The generation of the hierarchy starts from the assumption that terms appearing in more documents are more general than others, thus the algorithm places them in a higher position within the hierarchy. Murtagh also applied Correspondence Analysis to study the distribution of concepts within Aristotle's "Categories," following the semantic evolution of Aristotle's work in its 15 different parts; for instance, he found that parts 6, 8, 9 deal with some common concepts such as "category," "quality" and "degree." Parts 7, 10, 11, and 14, instead, appeared, in their distribution, very far from the others. The main limit of Murtagh's approach is that, in the end, the inferred information is about how the text is organized while no real semantics is extracted, i.e., we have represented semantics about documents (or parts of them), and not about concepts expressed by the corpus itself. This is also true for other studies on linguistics presented by Murtagh (2005), because the distribution of terms is always studied across the documents.

For what concerns *bootstrapping* approaches, many methods have been developed which are based on distributional similarity (Hearst, 1993; Schutze, 1993; Alfonseca, 2002; Maedche, 2003). Their common approach is to evaluate the similarity between a word appearing in a corpus of documents and other words (concepts) in an ontology. Then, the word becomes a sub-concept of the concept whose children are more similar to it.

Formal Concept Analysis

Formal Concept Analysis, as described by Philipp Cimiano (2006), is an approach to extract concept hierarchies from text that departs from distributional similarity. It is based on different assumptions and largely relies on Natural Language Processing (NLP) algorithms. One of the main advantages of distributional similarity is that, in most cases, its algorithms can be largely considered to be language-independent, while this is not the case of FCA approaches (actually, the algorithms we previously described relying on Hearst patterns are language dependent; however changing patterns with their equivalents in other languages is a trivial task).

The main idea in FCA is to identify the actions that a concept can do or undergo. Words are organized in groups according to the actions they share; then they are ordered in a hierarchy according to these actions (i.e., the group of entities that can run and eat and the group of entities that can fly and eat are put together under the more general group of entities that can eat). Finally, the user is asked to label every node of the hierarchy (or other automatic methods can be used to perform this operation), then the final hierarchy is ready. Cimiano's paper also describes an approach to generate hierarchies from text by using, as a sort of prompter, a pre-constructed ontology. This algorithm does not obtain an extension of the pre-existent ontology (as it happens with bootstrapping methods), but a new and independent one, not necessarily containing all the entities and relationships of the original one.

Ontology Learning Frameworks

In this section we describe other frameworks which, like ours, aim at modelling the whole ontology learning process, embedding different algorithms and possibly allowing researchers to easily add new ones.

The most relevant work in this field is the one performed at the University of Karlsruhe, Germany. Maedche & Staab (2001) introduce both a theoretical model for the ontology learning process (which is organized as a cycle) and a framework, called Text-To-Onto, organized in different modules whose purposes range from system management to the extraction of knowledge with an NLP system and a tool for ontology editing. This work is later refined in Maedche & Staab's KAON Text-To-Onto (2004), organized

in four main modules: the *ontology management* component, the *resource processing* component, the *algorithm library* component, and the *coordination* component. A further evolution of this framework can be seen in Text2Onto (Cimiano & Völker, 2005), where learned ontological structures are represented as modelling primitives, making them independent from any specific knowledge representation language. Moreover, *Probabilistic Ontology Models* (POM) are applied to attach probability values to system's results (a very useful feedback for ontology managers) and *data-driven change discovery* is introduced to detect changes in the corpus, calculating POM differences with respect to the changes, without the need of recalculating them for the whole collection of documents.

Other works, even if not aimed at providing a framework as general and complete as the ones in the Text-To-Onto family, present modules that might be interesting to be employed in such a kind of system. El Sayed et al. (2008), for instance, introduce a *relevance feedback* module into their tool. Keyword-based queries are expanded with their related terms by means of the synonymy and hypernymy relationships. Then, user interactions with the system are taken into account to update the taxonomy by means of a relevance feedback mechanism.

A MODULAR FRAMEWORK TO LEARN SEED ONTOLOGIES FROM TEXT

Heuristics for the automatic extraction of ontologies from text often return inaccurate results that need to be validated by users. Actually, no single solution is always better or worse than the others, rather the performance of each heuristic can be influenced by different factors: for instance, the number of documents taken into account, their length, or their language. As a result, there is no "one size fits all" solution that could be efficiently applied in this field. Learning which solution might be better for a specific problem is an interesting research question per se, and having a system which allows to test different heuristics on the same data might prove useful both for the comparison of results and for the generation of the final ontology.

Another point in favour of a modular approach is the fact that the ontology extraction process can be usually split into different steps which can be individually tweaked to obtain different results. And, since making two people agree on an ontology defined by only one of them is already a difficult task, we cannot expect a machine to get the right solution out of the box, without allowing an ontology manager to check its partial results and possibly refine them. Possible reasons for user intervention are, for instance, *simplification* (i.e., the number of extracted terms/concepts needs to be reduced), *customization* (i.e., some concepts are missing and need to be added, or some equivalences between concepts need to be defined), and *integration* (i.e., the ontology manager might need to work on an existing ontology, so she has to provide one as an input to the system).

As a direct consequence of these considerations, the objective of this work was to provide a modular framework for ontology extraction from text. The main requirements for this framework were the following two: (1) allowing users to easily plug their own metrics in the system and test them; (2) organizing the ontology extraction process as a sequence of steps, each one with well-defined inputs and outputs, and allow the process to be interrupted and its results to be inspected at each different stage. To accomplish this goal we designed our system to support a specific multi-step process, having at each step a well-defined set of inputs and outputs (see Figure 1). All the different stages of the process are accessible as methods of a container "Extraction" object, which can be easily embedded within another application. The description of each stage follows:

1. **Document indexing**. This step transforms a generic set of documents in a quickly accessible document index. The only constraint we put was that the documents had to be located in the same place, for instance inside a directory in the file system. As most of available document indexers (and in particular Lucene, the one we chose for our implementation) require input documents to be in plain text format, the document indexing module should also take care of the detection and conversion of different file types to text. The output produced at this step is a document index. To allow ontology managers to verify the results of the indexing process (i.e., if words in documents are correctly stemmed, or if terms that should be added to the stopwords list appear in the index instead), the index should be easy to open and inspect even using third-party applications. Moreover, the indexing process tends to be very expensive in terms of time. For this reason, this module should not only be able to make the index available to the following steps in the pipeline, but also to save it to disk in a standard (or, at least, widely known) format.

2. **Relevant terms extraction**. The expected output for this step is a weighted list of terms, appearing in the corpus of documents and considered relevant according to a chosen algorithm. Different implementations of these algorithms could be plugged in, provided they all receive as their input the document index generated in the previous step and return, as output, the weighted list of terms. While term relevance calculation can be considered as the main operation performed at this stage, the management of its output is nevertheless very important: as we want to allow users to inspect the tool's results at each step, it is essential to provide this information so that it can be used in different ways. In our case (see next sec-

tion for details), we chose to return relevant terms as simple text for direct inspection, as RDF/OWL to be opened with an ontology editor, and as JSON to be easily consumed by external applications.

3. **Similarity computation**. Most of the approaches we have studied for the automatic detection of subsumption relationships rely on some measures of similarity (or, conversely, distance) between terms. We have designed a specific module for this, whose inputs are both the document index and the list of relevant terms. The reason for this double input is that, on the one hand, term similarities are related to the number of their occurrences in one or more documents, while on the other hand we are interested in analyzing only the subset of terms which have been chosen as the most relevant ones. Again, different approaches to the calculation of similarities can be implemented and added to the system. The expected output is a matrix of distances between terms.

4. **Relationships suggestion**. In this last step the different algorithms for the detection of relationships are implemented. Even if most of these algorithms are aimed at detecting subsumption relationships, we preferred to talk here about generic ones, leaving the possibility for other types of algorithms (such as the "action/affection" we will introduce in the next section) to be plugged in. The main input is the matrix of distances between terms returned by the previous step. However, as we wanted the system not only to create new ontologies but also to enrich the already existing ones, it is also possible to provide an ontology as an additional input. The output of this step is a new or enriched ontology, containing as concepts the top relevant terms extracted in step 2 (and possibly the ones already present in the input ontology), and

as relationships between concepts the ones identified in this very step. Input and output ontologies should follow the OWL (Web Ontology Language, see http://www.w3.org/TR/owl-ref/) format, making it possible to open them with an ontology editor such as Protégé (http://protege.stanford.edu/).

Figure 1. The four stages of the extraction process and the data they exchange with each other

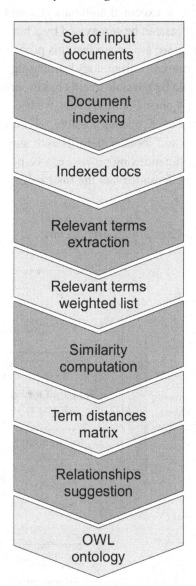

According to this design, at the end of each step the user can choose to interrupt the process and inspect the generated data. However, it is important to note that this interruption, though useful, should not be compulsory. In the implementation phase, it is important to allow this process (or some parts of it) to be also completed automatically. According to the task the user has to perform (i.e., create a new ontology or enrich an existing one) and the quality/time constraints she has, it will then be possible to choose which parts will be executed automatically and which ones will instead be supervised by a human.

Finally, we are aware that this process might not be common to all ontology learning algorithms, so it should be possible to either skip some steps or add new ones. For this reason, we tried to keep the framework as open as possible, relying on open standards and tools at the different stages. For instance, the indexing process can be performed separately, provided that the final index is saved in a format which is compatible with Lucene. As another example, different modules for relationship suggestion have already been developed, and not all of them require the similarity computation step to be performed.

THE EXTRACTION TOOL

In this section we describe the implementation of our framework. The general architecture of our system, called *Extraction*, closely follows its design (see Figure 2).

Extraction has been developed as a Java application and its code is available online at http://davide.eynard.it/SAOD/. The whole system is accessible through one container class, called *Extractor*. This class manages input data (document corpora, document indexes, and, optionally, ontologies to be enriched) and makes them available to the other modules. As the other modules

Figure 2. Extraction's architecture

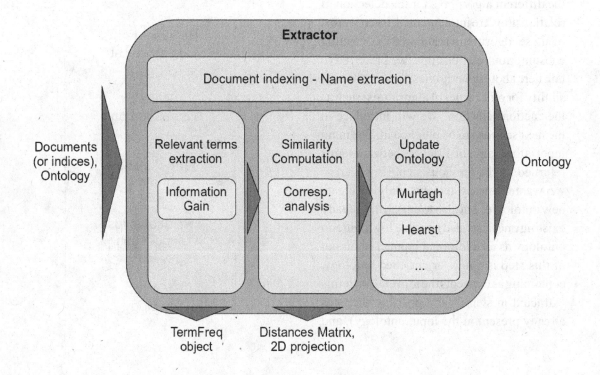

require documents to be indexed, the Extractor class also takes care of document indexing. At the end of the process, an ontology containing the most relevant terms extracted from the document collection and the relationships found between them is returned.

The following subsections describe in detail the choices we made during the development of the different system components: indexing and data filtering, relevant term identification, similarity computation, and relationship suggestion (divided into suggestion of subsumption relationships and action/affection identification). In each subsection, when a specific algorithm is used, we also describe how it works and how we implemented it.

Indexing and Data Filtering

The indexing and data filtering process is taken care of by the main Extractor class. Documents are indexed using Apache Lucene (http://lucene.apache.org), which takes care of tokenization, indexing, and stopwords filtering. Different applications are then available to visually inspect or automatically analyze the indexes generated by Lucene (i.e. the ones available at http://wiki.apache.org/lucene-java/CommunityContributions).

The process taking place in this phase can be divided into different sub-steps: first of all, documents which have not been saved as plain text are converted into this format; then, Lucene performs the document analysis, splitting texts into tokens and applying different transformations on them; finally, the index is built and optionally saved to disk.

Document conversion has been inspired by the architecture described in Gospodnetic et al. (2005): different document handlers have been developed, each one for a specific format; a file indexer class checks a file extension and then chooses the appropriate document handler; the mapping between extensions and handlers classes is done in a plain text file, therefore at any time it

is possible to create a handler for a new type of document and upgrade the system just by updating the text file. Currently we have handlers for:

- **plain text** files;
- **HTML** files, which are parsed using CyberNeko (http://nekohtml.sourceforge.net/);
- **Word** documents, converted with Apache POI (http://poi.apache.org/), the Java API for Microsoft documents;
- **PDF** documents, converted with Apache PDFBox (with http://pdfbox.apache.org/);
- **RTF** files, using the Swing class RTFEditorKit.

During the analysis phase, the text is split into tokens and Lucene performs a number of optional operations on them. Some examples are the elimination of stopwords, lowercasing, and stemming. As stemming is language-specific, different analyzers exist according to the language that needs to be parsed: some examples are the GermanAnalyzer, the RussianAnalyzer, and the SnowballAnalyzer, which implements a whole family of stemmers and is able to support many European languages. For simplicity, we decided to restrict our system to the English language in this phase, and we just used Lucene's default StandardAnalyzer to perform document analysis.

At this stage, additional custom filters can be applied to the single tokens: for instance, as concepts are typically names, we are interested in applying a name detector to automatically discard non-name terms before indexing. Extraction provides two such filters: the former is based on Wordnet, using the JWNL library (http://jwordnet.sf.net), while the latter uses the OpenNLP natural language processing library (http://opennlp.sf.net) to detect terms. Another filter we developed discards all the terms which are composed by less than *n* letters (usually, very short terms rarely represent relevant concepts, even if there are some exceptions such as acronyms). Applying these filters is optional, however it improves the results of the relevant term identification step by removing in advance all those terms which are likely to represent not relevant, if not invalid, concepts.

After the analysis has been performed, the converted terms which survive filtering are saved inside an inverted index, which relates words to all the documents they appear in. The indexing process is usually very time-consuming, so users are allowed to save the generated indexes and reuse them through different executions.

Relevant Term Identification

To extract relevant terms from text, we chose to calculate the Information Gain (IG hereafter) of indexed terms with respect to the common knowledge represented by a training set. Even if the calculation of IG is not the most common approach to detect relevant terms from a set of documents, it has an advantage over other techniques (i.e. TF-IDF) which only rely on term frequencies: the training set is used as a reference corpus and, to be considered relevant, a term needs to have, at the same time, many occurrences in the test set and few in the reference set. Thus, an accurate choice of both can provide better results with respect to classic approaches based on a single corpus. The training set might contain generic documents to automatically detect terms in the test set that are domain-specific (i.e. a collection of news articles vs. documents related to Semantic Web). Dually, the training set might be built with domain-specific documents to only extract those terms which are related to another domain (i.e. a set of Wikipedia-related pages can be used to automatically discard words belonging to this domain –for an application of this example see the Evaluation section). For every term appearing in the test corpus the score of Information Gain is computed. At the end of the process, terms are ordered by their IG and the top n ones are taken as potentially relevant concepts.

Information Gain measure is based on the concept of entropy. In our case, we want to calculate how the total entropy changes for the two training and test corpora by knowing that a specific term is more or less common within these sets. We can identify the $p(i)$ function as the probability for a document to appear in a corpus i, computed as the number of the documents in i divided by the total number of documents:

$$p(i) = \frac{documentsIn(i)}{totalDocuments}$$

Here i can be either the training or the test set. Entropy for a group of documents D_g distributed in the two corpora is calculated as:

$$H_{D_g} = -\sum_i p(i) \cdot log(p(i))$$

We now identify three different groups of documents:

- the group of all documents, D_{total};
- documents presenting the term t in them, D_t;
- and documents not presenting the term t in them, $D_{\neg t}$.

The Information Gain score of term t is then calculated as:

$$IG(t) = H_{D_{total}} - \frac{|D_t|}{|D_{total}|} H_{D_t} - \frac{|D_{\neg t}|}{|D_{total}|} H_{D_{\neg t}}$$

Information Gain has low values for terms that are very common in both training and test corpora. Terms that, instead, are very common in just one of the two corpora have a high Information Gain. In this context, the training corpus has the role of a reference for the test corpus: terms that are frequent in test corpus can both be characterizing terms of the corpus, or very common and uninteresting terms. If a term *t* is also very frequent in the training corpus, which refers to a topic different from the test corpus, then it is supposed to be a useless term, and in fact it will receive a lower IG value. Vice versa, if *t* is very frequent in the test corpus, but not in the training one, it is supposed to be a characterizing term of the test corpus, thus it will receive a higher IG value.

At the end of this process, a set of *n* (with *n* specified by the user) relevant terms is collected, as the top *n* terms ranked by their IG. The weighted list of terms is contained within a *TermFreq* object, which is basically an extension of a HashMap object that can be serialized in different formats. The formats we implemented are:

- **simple text**, for direct inspection during debugging;
- **JSON**, for an easy access within Web-based frontends;
- and a customizable **OWL/RDF ontology**, based on a template whose T-Box defines the vocabulary and whose A-Box is created at serialization time.

Similarity Computation

This step can be seen as propaedeutical to the extraction of relationships between words. In our case, the approach of Correspondence Analysis (Murtagh, 2005) is used to project the relevant terms in a *k*-dimensional euclidean space according to their distributional behaviour over the documents. The closer two terms are in this space (in Euclidean sense), the more their distributional behaviour over the documents of the corpus is similar. The more the distributional behaviour is similar, the more we are allowed to infer a semantic similarity between the terms.

Correspondence Analysis starts from a *(test documents)×(relevant terms)* matrix, where the

cell $n_{i,j}$ holds the number of occurrences of the *j*-th term in the *i*-th document, as shown in Table 1.

In order to create the Euclidean space, Correspondence Analysis applies different matrix transformations. The first step is to calculate the grand total of the individual observations and divide the value of every cell by this grand total. This is done in order to have a matrix M_{prob} expressing, in each cell $n_{i,j}$, the co-occurrence probability of the two (i, j) modalities (i.e., documents and terms). In this simple example, the grand total is 376, and the probability matrix becomes like the one shown in Table 2. Here one more column and one more row appear: they represent the *marginal distributions* of the two modalities, which are calculated in the following step. For every row *i*, the marginal distribution F_i is the sum of all the values appearing in that row; for every column *j*, the marginal distribution F_j is the sum of all the values appearing in that column.

Being $\sum_{n=0}^{i} F_i = 1$ and $\sum_{n=0}^{j} F_j = 1$, we prefer to show F_i and F_j as percentages. Every percentage represents the contribution of the *i*-th or *j*-th

Table 1. Observations of terms across documents

	Caligula	city	group
D1	60	12	60
D2	20	54	5
D3	32	3	2
D4	1	2	5

Table 2. The probability matrix with marginal distributions F_i and F_j

M_{prob}	caligula	city	group	F_i
D1	0.159	0.031	0.159	35%
D2	0.053	0.143	0.013	21%
D3	0.085	0.007	0.005	10%
D4	0.002	0.005	0.332	34%
F_j	30%	19%	51%	

modality to the total of the occurrences. Now, let us consider the columns of our M_{prob} matrix: the algorithm divides every $n_{i,j}$ probability by the F_j value. What we obtain is the matrix whose columns are called *column profiles* (see Table 3).

Column profiles are an important element of Correspondence Analysis because they represent the pure distributional behaviour of column modalities (the terms, in our case), independently from the original amount of occurrences we started with.

The last column F_i represents the average behaviour of the different column profiles. The divergences of the single column profiles from this average profile can be evaluated with the χ^2 test of independence, and the χ^2 distance between two column profiles l and k can be computed as

$$\chi^2(l,k) = \sqrt{\sum_j \frac{(n_{l,j} - n_{k,j})^2}{F_j}}$$

The sum of all the χ^2 tests applied to all column profiles with respect to the average profile represents the total inertia of the matrix with respect to its columns. Inertia represents the total amount of divergence of the column profiles from the assumption of independence. The higher this number, the higher the probability of an interdependence between rows and columns. There is also something more to say about the χ^2 distance between two different column profiles. The obtained value represents how much two different rows differ in their distributional behaviour: the more similar this behaviour, the more there should be a similarity between the entities represented by the two columns (in our case these entities are the terms appearing in the documents). What Correspondence Analysis does, starting from the column profiles matrix, is to provide a compact representation of the similarities between the column modalities. In order to do so we project them into an Euclidean space of k dimensions,

Table 3. The column profile matrix

$M_{colprof}$	caligula	city	group	F_i
D1	53%	17%	31%	35%
D2	18%	76%	3%	21%
D3	28%	4%	1%	10%
D4	1%	3%	65%	34%

where $k < min(i-1, j-1)$. This space has the following properties:

The Euclidean distance between the column modalities in this space of representation is exactly equal to the χ^2 distance between their column profiles. Calling the α-th dimension of the j-th column $F_\alpha(j)$ we can state:

$$\chi^2(l,k) = \sqrt{\sum_i \frac{(n_{i,l} - n_{i,k})^2}{F_i}} = \sqrt{\sum_\alpha (F_\alpha(l) - F_\alpha(k))^2}$$

- The origin of the axes is placed in the barycentre of the different column profiles with respect to the χ^2 distance measure, that is, as we said, the average column profile;
- Axes are selected to have along them, in decreasing order from the first to the k-th, the maximum possible variance of the projected elements.

The creation of the space is done with the application of different operations over the column profiles matrix. The most important between them is the eigenvalue decomposition applied to translate the cloud of modalities into a different coordinate system, whose axes follow the directions of maximum variance of the points. Knowing that the axes are ordered according to the variance of the elements, we can reduce the complexity of the representation by discarding as many dimensions as we want, starting from the last one. In this way, we know that we always keep the dimensions with the highest variance, that is the dimensions carrying the higher amount of distributional information. As an example, the plot in Figure 3 was obtained just keeping the two main dimensions in the *k*-dimensional space.

Subsumption Relationships

Subsumption relationships between the concepts identified in the previous steps are built using three different algorithms: hierarchy generation from hierarchical clustering representation (as in Murtagh's approach), search for Hearst Patterns on the Web, and bootstrapping.

Murtagh's Algorithm

This approach applies the technique presented by Fionn Murtagh (2007) for the generation of a hierarchy of concepts from a hierarchical clustering

representation. Having used the Correspondence Analysis technique, adopted in many works by Murtagh, it was natural for us to experiment with his solution for the generation of hierarchies of concepts, although we obtained better results with other techniques.

A Hierarchical Clustering tree (or *dendrogram*) is created according to term proximity in the Euclidean space. Murtagh's algorithm starts from this representation to build the concept hierarchy. As a first step, it transforms the dendrogram into its *canonical representation*, where later agglomerations are always represented by right child nodes (see Figure 4). Starting from the bottom-left cluster (i.e. the pair of nearest terms), then, the right sibling in the tree is always considered as a hypernym of the left one. In our example, for instance, *emperor* would be considered as a hypernym of *caligula* and *pompey*, and *troop* as a hypernym of *soldier* and

Figure 3. Philosophers and philosophical movements plotted in a 2D Euclidean space

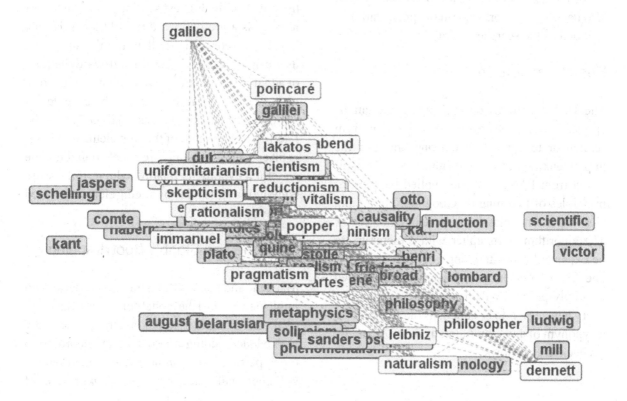

Figure 4. Result of hierarchical clustering over a set of terms from a corpus about Roman empire

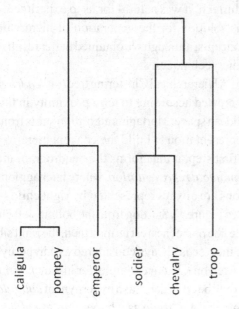

1. Five different pre-defined strings based on Hearst patterns are built:
   ◦ hp_1: pluralize(t_i) such as t_n
   ◦ hp_2: pluralize(t_i) including t_n
   ◦ hp_3: pluralize(t_i) especially t_n
   ◦ hp_4: pluralize(t_i) like t_n
   ◦ hp_5: t_n is a/an t_i
2. Six Google queries are executed (the five Hearst patterns plus the single term t_n), obtaining the number of Google hits for each query;
3. The score of every string is defined as the ratio between the number of its Google hits and the number of Google hits of the hyponym when searched by itself:
   ◦ $score_{hpi} = googleHits(hp_i) / googleHits(t_n)$
4. The total score is obtained as a sum of the five different scores.

Once the hypernym scores have been calculated for every t_i in the hierarchy, t_n is saved as a hyponym of the highest scoring t_i, provided that it exceeds a pre-defined threshold level. If no t_i hypernym scores higher than the threshold, the user can manually suggest one, discard the term or add it in the hierarchy as a hyponym of the root element. The algorithm can also be executed in an automatic way: in this case, it directly puts the t_n term as a hyponym of the root element. After t_n is placed, all its siblings are checked in the same way for a hyponymy relation with it; if the score is above the threshold, the sibling element is saved as a hyponym of t_n.

chevalry. Finally, the cluster dominated by *troop*, being the right sibling of the other one, would also be its dominator. This final representation is returned as the searched hierarchy.

Hearst Patterns on Web

The Hearst Patterns on Web approach can be applied both for the creation of a hierarchy from scratch or to expand an existing one. For the implementation of the algorithm we took inspiration from PANKOW and applied the general principles of Learning by Googling, pluralizing Hearst patterns' classes as in (Cimiano, 2004). The algorithm starts either with a hierarchy to be expanded (bootstrapping), or with an empty one. In the latter case, the first term t_i to be added is simply put under the root element. Then, for every new term t_n to be added, its likelihood to be a hyponym of any term t_i already in the hierarchy is checked as follows:

Maedche and Staab's Bootstrapping

Maedche and Staab's Bootstrapping Process is an implementation of the model defined in (Maedche, et al., 2003). In this model, a concept hierarchy is expanded adding a new t_n term according to the hypernyms of its m nearest neighbors in the k-dimensional space, where m is a parameter of the algorithm. The score for every f candidate hypernym is calculated as follows.

The Least Common Superconcept between two concepts a and b in a hierarchy is defined as:

$$lcs(a,b) = \operatorname*{argmin}_{c} \; \delta(a,c) + \delta(b,c) + \delta(root,c)$$

where $\delta(a, b)$ is the distance between a and b in terms of the number of edges which need to be traversed. Then the taxonomic similarity σ between two concepts in a hierarchy is defined as:

$$\sigma(a,b) = \frac{\delta(root,c)+1}{\delta(root,c) + \delta(a,c) + \delta(b,c) + 1}$$

where $c = lcs(a, b)$. The score $W(f)$ for a given candidate hypernym f is finally computed as:

$$W(f) = \sum_{h \in H(f)} sim(t_n, h) \cdot \sigma(n, h)$$

where t_n is the term to be classified and $H(f)$ is the set of hyponyms of candidate hypernym f that are also nearest neighbors of t_n in the k-dimensional space. The $sim()$ function is the similarity between two concepts as obtained from the k-dimensional space. If no hypernyms are found, the user can manually suggest one, discard the term or add it in the hierarchy as a hyponym of the root element. The algorithm can also be executed in an automatic way: in this case, it directly puts the t_n term as a hyponym of the root element.

Combination of Hearst Patterns on Web and Bootstrapping Algorithms

This approach works by combining the two algorithms we previously described. The pre-existing hierarchy could be huge, and adding a new term t_n with the Hearst patterns algorithm would generate too many connections to the search engine servers. Depending on the Internet connection speed, the execution of a very large number of HTTP requests could be very time consuming. In this case, we look for the n nearest neighbors in the k-dimensional space of t_n in the pre-existing hierarchy, and collect all their ancestors. These ancestors are considered as the candidate hypernyms for t_n and they are evaluated according to the Hearst Patterns on Web algorithm.

As with the previous algorithms, if no hypernyms are found, the user can manually suggest one, discard the term or add it in the hierarchy as a hyponym of the root element. The algorithm can also be executed in an automatic way: in this case, it directly puts the t_n term as a hyponym of the root element.

Action/Affection Identification

In 340 BC Aristotle wrote his "Categories," a treatise whose purpose was to classify all the possible propositions about a being. This subject is still referential today for many works on logics. In the context of our work we are interested in learning from natural text knowledge about two of these categories of attributes:

- an *action* attribute for a concept, defined as the action expressed by the verb of the sentence where the concept appears as subject. Roughly said, it specifies what the subject can do;
- an *affection* attribute for a concept, defined as the action expressed by the verb of the sentence where the concept appears as object. Roughly said, it specifies what can be done with (or to) the object.

In this case we cannot only rely on distributional similarity, but we also use NLP algorithms over a corpus of documents in order to build a table of occurrences of nouns that do or undergo given actions. Correspondence Analysis can be used to project all the nouns and verbs in a

Euclidean space of two or more dimensions (the more the dimensions, the more the precision of the information encoded by that representation). What we expect is that entities (nouns or verbs) that are more likely to be related are also close in this space. As an example, let us suppose that, as a result of document indexing, we create the matrix M shown in Figure 5 (top left). Following the steps of Correspondence Analysis algorithm, we can then calculate the matrix M_{prob} (Figure 5, top right), containing the probabilities for the different events, and its row and column profiles $M_{rowprof}$ and $M_{colprof}$ (Figure 5, bottom).

Figure 6 shows an example of 2-dimensional representation for the analyzed data. This representation leads to three different kind of interpretations:

- *semantic similarity between nouns*: the analysis of the distribution of nouns with respect to done or undergone actions can provide information about their semantic similarity. According to Aristotle's Categories, the more two beings share the same attributes (in this case, action and affection are analyzed), the more they can be classified as similar. So, the more two nouns are seen as near in the plot, the more we expect them to be semantically similar;
- *semantic similarity between verbs*: as for the nouns, we expect that the more two verbs share a similar distribution with respect to the nouns, the more they can be considered semantically similar;
- *cross-distance between a noun and a verb*: in this representation the distance between a noun and a verb is significant in the sense that the more an attribute (action or affection) is seen to be referred to a noun in the corpus of documents, the more the noun is expected to be near that attribute in the Euclidean space.

The last point represents the most interesting and innovative kind of information that Correspondence Analysis is able to provide in this context: from a huge corpus of documents we can obtain an *n*-dimensional map of concepts, and of actions done and undergone by those concepts. This map can then be used to have a compact (and, if 2 or 3 dimensions are used, also graphical) representation of the likelihood of a concept to be involved in a given action. As an example, Figure 6 shows a 2-dimensional plot of the previously described entities. Looking at the picture we can conclude that a gun is much more likely to be involved in shooting than in eating, while a man can be equally involved in both; a chicken is often either subject or object of the "eat" verb, while a cat mostly plays (at least according to the data we provided).

As a last note, in our work we chose to extract only action and affection attributes, however other techniques could be applied to extract different types of attributes, with the possibility to build more complete knowledge repositories.

QUANTITATIVE EVALUATION OF THE APPROACHES

Ontology evaluation, in the software developing process, is part of the quality assurance subprocess. Dellschaft and Staab (Dellschaft, et al., 2008) suggest to evaluate ontologies in two different dimensions: a functional and a structural one. The functional dimension (according to which an ontology is generally required to be [1] consistent, [2] complete, [3] concise, and [4] expandable) tries to evaluate the quality and usability of an ontology *with respect to the software environment* in which the ontology is employed. The main limit of this dimension is that it does not give us a general and unambiguous method to evaluate ontologies, but is rather dependent on the specific use the ontology has been designed for.

Figure 5. The different steps of the CA algorithm using nouns and verbs related to them

M	eat	play	Shoot
man	60	12	60
cat	20	54	5
chicken	32	3	2
gun	1	2	125

M_{prob}	eat	play	Shoot	F_i
man	0.159	0.031	0.159	35%
cat	0.053	0.143	0.013	21%
chicken	0.085	0.007	0.005	10%
gun	0.002	0.005	0.332	34%
F_j	30%	19%	51%	

$M_{rowprof}$	eat	play	Shoot
man	45%	10%	45%
cat	25%	68%	7%
chicken	85%	7%	5%
gun	1%	1%	98%
F_j	30%	19%	51%

$M_{colprof}$	eat	play	Shoot	F_i
man	53%	17%	31%	35%
cat	18%	76%	3%	21%
chicken	28%	4%	1%	10%
gun	1%	3%	65%	34%

Figure 6. A 2-dimensional representation of the data shown in Figure 5

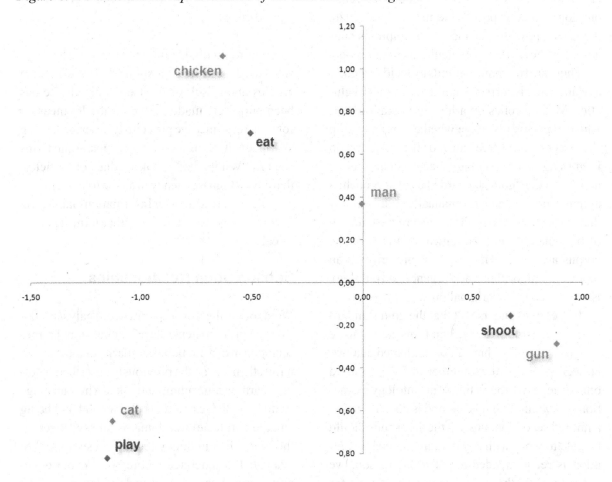

The structural dimension fulfills this requirement, evaluating the ontology logical structure. This is the approach we took for this work, as we wanted to evaluate ontologies generated by different algorithms, without actually being interested in how they could be used in a given software environment. Structural evaluation of an ontology usually foresees two different measures of evaluation, *precision* and *recall*. Precision is computed as the number of correct relationships found divided by the total number of the relationships in the ontology. Recall is the number of correct relationships found divided by the total number of correct relationships. While precision calculation can be performed without a reference ontology (i.e. it is possible to manually evaluate the correctness of the single subsumptions suggested by the tool), recall calculation requires one.

There are two main methods to decide whether a relationship is correct or not. The Manual Evaluation Method relies on a human domain expert who can personally judge whether a relationship is correct or not (precision), or if a relationship is missing in the ontology (recall). The second method is the "gold standard" based approach: a corpus of documents and a manually built ontology that is considered to be the correct representation of the concepts and the logical relations of the corpus are given. The corpus is provided as an input to the algorithm, and the generated ontology is compared to the original one.

It is easy to understand that the gold standard test provides us a general and unique measure which every algorithm can be evaluated against. However, as a limited number of gold standard ontologies exist, the testing of an ontology extraction algorithm with this method is constrained to a limited set of domains. As the algorithm should be able to work with any domain, manual evaluation is recommended too: for this reason, we chose to adopt the manual approach, at least for the evaluation of the computed hierarchies. For the experiments concerning relations different

from subsumption, we have chosen other evaluation approaches that are described in detail in the related section.

Datasets Details

For our evaluation three different document corpora have been selected:

- A set of 847 Wikipedia articles about Artificial Intelligence and related topics;
- A set of 1464 Wikipedia articles about Roman Empire and related historical articles;
- A set of 1364 Wikipedia articles about Biology.

As a referential training corpus we have always used the same collection of 1414 Wikipedia articles about Wikipedia itself. This choice has been purposely made to exploit the IG measure for term relevance we previously described: using Wikipedia itself as a training corpus, some terms such as "Wikipedia," "Wikimedia," or "article," that have a high frequency in all the four document corpora, received a lower Information Gain score, becoming less relevant than other terms specific of each test corpus.

Subsumption Relationships

We applied the Correspondence Analysis algorithm in order to generate a 2-dimensional representation of distributional similarity of the relevant terms, then we ran the previously described ontology learning algorithms and asked a human judge (with knowledge about ontologies and, not being an expert in all the three domains, allowed to search the Web when in doubt about a subsumption) to evaluate the generated hierarchies. As our document corpora contain hundreds of documents, the manual creation of reference ontologies for the three different domains we took into consideration was too expensive to be performed. Thus, while precision has been calculated for all the corpora, we performed the recall calculation only for one domain (the Roman Empire). We have built the reference ontology using the top 200 terms from the corpus and manually adding subsumption relationships. Then we have compared the generated ontology with the one we built, obtaining a low recall value (3.5%). This is somehow expected, as Hearst Patterns are characterized by having a high precision and low recall. In Table 4 the average precision measures of the ontologies are summarized. While Murtagh's algorithm does not seem to perform well, the research for Hearst patterns on the Web seems to be a good option for the generation of concept hierarchies. Its semi-automatic version provides nearly ready-to-go ontologies, producing hierarchies such as the one shown in Figure 7. Maedche' and Staab's Bootstrapping algorithm and its combination with Hearst Patterns on the Web were designed to expand large concept hierarchies, and, as we did not have one available, no valid attempts have been done to test them. Early tests with small ontologies showed that the combination of Maedche and Staab's algorithm with Hearst Patterns on the Web improves the precision of Maedche and Staab's algorithm by itself of about 10%. These results, however, should be considered only as preliminary, so their details are not shown here.

Action/Affection Identification

The evaluation of the action/affection extraction module has been performed with two different tests: evaluation of the 20 nearest attributes, and evaluation of the best concept extracted for a group of attributes.

20 Nearest Attributes

In this group of tests a set of concepts has been chosen from the ones extracted by the algorithm, and the 10 nearest action attributes and 10 nearest affection attributes have been identified for each one. The concepts for the test have been selected as follows: terms were extracted at random from the set of concepts, then a human expert evaluated whether they were actually important concepts for that domain of knowledge or not. If a term did not pass the test, another random one was selected and evaluated. Three independent human judges not involved in research evaluated whether the attributes found with our algorithm could represent typical actions that the term can do (action) or undergo (affection). The tests have been performed with a single-blind control procedure, with the human judge unaware of the origin of the data and of the purposes of the test: the judge had been only informed about the domain of knowledge of origin of names and attributes (necessary to better understand the semantics of the propositions). The judges graded each attribute with an integer value between 0 (impossible to match the attribute with the concept) and 5 (attribute typically matches the concept well). The ratio between the average of the three votes obtained and the maximum vote obtainable (5) has been considered as a partial score for a concept. Then, the final score for each concept has been computed as the average of its

Table 4. Precision measures obtained from the evaluation of the different ontology learning algorithms

Algorithm	AI	Rome	Biology	Average
Murtagh	6.6%	5.22%	1.87%	**4.56%**
Hearst Patterns on Web	60.00%	75.00%	37.50%	**57.50%**
Hearst Patterns on Web (assisted)	90.00%	94.52%	85.07%	**89.86%**

partial scores. The final scores obtained by the chosen concepts are summarized in Table 5. The total average score is 69.485%, which appears as a positive result: for affection attributes the scores are slightly lower, however we can state that the knowledge representation generated by the tool is able to recognize action and affection attributes of concepts with a confidence of about 2/3. Anyway, having no other referential works, we cannot state whether these results are good with respect to other approaches or not.

Best Concept from Attributes

This test has been designed as a sort of game: the user takes the role of an entity, and provides the tool some information about what this entity can do (action), or what can be done with it (affection). The tool, just based on what it extracted from the corpus of documents, tries to guess the entity. This is done by looking in the Euclidean space for the concept that minimizes the sum of the squares of the distances between it and all

Figure 7. A hierarchy generated by the semi-automatic version of Hearst Patterns on the Web, with terms extracted from a corpus about the Roman Empire

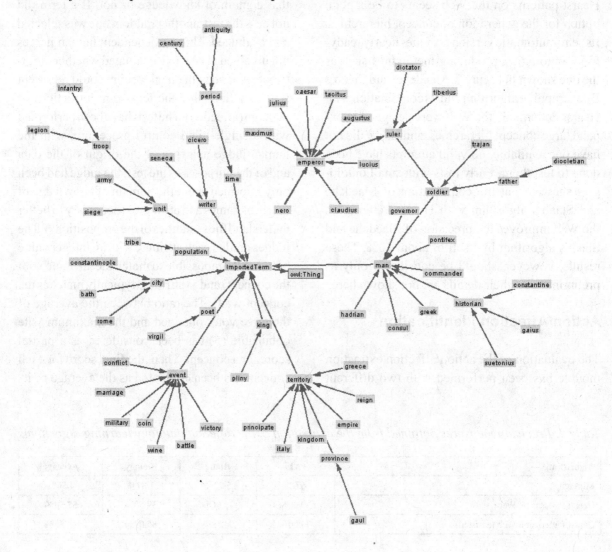

Table 5. Summary of the average scores obtained from tests on extracted terms and their nearest attributes

Concept	Action attributes score	Affection attributes score
city	70.4%	57.2%
attila	87.2%	80.0%
senate	79.2%	76.8%
troop	79.0%	58.8%
Roman Empire average	**78.95%**	**68.2%**
computer	70.2%	69.4%
chess	42.0%	53.2%
intelligence	68.6%	61.8%
newton	68.4%	80.0%
IA average	**62.3%**	**66.1%**
fish	79.4%	50.8%
bird	75.4%	67.0%
extinction	69.8%	72.8%
protein	75.8%	74.4%
Biology average	**75.1%**	**66.25%**
Attribute type average	**72.12%**	**66.85%**

the attributes given as input. Thus, every term t_i is given a score calculated as:

$$score(t_i) = \frac{1}{\sum_n distance(t_i, a_n)^2}$$

The term with the highest score is then returned, together with the five top concepts and their scores. Some examples follow:

Corpus about Roman Empire:

User: I can persecute, I can burn, I can conquer, I can command, I can lead, I can decide, I can kill, who am I?

Tool: You are pompey (5 top concepts found: pompey, score: 5.097; vespasian, score: 2.548; valentinian, score: 2.430; caesar, score: 2.115; sassanid, score: 1.839)

(Note: Pompey is the Roman General, do not mistake him for the Italian city. The user had

Nero in mind, but all those attributes related to war influenced the answers to be more directed towards commanders).

Corpus about Artificial Intelligence:

User: I can think, I can evolve, I can play, I can grow, I can infer, who am I?

Tool: You are a neuron (5 top concepts found: neuron, score: 9.070; intelligence, score: 2.731; predicate, score: 1.909; mechanic, score: 1.470; process, score: 1.469)

(Note: the user did not have a specific concept in mind, but just wanted to find the one which minimized the distance with all the others).

Corpus about Biology:

User: I can be killed, I can be observed, I can be fighted, I can be born, I can be fed, who am I?

Tool: You are a sponge (5 top concepts found: sponge, score: 8.238; tree, score: 2.898; fish, score: 1.874; soil, score: 1.742; clade, score: 1.461)

(Note: here the user thought about a human, but, despite being informed about the domain, she did not choose the most proper attributes to describe a human in biological terms).

As the examples show, the evaluation returned both good and bad results. The tests have been performed with different numbers of action and affection attributes. These attributes have not been chosen at random, but we employed a human judge aware of the fact that the corpus would have dealt with concepts related with them.

In 30 conversations, providing 4-5-6 concepts, the algorithm showed about 35% of the times a valid concept for the given attributes as the first word, and about 60% of the times at least one valid concept in the top 5. Providing fewer attributes led to worse results, but it is understandable, because fewer attributes are not enough to characterize a specific entity, increasing the number of wrong answers.

The results are encouraging: this last interaction example with the user, in particular, is not a trivial game but it represents a well-founded rough draft of a Natural Language Understanding application: the tool here simulates an intelligent agent that in a short time can read thousands of documents and proves to be able to express learned semantics. It is thus understandable that this model could represent a good source of knowledge for complex semantic applications.

CONCLUSION AND FUTURE WORK

In this chapter we have described the Extraction system, a modular framework for the semi-automatic extraction of ontologies from natural text. The system design is based on a model of the ontology extraction process, with the purpose of allowing its users (i.e. ontology experts and programmers) to plug-in their own metrics and algorithms and to interrupt the process at any time to inspect the results of the tool analyses.

The steps that form this process are document indexing, relevant term extraction, similarity computation and relationship suggestion. The system architecture strictly follows this design, and choices have been made in the implementation phase to (1) rely on open source solutions for the framework components which were not developed from scratch, and (2) provide intermediate results in standard formats which could easily be opened and inspected within the system or with third-party applications. Having a predetermined model of the ontology extraction process is of course a limit and a constraint, as not everyone follows the same steps to perform this activity. Thus, our effort has been directed towards easing the integration of our tool with others by using open standards when available and leaving users/developers the possibility of adding, skipping, or merging steps inside the process.

Algorithms for the extraction of the most relevant terms and their relationships from a document corpus have been developed and integrated within the system. The framework is versatile enough to allow us to compare the results of different algorithms for the creation of the hierarchy, both in an automatic and in a supervised execution. The final results showed us that the best-performing algorithm for the generation of a hierarchy of concepts (assisted Hearst Patterns on the Web) obtained a precision higher than 80%, which is quite satisfying if we consider it as a seed ontology which will then be polished by an ontology manager. As a limit, the tool still requires the document corpus to be in English. However, switching to a different language is possible as far as it is supported by Lucene (see http://lucene.apache.org/java/3_3_0/api/contrib-analyzers/index.html), OpenNLP (see http://opennlp.sourceforge.net/models/), and WordNet. The switch can be done in few steps: substitution of the current Lucene analyzer, modification of the language parameter passed to the OpenNLP library, and choice of the desired WordNet vocabulary. Finally, Hearst Patterns should also be updated to reflect the chosen language, but this is a really simple operation.

Extraction also provided us some useful and interesting byproducts. First of all, the possibility of plotting extracted terms in the 2D Euclidean space where they are projected (space which is also the same for documents) allows users to actually see the semantic similarity between words in a document corpus. Another interesting example is the application of the same framework to identify relations between words different from subsumption, such as the Action/Affection relationships described earlier and others that could be inferred by the straightforward application of NLP techniques. We think these byproducts deserve more investigation and represent a good starting point for the (near) future work. More long-term plans, instead, include the evolution of the user interface (which is already present in a graphical format but is still not mature) and the integration of other algorithms, plus a new set of experiments to make it more easily comparable to other systems of its kind. Finally, as the tool grows in features, simple ontology extraction might easily move towards ontology evolution, thus requiring the integration of newly extracted pieces of knowledge within the existing knowledge base. For this reason, our architecture should be extended with an integration module, with features such as the ones provided by SOFIE (Suchanek, 2009).

REFERENCES

Alfonseca, E., & Manandhar, S. (2002). Extending a lexical ontology by a combination of distributional semantics signatures. *Lecture Notes in Computer Science, 2473*, 1–7. doi:10.1007/3-540-45810-7_1

Alshawi, H. (1987). Processing dictionary definitions with phrasal pattern hierarchies. In *Computational Linguistics* (*Vol. 13*, pp. 195–202). Cambridge, MA: MIT Press.

Amsler, R. (1981). A taxonomy for English nouns and verbs. In *Proceedings of the 19th Annual Meeting of the Association for Computational Linguistics,* (pp. 133-138). Stanford, CA: ACL Press.

Benzécri, J.-P. (1976). *L'analyse des donnes.* Paris, France: Dounod.

Benzécri, J. P. (1990). Programs for linguistic statistics based on merge sort of text files. In *Les Cahiers de l'Analyse des Données* (*Vol. XIV*). Paris, France: Dounod.

Calzolari, N. (1984). Detecting patterns in a lexical database. In *Proceedings of the 10th International Conference on Computational Linguistics,* (pp. 170-173). Stroudsburg, PA: ACL Press.

Caraballo, S. (1999). Automatic construction of a hypernym-labeled noun hierarchy from text. In *Proceedings of the 37th Annual Meeting of the Association for Computational Linguistics,* (pp. 120-126). Morristown, NJ: Association for Computational Linguistics.

Caraballo, S., & Charniak, E. (1998). New figures of merit for best-first probabilistic chart parsing. *Computational Linguistics, 24*, 275–298.

Cimiano, P. (2006). *Ontology learning and population from text: Algorithms, evaluations, and applications*. New York: Springer.

Cimiano, P., Handschuh, S., & Staab, S. (2004). Towards the self-annotating web. In *Proceedings of the 13th World Wide Web Conference,* (pp. 462-471). New York, NY: ACM.

Cimiano, P., & Völker, J. (2005). Text2Onto - A framework for ontology learning and data-driven change discovery. In *Proceedings of the 10th International Conference on Applications of Natural Language to Information Systems (NLDB),* (pp. 2270238). Springer.

Dellschaft, K., & Staab, S. (2008). Strategies for the evaluation of ontology learning. In *Bridging the Gap between Text and Knowledge*. Amsterdam: IOS Press.

Dolan, W., & Vanderwende, L. R. S. (1993). Automatically deriving structured knowledge bases from online dictionaries. In *Proceedings of the Pacific Association for Computational Linguistics*. PACL Press.

El Sayed, A., Hacid, H., & Zighed, D. (2008). A new framework for taxonomy discovery from text. In *Proceedings of the 12th Pacific-Asia conference on Advances in Knowledge Discovery and Data Mining*, (pp. 985-991). Berlin, Germany: Springer-Verlag.

Etzioni, O., Cafarella, M., Downey, D., Kok, S., Popescu, A., & Shaked, T. … Yates, A. (2004). Web-scale information extraction in knowitall: Preliminary results. In *Proceedings of the 13th International Conference on World Wide Web*, (pp. 100-110). New York, NY: ACM.

Faure, D., & Nédellec, C. (1998). A corpus-based conceptual clustering method for verb frames and ontology. In *Proceedings of the LREC Workshop on Adapting Lexical and Corpus Resources to Sublanguages and Applications*, (5-12). Granada, Spain: Springer.

Firth, J. R. (1957). A synopsis of linguistic theory 1930-55. In *Studies in Linguistic Analysis 1952-59* (pp. 1–32). Oxford, UK: Blackwell.

Gospodnetic, O., & Hatcher, E. (2005). *Lucene in action*. Greenwich, CT: Manning.

Grefenstette, G. (1994). *Explorations in automatic thesaurus construction*. Berlin, Germany: Kluwer.

Harris, Z. (1968). *Mathematical structures of language*. New York: Wiley.

Hearst, M. (1992). Automatic acquisition of hyponyms from large text corpora. In *Proceedings of the 14th International Conference on Computational Linguistics*, (pp. 539-545). ACL Press.

Hearst, M., & Schütze, H. (1996). *Customizing a lexicon to better suit a computational task*. Paper presented at the ACL SIGLEX Workshop on Lexical Acquisition. Columbus, OH.

Maedche, A., Pekar, V., & Staab, S. (2003). *On discovering taxonomic relations from the web. Technical Report*. Karlsruhe, Germany: University of Karlsruhe.

Maedche, A., & Staab, S. (2001). Ontology learning for the semantic web. *IEEE Intelligent Systems*, *16*(2), 72–79. doi:10.1109/5254.920602

Maedche, A., & Staab, S. (2004). Ontology learning. In *Handbook on Ontologies* (pp. 173–189). Berlin, Germany: Springer.

Markert, K., Modjeska, N., & Nissim, M. (2003). Using the web for nominal anaphora resolution. In *Proceedings of the EACL Workshop on the Computational Treatment of Anaphora*, (pp. 39-46). EACL Press.

Miller, G. (1995). Wordnet: A lexical database for English. *Communications of the ACM*, *38*, 9–41. doi:10.1145/219717.219748

Murtagh, F. (2005). *Correspondence analysis and data coding with Java and R*. New York: Chapman & Hall.

Murtagh, F. (2007). *Ontology from hierarchical structure in text. Technical Report*. London, UK: University of London Egham.

Pasca, M. (2004). Acquisition of categorized named entities for web search. In *Proceedings of the 13th ACM International Conference on Information and Knowledge Management*, (pp. 137-145). New York, NY: ACM.

Ritter, A., Soderl, S., & Etzioni, O. (2009). What is this, anyway: Automatic hypernym discovery. In *Proceedings of the AAAI 2009 Spring Symposium on Learning,* (pp. 88-93). AAAI Press.

Schutze, H. (1993). Word space. *Advances in Neural Information Processing Systems, 5,* 895–902.

Suchanek, F. (2009). *Automated construction and growth of a large ontology.* Unpublished Doctoral Dissertation. Saarbrücken, Germany: Saarland University.

Chapter 3
SODA:
A Service Oriented Data Acquisition Framework

Andreea Diosteanu
Bucharest Academy of Economic Studies, Romania

Armando Stellato
University of Roma Tor Vergata, Italy

Andrea Turbati
University of Roma Tor Vergata, Italy

ABSTRACT

In this chapter, the authors present Service Oriented Data Acquisition (SODA), a service-deployable open-source platform for retrieving and dynamically aggregating information extraction and knowledge acquisition software components. The motivation in creating such a system came from the observed gap between the large availability of Information Analysis components for different frameworks (such as UIMA [Ferrucci & Lally, 2004] and GATE [Cunningham, Maynard, Bontcheva, & Tablan, 2002]) and the difficulties in discovering, retrieving, integrating these components, and embedding them into software systems for knowledge feeding. By analyzing the research area, the authors noticed that there are a few solutions for this problem, though they all lack in assuring a great level of platform independence, collaboration, flexibility, and most of all, openness. The solution that they propose is targeted to different kinds of users, from application developers, benefiting from a semantic repository of inter-connectable information extraction and ontology feeding components, to final users, who can plug and play these components through SODA compliant clients.

DOI: 10.4018/978-1-4666-0188-8.ch003

INTRODUCTION

While the Semantic Web (Berners-Lee, Hendler, & Lassila, 2001) is finally becoming a concrete reality, thanks to bootstrapping initiatives such as Linked Open Data (Bizer, Heath, & Berners-Lee, 2009) and assessment of W3C standards for expressing, querying, and accessing distributed knowledge, a large part of the information available from the web is still made available by traditional means: web pages and multimedia content.

To be able to cope with this huge volume of information, Information Extraction (IE) engines are allowed to lift relevant data from heterogeneous information sources and project it towards predefined knowledge schemes, thus enabling higher-level access based on semantic rather than textual indexing.

The purpose of such systems is actually two-fold: if documents (and media in general) are the focus, then these systems may support systems for document management, advanced semantic search, smart document tracking, etc. by identifying references to entities already available in knowledge bases and indexing these documents with them; on the contrary, if the focus is on knowledge production, they may extract the information which is contained inside information sources and compose it into semantic compound resources that can then be fed to knowledge bases.

The success of semantic search engines such as Eqentia[1] or Evri[2] and Information Extraction and services such as OpenCalais[3] and Zemanta[4] show that there is large demand for this kind of solutions. However, all of them—while promising to break the old-fashioned concept of knowledge-silos by providing services and API for producing knowledge modeled according to open standards—still represent silos in their own offer, as users are not allowed to participate in the definition of new content lifters, nor can they access the code (or runnable instances) of the engines implicitly available through the provided services.

In this chapter we present a novel framework which aims to overcome the above limitation, being completely based on standard technologies (such as UIMA for Unstructured Information Management) and models (from RDF to Web Ontology Language [W3C, 2004] and Simple Knowledge Organization Systems [W3C, 2009]) and offering an open architecture and platform for provisioning of IE components, which may help in composing systems for semi-automatic development and evolution of ontologies by lifting relevant data from unstructured information sources and projecting it over formal knowledge models.

BACKGROUND

Related Works

Applications such as the ones described above are becoming more and more popular because they provide many advantages like: facilitating communication between computers, creating standardized metadata, and facilitating the management and processing of various document formats. However, the development of such applications requires lot of time and development effort.

Development-free solutions are based on services: this is the case of Thomson Reuters' OpenCalais. OpenCalais offers valid and robust services for tagging documents. However, the main drawbacks of its offer consist in the limitations of a completely web-based approach: it does not assure user document privacy[5] and also it does not offer any possible vertical customization to different domains. Under a certain point of view, we could say that Open-Calais is much closer than what its name would suggest.

Other approaches have been proposed in the scientific literature, describing less-opaque frameworks for composition of NLP components. In Wilkinson, Vandervalk, & McCarthy (2009), SADI—Semantic Automated Discovery and Integration—an open SOA framework for discovery of—and interoperability between—distributed data and analytical resources, is presented. The intent of SADI is very close to the one of Open-Calais, that is, to make service consumption of data analytics very simple: avoid the creation of further languages/technologies, remain tight to standard stateless GET/POST-based Web Services, combine them with W3C Semantic Web knowledge representation languages, and provide something in the middle between best-practices and an available implementation to prove its success. With respect to openness, SADI (as well as Open-Calais) services completely hides the details of the analytical components, though this is just a requirement of its completely service-based architecture, which is focused on the description of the provided data rather than on the process to obtain it (thus allowing for any kind of analysis to be adopted and not constraining itself to any technology nor standard); however, different than Open-Calais, SADI releases as open source the whole service framework (i.e. including the server and service orchestration).

Semantic Assistants (Witte & Gitzinger, 2009) provides web services specifications for consumption of data analysis (IE and IR) services. The services may be defined as pipelines of components based on the GATE (General Architecture for Text Engineering) architecture. A Semantic Assistants Ontology allows for a clear specification of actors in the service consumption, by defining the kind of *artifact* which is being processed and its *format*, the *user*, the *language* (both describing the language of the document to be processed and the language understandable by the user), and the *task* which is requested to be performed on the given artifact. The authors also advocate a wider diffusion of desktop assistants to bring the power of text analytics in daily applications: their text engineering web service suite is thus complemented by dedicated client applications (Witte & Papadakis, 2009) developed as plug-ins

for common tools such as email browsers and word processors.

A wider investigation on ontological descriptions for NLP architectures is provided in Buyko, Chiarcos, & Pareja Lora (2008), where a modular ontology describes various aspects of an NLP pipeline, with particular relevance given to the linkage between annotations from standard processing environments (such as UIMA) and ontological definitions from different linguistic vocabularies. A similar approach has also been introduced in Cerbah and Daille (2007), where a service-oriented architecture geared towards terminology acquisition is defined. The described architecture wraps NLP components as Web services with clearly specified interface definitions: language engineers can thus easily create and alter concatenations of such components.

Reference Frameworks

Probably, the two most quoted frameworks for NLP systems are the General Architecture for Text Engineering: GATE (Cunningham, 2002) and the Unstructured Information Management Architecture: UIMA[6] (Ferrucci & Lally, 2004).

GATE was first released in 1996, inspired by the architecture for Text Engineering defined in the DARPA TIPSTER Project (Harman, 1992). Completely re-designed, rewritten, and re-released in 2002, the system is now one of the most widely-used systems of its type and is a relatively comprehensive infrastructure for language processing software development.

UIMA has originally been developed by IBM Research. In 2005, the US government sponsored the creation of the UIMA Working Group, a consortium of companies and universities committed to the exploration of UIMA as a framework for solving important NLP problems. As a result of the Working Group's activities, some existing NLP resources (such as Stanford's NLP library[7] and OpenNLP[8] toolkit) were integrated with UIMA. In early 2006, IBM published the UIMA source code on Source Forge and lately, in the same year, a new version of UIMA (Apache UIMA) had been made available as an open source project[9] (hosted as an incubator) by the Apache Software Foundation, recently graduating for a position inside list of supported Apache projects, on 18th of March, 2010.

UIMA is also the name of an OASIS specification (Ferrucci, 2009) for a standard architecture for Unstructured Information Management; former UIMA is now known as UIMA Framework/ Implementation or simply Apache UIMA.

Today, UIMA support can count on a wide open source community made up of developers (contributing to the main project) and users (in turn, developers too, who, however, contribute with NLP software released under UIMA specifications). Conversely, GATE benefits from 15 years of maturity and a plethora of available software (free open-source as well as commercial off-the-shelf products) compatible with its architecture which has been written in these years, and from the availability of analysis and manipulation components, such as the JAPE transducer (Java Annotation Patterns Engine), able to manage elements extracted over annotations based on regular expressions.

Other frameworks which have close commonalities with our environment are those related to software provisioning and dependency resolution, such as Apache Ivy[10], Maven[11], or Orbit[12].

Orbit is a project developed inside the Eclipse community to provide a repository of bundled versions of third party libraries that are approved for use in one or more Eclipse projects. Ivy is focused on dependency management of software components (from libraries to elaborated components or DB resources) inside the popular build system Apache ANT[13] while Maven is the current standard-de-facto for software description and provisioning, featuring a rich model for the describing software projects (the POM: Project Object Model) and a powerful dependency resolution mechanism.

Component description and dependency resolution (in this case, component-component as well as task-component and task-task are being considered) are two key features of the presented work too.

Ontology Development, Learning, and Evolution Frameworks

Nowadays, basic architectural definitions and interaction modalities have been defined in detail fulfilling industry-standard level for processes such as:

- Ontology development with most recent ontology development tools following the path laid by Protégé (Gennari, et al., 2003)
- Text analysis (see previous section).

A comprehensive study and synthesis of an architecture for supporting ontology development driven by knowledge acquired from external resources, has not been formalized until now.

What lacks in all current approaches is an overall perspective on the task and a proposal for an architecture providing instruments for supporting the entire flow of information (from acquisition of knowledge from external resources to its exploitation) to enrich and augment ontology content. Just looking at ontology learning, OntoLearn (Velardi, Navigli, Cucchiarelli, & Neri, 2005) provides a methodology, algorithms, and a system for performing different ontology learning tasks, OntoLT (Buitelaar, Olejnik, & Sintek, 2004) provides a ready-to-use Protégé plugin for adding new ontology resources extracted from text, while the sole Text2Onto (Cimiano & Völker, 2005) embodies a first attempt to realize an open architecture for the management of ontology learning processes.

If we consider ontology-lexicon integration, previous studies dealt with how to represent this integrated information (Peters, Montiel-Ponsoda, Aguado de Cea, & Gómez-Pérez, 2007; Buitelaar, et al., 2006; Cimiano, Haase,

Herold, Mantel, & Buitelaar, 2007), other have shown useful applications exploiting onto-lexical resources (Basili, Vindigni, & Zanzotto, 2003; Peter, Sack, & Beckstein, 2006) though only few works (Pazienza, Stellato, & Turbati, 2008) dealt with comprehensive framework for classifying, supporting, testing and evaluating processes for integration of content from lexical resources with ontological knowledge.

MOTIVATION

In our exploration of current state-of-the-art on semi-automatic development of structured data, we shared the same perspective and considerations expressed in Witte and Gitzinger (2009): "While more advanced semantically-oriented analysis techniques have been developed in recent years, they have not yet found their way into commonly used desktop clients, be they generic (e.g. word processors, email clients) or domain-specific (e.g., software IDEs, biological tools)."

Also, we agree with their perspectives on ideal directions for future development: "Instead of forcing the user to leave his current context and use .. external application(s) …", it is way better to leave users adopt their usual applications, possibly enriched with extensions and plugins for invoking "analysis services relevant for [their] current task". However, another consideration drove our research effort: current hit and consume services provide very simple and no-customizable-at-all data acquisition from documents, whereas the full potential of natural language processing could demand for a wider support on the web, embracing final users as well as developers (sitting on various and different steps of the development stairway…) in a more comprehensive and global experience. In this sense, we foresee the existence of environments for component provisioning and composition, much in the spirit of Maven and Ivy (and possibly sitting on top of them), but targeted towards the more specific area of Unstructured

Information Management and Data Acquisition. Components could then be easily downloaded and aggregated by developers through dedicated IDEs exploiting the provisioning services, or be immediately used by final users through dedicated and compliant service-consumers embedded in desktop applications as well.

Objectives

The solution that we are addressing should cover the motivations expressed above, by pursuing the following objectives:

1. Adopting a standard for Unstructured Information Management (UIM)
2. Providing (or adopting) a standard for cataloguing UIM components
3. Providing a standard for expressing the necessary transformations to project semantically annotated information into the desired data structures (e.g. projecting text annotations over the data structures of a given ontology)
4. Enabling data-driven semi-automatic composition of UIM and Data Projection components (e.g. the user defines the ontology for which they want to produce data, and the system is able to define a set of components properly composed—they may operate in a chain, or simply sum-up their different kind of extraction capabilities, or a combination of both—to extract data from unstructured information sources and project it towards the given ontology).
5. Provisioning components according to the composition modalities defined above

THE SODA ARCHITECTURE AND FRAMEWORK

Considering the objectives above, we found there is need for plenty of models, formats, and technologies going from the analysis of unstructured

Figure 1. SODA technology stack

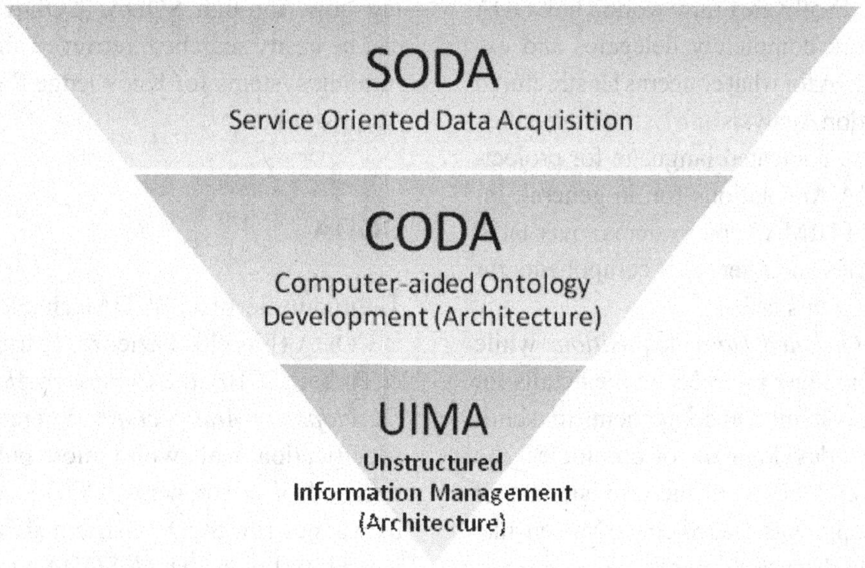

information up to the acquisition of knowledge for structured data sources, and that these would better be organized in separate layers rather than in an intricate forest of specifications (or, even worse, in an underspecified technology melting pot).

Thus, as a first action, we laid up a technology layer cake addressing our requirements and providing independent levels of application (i.e. starting bottom-up, each layer may be considered as a contribution to information management which is complete in its objectives and does not need to be motivated by its role in higher layers). The layer-cake, which is shown in Figure 1, is composed of:

1. *Unstructured Information Management*: supports creation, integration, and deployment of unstructured information management solutions from combinations of semantic analysis and search components. Comprehends, but is not limited to, text analysis and understanding, audio and video processing, etc. with the intent of providing structured chunks of information extracted

from the unstructured information streams, which can then be searched, reused, transformed etc. For this layer, we decided to stand on top of mature results available from state-of-the-art technologies in UIM, and have chosen the OASIS standard UIMA embracing its information models (e.g. Feature Structures, Type Systems) and the whole software architecture and framework as well.

2. *Computer-Aided Ontology Development*: this layer deals with the enrichment and evolution of ontology content through exploitation of unstructured information sources, by using (semi)automatic approaches. While the first layer provides resources analysis and sensible information extraction, the specifications in this layer allow for the reuse and transformation of the above extracted information to populate ontologies[14]. For this layer, we have worked on the definition of an Architecture, CODA: Computer-Aided Ontology Development Architecture (Fiorelli, Pazienza, Petruzza, Stellato, &

Turbati, 2010) and in the development of an associated Software Framework. The CODA Framework completely delegates and exploits UIMA for what concerns Unstructured Information Analysis and Extraction; it then provides a dedicated language for projecting UIMA Annotations (or, in general, instances of UIMA Type Systems) over RDF repositories and a series of components for supporting this task.

3. *Service Oriented Data Acquisition:* while the second layer provides all the details for building systems and components for semi-automatic development of ontologies, the third layer focuses on the provisioning of such components. Based on the Maven-like approach discussed in previous sections, but tailored versus CODA, the Service Oriented Data Acquisition Framework establishes services and specifications for searching, retrieving and plugging CODA components. The search specification should be considered as simple as possible, completely abstracting from the details of the needed components and only focusing on the knowledge need (e.g. the ontology/thesaurus/conceptual scheme for which the information need to be provided) and on the context of the subject of analysis (e.g. the processed media, their format etc…). The SODA provisioning system can also be seen as a developer's open library, providing a component repository to be inspected and consumed by development environments, where users can search, download and compose components to rearrange new analysis engines, possibly contributing with their own developed components, again, much in the spirit of similar solutions for library provisioning, such as Maven (Dodinet, 2005)

In the following sections we first describe the CODA architecture and framework for supporting Semi-Automatic Development of Ontologies, and consequently move to the following layer, showing how, through SODA, CODA components can be easily searched, retrieved and plugged to running systems for Knowledge Processing and Acquisition.

CODA

The middle tier of the SODA technology layer cake is CODA (Fiorelli, Pazienza, Petruzza, Stellato, & Turbati, 2010), the *Computer-Aided Ontology Development Architecture*. Whereas the SODA specification deals with remote publication and retrieval of components, CODA acts as a core backbone of the SODA distributed framework and is the Interlingua that all SODA compliant client machines must be able to understand.

Though the objectives of the full CODA+SODA framework have already been provided, we define here the specific expression "Computer-aided Ontology Development" as to include all processes for enriching ontology content through exploitation of external resources, by using (semi)automatic approaches.

COD tasks cover:

1. **(Traditional) Ontology Learning** tasks, devoted to augmentation of ontology content through discovery of new resources and axioms. These include discovery of new concepts, concept inheritance relations, concept instantiation, properties/relations, domain and range restrictions, mereological relations, equivalence relations etc.

2. **Population of ontologies with new data**: a rib of the above, this focuses on the extraction of new ground data for a given (ontology) model (or even for specific concepts belonging to it)

3. **Linguistic enrichment of ontologies**: enrichment of ontological content with linguistic information coming from external resources (e.g. text, linguistic resources etc.)

Figure 2. CODA architecture

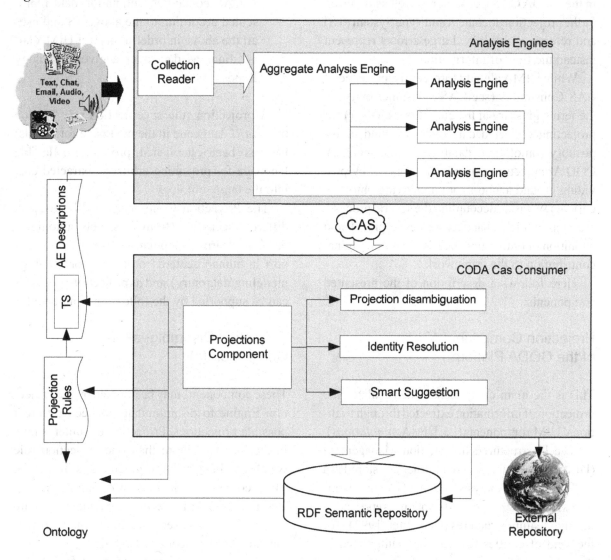

As for UIMA, CODA is the given name of both an architecture and of its associated platform; for this reason we use the whole name CODA even when referring to its architecture (whereas the final "A" stands for "Architecture") instead of just COD.

CODA Architecture

The Architecture of CODA defines the components and their interaction at an abstract level, which are then implemented in the homonymous framework.

This architecture builds on top of the industry standard UIMA (tasks 1 and 2) and, for task 3, on the Linguistic Watermark (Pazienza, Stellato, & Turbati, 2008) suite of ontology vocabularies and software libraries for describing linguistic resources and the linguistic aspects of ontologies. Figure 2 depicts the part of the architecture supporting tasks 1 and 2. Tiny arrows represent the *use/depends on* relationship, so that the Semantic Repository (bottom part of the figure) owl:imports the reference ontologies, the projection component *invokes* services from the other three components in the CODA CAS Consumer as well as *is driven by* the projection document and Type System (TS) and reference ontology. Large arrows represent instead the flow of information.

While UIMA already foresees the presence of CAS Consumers (see CAS Consumer entry on the terms glossary at the end of this chapter) for projecting collected data over any kind of repository (ontologies, databases, indices etc…), COD Architecture expands this concept by providing ground anchors for engineering ontology enrichment tasks, decoupling the several processing steps which characterize development and evolution of ontologies. This is our main original contribution to the framework.

Here follows a description of the presented components.

Projection Component (Core of the CODA Platform)

This is the main component which realizes the projection of information extracted through traditional UIM components (i.e. UIMA *Annotations*).

The Unstructured Information Management (UIM) standard foresees data structures stored in a CAS (Common Analysis System). CAS data comprises a *type system*, i.e. a description—represented through feature structures (Carpenter, 1992)—of the kind of entities that can be manipulated in the CAS, and the *data* (modeled after the above type system) which is produced over processed information stream (see also the key terms at the end of this chapter).

This component thus takes as input:

- A Type System (TS from now on)
- A reference *ontology* (we assume the ontology to be written in the RDFS or OWL W3C standard)
- A projection document containing projection rules from the TS to the ontology

- A CAS containing annotation data represented according to the above TS and uses all the above in order to project UIMA annotations as data over a given Ontology Repository.

A projection rule specification (see section on *PEARL* language in the next page for details) has also been established, providing a flexible language for projecting arbitrary extracted data into the target ontology.

The Projection Component can be used in different scenarios (from massively automated ontology learning/population scenarios, to support in human centered processes for ontology modeling/data entry), and its projection processes can be supported by the following components.

Projection Disambiguation Component(s)

These components may be invoked by the Projection Engine to disambiguate between different possible projections. Projection documents may in fact describe more than one projection rule which can be applied to given types in the TS. These components are thus, by definition, associated to entries in Projection Documents and are automatically invoked when more than a rule is matched on the incoming CAS data.

This component has access by default to the managed Semantic Repository (and any reference ontology for the Projection rules), to obtain a picture of the ongoing process which can contribute to the disambiguation process.

Identity Resolution

Whenever an annotation is projected towards ontology data, the services of this component are invoked to identify potential matches between the annotated info which is being reified into the semantic repository, and resources already present inside it.

If the Identity Resolution (IR) component discovers a match, then the new entry is suggested to be the same as the pre-existing one; that is, any new data is added to the resource description while duplicated information (probably the one which helped in finding the match) is discarded.

The IR component may look up on the same repository which is being fed by CODA though also external repositories of LOD (linked open data) can be accessed. Eventually, entity naming resolutions provided by external services—such as the Entity Naming System (ENS) OKKAM (Bouquet, Stoermer, & Bazzanella, 2008)—may be combined with internal lookup on the local repository. The component interface is agnostic with respect to the algorithms used to compute the identity, and are used instead for properly informing the system whenever matching identities are found during resource generation.

The Input for this component is composed of:

- External RDF repositories (providing at least search functionalities over their resources)
- Entity Naming Systems access methods
- Other parameters needed by specific implementation of the component

Smart Suggestion Component(s)

These components help in proposing suggestions on how to fill empty slots in projection rules (such as subjects in datatype property projections or free variables in complex FS to graph-pattern projections). As for Disambiguation Components, these components can be written for specific Projection Documents and associated to the rules described inside them, as supporting computational objects.

PEARL: The ProjEction of Annotations Rule Language

One of the main features of CODA is PEARL, the ProjEction of Annotations Rule Language: a language used to describe projections from annotations taken after UIMA Type Systems towards RDF. A simplified version of the language grammar, expressed in Backus-Naur form, can be seen in Figure 3.

Core elements of the language are the Projection Rules, which enable users to describe matches over a set of annotations taken by UIMA components over streams of unstructured information, and to specify how the matched annotations will be transformed into sensible information which will be in turn imported inside the target ontology. The concept is very close to XSL Transformations over XML: template + rewrite rules. The main difference resides in the applicability of its templates at model level (RDF) instead of syntactic level (XML syntactic patterns).

We describe here the structure of a typical projection document, namely a document containing a set of projection rules.

Structure of a Projection Document

Each projection document (a document containing PEARL rules) can be considered as divided into two main parts: in the upper part there is a listing of all the namespace prefixes that will be used in the projection rules for what concerns ontology resources, and the second part, which is normally longer, contains the projection rules. An example of a Projection Document with two rule declarations is provided in Figure 4.

Prefix Declaration

The first part of a projection document contains all the ontology prefixes (my, xsd, bibo, and foaf in the example) being used in the projection rules.

Figure 3. BNF of (part of) the grammar used in the projection rule file

```
prRules := prefixDeclaration* prRule+ ;
prefixDeclaration := prefix '=' namespace ';';
prRule := 'rule' uimaTypePR (ID ':' idVal)? Conf? ('dependsOn'
         (depend)+)? '{' alias? nodes? graph where? parameters? ';'? '}';
depends := DependType '(' idVal ')';
alias := 'alias' '=' '{' singleAlias+ '}' ;
singleAlias := idAlias uimaTypeAndFeats ;
nodes := 'nodes' '=' '{' node+ '}' ;
node := idNode type (uimaTypeAndFeats | condIf);
condIf := 'if' condValueAndUIMAType condElseIf* condElse?;
condValueAndUIMAType := '(' condBool ')' '{'uimaTypeAndFeats | OntoRes'}';
condElseIf := 'else if' condValueAndUIMAType ;
condElse := 'else' '{'uimaTypeAndFeats | OntoRes'}' ;
graph := 'graph' '=' '{' triple+ '}' ;
triple := tripleSubj  triplePred  tripleObj
        | 'OPTIONAL' '{' tripleSubj  triplePred  tripleObj '}';
where := tripleSubj  triplePred  tripleObj
        | 'OPTIONAL' '{' tripleSubj  triplePred  tripleObj '}';parameters :=
'parameters' '=' '{' (parameterNameValue (','
parameterNameValue)*)?   '}';
parameterNameValue := parameterName ('=' val=parameterValue)? ;
```

Note that these prefixes may not be the same (though they may overlap) of those which have been declared inside the target ontology and are independent from that declaration. They thus are local to the projection process, are used to expand prefixed names inside the document into valid RDF URIs and no trace of them is left in the target ontology.

Projection Rules

After the prefix declaration, the projection document lists the projection rules and their descriptions (2 projection rules in the example).

Each Projection Rule is divided into the following parts (some of them are optional): a *rule*

declaration, followed by its *definition*, which is in turn composed of the following sections: *nodes*, *graph*, *where* and *parameters*.

Rule Declaration

Each rule starts with a declaration, expressed through the keyword "rule" and concluding with a curly bracket "{" initiating its definition. The first element in the declaration is the UIMA type from the adopted UIMA Type System: any UIMA annotation taken after that type (written following the UIMA standards regarding types, as a dot-separated package name followed by a capitalized word referring to the Type in the UIMA Type System) will trigger the rule. After the type

Figure 4. Example of a projection rule file

```
my=http://Publication#;
xsd=http://www.w3.org/2001/XMLSchema#;
foaf=http://xmlns.com/foaf/0.1/;
bibo= http://purl.org/ontology/bibo/;


rule it.uniroma2.Book id:book1 0.9 {

    nodes = {
        book          uri                    _it.uniroma2.Book:title
        title         plainLiteral           _it.uniroma2.Book:title
        author        uri                    _it.uniroma2.Book:author
        authorName    literal(xsd:String)    _it.uniroma2.Book:author
        editor        uri                    _it.uniroma2.Book:editor
        isbn          literal(xsd:String)    _it.uniroma2.Book:isbn
    }

    graph= {
        $book         a                      bibo:Book       .
        $book         <bibo:title>           $title          .
        $book         bibo:author            ?author         .
        ?author       foaf:name              $authorName     .
        $book         bibo:editor            $editor         .
        $book         bibo:isbn              $isbn           .
    }

    where = {
        ?author       foaf:name              $authorName .
    }

    parameters={mandatory,reference=false};

}


rule it.uniroma2.Site dependsOn last(book1) {

    nodes={
        site          literal(xsd:anyURI)      it.uniroma2.Site
    }

    graph = {
        $book1:book my:site                  $site
    }
}
```

declaration, there is an optional rule identifier that can be used to make references to a rule from other rules, according to different relationships of dependency. Then we have a number in the range of 0..1, representing a confidence value which can be used by to rank different rules of the same type. Decision whether to apply all rules, only the first one or, for example, letting the users make their choice, is up to the external application exploiting CODA. The declaration may end with a list of dependencies to other rules. Each dependency must specify the *relationship* which is being established (e.g. the second rule in the example in Figure 4 states that when this rule will be used it will have a dependency with the *last* occurrence of the first rule).

Alias

This optional section is used to define aliases that will be used in the Nodes part (see next section). An alias is a compact way to use a value which is present inside a feature of the given annotation type. This means that by using an alias ('$'+alias_name) in the Nodes part we mean the value, if present, contained in that particular feature.

Nodes

The third part, which is optional only if the rules depends on another one, provides a list of placeholders for ontology nodes. These placeholders are used to state which features of the triggered UIMA type are important for the target ontology, and to specify which kind of RDF nodes (URI, typed literal, plain literal) will be used as recipients to host the information that will be projected from them. For instance, in the first rule in Figure 4, the UIMA feature *it.uniroma2.Book:title* will be projected both as an RDF named resource (URI) and as a simple string (plainLiteral): in the first case an URI is created after the feature's content (book placeholder), and will be used as the resource identifying the extracted book, while in the second case a literal value (title placeholder) is generated to populate a property of the book (see next *Graph* section for details about the projection). A set of operators are available for applying different transformations to the features, converting them into valid RDF nodes. Default conversions are applied when no operator is specified, and are inferred on the basis of the specified node type (e.g. if the node type is an URI, the feature value is first "sanitized," to remove characters which are incompatible with the URI standard, and then used as a local name and concatenated to the namespace of the target ontology to create an URI).

In UIMA it is possible for a value of a particular feature to be a type itself, thus containing other features and so on recursively, as stated in the feature structure theory: *Feature Path* is a standard notation introduced in UIMA to identify arbitrary values in complex feature structures by describing navigation of nodes into up to the desired value, much in the spirit of XPath for XML.

Sometimes it may be necessary to assign one feature (its value) or statically an RDF resource (e.g. a given OWL Class/Property) depending on the value of another feature. This can be done using the *alias* mechanism and a simple if/else construct as explained in the grammar (the alias is used in the "condBool"). So for example it is possible to assign to the placeholder 'gender' the OWL class 'Male' or 'Female' by checking a value of a feature (if that feature has the value 'mr.' we may assign 'Male', conversely, 'Female' will be assigned for the value 'mrs.'). This can be useful because in the GRAPH part of a rule (see next section on graphs) we can have the triple '$person a $gender', which is more specific than '$person a foaf:Person'

Graph

The graph section contains the true projection over the target ontology graph, by describing a graph pattern which is dynamically populated with grounded placeholders and variables (see next paragraph on the where section). The graph pattern[15] consists in a set of triples, where the first element is the subject, the second is the predicate and the third the object of an RDF statement. Each single element in the graph may be one of the following: a *placeholder*, a *variable*, an *RDF node* or an *abbreviation*. Inside a graph pattern, placeholders (defined in the nodes section) are identified by the prefixed symbol "$". Getting back to the example discussed in the previous paragraph, the book placeholder is used in five different triples, always as the subject, since it is the main resource which is being described through other features extracted with UIMA, the title placeholder, which originated from the same feature (but has been converted in a different way, providing a human readable label instead of a formal URI), is instead used to populate the bibo:title property linked to the previous URI. RDF nodes can be references in graph patterns through the usual notation for URIs ("< >" delimited standard URIs) or by prefixed local names. The abbreviations are represented by a finite list of words that can be used in place of explicit reference to RDF resources. For example we included in this list the standard abbreviation from the RDF Turtle format (Beckett & Berners-Lee, 2008)—also adopted in the SPARQL query language—which assumes the character "a" to be interpreted as rdf:type.

Finally, it is possible to use *variables* (by prefixing their names with a "?" symbol) when there is a need to dynamically reference an RDF node already existing in the target ontology, which is not known in advance (i.e. it is not statically added in the rule, but dynamically retrieved from the ontology by means of unification, see next paragraph for more details).

Where

As for *graph* section, the *where* section contains a graph pattern: this pattern is matched over the target ontology to retrieve nodes already existing in it by means of variable unification (variables are identifiable by a prefixed "?" symbol), so that the variables substitutions can be reused in the *graph* section. The purpose of this graph is to be able to link newly extracted data with information which is already present in the target ontology. In this sense, it is much close to the purpose of the *where* statement in a SPARQL CONSTRUCT[16] query. The unification mechanism allows values to be assigned to variables by constraining them on the basis of information which is thought to be present in the ontology: these substitutions are then applied to the graph pattern of the graph section to project the data in the over target ontology. New operators can be introduced by custom Identity Resolution components (PEARL is extensible

much in the same way as SPARQL), to search values over the target ontology (or external data such in the case of Entity Naming Systems) instead of just unifying them.

Parameters

The fifth and last part, optional, consist of a list of parameters. A parameter can be in the form of a <name,value> pair or just a name. There is no pre-assigned semantics to any parameter, they are just outputted by any rule when it is being applied, and their meaning is properly interpreted by specific CODA component implementations which may be associated to a given projection document. These parameters can thus be seen as flexible extension points for the language, requiring no dedicated syntax, and conveying specific information (parameter values can contain placeholder/variable assignments) for the appropriate listener.

Rule Execution

The execution flow of a rule is shown in Figure 5: the depicted status of placeholders and variables is considered to represent their assignment at the start of each phase. The execution starts by parsing and replacing all prefixes and assigning them to namespaces, then it moves to the *nodes* section, by creating values for the placeholders; these values are then assigned to placeholders appearing in the graph of the *where* section (and forwarded to the *graph* too), which is then matched over the target ontology graph, by unifying the variables contained into it. Ground values assigned to variables after the graph match and the already calculated placeholders are then replaced in the graph pattern of the *graph* section, the content of which is finally added to the target ontology.

Both the *WHERE* and *GRAPH* graph patterns applications can fail. In the first case, the *WHERE* graph application is a match against the target

Figure 5 PEARL execution flow

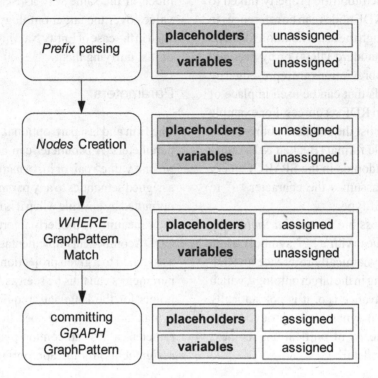

ontology: a failed match is always considered as having a result-set of a single tuple with all variables unbound. All of SPARQL operators can be used in the *WHERE* clause to alter the matching strategy.

The application of the *GRAPH* graph pattern (that is, writing triples to the target ontology) is different: the graph does not need to be matched against the target ontology, but instead to be written into it; in this case, satisfying the graph is considered as satisfying the set of all write operations on each triple. A write operation succeeds if all the three elements of its triple are bound (instantiated). The OPTIONAL modifier here is similar to the one in the *WHERE*: the whole writing of the graph pattern is not compromised if the triples inside an OPTIONAL clause fails to be written (they are not completely instantiated), and these are simply left out from the global write of the graph.

If the application of a *GRAPH* graph pattern write fails, no triple is written to the target ontology (for that rule application).

It is possible to note how, in the example in Figure 4, the placeholder $author is never used in the rule, though it is being created inside the *nodes* rule fragment. This brings in another feature of the variable assignment process: whenever a variable in the final *GRAPH* pattern is not bound, before declaring that write to be failed, the processor tries to match it with a placeholder of identical name. In the case of the example, the variable ?author is used two times: the first time as the object of the property bibo:author and the second time as the subject of the property foaf:name. The value of that variable is bound to a match in the target ontology, looking for already existing authors with the same name: if the match succeeds, then the variable is bound and initialized with the URI already assigned to the author with that name, conversely, if the match fails, the variable is not bound, but a placeholder with the same name is found, so its value will be used in place. The idea is that if the author already exists in the target ontology, then its URI is retrieved, otherwise a URI is generated for it.

Templates

Templates are a useful feature of the PEARL language which allow, very closely to programming languages such as C++, to create parametric definitions of rules which can be saved into libraries of projections and then be easily identifiable and reusable in different contexts. A template projection rule can thus be identified by a simple *template signature*, which is composed of the template name and by its set of parameters (which occur in the template rule definition). New rules can then be generated by referring the opportune template and by assigning values to the parameters. Rule resolution does not change; it is handled as a pre-processer macro expansion: simply a projection document containing reference to templates is rewritten by expanding the template references in their rule definitions, by replacing the parameters with their assigned values, and then the normal PEARL execution flow is activated.

Here we provide two simple examples of rule templates:

- *Projecting CAS Feature Structures (FS) as instances of a given class*. A single entity from a UIMA type system can be projected as an instance of a given class
- *Projecting FSs as values of datatype properties*. This requires ontology instances to be elected as subjects for each occurrence of this projection, usually by specifying a reference to another rule.

Another relevant feature of rule templates is the possibility to specify *decorators* for parameters:

decorators may be used to convey semantics to external applications about the nature of the objects to be projected. For instance, an interactive annotation tool recognizing a given parameter to be recognized as a *class* resource, would allow the user—anytime a given template rule implementation is being applied—to choose the proper class among the subclasses of the one assigned to the parameter, by showing a *class tree* rooted on it.

The CODA Framework and Its Objectives

CODA Framework is an effort to facilitate development of systems implementing the COD Architecture, by providing a core platform and highly reusable components for realization of COD tasks.

Main objectives of this architectural framework are:

1. Orchestration of all processes supporting COD tasks
2. Interface-driven development of COD components
3. Maximizing reuse of components and code
4. Tight integration with available environments, such as UIMA for management of unstructured information from external resources (e.g. text documents) and Linguistic Watermark (Pazienza, Stellato, & Turbati, 2008) for management of linguistic resources
5. Minimizing required LOCs (lines of code) and effort for specific COD component development, by providing high level languages (and implementations for associated processors) for matching/mapping components I/O specifications instead of developing software adapters for their interconnection
6. Providing standard implementations for components realizing typical support steps for COD tasks, such as management of cor-

pora, user interaction, validation, evaluation, production of reference data (oracles, gold standards) for evaluation, identity discoverers etc…

With respect to components described in the previous section, the CODA Framework provides the main Projection Component (and its associated projection language), a basic implementation of an Identity Resolution Component, and all the required business logic to fulfill COD tasks through orchestration of COD components.

Possible Application Scenarios

In our attempt to fulfill the above objectives, we envision several application scenarios for CODA. We provide here descriptions of a few of them.

Fast Integration of Existing UIMA Components for Ontology Population

By providing projections from CAS type systems to ontology vocabularies via PEARL, one could easily embed standard UIMA AEs (Analysis Engines) and make them able to populate ontology concepts pointed by the projections, without requiring development of any new software component. Moreover (number 6 above), standard or customized identity discoverers will try to suggest potential matches between entities annotated by the AE and already existing resources in the target ontology, to keep identity of individual resources and add further description to them. In this scenario, given an ontology and an AE, only the projection from the CAS type system of the AE to the ontology is needed (and optionally, a customized identity discoverer). Everything else is assumed to be automatically embedded and coordinated by the framework.

Rapid Prototyping of Ontology Learning Algorithms

This is the opposite situation of the scenario above. CODA, by reusing the same chaining of UIMA components, ontologies, CAS-to-Ontology projections, identity discoverers etc., may provide:

- A preconfigured CAS type system (Ontology Learning CAS Type System) for representing information to be extracted under the scope of standard ontology learning tasks
- Preconfigured projections from above CAS type system to learned ontology triples, in the form of PEARL templates (see subsection on PEARL templates) dedicated to Ontology Learning
- Extended interface definitions for UIMA analysis engines dedicated to ontology learning tasks: available abstract adapter classes will implement the standard UIMA AnalysisComponent interface, interacting with the above Ontology Learning CAS type system and exposing specific interface methods for the different learning tasks

In this scenario, developers willing to rapidly deploy prototypes for new ontology learning algorithms, will be able to focus on algorithm implementation and benefit of the whole framework, disburdening them from corpora management and generation of ontology data. This level of abstraction far overtakes the *Modeling Primitive Library* of Text2Onto (i.e. a set of generic modeling primitives abstracting from specific ontology model adopted and being based on the assumption that the ontology exposes at least a traditional object oriented design, such as that of OKBC (Chaudhri, Farquhar, Fikes, Karp, & Rice, 1998)). In fact in CODA ontology learning tasks are actively defined in terms of reusable projection rules, which just provide UIMA anchors for Analysis Engines to be developed by researchers. For instance, pairs of terms could be produced by taxonomy learners, which are then be projected as IS-A or type-of relationships by the framework.

Plugging Algorithms for Automatic Linguistic Enrichment of Ontologies

In such a scenario, the user is interested in enriching ontologies with linguistic content originated from external lexical resources. The Linguistic Watermark library—which is already been used in tools for (multilingual) linguistic enrichment of ontologies (Pazienza, Stellato, & Turbati, 2010) and which constitutes a fundamental module of CODA—supports uniform access to heterogeneous resources wrapped upon a common model for lexical resource definition, allows for their integration with ontologies and for evaluation of the acquired information. The objective is to relieve developers from technical details such as resource access, ontology interaction and update, by providing standard facilities associated to tasks for ontology-lexicon integration/enrichment, and thus leaving up to them the sole objective of implementing enrichment algorithms.

User Interaction for Knowledge Acquisition and Validation

User interaction is a fundamental aspect when dealing with decision-support systems. Prompting the user with compact and easy-to-analyze reports on the application of automated processes, and putting at his hands instruments for validating choices made by the system can dramatically improve the outcome of processes for knowledge acquisition as well as support supervised training of these same processes. CODA front-end tools should thus provide CODA specific applications supporting training of learning-based COD components, automatic acquisition of information from web pages visualized through the browser

(or management of info previously extracted from entire corpora of documents) and editing of main CODA data structures (such as UIMA CAS types, projection documents and, obviously, ontologies). Interactive tools should support iterative refinement of massive production of ontology data as well as human-centered process for ontology development/evolution.

This last important environment is a further very relevant objective, and motivated us to develop UIMAST (Fiorelli, Pazienza, Petruzza, Stellato, & Turbati, 2010), an extension for Semantic Turkey (Griesi, Pazienza, & Stellato, 2007)—a Semantic Web Knowledge Acquisition and Management platform[17] hosted on the Firefox Web Browser—to act as a CODA front-end for doing interactive knowledge acquisition from web pages. Figure 6 displays a screenshot from UIMAST, where a standard PEARL template for populating classes with instances is applied to a UIMA Named Entity Recognizer: UIMAST prompts the user with a cascade of classes rooted on the class which is being mapped to the Named Entry Recognizer (Person), taken from the currently edited ontology. In this scenario, the user has yet full control of the Knowledge Acquisition process, yet their effort is incredibly lessened as their choices are strongly driven by constraints of the imported projection rules.

SODA

The upper layer of the whole SODA layer cake (called SODA itself) is the true part dedicated to Service-Oriented Data Acquisition, so it is focused on an open architecture and framework for provisioning of CODA components. In short, with respect to available extraction-on-demand services, SODA provides the required components that a SODA compliant client can assemble to semi-automatically compose data acquisition systems. This process, as already discussed, has a series of advantages, such as:

Figure 6. Knowledge acquisition with UIMAST

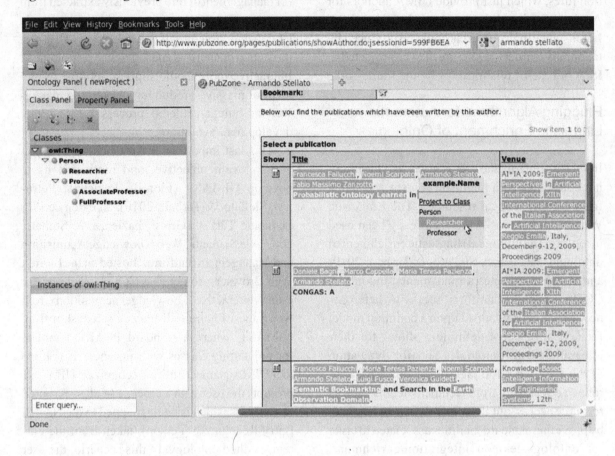

1. *Total data protection guaranteed at physical level*: unstructured information is processed on the client machine and is never sent to the service. There is no need of any security infrastructure nor of trusting the SODA provider[18]

2. *support for very large corpora and heavy-processing*: again, thanks to the downloaded components being activated on the client machine, users are free to setup heavy-processing hardware and just get the business logic (CODA components) from the web. This does not prevent the creation of OpenCalais-like solutions based on SODA, i.e. where the service takes care of all the processing, acquires the unstructured information and returns result to the client.

Simply, the system is truly open, and all options in this sense are viable.

3. *an increased level of flexibility*. SODA is a provider of CODA/UIMA components and of CODA projection documents as well. The SODA search services can be used to download the components and projections which mostly reflect user needs, and customize them to exactly fit these needs, for instance, by adapting projections for a given "famous" vocabulary, to a specific vocabulary which is not supported by SODA or by replacing one UIMA component with a locally improved version (by using the same UIMA Type System or by adapting the projections to the one which is being adopted by the replacing component)

The main services provided by SODA are:

- *retrieval of CODA projection documents* for a given vocabulary specified by the user
- *download of UIMA components*, by inspecting available UIMA AEs and matching them with those required by available projection documents for the specified ontology

Further services are then built around this platform, still with the intention of satisfying specific needs and exigencies related to the provisioning of data acquisition components. For instance, whenever no projection document is available for a given vocabulary, the system provides a semantic matching service which looks for projection documents available for ontologies having a domain overlap with the desired one. If one or more candidates are found, a new projection document is dynamically produced by properly readapting those which have been retrieved, to project towards the desired target vocabulary. Results of the above process are also cached, and can be proposed to the next user requesting CODA setups for the same vocabularies, while specifying that they have been automatically produced (for purposes of assessing quality of extraction components).

SODA Architecture

SODA is flexible and scalable service oriented platform-independent solution. The functionalities of the platform may be extended by integrating further components, such as new web services or API calls.

At the time being SODA Architecture is composed of the modules described in Figure 7. The following sections provide detailed descriptions for all of them.

Figure 7 SODA: general view of the architecture

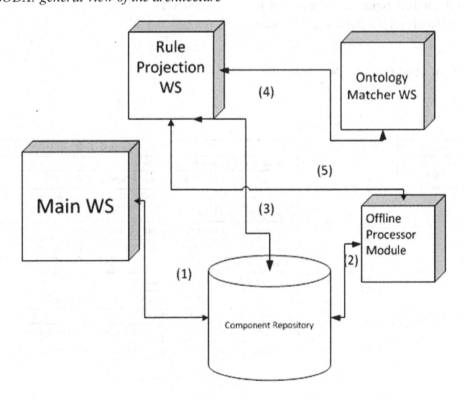

Main Web Service Module

The scenario for consuming this service is the following one: a SODA enabled client is looking for appropriate Information Extraction components to populate the ontology it is being managing (we refer to it as the *target ontology* from now on) and thus sends a request to this service, specifying the namespace of the target ontology.

The role of this web service is thus to establish communication with the client, that is to register SODA enabled clients' requests (in the form of the namespace of their target ontology) and to return to them the UIMA Pear Component and the Projection Rule Document which are most appropriate for the client's target ontology. The output containing all the previously mentioned components is returned to the client either immediately or after required offline processing (such as the above mentioned semantic matching) has been concluded, by means of a ticket mechanism.

Whenever the ontology URI submitted by the client application as part of the request is available on the SODA repository, the output is returned immediately (or if a request for the same URI was previously processed by the system, the caching mechanism guarantees an immediate reply as well).

Otherwise, in the case of a newly introduced ontology URI, the system responds to the client by sending a ticket, which represents a unique identifier of the request (UID). By using this ticket the client can resubmit a query to the server from time to time to check if its request has been satisfied or not. In this case, when having a newly registered ontology, the system immediately passes on the request to a dedicated semantic coordination service in charge of processing the request and of interacting with other specialized components to accomplish the task.

The interface of this web service is presented in Figure 8; here we provide a detailed description of all of its methods:

registerClientInformation

The *registerClientInformation* method has the following elements:

INPUT:

Figure 8. SODA: main web service module interface

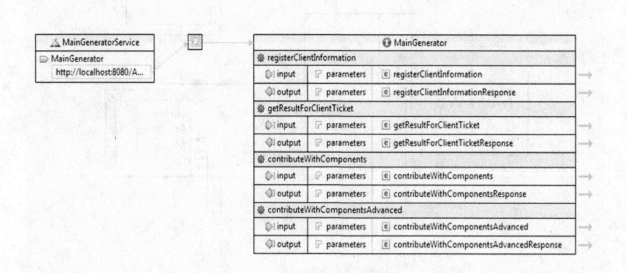

- *requestType* – indicates weather the client is a *lazy* client or a *developer*. We will discuss more in the next section the importance of such a parameter.
- *operatingSystem* – indicates the operating system of the client platform. This parameter is important because some components that are stored in the repository might have restrictions regarding some Operating Systems.
- *ontologyURI* – the URI of the client's *target ontology*.

OUTPUT:

- *URIList* – represents the list of URIs of the individual UIMA Pear components. The list is returned as a comma separated string.
- *aggregatedDescriptor* – returns the content of the aggregated UIMA Analysis Engine (AAE). The AAE is obtained based on the individual components.
- *projectionRules* – represents the projection rules associated to the identify components, that project UIMA Features or TypeSystem into the classes of the client ontology.
- *prefixNamespaces* – the list of namspace prefixes, returned as a string.
- *clientTicket* – unique identifier for client request. If the ontology was not previously processed than the client can return in the system by using this UID to check if its request was completed.

ROLE:

This method records the information regarding the client request in the database. Afterwards, checks if the ontology URI was processed. In case it appears in the database, the associated components are retrieved and sent to the client under the format presented above. Otherwise, the request is recorded in the database with the status "Pending". From time to time (10 minutes), the offline processor module checks the database and retrieves all the pending requests and processes them offline (through the Semantic Matching process cited above).

getResultForClientTicket

the *getResultForClientTicket* method is characterized by the following:

INPUT:

- *IdClientRequest* – represents the ticket received by the client when registering its request

OUTPUT:

- the same type of output as for the method presented above

ROLE:

The method queries the database and checks the status of the client request. If the status is "Processed" than the client receives the complete output (as presented in the method above), otherwise it is informed that the request has not yet been processed and is requested to retry after a while.

contributeWithComponent

The *contributeWithComponent* method enables users to contribute to the repository by uploading UIMA Pear components. Uploading a component does not require any projection document to be associated to it. The SODA repository is actually also a UIMA component repository and new UIMA components can be registered and stored in the SODA repository, independently from their use in SODA. Contributed UIMA components can later be associated to projection rules by other SODA contributors.

INPUT:

- *componentURI* – a string representing the URI of the component
- *componentDesc* – a string containing the description of the component.

OUTPUT:

- *feedback* – a string that informs the contributor whether the upload was performed successfully or not, or if the component is valid or not.

ROLE:

This method is targeted to extend the system's data repository and to involve the UIMA community into the creation of a component repository. The contributor introduces into the system the URI of their UIMA Pear component and a short description of its functionalities. The system validates the component by trying to download and install it. If no errors occur and the component is valid the contributor is informed that their contribution was successfully recorded, otherwise they receive an error message and are asked to resubmit.

contributeWithComponentAdvanced

The *contributeWithComponentsAdvanced* method enables CODA clients to contribute to the repository by providing an ontology (referenced through its URI) and a set of projection rules and associated UIMA Component Pears for extracting and projecting data over it.

INPUT:

- *ontologyURI* – a string representing the URI of the client ontology
- *componentElementVector* – a string containing the serialized vector of UIMA Components URIs and their description and also the associated Projection rule.

OUTPUT:

- *feedback* – a string that informs the contributor whether the upload was performed successfully or not, or if the component is valid or not.

ROLE:

The purpose of this method is to allow a community of users to contribute the repository with new ontologies, extraction components and projection documents.

The system validates the components by trying to download and install them. If no errors occur and the components are valid then the contributor is informed that their contribution was successfully recorded, otherwise they receive an error message and are asked to resubmit. Figure 9 presents a screenshot of the application dedicated to the components contributors.

Offline Processing Module

This module is in charge of processing clients' requests offline. It queries from time to time the database and retrieves all the pending requests. For each request, it first downloads the requested vocabulary (we assume the vocabulary is expressed in one of the W3C standards of the RDF family: RDF/RDFS/OWL/SKOS) and identifies all the concepts[19] of the vocabulary.

Afterwards, based on the analyzed concepts from the ontology/thesaurus, the module tries to identify which UIMA components might be identified as possible matches based on the component description (in particular, on their *Type System*) and, if available, on the ontologies already associated to these components. For each identified component it retrieves from the database the ontology URI that was previously matched with it, in case there is one. For every ontology URI that was identified as a possible match, the system performs a check. The check is done by submitting

Figure 9. A screenshot of the service page for contributing new components

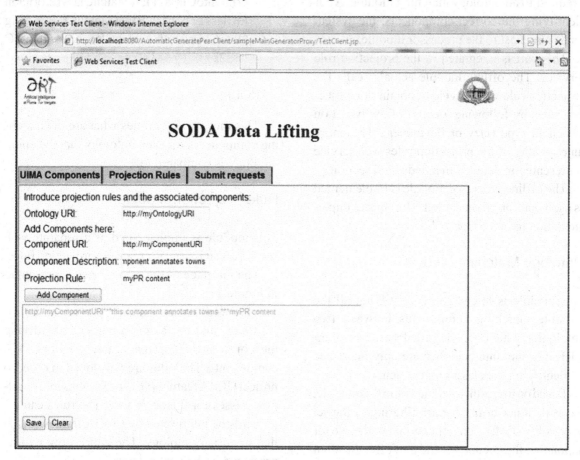

Figure 10. SODA ontology matching web service interface

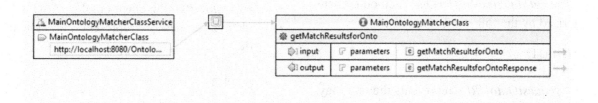

Figure 11. SODA-rule projector web service

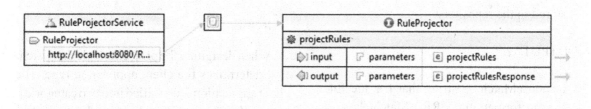

a request to an ontology matching module. After identifying the correct components, the system sends a request to the processor module.

This part is integrated in the projection rule services. The offline module actually calls the projection rule web service to obtain the projection rules by following a certain flow based on the client type (lazy or developer). The entire functionality of the projection rules web service is presented in detailed in a dedicated section.

The offline processor module is implemented as a job that can be scheduled. The current implementation uses the Quartz library.

Ontology Matching Module

This module is in charge of identifying all the possible matching components between two ontologies which are identified based on their URL. For the time being we are only interested in identifying the classes that match.

Based on the results obtained from this module, the system performs an extra filtering of the set of possible UIMA Components that will serve for annotating the documents and also offer the input for the rule projection flow.

The interface of the web service is presented in Figure 10.

The *getMatchResultsforOnto* method is characterized by the following elements:

INPUT:

- *requestOntoURI* – represents the ontology URI that the client uses
- *commaSeparatedPossibleOnto-* represents a comma separated string containing all the possible matching ontologies that are stored in the repository.

OUTPUT:

- responseMatch –a string that has the following format: ont1URI|_|(MatchClass11,

origOntoClass11)!#(MatchClass12,origOntoClass12);ont2URI|_|(MatchClass21,origOntoClass21)!#(MatchClass22,origOntoClass22)

ROLE:

This method determines what are the matching components for each ontology that the client ontology is compared to.

Rule Projection Module

This module is implemented as a separate web service and it is used to create the projection rules.

The interface of the web service is presented in Figure 11.

This web service has only one method, *projectRules*, that has as main purpose identifying the projection rules or creating new ones for UIMA components. The rules are developed in order to project UIMA features or TypeSystems into ontology classes for the beginning. The rules can afterwards be interpreted by CODA framework so that to enrich ontology. The entire flow will be presented in the next section.

INPUT:

- *reqOntoURI* – the client ontology URI
- idClientRequest – represents the client ticket

OUTPUT:

- *projectionRule* – the projection rule created by the system according to the business rules that will be presented below.

ROLE:

When designing the projection rule the system first determines the client application type. The client application is classified into two categories: lazy or developer. If the client is a lazy one than the rules that will be sent to him will be only the ones that were previously validated, that is the ones that were already in the repository for the components identified as matching.

This method makes a call to the "Ontology Matching Web Service." After retrieving the response, it parses it. For every component that was identified as a match, the system retrieves the rules from the database and changes the ontology class name within the rule. If the existing rule was a validated rule and the client was lazy or developer than the rule is saved in the database as associated to the client request. Otherwise, if the existing rule was not validated and the client was a lazy one, than the rule is not associated and the rule projection algorithm continues to investigate the other components.

For the components that were identified by the windows service as suitable for the ontology, but were not selected as matching components with other already existing ontology, the system creates new projection rules only if the client request was "developer". The creation of the new rule consists in extracting the type systems, or the features that are present within the UIMA Analysis Engine from the UIMA Pear component. Afterwards, the features are projected into an ontology class. A simple sample rule can be seen below:

```
my=http://art.uniroma2.it/ontologies/
st_example#;
rule it.uniroma2.art.uima.Author
id:author1 0.9 {
        nodes = {
                person     uri
it.uniroma2.art.uima.Author:name
        }
        graph = {
                ?person    a
my:Person    .
        }
}
```

The rule above can be interpreted as follows: the entity annotated as *it.uniroma2.art.uima. Author* is projected into the target RDF, with a confidence of 0.9. The feature that is projected is *name*, the class to which it is projected is my:Person

FUTURE RESEARCH DIRECTIONS

The ambitions of such a complex framework as SODA is to embrace a wide community of users, establishing a milestone for industry-level Text Analysis and Content Management by fostering component re-use and fast deployment of information processing systems. In this sense, much of the future effort should be spent on actively supporting its adoption (e.g. by providing a bootstrapped repository of SODA projection rules and UIMA components accessible via SODA services, by documenting all the layers both at user and developer level to enable further contributions by communities of developers etc…).

However, the purpose of such an architecture, as a research effort, is also to lay the path for other approaches acting in the same direction, by riding state-of-the-art research and industry-level solutions to feed new ideas in it. In this sense, one of the foreseen actions for the future is to improve the semantic search functionalities based on semantic matching (currently based on naïve implementations of these techniques), by applying clustering and recommendation algorithms to the description of UIMA components, and to take into account the constraints imposed by the client systems, specified through the client request. The objective is to avoid the typical "go-off-from-your-working-environment-and-Google search your components" to enable instead fully-fledged semantic search services enabling components search and browsing of components which are semantically connected according to common purposes, data formats being used and other contradistinguishing features.

Another aspect which has to be improved is the relationship with other software provisioning frameworks, such as Maven: combining both efforts, probably reusing traditional provisioning frameworks for dependency resolution and physical provisioning while demanding to SODA search and component/rule harmonization can even better separate the specifications and have SODA benefit of already available solutions.

CONCLUSION

In this work we have introduced SODA, an architecture and a platform for supporting and automatizing the creation and population of semantic repositories and ontologies based on models of the RDF family. One characterizing aspect of SODA, which distinguishes it from other systems of this kind, is its real total openness: from component provisioning to extraction services, all of the layers which constitute SODA can be re-elaborated to suit specific needs and fit into different scenarios. This also assures data protection and privacy, where components contributed by the community may be downloaded and coordinated into private deployments of semantic data acquisition systems.

The objective of this contribution lies in the engineering of data acquisition processes, by offering formal languages and tools for driving information management from core raw sources to structured data, and by providing specifications and concrete frameworks for the realization of content processing and knowledge elicitation systems.

REFERENCES

Basili, R., Vindigni, M., & Zanzotto, F. (2003). *Integrating ontological and linguistic knowledge for conceptual information extraction*. Paper presented at the IEEE/WIC International Conference on Web Intelligence. Washington, DC.

Beckett, D., & Berners-Lee, T. (2008). *Turtle - Terse RDF triple language*. Retrieved from http://www.w3.org/TeamSubmission/turtle/.

Berners-Lee, T., Hendler, J. A., & Lassila, O. (2001). The semantic web: A new form of web content that is meaningful to computers will unleash a revolution of new possibilities. *Scientific American*, *279*(5), 34–43. doi:10.1038/scientificamerican0501-34

Bizer, C., Heath, T., & Berners-Lee, T. (2009). Linked data - The story so far. *International Journal on Semantic Web and Information Systems*, *5*(3), 1–22. doi:10.4018/jswis.2009081901

Bouquet, P., Stoermer, H., & Bazzanella, B. (2008). An entity naming system for the semantic web. In *Proceedings of the 5th European Semantic Web Conference (ESWC 2008)*. Springer Verlag.

Buitelaar, P., Declerck, T., Frank, A., Racioppa, S., Kiesel, M., Sintek, M., et al. (2006). *LingInfo: Design and applications of a model for the integration of linguistic information in ontologies*. Paper presented at OntoLex06. Genoa, Italy.

Buitelaar, P., Olejnik, D., & Sintek, M. (2004). A protégé plug-in for ontology extraction from text based on linguistic analysis. In *Proceedings of the 1st European Semantic Web Symposium (ESWS)*. Heraklion, Greece: ESWS Press.

Buyko, E., Chiarcos, C., & Pareja Lora, A. (2008). Ontology-based interface specifications for an NLP pipeline architecture. In *Proceedings of the 6th International Conference on Language Resources and Evaluation*. Marrakech, Morocco: LREC Press.

Carpenter, B. (1992). *The logic of typed feature structures: Cambridge tracts in theoretical computer science* (*Vol. 32*). Cambridge, UK: Cambridge University Press. doi:10.1017/CBO9780511530098

Cerbah, F., & Daille, B. (2007). A service oriented architecture for adaptable terminology acquisition. In Kedad, Z., Lammari, N., Métais, E., Meziane, F., & Rezgui, Y. (Eds.), *Natural Language Processing and Information Systems* (*Vol. 4592*, pp. 420–426). Berlin, Germany: Springer. doi:10.1007/978-3-540-73351-5_40

Chaudhri, V. K., Farquhar, A., Fikes, R., Karp, P., & Rice, J. P. (1998). OKBC: A programmatic foundation for knowledge base interoperability. In *Proceedings of the Fifteenth National Conference on Artificial Intelligence (AAAI-98)*, (pp. 600-607). Cambridge, MA: MIT Press.

Cimiano, P., Haase, P., Herold, M., Mantel, M., & Buitelaar, P. (2007). LexOnto: A model for ontology lexicons for ontology-based NLP. In *Proceedings of the OntoLex07 Workshop*. ISWC Press.

Cimiano, P., & Völker, J. (2005). Text2Onto - A framework for ontology learning and data-driven change discovery. In *Proceedings of the 10th International Conference on Applications of Natural Language to Information Systems*, (pp. 227-238). Alicante, Spain: NLIS Press.

Cunningham, H. (2002). GATE: A general architecture for text engineering. *Computers and the Humanities*, *36*, 223–254. doi:10.1023/A:1014348124664

Cunningham, H., Maynard, D., Bontcheva, K., & Tablan, V. (2002). GATE: A framework and graphical development environment for robust NLP tools and applications. In *Proceedings of the 40th Anniversary Meeting of the Association for Computational Linguistics (ACL 2002)*. Philadelphia, PA: ACL Press.

Dodinet, G. (2005). *Exploiting maven in eclipse*. Retrieved from http://www.ibm.com/developer-works/.

Ferrucci, D. (2009). Unstructured information management architecture (UIMA) version 1.0. In A. Lally, K. Verspoor, & E. Nyberg (Eds.), *OASIS Standard*. Retrieved from http://www.oasis-open.org/.

Ferrucci, D., & Lally, A. (2004). Uima: An architectural approach to unstructured information processing in the corporate research environment. *Natural Language Engineering*, *10*(3-4), 327–348. doi:10.1017/S1351324904003523

Fiorelli, M., Pazienza, M. T., Petruzza, S., Stellato, A., & Turbati, A. (2010). *Computer-aided ontology development: An integrated environment*. Paper presented at New Challenges for NLP Frameworks 2010. La Valletta, Malta.

Gennari, J., Musen, M., Fergerson, R., Grosso, W., Crubézy, M., & Eriksson, H. (2003). The evolution of Protégé-2000: An environment for knowledge-based systems development. *International Journal of Human-Computer Studies*, *58*(1), 89–123. doi:10.1016/S1071-5819(02)00127-1

Griesi, D., Pazienza, M., & Stellato, A. (2007). Semantic turkey - A *Semantic Bookmarking tool: System description*. *Lecture Notes in Computer Science*, *4519*, 779–788. doi:10.1007/978-3-540-72667-8_56

Harman, D. (1992). The DARPA TIPSTER project. *SIGIR Forum*, *26*(2), 26–28. doi:10.1145/146565.146567

Pazienza, M., Scarpato, N., Stellato, A., & Turbati, A. (2008). *Din din! The (semantic) turkey is served!* Semantic Web Applications and Perspectives, 5th Italian Semantic Web Workshop (SWAP2008) Rome, Italy December 15-17.

Pazienza, M., Stellato, A., & Turbati, A. (2008). *Linguistic watermark 3.0: An RDF framework and a software library for bridging language and ontologies in the semantic web*. Paper presented at the Semantic Web Applications and Perspectives, 5th Italian Semantic Web Workshop (SWAP2008). Rome, Italy.

Pazienza, M. T., Stellato, A., & Turbati, A. (2010). A suite of semantic web tools supporting development of multilingual ontologies. In Armano, G., de Gemmis, M., Semeraro, G., & Vargiu, E. (Eds.), *Intelligent Information Access*. Berlin, Germany: Springer-Verlag. doi:10.1007/978-3-642-14000-6_6

Peter, H., Sack, H., & Beckstein, C. (2006). *SMARTINDEXER – Amalgamating ontologies and lexical resources for document indexing*. Paper presented at the Workshop on Interfacing Ontologies and Lexical Resources for Semantic Web Technologies (OntoLex2006). Genoa, Italy.

Peters, W., Montiel-Ponsoda, E., Aguado de Cea, G., & Gómez-Pérez, A. (2007). Localizing ontologies in OWL. In *Proceedings of the OntoLex07 Workshop*. ISWC Press.

Velardi, P., Navigli, R., Cucchiarelli, A., & Neri, F. (2005). Evaluation of ontolearn: A methodology for automatic population of domain ontologie. In *Ontology Learning from Text: Methods, Applications and Evaluation*. IOS Press.

W3C. (2004). *OWL web ontology language*. Retrieved from http://www.w3.org/TR/owl-features/.

W3C. (2009). *SKOS simple knowledge organization system reference*. Retrieved from http://www.w3.org.

Wilkinson, M., Vandervalk, B., & McCarthy, L. (2009). SADI semantic web services - Cause you can't always get what you want! In *Proceedings of the IEEE International Workshop on Semantic Web Services in Practice*, (pp 13-18). Singapore: IEEE Press.

Witte, R., & Gitzinger, T. (2009). Semantic assistants -- User-centric natural language processing services for desktop clients. In *Proceedings of the 3rd Asian Semantic Web Conference (ASWC 2008)*, (vol 5367), (pp. 360-374). Bangkok, Thailand: Springer.

Witte, R., & Papadakis, N. (2009). *Semantic assistants: SOA for text mining*. Paper presented at the CASCON 2009 Technical Showcase. Markham, Canada.

KEY TERMS AND DEFINITIONS

Analysis Engine: A program that analyzes different kinds of documents (text, video, audio, etc) and infers[20] information about them, and which implements the UIMA Analysis Engine interface Specification

Annotator Components Repository: Environment that assures safe storage of different annotator components and also enables the retrieval and editing processes.

CAS Consumer: A component that receives each CAS in the collection, usually after it has been processed by an Analysis Engine. It is responsible for taking the results from the CAS and using them for some purpose, perhaps storing selected results into a database, for instance. The CAS Consumer may also perform collection-level analysis, saving these results in an application-specific, aggregate data structure.

CAS: The UIMA Common Analysis Structure is the primary data structure which UIMA analysis components use to represent and share analysis results. It contains: The artifact. This is the object being analyzed such as a text document or audio or video stream. The CAS projects one or more views of the artifact. Each view is referred to as a *Sofa* (*Subject OF Analysis*); A type system description – indicating the types, subtypes, and their features; Analysis metadata – "standoff" annotations describing the artifact or a region of the artifact; An index repository to support efficient access to and iteration over the results of analysis.

Platform Independence: A model of a software system, that is independent of the specific technological platform used to implement it.

UIMA Pear: An archive file that packages up a UIMA component its code, descriptor files and other resources required to install and run it in another environment

Web Service: A software system designed to support interoperable machine-to-machine interaction over a network which exposes a standard interface in WSDL.

ENDNOTES

[1] http://www.eqentia.com/

[2] http://www.evri.com/

[3] http://www.opencalais.com/

[4] http://www.zemanta.com/

[5] OpenCalais privacy policy reported on http://www.opencalais.com/privacy fully respects the privacy of users with respect to their submitted documents, though strictly-secured documents are clearly not allowed to pass through a web service like that. This is just one of the many cases in which strict privacy policies on the user side end up in the demand for in-house solutions because those offered by free and open services on the web are not able to meet high-privacy requirements.

[6] http://uima.apache.org

[7] http://nlp.stanford.edu/software

[8] http://incubator.apache.org/opennlp/

[9] http://uima.apache.org/

[10] http://ant.apache.org/ivy/

[11] http://maven.apache.org/

[12] http://www.eclipse.org/orbit/

[13] http://ant.apache.org/

[14] The term ontology here is used in a wide sense, covering every data structures from simple vocabularies/thesauri to highly structured content such as OWL ontologies.

[15] See graph pattern specification at: http://www.w3.org/TR/rdf-sparql-query/#GraphPattern

[16] See http://www.w3.org/TR/rdf-sparql-query/#construct for more details.

[17] https://addons.mozilla.org/it/firefox/addon/8880 is the official page on Firefox add-ons site addressing Semantic Turkey extension, while http://semanticturkey.uniroma2.it/ provides an inside view about Semantic Turkey project, with updated downloads, user manuals, developers support and access to ST extensions.

[18] Obviously, this does not prevent from the upload (and consequent download from users) of malicious components sending information to a remote server. On the other hand, the user is free to disconnect the processing machine from the web (or block SODA through a firewall) and thus prevent any undesired flow of information.

[19] In this context, with the term concept we refer to RDFS/OWL *classes* and SKOS *concepts*.

[20] We preferred to leave the definition from the UIMA Glossary, from the Overview and Setup guide available at: http://uima.apache.org/documentation, though we disagree with the use of the term "infers", as such terminology may evoke processes of formal inference, which are mostly distant from the kind of approaches followed in building Analysis Engines.

Section 2
Resource Adoption and Reuse to Build Ontologies and Semantic Repositories

Chapter 4
Mining XML Schemas to Extract Conceptual Knowledge

Ivan Bedini
Alcatel-Lucent Bell Labs, Ireland

Benjamin Nguyen
University of Versailles, France

Christopher Matheus
Alcatel-Lucent Bell Labs, Ireland

Peter F. Patel-Schneider
Alcatel-Lucent Bell Labs, USA

Aidan Boran
Alcatel-Lucent Bell Labs, Ireland

ABSTRACT

One of the promises of the Semantic Web is to support applications that easily and seamlessly deal with heterogeneous data. Most data in the Web, however, is in the Extensible Markup Language (XML) format, but using XML requires applications to understand the format of each data source that they access. Achieving the benefits of the Semantic Web involves transforming XML into the Semantic Web languages, OWL (the Web Ontology Language) and RDF (the Resource Description Framework), a process that generally has manual or only semi-automatic components. In this chapter, the authors present a set of patterns that enable the automatic transformation from XML Schema into RDF and OWL, enabling the direct use of much XML data in the Semantic Web. They focus on a possible logical representation of the first language and present an implementation, including a comparison with related works.

INTRODUCTION

In the last decade, the formalism of eXtensible Markup Language (XML) (Bray, 1998) has reached consensus among the most standards bodies, becoming the de facto standard format for data interchange. Several reasons motivated this choice, the first of them being that XML provides a format that is at the same time both human readable and machine interpretable. Another reason is its simplicity and suppleness of usage that fits well with the greater part of application information exchange requirements. Furthermore, the introduction of the Document Type Definition

DOI: 10.4018/978-1-4666-0188-8.ch004

(DTD) and XML Schema (XSD) (Fallside, 2004) formalisms permits a clean separation between meta-data and instances containing the actual data to be exchanged. Nevertheless, XML still remains, in a certain sense, too open and permits an excess of dialects that tend to overload its basic usage and meanings.

The more recent Web Ontology Language (OWL), along with the Resource Description Framework (RDF) on which it is based, has become another popular standard for data representation and exchange. Being able to translate XML Schema models to OWL ontologies through an automated process offers a significant advantage that can reduce the human work necessary when designing an ontology and the effort required to transform the Web into a Semantic Web.

Throughout this chapter we provide a pragmatic view of XML Schema practices based on a detailed analysis of Business to Business (B2B) standard specifications that, as shown in (Bedini, 2010), describes a large fraction of the usage of this technology. Our goal is to identify practical patterns for demonstrating how XML Schemas can be mined to extract ontological assertions automatically and to provide a concrete and implementable approach that improves existing systems. We show that it is not a simple process, but that this operation requires precise attention on design practices. Moreover we provide some considerations on how to best exploit the semantics given by XML Schema sources to provide labels composed by dictionary word as ontology entities names.

After this first step, we present our implementation to validate our approach and we compare the resulting data transformations with those of other systems. Indeed, as we show, some systems can already derive an OWL ontology from XML Schemas. More often the ontology is obtained with ad hoc mapping of XSD components either to OWL entities or to an intermediate data model. Rather than providing a closed set of mapping procedures, the approach we provide is based on pattern recognition. The 40 patterns we have defined are capable of mapping the most part of XSD constructions by integrating several specific design practices. This behaviour ensures a better interpretation of XML schema sources with the possibility of improving the derivation of the conceptual information handling exceptions. Our pattern-based system can also be extended simply by adding new patterns to fit other specific requirements.

This chapter is organized as follows. First, we introduce some of the main concepts on XML components, focusing on XML Schema. We continue presenting a brief analysis of XML Schema design practices based on B2B standard specifications seen as XML sources. The next sections present XML components and detail 40 transformation patterns. Then we present the prototype we have developed to validate the approach. Afterwards we provide some elements to evaluate our transformations and compare our system and approach with other systems. Finally, we conclude this chapter with a discussion of future works and research directions.

XML DOCUMENTS AND XML SCHEMAS

An XML Schema (Fallside, 2004) formally describes what a given XML document (Bray, 2008) contains, in the same way a database schema describes the data that can be contained in a database (tree structures, data types, integrity constraints, etc.). An XML Schema describes the coarse shape of the XML document. It can be used to express a set of rules to which an XML document must conform to be considered as 'valid' according to that schema, as depicted in Figure 1. Rules can define what fields or sub-element an element can contain. An XML Schema can also describe the values that can be placed into any element or attribute. At present, there exist several XML languages to describe XML documents.

Figure 1. Validating XML data

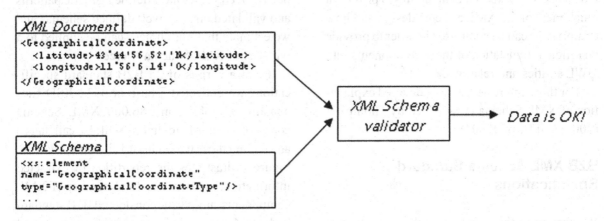

While the primary reason for defining an XML schema is to formally describe the data in a collection of related XML documents an XML Schema can also be useful for other tasks that go beyond simple validation. Indeed the schema can be used to generate human readable documentation (especially useful where the authors have made use of annotation elements) and to generate code (this is referred to as XML Data Binding). From the automatic ontology generation standpoint, the XML Schema data model already includes the vocabulary (named components like elements and attributes), the content model (relationships and structure) and the data types. This allows the extraction of information necessary to define ontology entities and properties.

In the following sub-sections we provide a description of XML Schema components and some figures about their practical adoption in the B2B domain.

XML Schema Components

Technically, an XML Schema is an abstract collection of metadata. This collection is usually created by processing a collection of XML Schema documents, which contains the source language definitions (also known as XML Schemata) of the metadata components. In popular usage, however, a schema document is often referred to as a schema.

Thus for the sake of simplicity, throughout this document XSD, the schema definition language format, will often be the name used to refer to a schema itself.

The W3C XML Schema recommendation (Fallside, 2004) defines an XML Schema as a set of building blocks, also referred to as schema components, that comprise the abstract data model of the schema. There are 13 different components, falling into three groups:

Primary components which may (in case of type definitions) or must (in case of element and attribute declarations) have names: simple type definitions, complex type definitions, attribute declarations and element declarations.

Secondary components, which must have names: attribute group definitions, identity-constraint definitions, model group definitions and notation declarations.

Helper components, which provide small parts of other components and are dependent on their context: annotations, model groups, particles, wildcards and attribute uses.

XML Schema proposes several ways to declare and compose components in a schema declaration. For example we can find at least 17 ways to declare elements (e.g. global/local element, references to a global element, a global/local element which defines a simple/complex type inline declaration, …) and 20 different ways to declare attributes. This makes it challenging to provide a quick view of the XML Schema design and how components can be composed in order to provide an efficient translation of these components into OWL entities and relations.

For those interested, a more detailed explanation of XML Schema is described by Thompson (2004) and Biron (2004).

B2B XML Schema Standard Specifications

We present in this sub-section the analysis of a representative example of XSD source corpus we collected in the B2B domain. We provide here elements to quantify the information we collected and secondly an analysis of some design practices to profile the conceptual knowledge extraction from this kind of source. The result is a tailoring for the extraction operation to XML sources for the B2B domain. However even though it has not

been proved yet we have defined generic patterns and validated on such well defined schemas and we estimate that our choices can be applied to a wide set of XML Schema sources.

From a corpus of 25 B2B standard specifications we collected a base of 3432 XSD files containing more than 586.000 XML Schema components (that hereafter we will also call 'tags') and among these tags at least 170.000 are named. Figure 2 illustrates the repartition of extracted information, measured as total number of XML components, among the considered B2B standard bodies. More detailed information can be found in (Bedini, 2010).

From the *camembert* graph in Figure 2, we observe that Mismo[1] is the more prolific standard body, a few others each provide between 5 and 10% each and around 30% is shared between the remaining standards.

Figure 3 provides a global view of the usage of XML Schema components we have considered.

Figure 2. B2B standard bodies' specifications extraction

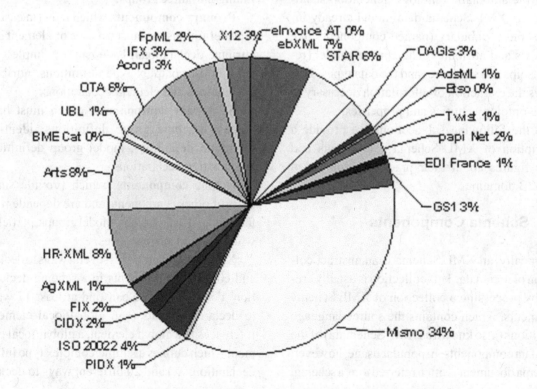

It clearly shows that standard bodies include a considerable amount of documentation. Moreover XSD *element* and XSD *attribute* are the most used components, while others like *union*, *all*, *any* and *substitutionGroup* are very few adopted. Here again, the figure only provides a statistical measure of the component adoption and simply gives us a list of those components that should be included in the extraction of information from XML Schemas.

In the following sections we describe a set of 40 transformation patterns and the extraction of semantics useful to extract ontological knowledge from a XML Schema source.

DERIVATION OF LOGICAL ASSERTIONS FROM XML SCHEMAS

As stated by Klein *et al.* (2003), ontologies and XML schemata serve very different purposes. Ontology languages are a means to specify domain theories based on logical representation and XML schemata are a means to provide integrity constraints for information sources (i.e., documents and/or semi-structured data). It is therefore not surprising to encounter differences when comparing XML schema with ontology languages. However, XML schema and OWL ontologies have one main goal in common: both provide vocabulary and structure for describing information about data.

Indeed it is simple to imagine equivalences between OWL classes and XSD elements, like *Person* or *Employee* presented below in Box 4, or even derive hierarchical information such as *rdfs:subClasseOf* between *CreditPostalAddress* and *PostalAddress* shown in Box 2 and *owl:ObjectProperty* (like *hasLongitude* and *hasLatitude* for *Coordinate* in Box 1). These simple equivalences between OWL and XSD permit the provision of not only basic information for a target ontology, but also interesting properties and restrictions relating entities.

From these considerations, given a non empty set of XML Schema source, we define the extracted conceptual knowledge from XML Schemas as a domain conceptualization. We assume that given a set of XSD files X, it is possible to retrieve a complete set of related concepts O by a surjective mapping m^2, $m: X \rightarrow O$.

Figure 3. XML schema components extraction

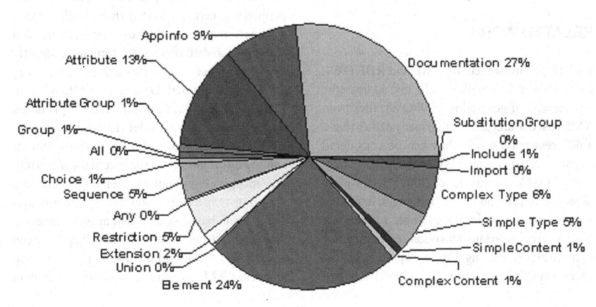

Box 1. Example of simple type component definitions

```
1.
<xsd:complexType name="CoordinateType">
<xsd:sequence>
<xsd:element name="longitude" type="xs:string"/>
<xsd:element name="latitude" type="xs:string"/>
</xsd:sequence>
</xsd:complexType>
2.
<xsd:simpleType name="DispositionType">
<xsd:union memberTypes="CriminalDispositionTypes xsd:string"/>
</xsd:simpleType>
```

The automation of the domain conceptualization presents different problems. Among them we have found the interpretation of XML Schema design as logical assertions and the derivation of correct names and structures not trivial. The interpretation of logical structures from XML constructs not a direct mapping except in very limited and ad-hoc use cases. The formalization of the resulting ontology is not satisfactory. Throughout this Chapter we argue all this problems and provide our solution and motivate the choices of our approach along with its applicability and limitations.

RELATED WORK

With the establishment of XML and RDF/OWL several tools and methods already address the problematic of generating RDF/OWL files from XML based sources. Although many of them have a different main scope, they can be considered as part of the mapping XML sources to ontology tools. COMA++ (Aumueller, 2005) has the main objective to provide several automatic matching algorithms. It permits for example to compare XML sources with target taxonomies running one or more algorithms suggesting mappings that the user must validate. It can produce an RDF output

from this mapping. This ability of COMA++ is really interesting since it attenuates the manual mapping processes and permits to obtain a final ontology, but have the inconvenience of being time consuming, tedious and error-prone. Although COMA++ can be considered as part of the mapping tools, being focused on matching element and relying on human intervention it does not really intend to map XML Schemas to ontologies. Indeed it does not consider specific XML Schema structures and result limited and poorly extensible to this scope.

Similarly to COMA++, the approach in (Beneventano, 2008) has a different focus but permits to generate ontologies from XML sources. It targets the integration of heterogeneus data coming from different source formats. Currently the system already provides a transformation to OWL of Relational Database, XML-schema, EDIFACT, and Flat File formalisms. It is based on the Logical Data Model (LDM) ontology as a neutral representational format to represent incoming information from an external schema into their mapping environment. Their implementation permits to map a large amount of XML constructs using a rule based system that at some extent is comparable to our. Indeed even their approach can be extended by adding new rules to be able to map a specific XML construct. Actually this system

Box 2. Examples of extension with simple and complex content (excerpts from GSl[3] [1], HR-XML[4] [2] and eInvoiceAt [3])

```
1.
<xsd:complexType name="NoteType">
  <xsd:simpleContent>
    <xsd:extension base="DescriptionType">
      <xsd:attribute name="author" type="StringType" use="optional"/>
      <xsd:attribute name="entryDateTime" type="DateTimeType" use="optional"/>
      <xsd:attribute name="status" type="StringType" use="optional"/>
    </xsd:extension>
  </xsd:simpleContent>
</xsd:complexType>
2.
<xsd:complexType name="CreditPostalAddressType">
  <xsd:complexContent>
    <xsd:extension base="PostalAddressType">
      <xsd:sequence>
        <xsd:element name="ReportedDate" type="ReportedDateType" minOc-
curs="0"/>
        <xsd:element name="LastReportedBy" type="xsd:string" minOccurs="0"/>
      </xsd:sequence>
      <xsd:attribute name="current" type="xsd:boolean" use="optional"/>
      <xsd:attribute name="enteredOnInquiry" type="xsd:boolean"
use="optional"/>
      <xsd:attribute name="timesReported" type="xsd:string" use="optional"/>
      <xsd:attribute name="validFrom" type="AnyDateTimeNaType" use="optional"/>
      <xsd:attribute name="validTo" type="AnyDateTimeNaType" use="optional"/>
    </xsd:extension>
  </xsd:complexContent>
</xsd:complexType>
3.
<xsd:simpleType name="CountryCodeType">
  <xsd:restriction base="xsd:token">
        <xsd:enumeration value="AF"/>
        <xsd:enumeration value="AL"/>
        <xsd:enumeration value="DZ"/>
    ...
  </xsd:restriction>
</xsd:simpleType>
<xsd:element name="CountryCode" type="CountryCodeType"/>
```

provides a larger scope and coverage than our, but has the drawback to have the resulting ontology tailored on the LDM ontology rather than being a logical interpretation of the source schema.

Always related to our field, some works provide a tool that allow the automatic transformation of XML sources to existing OWL ontology. The process generally requires an initial task, provided by a user, aiming to define the mapping. Among them JXML2OWL (Rodrigues, 2008; An, 2005) and XSPARQL (Polleres, 2009; Bishof, 2011). XSPARQL also permits to define a transformation in both directions, from XML to RDF/OWL and viceversa. These tools have a practical approach and are very interesting from a user perspective because they permit to automatically transform XML sources to RDF/OWL format. The inconvenient is that they require the presence of a reference/target ontology and the user provided set of correspondences. Their scope is not to generate a new ontology from XML Schema sources, but to transform XML Schema instances, data, to RDF.

Closer to our main scope there are XML2OWL (Bohring, 2005), OWLMAP (Ferdinand, 2004) and XSD2OWL (Garcia, 2006). However their approach is based on a close table of mapping, generally expressed with simple pairs (XML schema element, OWL entity) and implemented using XSL (XML Style Sheet) technology to perform a partial mapping from XML Schema components to OWL entities. These approaches do not allow to extend the mapping.

With respect to all cited works our approach and implementation present some innovative advantages. The consideration and improvement of semantics used to name OWL entities, to show a simple way to define specific interpretations of XML constructs to OWL2, to be easily extensible and to provide a concrete and explicit OWL syntax as resulting mapping.

Sub-sections below detail our pattern based approach to the transformation from XML Schema constructs to OWL entities. We also highlight the fact that for retrieving ontological knowledge the following patterns not only considers XML Schema natural components, but also specific combinations of them.

TRANSFORMATION PATTERNS

Patterns are used in many areas as "templates" or abstract descriptions encoding best practices of some field. In this section we provide a set of 40 patterns to transform XSD constructs to OWL2-RL profile (Motik, 2009) for helping construct axiom-rich, formal ontologies, based on identifying recurring patterns of knowledge in the XML Schemas, and then stating how those patterns map onto concepts in the ontology. From a modelling perspective, we are not designing specific logic representations; instead we are making an interpretation of XML constructs to get the maximum logical expression derivable from that formalism.

In the interpretations below, selected XML patterns are written using XML Schema syntax, while RDF/OWL correspondences are expressed using Turtle syntax (Beckett, 2008). Table 1 presents all generic names used in pattern descriptions, while Table 2 lists all prefixes used in the generated turtle ontology.

One must be aware that we work only on XSD, thus we target TBox statements and we do not integrate XML instances (that may be better compared to ABoxes). Each sub-section below presents a short introduction of the XML components with their transformation patterns to OWL.

Simple and Complex Types

Simple and complex type components are defined and used only within the schema document(s) and thus have no representation in an XML instance.

The XSD *complexType* component is normally used to define components with child elements and/or attributes. The *simpleType* is used to create a new datatype that is a refinement of a built-in XSD type (e.g., string, date, gYear, etc). In particular,

Table 1. List of abbreviations/variables used in patterns

Abbreviation/Variable	Description
ct_name	Complex type name (e.g. *Person*)
st_name	Simple type name (e.g. *amount*)
nativeDataType	Represents any datatypes as defined in XML Schemas Part 2 (Biron, 2004) (e.g. *xsd:string, xsd:Boolean, etc.*)
basedDT	Data type on which the restriction/extension is based, it can be an xsd native data type or a specific defined rdfs datatype
has_*ct_name*	Object or datatype property given name adding the prefix 'has_' plus the name of the associated complex type (e.g. *has_coordinate*)
has_*st_name*	Object or datatype property given name adding the prefix 'has_' plus the name of the associated simple type (e.g. *has_monetaryAmount*)
ct_name_dt	Name of a datatype derived by a complex type (e.g. *author*)
elt_name	Name of the element (e.g. *Customer*)
elt_type	Name of the type of the element that can be a simple type, xsd native data type or a complex type.
Elt_name_Ct_name	Derived name for an OWL class composed by the name of the complex type name plus the element name (if different) (e.g. *Domiciliation_Address*)
has_*elt_name*	Object or datatype property given name adding the prefix 'has_' plus the name of the associated element
has_*elt_name_ct_name*	Object or datatype property given name adding the prefix 'has_' plus the names of associated complex type and element to prevent the creation of more properties with different domains
attr_name	Name of the attribute
has_*attr_name*	Object or datatype property given name adding the prefix 'has_' plus the name of the associated attribute
has_*ct_name_attr_name*	Object or datatype property given name adding the prefix 'has_' plus the names of associated complex type and attribute to prevent the creation of more properties with different domains
group_name	Name of the group
has_*group_name*	Object property given name adding the prefix 'has_' plus the name of the associated group
attr_group_name	Name of the attribute group component
attr_type	Name of the type of the attribute that can be a simple type or a native xsd datatype
language_code	Code of the language (e.g. *en, fr, it, …*)

we can derive a new simple type by restricting an existing simple type; in other words, the legal range of values for the new type is a subset of the existing type range of values.

Type components can be anonymous (without name) when used locally for an element, but they must be named for a global definition. Box 1 (1) provides as example the definition of a global complex type CoordinateType. In addition to the so-called *atomic* types, XML Schema simple types have also the concept of *list* and *union* types. Atomic types and list types enable an element or an attribute value to be one or more instances of one atomic type. In contrast, a union type enables an element or an attribute value to be one or more instances of one type drawn from the union of multiple atomic and list types. Box 1 (2) illustrates an example of a simple type declaration with *union* definition, where the DispositionType union type is built from one atomic type, xsd:string in this case, and one simple type, CriminalDispositionTypes which is a closed list of allowed string values, called *enumeration*, shown in Box 1 (2).

Table 2. List of prefix and correspondent namespace URI used in the derived OWL ontology

Prefix	Namespace URI
:	http://www.alcatel-lucent.com/ontologies/2011/03/xsd2owl#*(Default namespace)*
xsd:	http://www.w3.org/2001/XMLSchema#
rdf:	http://www.w3.org/1999/02/22-rdf-syntax-ns#
rdfs:	http://www.w3.org/2000/01/rdf-schema#
owl:	http://www.w3.org/2002/07/owl#

As we observed in XML Schema design practices analysed above all simple types are used in defining concrete datatype, i.e. binary predicates relating individuals with values. For this reason simple types are always mapped to rdfs datatype. Conversely Complex types can be used to define a sort of composed datatype to which is added meta-data information, like author for a comment or detail of a specific code list used to define the data value, or again supplementary details on the data itself like the unit of measure. However even in OWL there is not a clear representation for such complex datatype. Therefore all named complex type here are directly mapped to owl classes and further assertions and relations to datatypes are exposed in sections below.

Transformation patterns for simple and complex type declarations are presented in Table 3.

Derived Types

XSD provides two forms of sub-classing type components, called **derived types**. The first form derives by extension from a parent complex type with more elements (i.e. properties for the ontology), while the second form can be obtained by restriction of the base type, creating a type as a subset. The restriction for simple types operates with the application of constraints on predefined simple types or with the help of regular expressions. Restriction of complex types is conceptually the same as restriction of simple types, except that the restriction of complex types involves a type's declarations rather than the acceptable range of a simple type values. A complex type derived by restriction is very similar to its base type, except that its instances are more limited than the corresponding declarations in the base type.

XML Schema provides two components to derive types. The *complexContent* component signals that we intend to restrict or extend the content of a complex type. A *simpleContent* component indicates that the content of the new complex type contains only simple data and no element. In other words, *simpleContent* provides a solution for adding attributes to simple types.

Box 2 illustrates two extensions for a complex type and precisely in (1) with the simple content component we provides more attributes to DescriptionType, which is defined as a string (not shown in the example). While in (2) with complex content component we extend PostalAddressType base complex type with more sub-elements and attributes at the same time. And (3) shows an example of simple type restriction.

Although the two derivations are called extention and restriction, conceptually they both represent a possible restriction of the set of individuals of the base ontological entity. Indeed the extension just adds property to a class, consequently only individuals having all these properties asserted belong to the "extension," As such, derived types generate either sub-classes or sub-propertiesof the base entity. Table 4 details most of the possible patterns for derived types.

Table 3. Simple and complex type transformation patterns

#	XSD	OWL
1	<simpleType name="st_name">	:st_name rdf:type rdfs:Datatype .
2	<simpleType name="st_name"> <union memberTypes="st_name1 xsd:nativDataType ..."/> </simpleType>	:st_name owl:equivalentClass:st_name1 ; owl:equivalentClass xsd:nativeDataType; owl:equivalentClass ... .
3	<complexType name="ct_name">	:Ct_name rdf:type owl:Class .

XSD Elements

XSD *element* is the most used component (see Figure 3 for more details). More than attributes, the element component allows the description of simple and complex entities to define different kind of concepts for the ontology to build, like classes, datatypes or properties. Elements can be declared via several different methods. Box 3 shows three examples of possible declarations for an element. The first one is a global element with a declared type. In the second example, the element is declared with an inline *complexType* and inline sub-elements. It also defines the expected minimal occurrence that in this case is 1, i.e., the element is not optional. The latter is declared with inline *simpleType* that refines an XSD built-in data type.

Global elements and global types are element declarations/definitions that are immediate children of the root *<schema>* element. Local elements, local types, and inline types are declarations/definitions that are nested within other elements or types. Although inline and local declarations, like those presented in Box 3, result in a much more compact schema, they have the disadvantage of being not reusable by other elements.

XML Schema specifications do not outline preferences to follow, but as general rule the global declaration is often preferred to local and inline declarations. As illustrated in Box 4, a global element can be reused by other component definition simply using the element *ref* declaration. This makes definition of elements and their usage clearly separated, which is generally simpler to understand and reuse.

The wide usage of XSD element means that they correspond with multiple OWL entities (i.e. classes, object properties, datatype properties and even datatypes) and patterns must consider also the referred constructs of the element declaration. We first differentiate local and global declarations, where from global declarations we generally derive classes and datatypes, while from local and inline declaration we derive object and datatype properties. Moreover as mentioned above a local declaration can not be reused by other elements in the XSD source. Conversely a global declaration can be reused in different cases and thus can define a more generic entity for the ontology. This brings to a specific pattern for element *ref* declarations as presented in #18 and #23 of Table 5. In this pattern we differentiate the derived object property name from the element using a compound name composed by the element name itself plus the name of the component enclosing it. This because in automated transformation the control over the uniqueness of the property can not be always guaranteed and a double declaration of a property with two different domains can lead to a misleading design, with the resulting property domain formed by the intersection of two classes. Table 5 details all defined patterns for the element declaration.

Attributes

XML Schema *attribute* component is used to declare simple values for a given complex ele-

Table 4. Derived types transformation patterns

#	XSD	OWL

4	`<simpleType name="st_name">`
	`<restriction base="xsd:nativDataType">`
	`<enumeration value="value1">`
	…
		`:st_name owl:equivalentClass`
		`[ rdf:type rdfs:Datatype;`
		`owl:oneOf ("value1"^^xsd:nativDataType ...)`
		`] .`

5	`<simpleType name="st_name">`
	`<restriction base="basedDT">`
	`<minInclusive value="value1"/>`
	`<maxInclusive value="value2"/>`
	`</restriction>`
	`</simpleType>`
		`:st_name owl:equivalentClass`
		`[ rdf:type rdfs:Datatype;`
		`owl:onDatatype :basedDT;`
		`owl:withRestrictions (`
		`[ xsd:minInclusive "value1"^^:basedDT ]`
		`[ xsd:maxInclusive "value2"^^:basedDT ]`
		`) ] .`

6	`<complexType name="ct_name">`
	`<simpleContent>`
	`<extension base="xsd:nativeDataType">`
	…
		`:Ct_name rdf:type owl:Class .`
		`:has_ct_name rdf:type owl:DatatypeProperty ;`
		`rdfs:domain:Ct_name ; rdfs:range xsd:nativeDataType .`

7	`<simpleType name="st_name">`
	`<restriction base="basedDT">`
	`<minExclusive value="value1"/>`
	`<maxExclusive value="value2"/>`
	`</restriction>`
	`</simpleType>`
		`:st_name owl:equivalentClass`
		`[ rdf:type rdfs:Datatype;`
		`owl:onDatatype:basedDT;`
		`owl:withRestrictions (`
		`[ xsd:minExclusive "value1"^^:basedDT ]`
		`[ xsd:maxExclusive "value2"^^:basedDT ]) ] .`

8	`<complexType name="ct_name">`
	`<simpleContent>`
	`<extension base="st_name">`
	…
		`:Ct_name rdf:type owl:Class .`
		`:has_ct_name rdf:type owl:DatatypeProperty ;`
		`rdfs:domain:Ct_name ; rdfs:range:st_name ;`
		`rdfs:subPropertyOf:has_st_name .`

9	`<complexType name="ct_name">`
	`<simpleContent>`
	`<extension base="ct_name2">`
	`(see #26, 27, 28)…`
		`Same than #8 +`
		`:Ct_name rdfs:subClassOf:Ct_name2 .`

10	`<complexType name="ct_name">`
	`<simpleContent>`
	`<restriction base="xsd:nativDataType">`
	`(cf #4,5,6)…`
		`:Ct_name rdf:type owl:Class .`
		`:ct_name_dt owl:equivalentClass`
		`[ rdf:type rdfs:Datatype; (cf#4,5,6)] .`
		`:has_ct_name rdf:type owl:DatatypeProperty ;`
		`rdfs:domain:Ct_name ; rdfs:range:ct_name_dt .`

11	`<complexType name="ct_name">`
	`<simpleContent>`
	`<restriction base="st_name">` …
		`Same than #10 +`
		`:has_ct_name rdfs:subPropertyOf:has_st_name .`

12	`<complexType name="ct_name">`
	`<simpleContent>`
	`<restriction base="ct_name2">`
	…
		`Same than #11 +`
		`:Ct_name rdfs:subClassOf:Ct_name2 .`

13	`<complexType name="ct_name">`
	`<complexContent>`
	`<extension base="ct_name2">`…
		`:Ct_name rdf:type owl:Class ;`
		`rdfs:subClassOf:Ct_name2 .`

14	`<complexType name="ct_name">`
	`<complexContent>`
	`<restriction base="ct_name2">`…
		`:Ct_name rdf:type owl:Class ;`
		`rdfs:subClassOf:Ct_name2 .`

Box 3. Elements declarations

```
1. Global element declaration (direct child of schema component)
<xsd:element name="MonetaryAmount" type="AmountType"/>
2. Local declarations
<xsd:element name="GeographicalCoordinate">
  <xsd:complexType>
    <xsd:sequence>
      <xsd:element name="longitude" type="xsd:string" minOccurs="1"/>
      <xsd:element name="latitude" type="xsd:string" minOccurs="1"/>
    </xsd:sequence>
  </xsd:complexType>
</xsd:element>
3. Inline anonymous simple type declaration
<xsd:element name="Amount">
<xsd:simpleType>
<xsd:restriction base="udt:amountType">
...
</xsd:restriction>
</xsd:simpleType>
</xsd:element>
```

ment (attributes cannot have child elements). Attribute declarations can appear at the top level of a schema document, or within complex type definitions, either as complete (local) declarations, or by reference to top-level declarations, and also within attribute group definitions. For complete declarations, top-level or local, the type attribute is used when the declaration can use a built-in or pre-declared simple type definition. Otherwise an anonymous simple type is provided inline.

Box 5 shows an example of inline attributes declaration for a complex type component. We can also observe that at data content level, this definition of GeographicalCoordinateType and that one provided in Box 3(2) are equivalent. Here again XML Schema specifications do not provide any recommendation about the usage of one declaration rather than another. Generally attributes are indicated for transmitting metadata information, like an internal identifier or a specific detail on the value. For the geographical coordinate it could be the specific coordinate system (e.g. cartesian or polar). Nevertheless in evaluated practices, attribute declarations are often preferred simply because of their lower verbosity in XML instances, so reducing the size of large data sets.

Table 6 details transformation patterns for the attribute components. Similarly to elements we differentiate global declaration and local and inline ones. The former produces a datatype while the two latter produce datatype properties.

Grouping XML Entities

XML Schema enables groups of elements to be defined and named, so that the elements can be used to build up the content models of complex types. Thus to provide more information about an element, XML Schema permits to create a named *group* global component that permits to assembly together more elements that can be simply referenced in complex elements. The same

Table 5. Element transformation patterns

#	XSD	OWL
15	`<element name="elt_name" type="xsd:nativeDataType">`	`:elt_name rdf:type rdfs:Datatype ;` `owl:equivalentClass xsd:nativeDataType .`
16	`<element name="elt_name" type="st_name"/>`	`:elt_name rdf:type rdfs:Datatype ;` `owl:equivalentClass:st_name .`

17	`<complexType name="ct_name">`
	`<sequence>`
	`<element name="elt_name" type="st_name">...`
		`:has_elt_name rdf:type owl:ObjectDatatype ;`
		`rdfs:domain:ct_name ; rdfs:range:st_name .`

18	`<complexType name="ct_name">`
	`<sequence>`
	`<element ref="elt_name"/> (referring to a simple type)...`
		`:has_elt_name_ct_name rdf:type owl:ObjectDatatype ;`
		`rdfs:domain:ct_name ; rdfs:range:elt_name .`

19	`<element name="elt_name">`
	`<simpleType>`
	`<restriction base="xsd:nativeDataType">`
	`...`
		`:elt_name owl:equivalentClass`
		`[ rdf:type rdfs:Datatype; (cf #4,5,6)`
		`] .`
		`:has_elt_name rdf:type owl:DatatypeProperty ;`
		`rdfs:range:elt_name .`

20	`<element name="elt_name">`
	`<simpleType>`
	`<restriction base="st_name">`
	`...`
		`:has_st_name rdf:type owl:DatatypeProperty ;`
		`rdfs:range:st_name .`
		`:elt_name owl:equivalentClass`
		`[ rdf:type rdfs:Datatype; (cf #4,5,6)`
		`] .`
		`:has_elt_name rdf:type owl:DatatypeProperty ;`
		`rdfs:range:elt_name ;`
		`rdfs:subPropertyOf:has_st_name .`

21	`<element name="elt_name" type="ct_name"/>` `(global declaration)`	`:Elt_name rdf:type owl:Class ;` `rdfs:subClassOf:Ct_name .`

22	`<complexType name="ct_name">`
	`<sequence>`
	`<element name="elt_name" type="ct_name1"/> ...`
		`:has_elt_name rdf:type owl:ObjectProperty ;`
		`rdfs:domain:ct_name ; rdfs:range:ct_name1 .`

23	`<complexType name="ct_name">`
	`<sequence>`
	`<element ref="elt_name"/> (referring to a complex type)...`
		`:has_elt_name_ct_name rdf:type owl:ObjectProperty ;`
		`rdfs:domain:ct_name ; rdfs:range:elt_name .`

24	`<element name="elt_name" type="xsd:nativeDataType ">`	`:elt_name rdf:type owl:DatatypeProperty ;` `rdfs:range xsd:nativeDataType .`
25	`<element name="elt_name1" type="elt_type"/>` `<element name="elt_name2" substitutionGroup="elt_name1"/>`	`:elt_name2 rdfs:subClassOf:elt_name1 .`

is done with the *attributeGroup* containing all the desired attributes of an item element that can be referenced by name in more elements declarations. Moreover the definitions of complex types are declared using sequences of elements that can appear in the document instance. XML Schema provides three different constructors to allow the definition of sub-elements sequences:

- *sequence* corresponds to an order collection of typed sub-elements;

- *choice* groups element using an exclusive-or, i.e., only one of its children can appear in an instance;

- *all* contains at most one of each element specified as sub-elements. It means that all the elements in the group may appear once or not at all (i.e. the permissible values of *minOccurs* and *maxOccurs* are 0 and 1) and they may appear in any order.

Box 4. Example of element ref usage (from HR-XML standard)

```
<xsd:complexType name="Someone">
  <xsd:sequence>
   <xsd:choice>
     <xsd:element ref="Person" minOccurs="0"/>
       <xsd:element ref="Contact" minOccurs="0"/>
       <xsd:element ref="Employee" minOccurs="0"/>
     </xsd:choice>
  </xsd:sequence>
</xsd:complexType>
<xsd:element name="Person" type="Person"/>
<xsd:element name="Employee" type="Employee"/>
<xsd:element name="Contact" type="Contact"/>
```

Any element in a group can be restricted using *minOccurs* and *maxOccurs* occurrence indicators that are used to define how often an element can occur in an instance. The default value for these indicators is 1, which means that the element is required and can appear only once.

Box 6 illustrates the definition of Telecom-NumberType complex type, where sub-elements can be either FormattedNumber or the ordered sequence of elements grouped by TelecomNumberGroup.

Table 7 details the defined transformation patterns for grouping components. All inline and local declaration of element described in Table 7 just complete patterns already defined in Table 5, where to each element corresponds either a datatype or object property depending on the nature of the related element type. Pattern #31 tries to translate the exclusive-or carried by the *choice* component. Indeed differently from XML Schemas it is not possible to represent such integrity constraints on properties in OWL. Thus

Box 5. Example of usage of attributes

```
<xsd:complexType name="GeographicalCoordinateType">
  <xsd:attribute name="longitude" type="xsd:string"/>
  <xsd:attribute name="latitude" type="xsd:string"/>
</xsd:complexType>
```

Table 6. Attributes transformation patterns

#	XSD	OWL
26	`<attribute name="attr_name" type="xsd:nativDataType"/>`	:attr_name rdf:type rdfs:Datatype ; owl:equivalentClass xsd:nativDataType.
27	`<complexType name="ct_name">` `<attribute name="attr_name" type="st_name"/> ...`	:has_attr_name rdf:type owl:DatatypeProperty ; rdfs:domain:Ct_name ; rdfs:range:st_name .
28	`<complexType name="ct_name">` `<attribute ref="attr_name"/>` ...	:has_ct_name_attr_name rdf:type owl:DatatypeProperty ; rdfs:domain:Ct_name ; rdfs:range:attr_name .

Box 6. Example of components to group entities (from OAGIS[5] 9.0) with occurrence indicators

```
<xsd:complexType name="TelcomNumberType">
  <xsd:choice>
    <xsd:element ref="FormattedNumber"/>
    <xsd:group ref="TelcomNumberGroup"/>
  </xsd:choice>
</xsd:complexType>

<xsd:group name="TelcomNumberGroup">
  <xsd:sequence>
    <xsd:element ref="InternationalCountryCode" minOccurs="0" maxOccurs="1"/>
    <xsd:element ref="NationalNumber" minOccurs="0" maxOccurs="1"/>
    <xsd:element ref="AreaCityCode" minOccurs="0" maxOccurs="1"/>
    <xsd:element ref="SubscriberNumber"/>
    <xsd:element ref="Extension" minOccurs="0" maxOccurs="1"/>
  </xsd:sequence>
</xsd:group>
```

we have created a consistency check that arises if concurrent triples appear in the ontology. This has been done by creating fictitious complex classes definitions using the *owl:onProperty* property restrictions that permits to define a class as the set of all individuals that are connected via a particular property to another individual. Thus we define a subclass for each element of the group with only one property of the complex component and declared all this classes disjoint. Doing that, we assert that we cannot have individuals having more than one property at once at the same time.

Pattern #32 and #34 respectively for group and *attributeGroup* do not present a great difference. Conceptually they define a class with enclosed elements as properties. Just the attribute types are all datatype properties and datatypes.

A particular attention must be done over the #38 that for maintaining compliancy with Owl2-RL profile the value of occurrencies can be only 1.

Annotations

XML Schema provides three elements for annotating schemas for the benefit of both human readers and applications. One is a basic schema description information, the *documentation* component, which is the recommended location for human readable material. The second is *appinfo* component that can be used to provide information for tools, style-sheets and other applications. Both *documentation* and *appinfo* appear as sub-elements of *annotation*, which may itself appear at the beginning of most schema constructions. To illustrate, Box 7 shows a documentation annotation element appearing at the beginning of a complex type definition.

Table 8 provides two elementary transformation patterns for XSD annotations.

Pattern Recognition Limitations

Because OWL is more generally expressive than XML Schema, it is not possible to derive a direct transformation pattern for each OWL

Table 7. Grouping components transformation patterns

#	XSD	OWL

29	`<complexType name="ct_name">`
	`<sequence>`
	`<element name="elt_name1" type="elt_type1"/>`
	`<element name="elt_name2" type="elt_type2"/> ...`
	`</sequence>`
	`</complexType>`
		:has_elt_name1 rdfs:domain:Ct_name; rdfs:range:elt_type1 .
		:has_elt_name2 rdfs:domain:Ct_name; rdfs:range:elt_type2 .

30	`<complexType name="ct_name">`
	`<all>`
	`<element name="elt_name1" type="elt_type1"/>`
	`...`
	`</all>`
	`</complexType>`
		:has_elt_name1 rdf:type owl:FunctionalProperty ;
		rdfs:domain:Ct_name ;
		rdfs:range [rdf:type owl:Restriction ;
		owl:onProperty:has_elt_name1 ;
		owl:onClass:Elt_type1 ;
		owl:maxQualifiedCardinality "1"^^xsd:nonNegativeInteger] ....

31	`<complexType name="ct_name">`
	`<choice>`
	`<element name="elt_name1" type="elt_type1"/>`
	`<element name="elt_name2" type="elt_type2"/>`
	`</choice>`
	`</complexType>`
		:Elt_name_Ct_name1 owl:equivalentClass
		[rdf:type owl:Restriction ;
		owl:onProperty:has_elt_name1 ;
		owl:someValuesFrom:elt_type1] ;
		rdfs:subClassOf:Ct_name .
		:Elt_name_Ct_name2 owl:equivalentClass
		[rdf:type owl:Restriction ;
		owl:onProperty:has_elt_name2 ;
		owl:someValuesFrom:elt_type2] ;
		rdfs:subClassOf:Ct_name .
		[] rdf:type owl:AllDisjointClasses ;
		owl:members (:Elt_name_Ct_name1:Elt_name_Ct_name2) .

32	`<group name="group_name">`
	`<sequence>`
	`<element name="elt_name1" type="elt_type1"/>`
	`<element name="elt_name2" type="elt_type2"/>`
	`</sequence>`
	`</group>`
		:Group_name rdf:type owl:Class .
		:has_elt_name1 rdf:type owl:ObjectProperty;
		rdfs:domain:group_name ; rdfs:range:elt_type1 .
		:has_elt_name2 rdf:type owl:ObjectProperty;
		rdfs:domain:Group_name ; rdfs:range:elt_type2 .

33	`<complexType name="ct_name">`
	`<sequence>`
	`<group ref="group_name"/>`
	`</sequence>`
	`</complexType>`
		:has_group_name rdf:type owl:ObjectProperty ;
		rdfs:domain:Ct_name ; rdfs:range:Group_name .

34	`<attributeGroup name="attr_group_name">`
	`<attribute name="attr_name1" type="attr_type1"/>`
	`<attribute name="attr_name2" type="attr_type2"/>`
	`</attributeGroup>`
		:Attr_group_name rdf:type owl:Class .
		:has_attr_name1 rdf:type owl:ObjectProperty;
		rdfs:domain:Attr_group_name ; rdfs:range:attr_type1 .
		:has_attr_name2 rdf:type owl:ObjectProperty;
		rdfs:domain:Attr_group_name ; rdfs:range:attr_type2 .

35	`<complexType name="ct_name">`
	`<attributeGroup ref="attr_group_name"/>`
	`</complexType>`
		:has_attr_group_name rdf:type owl:ObjectProperty ;
		rdfs:domain:Ct_name ; rdfs:range:attr_group_name .

36	`<complexType name="ct_name">`
	`<sequence>`
	`<element name="elt_name" minOccurs="value1"/>`
	`</sequence>`
	`</complexType>`
		:Ct_name owl:equivalentClass
		[rdf:type owl:Restriction ;
		owl:minCardinality "value1"^^xsd:nonNegativeInteger ;
		owl:onProperty:has_elt_name
		] .

37	`<complexType name="ct_name">`
	`<sequence>`
	`<element name="elt_name" maxOccurs="value2"/>`
	`</sequence>`
	`</complexType>`
		:Ct_name owl:equivalentClass
		[rdf:type owl:Restriction ;
		owl:maxCardinality "value2"^^xsd:nonNegativeInteger ;
		owl:onProperty:has_elt_name
		] .

continued on following page

Table 7. Continued

#	XSD	OWL
38	<complexType name="ct_name"> <sequence> <element name="elt_name" minOccurs="valueX" maxOccurs="valueX"/> </sequence> </complexType>	:Ct_name owl:equivalentClass [rdf:type owl:Restriction ; owl:cardinality "valueX"^^xsd:nonNegativeInteger ; owl:onProperty:has_elt_name] .

logical construct. As an example it is not possible to derive automatically a pattern from XML Schema for describing binary relations like inverse, transitive and symmetric properties. The same for other construct like *owl:differentFrom*, *owl:NegativePropertyAssertion* and *owl:PropertyChainAxiom*.

It is also not possible to convert all XML Schema integrity constraints into OWL, as there are areas where XML Schema is more expressive than OWL. For example pattern and length constraints on data values, (e.g. *<pattern value="[a-z] [a-z] [0-9]"/>*, *<xs:length value="8"/>*, *<xs:minLength value="5"/>*, *<xs:maxLength value="8"/>*), have no direct mapping into OWL.

DERIVATION OF NAMES FOR OWL ENTITIES

In this sub-section, we focus on adequacy of extracted labels from named XML schema components to provide semantically correct names for OWL ontology entities. Although this step is not indispensable for an acceptable automatic transformation process, derived benefits by paying close attention to entity names are considerable. A good semantic can improve the transformation process if more sources are involved; provide a meaningful ontology; and simplify the automatic, but even human, matching of concepts with other ontologies or external resources.

However as we will show in the related section this is still an under considered research topic. If the derivation of correct names (i.e. the adoption

of meaningful words) is intuitively simple for automatic process from text documents sources, it is not always the case for XML Schemas. As we observed, several XSD specifications have different practices on naming conventions that not always are of direct understanding. Thus their automatic interpretation is not always a trivial task.

For example, XML Schema named components (that we can refer to also as XML tags) are often compound words that can be expressed using the common *Camel Case* convention with known terms (that we also call **dictionary terms**), like *OfficeLocation*, or using abbreviations to reduce the length of the tag like *amt_ccy* (which should stand for *amount currency*). In addition, tags can contain compound words (like *cashflow*), acronyms, bad spelled words, no separator between terms (like *foodservice*), specific terms, unrelated words with the meaning of the element (like *UnitOfMeasureBBIECommonData*), etc.... This is another important feature to analyse in the automatic derivation of an ontology from this format. Indeed it is our strong believe that an ontology must have correct semantics for naming entities. For this reason, what follow are few simple considerations on which we must pay special attention when deriving automatically an ontology, independently from the adopted method.

As shown in (Bedini, 2010) 71% of tags are composed by recognized dictionary words, 14% contain recognized abbreviations that can be related to dictionary words, and only 15% of total tags contain unknown words. However, even though this is a good partial result, a satisfactory extraction system could be aware of these prob-

Box 7. Example of UBL annotations following CCTS format for annotations

```
<xsd:complexType name="AmountType">
  <xsd:annotation>
    <xsd:documentation xml:lang="en">
      <ccts:UniqueID>UDT000001</ccts:UniqueID>
      <ccts:CategoryCode>UDT</ccts:CategoryCode>
      <ccts:DictionaryEntryName>Amount. Type</ccts:DictionaryEntryName>
      <ccts:VersionID>1.0</ccts:VersionID>
      <ccts:Definition>A number of monetary units specified in a currency
where the unit of the currency is explicit or implied.</ccts:Definition>
      <ccts:RepresentationTermName>Amount</ccts:RepresentationTermName>
      <ccts:PrimitiveType>decimal</ccts:PrimitiveType>
      <xsd:BuiltinType>decimal</xsd:BuiltinType>
    </xsd:documentation>
  </xsd:annotation>
  <xsd:simpleContent>
...
  </xsd:simpleContent>
</xsd:complexType>
```

lematic tags. In specific cases, the introduction of such a noise can lead to bad extraction/transformation conclusions. To get optimal results, a system should execute this kind of test for each source to be included. On the basis of a predefined threshold, it should decide to use specific terms recognition algorithms, or in the worst case exclude a source from the corpus to be considered to generate the ontology.

A task achieving preliminary normalisation of labels from named XML components (i.e. complex/simple types, elements, attributes, attribute groups and groups) is indispensable. Concerning XML types declaration we observed that almost all of them contain a prefix or a suffix indicating

Table 8. Annotations transformation patterns

#	XSD	OWL

39	`<xs:element name="elt_name" type="elt_type">`
	`<xs:annotation>`
	`<xs:documentation xml:lang="lang_cd" source="anyURI">`
	Text of the comment
	`</xs:documentation>`
	`</xs:annotation>`
	`</element>`
		:Elt_name rdfs:comment "xsd:documentation Text of the comment"@ lang_cd ;
		rdfs:seeAlso "anyURI"^^xsd:string .

40	`<xs:element name="elt_name" type="elt_type">`
	`<xs:annotation>`
	`<xs:appinfo>`
	Text of the annotation
	`</xs:appinfo>`
	`</xs:annotation>`
	`</element>`
		:Elt_name:appinfo "xsd:appinfo Text of the annotation"^^xsd:string .

that it is a type. In our analysis we have been able to detect practically all of them and normalize the label by dropping the following patterns: *_type, _Type, _TYPE, type, Type, TYPE, _tp, _Tp, _t, _T, type_, Type_, TYPE_*.

Since the type concept is not recognizable in ontology as part of the name, the elimination of such parts guarantees a more meaningful name for ontology entities.

Another design practice we have observed is that although elements and attributes define the tag syntax for XML documents, the better semantic can be often extracted from related complex and simple types. However this is not a general rule that can be applicable to any source, therefore in our patterns we have considered names for our entities derived from both kinds of components.

Problematic Words

As mentioned above, a discrete number of unrecognised words still remain, at least at first sight. The analysis shows that these problematic words are of the following type: mostly abbreviations (about 50%); about 30% are compound words not split by the system (for example compound words not written in UCC form like *worktime* or *preowned*); about 10% are words not included in the external dictionary; and another 10% are acronyms.

Several techniques can be implemented to improve the detection of hidden words. In our implementation, presented below, the abbreviation discovery, based on a specific adaptation of the N-Gram algorithms, is able to detect more than 60% of them automatically. This in reality corresponds to 70% of total occurrences (for example *amt => amount* has 958 occurrences thus more important than *lqdty* with just one occurrence). Improving these results means: (a) adopting a more complex management of abbreviations to detect different words having the same abbreviation, (b) implementing NLP techniques to mine text documents that often come with XML files and;

(c) improving the external dictionary capabilities. For the moment, these improvements have not been yet implemented.

In summary, we can say that solutions improving the quality of the extraction exist, but in order to fully exploit the potential of semantic technologies, a source document should be somehow *semantically correct* alone. No semantic/linguistic algorithm will be able to understand the sense behind tags such as *AmortMktValDiffPct* or *setr.100.101*. The adoption of XML based standards has already notably improved the opportunity of automating the extraction of useful information, made this issue more apparent, and accelerated the drive towards convergence.

Input XSD Semantics and Structures

Before concluding this section, we like to stress out the importance of input sources. This issue reflects the well known phrase *"Garbage In, Garbage Out (GIGO)[6]"* in computer science. Computers will unquestioningly process the most nonsensical of input data and produce nonsensical output. Indeed, to automate the ontology generation as best as possible, the quality of the output is directly dependent on the definition of input elements. So when retrieving information it is important to know how sources are built to be able to decide if a source can be included in the corpus or not. In our use case, we are building a semantic network of concepts, thus it is obvious that having correct semantics and structure is an essential condition to get better quality results.

Regarding XML Schema instances, XML specifications already provide a definition of *well-formedness* of XML documents. But it focuses on syntax and XML entities as logical and physical structures that in an XML document must be properly nested. This is limited to the fact that no start-tag, end-tag, empty-element tag, element, comment, processing instruction, character reference, or entity reference can begin in one entity and end in another. No concerns are

Figure 4. Overall architecture of transformation patterns and normalisation implementation

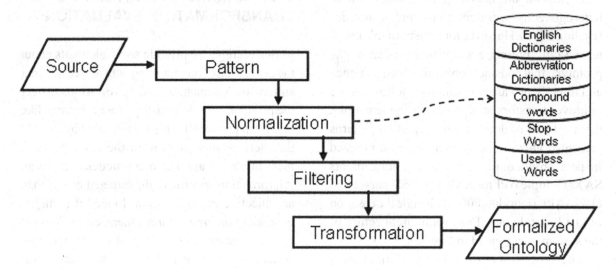

done over semantics and conceptual structures of XML entities.

In our approach we add the definition of **XML documents semantically well structured** in order to define some basic rules to have real semantics and concepts defined in an XML schema document. This kind of classification of such documents can be used to settle on the adoption of either a specific algorithm or excluding it, thus to be able to evaluate input source quality before adding them to the input corpus. Thus we say that a concept *c* derived from an XML Schema source is **semantically valid** if its label is composed by clearly identifiable words belonging to a standard common dictionary (like the English Oxford dictionary for the English language), rather than unrecognized abbreviations, acronyms or any other sequence of chars.

On the same line we say that a set of extracted concepts *C* is **well structured** if the ratio between obtained properties (#*Rs*) and the total number of extracted concepts (#*C*) is higher of a predefined threshold (α). This last definition prevents the integration of only flat definition of XML elements. For example, applying this test we were able to discard some XBRL[7] files. Indeed their specifications are defined with the help of XLink

constructs that our system was not able to detect. As consequence, retrieved information presented some inconsistencies that produced some bad concept definitions.

Finally, following the definitions above we say that a non empty set of concepts *C*, obtained from a given source, is **semantically well structured** if at least a considerable number of its concepts are semantically valid (on the basis of a predefined threshold β) and *C* itself is well structured. We adapted this measures to our corpus using $\alpha = 0,75$ and $\beta = 0,5$ following some empirical observations and we were able to slightly improve the acquisition step. This is at the price of losing some information that in certain cases could be integrated with simple human intervention.

SYSTEM IMPLEMENTATION

To validate our approach we have developed a prototype that aims to generate an ontology from a large source corpus of XML Schemas, called Janus, like the one presented above concerning the B2B domain. This system integrates sources incrementally and produces an intermediary conceptual model compatible to OWL to add flexibility on the matching and integration of heterogeneous representations and semantics (Bedini, 2010). However for the aim of this chapter we only present a simplified version of the prototype that considers only one schema at once and directly produces an ontology following the improved transformation approach, implementing the most part of defined transformation patterns presented above. The system has been realized in java programming language. It implements SAX[8] (Simple API for XML) as XSD parser and OWL-API[9] (Horidge, 2009) to handle the creation of OWL ontologies. The overall architecture of the system is presented in Figure 4.

The process realizing the transformation is composed by a first step that parses XSD sources and, implementing specific java algorithms, recognise selected patterns and stores candidate ontology entities in an organized internal data model based on multiple hash-tables.

The second step aims to normalize extracted labels and produces real semantics. For this reason the prototype integrates different dictionaries. The English dictionary is based on WordNet (Miller, 1995) version 3.0 using JWNL[10] (Java WordNet Library). Other dictionaries are specific lists of abbreviations and acronyms, stop-words[11], *compound words* and the so called *useless words* that we have tailored for the B2B domain. All these specific dictionaries are based on either java property files or simple text files that can be simply replaced and adapted to another specific domain.

The following filtering step aims to identify more abbreviations eventually not detected previously and to purge sources that do not produce a semantically well structured output, as explained in section above. The last step simply translates the normalised internal data model to OWL.

An evaluation of the prototype is provided below with the comparison with other systems

COMPARISON AND AUTOMATIC TRANSFORMATION EVALUATION

In this section, we provide some elements about the evaluation of our mapping with respect to other similar implementations. We have not looked over the produced ontology using exact measures like precision and recall. This is motivated by the fact that defined mappings from the XML Schema meta-model to another meta-model is more an interpretation specific to the targeted model then an objective transformation. Indeed it is highly dependent on input sources themselves. At most we can measure the number of considered constructs, to estimate if there is information lost in the translation. Another way to measure the quality could be done at the usage of the resulting ontology itself, like how many reasoning elements can be calculated from it. This is a preliminary step of the whole generation process difficult to evaluate. Thus, until now no one has provided such test cases.

Further we have evaluated some available systems providing a detailed XML Schema transformation, which are XML2OWL (Bohring, 2005), OWLMAP (Ferdinand, 2004), LDM (Beneventano, 2008) with our system. Mainly our analysis highlights the following aspects of the different systems:

- *Number of XSD constructs*, that permit to appreciate the completeness of the map with the possibility to maintain as much information as possible;
- *XML instances*, which normally means that the resulting ontology is directly populated with OWL individuals. However as far as we know we remark that no systems further investigate the possibility to use instances knowledge to extend the ontology expressivity. At most XML instance with a back engineering is transformed in pseudo XML Schema and used to produce the mapping to OWL;

- *Extensibility* just says if the system can be simply extended to add more XSD constructs or rules;
- *Exception management* tells if a system is able to look forward the simple direct mapping and manage exception of specific design practices;
- *Semantic normalisation* looks at the capacity of the system to resolve linguistic and semantic normalisations (like abbreviations, tag lemmatisation and so on);
- *Concept structures* evaluates the possibility to resolve hierarchical, properties and datatype relations;
- *Concept relations* provides a quality measure about the richness of semantic relations extracted like equivalent classes, functional properties and other specific relations that can subsist among constructs
- *OWL expressivity* is a theoretical interpretation of the retrieved information expressivity using the DL naming convention (Baader, 2003) (the corresponding value is an evaluation we made on the basis of the available documentation).

Table 9 resumes the evaluation described above.

Table 10 details the XML Schema constructs that are considered for the information extraction of each system.

As we can see, our system improves existing solutions. This is thanks to the integration of more XSD constructs and of specific extensible rules. As already mentioned at this level, we cannot provide real quality estimation because of the objectivity of the resulting mapping of XSD constructs. Nevertheless we can at least be sure that our approach provides a satisfactory transformation.

CONCLUSION AND FUTURE WORK

This chapter has presented our contribution on the transformation of XML schemas into RDF/OWL. We prove to be more complete than others, and particularly highly improve the number of direct transformation patterns, with respect to similar approaches like XML2OWL, and being simpler and at the same time equivalent in transformation capacity to other systems implementing more complex approaches with the integration of intermediary and dedicated model, like LDM. We also provide important elements and guidelines to transform XML Schema sources, based on an initial set of 40 transformation patterns formalised using direct OWL syntax in Turtle format. We show that it is possible to mine XML Schema sources to extract enough knowledge for building semantically correct ontologies with a considerable expressivity. Furthermore we have provided

Table 9. XML schema information extraction considerations

	XML2OWL	OWLMAP	LDM	Janus
N. of XSD construct	8	9	18	19
XML instances	✓	✓		
Extensible			✓	✓
Exception management	limited	limited	✓	✓
Semantic normalisation			·	✓
Concept structures	limited	✓	✓	✓
Concept relations	limited	✓	limited	✓
OWL expressivity	ALUHN	tbd	tbd	*ALHONQF*(D)

Table 10. Details on the extracted XSD constructs for the transformation to ontology

[XSD construct]	XML2OWL	OWLMAP	LDM	Janus
All	✓	✓	✓	✓
Annotation	·	·	✓	·
Any	·	·	✓	✓
Appinfo	·	·	·	·
Attribute	·	✓	✓	✓
AttributeGroup	·	✓	✓	✓
Choice	✓	✓	✓	✓
ComplexContent	·	·	·	✓
ComplexType	✓	✓	✓	✓
Documentation	·	·	·	✓
Element	✓	✓	✓	✓
Extension	·	✓	✓	✓
Group	·	✓	✓	✓
Import	·	·	✓	✓
Include	·	·	✓	✓
Restriction	·	✓	✓	✓
Sequence	✓	✓	✓	✓
SimpleContent	·	·	·	✓
SimpleType	✓	✓	✓	✓
SubstitutionGroup	·	✓	·	✓
Union	·	·	✓	✓
List	·	·	✓	·
Min/Max Occurs	✓	✓	✓	✓
Namespace	·	✓	·	·

a simple and complete way to define direct transformation patterns that can be easily implemented by any system and simply extended to augment the number of XML components and construct to be included. The prototype we have developed has been proved to be reliable, straightforward to implement and extensible as well.

In future work we aim to improve the number of patterns to be able to map all possible XSD components and other specific constructs. About the implementation the prototype can be improved and built as a reusable API to be easily integrated in other systems.

Further research is still needed in order to improve the capacity to detect valid semantics. Furthermore the real challenge of these kinds of applications still remains the extraction from multiple sources and the incremental integration of new sources. Indeed although our approach and implementation are of simple realisation, as such, they are limited capacity in integration and merging. However our implementation approach is a concrete input to the automatic generation of ontology from XML Schemas, reduces the effort to convert the Web into a Semantic Web and can provide a useful input to more complex and ambitious systems.

REFERENCES

An, Y., Borgida, A., & Mylopoulos, J. (2005). Constructing complex semantic mappings between XML data and ontologies. In Y. Gil, E. Motta, V. R. Benjamins, & M. A. Musen (Eds.), *Proceedings of ISWC 2005*, (vol 3729), (pp. 6–20). Berlin, Germany: Springer.

Aumueller, D. Do. H., Massmann, S., & Rahm, E. (2005). Schema and ontology matching with COMA++. In *Proceedings of International Conference on Management of Data* 2005, (pp. 906-908). Baltimore, MD: ACM Press.

Baader, F., Calvanese, D., McGuinness, D. L., Nardi, D., & Patel-Schneider, P. F. (2003). *The description logic handbook: Theory, implementation, applications*. Cambridge, UK: Cambridge University Press.

Beckett, D., & Berners-Lee, T. (2008). *Turtle - Terse RDF triple language*. W3C Team Submission, 14 January 2008. Retrieved from http://www.w3c.org.

Bedini, I. (2010). *Deriving ontologies automatically from XML schemas applied to the B2B domain*. Doctoral dissertation. University of Versailles. Retrieved April 15, 2011 from http://bivan.free.fr/Janus/Docs/PhD_Report_IvanBedini.pdf.

Beneventano, D. (Ed.). (2008). *Semantic and ontology language specification*. STASIS Project Deliverable 2.3.2, Version 10.

Biron, P. V., & Malhotra, A. (2004). *XML schema part 2: Datatypes* (2nd ed). W3C Recommendation 28 October 2004. Retrieved from http://www.w3c.org.

Bischof, S., Lopes, N., & Polleres, A. (2011). Improve efficiency of mapping data between XML and RDF with XSPARQL. In *Proceedings of the The Fifth International Conference on Web Reasoning and Rule Systems*. Springer.

Bohring, H., & Auer, S. (2005). *Mapping XML to OWL ontologies*. Leipzig, Germnay: Leipziger Informatik-Tage.

Bray, T., Paoli, J., Sperberg-McQueen, C. M., Maler, E., & Yergeau, F. (2008). *Extensible markup language (XML) 1.0* (5th ed). W3C Recommendation 26 November 2008. Retrieved from http://www.w3c.org.

Fallside, D. C., & Walmsley, P. (2004). *XML schema part 0: Primer* (2nd ed). W3C Recommendation 28 October 2004. Retrieved from http://www.w3c.org.

Fallside, D. C., & Walmsley, P. (2004). *XML schema Part 0: Primer* (2nd ed). W3C Recommendation 28 October 2004. Retrieved from http://www.w3c.org.

Ferdinand, M., Zirpins, C., & Trastour, D. (2004). Lifting XML schema to OWL. In *Proceedings of Web Engineering, 4th International Conference, ICWE 2004*, (pp. 354-358). Munich, Germany: Springer.

García, R. (2006). *A semantic web approach to digital rights management*. Doctoral Dissertation. University of Versailles. Retrieved June 23rd, 2011, from http://rhizomik.net/html/~roberto/thesis/.

Hitzler, P., Krötzsch, M., Parsia, B., Patel-Schneider, P. F., & Rudolph, S. (2009). *OWL 2 web ontology language primer*. W3C Recommendation 27 October 2009. Retrieved from http://www.w3c.org.

Horridge, M., & Bechhofer, S. (2009). *The OWL API: A Java API for working with OWL 2 ontologies*. Paper presented at OWLED 2009, 6th OWL Experienced and Directions Workshop. Chantilly, VA.

Klein, M. C. A., Broekstra, J., Fensel, D., Van Harmelen, F., & Horrocks, I. (2003). Ontologies and schema languages on the Web. In *Spinning the Semantic Web* (pp. 95–139). Cambridge, MA: MIT Press.

Miller, G. A. (1995). WORDNET: A lexical database for English. *Communications of the ACM*, *11*, 39–41. doi:10.1145/219717.219748

Motik, B., Grau, B. C., Horrocks, I., Wu, Z., Fokoue, A., & Lutz, C. (2009). *OWL 2 Web ontology language profiles*. W3C Recommendation 27 October 2009. Retrieved from http://www.w3c.org.

Polleres, A., Krennwallner, T., Lopes, N., Kopecký, J., & Decker, S. (2009). *XSPARQL language specification*. W3C Member Submission, January 2009. Retrieved from http://www.w3c.org.

Rodrigues, T., Rosa, P., & Cardoso, J. (2008). Moving from syntactic to semantic organizations using jxml2owl. *Computers in Industry*, *59*(8), 808–819. doi:10.1016/j.compind.2008.06.002

Thompson, H. S., Beech, D., Maloney, M., & Mendelsohn, N. (2004). *XML schema part 1: Structures* (2nd ed). W3C Recommendation 28 October 2004. Retrieved from http://www.w3c.org.

KEY TERMS AND DEFINITIONS

XML Schema: XML Schema is an abstract collection of metadata usually created by processing a collection of XML Schema documents, which contains the source language definitions (also known as XML Schemata) of the metadata components.

XML Schema Component: An XML Schema component is a building block that defines an abstract data model of a schema. Components can be of three groups: Primary components, Secondary components, and Helper components.

OWL: Ontology Web Language

Transformation Pattern: A pattern is used in many areas as "template" or abstract descriptions encoding best practices of some field. We define Transformation Pattern as a clear and formal transformation of XSD components and related constructs into OWL2-RL profile.

Dictionary Term: Clearly identifiable word belonging to a standard common dictionary (like the English Oxford dictionary for the English language), rather than unrecognized abbreviations, acronyms or any other sequence of chars.

Semantically Valid Concept: A concept c derived from an XML Schema source is semantically valid if its label is composed by only dictionary terms.

Well Structured Concept: A concept c is well structured if the ratio between obtained properties (#Rs) and the total number of extracted concepts (#C) is higher of a predefined threshold (α).

Semantically Well Structured Concepts: A non empty set of concepts C is semantically well structured if its concepts are semantically valid (on the basis of a predefined threshold β) and C itself is well structured

ENDNOTES

1. Mortgage Industry Standards Maintenance Organization, (MISMO) http://www.mismo.org/

2. A mapping from set A onto B is called surjective (or 'onto') if every member of B is the image of at least one member of A. ➔ $f: A \rightarrow B$ is surjective if $\forall b \in B$ ($\exists a \in A$ ($f(a)=b$))

3. GS1 – Global Standard and solutions http://www.gs1.org/

4. e-business human resources-related data exchanges standard http://www.hr-xml.org/

5. Open Applications Group http://www.oagi.org/

6. http://en.wikipedia.org/wiki/Garbage_In,_Garbage_Out

[7] XBRL (eXtensible Business Reporting Language) http://www.xbrl.org

[8] http://sax.sourceforge.net/

[9] http://owlapi.sourceforge.net/

[10] http://sourceforge.net/projects/jwordnet/

[11] A stop word is a word, usually one of a series in a stop list, that is to be ignored because considered as non influential to the semantic meaning of a sentence (like prepositions or conjunctions)

Chapter 5
LMF Dictionary–Based Approach for Domain Ontology Generation

Feten Baccar Ben Amar
University of Sfax, Tunisia

Bilel Gargouri
University of Sfax, Tunisia

Abdelmajid Ben Hamadou
University of Sfax, Tunisia

ABSTRACT

In this chapter, the authors propose an approach for generating domain ontologies from LMF standardized dictionaries (ISO-24613). It consists, firstly, of deriving the target ontology core systematically from the explicit information of the LMF dictionary structure. Secondly, it aims at enriching such a core, taking advantage of textual sources with guided semantic fields available in the definitions and the examples of lexical entries. The originality of this work lies not only in the use of a unique and finely-structured source containing multi-domain and lexical knowledge of morphological, syntactic, and semantic levels, lending itself to ontological interpretations, but also in providing ontological elements with linguistic grounding. In addition, the proposed approach has addressed the quality issue that is of a major importance in ontology engineering. They have integrated a validation stage along with the extraction modules in order to maintain the consistency of the generated ontologies. Furthermore, the proposed approach was applied to a case study in the field of astronomy and the experiment has been carried out on the Arabic language. This choice is explained both by the great deficiency of work on Arabic ontology development and the availability within the research team of an LMF standardized Arabic dictionary.

DOI: 10.4018/978-1-4666-0188-8.ch005

INTRODUCTION

Over the last decades, ontologies have gained growing interest opening fascinating possibilities in several applications such as Natural Language Processing (NLP), Information Retrieval, Semantic Web (SW) and Question Answering. Indeed, Guarino (1998) defines ontology as an "engineering artifact," constituted by a specific vocabulary used to describe a certain reality in a formal way. Hence, research on ontology development and construction process improvement has become increasingly widespread in computer science community. In fact, the nature of ontologies as reference models for a domain requires a high quality degree of the respective model. Although several approaches have been considered in literature to assess ontology construction methodologies (Gómez-Pérez, 1994, 2004; Guarino & Welty, 2002; Porzel & Malaka, 2004; Brewster, et al., 2004; Gangemi, et al., 2006), a comprehensive and consensual standard methodology seems to be out of reach. Yet, evaluating the ontology as a whole is a costly and challenging task especially when the reduction of human intervention is sought. This can be deemed as a major impediment that may elucidate the ontologies' failure not only to be reused in others but also to be exploited in final applications (M. B. Almeida, 2009).

Moreover, even though an ontology may be constructed manually or semi-automatically, it is never a trivial task. Actually, the absence of common consensus and structured guidelines has hindered the development of ontologies within and between research teams. Indeed, although the area of ontology learning aiming to automate the ontology creation process has been dealt with by plenty of work, it is still a long way from being fully automatic and deployable on a large scale. This is essentially because it is a time-consuming and painstaking endeavor that requires significant human (expert) involvement for the validation of each step throughout this process (Lonsdale, et al., 2010).

In order to reduce the costs, research on (semi-) automatic ontology building from scratch has been conducted using a variety of resources, such as raw text (Aussenac-Gilles, et al., 2008; Li, et al., 2005; Navigli, et al., 2003), Machine-Readable Dictionaries (MRDs) (Kurematsu, et al., 2004; Kietz, et al., 2000; Rigau, et al., 1998), and thesauri (Christment, et al., 2008; Soergel, et al., 2004). Obviously, these resources have different features, and therefore, each proposed process is based on a different approach with respect to principles, design criteria, NLP techniques, etc.

On the other hand, as linguistic information is increasingly required in ontologies, mainly in SW and NLP communities (Buitelaar, et al., 2009; Pazienza, et al., 2007), among the considered terminological resources, MRDs represent one of the most likely and suitable sources promoting the knowledge extraction both at ontological and lexical levels. However, since much information has not yet been encoded, the access to the potential wealth of information in dictionaries remains limited to software applications.

Recently, Lexical Markup Framework (LMF) (ISO 24613, 2008), which is a standard for the representation and construction of lexical resources, has been defined. Its meta-model basically provides a common and shared representation of lexical objects that allows the encoding of rich linguistic information, including morphological, syntactic, and semantic aspects (Francopoulo & George, 2008). Thanks to its encompassing of both ontological and lexical information, an LMF standardized dictionary offers a very suitable primary knowledge resource to learn domain ontologies and above all to provide the ontology elements with linguistic grounding or structure (Baccar, et al., 2010).

This chapter presents an approach for generating domain ontologies from LMF standardized dictionaries. Indeed, it consists in deriving the target ontology core systematically from the explicit information of the LMF dictionary structure. Besides, it aims at enriching such core taking advantage of textual sources available in the definitions and examples of lexical entries. Since one of the challenges in ontology engineering is the preservation of the quality of the produced ontology throughout its development life cycle, a validation phase had to be integrated into this process. This validation phase uses a set of constraints to anticipate errors and prevent their occurrence.

In order to illustrate the reliability of the proposed approach, we present a detailed case study pertaining to the astronomy domain, whose experiment was performed using an LMF standardized dictionary of the Arabic language. This choice was highly motivated by the great deficiency of work on Arabic ontology building as well as the availability within our research team of an LMF standardized Arabic dictionary (Baccar, et al., 2008).

The remainder of this chapter is structured as follows. Section 2 presents the state-of-the art and motivations of this work. Then, Section 3 describes the fundamentals of the proposed approach for domain ontology generation from LMF standardized dictionaries. Section 4 gives details of the tool implementation. Section 5 describes a case study relating to the astronomy domain investigating the LMF standardized dictionary of Arabic language. As for Section 6, it is devoted to discuss the approach evaluation. Finally, Section 7 concludes the chapter with opening perspectives for future work.

STATE-OF-THE-ART AND MOTIVATIONS

Ontology engineering has always been a tedious task requiring considerable human involvement and effort especially with regard to the activity of knowledge acquisition. During the three last decades, there have been some efforts to automate ontology construction process by exploiting (semi-) structured knowledge content like the one pro-

vided by Machine-Readable Dictionaries (MRDs). In fact, early work on extraction taxonomies from MRDs goes back to the 80s and early 90s (Michiels, et al., 1980, Amsler, 1981, Calzolari, 1984, Chodorow, et al, 1985, Dolan, et al., 1993). Bearing in mind that MRDs can be exploited to obtain rich and explicit semantic information between lexical entries, these researchers have attempted to make explicit the implicitly embedded knowledge in the definitions texts. The basic idea is to exploit the regularity of dictionary entries to initially find a suitable *hypernym* for the defined word (For more details, we refer the reader to Cimaino [2006]).

Furthermore, considered as a large repository of semi-structured knowledge about language and the knowledge of real world, MRDs have been the backbone for generating conceptual structures ranging from concept hierarchies (Jannink & Wiederhold, 1999; Yamaguchi, 1999), thesauri (Jannink, 1999) to ontologies (Kurematsu, et al., 2004; Nichols, et al., 2005). Indeed, the main advantage of using existing human-oriented knowledge resources such as MRDs is the possibility to exploit their partial structure. Actually, word senses, separately defined in MRDs, can be seen as the equivalent of ontological categories, and semantic relations (e.g. *synonymy*, *antonymy*, *hyponymy*, *meronymy*) between different senses would correspond to ontological relations (for example, *hypernymy* would stand for *subsumption*) (Hirst, 2004). Another important aspect is that ontological relationships are learned between word senses (i.e. concepts) rather than between the words themselves (Cimaino, 2006).

Nevertheless, since the MRDs are oriented towards human reader, much information is not well-structured and subsequently its machine interpretation might not be evident. Consequently, systems relying on MRDs encounter two major problems. While the first inherent problem is their need for massive human intervention, the second is their confinement to limited relations in almost all but the taxonomic cases (Vaquero, et al., 2007).

Recently, a common and unified model for the creation and use of computational lexicons, baptized Lexical Markup Framework (LMF), has been defined (ISO 24613). Notice that even though its main goals are to manage the exchange of data among lexical resources and enable their merging at small or large scale (Francopoulo & Georges, 2008), the LMF meta-model allows for rendering MRDs' content into a finely-structured and more explicit knowledge format, thus facilitating the access to its manifold lexical information. Indeed, covering all natural languages (including languages with rich and complex morphology such as Arabic), the LMF meta-model contains much explicit linguistic information (inflectional and variant forms, synonyms, part-of-speech, definitions, usage domain, grammatical properties, etc.) as well as a lot of semantic knowledge disseminated in the definitions and examples.

From another standpoint, the growing awareness of the benefits of the linguistically grounded ontologies, especially in semantic web and NLP communities, has led to the creation of a number of models attempting to extend ontological objects with linguistic grounding (Pazienza, et al., 2008; Aussenac-Gilles, et al., 2008). Moreover, after the introduction of LMF standard, a good deal of active work, among which we can mention LexInfo (Buitelaar, et al., 2009) and Linguistic Information Repository (LIR) (Montiel-Pensoda, et al., 2008), has been undertaken in response to the need for increasing the linguistic expressivity of given ontologies. The proposed models try to associate lexical information with ontological entities, which is a heavy and time consuming activity considering the plurality and the heterogeneity of the resort sources. In addition, some complexity rises when linguistic information is involved in ontology reasoning (Ma, et al., 2010).

Since an undeniable contribution of the LMF standard lies in its ability of rich representation of MRD and NLP lexica, thus allowing to direct and selective access to various lexical objects in the linguistic resources, we have asserted that an LMF standardized dictionary offers a very suitable primary knowledge resource to learn domain ontologies. Indeed, thanks to its encompassing of both ontological and lexical information, such a resource is interesting to get all the elements (i.e. concepts, relationships and individuals) required in the domain ontologies and above all to provide them with linguistic grounding or structure. In this chapter, we detail of the proposed approach for generating domain ontologies from LMF standardized dictionaries. Therefore, the way how to exploit LMF-standardized dictionaries as well as the assessment of the proposed approach will be the topic of the rest of this chapter.

GENERATING DOMAIN ONTOLOGIES FROM LMF STANDARDIZED DICTIONARIES

The Proposed Approach: Originality and Principles

Our preliminary studies based on LMF standardized dictionary show promising results and prove that much can be learned through its structure and text analysis. Indeed, based on the LMF meta-model subtlety and power, lexical knowledge is expressed either directly, through the fields (e.g. *Context, SubjectField, SenseRelation*) related to the lexical entries or indirectly, through the text included in the semantic knowledge (e.g. definitions and examples). The main advantage of using such a finely-structured resource lies in reducing the considerable effort and time required in the activity of knowledge acquisition that constitutes one of the most important steps at the beginning of the ontology development process, and above all to provide the ontology elements with linguistic grounding or structure.

Although the whole lexical data in LMF standardized dictionaries cannot be directly accessed, its definitions contain a profusion of semantic knowledge included in a more or less regularly-structured text, thus facilitating the natural language processing in the enrichment stage. Here, the pattern-based approach is proven to be significant for two reasons. First, the patterns are typically specified because the text dealt with is quite particular (language regularity), hence reducing the cost of their definition and augmenting their robustness. Second, almost all concepts revealed in the definitions are closely dependent on the domain in question, so the human intervention for deciding concept relevance is not compulsory. Besides, the pattern-matching which focuses on quality and fine-grained analyses yields more certain results than those of co-occurrence context clustering or other statistical approaches especially when handling a few texts (Aussenac-Gilles & Jacques, 2008).

In addition, being more and more available in the linguistic community, an LMF-compliant dictionary would certainly be an extendable resource that could greatly be fed with other sources (e.g. lexicons, text corpora) thanks to the modular structure of LMF meta-model. Thus, the richness of the generated ontologies can be guaranteed if the primary resource contains a large amount of domain-specific knowledge. It should be pointed out that even a very large corpus may not include all the familiar words of a language.

Accordingly, we propose an approach, whose overall process is depicted in Figure 1, for automatically generating domain ontologies from LMF standardized dictionaries. It consists mainly of three stages. Firstly, we extract a dictionary fragment corresponding to a selected domain from the whole dictionary. Secondly, we aim at digging out the basic elements of the chosen domain from the previously-created dictionary fragment in order to build a core of the target ontology. Finally, the obtained ontology will be greatly enriched by exploiting the semantics conveyed by the textual fields of the dictionary. In order to ensure the high quality of the produced ontology, a verification step is performed along with the identification of ontological entities (core and enrichment components). We describe these stages in more details in the sections that follow.

Domain Selection

In the initial stage, we begin with the creation of a dictionary fragment, also called a domain dictionary, by extracting the relevant part of the whole dictionary. Such a dictionary fragment firstly gathers the lexical entries of related senses to the domain of interest as well as their semantically related words by accessing to the explicit information corresponding to the usage domain in the dictionary (i.e., *SubjectField* in LMF). Then, all along the building process, this dictionary fragment is extended by importing new lexical entries pertaining to concepts revealed by the text analysis. Therefore, the interest of the domain dictionary is twofold. First, it represents the privileged initial source for generating the target domain ontology. Second, when tackling the obtained ontology conceptual nodes always keep reference (i.e. through simple reference pointer) to linguistic structures that are kept separate from the domain ontology, thanks to the univocity between them.

LMF Structure-Based Ontology Acquisition: The Core Building

The second stage consists in building the core of the target ontology. The ontological core within our context stands for all possible sets of basic objects in a specific domain that could be directly derived from the systematic organization of linguistic objects in an LMF standardized dictionary. It has also become evident that ontology elements in turn would benefit from an easy access to the linguistic information pertaining to these lexical entries. The core building process consists of the (1) identification of ontology candidates, (2) duplication check and (3) validation stage (Figure 2).

Figure 1. The architecture of the proposed approach for domain ontology generation

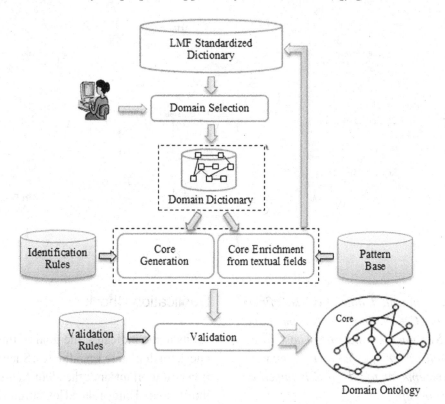

Concepts and Relations Identification

During this stage, the concepts and their relationships are identified from the lexical entries in the LMF standardized dictionary. According to our investigation on LMF structure and as it is shown in Figure 3, we managed to define a set of identification rules allowing for the elicitation of ontological entities. It is worth noting that the choice of using rules is explained by two main motives. The first one is their lucidity in describing the assigned actions and the second is their simple representation of solutions. These rules can be divided into two types: those of concepts identification and those of relations identification. For each dictionary entry, concepts identification rules are applied and followed by those of the relationships identification. It goes without

saying that the relations identification may also bring out concepts candidates. For instance, since a concept corresponds to a meaning of a word, we can directly deduce the concepts of the domain ontology from the particular instances (e.g. *Context*, *SenseExample*) attached to the *Sense* class. Another example of rules can be illustrated by the fact that a semantic relationship (e.g. *synonymy*, *hypernymy*, *meronymy*) between the senses of two or several lexical entries by means of the *SenseRelation* class gives birth to an ontological relation linking the corresponding concepts.

As a result of the initial stage, all the candidates of the core elements (i.e. concepts and relationships) are acquired; each of which is assigned to a given signature. In the present work, we formally define a signature of a candidate concept and a candidate relation as follows:

Figure 2. The core domain ontology generation process

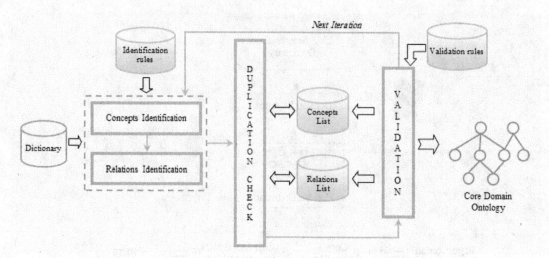

Definition 1. *A concept, denoted by C, is defined as a couple, C = (N, S), where N is the name of C and S denotes its binary tag whose value is equal either "0" if C has no relation with other concepts, or to "1" if C is linked to another concept.*

Definition 2. *A relation, denoted by R, is defined by a triplet, R = (N, CD, CR), where N is the name of the relation, CD is the domain of R and CR is the range of R, (where CD and CR are two concepts).*

Duplication Check

As its name indicates, the goal of this stage is to check for duplicated candidates. Such verification is very important since the identification task may imply several inter-related lexical entries per iteration. In order to detect duplicated candidates, the proposed process is based on two lists of concepts and relations, which are initially empty. They are intended to contain signatures of the concepts and relations, emanated from the valid introduction

Figure 3. Correspondences between the LMF standardized dictionary elements and the domain ontology entities. R1, R2, ..., R9 refer to the identification rules.

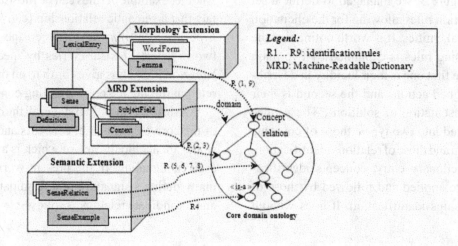

Box 1.

* Let $< C1 = (Name\_1, ?) >$ and $< C2 = (Name\_2, 0) >$ be concept candidates,

$$\begin{cases} < C2 = (Name\_2, 0) > \ \equiv \ < C1 = (Name\_1, ?) > \ \textbf{Iff} \\ \qquad Name\_1 = Name\_2 \end{cases}$$

* Let $< R_q = (relation_q, C1_q, C2_q) >$ and $< R_p = (relation_p, C1_p, C2_p) >$ be two relation candidates and $<C1_q = (Name\_1_q, 1) >, < C2_q = (Name\_2_q, 1) >, <C1_p = (Name\_1_p, 1) >$ and $< C2_p = (Name\_2_p, 1) >$ be its two arguments, respectively,

$$\begin{cases} < R_q = (relation_q, C1_q, C2_q) > \ \equiv \ < R_p = (relation_p, C1_p, C2_p) > \ \textbf{Iff} \\ \qquad < C1_p = (Name\_1_p, 1) > \ \equiv \ < C1_q = (Name\_1_q, 1) > \ \textbf{and} \\ \qquad < C2_p = (Name\_2_p, 1) > \ \equiv \ < C2_q = ((Name\_2_q, 1) > \ \textbf{and} \\ \qquad relation_p = relation_q \end{cases}$$

of new concepts and/or relations into the resulting core. In addition, we distinguish three types of duplication: exact duplication, quasi-exact duplication and implicit duplication.

Let L_C and L_R be the lists of concepts and relations, respectively.

- **Exact duplication**. It refers to the identification of the same copy of a previously identified candidate. This type of duplication is denoted by the ' $\equiv$ ' symbol which is formally stated in Box 1.
- **Quasi-exact duplication**. This duplication denoted by the ' $\cong$ ' symbol concerns only relation candidates. A quasi-exact duplicated relation candidate might not be identical to an already identified candidate but it represents an equivalent one. Formally, it is represented in Box 2.

To illustrate the quasi-exact duplication with a concrete example, we consider the case of "*married-to*" symmetric relationship, for instance **R1** = (*married-to*, Man, Woman). Hence, a candidate relation with the **R2** = (*married-to*, Woman, Man) signature is considered as a quasi-exact duplicated relationship and should be ignored.

- **Implicit duplication**. It also concerns only relation candidates. An implicit duplicated candidate is a completely different candidate but whose knowledge can be inferred from existing core elements. Formally, it is represented in Box 3.

For example, if we have two identified relations, **R1** = (*is-a, Dog, Pet*) and **R2** = (*is-a, Pet, Animal*), then we can derive the **R3** = (*is-a, Dog, Animal*) relation candidate. Hence, a candidate

Box 2.

Let $< R_p = (relation_p, C1_p, C2_p) >$ and $< R_q = (relation_q, C1_q, C2_q) >$ be two relation candidates and $< C1_p = (Name\_1_p, 1) >, < C2_p = (Name\_2_p, 1) >, < C1_q = (Name\_1_q, 1) >$ and $< C2_q = (Name\_2_q, 1) >$ be its two arguments, respectively,

$$\begin{cases} < R_q = (relation_q, C1_q, C2_q) > \ \cong \ < R_p = (relation_p, C1_p, C2_p) > \ \textbf{Iff} \\ \qquad < C1_p = (Name\_1_p, 1) > \ \equiv \ < C2_q = (Name\_2_q, 1) > \ \textbf{and} \\ \qquad < C1_q = (Name\_1_q, 1) > \ \equiv \ < C2_p = (Name\_2_p, 1) > \ \textbf{and} \\ \qquad (relation_p = relation_q = relation) \ \textbf{and} \ \textit{\textbf{symmetric}}^i \ (relation) \end{cases}$$

Box 3.

Let $< R_p = (relation_p, C1_p, C2_p) >$, $< R_q = (relation_q, C1_q, C2_q) >$ and $< R_u = (relation_u, C1, C2) >$ be three relation candidates and $< C1 = (Name\_, 1) >$ and $< C2 = (Name\_2, 1) >$ be the arguments of R_u,

$$\left[\begin{array}{l} < R_u = (relation_u, C1, C2) > \text{ is an implicit duplicated relation } \textbf{Iff} \\[2ex] \dfrac{R_p \quad R_q}{R_p \wedge R_q \Rightarrow R_u} \end{array} \right.$$

with **R3** signature is an implicit duplicated relationship that must be removed from the relations list.

In all duplication types, the duplicated candidates should be ignored. Therefore, the constructed core domain ontology does not store unnecessary or useless entities. This quality criterion is also called *conciseness* (Gómez-Pérez, 2004).

It is worth mentioning that the final lists of concepts and relations are very helpful not only for the core construction, but also for its enrichment. Particularly, in the enrichment task, we will consider only the orphan concepts (i.e. whose binary tag is equal to 0) in order to link them to either old or new concepts. Indeed, the first stage of this process may introduce a good number of concepts that are not involved in any relations. Likewise, the list of relations is needed for the enrichment stage so as to check the coherence of the whole ontology (i.e. the core-part plus elements of the enrichment module(s)).

Once duplication check is performed, a further validation stage is required to verify whether the resulting core remains coherent when the candidate is added to it.

Validation Stage

The automatic addition of non-duplicated ontological entities to the ontology core could bring about errors. In order to maintain the coherence of the built core, the integration of a validation stage into the proposed process is necessary. In other words, a concept or a relation is automatically added to the output core structure only when the latter is still coherent. Gómez-Pérez (1999) has identified and classified different kinds of errors in taxonomies: inconsistency, incompleteness, and redundancy errors.

Incompleteness error. It occurs if the domain of interest is not appropriately covered. Typically, an ontology is incomplete if it does not include all relevant concepts and their lexical representations. Moreover, partitions are incompletely defined if knowledge about disjointedness or exhaustiveness of a partition is omitted.

Redundancy error. It is a type of error that occurs when redefining expressions that were already explicitly defined or that can be inferred using other definitions.

Inconsistency error. This kind of errors can be classified in circularity errors, semantic inconsistency errors, and partition errors.

- **Circularity error.** A circularity error is identified, if a defined class in an ontology is a specialization or generalization of itself. For example, the concept Woman is a subclass of the concept Person which is a subclass of the concept Woman.
- **Semantic inconsistency error.** It refers to an incorrect semantic classification, for example, the concept Car is a subclass of the concept Person.

- **Partition error.** A class partition error occurs, if a class is defined as a common subclass of several classes of a disjoint partition. For example, the concept Dog is a subclass of the concepts Pet_Animal and Wild_Animal which are disjoint subclasses of the concept Animal.

In the current stage, we are interested in the kinds of errors that can be automatically detected (i.e. without human expert involvement). The redundancy verification has already been dealt with in the second stage of this process. As to the completeness assessment, it could not be done at this early stage of domain ontology development. Therefore, only inconsistency errors, particularly those of circularity and partition types, are addressed in the present work. After the check of the resulting core, we proceed to the update of the concepts and relations lists as well as the core ontology.

The Ontology Enrichment

Pattern-Based Identification Solution

The objective of the final stage is to enrich an existing ontology by new elements. Relations can be efficient means to rapidly structure ontologies. Moreover, they play a major role to identify concepts along with their properties (Aussenac-Gilles & Jacques, 2008).

Yet, the text of definition in the dictionary is the best way to extract semantic relations between the concepts of a specific domain. Indeed, this sort of knowledge is endowed with a regular structure, thus allowing us to specify a finite set of patterns in the form of regular expressions. Patterns are then abstractions of these regularities. This trend of research has been opened by the seminal work of (Hearst, 1992), who used automatically-extracted patterns. This method includes a kind of weak supervision, since it relies on an *a priori* list of

patterns deciding which patterns are associated with which semantic relations. The increasing popularity of pattern-based methods (Berland & Charniak, 1999; Widdows & Dorow, 2002; Almuhareb & Poesio, 2004; Cimiano & Wenderoth, 2007; among many others) is due to the fact that they are very promising in allowing the explicit typing of the extracted knowledge. It is also worth mentioning that such a pattern-based approach works well provided that it is possible to identify easy-to-mine patterns univocally associated with the target knowledge type. In other words, it assumes that linguistic regularities always characterize the same kind of knowledge.

Over the last ten years, patterns have been widely used effectively for information extraction or relation extraction (Reinberger & Spyns, 2004). However, according to the literature, such an approach based on lexico-syntactic patterns presents a shortcoming when learning lexical relations between word forms rather than between senses of words or concepts. In order to mitigate this problem and reduce the risk of errors especially as the proposed process is intended to be fully automatic, we decided to exploit the core concepts that were previously generated in the ontology and annotate the text by their means. Consequently, in almost all cases, when examining a given relation, we dispose already of one argument (i.e. annotated with a core concept) and we have only to look for the second argument. Next, the state-of-the-art NLP tools are applied in order to specify the grammatical category of each word (e.g. part-of-speech tagger, anaphora resolution tool, Named Entity Recognition).

Therefore, once the set of patterns and rules are fixed, and based on an entirely automatic and non-supervised process, the proposed solution is able to discover any kind of relationship; both taxonomical and non-taxonomical. Furthermore, it can be applied to any field for which the ontology will be designed, relying on a pattern base that was previously established.

Process Overview

In order to carry out the ontology enrichment, we propose the process depicted in Figure 4. It consists in (1) annotating the text with the core concepts as well as grammatical categories, (2) performing a pattern-matching stage in order to find out ontological entities, (3) checking its duplication check and (4) validating its addition in the resulting ontology if the latter remains coherent.

- **Text annotation.** In a first stage, we collect definitions available in the dictionary and associate each one to its concept. Knowing that the concept may occur in a sentence under different forms (e.g. flexional forms), it is necessary to expand the list of the previously obtained concepts, by generating their possible forms. A considerable number of these forms can be acquired directly

from the dictionary itself. For instance, the concept car can be found in a sentence under its plural form, cars. The fact that an overlap may occur, due to the common words in many concepts (for example, sun and sun eclipse), is taken into consideration (i.e. an occurrence of *"sun eclipse"* in the text is tagged with sun eclipse and not with sun only).

Once the first annotation is done, the non-annotated tokens in the text are part-of-speech (POS) tagged using a dedicated tool. Next, the linguistic information assigned to each token will stipulate its role in the ontology. For linguistic phenomena resolution, like ellipsis and anaphora, we use NLP specialized tools available in our laboratory, for instance, AnATAr for Arabic anaphora resolution tool (Hammami et al., 2010).

Figure 4. The ontology enrichment process

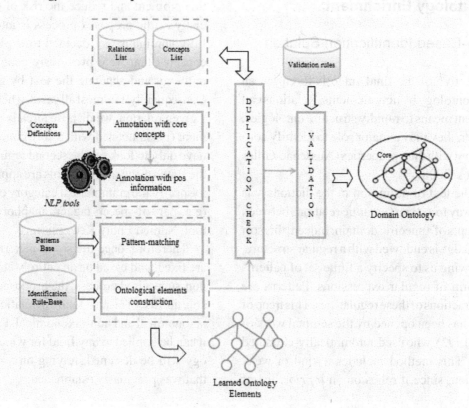

Learned Ontology Elements

- **Pattern-matching and Ontological entities identification.** During this stage, the system performs the pattern-matching procedure in order to identify ontological entities (i.e. to mark them with concept, relation and property). Based on a set of rules, it brings about the constructed elements and owing to the regularity of definitions, the set of rules is finite. In the case of narration style change or missing word or a rarely used style, the system will suggest to the expert how to define the necessary rule.

In the proposed process for core domain ontology generation, we have elaborated two stages for duplication checking and validation. Likewise, these sub-stages (§ subsections 2 and 3) are needed in the enrichment stage.

IMPLEMENTATION DETAILS

The approach for domain ontology generation from LMF standardized dictionaries is implemented in a Java-based tool that enables users to automatically build the ontologies formalized in OWL-DL, a sublanguage of OWL (Dean & Schreiber, 2004). Indeed, an OWL-DL formalized ontology can be interpreted according to description logics, and DL-based reasoning software (e.g., RacerPro[1] or Pellet[2]) can be applied to check its consistency or draw inferences from it. To take advantage of this, we have decided to incorporate the Pellet reasoner into our system. It is an open-source Java-based OWL-DL reasoning tool (Sirin, et al., 2007). Its consistency checking ensures that the produced ontology core does not contain any contradictory facts. After the loading of the built OWL file, Pellet determines if the ontology is actually consistent by calling the isConsistent() method, whereby its boolean return would decide whether the addition operation could be performed in the resulting core. Regarding NLP tools used for the purpose of text analysis, we have tested

the implemented system for the Arabic language. Actually, we have successfully integrated MOPH2 (Chaâbane, et al., 2010) and AnATAr (Hammami, et al., 2010) into our system. Moreover, in order to visualize the created OWL domain ontology, we have utilized the Protégé ontology editor[3] with its jambalaya plug-in which allows displaying Arabic text.

A CASE STUDY: THE ASTRONOMY DOMAIN

In this section, we describe the proposed process for domain ontology generation through an illustrative case relating to the astronomy domain. In what follows, we firstly define the domain of interest as well as the dictionary of the experiment. Secondly, we report examples and results of each stage in the approach.

Arabic Dictionary Use Case and Domain Definition

In order to illustrate the proposed process, a series of experiments has been conducted on different domains using an LMF standardized Arabic dictionary. This choice is explained by two main motives. The first one is the great deficiency of work on Arabic ontology development and the second is the availability within our research team of an LMF standardized Arabic dictionary (Baccar, et al., 2008). This dictionary is covering various domains, of which animals, plants, astronomy and sports are but a few. Besides, it contains about 40.000 lexical entries and about 30.000 relationships among which the most frequent are synonymy, antonymy and hypernymy. In addition, due to the specificities of Arabic and the presence of different tools for its natural language processing (Chaâbane, et al., 2010; Hammami, et al., 2010), we consider that going through ontology learning issue for Arabic language represents another big challenge.

In the remainder of this section, we report an illustrative case study pertaining to the astronomy field, whose choice is based on two main reasons. Firstly, Arabic scientists have soundly described the astronomy science « علم فلك » thanks to the richness in terms of concepts and relations of such domain. Secondly, it is quite popular in the ontology learning community. For the illustration, we consider a fragment of an LMF standardized dictionary corresponding to the domain of interest, which deals with the study of celestial objects (such as stars, planets, comets, nebulae, star clusters and galaxies) and phenomena that originate outside the Earth's atmosphere (such as the cosmic background radiation). It is concerned with the evolution, physics, chemistry, meteorology, and motion of celestial objects, as well as the formation and development of the universe.

Let us remind that the proposed approach consists in automatically extracting explicit knowledge from the LMF structure in order to build the target ontology core. Such core stands for an initial ontology involving a set of basic concepts and their taxonomic relationships. Based on natural text processing and pattern-matching techniques, the obtained ontology is greatly enriched with new concepts, semantic relations that were not stated explicitly in the handled dictionary, as well as attributes of concepts.

Domain Selection

Starting from an LMF standardized dictionary of the Arabic language comprising thousands of muti-domain lexical entries, we collect those corresponding to the domain of interest. Then, we build our dictionary fragment comprising a hundred or so of lexical entries (around 350 senses). The extraction of all relevant senses is based on the explicit information associated with the domain-specific senses of lexical entries (i.e. *SubjectField* class) to describe their meaning in a given domain. Subsequently, only the senses (or concepts) that are directly connected to the

domain of the astronomy were considered (i.e. the concepts of mathematical, chemistry, physics, etc. domains were disregarded). It is to be noted the overlooked senses, even tagged with other domain, would be revealed at the core enrichment stage. For example, the concept "خَطُّ الاسْتِواءِ" ("Equator") which is assigned to the geographical domain, can be deduced from the definition of the concept "الدَّائِرَةُ القُطْبِيَّةُ" ("Polar_ Circle") belonging to the astronomy domain.

Core Construction

For each lexical entry in the dictionary, the identification rules are applied on its structure in order to deduce the candidates of concepts and relationships held between them. As already mentioned above, in the LMF standardized dictionary, a concept or a sub-concept can be denoted by numerous fields in the LMF-compliant dictionary. Typical examples are provided in order to show the rule identification process. For example, in the simplest case where a lexical entry has one sense, we deduce a concept labeled with either the *Lemma* class string or the *Context* class expression. For instance, in the case of the lexical entry "ثُرَيَّا" (resp. "زُحَلّ"), we deduce the concept "الثُّرَيَّا" ("Pleiades") (resp. "زُحَلّ" ["Saturn"]). In the case of more than one context, an "is-a" relationship should also be created between each concept derived from Context class and that derived from Lemma class. For example, the sense in the lexical entry "أَشِعَّةُ" ("Rays") has two *Context* instances, thus classifying the two following sub-concepts: "أَشِعَّةُ الشَّمْسِ" ("Solar_Radiation") and "أَشِعَّةٌ نَجْمِيَّةٌ" ("Stellar_Radiation") under the common super-concept ("Rays").

It is worthwhile to note that numerous lexical entries contain many senses corresponding to the astronomy domain, as in the case of the lexical entry "دَائِرَةٌ" ("Circle"), which has four senses related to the astronomy domain. Starting from the rules of concept identification, we deduce these concepts: "دَائِرَةُ الانْقِلاب" ("Solstice"), "دَائِرَةُ الإرْتِفَاع" ("Parallel_Of_Altitude"), "الدَّائِرَةُ القُطْبِيَّةُ الجَنُوبِيَّة" ("Antarctic_Circle"),

"الشَّمَالِيَّةُ" ("Arctic_Circle").

As for the lexical entry of "كَوْكَبَةٌ" ("Constellation"), we deduce the concept "كَوْكَبَةُ النُّجُوم" ("Asterism") from the *Context* class. In fact, such concept has two instances of *SenseExample* class, which lead to the generation of two sub-concepts: "النَّسْرِ" ("Vega") and "النَّسْرِ الوَاقِعِ" ("Aquila").

As a result, in this stage, a significant number of core concepts are defined after achieving several iterations. Similarly, taxonomic relationships among concepts, which are the simplest and the most fundamental relations, are revealed through different lexical objects related to the lexical entries. Indeed, synonymy leads to the identification of an "is-a" relation. For instance, the lexical entry "اِحْتِجَابٌ" has a sense related to the astronomy domain having "اِحْتِجَابُ القَمَرِ" ("Occultation") as Context, and which means the sense of "كُسُوفٌ" ("Eclipse") attached to the corresponding lexical entry. Therefore, we create the following relation candidate <is-a, *Occultation, Eclipse*). In the particular case, when the synonymy link is bidirectional, then we deduce an equivalence relationship between the corresponding concepts.

Furthermore, a *hypernymy* relationship in the dictionary that connects two or more *Sense* class instances lead to the generation of an "is-a" relation between the corresponding concepts. For example, in the case of the sense of "دَائِرَةُ الاِنْقِلاب" ("Solstice"), we have two senses related to it by a *hypernym* relation. Hence, we create

its two sub-concepts: "دَائِرَةُ الاِنْقِلاب الشَّتَوِيُّ" ("Winter_Solstice") and "دَائِرَةُ الاِنْقِلاب الصَّيْفِيُّ" ("Summer_Solstice"), respectively.

What should be mentioned is that 144 concepts are derived from the structure analysis of the handled dictionary. Based on a variety of experiments carried out on the dictionary at hand and an expert census, we estimate that, in almost all cases, this number of concepts would represent around 85% of the total number of concepts. The rest cannot be identified in the core construction stage for two reasons. On the one hand, though tagged with another domain such as physics many concepts are relevant to the astronomy domain. On the other hand, certain entries of the dictionary have senses without usage domain indication. While a considerable number of concepts has been identified, a small number of relations are revealed in this stage. Indeed such a shortage is due to the lack of explicit semantic relations in the current release of the handled dictionary. What is worth emphasizing is that the overlooked concepts as well as relations will be deduced from the text analysis in the enrichment stage.

Ontology Enrichment

As mentioned earlier, this stage relies on a set of patterns in order to identify ontological entities from the text. At present, we dispose of a pattern-base that includes about 40 patterns for Arabic.

Table 1. Examples of relation extraction patterns (verbal patterns)

Pattern	Examples	English equivalent
فعل VERB	"تَخْتَرِقُ" ، "تُؤَلِّفُ"، "يُسَمَّى"	*"penetrate," "composes," "is named as"*
فعل + (حرف جر| ظرف) VERB + (PREP | ADV)	"يَبْتَدِئُ مِنْ"، "يُسَمَّى أيضاً"، "تَدُورُ حَوْلَ"، "تَمُرُّ بِ"	*"starts from," "is also named as," "turns around," "passes by"*
فعل + ... + حرف VERB + ... + PREP	"يَتَكَوَّنُ ... مِنْ"	*"consists of"*
فعل + حرف + ضمير + حرف VERB + PREP + PRON + PREP	"يُبْحَثُ فيهِ عَنْ"	*"is searched in about"*

Table 2. Examples of relation extraction patterns (nominal patterns)

Pattern	Examples	English equivalent
اسم فاعل + (حرف جر | ظرف) ACTIVE PARTICIPLE + (PREP | ADV)	"قَائِمٌ بَيْنَ "، "مُحِيطٌ بِـ"، "مُوَازِيَةٌ لِـ"	"existing between" "surrounding," "parallel to,"
اسم مفعول + (حرف جر | ظرف) PASSIVE PARTICIPLE + (PREP | ADV)	"مُحَاطٌ بِـ"، "مُزَوَّدٌ بِـ"، "مُلْتَفَّةٌ حَوْلَ "	"supplied with," "surrounded by," " spiral around"
نسبة + (حرف جر | ظرف) NISBA + (PREP | ADV)	"عَمُودِيَّةٌ عَلَى "	"be vertical on"
حرف جر + مصدر PREP + DEVERBAL NOUN	"بِاسْتِثْنَاء"، "لِلرُّؤْيَةِ"، "لِرَقْبِ"	"except the," "to view," "keep watch over"
حرف جر + مصدر + حرف جر PREP + DEVERBAL NOUN + PREP	"فِي تَقَاطُع عَلَى "	"in an intersection on"
اسم عدد ترتيبي + حرف جر ORDINAL NUMBER + PREP	"الرَّابِعُ فِي "	"the fourth in"
اسم تفضيل + حرف جر COMPARATIVE ADJ + PERP	"أَصْغَر مِن"	"smaller than"

Table 3. Examples of concept extraction patterns

Pattern	Examples	English equivalent
اسم NOUN	"عِلْمٌ"، "مَارِس"، "الأَوْجُ"، "الأُفُق"	"Science," "Mars," "Perihelion," "Horizon"
اسم + اسم NOUN + NOUN	"خَطُّ الاسْتِوَاءِ" ، "طَرَفُ المِحْوَر"	"equator," "pole extremity" "equator," "pole extremity"
اسم + نسبة NOUN + NISBA	"الكُرَةُ الأَرْضِيَّةُ" ، "جُرْمٌ سَمَاوِي"	"Globe," "Celestial object" "Globe," "Celestial object"
صفة + اسم + نسبة ADJ + NOUN + NISBA	"نِصْفُ الكُرَةِ الجُنُوبِيُّ" "نِصْفُ الكُرَةِ الجُنُوبِيُّ"	"Southern hemisphere" "Southern hemisphere"
مصدر + اسم DEVERBAL NOUN + NOUN DEVERBAL NOUN + NOUN	"تَجَمُّعُ نُجُوم"، "تَوَسُّطُ الأَرْض"، "مُرَاقَبَةُ النُّجُوم"، "مُرَاقَبَةُ النُّجُوم"	"Star assembly," "Intermediacy of the Earth," "Watching the stars"
اسم مفعول + اسم PASSIVE PARTICIPLE + NOUN	"مَجْمُوعَةُ نُجُوم" ، "مَدَارُ الأَرْض"	"Star constellation," "Earth orbit"
اسم مفعول + نسبة PASSIVE PARTICIPLE + NISBA	" المجموعة الشمسية "	"Solar System"
اسم فاعل + نسبة ACTIVE PARTICIPLE + NISBA	"ظَاهِرَةٌ طَبِيعِيَّةٌ فَلَكِيَّةٌ"	"Astronomical natural phenomenon"
اسم + مصدر + اسم NOUN + DEVERBAL NOUN + NOUN	"أَحْوَالُ حَرَكَاتِ الكَوَاكِبِ"	"planets movements conditions"

They are expressed with Part-Of-Speech (POS) tags and among which; two types of patterns are used to extract relations: verbal patterns and nominal patterns. On the other hand, certain patterns lead to the concept identification as well as their properties. For this purpose, we used the POS tag set provided by Tim Buckwalter and his colleagues (Hajič, et al., 2005). Some examples of patterns are given in Table 1, Table 2, Table 3, and Table 4.

Table 4. Examples of property extraction patterns

Pattern	Examples	English equivalent
صفة مشبهة/ صيغة مبالغة ADJ	"رئيس" ، "نير" ، "ثقافة"	*"pellucid," "luminous," "principal,"*
اسم فاعل ACTIVE PARTICIPLE	"مُشِعَّة" ، "مُضيء" ، "مُسْتَقِيمٌ"	*"straight," "lighted," "radioactive"*
صفة + اسم ADJ + NOUN	"شَدِيدَةِ الحَرَارَةِ"، "خَفِيفُ الضَّوْءِ"	*"with light brilliance," "with high temperature"*

Table 5. Examples of key words

Patterns	Key word (kw)	English equivalent
is-a $<N_1> +/kw/+<N_2>$	"أَخُ" ، "مِثْلَ" ، "وَ هُوَ نَوْعٌ مِنْ"	*"is a kind of," "such as," "one of"*
part/whole $<N_1> +/kw/+<N_2>, \ldots <N_n>$	"جُزْءٌ مِنْ" "يَتَكَوَّنُ مِنْ"	*part of* *Includes/consists of*
Equivalent $<N_1> +/kw/+<N_2>$	"أَوْ" ، "أَيْ"	*"i.e.," "or"*

The above patterns are part-of-speech-composed expressions simply written in conformity with the following grammars (Figure 5, Figure 6, and Figure 7). Each defined grammar **G** is composed of a set of terminals Σ, a set of non-terminals V, an *axiom S* and a set of transformation rules P. Concepts, relations and properties occurring in text will be marked with $[string(s)]_{concept}$, $[string(s)]_{relation}$, $[string(s)]_{property}$, respectively.

Moreover, in particular ontological relations, we dispose of some lexical items or key words revealing these particular relations such as *hypernymy* (is-a), *meronymy* (part/whole) and *equivalent* relations (Table 5).

As an illustration, let us consider the definition of "مِرِّيخ" mrīkh (Mars) concept given in the top-part of Figure 8a.

A preliminary step consists in the definition splitting according to punctuation marks (full stop and comma) (Figure 8a). Then, each sentence is annotated with the core concepts (Figure 8b). Next, POS linguistic information are assigned to

each token (Figure 8c) in order to identify potentially interesting information (i.e. concept, relation, property) for ontology building (Figure 8d).

The following rules show the transformation when encountering the corresponding situation. Figure 9 depicts the constructed elements after applying these rules.

Rule 1:

$[token]_{concept} : [token]^* [token]_{concept} \rightarrow$
$\quad < is\text{-}a, concept_1, concept_2 >$

Rule 2:

$[token]_{concept} [token]^* [token]_{property} \rightarrow$
$\quad < has\text{-}property, concept, property >$

Rule 3:

$[token]_{concept} : [token]^* [token]_{relation} [token]_{concept} \rightarrow$
$\quad <relation, concept_1, concept_2 >$

Figure 5. Relations extraction grammars

$G = (\Sigma, V, S, P)$
$\Sigma = \{$ جر, مصدر, ظرف, فعل, ضمير $\}$
$V = \{S, F1, VAV, VAP\}$
$P = \{$
     S → فعل | F1
     F1 → VAV S | S VAP
     VAP → مصدر | ضمير | جر | ظرف
     VAV → ظرف ضمير | جر ضمير
$\}$

$G = (\Sigma, V, S, P)$
$\Sigma = \{$ جر, مصدر, ترتيبي, تفضيل, نسبة, مفعول, فاعل, ضمير, ظرف $\}$
$V = \{S, PC, F1\}$
$P = \{$
     S → F1 PC | PC مصدر PC | مصدر PC
     F1 → مصدر | ترتيبي | تفضيل | نسبة | مفعول | فاعل
     PC → ضمير | ظرف | جر PC
$\}$

Figure 6. Concepts extraction grammar

$G = (\Sigma, V, S, P)$
$\Sigma = \{$ تفضيل, نسبة, مصدر, مفعول, فاعل, اسم $\}$
$V = \{S, F1, F2, F3, F4, VAV, VAP\}$
$P = \{$
     S → F1 | F2 | F3 | F4 | اسم
     F1 → VAV S | S VAP
     VAV → اسم | مصدر | مفعول | فاعل
     VAP → تفضيل | مصدر | اسم | نسبة
     F2 → مصدر
     F3 → مفعول + نسبة

Figure 7. Property extraction grammar

$G = (\Sigma, V, S, P)$
$\Sigma = \{$ نسبة, فاعل, مبالغة, صفة, *concept* $\}$
$V = \{S, F1, VAP\}$
$P = \{$
     S → فاعل | مبالغة | صفة | F1
     F1 → S VAP
     VAP → نسبة | concept
$\}$

Figure 8. Enrichment steps applied to the definition of the "مرّيخ" mrīkh (Mars) concept

(a)	مرّيخ :كَوْكَبٌ سَيّارٌ وَهُوَ الرّابِعُ في النّظَامِ الشّمْسيِّ، أصْغَرُ مِنَ الأرْضِ وَيُعْرَفُ بِمَارِس (مرّيخ) mrīkh: the fourth planet in the solar system, smaller than Earth and is known as Mars
	مرّيخ :كَوْكَبٌ سَيّارٌ وَهُوَ الرّابِعُ في النّظَامِ الشّمْسيِّ مرّيخ : أصْغَرُ مِنَ الأرْضِ وَيُعْرَفُ بِمَارِس
(b)	concept[مرّيخ] :concept[كَوْكَبٌ] سَيّارٌ وَهُوَ الرّابِعُ في concept[النّظَام الشّمْسيّ] concept[مرّيخ] : أصْغَرُ مِنْ concept[الأرْض] وَيُعْرَفُ بِمَارِس
(c)	concept[مرّيخ] :concept[كَوْكَبٌ] سَيّارٌ وَهُوَ الرّابِعُ في concept[النّظَام الشّمْسيّ] cc_1+ : cc_2 + صفة + حرف عطف + اسم اشارة + ترتيب + حرف جر + cc_3 cc_1+ : +cc_2 + ADJ + PART + DEM_PRON + ORDINAL NUMBER + PREP + cc_3 concept[مرّيخ] : أصْغَرُ مِنْ concept[الأرْض] وَيُعْرَفُ بِمَارِس cc_1+ : + اسم تفضيل + حرف جر + cc_2 + حرف عطف + فعل + حرف جر + اسم cc_1+ : +COMPARATIVE ADJ + PREP + cc_2 + PART + VERB + PREP +NOUN
(d)	concept[مرّيخ] concept[كَوْكَبٌ] property سَيّارٌ وَهُوَ relation الرّابِعُ في concept[النّظَام الشّمْسيّ] concept[مرّيخ] : relation أصْغَرُ مِنْ concept[الأرْض] وَ relation يُعْرَفُ بِـ concept[مارس]

Results

We can firstly point out that all the ontology concepts as well as their properties are relevant to the considered domain. Apart from their satisfactory quality, the results of the developed process are very encouraging. Indeed, having done a first evaluation illustrated in Table 6 in order to highlight the importance of the core construction stage, we found out that about 85% of all concepts are directly deduced within the core component. In addition, about 30% of taxonomic relationships can be easily identified with the help of the dictionary structure.

Added to the estimation of the core component proportion in comparison with the enrichment parts, we need to assess how good the automatically learned ontologies are to reflect a given domain. To achieve this goal, we established a comparison between the obtained ontology and a hand-crafted corresponding ontology, manually created by ontology engineers, to reach the conclusion that all acquired ontological items are relevant to the considered domain. Moreover, it is worth to state that 100% of concepts and taxonomic relationships are acquired while 12% of semantic relations are not. Actually, these results seem to be quite promising.

EVALUATION AND DISCUSSION

Brief Outline on Ontology Evaluation Approaches

According to Brank et al. (2005), most evaluation approaches fall into one of the subsequent categories. The first one covers those based on

Figure 9. The generated ontological items from the definition of the "مِرّيخ" mrīkh (Mars) concept

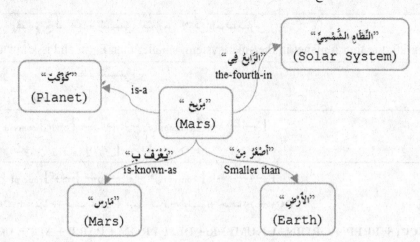

comparing the ontology to a "golden standard" (which may also be an ontology [Maedche & Staab, 2002]). The main drawback of this approach is the high costs of developing the "golden standard." As for the second category, it pertains to those based on using the ontology in an application and evaluating results (Porzel & Malaka, 2004). However, application-based approach to ontology evaluation has also several drawbacks. Indeed, an ontology is seen as good or bad only when it is used in a particular way for a particular task, but it is difficult to generalize this observation. Next, the ontology could only be a small component of the application and its effect on the outcome may be relatively small and indirect. Last, comparing different ontologies is possible only if they can all be plugged into the same application. Concern-

ing the third category, it relates to those based on the evaluation of different levels of the ontology separately (e.g. lexical/vocabulary, context, hierarchy and application). It seems that the step by step or level by level evaluation is more practical than trying to directly evaluate the ontology as a whole, especially when the reduction of human intervention in the evaluation task is sought.

Evaluation of the Proposed Approach

As far as the evaluation of the proposed approach is concerned, it can be seen, even in the above case study, that besides the fully automated level, many important benefits are noticeable. However, it goes without saying that the quality of the pri-

Table 6. Results of the core construction and its enrichment

	Core Component	Enrichment component	Total
Number of concepts	144	29	173
Taxonomic relation	20	58	78
Other semantic relations	0	93	93
Properties	0	24	24
Incorrect semantic links	0	3	3

mary resource influences the results. In the following, we discuss experimental results against some evaluation criteria: degree of automation, generality of the proposed approach and quality of the generated ontologies.

Degree of Automation

It is generally accepted that building ontologies from scratch is a challenging, time-consuming and error-prone task. That is why one of our primary goals is to alleviate this undertaking through the reuse of existing linguistic resources. According to our experiences carried out on LMF-standardized dictionaries (ISO-24613), we argue that reusing such a sort of resources was profitable for ontology generation. Indeed, as we have previously pointed out, we could certainly benefit from some particular information (i.e. domain tags and lexical relations) that is explicitly encoded by the LMF standard, thereby allowing the extraction automatically the relevant part from the whole dictionary. Moreover, we propose to systematically generate the target ontology core using the LMF structure. The resulting preliminary ontology can serve as a basis for further enrichment and thus shorten the time and efforts required to identify concepts. Additionally, many experiments carried out on various domains have shown the efficiency of the proposed enrichment solution. Finally, besides the fully automated level of generating domain ontologies from LMF standardized dictionaries, the latter are undeniably widely-accepted and commonly-referenced resources; thereby they simplify the task of labeling concepts and relationships.

General Approach

In contrast with almost all approaches of ontology learning, the one proposed here rather suggests domain and language independent ontology engineering process. Indeed, the LMF structure would play a major role in supporting multi-domain and

rich lexical information that serve to select the domain of interest as well as the needed linguistic data (e.g. word senses, semantic relation, morphological variants and part-of-speech). Indeed, LMF is able to cover all natural languages and represent most of the lexicons (e.g. WordNet, EDR, and PAROLE) (Francopoulo & George, 2008).

Quality of Generated Ontologies

Coherence. Let us remind that one of the main issues of this work is to be interested with the quality of the generated ontologies alongside the building process. To this purpose, we propose an automatic and iterative process including a validation stage to bring out ontologies of a good quality. As mentioned earlier, it consists in taking into account some criteria proposed by Gómez-Pérez in Gómez-Pérez (1999) to check a given ontologies for consistency, redundancy and completeness. In fact, there are no redundancy errors insofar as we check the preexistence of the constructed elements as well as no inferred knowledge is explicitly represented. Moreover, there are no consistency errors since we managed to check the coherence of the generated ontology with an OWL-DL reasoner, which is Pellet (Sirin, et al., 2007).

Richness and domain coverage. Another important aspect related to the quality of obtained results is the amount of conceptual information retained in the resulting ontology. Evaluating results of an automatic learning process is not a trivial task. In general, either an expert opinion is needed to check the results manually, or a repository is required to assess the coverage of the yielded ontology. Since there is neither a standard to perform systematically this comparison nor a reference resource for Arabic language, quantitative analysis has been performed by human experts (i.e. domain specialists) who carry out the manual census of ontological entities generated from a significant LMF dictionary fragment. Actually, they believe that yielded ontologies are enough rich in the sense that a lot of knowledge in the dictionary is modeled in the ontology. Moreover, almost all concepts are identified while some relationships might be failed. This estimation is related to the robustness of NLP tools within reach as well as the coverage of investigated patterns.

CONCLUSION

The main contribution of the current research work is to propose an approach for the domain ontology generation starting from an LMF standardized dictionary (ISO-24613). Firstly, it consists in building an ontology core which in turn will be further enriched with additional knowledge included in the text available in the dictionary itself. The originality of this approach lies in the use of a unique and finely-structured source, which is rich in lexical and conceptual knowledge. We have also addressed another challenging task of a major importance, which is ontology quality. For this reason, we have decided to focus on error detecting during the building process. Therefore, we have proposed an automatic and iterative process, whose ultimate goal is to produce coherent ontologies that are formalized and capable of reasoning.

Furthermore, the proposed approach is proven to be reliable through the case study carried out on astronomy domain. In reality, more experiments have been conducted on different domains using an LMF standardized Arabic dictionary, but without lack of generality, we choose the astronomy domain in the present study illustrations. The choice of the Arabic language is explained by two main motives. The first one is the great deficiency of work on building of Arabic ontologies and the second is the availability within our research team of an LMF standardized Arabic dictionary as well as NLP tools (e.g. morphological analyzer MOPH2 [Chaâbane, et al., 2010], AnATAr for anaphora resolution tool [Hammami, et al., 2010]). In addition, both qualitative and quantitative evaluations have shown that the generated ontologies seem to be promising and valuable semantic resources that are suitable for NLP tasks.

The next challenges will be the focus on the use of an inference engine (e.g. API of Pellet reasoner) that can be used either to enrich the obtained ontologies or check for potential semantic inconsistencies. We also plan to apply the proposed approach on other available linguistic resources for Arabic such as Arabic WordNet.

REFERENCES

Almeida, M. B. (2009). A proposal to evaluate ontology content. *Applied Ontology*, *4*(3-4), 245–265.

Almuhareb, A., & Poesio, M. (2004). Attribute-based and value-based clustering: An evaluation. In *Proceedings of EMNLP, 2004*, 158–165. Barcelona, Spain.

Alshawi, H. (1989). Analysing the dictionary definitions. In *Computational Lexicography for Natural Language Processing* (pp. 153–169). New York, NY: Longman.

Amsler, R. A. (1981). A taxonomy for English nouns and verbs. In *Proceedings of the 19th Annual Meeting on Association for Computational Linguistics,* (pp. 133-138). Morristown, NJ: ACL Press.

Antoniou, G., & van Harmelen, F. (2004). Ontology engineering. In *A Semantic Web Primer* (pp. 205–222). Cambridge, MA: Massachusetts Institute of Technology Press.

Aussenac-Gilles, N., Despres, S., & Szulman, S. (2008). The TERMINAE method and platform for ontology engineering from texts. In Buitelaar, P., & Cimiano, P. (Eds.), *Bridging the Gap between Text and Knowledge* (pp. 199–223). Amsterdam, The Netherlands: IOS Press.

Aussenac-Gilles, N., & Jacques, M.-P. (2008). Terminology. *Pattern-Based Approaches to Semantic Relations, 14*(1), 45–73.

Baccar Ben Amar, F. Khemakhem. A., Gargouri. B., Haddar. K., & Ben Hamadou, A. (2008). LMF standardized model for the editorial electronic dictionaries of Arabic. In *Proceeding of Natural Language Processing and Cognitive Science Workshop*, (pp. 64-73). Barcelona, Spain: NLPCSW Press.

Baccar Ben Amar, F., Gargouri, B., & Ben Hamadou, A. (2010). Towards generation of domain ontology from LMF standardized dictionaries. In *Proceedings of the 22nd International Conference on Software Engineering and Knowledge Engineering,* (pp. 515-520). Redwood City, CA: IEEE Press.

Berland, M., & Charniak, E. (1999), Finding parts in very large corpora. In *Proceedings of the 37th Meeting of the Association for Computational Linguistics,* (pp. 57-64). ACL Press.

Brank, J., Grobelnik, M., & Mladenic, D. (2005), A survey of ontology evaluation techniques. In *Proceedings* of *the Conference on Data Mining and Data Warehouses* (SiKDD 2005). IEEE Press.

Brewster, C., Alani, H., Dasmahapatra, S., & Wilk, Y. (2004). Data driven ontology evaluation. In *Proceedings of the International Conference on Language Resources and Evaluation,* (pp.164-168). Lisbon, Portugal: ACL Press.

Buitelaar, P., Cimiano, P., Haase, P., & Sintek, M. (2009). Towards linguistically grounded ontologies. In *Proceedings of the 6th Extended Semantic Web Conference,* (pp. 111-125). Heraklion, Greece: ACM Press.

Calzolari, N. (1984). Detecting patterns in a lexical data base. In *Proceedings of the 22nd Annual Meeting on Association for Computational Linguistics*, (pp. 170-173). Morristown, NJ: ACL Press.

Chaâben-Kammoun, N., Hadrichn Belguith, L., & Ben Hamadou, A. (2010). *The MORPH2 new version: A robust morphological analyzer for Arabic texts*. Paper presented at JADT 2010. Rome, Italy.

Chodorow, M. S., Byrd, R. J., & Heidorn, G. E. (1985). Extracting semantic hierarchies from a large on-line dictionary. In *Proceedings of the 23rd annual meeting on Association for Computational Linguistics*, (pp. 299-304). Morristown, NJ: ACL Press.

Chrisment, C., Haemmerlé, O., Hernandez, N., & Mothe, J. (2008). Méthodologie de transformation d'un thesaurus en une ontologie de domaine. *Revue d'Intelligence Artificielle, 22*(1), 7–37. doi:10.3166/ria.22.7-37

Cimiano, P. (2006). *Ontology learning and population from text: Algorithms, evaluation and applications*. Berlin, Germany: Springer Verlag.

Cimiano, P., & Wenderoth, J. (2007). Automatic acquisition of ranked qualia structures from the Web. In *Proceedings of the 45th Annual Meeting of the Association of Computational Linguistics,* (pp. 888-895). Prague, Czech Republic: ACL Press.

Dean, M., & Schreiber, G. (2004). *OWL web ontology language reference*. W3C recommendation. Retrieved from http://www.w3c.org.

Dolan, W., Vanderwende, L., & Richardson, S. (1993). Automatically deriving structured knowledge bases from online dictionaries. In *Proceedings of the Pacific Association for Computational Linguistics,* (pp. 5-14). ACL Press.

Francopoulo, G., & George, M. (2008). *Language resource management - Lexical markup framework (LMF). Technical Report, ISO/TC 37/ SC 4 N453 (N330 Rev.16)*. Washington, DC: US Government Press.

Gangemi, A., Catenacci, C., Ciaramita, M., & Lehmann, J. (2006). *Qood grid: A metaontology-based framework for ontology evaluation and selection*. Paper presented at the 4th International Workshop on Evaluation of Ontologies for the Web (EON 2006) at the 15th International World Wide Web Conference. Edinburgh, UK.

Gomez-Perez, A. (1994). *Some ideas and examples to evaluate ontologies*. Palo Alto, CA: Stanford University Press.

Gómez-Pérez, A. (1999). Evaluation of taxonomic knowledge on ontologies and knowledge-based systems. In *Proceedings of the North American Workshop on Knowledge Acquisition, Modeling, and Management*. KAW Press.

Gómez-Pérez, A. (2004). Ontology evaluation. In Staab, S., & Studer, R. (Eds.), *Handbook on Ontologies in Information Systems* (1st ed., pp. 251–274). Berlin, Germany: Springer.

Guarino, N. (1998). Formal ontology in information systems. In Guarino, N. (Ed.), *Formal Ontology in Information Systems* (pp. 3–15). Amsterdam, The Netherlands: IOS Press.

Guarino, N., & Welty, C. (2002). Evaluating ontological decisions with OntoClean. *Communications of the ACM, 45*(2), 61–65. doi:10.1145/503124.503150

Hajič, J., Smrž, O., Buckwalter, T., & Jin, H. (2005). Feature-based tagger of approximations of functional Arabic morphology. In Civit, M. A. M. M., & Kübler, S. (Eds.), *Proceedings of Treebanks and Linguistic Theories (TLT)* (pp. 53–64). Barcelona, Spain: TLT Press.

Hearst, M. (1992). Automatic acquisition of hyponyms from large text corpora. In *Proceedings of the 14th International Conference on Computational Linguistics*, (pp. 539-545). ACL Press.

Hirst, G. (2004). Ontology and the lexicon. In Staab, S., & Studer, R. (Eds.), *Handbook on Ontologies and Information Systems*. Berlin, Germany: Springer.

ISO 24613 (2008). *Lexical markup framework (LMF) revision 16*. ISO FDIS 24613:2008. Washington, DC: US Government Press.

Jannink, J. (1999). Thesaurus entry extraction from an on-line dictionary. In *Proceedings of Fusion 1999*. ACL Press.

Jannink, J., & Wiederhold, G. (1999). Ontology maintenance with an algebraic methodology: A case study. In *Proceedings of AAAI Workshop on Ontology Management*. AAAI Press.

Kietz, J. U., Maedche, A., & Volz, R. (2000). A method for semi-automatic ontology acquisition from a corporate intranet. In *Proceedings of Workshop Ontologies and Text*. KAW Press.

Kurematsu, M., Iwade, T., Nakaya, N., & Yamaguchi, T. (2004). DODDLE II: A domain ontology development environment using a MRD and text corpus. *IEICE(E). E (Norwalk, Conn.), 87-D*(4), 908–916.

Li, S., Lu, Q., & Li, W. (2005). Experiments of ontology construction with formal concept analysis. In *Proceedings of the OntoLex Workshop IJCNLP*, (pp. 67–75). Korea: IJCNLP Press.

Lonsdale, D., Embley, D., Ding, D., Xu, L., & Hepp, M. (2010). Reusing ontologies and language components for ontology generation. *Journal of Data & Knowledge Engineering, 69*(4), 318–330. doi:10.1016/j.datak.2009.08.003

Maedche, A., & Staab, A. (2002). Measuring similarity between ontologies. In *Proceedings of the European Conference on Knowledge Acquisition and Management*, (vol 2473), (pp. 251-263). Berlin, Germany: Springer.

Mezghanni Hammami, S., Hadrich Belguith, L., & Ben Hamadou, A. (2009). Anaphora resolution: Corpora annotation with coreferential links. *International Arab Journal of Information Technology, 6*(5), 481–489.

Michiels, A., Mullenders, J., & Noël, J. (1980). Exploiting a large data base by Longman. In *Proceedings of the 8th Conference on Computational linguistics,* (pp. 374-382). Morristown, NJ: ACL Press.

Navigli, R., Velardi, P., & Gangemi, A. (2003). Ontology learning and its application to automated terminology translation. *IEEE Intelligent Systems, 18*, 22–31. doi:10.1109/MIS.2003.1179190

Nichols, E., Bond, F., & Flickinger, D. (2005). Robust ontology acquisition from machine-readable dictionaries. In *Proceedings of the International Joint Conference on Artificial Intelligence IJCAI-2005,* (pp. 1111–1116). Edinburgh, UK: IEEE Press.

Pazienza, M. T., Sguera, S., & Stellato, A. (2007). Let's talk about our "being": A linguistic-based ontology framework for coordinating agents. In R. Ferrario & L. Prévot (Eds.), *Applied Ontology, 2*(3-4), 305-332.

Pazienza, M. T., Stellato, A., & Turbati, A. (2008). Linguistic watermark 3.0: An RDF framework and a software library for bridging language and ontologies in the semantic web. In *Proceedings of the 5th Workshop on Semantic Web Applications and Perspectives*. Rome, Italy: IEEE Press.

Porzel, R., & Malaka, R. (2004). A task-based approach for ontology evaluation. In *Proceedings of ECAI 2004 Workshop on Ontology Learning and Population,* (pp. 7-12). ECAI Press.

Reinberger, M.-L., & Spyns, P. (2004). Discovering knowledge in texts for the learning of dogma-inspired ontologies. In P. Buitelaar, S. Handschuh, & B. Magnini (Eds.), *Proceedings of the ECAI Workshop on Ontology Learning and Population,* (pp. 19-24). ECAI Press.

Rigau, G., Rodríguez, H., & Agirre, E. (1998). Building accurate semantic taxonomies from monolingual MRDs. In *Proceedings of the 17th International Conference on Computational Linguistics and 36th Annual Meeting of the Association for Computational Linguistics COLING-ACL 1998*. Montreal, Canada: ACL Press.

Sirin, E., Parsia, B., Grau, B., Kalyanpur, A., & Katz, Y. (2007). Pellet: A practical OWL DL reasoner. *Journal of Web Semantics, 5*(2), 51–53. doi:10.1016/j.websem.2007.03.004

Soergel, D., Lauser, B., Liang, A., Fisseha, F., Keizer, J., & Katz, S. (2004). Reengineering thesauri for new applications: The AGROVOC example. *Journal of Digital Information, 4*(4).

Vaquero, A., Sáenz, F., & Álvarez, F. J. (2007). A review of common problems in linguistic resources and a new way to represent ontological relationships. *Electronic Journal of Argentine Society for Informatics and Operations Research, 7*(1), 1–11.

Widdows, D., & Dorow, B. (2002). A graph model for unsupervised lexical acquisition. In *Proceedings of the 19th International Conference on Computational Linguistics,* (pp. 1093-1099). Taipei, Taiwan: ACL Press.

Yamaguchi, T. (1999). Constructing domain ontologies based on concept drift analysis. In *Proceedings of IJCAI 1999 Workshop on Ontologies and Problem-Solving Methods: Lessons Learned and Future Trends*. Stockholm, Sweden: ACL Press.

KEY TERMS AND DEFINITIONS

Core component: Stands for all possible set of basic objects in a specific domain that could be directly derived from systematic organization of linguistic objects in an LMF standardized dictionary.

Domain Ontology: It is basically a formal representation of knowledge as a set of concepts within a domain, and the relationships between them.

Enrichment Parts: Are the ontological elements deduced from the concepts definitions in order to complete the core component of the target ontology.

LMF Standardized Dictionary: It is an electronic version of dictionary which is compliant to the LMF standard.

LMF: A standard for the representation and construction of lexical resources. Its meta-model provides a common and shared representation of lexical objects that allows the encoding of rich linguistic information, including morphological, syntactic, and semantic aspects.

Ontology Learning: Automatic processing techniques of existing resources (e.g. text, dictionary, thesaurus) towards ontology building.

Quality: An ontology is of a quality if it is coherent (i.e. without errors of consistency or contradictory semantic links), and also, if it suitably reflect the given domain.

ENDNOTES

[1]   http://www.racer-systems.com
[2]   http://pellet.owldl.com
[3]   http://protege.stanford.edu/

Chapter 6
OntoWiktionary:
Constructing an Ontology from the Collaborative Online Dictionary Wiktionary

Christian M. Meyer
Technische Universität Darmstadt, Germany

Iryna Gurevych
Technische Universität Darmstadt, Germany

ABSTRACT

The semi-automatic development of ontologies is an important field of research, since existing ontologies often suffer from their small size, unaffordable construction cost, and limited quality of ontology learning systems. The main objective of this chapter is to introduce Wiktionary, which is a collaborative online dictionary encoding information about words, word senses, and relations between them, as a resource for ontology construction. The authors find that a Wiktionary-based ontology can exceed the size of, for example, OpenCyc and OntoWordNet. One particular advantage of Wiktionary is its multilingual nature, which allows the construction of ontologies for different languages. Additionally, its collaborative construction approach means that novel concepts and domain-specific knowledge are quick to appear in the dictionary.

For constructing their ontology ONTOWIKTIONARY, the authors present a two-step approach that involves (1) harvesting structured knowledge from Wiktionary and (2) ontologizing this knowledge (i.e., the formation of ontological concepts and relationships from the harvested knowledge). They evaluate their approach based on human judgments and find their new ontology to be of overall good quality. To encourage further research in this field, the authors make the final ONTOWIKTIONARY publicly available and suggest integrating this novel resource with the linked data cloud as well as other existing ontology projects.

DOI: 10.4018/978-1-4666-0188-8.ch006

INTRODUCTION

To date, many knowledge-based tasks utilize ontologies as a source of background knowledge. This includes, for example, the calculation of semantic relatedness, automatic word sense disambiguation, or machine translation systems. Ontologies also represent the backbone of the Semantic Web (Berners-Lee et al., 2006). It turns, however, out that existing ontologies are either small or show only limited quality, which prompts further research in this direction. In particular, the (semi-)automatic development of ontologies is still a significant challenge and a yet unsolved research question.

Recent developments in the World Wide Web actuate a large number of collaborative online projects, such as Wikipedia. These collaborative resources have the potential to form huge ontologies, since they can attract a large community of contributors. At the same time, they also ensure a reasonably good quality, as their content has been defined and verified by humans. It has been found that this type of resource can surmount the shortcomings of both expert-built resources, which are often fairly small and hard to keep up to date, and of data-driven ontology learning approaches, which are usually prone to noise and errors.

In this particular work, we focus on constructing an ontology from Wiktionary, which is a freely available, collaboratively built online dictionary. Although Wiktionary is still dramatically under-researched, it has proven to have enormous potential within a natural language processing system measuring the semantic relatedness between words (Zesch, et al., 2008a). Wiktionary encodes a huge number of words, word senses, and semantic relations, which is an ideal basis for constructing ontologies. Therefore, we will explore how large amounts of knowledge can be harvested from Wiktionary and how this knowledge can be "ontologized"—i.e., transformed into an ontological structure. As a result of our work, we present ONTOWIKTIONARY, which is a novel ontology consisting of concepts and relations harvested from Wiktionary. ONTOWIKTIONARY has several advantages over existing ontologies, as it contains a large number of concepts and lexicalizations, which include both commonly used ones as well as rare and domain-specific ones. Additionally, the collaborative construction process of Wiktionary allows it to quickly reflect usage trends and newly occurring concepts. The multilingual nature of Wiktionary moreover puts us in the position of constructing ontologies for a large number of languages. We make ONTOWIKTIONARY publicly available to foster integration with existing ontologies, as well as the development of knowledge-rich applications that can benefit from employing it as a source of background knowledge.

The remainder of this chapter is structured as follows: We will first discuss previous work in the area of ontology construction in general as well as using collaboratively created resources in particular. We then provide a comprehensive introduction to Wiktionary and the knowledge encoded therein. In order to harvest ontological knowledge from Wiktionary, we first need to discuss the structure of Wiktionary articles and explain how to deal with structural errors and inconsistencies pertinent to Wiktionary data. Then, we describe how we construct and evaluate ONTOWIKTIONARY by ontologizing the extracted Wiktionary knowledge. The ontologizing step consists of three tasks—namely, the anchoring of relations, the formation of ontological concepts, and the formation of relations between these concepts. We conclude our chapter with a discussion of our findings and outline some open issues and future research directions.

BACKGROUND

Before taking a deeper look at Wiktionary and our ontology construction architecture, we introduce the notation used throughout the chapter and relate our approach to previous work in the area of both ontology construction in general and particularly in the context of collaborative resources.

Notation

Over time, a broad variety of terms has emerged in the area of ontology construction. We therefore introduce the notation that we will use throughout the chapter. Our definitions are mainly based on the work by Guarino et al. (2009). By *ontology*, we refer to a computer artifact that is able to model everything that exists in a certain universe (not necessarily the real world). The process of building ontologies (i.e., the definition and population of the computer artifact with knowledge) is usually called *ontology construction* or *ontology development*. A more specialized term is *ontology learning*, which focuses on automatic ontology construction, usually using methods from machine learning or information extraction. Note that these terms are sometimes used synonymously or defined differently, so we will use the term *ontology construction* henceforth to denote the general building process of ontologies, including manual, semi-automatic, and fully automatic approaches.

According to Guarino et al. (2009), the building blocks of an ontology are *concepts* and *relations*. The former is a conceptualization of a phenomenon observed in the universe. An example is the idea of a dog — i.e., the animal of the genus *Canis*. Note that this concept 'Dog' comprises all dogs observed in the universe. Individual dogs (like 'Lassie') are, in contrast, called *instances*, which can also be modeled in an ontology. In the following, we will not consider instances any further, but focus on concepts. While a concept has a certain meaning, it can be referred to by multiple words of our language, which we call *lexicalizations*. The 'Dog' concept might, for instance, have the lexicalizations 'dog' and 'hound.' The backbone of an ontology are subsumption relations between concepts — i.e., a relationship that forms a hierarchy of concepts, which is also known as *generalization*, *specialization*, or *taxonomy*. The concept 'Dog' can, for example, be subsumed by a superconcept 'Animal' that represents any type of animal.

Note that we use single-quoted words starting with an upper case letter (e.g., 'Dog') to identify concepts, and single-quoted words starting with a lower case letter to refer to lexicalizations (e.g., 'dog'). Since word senses are used as lexicalizations in our approach, we use the same markup for them. Sets of concepts, lexicalizations, and word senses are denoted by curly brackets; for example, {dog, hound}. Relations between concepts, lexicalizations, and word senses are, in contrast, surrounded by round brackets — e.g., (dog, hound), which denotes a certain relation between 'dog' and 'hound.'

General Ontology Construction Approaches

In the past, very different ways of constructing ontologies have been proposed and, accordingly, there has been a variety of classifications and surveys on this topic. Following Russel and Norvig (2010), we distinguish four general approaches based on:

1. the *manual modeling of experts*, such as lexicographers, ontology engineers, or domain specialists, which is the case with (inter alia) Cyc (Lenat, 1995) and OpenCyc.[1]
2. *information extraction* from large amounts of unstructured documents—e.g., using the TextRunner system (Banko, et al., 2007) on a large corpus of Web documents. An overview of such systems can be found in Maynard et al. (2008).
3. existing *(semi-)structured resources* that are either restructured to form a novel ontology, or used to populate an ontological model, or aligned with existing ontologies (Prévot, et al., 2005). Such resources can be, for example, linguistic resources (Gangemi,

et al., 2003), or domain-specific resources (Reed & Lenat, 2002).

4. a *collaborative annotation effort*, such as the OpenMind project (Singh, 2002), which provides a platform for non-experts to propose machine-readable common-sense knowledge on a voluntary basis.

Each of these approaches has its unique advantages and limitations that we discuss in the following and summarize in Table 1:

Expert-built ontologies, as described in (1), can be very consistent and of high quality; their size, however, is usually subject to time and budget considerations. This often yields rather small ontologies. OpenCyc 2.0 encodes, for example, only 56,000 concepts, although its creation required an enormous effort for years. Another problem with the manual construction process is the need for continuous revisions and updates. Human language is constantly changing and evolving, which introduces new concepts and lexicalizations that are not yet represented within an ontology. Expert-built ontologies are usually released at certain fixed dates and thus unable to integrate novel concepts until their next release.

The parsing of unstructured document collections that is proposed in (2) allows the construction of huge ontologies, though often of limited quality. The main reason is the lack of structure and ontological properties within the variety of documents used for the information extraction method, which causes noise in the resulting ontology. The most prominent approaches in this line of research rely on the redundant nature of a large number of documents, usually acquired from the Web. They try to infer semantic knowledge from a large set of input data, while only a small fraction of it contains evidence (e.g., for a certain relation). A well-known example is the TextRunner system (Banko, et al., 2007). Although such systems have recently shown impressive progress in their precision, they still cannot reach the quality of human judgments. An additional problem is that unstructured document collections might be highly biased to certain topics, styles, registers, or genres. The same applies to the Web as a corpus, which is known to contain errors, sublanguages, and topics that are predominant within the World Wide Web (Kilgarriff & Grefenstette, 2003).

While ontology learning systems operating on a large amount of unstructured text data usually yield low precision, better structured resources as in (3) appear to be a viable option. Most of these structured or semi-structured resources that have been proposed for creating or populating an ontology are very focused on a certain purpose or domain and thus ill-suited for constructing a general ontology. Reed and Lenat (2002) report, for instance, on the integration of the Open Directory Project,[2] the CIA World Factbook,[3] and the Unified Medical Language System[4] into

Table 1. Summary of advantages and limitations of different ontology construction approaches

	(1) Manual modeling of experts	(2) Information extraction	(3) Semi-structured resources	(4) Collaborative effort
Size	−	+ +	o	+ +
Quality of contents	+ +	−	+	+
Development effort	− −	+ +	−	+
Coverage of novel concepts	− −	+	−	+ +
Coverage of domain and rare concepts	+	o	+ +	+ +
Available languages	−	+ +	−	+ +

Cyc, which is a good starting point for enriching general ontologies. Their integration, however, still requires the judgment of experts in order to identify overlapping concepts. This human effort might be feasible for a small number of resources, but does not scale to a larger resource collection. Apart from this, changes in the resources, such as new categories within the Open Directory Project, require new judgments, which turns out to be a very time-consuming process in the long run.

Amongst others, Gangemi et al. (2003) suggest linguistic resources, like dictionaries, lexicons, or semantic networks, as a source for constructing ontologies. They usually cover general language and are thus not limited to certain domains. The Princeton WordNet (Fellbaum, 1998) is the de facto standard resource in the natural language processing community, and it is straightforward to use this resource for populating an ontology. Word-Net has the advantage of being clearly structured, which avoids noise in the ontology construction process. Gangemi et al. (2003) present a semi-automatic method for constructing an ontologized version of WordNet called OntoWordNet. A different approach is introduced by Martin (2003), who proposes multiple transformation steps within WordNet to allow using it as an ontology directly. But since WordNet has been created by a small group of linguists, it shows — although encoding more concepts than OpenCyc—the same problems as the manually created ontologies described in (1), such as the time-consuming development and update process, which is restricted to a fixed release cycle. For languages other than English, the problems pertinent to expert-built resources are even more severe, as resources such as Euro-WordNet (Vossen, 1998) are usually a lot smaller (if they exist at all).

A promising and emerging field of research makes use of collaboratively constructed knowledge resources as described in (4). While the phenomenon of collective intelligence—often denoted as the 'wisdom of the crowds'—has been found to be competitive to expert knowledge (Sur-

owiecki, 2005), the advent of the socio-semantic Web gave rise to a large number of Web projects fostering collaborative text and knowledge editing, including blogs, forums, social tagging sites, and wikis. Such collaborative resources have the potential to be a source of extensive ontological knowledge due to the usually large user communities. At the same time, they ensure fairly good quality, as their content has been explicitly defined by humans rather than automatically extracted from heterogeneous text collections. The broad variety of authors in collaborative resources opens up new opportunities for harvesting knowledge from multiple languages, including both general and domain-specific concepts, as well as rare ones. Additionally, the construction costs of an ontology based on collaborative resources are rather small, since their contents can be freely accessed. This brings us to focus on this approach to constructing ontologies here. In the following section, we will review previous approaches from this strand of research in more detail and illustrate how Wiktionary can surmount limitations of alternative resources.

Collaborative Resources as a Source for Ontologies

The most prominent types of collaborative resources are blogs, forums, social tagging websites, and wikis. Naturally, there are large differences amongst such projects, which we will discuss in the following and summarize in Table 2.

Regarding blogs and forums, which are mainly based on free text, automatic information extraction methods can be used for constructing ontologies. This raises again the problem of noise and errors discussed in the previous section. The inference of relations and the identification and disambiguation of concepts are the main source for errors here. The use of folksonomies (i.e., social tagging websites such as Del.icio.us[5] or Flickr[6] that encourage people to tag images, places, bookmarks, etc. with keyword tags)

Table 2. Summary of advantages and limitations of different ontology construction approaches based on collaborative resources

	Blog- and forum-based ontologies	Folksonomy-based ontologies	Collaborative ontology projects	Wikipedia-based ontologies	Wiktionary-based ontologies
Community size	++	+	--	++	+
Ontology size	++	+	-	++	+
Sense-disambiguated concepts	-	-	o	+	+
Instances	o	+	o	+	-
Abstract concepts	o	o	+	-	+
Lexicalizations	-	+	o	o	+
Clear-cut subsumption hierarchy	-	-	+	o	++

poses similar challenges: Gruber (2007) examines the differences between an ontology and a folksonomy and proposes a general ontological model for them, which is populated by (among others) Echarte et al. (2007). In folksonomies, the tags can be processed automatically without the necessity of information extraction methods. However, no explicit relations between tags are usually encoded, and the individual tags are not per se sense disambiguated (Mika, 2007). The tag 'tree' can, for instance, be used for tagging both botany-related objects as well as computer science-related ones.

Singh (2002) presents the collaborative ontology OpenMind,[7] whose website asks volunteers to add machine-readable common-sense knowledge that can directly be used for creating ontologies. The users first choose a predefined relationship and then insert the concepts for this relationship (e.g., that 'shoes' are made of 'leather'). This directly models ontological relations without the necessity of an extraction or learning step that would introduce noise. A problem is, though, that OpenMind does not really model concepts, but rather uses individual words only. Thus, there might be different relations for the synonymous words 'pullover' and 'sweater,' which denote a single concept. An additional problem is ambiguity. Relationships including, for instance, 'bass' do not distinguish the concept of a fish from that of the music instrument. Moreover, the community of the platform is rather small, which might be due to the specialized focus of the project. Ordinary Web users can hardly benefit from the knowledge encoded in OpenMind and might thus be less motivated to contribute.

Large wikis, such as Wikipedia and Wiktionary have, in contrast, become more and more popular and manage to attract a huge community of contributors. The ease of editing the content of a wiki page and the direct usefulness of the encoded contents for the users are crucial for their success. In the following sections, we will therefore focus on this type of collaborative resource and discuss Wikipedia-based as well as Wiktionary-based ontologies, which will be the main objective of this chapter.

Wikipedia-Based Ontologies

Of particular research interest in both the natural language processing community and the Semantic Web community is Wikipedia,[8] which quickly became the largest encyclopedia in the world. Since Wikipedia is consulted by thousands of Web users every day, many people are motivated to contribute to the project by writing new articles or editing and correcting existing ones. The Wikipedia community is indeed three orders of magnitude larger than the OpenMind community and provides over three million articles in English that can be used to represent the concepts of an ontology. But not only is the size of such an ontology so huge; Wikipedia has also been found to be of competitive quality to expert-defined encyclopedias (Giles, 2005).

The most influential works in the area of Wikipedia-based ontologies are YAGO (Suchanek, et al., 2008) and DBpedia (Bizer, et al., 2009). The goals of these works are the transformation of Wikipedia into an ontology and the interlinking of its concepts with the Linked Data cloud (Bizer, et al., 2009a)—i.e., the transformation of Wikipedia data into standardized RDF models and relating it to other Linked Data by means of unique URIs. Both YAGO and DBpedia are nowadays well known and have been successfully used in various applications. However, there is some potential for improvement regarding these works: Typically, redirects, disambiguation pages, hyperlinks, categories, geographic coordinates, and infoboxes serve as a source for extracting the relationships between concepts. In this context, category labels are used to create a subsumption hierarchy. Although this yields a densely connected taxonomy of concepts, Ponzetto and Strube (2007) point out that the Wikipedia categories "do not form a taxonomy with a fully-fledged subsumption hierarchy." Both the YAGO and the DBpedia concept 'Iron (appliance)' is, for instance, not only a subsumption of 'Home appliance,' but also of 'Laundry.' This is not a generalization of 'Iron,' but represents the domain the concept is used in.

Another problem of a Wikipedia-based ontology lies in the lexicalizations of concepts. In order to reduce redundancy, each concept is encoded only once within Wikipedia and thus described within the article with the most common lexicalization of the concept. The concept 'Iron' in the sense of the 26th chemical element is, for example, described within the article 'Iron.' Additionally, Wikipedia allows one to define redirects from one article title to another; for example, the redirects

from 'Fe,' 'Ferryl,' and 'Element 26' to the article 'Iron.' These redirects are also used as lexicalizations of the concept in DBpedia. Although such lexicalizations are generally correct, redirects are not always used for defining synonymous terms, but also for spelling errors (e.g., 'Iorn') and related concepts (e.g., 'Iron rope' or 'Iron compounds') that should not serve as lexicalizations for the concept 'Iron.' Of the fifteen redirects to the article 'Iron' in the current version of the English Wikipedia, only six represent valid lexicalizations of this concept.

Wiktionary-Based Ontologies

Wiktionary[9] is a free online dictionary that is organized similarly to Wikipedia, but which focuses on linguistic rather than encyclopedic knowledge. It encodes knowledge about words, word meanings, and semantic relations between them (Zesch, et al., 2008). Wiktionary is much more structured than Wikipedia, which allows us to harvest the encoded knowledge in a more precise way than is the case with Wikipedia. In particular, synonymous terms and subsumption relations between word meanings are explicitly encoded in Wiktionary and can thus be acquired more accurately. Such relations are crucial for constructing ontologies with rich lexicalizations, which we will discuss in this chapter.

Additionally, Wiktionary is similar to WordNet as both resources encode linguistic knowledge in the form of word meanings and semantic relations, such as synonymy, hyponymy, and hypernymy. Wiktionary, however, comes with four major advantages over WordNet:

1. Wiktionary is far larger in size than WordNet. The English Wiktionary edition currently encodes knowledge for over 375,000 English words,[10] while WordNet's lexicon contains only about 155,000 words.

2. The data of Wiktionary is constantly updated by its community and thus, rather than re-

lying on certain fixed release dates as it is the case for WordNet, neologisms and new concepts are quick to appear in the resource.

3. Wiktionary has been found to encode a large number of domain-specific entries (Meyer & Gurevych, 2010a), which enables the creation of domain-specific ontologies or the enrichment of a general ontology with very specialized concepts from science, medicine, sports, etc.

4. Wiktionary is available in over 145 languages and thus can yield ontologies for languages where no expert-defined ontology or wordnet is yet available. This is particularly valuable for research in the context of machine translation and cross-lingual natural language processing.

As mentioned above, WordNet has been used as a basis to construct the ontology OntoWordNet (Gangemi, et al., 2003). We follow this principle and construct the novel ontology ONTOWIKTION-ARY from linguistic knowledge harvested from Wiktionary. We expect our ontology to improve OntoWordNet with regard to (1)—(4) and especially focus on the formation of concepts, which are associated with a large number of lexicalizations, and on a more accurate subsumption hierarchy than present in DBpedia and YAGO. Besides the English Wiktionary, we will employ the German and Russian Wiktionary editions to demonstrate the possibility of constructing Wiktionary-based ontologies for a large number of languages. We make ONTOWIKTIONARY publicly available on our website to encourage other researchers to build upon this ontology, integrate it with other knowledge repositories, and utilize it in different natural language processing applications. In the next section, we introduce Wiktionary in more detail and outline the architecture of our Wiktionary-based ontology construction method.

ONTOWIKTIONARY

In order to use Wiktionary as a source for constructing a new ontology, we first need to understand what kind of knowledge is encoded therein and how this resource is structured. In this section, we therefore provide an overview of Wiktionary's basic organization and some example entries illustrating it. Then, we introduce our architecture for constructing an ontology from Wiktionary.

Wiktionary: A Collaborative Resource for Linguistic Knowledge

The goal of Wiktionary is to create a large, multilingual online dictionary that is both freely available and editable by volunteers. The project started in 2002 with the English Wiktionary. By 2004, the community began to set up Wiktionary editions for other languages. Since there are no special requirements for contributing to the project, the community of Wiktionary editors grew very quickly — by the beginning of 2011, about 460,000 users have created over 2,200,000 articles in the English edition.

Currently, there are 145 active language editions of Wiktionary.[11] The primary building blocks of each Wiktionary edition are article pages that contain lexical semantic information about a certain word or phrase—e.g., 'boat,' 'sleep,' or 'trace element.' Figure 1 shows the article 'boat' of the English Wiktionary as an example. A single Wiktionary language edition is not limited to encoding only those words of its own, native language. It is rather the vision of Wiktionary that every language edition contains information about words of any language. In each article, multiple language entries can thus be distinguished. The article 'sensible' within the English Wiktionary, for example, encodes linguistic knowledge about the corresponding English and French words. It should be noted that these two words only share the same written form rather than the same meaning (the French *sensible* means sensitive in English). For each language entry, there are multiple sections for encoding the word's part of speech, etymology, pronunciation, grammatically inflected word forms, and lots of other linguistic information.

Most important for our purpose is the section encoding a word's meaning, which is represented as a list of different word senses for the word described by the article. The enumeration of distinct word senses corresponds to common practice in printed and electronic dictionaries where words are divided into a number of distinct senses for pragmatic reasons (Atkins & Rundell, 2008). Each word sense is represented by a short definition text that might be accompanied by some example sentences or quotations illustrating the usage of the word sense. Meyer and Gurevych (2010a) note that the nature of word senses in

Wiktionary is unique, since the collaborative construction approach leads to constant revision and discussion about the composition of word senses. This yields a consolidation of the different opinions of the speakers. The granularity of a word sense definition—i.e., where to split or lump two nuances of the meaning—is an open discussion that has previously almost solely been the province of a small number of expert lexicographers but is now transferred to a large community of ordinary speakers of a language. Constructing an ontology from these collaboratively defined word senses can help us to understand the different semantics of collaborative language resources such as Wiktionary and expert-built resources like WordNet.

In Wiktionary, there are also sections for encoding semantic relations, such as "Synonyms," "Hypernyms," "Hyponyms," "Meronyms," "De-

Figure 1. Wiktionary article for the word 'boat'

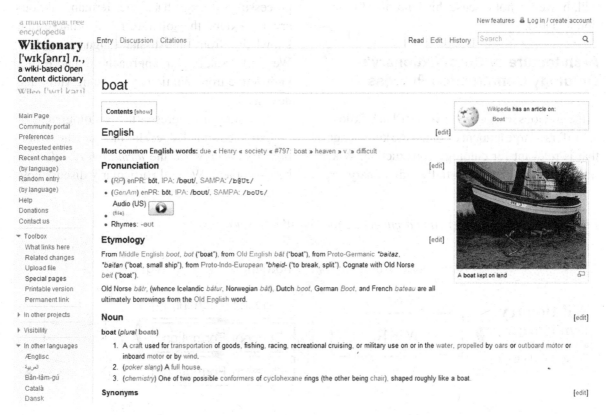

rived from," "See also," etc. Semantic relations are represented by a hyperlink to another Wiktionary article. The article 'boat' contains, for example, a link to the article 'vessel' within its "Synonyms" section, and a link to the article 'canoe' within its "Hyponyms" section. This notation puts us in the position of harvesting relations between concepts that we will explain in the main part of the chapter.

Besides words, word senses, and semantic relations, which we use for the construction of ONTOWIKTIONARY, there is lots of other linguistic information that is attached to the encoded words and word senses. This includes a word's pronunciation, hyphenation, etymology, alternative spellings, or rhyme schemes, as well as a word sense's semantic domain, translation, or image that illustrates the meaning. Such information can be used to enrich the ontology. Translations in particular offer interesting future research questions in the context of interlinking ontologies across multiple languages. Since we focus on the general ontology construction process here, we will, however, not discuss this kind of information in detail.

Architecture of OntoWiktionary's Ontology Construction Process

In the previous section, we have seen that Wiktionary offers a large amount of linguistic knowledge that is relevant for ontology construction. Wiktionary is, however, essentially a dictionary for human readers rather than an ontology. We thus need an ontology construction process to transform the knowledge encoded in Wiktionary into the concepts and relations of an ontology. Figure 2 outlines our architecture, which will be explained within the subsequent sections.

Following Pantel and Pennacchiotti (2008), we divide our process into two parts: (1) *harvesting knowledge*, and (2) *ontologizing knowledge*. The former addresses obtaining the data from Wiktionary and extracting its knowledge in a structured and machine-readable manner. Since Wiktionary is a semi-structured resource, a carefully crafted system needs to be developed that is able to deal with noise induced by errors of the data extraction process on the one hand and with constant changes by the community pertinent to Wiktionary on the other hand. In particular, we address the extraction of words, word senses, and semantic relations from Wiktionary, which are required in our ontologizing step. Therefore, we use the JWKTL (Zesch, et al., 2008) software for processing the English and the German Wiktionary and extend the software for also harvesting knowledge from the Russian language edition. We will explain our approach of harvesting knowledge from Wiktionary in detail within the next section.

The latter part addresses the "ontologizing" of the extracted knowledge. This includes the *formation of concepts* and the *formation of relations* between them. We will particularly discuss how

Figure 2. Ontology construction architecture for ONTOWIKTIONARY

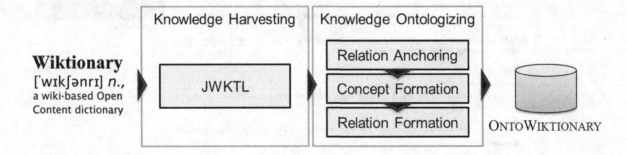

Wiktionary word senses can be used to induce ontological concepts and how hyperlinks between different Wiktionary articles may be treated as conceptual relations. A central point is thereby the *relation anchoring*—i.e., the association of a relation's endpoint with the correct concepts of the ontology—which is done in a separate preprocessing step. The explanation of the knowledge ontologizing part will be the subject of the section after the next one.

HARVESTING KNOWLEDGE FROM WIKTIONARY

Wiktionary is intended to fulfill linguistic information needs of humans—i.e., to provide information about words, word senses, and semantic relations amongst them in a similar way as printed dictionaries do. Therefore, a focus has been put on providing a graphical user interface that is optimized for human perception rather than automatic data processing. Harvesting the knowledge encoded in Wiktionary thus raises the challenge of creating extraction software that processes Wiktionary's semi-structured content and transforms it into a machine-readable format for further processing. In the following section, we will first discuss the problem of noise pertinent to the data extraction process and how to deal with it, and then introduce existing software libraries and our extensions to them.

Dealing with Noise and Errors

A main characteristic of Wiktionary is its openness—that is, the possibility for every Web user to add, modify, and delete content from the articles. While this openness is a key for the success of Wiktionary, it also presents a major challenge for the computational exploitation of this resource. The structural openness in particular turns out to be very challenging, as this includes missing sections, constant restructuring of the articles,

malformation, and spam, as well as previously unseen types of knowledge, such as totally new sections.

An important feature of Wiktionary is the notion of templates. Templates are reusable patterns that can be defined in a central place and then invoked by a large number of articles. Each template is identified by a unique name. Invoking a template means that this name is added to the article text and enclosed by two curly brackets. Upon formatting the article to HTML, which is done when reading the article on the Wiktionary website, the invoked template is substituted with the template's text. The template may be further parameterized with different user inputs. For example, invoking the template {{rfe}} on an article page, causes the insertion of a box "This entry lacks etymological information […]" when the article is formatted, as well as a category tag "Requests for etymology" to allow searching for such entries easily. Another example is the template {{sense|<reference>}}, which is used to associate semantic relations to a certain word sense. This "sense" template is parameterized with a <reference> to the corresponding word sense, which is a shortened version of the sense's textual description. Figure 3 shows an example usage of (a) the "sense" template for the article 'boat,' and (b) the HTML-formatted result of this syntax. We will take a deeper look at the "sense" template later in the chapter when the semantic relations are anchored.

While the "RFE" template is primarily used to abbreviate an oft-used structure, the "sense" template is obviously used for different reasons, since the template syntax is actually longer than adding the formatted result directly. It is rather Wiktionary's way of adding structure and encouraging consistent encoding of the entries. Templates such as "sense" are not only useful for the community to quickly modify the formatting of all entries at once (e.g., using square brackets for the sense reference instead of round ones), but also allow for easy perception of the encoded knowl-

Figure 3. Wiki syntax of (a) the "sense" template, and (b) its corresponding HTML format

```
====Synonyms====
* {{sense|A craft on or in water}} [[craft]],
[[ship]], [[vessel]]

====Hyponyms====
* {{sense|A craft on or in water}} [[ark]],
[[bangca]], [[barge]],
```

(a)

Synonyms

- *(A craft on or in water)*: craft, ship, vessel

Hyponyms

- *(A craft on or in water)*: ark, bangca, barge,

(b)

edge, since all semantic relations follow a similar notation. Each article page in Wiktionary is usually a composition of many different templates and thus follows a common layout. At the same time, templates are a viable option to extract the data automatically, because it is easier to identify the "sense" template in front of a hyperlink than to rely on a certain combination of brackets and font styles that might be slightly varying for each article page.

In general, there is, however, no set of rigid rules for what an article page should look like. Rather, an author can extend or manipulate the proposed structure to better fit his or her needs. The Wiktionary guidelines[12] explain: "You may experiment with deviations, but other editors may find those deviations unacceptable, and revert those changes. They have just as much right to do that as you have to make them." An extraction system for Wiktionary is therefore required to deal with additional, modified, or missing structures. In the following section, we will introduce different software systems that can be used to harvest knowledge from Wiktionary.

Obtaining and Extracting Wiktionary Data

Human readers use Wiktionary's Web front end to browse the encoded contents. An obvious way of obtaining the data automatically would thus be to crawl it from the front end. This would, however, imply extracting knowledge from the formatted HTML pages, which causes a loss of the encoded entry's structure in form of templates that we introduced in the previous section. As shown in Figure 3, templates such as "sense" are important to associate semantic relations to word senses. A formatted HTML page, on the other hand, contains only a remark in round brackets, which may be interpreted as a "sense" template or any other remark added to a semantic relation, such as a label denoting a register of language (such as "formal," or "colloquial"). Fortunately, the Wiktionary data is also available as an XML database dump, which contains the original wiki markup in the form of templates.[13] Although these dumps were originally intended for developing alternative user interfaces and hosting mirror sites, they are also an ideal starting point for extracting the encoded knowledge and using it to construct ontologies.

To date, we are aware of four software libraries that allow extracting Wiktionary's knowledge based on the XML dump files: The *Java-Based Wiktionary Library*[14] (JWKTL) introduced by Zesch et al. (2008), the *Wiki tool kit*[15] (Wikokit) by Krizhanovsky and Lin (2009), *WIktionarieS Improvement by Graphs-Oriented meTHods*[16] (WISIGOTH) introduced by Sajous et al. (2010), and *Zawilinski*[17] by Kurmas (2010). We discuss the differences between these software libraries very briefly here, but refer the reader to the original works for further details. Aside from Zawilinski, which concentrates on the extraction of inflected word forms, all software libraries are able to extract words, word senses, and semantic relations, which represent the required information to construct ONTOWIKTIONARY. An important property of Wiktionary is that each language edition has its own structure and format.[18] It is thus necessary to create a new extraction system for each language edition—or at least to adapt an existing one. As this is a time-consuming process, it is not surprising that each of the software libraries focuses on certain language editions: JWKTL allows one to process the English and the German Wiktionaries, Wikokit is able to process the Russian and English editions, WISIGOTH is suitable for the French and English editions, while Zawilinski has been built for the Polish Wiktionary.

For the construction of ONTOWIKTIONARY described in this chapter, we utilize JWKTL for processing the English and German Wiktionaries. Additionally, we create a novel JWKTL adapter to Wikokit and thus also extract the knowledge from the Russian Wiktionary using the same software system. This choice of languages allows for studying the ontology construction process for a very large Wiktionary (the English one), for a medium-sized Wiktionary (the German one), and for a Wiktionary having a script different from Latin (namely the Cyrillic alphabet in the Russian Wiktionary). As future work, we also plan to include other Wiktionaries, such as the French edition that is also one of the largest ones. At the time of writing, WISIGOTH is, however, subject to revision and thus prevents us from analyzing the French Wiktionary. The XML dump files processed with JWKTL are from February 2, 2011 for the English Wiktionary; February 1, 2011 for the German Wiktionary; and April 4, 2011 for the Russian Wiktionary. Any numbers reported in this chapter refer to these dates unless otherwise indicated.

Although each Wiktionary language edition encodes words from multiple languages, we focus on only those words that are "native" to a language edition (i.e., the English words in the English edition, the German words in the German edition,

etc.). According to Meyer and Gurevych (2010a), these native entries represent the vast majority of a language edition. There is, for instance, an entry about the German word 'Boot' (English 'boat') within the English Wiktionary which is not considered by our approach.

ONTOLOGIZING THE KNOWLEDGE IN WIKTIONARY

In the previous section, we focused on the knowledge harvesting step (i.e., obtaining and extracting the knowledge from Wiktionary). In order to build ONTOWIKTIONARY, we need to transform this knowledge into ontological structures—that is, to define concepts and relations between them. Pantel and Pennacchiotti (2008) call this step "ontologizing" the harvested knowledge.

The basic building blocks of ONTOWIKTIONARY are concepts and relations between them. We therefore address the formation of concepts and relations as two separate tasks of the ontologizing step. But before being able to form the concepts and relations, we need to apply a necessary preprocessing step that aims at associating the encoded hyperlinks to word senses. This process is called relation anchoring and will be the subject of the following subsection.

Relation Anchoring

An important type of linguistic information encoded in Wiktionary is semantic relations between word senses. A Wiktionary entry may contain sections labeled "Synonyms," "Hypernyms," "Hyponyms," "Derived terms," etc. that allow for the inclusion of hyperlinks to other articles. The noun entry of 'boat,' for example, encodes a link to the article 'ship' within the "Synonyms" section, since 'boat' and 'ship' denote (roughly) the same meaning. Additionally, it contains a link to 'canoe' within the "Hyponyms" section, because a canoe is a special kind of boat. While these relations are linguistically motivated to denote words with the same (synonym), a broader (hypernym), or a narrower (hyponym) meaning, we note that they are an ideal basis for forming concepts based on synonymy links and for defining subsumption relations between them based on hypernymy and hyponymy links.

An inherent problem of Wiktionary's encoding format for these semantic relations is that the hyperlinks connect words rather than word senses. For example, from a hypernymy link pointing from 'flower' to 'plant,' it remains unspecified whether 'flower' is a narrower term of 'plant' in the biological sense or in the sense of an industrial facility. Accordingly, 'flower' not only refers to the botanical organism, but is also used to denote the finest part of something, as in the phrase "in the flower of her youth." This is especially a problem if chains of relations are considered: from the two hyponymy relations (smallmouth bass, bass) and (bass, music instrument) one could infer that 'smallmouth bass' and 'music instrument' are closely related, which is obviously wrong. In order to create a precise ontology, this issue needs to be tackled by our approach, which requires the anchoring of the encoded hyperlinks. This means that the correct word senses connected by the semantic relation need to be identified from the corresponding words in Wiktionary.

The necessity of anchoring relations has been observed before by Pantel and Pennacchiotti (2008). In particular, they mine a large amount of ontological relations from the Web using their Espresso system. Both the source and the target (i.e., the two endpoints of a relation) are thereby words that need to be "ontologized." In their approach, all possible word senses from WordNet serve as candidates for the relation's source and target word sense. These candidates are then disambiguated using measures based on distributional similarity. In this setting, the anchoring of relations is a fairly complex task, since both the source and the target word senses need to be disambiguated. Consider for instance

the hyponymy relation (boat, canoe). If there are three word senses for 'boat' and two word senses for 'canoe,' all six possible combinations have to be compared by the anchoring method.

In the previous section, we introduced Wiktionary's template mechanism, which is commonly used by the Wiktionary community to associate a relation link with a so-called sense marker. A sense marker is—depending on the language of the Wiktionary edition—a numerical index or a shortened version of the textual description of a word sense, which identifies the corresponding word sense of a relation. The hyponym link 'canoe' in the article 'boat' is, for example, preceded by the sense marker "(a craft on or in water)," which associates this hyponymy relation with the first word sense of 'boat,' namely "a craft used for transportation of goods, [...]." The German Wiktionary uses numerical indices as sense markers instead. The hyponymy link 'Kanu' (English 'canoe') in the German Wiktionary is, for instance, preceded by the sense marker "[1]," which associates it with the first word sense of 'Boot' (English 'boat').

By considering the sense markers, we are able to extract the word sense of a relation's source directly from the encoded data. Given the word sense of the source, only the word sense of the relation's target remains to be found. Following this procedure, we are able to simplify the relation anchoring task by one degree of freedom, as only the two word senses of the target word 'canoe' need to be processed for anchoring our example relation (boat, canoe). This approach not only reduces the computational complexity, but also allows for a higher quality at the same time: Since the sense markers are defined by humans, no automatic disambiguation task is involved, which would introduce noise to the relation anchoring results. In the following subsection, we describe our approach to anchor Wiktionary's semantic relations. The evaluation of this approach is then discussed in the subsequent subsection.

Word Sense Disambiguation-Based Relation Anchoring

Meyer and Gurevych (2010) introduce a word sense disambiguation method for Wiktionary relations, which we can directly apply for the anchoring of relations. In the following, we will briefly review this work, before we apply it to our setting. The hypothesis of the method is that the textual description of the target word sense is semantically related to the description of the source word sense. This is a direct consequence of the relatedness of the source and target word senses themselves. Consider the hyponymy relation between 'boat' and 'canoe'; the corresponding textual definitions are:

Boat:

1. A craft used for transportation of goods, fishing, racing, recreational cruising, or military use on or in the water, propelled by oars or outboard motor or inboard motor or by wind.

Canoe:

1. A small long and narrow boat, propelled by one or more people (depending on the size of canoe), using single-bladed paddles. The paddlers face in the direction of travel, in either a seated position, or kneeling on the bottom of the boat. Canoes are open on top, and pointed at both ends.
2. (slang) An oversize, usually older, luxury car.

From this example, we immediately observe that a disambiguation method based on word overlap (i.e., choosing the target word sense with the highest number of shared words) will not work very well, since only the word 'propelled' is present in more than one description (we ignore stop words such as 'the,' 'of,' etc. in the following). We though observe many pairs of related words (e.g., 'water' and 'boat,' 'oar' and 'paddle,' 'transportation' and 'people'). that are shared by the first word senses of 'boat' and 'canoe.' This motivates the application of methods based on the semantic relatedness of each pair of textual descriptions. It should be noted that there are also some related words shared by the first word sense of 'boat' and the second word sense of 'canoe,' like 'transportation' and 'car,' 'motor' and 'car,' etc. There is thus a need for carefully evaluating this method, which we will address in the next section.

For calculating the semantic relatedness between each possible pair of textual descriptions, we use Explicit Semantic Analysis (Gabrilovich & Markovitch, 2007), which is a state-of-the-art method for this task. In a preprocessing step, each textual description is tokenized and lemmatized using Helmut Schmid's (1994) TreeTagger. To avoid noise in the relatedness calculation, we also remove stop words from the descriptions. Then, we represent each token t as a concept vector—i.e., a vector $c(t) = (w_i(t))$, where $w_i(t)$ denotes the degree of how well t is represented by a concept i. Note that the concepts used here can be taken from any semantic space. Following Gabrilovich and Markovitch (2007), we use Wikipedia as a semantic space here, which has shown very good results on reference datasets for semantic relatedness, such as the WordSimilarity-353 collection (Finkelstein, et al., 2002). Thus, $w_i(t)$ denotes the degree of how well t is represented by the ith article in Wikipedia. The values of $w_i(t)$ are calculated using the term frequency—inverse document frequency (tf–idf) schema. The token 'boat,' for instance, would receive a high $w_i(t)$ for the Wikipedia concepts 'Boat,' 'Ship,' 'Watercraft rowing,' 'Lighthouse,' etc., as it appears frequently on the corresponding article pages, and a low $w_i(t)$ for the articles 'Syntax,' 'Trumpet,' or 'Formula' that do not contain 'boat.' In order to obtain a semantic relatedness score $r(A, B)$ for two textual descriptions A and B, we add up the concept vectors for all tokens $t_{A,i} \in A$ and $t_{B,j} \in B$, and calculate the cosine of the angle between them within our semantic space:

$$r(A, B) = \frac{c_A \cdot c_B}{\|c_A\| \cdot \|c_B\|}$$

with

$$c_A = \sum_{t_{A,i} \in A} c(t_{A,i})$$

and

$$c_B = \sum_{t_{B,j} \in B} c(t_{B,j}).$$

Using Explicit Semantic Analysis, the descriptions of the maritime word senses of 'boat' and 'canoe' have nearly the same concept vectors and thus a high relatedness score $r(A, B)$. The word sense of the relation's target word with the highest semantic relatedness score is returned by the method and serves as the target word sense of our anchored relation. Note that this approach goes substantially beyond word-based cosine similarity in which the tokens are not represented in a semantic space.

Evaluation

To evaluate our approach, we have randomly chosen 250 relations from the "Synonymy," "Hyponymy," and "Hypernymy" section of Wiktionary, and annotated each of the 920 possible pairs of word senses as positive (the two word senses are directly related by means of the semantic relation) or negative (the two word senses are not directly related—i.e., there should not be a semantic relation between them). The annotators were also allowed to annotate multiple target word senses for a given source word sense as positive, provided a relation holds between more than one

pair of word senses. An example for such a case is the hypernymy relation from 'drinking water' to 'water,' for which the two word senses "mineral water" and "a serving of water" are suitable relation targets. The dataset has been annotated independently by two human raters.

In order to ensure the reliability of our annotations, we measured the inter-rater agreement, which turned out to be $A_o = 0.88$ in a non-chance-corrected setting and $\kappa = 0.72$ using the chance-corrected kappa measure. Since almost two thirds of our dataset (597 items) are marked with a negative annotation, the dataset is skewed, which, in general, causes lower kappa values (Artstein & Poesio, 2008). Therefore, we also measured the agreement in a set-based setting using Krippendorff's α and the MASI distance function (Passonneau, 2006). This approach compares the annotations of both raters for each of the 250 relations rather than the 920 annotation pairs. For each relation, the set of positively annotated word senses is compared. Using this third measure of inter-rater agreement, we measured $\alpha = 0.86$, which indicates good agreement and allows us to draw conclusions from our results (Krippendorff, 1980).

We refrained from removing or re-annotating those cases where no agreement was found to preserve the hard cases that our relation anchoring method needs to tackle. Therefore, we are not providing precision and recall values but rather the inter-rater agreement between our approach (denoted by M in the following) and the individual human raters (denoted by A and B). This also allows the comparison of our method's result with the agreement amongst the human raters that serves as an upper bound for our algorithm. As a baseline approach (denoted by 0), we always choose the first word sense of the target word, which is usually the most frequently used one. This kind of baseline is common practice in word sense disambiguation evaluations and is known to be difficult to surpass.

Table 3. Evaluation results of our relation anchoring method of Wiktionary relations

	0–A	0–B	M–A	M–B	A–B
A_O	0.791	0.780	0.820	0.791	0.886
κ	0.498	0.452	0.567	0.480	0.728
α	0.679	0.620	0.726	0.649	0.866

Table 3 shows the agreement of our method compared to the baseline and the upper bound. Our method exceeds the baseline in every case. There is, however, still room for improvement with respect to the upper bound A–B. In our error analysis, we observe large differences in the length of the textual descriptions. Although the semantic relatedness scores are normalized, this can significantly influence the performance. Very short descriptions in particular have been found to often yield errors. We also observed differences in the textual descriptions for each part of speech, which we plan to analyze in a separate study using a well-balanced dataset that covers each part of speech and relation type equally well. Another type of error is due to references to other word senses within the textual descriptions. The second word sense of 'tomato' (the fruit), for example, refers to its first sense (the plant): "[2] the fruit of [1]." Such references limit the number of words that can be used for calculating our semantic relatedness score. A future approach should take these cases into account by either augmenting them with words from the referenced description or by treating the distinctive feature (like "the fruit of sth.") in a special way. We also notice that the agreement of our method and rater A is systematically higher than the agreement with rater B. It turns out that rater A tended to rate a relation target as positive when in doubt, while rater B tended to rate the target as negative. Although the overall agreement between the two raters is fairly good, subsequent annotation studies of Wiktionary relations should further improve the annotation guidelines based on these results.

We now use the described method to anchor all harvested Wiktionary relations. This is a necessary preprocessing step for the formation of concepts and ontological relations in ONTOWIKTIONARY that we describe in the following.

The Formation of Concepts

The data encoded in Wiktionary is based on the notion of word senses. The noun 'dog' has, for instance, the word senses "An animal, member of the genus *Canis* [...]" and "(*slang*) A coward." The basic building blocks of an ontology are, in contrast, concepts — i.e., a model of an entity observed in the universe. A concept also has a certain meaning, but might be represented by multiple words, which we call lexicalizations. The concept 'Dog' could, for example, be modeled for representing all instances that are denoted by the word 'dog' in our universe. The noun 'dog' (in the animal sense) then serves as a lexicalization of 'Dog.' Additionally, 'Dog' might also be represented by a second lexicalization using the noun 'hound' (in a general word sense).

From this example, we observe that both the Wiktionary word senses of 'dog' and 'hound' should be combined to form a concept 'Dog' with the two lexicalizations 'dog' and 'hound.' We thus need a method for identifying word senses representing the same meaning in order to form the concepts of our novel ontology ONTOWIKTIONARY. We will outline our approach in the following section.

Concepts Based on Synonymy Links

In linguistics, word senses with the same meaning are considered to be synonyms. This also applies to 'dog' and 'hound' (in their sense of a member of the genus *Canis*). The definition of synonymy can directly be used to form concepts — namely, by combining those word senses that are connected by a synonymy relation. This approach has been followed for the construction of the Princeton WordNet, which organizes its contents in so-called synsets—i.e., sets of synonymous word senses. The synsets in WordNet may directly be used as the concepts of an ontology, as in OntoWordNet (Gangemi, et al., 2003), for instance.

Synonymy relations are also present in Wiktionary. They are defined within the "Synonyms" section by means of hyperlinks from one article to another. There is, for example, a hyperlink within the article 'dog' pointing to the article 'hound.' In the previous section, we have seen that these synonymy hyperlinks need to be anchored—i.e., associated with the correct word senses. We accomplish this task by extracting sense markers and disambiguating the link target using a method based on the semantic relatedness of short texts as explained above. Our idea is now to form ontological concepts using these anchored synonymy relations from Wiktionary.

In WordNet, the synonymy relation is assumed to be transitive—that is, if a and b are synonymous, and b and c are synonymous, then a and c are likewise synonymous. This is accounted for by the fact that a, b, and c are in the same synset. For instance, 'CV' is a synonym of 'curriculum vitae,' which in turn is a synonym of 'resume.' Consequently, 'CV' and 'resume' can also be considered synonymous. Additionally, it is obvious that WordNet's definition of synonymy is also symmetric: If 'CV' is a synonym of 'resume,' then 'resume' is also a synonym of 'CV.'

In Wiktionary, there is no such synset structure, which would make the synonymy-based formation of concepts a trivial task. Rather, synonyms are encoded for each word sense individually and thus are not necessarily required to have a symmetric or transitive counterpart. There is, for example, a synonymy link from 'curriculum vitae' to 'CV,' but not vice-versa. A viable option, therefore, is to first create a synset-like structure and then use these synsets as the concepts for OntoWiktionary. We obtain this synset structure by adding the missing symmetric and transitive counterparts of the synonymy relation. This makes Wiktionary's synonymy relation an equivalence relation, whose transitive closure contains all inferred symmetric and transitive relations. There are, for instance, the synonymy relations (island, oasis), (oasis, island), and (oasis, refuge) that can be found in Wiktionary. By considering the transitive closure, the three additional relations (refuge, oasis), (island, refuge), and (refuge, island) are added. The corresponding concepts can now be formed from the equivalence classes of this transitive closure. In our example, the set {island, oasis, refuge} represents one equivalence class and thus forms a concept with three lexicalizations within OntoWiktionary.

Table 4 shows the number of concepts in OntoWiktionary generated from the synonymy relations encoded in the English, German, and Russian Wiktionaries. The largest ontology is obtained from the English Wiktionary. This is not surprising, since the English Wiktionary edition is currently the largest available one.[19] With its 456,638 concepts, the English OntoWiktionary is about three times larger than OpenCyc (153,920 concepts) and WordNet (117,659 synsets), as well as seven times larger than OntoWordNet (about 60,000 concepts).[20] The Wikipedia-based ontology DBpedia contains about 1.6 million entries, which are, however, mostly instances (i.e., proper names like places, organizations, people, etc.) Wiktionary focuses on common words rather than proper names and thus encodes a different type of concepts.

From the German and Russian Wiktionaries, a considerably lower number of concepts can be

Table 4. Number of concepts, lexicalizations, and relationships within ONTOWIKTIONARY

	English Wiktionary	German Wiktionary	Russian Wiktionary
Ontologized concepts	456,638	64,335	72,390
Lexicalizations	469,025	72,157	80,618
Ontologized relations	8,026	153,685	66,192

formed. These language editions are much smaller than the English Wiktionary: there are 2.3 million articles in the English edition, but only about 158,000 in the German and 289,000 in the Russian edition, so there are many more word senses available for the formation of the concepts in the English ONTOWIKTIONARY. However, we observe a greater number of synonymy relations in both the German and Russian Wiktionaries. This yields a higher number of lexicalizations provided for each concept: while a concept has only 1.03 lexicalizations on average in our English ontology, there are 1.11 in the Russian version and 1.12 in the German ONTOWIKTIONARY. Since the English Wiktionary is rather sparse in the number of encoded synonymy relations, we plan to incorporate systems for synonymy identification into the concept formation step as part of our future work.

Evaluation

The induction of a synset-like structure in Wiktionary might introduce errors into our final ontology that can be traced back to either errors in the relation anchoring step or inconsistencies in the encoded synonymy relations, which are not as rigidly structured as it is the case for WordNet. An evaluation of the relation anchoring step was presented in the previous section. Although the vast majority of relations could successfully be associated to the correct word senses, errors of this approach also affect the concept formation.

Since the synonymy relations in Wiktionary are added by humans rather than by an automatic system, we expect them to be generally correct.

However, we can still expect to encounter errors due to extraction errors within the knowledge harvesting step or differences in the granularity of the word sense definition. For instance, Wiktionary encodes two word senses for the term 'New York,' namely the state within the U.S. and the city therein. Accordingly, there are synonyms listed for each sense: 'Empire State' and 'New York State' for the former and 'Big Apple,' 'New York City,' and 'NYC' for the latter. The abbreviation 'N.Y.' that is being used to refer to both of them—depending on the context—is additionally listed for both word senses. We would require (and expect) to find two word senses for 'N.Y.' denoting the abbreviation for the state on the one hand and the abbreviation for the city on the other hand. But Wiktionary encodes only a single word sense that covers both meanings. This distracts our word sense disambiguation algorithm, which chooses this more general word sense for anchoring both 'N.Y.' synonymy relations. The result is a lumped concept with the lexicalizations {Empire State, New York State, Big Apple, New York City, NYC, N.Y.}, which is clearly wrong.

Therefore, in order to analyze the quality of our concept formation step, we carried out another evaluation experiment that relies on human judgments. We have chosen 100 concepts from the English version of ONTOWIKTIONARY and 100 concepts from the corresponding German version. We considered only those concepts with at least three lexicalizations, because concepts with fewer lexicalizations are not influenced by the problem of lumped concepts described above; rather, they are directly formed from independent, explicitly encoded synonymy links and thus inherently correct. For both datasets, we asked two human raters to annotate the concepts as "consistent" (1), "lexically consistent" (2), or "inconsistent" (0). A concept is thereby represented by its lexicalizations, which consist of the corresponding word and the textual definition that is extracted for the corresponding word sense. Consider the following three examples:[21]

1. **Bass:** A male singer who sings in the bass range.
   Basso: A bass singer, especially in opera.
2. **Bass:** A male singer who sings in the bass range.
   Basso: A bass singer, especially in opera.
   Singer: Person who sings, is able to sing, or earns a living by singing.
3. **Bass:** The perch; any of various marine and freshwater fish resembling the perch.
   Basso: A bass singer, especially in opera.

In example (1), both lexicalizations refer to the same meaning, namely a singer in the bass range, although there are subtle differences, such as that 'basso' is used especially when talking about opera. As Hirst (1995) points out, many words that occur to be synonyms at first sight turn out at closer examination to be plesionyms (i.e., near-synonyms). A "statement that does not conform to the truth" can, for instance, be lexicalized as 'lie,' 'falsehood,' 'untruth,' 'fib,' or 'misrepresentation,' which have—although they share the same meaning—subtle differences. A 'lie,' for example, usually implies deceiving someone, while a 'misconception' can be simply due to ignorance (Hirst, 1995). For our concept formation step, we asked the annotators to ignore these subtle differences in order to obtain a rather coarse-grained ontology. The words 'lie,' 'falsehood,' 'untruth,' 'fib,' and 'misrepresentation' should thus form a single concept with multiple lexicalizations. We therefore asked the raters to judge (1) as "consistent" (1).

Example (2) contains the same lexicalizations as (1), but has an additional lexicalization 'singer.' A 'bass' is a certain kind of 'singer'; we would thus not expect to find both lexicalizations as a representation for the same concept. Humans would rather model two independent concepts {bass, basso} and {singer} that are connected by a subsumption relation. We hence asked the raters to judge such cases as "inconsistent" (0).

Regarding (3), the textual definitions would indicate an "inconsistent" concept, as the fish 'bass' and the singer 'basso' do clearly not represent the same meaning. We, however, asked the raters to judge such concepts as "lexically consistent" (2), since there is a different word sense for 'bass' that refers to the male singer. For judging a concept as "lexically consistent," the rater should hence ignore the textual description and rather judge if the words ('bass' and 'basso' in this case) refer to the same concept. While "inconsistent" concepts yield errors in our final ontology, "lexically consistent" concepts are still useful, as they represent valid lexicalizations of a concept. A concept that is lexicalized as {bass, basso} induces a clear, consistent meaning regardless of the textual definitions mined from Wiktionary. Such a concept can particularly be used in a subsumption relation to, for example, {singer} without introducing inconsistencies per se.

Each rater had previous experience in linguistic annotation studies. The annotation task was explained in an annotation guidebook that contains multiple examples illustrating the task. The annotators were also encouraged to consult other knowledge resources such as books or the Web, but were not supposed to discuss the items with each other. Wiktionary in particular could be used to better grasp the possible meanings of the lexicalizations. To allow for reproducibility, we make the dataset and the guidebook available on our website.

In order to ensure the reliability of our data, we measure the inter-rater agreement of each dataset; this is shown in Table 5. We observe a slight trend or bias of rater A annotating a concept as "consistent" or "lexically consistent," while rater B seems to use "lexically consistent" or "inconsistent" more often. This caused us to look more closely at the agreement between the annotations of both raters. For the English dataset, we observed an overall agreement of $A_O = 0.89$ and likewise $A_O = 0.87$ for the German dataset. While the observed agreement A_O considers the absolute number of concepts that were annotated with the same class, some of these matches might be due to chance. We therefore also measured the chance-corrected inter-rater agreements $\kappa = 0.79$ for the English dataset and $\kappa = 0.71$ for the German dataset using Cohen's kappa (Artstein & Poesio, 2008). Both agreement scores are well above 0.67, which indicates substantial agreement and allows tentative conclusions to be drawn (Krippendorff, 1980).

As already mentioned for the anchoring of the relations, kappa is known to yield smaller values if the distribution of categories is skewed. From the distribution of the annotation categories shown in Table 5, we observe that most concepts have been rated as "consistent" (1), which indicates a skewed distribution of categories. We therefore analyzed each annotation category separately by measuring the observed agreement $A_{O,i}$ per category i and the kappa per category κ_i that has been introduced by Fleiss (1971). With the exception of the "lexically consistent" category of the Ger-

man dataset, all κ_i values are above 0.7; the "inconsistent" category of the English dataset is even above 0.9, which indicates perfect agreement. Hence, we consider our annotated dataset reliable.

Besides the inter-rater agreement, Table 5 also shows the actual annotations per class. As can be seen from the table, the vast majority of concepts (59–70% in the English and 65–77% in the German dataset) are judged as "consistent," which demonstrates the validity of our new ontology. Apart from that, the majority of the concepts not judged as "consistent" are considered "lexically consistent" by the raters. In the English dataset, 83% (rater A) and 80% (rater B) are annotated as either "consistent" or "lexically consistent." For the German dataset, even 94% (rater A) and 90% (rater B) of the concepts fall in these categories. As noted above, we only evaluated concepts with at least three lexicalizations. Concepts with only one lexicalization can be seen as consistent per se, as only one word sense is involved and concepts with two lexicalizations are at least "lexically consistent," since they only depend on the quality of the relation anchoring step. From these observations, we conclude that the concepts in OntoWiktionary are of good quality.

Our error analysis showed that most ill-formed concepts are due to errors in the relation anchoring step. Consider example (3) from the annotation task definition above. This concept is created from a synonymy relation between 'basso' and

Table 5. Evaluation of our concept formation step

	Rater A	Rater B	A_O	$A_{O,i}$	κ	κ_i
English data	**100**	**100**	**0.890**		**0.791**	
consistent (1)	70	59		0.915		0.760
lexically consistent (2)	13	21		0.765		0.717
inconsistent (0)	17	20		0.919		0.901
German data	**100**	**100**	**0.870**		**0.712**	
consistent (1)	77	65		0.915		0.709
lexically consistent (2)	17	25		0.762		0.699
inconsistent (0)	6	10		0.750		0.728

'bass,' whereby the relation target has been detected wrongly — i.e., the fish sense of 'bass' has been used rather than the 'singer' sense. Future improvements should thus concentrate on the relation anchoring step.

The Formation of Relationships

We have already observed that there are different types of relations encoded in a Wiktionary article. Besides synonymy relations, this includes, amongst others, hyponymy and hypernymy relations, which are particularly useful for constructing an ontology. Hyponyms are "narrower" terms: for example, 'canoe' is a hyponym of 'boat,' since it is a special kind of boat. Conversely, hypernyms are "broader" terms, such as 'vessel,' which is a hypernym of 'boat.' These relations are capable of creating a subsumption hierarchy of the concepts in ONTOWIKTIONARY.

In order to incorporate them, we need to ontologize Wiktionary's semantic relations, since they are defined between word senses rather than concepts. This can be done directly based on the previous steps of our ontologizing process: As discussed in the previous section, the concepts in ONTOWIKTIONARY consist of individual word senses—i.e., they have been defined as the equivalence classes of the transitive closure of the synonymy relation. We can thus infer the concepts unambiguously from the word senses of a relation. Consider the hypernymy relation (submarine, boat). After applying our ontologizing approach, we are able to add a subsumption relation ({submarine, U-boat}, {boat, craft, ship}) to ONTOWIKTIONARY, since the 'boat' word sense is included in the concept {boat, craft, ship} and likewise for 'submarine.'

While the synonymy relation is usually considered to be symmetric, the hyponymy and hypernymy relations are invertible. If a hypernymy relation holds between 'submarine' and 'boat,' then an inverse hyponymy relation should hold between 'boat' and 'submarine' (and vice-versa). The inverse counterpart of a relation is not always explicitly defined in Wiktionary. This is why we generate them by flipping the relation's source and target word sense, as well as inverting the relation type.

In addition to hyponymy and hypernymy relations, Wiktionary encodes hyperlinks to derived words, words with opposite meaning (antonymy), or words that appear often with another word (collocation). We also extract these relations, and anchor them within our ontology as related concepts. Each concept thus contains relations to concepts that it subsumes, that it is subsumed by, and that it is related to. The concept {micronutrient, micromineral, trace element}, for example, subsumes the concept {vitamin}, is subsumed by the concept {nutrient}, and is related to the concepts {electrolyte} and {macronutrient}. Figure 4 shows an excerpt of ONTOWIKTIONARY, which illustrates its structure.

Table 4 shows the number of relations in ONTOWIKTIONARY. The English Wiktionary encodes the fewest number of relations, which is surprising as it is the largest yet available Wiktionary. The reason is that the English Wiktionary's community has put a focus on the encoding of words and word senses for a long time. However, the recently started initiative Wikisaurus[22] addresses exactly the encoding of semantic relations. The Wikisaurus is a special part of the English Wiktionary which contains a list of hyperlinks to terms that are related to each other. The Wikisaurus entry for 'mountain' contains, for example, links to the synonymous terms 'mount' and 'hill,' as well as a hyponymy link to 'volcano' and many other links that are good semantic relations. However, since Wikisaurus is fairly new, it cannot be extracted by any of the Wiktionary extraction systems. We thus leave the inclusion of Wikisaurus to future work. The German ONTOWIKTIONARY encodes the most semantic relations, although it is the smallest Wiktionary edition regarding the

Figure 4. An excerpt of OntoWiktionary showing three concepts with their different lexicalizations. Both the OntoWiktionary data and the user interface shown in the figure are publicly available from our website.

Concept ID	Lexicalization ID	Lemma	Gloss
3784	322367:0:1	egocentric	selfish, self-centered
Subsumes (0) SubsumedBy (0) Related (2)	549591:0:1	idiocentric	characterized by or denoting interest centered upon oneself or one's own ways, rather than upon others or the ways of others; self-centered
	742106:0:2	individualistic	Interested in oneself rather than others; egocentric
3785	206262:0:1	micronutrient	A mineral, vitamin or other substance that is essential, even in very small quantities, for growth or metabolism
Subsumes (1) SubsumedBy (1) Related (3)	1582847:0:1	micromineral	A mineral of which only trace amounts are needed in the diet.
	550155:0:1	trace element	A chemical element present in a sample in very small quantities.
3786	294590:0:1	condescension	The act of condescending; voluntary descent from one's rank or dignity in intercourse with an inferior; courtesy toward inferiors.
Subsumes (0) SubsumedBy (0) Related (0)	1492758:0:1	condescendence	The act of condescending; voluntary descent from one's rank or dignity in intercourse with an inferior; courtesy toward inferiors, condescension.

number of concepts. In our future work, we plan to add additional relations to OntoWiktionary by, for example, integrating our ontology with previously existing ones.

FUTURE RESEARCH DIRECTIONS

There are multiple future research directions concerning the ontology construction process of OntoWiktionary. One crucial point is the development of the knowledge harvesting step, which relies on complex software systems that interpret Wiktionary's encoding format. Although much effort lies in the engineering of robust extraction software, emerging research in the field of Web-based information extraction and wrapper induction can help to improve the software components. This includes automatic detection of format changes and new sections, as well as the adaptation of the extraction software to a Wiktionary edition of another language. Particularly the latter is an important challenge, since Wiktionary currently utilizes different structures and guidelines for each language edition.

Furthermore, as regards the knowledge ontologizing step, our error analysis of the relation anchoring approach reveals some room for improvements in our algorithm. A future improvement we are working on involves the transfer of state-of-

the-art methods in word sense disambiguation to this problem. Refining the relation anchoring approach also enables other usages of Wiktionary which rely on lexical semantic information, such as machine translation, and thus increases the need for high-quality results for this task. Apart from that, the concept and relation formation steps offer multiple future directions. We observe that the English OntoWiktionary contains rather few lexicalizations for each concept, which is caused by a fewer number of semantic relations in the English Wiktionary compared to other language editions. The information encoded in the Wikisaurus part of Wiktionary might prove helpful here, as well as the incorporation of methods for synonymy mining.

Besides improvements to our ontology construction process, we want to point out several other future directions in the context of OntoWiktionary and ontologies in general. We see an important research question in the integration of different ontologies. As discussed in the "background" section, the different ontology construction approaches have their individual limitations, which might be alleviated by an integrated ontology. The integration of OntoWiktionary with OpenCyc, OntoWordNet, and DBpedia appears to be a promising option, since Wiktionary encodes a huge amount of lexical semantic information that cannot be found within the other ontologies. Another important task is the integration of ONTOWIKTIONARY into the linked data cloud which has proven to be an excellent platform for combining heterogeneous ontologies. A main challenge therein will be the modeling of stable identifiers in Wiktionary. Since word senses in Wiktionary are subject to change at basically any time, their indices in the scope of a Wiktionary page might change and thus the index is not a good identifier for integrating ONTOWIKTIONARY with other ontologies.

Finally, we see lots of applications in the field of natural language processing that can benefit from ONTOWIKTIONARY. Such applications might be (1) foundational algorithms like calculating semantic relatedness or performing word sense disambiguation, as well as (2) applications to real world problems (e.g., question answering, automatic summarization systems, or semantic search engines) that usually require huge ontologies as a source of background knowledge. We refer to some interesting applications that started to discover Wiktionary within our additional reading section. We are, however, not aware of any work that transforms Wiktionary data into an ontology. Thus, we expect substantial impact from providing a huge Wiktionary-based ontology of considerable quality.

CONCLUSION

The aim of this chapter is to explore the potential of the free online dictionary Wiktionary for constructing ontologies in a (semi-)automatic manner. Wiktionary is a collaborative wiki collecting knowledge about words, word senses, and semantic relations between words. The large community of voluntary editors has collected millions of individual facts in over 145 languages, which makes Wiktionary a hidden treasure for developing ontologies.

Employing Wiktionary as a source for ontology construction has several advantages: (1)

it is larger than many other existing resources such as OpenCyc or OntoWordNet; (2) its data is constantly edited and extended by the community, which allows it to quickly reflect trends and emerging topics; (3) it has good coverage of domain-specific terminology that can be used to develop domain ontologies; and (4) its data is multilingual and thus can be used to develop ontologies for resource-poor languages. As opposed to automatically created ontologies using information extraction systems, Wiktionary's knowledge can be of fairly high quality, since it has been explicitly encoded by humans, and is constantly reviewed by its community. Our intuition is that Wiktionary has a similar potential as Wikipedia, which gained great attention within the Semantic Web community. Wiktionary shows similar properties as its encyclopedic companion, although focusing on linguistic knowledge. The harvesting of lexicalizations of ontological concepts and a clear-cut taxonomy of subsumption relations are two main strengths that we observe in the Wiktionary data and that we exploit for constructing ontologies.

In this chapter, we proposed a two-step approach to construct the novel ontology ONTOWIKTIONARY that contains concepts, their lexicalizations, and relations harvested from Wiktionary. The first step applies a software system to transform a Wiktionary dump into a structured database. After reviewing different existing software systems for this purpose and the challenges they need to tackle, we used JWKTL and developed a new adapter to Wikokit, which allows us to extract data from the English, German, and Russian Wiktionary editions.

The second step addresses the ontologizing of the harvested knowledge—i.e., the formation of concepts and relations within our ontology. A necessary preprocessing task for achieving this goal is the anchoring of Wiktionary's relations. For this task, each relation needs to be associated with the correct word sense (which is used to form the concepts later on). For our setting, we adapted a method by Meyer and Gurevych (2010), which works well for our purposes. The error analysis reveals some remaining issues that we leave to future work, such as references within the textual definitions of senses. From the anchored synonymy relations, we then formed the concepts of ONTOWIKTIONARY. In particular, we followed the approach of OntoWordNet that uses the synsets of WordNet as a basis for the concepts of their ontology. Wiktionary has no explicitly encoded synsets, so we induced a synset-like structure by considering the synonymy relation as an equivalence relation and using its transitive closure as automatically induced concepts for ONTOWIKTIONARY. We evaluated our method by asking human raters whether the concepts we formed are consistent and found that about three quarters are considered consistent, while between 80% and 94% are at least lexically consistent (i.e., they have consistent lexicalizations) although their textual definition might not be fully correct due to errors in the relation anchoring preprocessing step. Finally, we augmented the encoded taxonomic relations between senses by adding subsumption relations and related concepts to ONTOWIKTIONARY.

From our evaluation, we conclude that ON-TOWIKTIONARY is of good quality. At the same time, it contains a large number of concepts and thus surmounts the size of OntoWordNet and OpenCyc in terms of concepts. The final ONTOWIKTIONARY for the English, German, and Russian language is available from our website.[23] The ontological data can be browsed using the Web-based user interface shown in Figure 4 or downloaded as a simple XML file for offline use. By making ONTOWIKTIONARY publicly available, we want to foster research in the field of Wiktionary and ontologies in general. One particular future task will be the integration of ONTOWIKTIONARY with existing ontologies as well as the linked data cloud.

ACKNOWLEDGMENT

This work has been supported by the Volkswagen Foundation as part of the Lichtenberg Professorship Program under grant N° I/82806. We would like to thank the anonymous reviewers for their valuable comments, our student Yevgen Chebotar for his contributions to this work, as well as our colleagues at the Ubiquitous Knowledge Processing Lab for many fruitful discussions about this chapter. Moreover, we thank Andrew Krizhanovsky for developing the Wikokit software library to access the Russian Wiktionary.

REFERENCES

Artstein, R., & Poesio, M. (2008). Inter-coder agreement for computational linguistics. *Computational Linguistics, 34*(4), 555–596. doi:10.1162/coli.07-034-R2

Atkins, B. T. S., & Rundell, M. (2008). *The Oxford guide to practical lexicography*. Oxford, UK: Oxford University Press.

Banko, M., Cafarella, M. J., Soderland, S., Broadhead, M., & Etzioni, O. (2007). Open information extraction from the web. In *Proceedings of the 20th International Joint Conference on Artificial Intelligence,* (pp. 2670–2676). IEEE Press.

Berners-Lee, T., Hall, W., Hendler, J., Shadbolt, N., & Weitzner, D. J. (2006). Creating a science of the web. *Science, 313*(5788), 769–771. doi:10.1126/science.1126902

Bizer, C., Heath, T., & Berners-Lee, T. (2009a). Linked data – The story so far. *International Journal on Semantic Web and Information Systems, 5*(3), 1–22. doi:10.4018/jswis.2009081901

Bizer, C., Lehmann, J., Kobilarov, G., Auer, S., Becker, C., Cyganiak, R., & Hellmann, S. (2009). DBpedia – A crystallization point for the web of data. *Journal of Web Semantics, 7*(3), 154–165. doi:10.1016/j.websem.2009.07.002

Echarte, F., Astrain, J., Córdoba, A., & Villadangos, J. (2007). *Ontology of folksonomy: A new modeling method*. Paper presented at the Semantic Authoring, Annotation and Knowledge Markup Workshop. Whistler, Canada.

Fellbaum, C. (Ed.). (1998). *WordNet: An electronic lexical database*. Cambridge, MA: MIT Press.

Finkelstein, L., Gabrilovich, E., Matias, Y., Rivlin, E., Solan, Z., Wolfman, G., & Ruppin, E. (2002). Placing search in context: The concept revisited. *ACM Transactions on Information Systems, 20*(1), 116–131. doi:10.1145/503104.503110

Fleiss, J. L. (1971). Measuring nominal scale agreement among many raters. *Psychological Bulletin, 76*(5), 378–381. doi:10.1037/h0031619

Gabrilovich, E., & Markovitch, S. (2007). Computing semantic relatedness using Wikipedia-based explicit semantic analysis. In *Proceedings of the 20th International Joint Conference on Artificial Intelligence,* (pp. 1606–1611). IEEE Press.

Gangemi, A., Navigli, R., & Velardi, P. (2003). The OntoWordNet project: Extension and axiomatization of conceptual relations in WordNet. In Meersman, R., Tari, Z., & Schmidt, D. C. (Eds.), *On the Move to Meaningful Internet Systems* (pp. 820–838). Berlin, Germany: Springer. doi:10.1007/978-3-540-39964-3_52

Giles, J. (2005). Internet encyclopaedias go head to head. *Nature, 438*(7070), 900–901. doi:10.1038/438900a

Gruber, T. (2007). Ontology of folksonomy: A mash-up of apples and oranges. *International Journal on Semantic Web and Information Systems, 3*(1), 1–11. doi:10.4018/jswis.2007010101

Guarino, N., Oberle, D., & Staab, S. (2009). What is an ontology? In Staab, S., & Studer, R. (Eds.), *Handbook on Ontologies* (pp. 1–7). Berlin, Germany: Springer. doi:10.1007/978-3-540-92673-3_0

Hirst, G. (1995). Near-synonymy and the structure of lexical knowledge. In *Proceedings of the AAAI Spring Symposium Representation and Acquisition of Lexical Knowledge: Polysemy, Ambiguity, and Generativity,* (pp. 51–56). Menlo Park, CA: The AAAI Press.

Kilgarriff, A., & Grefenstette, G. (2003). Introduction to the special issue on the web as corpus. *Computational Linguistics, 29*(3), 333–347. doi:10.1162/089120103322711569

Krippendorff, K. (1980). *Content analysis: An introduction to its methodology*. Thousand Oaks, CA: Sage Publications.

Krizhanovsky, A., & Lin, F. (2009). Related terms search based on WordNet / Wiktionary and its application in ontology matching. In *Proceedings of the 11th Russian Conference on Digital Libraries,* (pp. 363–369). RCDL Press.

Kurmas, Z. (2010). *Zawilinski: A library for studying grammar in Wiktionary*. Paper presented at the 6th International Symposium on Wikis and Open Collaboration. Gdańsk, Poland.

Lenat, D. B. (1995). Cyc: A large-scale investment in knowledge infrastructure. *Communications of the ACM, 38*(11), 33–38. doi:10.1145/219717.219745

Martin, P. (2003). Correction and extension of WordNet 1.7. In *Conceptual Structures for Knowledge Creation and Communication: 11th International Conference on Conceptual Structures,* (pp. 160–173). Berlin, Germany: Springer.

Maynard, D., Li, Y., & Peters, W. (2008). NLP techniques for term extraction and ontology population. In Buitelaar, P., & Cimiano, P. (Eds.), *Ontology Learning and Population: Bridging the Gap between Text and Knowledge* (pp. 107–127). Amsterdam: IOS Press.

Meyer, C. M., & Gurevych, I. (2010a). Worth its weight in gold or yet another resource – A comparative study of Wiktionary, OpenThesaurus and GermaNet. In A. Gelbukh (Ed.), *Computational Linguistics and Intelligent Text Processing: 11th International Conference,* (pp. 38–49). Berlin, Germany: Springer.

Meyer, C. M., & Gurevych, I. (2010b). *How Web communities analyze human language: Word senses in Wiktionary.* Paper presented at the Second Web Science Conference. Raleigh, NC.

Mika, P. (2007). Ontologies are us: A unified model of social networks and semantics. *Web Semantics: Science. Services and Agents on the World Wide Web*, 5(1), 5–15. doi:10.1016/j.websem.2006.11.002

Pantel, P., & Pennacchiotti, M. (2008). Automatically harvesting and ontologizing semantic relations. In Buitelaar, P., & Cimiano, P. (Eds.), *Ontology Learning and Population: Bridging the Gap between Text and Knowledge* (pp. 171–198). Amsterdam: IOS Press.

Passonneau, R. J. (2006). Measuring agreement on set-valued items (MASI) for semantic and pragmatic annotation. In *Proceedings of the Fifth International Conference on Language Resources and Evaluation,* (pp. 831–836). ACL Press.

Ponzetto, S. P., & Strube, M. (2007). Deriving a large-scale taxonomy from Wikipedia, In *Proceedings of the Twenty-Second AAAI Conference on Artificial Intelligence,* (pp. 1440–1445). Menlo Park, CA: AAAI Press.

Prévot, L., Borgo, S., & Oltramari, A. (2005). Interfacing ontologies and lexical resources. In *Proceedings of the IJCNLP 2005 Workshop Ontologies and Lexical Resources,* (pp. 91–102). IJCNLP Press.

Reed, S. L., & Lenat, D. B. (2002). Mapping ontologies into Cyc. In *Proceedings of the AAAI 2002 Workshop Ontologies and the Semantic Web,* (pp. 1–6). AAAI Press.

Russell, S., & Norvig, P. (2010). *Artificial intelligence: A modern approach.* Upper Saddle River, NJ: Prentice Hall.

Sajous, F., Navarro, E., Gaume, B., Prévot, L., & Chudy, Y. (2010). Semi-automatic endogenous enrichment of collaboratively constructed lexical resources: Piggybacking onto Wiktionary. In H. Loftsson, E. Rögnvaldsson, & S. Helgadóttir (Eds.), *Advances in Natural Language Processing: Proceedings of the 7th International Conference on NLP,* (pp. 332–344). Berlin, Germany: Springer.

Schmid, H. (1994). Probabilistic part-of-speech tagging using decision trees. In *Proceedings of International Conference on New Methods in Language Processing,* (pp. 44–49). ICLP Press.

Singh, P. (2002). The public acquisition of commonsense knowledge. In *Proceedings of AAAI Spring Symposium on Acquiring (and Using) Linguistic (and World) Knowledge for Information Access,* (pp. 47–52). Menlo Park, CA: The AAAI Press.

Suchanek, F., Kasneci, G., & Weikum, G. (2008). YAGO – A large ontology from Wikipedia and WordNet. *Web Semantics: Science. Services and Agents on the World Wide Web*, 6(3), 203–217. doi:10.1016/j.websem.2008.06.001

Surowiecki, J. (2005). *The wisdom of crowds.* New York, NY: Anchor Books.

Vossen, P. (1998). Introduction to EuroWordNet. *Computers and the Humanities, 32*(2–3), 73–89. doi:10.1023/A:1001175424222

Zesch, T., Müller, C., & Gurevych, I. (2008a). Extracting lexical semantic knowledge from Wikipedia and Wiktionary. In *Proceedings of the 6th International Conference on Language Resources and Evaluation,* (pp. 1646–1652). ACL Press.

Zesch, T., Müller, C., & Gurevych, I. (2008b). Using Wiktionary for computing semantic relatedness. In *Proceedings of the Twenty-Third AAAI Conference on Artificial Intelligence,* (pp. 861–867). AAAI Press.

ADDITIONAL READING

Bernhard, D., & Gurevych, I. (2009). Combining lexical semantic resources with question & answer archives for translation-based answer finding. In *Proceedings of the Joint Conference of the 47th Annual Meeting of the Association for Computational Linguistics and the 4th International Joint Conference on Natural Language Processing of the Asian Federation of Natural Language Processing,* (pp. 728–736). ACL Press.

Bouchard-Côté, A., Liang, P., Griffiths, T. L., & Klein, D. (2007). A probabilistic approach to diachronic phonology. In *Proceedings of the 2007 Joint Conference on Empirical Methods in Natural Language Processing and Computational Natural Language Learning,* (pp. 887–896). ACL Press.

Buitelaar, P., & Cimiano, P. (Eds.). (2008). *Ontology learning and population: Bridging the gap between text and knowledge.* Amsterdam: IOS Press.

Burfoot, C., & Baldwin, T. (2009). Automatic satire detection: Are you having a laugh? In *Proceedings of the ACL-IJCNLP 2009 Conference Short Papers,* (pp. 161–164). ACL Press.

Chesley, P., Vincent, B., Xu, L., & Srihari, R. (2006). Using verbs and adjectives to automatically classify blog sentiment. In *Proceedings of the AAAI Spring Symposium Computational Approaches to Analysing Weblogs,* (pp. 27–29). Menlo Park, CA: The AAAI Press.

De Melo, G., & Weikum, G. (2009). Towards a universal wordnet by learning from combined evidence. In *Proceedings of the 18th ACM Conference on Information and Knowledge Management,* (pp. 513–522). New York, NY: ACM.

De Melo, G., & Weikum, G. (2010). Providing multilingual, multimodal answers to lexical database queries. In N. Calzolari, et al. (Eds.), *Proceedings of the 7th International Conference on Language Resources and Evaluation,* (pp. 348–355). ACL Press.

Descy, D. E. (2006). The Wiki: True Web democracy. *TechTrends, 50*(1), 4–5. doi:10.1007/s11528-006-7569-y

Etzioni, O., Reiter, K., Soderland, S., & Sammer, M. (2007). *Lexical translation with application to image search on the Web.* Paper presented at the Machine Translation Summit XI. Copenhagen, Denmark.

Fišer, D., & Sagot, B. (2008). Combining multiple resources to build reliable wordnets. In *Proceedings of the 11th International Conference on Text, Speech and Dialogue,* (pp. 61–68). Berlin, Germany: Springer.

Garoufi, K., Zesch, T., & Gurevych, I. (2008). *Graph-theoretic analysis of collaborative knowledge bases in natural language processing.* Paper presented at the Poster Session of the 7th International Semantic Web Conference. Karlsruhe, Germany.

Gurevych, I., & Wolf, E. (2010). Expert-built and collaboratively constructed lexical semantic resources. *Language and Linguistics Compass, 4*(11), 1074–1090. doi:10.1111/j.1749-818X.2010.00251.x

Kann, V., & Rosell, M. (2006). Free construction of a free Swedish dictionary of synonyms. In S. Werner (Ed.), *Proceedings of the 15th Nordic Conference on Computational Linguistics,* (pp. 105–110). ACL Press.

Kulkarni, A., & Callan, J. (2008). Dictionary definitions based homograph identification using a generative hierarchical model. In *Proceedings of the 46th Annual Meeting of the Association for Computational Linguistics: Human Language Technologies,* (pp. 85–88). ACL Press.

Kurmas, Z. (2010). *Encouraging language students to contribute inflection data to Wiktionary.* Paper presented at the 6th International Symposium on Wikis and Open Collaboration. Gdańsk, Poland.

Matuschek, M., & Gurevych, I. (2010). *Beyond the synset: Synonyms in collaboratively constructed semantic resources.* Paper presented at the Workshop on Computational Approaches to Synonymy at the Symposium on Re-Thinking Synonymy. Helsinki, Finland.

Maxwell, M., & Hughes, B. (2006). Frontiers in linguistic annotation for lower-density languages. In *Proceedings of the COLING/ACL 2006 Workshop Frontiers in Linguistically Annotated Corpora,* (pp. 29–37). ACL Press.

Medero, J., & Ostendorf, M. (2009). *Analysis of vocabulary difficulty using Wiktionary.* Paper presented at the ISCA International Workshop on Speech and Language Technology in Education. Warwickshire, UK.

Müller, C., & Gurevych, I. (2009). Using Wikipedia and Wiktionary in domain-specific information retrieval. In C. Peters, et al. (Eds.), *Evaluating Systems for Multilingual and Multimodal Information Access: Proceedings of the 9th Workshop of the Cross-Language Evaluation Forum,* (pp. 219–226). Berlin, Germany: Springer.

Navarro, E., Sajous, F., Gaume, B., Prévot, L., Hsieh, S., Kuo, I., et al. (2009). Wiktionary and NLP: Improving synonymy networks. In *Proceedings of the ACL 2009 Workshop The People's Web Meets NLP: Collaboratively Constructed Semantic Resources,* (pp. 19–27). ACL Press.

Perera, P., & Witte, R. (2005). A self-learning context-aware lemmatizer for German. In *Proceedings of Human Language Technology Conference and Conference on Empirical Methods in Natural Language Processing,* (pp. 636–643). ACL Press.

Richman, A. E., & Schone, P. (2008). Mining Wiki resources for multilingual named entity recognition. In *Proceedings of the 46th Annual Meeting of the Association for Computational Linguistics: Human Language Technologies,* (pp. 1–9). ACL Press.

Sagot, B., & Fišer, D. (2008). Building a free French wordnet from multilingual resources. In *Proceedings of the LREC 2008 Workshop Ontologies and Lexical Resources,* (pp. 14–19).

Schlippe, T., Ochs, S., & Schultz, T. (2010). Wiktionary as a source for automatic pronunciation extraction. In *Proceedings of the 11th Annual Conference of the International Speech Communication Association,* (pp. 2290–2293). ISCA Press.

Walther, G., Sagot, B., & Fort, K. (2010). *Fast development of basic NLP tools: Towards a lexicon and a POS tagger for Kurmanji Kurdish.* Paper presented at the 29th International Conference on Lexis and Grammar. Belgrade, Serbia.

Wandmacher, T., Ovchinnikova, E., Krumnack, U., & Dittmann, H. (2007). Extraction, evaluation and integration of lexical-semantic relations for the automated construction of a lexical ontology. In T. Meyer & A. C. Nayak (Eds.), *Proceedings of the AI 2007 Workshop Third Australasian Ontology Workshop,* (pp. 61–69). AAOW Press.

Weale, T., Brew, C., & Fosler-Lussier, E. (2009). Using the Wiktionary graph structure for synonym detection. In *Proceedings of the ACL 2009 Workshop The People's Web Meets NLP: Collaboratively Constructed Semantic Resources,* (pp. 28–31). ACL Press.

Weber, N., & Buitelaar, P. (2006). *Web-based ontology learning with ISOLDE.* Paper presented at the ISWC 2006 Workshop Web Content Mining with Human Language. Athens, GA.

Zesch, T. (2010). What's the difference? Comparing expert-built and collaboratively-built lexical semantic resources. In N. Calzolari, P. Baroni, M. Monachini, & C. Soria (Eds.), *Proceedings of the 2nd European Language Resources and Technologies Forum Language Resources of the Future / the Future of Language Resources,* (pp. 91–92). ACL Press.

KEY TERMS AND DEFINITIONS

Concept: A model for objects/entities observed in a world (not necessarily the real world). Concepts are the building blocks of ontologies.

Hypernymy: A semantic relation between two word senses, whereby the target sense is broader (i.e., more general) than the source.

Hyponymy: A semantic relation between two word senses, whereby the target sense is narrower (i.e., more specific) than the source.

Ontologizing: The process of transforming knowledge into ontological structures – i.e., finding or creating concepts and relationships based on the given knowledge.

Semantic Relation: A binary relation between word senses that consists of a source, target, and relation type, which denotes a certain semantic relationship between the source and the target.

Synonymy: A semantic relation between two word senses that have an equivalent meaning.

Synset: A set of synonymous word senses — i.e., a set in which each pair of word senses are in a synonymy relation to each other.

Wiki: A software for collaborative text editing in the World Wide Web that is known for its simple and easy-to-use interface.

Word Sense: A certain aspect of meaning of a word that is usually found in dictionaries where it is defined by a brief textual description.

ENDNOTES

1   Cyc and OpenCyc – http://www.cyc.com
2   Open Directory Project – http://www.dmoz.org
3   CIA World Factbook – https://www.cia.gov/library/publications/the-world-factbook
4   Unified Medical Language System – http://www.nlm.nih.gov/mesh/umlsforelis.html
5   Del.icio.us – http://www.delicious.com
6   Flickr – http://www.flickr.com
7   OpenMind – http://www.openmind.org
8   Wikipedia – http://www.wikipedia.org
9   Wiktionary – http://www.wiktionary.org
10 Note that we only count entries about English words here, which largely deviates from the number of articles in the entire English Wiktionary (2.3 million). For the distinction between word, entry, and article; see section "Wiktionary: A Collaborative Resource for Linguistic Knowledge."
11 We only count active Wiktionary editions according to the list on http://meta.wikimedia.org/wiki/Wiktionary (April 1, 2011). There are about 35 additional editions, which have been newly created or are not maintained anymore, and are thus not considered an "active" Wiktionary edition
12 Wiktionary: Entry layout explained – http://en.wiktionary.org/wiki/Wiktionary:ELE (February 10, 2011)
13 Wikimedia database backup dumps – http://dumps.wikimedia.org

[14] Java-based Wiktionary Library (JWKTL) – http://www.ukp.tu-darmstadt.de/software/jwktl

[15] Wiki tool kit (Wikokit) – http://code.google.com/p/wikokit

[16] WIktionarieS Improvement by Graphs-Oriented meTHods (WISIGOTH) – http://redac.univ-tlse2.fr/wisigoth

[17] Zawilinski – http://www.cis.gvsu.edu/~kurmasz

[18] This is an important difference from Wikipedia, whose individual language editions are very similar.

[19] Note that the English and the French Wiktionary editions are head-to-head. While the French edition has been the largest one for several years, the English edition currently contains about 400,000 articles more than the French edition, cf. http://meta.wikimedia.org/wiki/Wiktionary (June 7, 2011)

[20] It should be noted that Meyer and Gurevych (2010a) mention that Wiktionary also encodes entries for inflected word forms, which are not part of comparable resources like OpenCyc or OntoWordNet.

[21] For brevity, we also use concepts with only two lexicalizations in our examples.

[22] Wikisaurus – http://en.wiktionary.org/wiki/Wiktionary:Wikisaurus

[23] ONTOWIKTIONARY – http://www.ukp.tu-darmstadt.de/data/lexical-resources/

Chapter 7
Creation and Integration of Reference Ontologies for Efficient LOD Management

Mariana Damova
Ontotext AD, Bulgaria

Atanas Kiryakov
Ontotext AD, Bulgaria

Maurice Grinberg
Ontotext AD, Bulgaria & New Bulgarian University, Bulgaria

Michael K. Bergman
Structured Dynamics, USA

Frédérick Giasson
Structured Dynamics, USA

Kiril Simov
Ontotext AD, Bulgaria & Bulgarian Academy of Sciences, Bulgaria

ABSTRACT

The chapter introduces the process of design of two upper-level ontologies—PROTON and UMBEL—into reference ontologies and their integration in the so-called Reference Knowledge Stack (RKS). It is argued that RKS is an important step in the efforts of the Linked Open Data (LOD) project to transform the Web into a global data space with diverse real data, available for review and analysis. RKS is intended to make the interoperability between published datasets much more efficient than it is now. The approach discussed in the chapter consists of developing reference layers of upper-level ontologies by mapping them to certain LOD schemata and assigning instance data to them so they cover a reasonable portion of the LOD datasets. The chapter presents the methods (manual and semi-automatic) used in the creation of the RKS and gives examples that illustrate its advantages for managing highly heterogeneous data and its usefulness in real life knowledge intense applications.

DOI: 10.4018/978-1-4666-0188-8.ch007

INTRODUCTION

Linking Open Data (LOD) (Linking Open Data, 2011) facilitates the emergence of a Web of linked data by publishing and interlinking open data on the web in RDF (Brickley & Guha, 2004). The current 203 datasets in LOD cover a wide spectrum of subject domains – biomedical, science, geographic, generic knowledge, entertainment, government, etc. (State of the LOD Cloud, 2011). As they constantly grow, we face the problem of conveniently accessing, manipulating, and further developing them. It is believed that this large set of interconnected data will enable new classes of applications, making use of more sophisticated querying, knowledge discovery, and reasoning. This calls for approaches for their efficient use and better integration.

At the same time, LOD are characterized by heterogeneity and inconsistency, which makes their use in automated ways via algorithms difficult. A lot of research effort nowadays has been focused on looking for methods to cope with and preserve the diversity of LOD, which can scale and manage their increasing growth rates. These methods bring experimental results, which show that the state of the art is still far from the performance necessary for real life applications.

Another perspective to LOD management, which we adopt in this chapter, relates to Master Data Management (MDM) as understood in the business enterprise and DBMS worlds (Wolter, & Haselden, 2006; Withbrock, 2007; Wikipedia, 2011a; Wikipedia, 2011b). In enterprise settings, the homogeneity of the data is a fundamental requirement, e.g. the entities in the data model and the tables in a physical database have to be identical with respect to their properties, behavior, and management needs (Wolter, & Haselden, 2006). Master data are data that are shared and used by many applications within the organization. MDM aims at ensuring consistency and control of the ongoing maintenance and use of this non-transactional information, critical for the business operation of the organization. Moreover, MDM develops a shared view across the organization by creating and maintaining consistent and accurate lists of master data. Master data usually include reference data, e.g. any kind of data that is used solely to categorize other data found in a database or to relate the data in a database to information outside the enterprise.

Highly heterogeneous contexts such as LOD and the Web need similar mechanisms to ensure consistency based on a set of data agreed upon or commonly acceptable, shared by various datasets, and make them interconnected.

Our main claim in this chapter is that a reference layer, consisting of ontologies with different degrees of generality built on top of LOD and interlinked with their schemata and instances, is a viable and optimal solution for coping with LOD heterogeneity at the present time. In our opinion, such an approach will lead to more efficient LOD management and dataset integration while preserving the diversity of the data. In the Semantic Web, the idea of having integrated global ontology extracting information from the local ontologies and providing a unified view through which users can query the local ontologies is unrealistic, as it is practically impossible to maintain this global ontology in a highly dynamic environment.

The reference layer we propose here, called the Reference Knowledge Stack (RKS), will provide reference points that will serve as bridges between the various views about things, described in the LOD cloud and on the Web.

The idea of building reference structures at the schema level has been advocated previously (e.g. see Jain et al., 2010). Jain et al. (2010) state that it would be valuable to have a schema describing the subject domain of the datasets in LOD. Moreover, the three big players in the Web space—Bing, Google, and Yahoo—recently embraced the same initiative and joint forces to build the so-called Web of Objects (Bing Google Yahoo, 2011).

However, to our knowledge, RKS is the first completed project of design and implementation of reference structures for LOD.

The main arguments supporting RKS are based on the characteristics of the linkages in the LOD cloud. Although the LOD cloud contains schemata, the linkage between the datasets is mostly performed at the instance level. This limits the inherent potential of deriving implicit facts and introduces inconsistencies in the available knowledge. RKS helps to deal also with the problematic situations when different properties refer to the same relation like for example DBpedia's properties place (http://dbpedia.org/property/place), location (http://dbpedia.org/ontology/location), and city (http://dbpedia.org/ontology/city) all refer to one and the same relation between an entity and the location it is located in. Our analysis of the ontologies, alias the schemata, of some LOD datasets shows that there can be many ways of conceptualizing one and the same thing e.g. the Geonames's concept Feature and the DBpedia's concept Location. In such cases, RKS can provide a consistent interoperability between the LOD datasets. Preserving the heterogeneity of the data in the LOD cloud and at the same time making them usable requires linking the datasets at the schema level as well as at the instance level. This ensures better exploitation of data, giving access to otherwise hidden implicit knowledge, and provides better degrees of interoperability.

But what are the schema properties needed to preserve the heterogeneity of the data and at the same time to provide a convenient access and interoperability between them? Where do they have to be stored, how do they have to be processed and what would be the best techniques to access them?

This chapter addresses these questions by presenting the process of designing and creating RKS, and the first explorations of the advantages it can provide.

We argue that this intermediary layer is the glue that makes the heterogeneous datasets of LOD optimally interoperable, available for most consistent use, and serve as pathways over the web of data. The success of this approach is tightly linked to answering the questions about the optimal number of concepts to be included in such reference structures, about their integration with existing ontologies and datasets in LOD, and about the number and characteristics of the layers necessary to provide the interoperability of data related to domain specific and general knowledge.

To face these challenges, we propose a two layered approach to reference ontologies. In this approach, the schemata of selected LOD datasets are first mapped to a specially created upper reference layer – UMBEL (Bergman & Giasson, 2011) designed to enable interoperability on the Web. This layer represents a subsumption hierarchy and covers a large amount (tens of thousand) of concepts. Although relatively small compared to LOD, such ontology is difficult to grasp by human users. That is why an additional, much more compact, upper level ontology of up to a thousand concepts, was found to be needed to provide the optimal basis for LOD coverage and at the same time to be humanly perceivable and easily adoptable. The upper level ontology PROTON (Terziev, Kiryakov, & Manov, 2005) initially designed for semantic annotation, indexing and retrieval, satisfies these requirements and was chosen to be the layer on top of UMBEL. Thus, PROTON is mapped to UMBEL, making LOD instances accessible through PROTON concepts at a first degree of granularity and through UMBEL concepts at a second degree of granularity. The interoperability of this reference layers at the instance level is achieved by assigning UMBEL classes to LOD instances, more precisely DBpedia instances. This composition of interconnected elements is at the core of RKS and is illustrated in Figure 1.

More specifically, the chapter discusses the implementation of RKS in a reason-able view of the web of data (Kiryakov, et al., 2009a), the only approach so far allowing for reasoning with LOD. The reason-able view presents a practical com-

Figure 1.The structure and integration of the reference knowledge stack

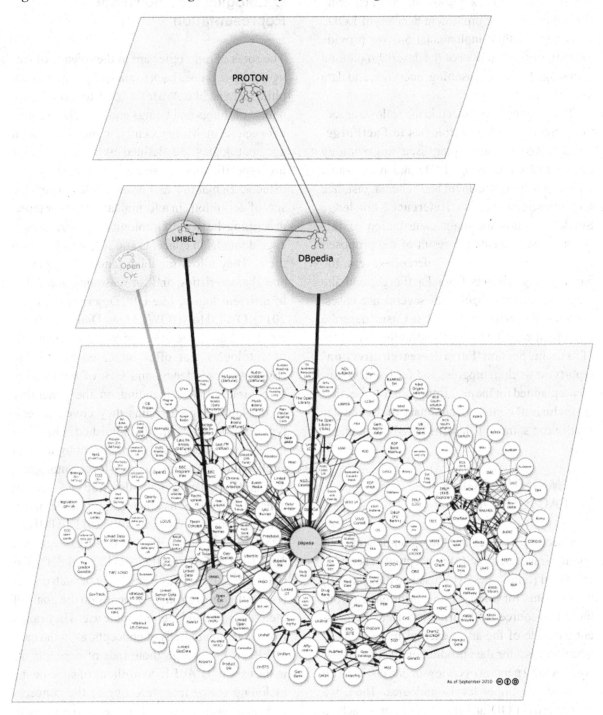

promise between the idea of the linked data openness and the rigidity of the requirements for sound and complete reasoning, and is a substantiation of the web of data. It offers a unified way of exploring and discovering knowledge, which sits in different datasets. The viability of the idea behind RKS was tested in a new instance of a reason-able view of the web of data, based on FactForge

(FactForge, 2011), a public service featuring several of the most prominent datasets of LOD.

Based on this implementation, we provide examples of actual uses of the described method to manage LOD for reasoning, querying, and data integration.

The chapter is organized in the following sections. Section **'From ontologies to FactForge'** sets the context of the chapter, discussing ontology design and engineering, LOD and reason-able views, ontology alignment and schema, instance level integration. Section **'Reference Knowledge Stack'** contains the main contribution of this chapter and presents the result of the proposed approach. It discusses the reference layers, the participating datasets from FactForge, and the mappings among them with several use cases. Sections **'Experiments'** and **'Use Cases'** describe the implementation the RKS and outline examples of its usage. Section **'Future research direction'** reports on work in progress and further developments planned for the near future. Finally, Section **'Conclusion'** contains a summary of the chapter results and some conclusions based on them.

FROM ONTOLOGIES TO FACTFORGE

This section outlines the three components our approach is based on: (a) conceptual schema of the world (ontologies); (b) instance data; and (c) mechanisms for inferring new information from these two sources of information. Here we present the state of the art in each of these areas as a background for the introduction of RKS. First, we provide a general overview of ontologies with emphasis on upper level ontologies. Then, we characterize LOD and describe an approach to using the LOD data with reasoning—the reason-able views. We finish the section by discussing ontology matching.

Ontologies for Knowledge Representation

The roots of ontologies are in the science of categorization. It goes back to antiquity, when Greek philosophers like Aristotle tried to explain the nature of things and beings and the relationships between them. More recently, in the information age, ontologies are defined as "a formal, explicit specification of a shared conceptualization" (Studer, Benjamin, & Fensel, 1998). They are sets of definitions in a formal language for terms describing the world. Ontologies organize knowledge domains in concepts and relations between them. They allow for inheritance of properties and characteristics, and for reasoning according to different logics, like DL (Description Logic, 2011), OWL-Horst (OWL Horst Dialects, 2010), etc. These are some of the powerful mechanisms of ontologies that offer increased knowledge coverage, consistency, and lack of redundancy or contradiction. Depending on the generality of the knowledge domains they cover, several types of ontologies are distinguished. These are upper-level ontologies, domain ontologies and application ontologies. Upper-level ontologies, or foundational ontologies, describe very general concepts that can be used across multiple domains; examples include Cyc (Cycorp, 2011), UMBEL (UMBEL 1.0, 2011), PROTON (Terziev, et al., 2005), SUMO (SUMO, 2011), and DOLCE (DOLCE, 2011). The optimal size of such upper-level ontologies strongly depends on the goals of their designers and their ultimate use. They range from several hundreds of concepts, as in the case of PROTON through thousands of concepts, as in the case of UMBEL, to millions of statements, including actual facts referring to the concepts and relationships defined in the ontology, as in the case of Cyc. Domain ontologies cover the conceptualization of given subject domains. They describe concepts and relationships representative for the subject domain like biology, vehicle sales, product types, etc. Application ontologies are the most specific ones and contain concepts that help realize the purposes of the application.

The most common ontology design principles include: defining the scope of the ontology, creating a balanced class hierarchy, providing methods to evaluate the concepts and properties, and consistency checking. The OntoClean method (Guarino, & Welty, 2002) is a very popular ontology design method. It recommends distinguishing between type and role when defining the concepts. It uses meta properties to check the consistency of the ontology with predefined constraints helping to discover taxonomic errors, and allowing to discover confusions between concepts and individuals, confusions at the levels of abstraction, e.g. object-level and meta-level, constraints violations, different degrees of generality. Other methods of ontology design pay close attention to the definition of the concepts requiring them to be fully disjoint (UMBEL 1.0), including axioms, and avoiding philosophical distinctions (Niles, & Pease, 2001) or allowing multiple inheritance (DOLCE, 2011). Data-driven ontologies such as the ontology of DBpedia (DBpedia, 2011) select the concepts based on the availability of data instantiating them.

SUMO (SUMO, 2011) is a very large formal ontology in First Order Logic (First Order Predicate Logic, 2009) with about 20,000 terms and about 70,000 axioms in which all domain ontologies are combined. It is well suited for linguistic processing as it is fully mapped to the largest lexical knowledge base Wordnet 3.0 (Wordnet, 2011). However, similarly to Cyc, it is too big and complex to be operational at the web of data scale.

DOLCE (DOLCE, 2011) is a foundational ontology, based on cognitive principles, intended to act as a starting point for comparing and elucidating the relationships with other future ontology modules as well as for clarifying the hidden assumptions, underlying existing ontologies or

linguistic resources such as WordNet. Its axioms are encoded in KIF (Knowledge Interchange Format, 1998) and its general representation follows First Order Logic. Although originally thought of as reference ontology for further ontology engineering, DOLCE is not suitable for the web of data due to its complexity.

These shortcomings motivate our choice of UMBEL and PROTON. UMBEL was built to become an abstract structure enabling interconnectedness of data on the Web and designed as a strict subset of Cyc (Cycorp, 2011). With initially 20,000 reference concepts, UMBEL has nearly an order of magnitude fewer concepts than Cyc, and adheres to an adaptive model that accommodates the diversity in LOD datasets. At the same time, it ensures straight connection to the rich representations of Cyc. PROTON, an upper-level lightweight ontology of a couple of hundred concepts and properties, provides a more general structure for the datasets in LOD to interoperate at a higher level, additionally it addresses not only subsumption hierarchies, but also properties.

We now thoroughly consider the core notions underlying our approach to RKS: LOD - instrumental in the transformation of the web into a "global giant graph" (Heath & Bizer, 2011), and Reason-able Views - the practical method providing the infrastructure for managing LOD (Linking Open Data, 2011).

Linked Open Data (LOD)

The notion of "linked data" is defined by Tim Berners-Lee (2006), as RDF graphs, published on the WWW so that one can explore them across servers by following the links in the graph in a manner similar to the way the HTML web is navigated. It is viewed as a method for exposing, sharing, and connecting pieces of data, information, and knowledge on the Semantic Web using URIs and RDF. "Linked data" are constituted by publishing and interlinking open data sources, following the principles of:

- Using URIs as names for things;
- Using HTTP URIs, so that people can look up these names;
- Providing useful information when someone looks up a URI;
- Including links to other URIs, so that people can discover more things.

In fact, most of the RDF datasets fulfill the first, second and fourth principles by design. The piece of novelty in the design principles above concerns the requirement for enabling Semantic Web browsers to load HTTP descriptions of RDF resources based on their URIs. To this end, data publishers should make sure that:

- The "physical" addresses of the pieces of data published are the same as the "logical" addresses, used as RDF identifiers (URIs);
- Upon receiving an HTTP request, the server should return a set of triples describing the resource.

LOD (Linking Open Data, 2011) initially began as a W3C SWEO (SWEO, 2011) community project aiming to extend the Web by publishing open datasets as RDF and by creating RDF links between data items from different data sources. LOD provide sets of referenceable, semantically interlinked resources with defined meaning. The central dataset of the LOD is DBpedia (DBpedia, 2011). Because of the many mappings between other LOD datasets and DBpedia, the latter serves as a sort of a hub in the LOD graph ensuring a certain level of connectivity. LOD is rapidly growing – as of September 2010 it contained more than 200 datasets, with total volume above 25 billion statements, interlinked with 395 million statements as illustrated in Figure 2.

It contains datasets from different subject domains, which can be seen in different color codes in Figure 2. The largest number of datasets in LOD belongs to the bio-medical domain. Another big subject area in the LOD cloud is scientific literature collection; entertainment data like Musibrainz, BBC Music, LastFM; government data like data.gov.uk, etc. Finally, some datasets contain general-purpose encyclopedic knowledge such as DBpedia and Freebase, and geographic knowledge such as Geonames, etc.

The use of LOD and the development of applications based on it are difficult because the different LOD datasets are rather loosely connected chunks of information, facts, and instances. They have varying levels of completeness and external linkages. They are mainly connected at the instance level, thus losing the benefits from the enrichment of the data with implicit factual knowledge, when ontologies and schema-level mappings are involved. Even the linkage between instances of different datasets in the LOD cloud, using the predicate `owl:sameAs` shows drawbacks due to the fact that the instances are not described in the same way in the different datasets. They are, strictly speaking, not the same. For instance New York's population in DBpedia is given as of July 2009, and counts 8,391,881, whereas in Freebase it is 8,363,710 as of 2008. Nevertheless, the two instances of New York from DBpedia and from Freebase are linked together with `owl:sameAs`, which implies that the two resources are fully identical. Yet, the "facts" for each instance differ. Another example points to the country of Kosovo. In DBpedia, it is described as a country, whereas in Freebase, it is denoted as a region. Still these two instances are reliably linked with `owl:sameAs`. Such divergences make the use of LOD data challenging in knowledge demanding applications or for reasoning tasks. We refer here to the discussions about the use of `owl:sameAs` in LOD (Jain et al., 2010). On the other hand, introducing schema-level alignment of LOD datasets would provide significant advantages in ensuring the consistency

Figure 2. LOD datasets[1]

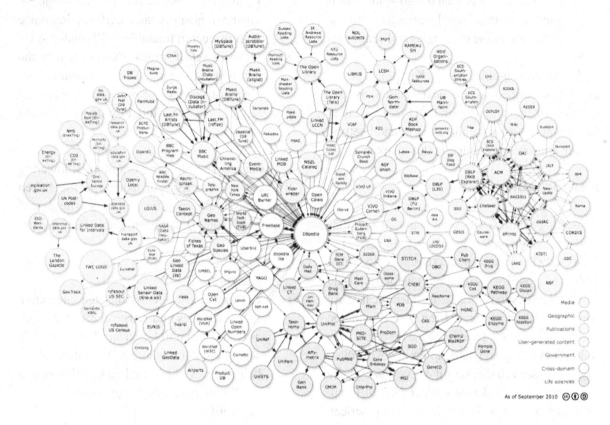

of linkages. Such linkages would enable applications that can answer queries requiring multiple and disparate information sources.

But the quality of the data in the LOD cloud and their linkage are not the only challenges when using it. The RDF datasets are supplied with vocabularies, which imply inference and generation of implicit facts, which considerably increases the overall number of facts available for exploration. This poses the question of managing LOD, and creating environments, which would allow one to make use of their full potential. Using linked data for data management is considered to have great potential for the transformation of the web of data into a giant global graph (Heath & Bizer, 2011). Still, there are several challenges that have to be overcome to make this possible, namely:

- LOD are hard to comprehend – the fact that multiple datasets are interlinked and accessible in the same data format is not enough to deal with hundreds of data schemata, ontologies, vocabularies and data modeling patterns;
- Diversity comes at a price – often there are tens of different ways of expressing one and the same piece of information even in a single dataset such as DBpedia;
- LOD is unreliable – many of the servers behind LOD today are slow and have down times higher than the one acceptable for most of the data management setups;
- Dealing with data distributed on the web is slow – a federated SPARQL query that uses, say, three servers within several joins can be very slow;

- No consistency is guaranteed – low commitment to the formal semantics and intended use of the ontologies and schemata.

Using reason-able views (Kiryakov, et al., 2009a), described in the next section, is one solution to the problem of LOD management. Reason-able views are the experimental setting for the approach presented in this chapter.

Reason-Able Views

Reasoning within LOD with standard methods of sound and complete inference with respect to First Order Predicate Calculus is practically infeasible. The closed-world assumption for sound and complete reasoning is practically inapplicable in a web context and has never been even considered for the web of data. Due to the nature of the data in LOD in its current state, inference with them in many cases is useless, as it derives many false statements. Having datasets dispersed in different locations makes reasoning with them impractical.

Reason-able views (Kiryakov, et al., 2009a) are an approach to reasoning with and managing linked data. *Reason-able view* is an assembly of independent datasets, which can be used as a single body of knowledge with respect to reasoning and query evaluation. The key principles of constructing reason-able views can be summarized as follows:

- Group selected datasets and ontologies in a compound dataset;
- Clean up, post-process and enrich the datasets if necessary. Do this conservatively, in a clearly documented and automated manner, so that (a) the operation can easily be performed each time a new version of one of the datasets is published; and (b) the users can easily understand the intervention made to the original dataset;

- Load the compound dataset in a single semantic repository and perform inference with respect to tractable OWL dialects;
- Define a set of sample queries against the compound dataset. These determine the "level of service" or the "scope of consistency" contract offered by the reason-able view.

Each reason-able view is aiming at lowering the cost and the risks of using specific linked data datasets for specific purposes. The design objectives behind each reason-able view are to:

- Make reasoning and query evaluation feasible;
- Lower the cost of entry through interactive user interfaces and retrieval methods such as URI auto-completion and *RDF search* (a search modality where RDF molecules are being retrieved and ranked by relevance to a full-text style query, represented as set of keywords);
- Guarantee a basic level of consistency – the sample queries guarantee the consistency of the data in the same way in which regression tests do for the quality of software;
- Guarantee availability – in the same way in which web search engines are usually more reliable than most of the web sites; they also do caching;
- Easier exploration and querying of unseen data – sample queries provide re-usable extraction patterns, which reduce the time for acquaintance with the datasets and their interconnections.

Reason-able views are built according to certain design principles, e.g.:

- All datasets in the view represent linked data;

- Single reasonability criteria is imposed on all datasets;
- Each dataset is connected to at least one of the others.

Reason-able views are implemented in two public services, namely, FactForge (FactForge, 2011) and LinkedLifeData (Linked Life Data, 2011), and integrated as the semantic knowledge base of The National Archive of Great Britain (SKB, 2011).

Similar approach to handling large amounts of linked data is featured in Bio2RDF (Bio2RDF, 2011). This project uses open-source Semantic Web technologies to provide interlinked life science data to support biological knowledge discovery. Its data integration methods differ from the methods applied in the reason-able views FactForge and LinkedLifeData, because Bio2RDF is using both syntactic and semantic data integration techniques, provide linkages mainly at the operational instance level, and define special identifiers for each resource in their knowledge base. FactForge and LinkedLifeData use the URIs (URI, 2011) from the original datasets included in the respective reason-able view.

Ontology Matching

Ontologies are increasingly seen as a key factor for enabling interoperability across heterogeneous systems and Semantic Web applications. Ontology matching ensures that the diverse conceptualizations will be able to function together in a consistent way. It refers to the activity of finding or discovering relationships or correspondences between entities in different ontologies or ontology modules.

Automated ontology matching consists in finding the correspondences of concepts and properties in two ontologies using automated methods and algorithms. Certain scholars categorize the mapping approaches according to the types of ontologies to be mapped together. Choi, Song,

and Han (2006) describe different types of ontology mapping such as between a global ontology and local ontologies, between local ontologies, or between ontology merge and alignment. Systems that use algorithms for local ontologies mapping are considered the most appropriate for the Semantic Web. They adopt approaches like C-OWL: contextualizing ontologies (Bouquet, et al., 2003). This approach consists in keeping the contents of ontologies local, e.g. not shared with other ontologies, and mapped with the contents of other ontologies with explicit mappings – bridge rules – that allow relating concepts, roles and individuals in different ontologies both at the syntactic and at the semantic level. The system GLUE (Doan, et al., 2003), on the other hand, creates ontology mapping semi-automatically using machine learning techniques by finding the most similar concepts between two ontologies and calculates the joint probability distribution of the concept using a multi-strategy learning approach for similarity measurement. MAFRA (Ontology Mapping framework for distributed ontologies in the Semantic Web) (Silva, & Rocha, 2003) provides a distributed mapping process that consists of five horizontal and four vertical modules, e.g. normalization, similarity discovery, execution (transforms instances from the source ontology into the target ontology), and post-processing. This algorithm uses semantic bridges for concepts and properties, which translate source instances and instance properties into target ones. Such approaches are efficient when there is mutual inconsistency of the two source ontologies. Still, the lack of common reference vocabularies makes the task of finding the accurate mappings impossible. Since it is not a trivial task, there are numerous methods attempting to perform it with highest precision, and at a low cost (Jain, et al., 2011; Lambrix & Tan, 2006; Sabou & Gracia, 2008). Also many automated and semi-automated matching techniques have been developed in the last couple of years (Li, et al., 2009; Jean-Mary & Kabuka, 2009; David, Guillet, & Briand, 2006).

Automated ontology matching approaches are evaluated at the automated matching competitions (OAEI, 2011) that were carried out annually with the purpose of measuring the state of the art in the field. These competitions maintain a few tracks with different evaluation parameters described in more detail in Caracciolo et al. (2008) and Euzenat et al. (2009). One of them, the benchmark track aims to measure the precision rates of the systems. It runs on one particular ontology describing a very precise and narrow subject domain such as bibliography, compared to a number of other ontologies of the same domain for which manual alignments are provided. The best result in this track for the 2009 matching competition was an F-measure value of 80% (Euzenat, et al., 2009). While relatively good, this result is not sufficient for a full interoperability in highly heterogeneous contexts. Extensive surveys of automated ontology matching methods can be found in (Shvaiko & Euzenat, 2005; Shvaiko & Euzenat, 2008).

Automated matching methods are considered the most promising strategy to deal with open environments such as LOD. However, such approaches currently "fail" when it comes to dealing with highly heterogeneous data and high precision requirements.

Achieving a high degree of interoperability, as in the case of a foundational backbone such as the RKS, requires high precision in the matching. That is why we have employed semi-automatic and manual methods in the matching between PROTON, UMBEL and the LOD datasets and schemata. The semi-automatic methods involve a preliminary selection of candidate matching concepts that is done automatically but the ultimate decisions are taken by human experts based on analyzing definitions and comparing the instances assigned to the classes from the two ontologies. In this process the interpretation of the definitions relies on the given supporting examples and not on the interpretations of the human experts.

Another distinction related to ontology matching is based on the type of matching performed.

Mainly, there are syntactic and semantic matching systems. In syntactic matching the relations are computed between labels at nodes and they are evaluated as true or false. In semantic matching the relations are computed between concepts at nodes and they are evaluated as set theoretic relations. The semantic matching discovers semantic relationships across distinct and autonomous generic structures and recognizes relationships between matched entities such as equivalence, subsumption, disjointness and intersection. Harmonizing semantics is one approach to model integration by formally mapping two domains in a heterogeneous context (El-Mekawy & Östman, 2010).

In the approach presented here, we have adopted a semantic matching with reference data from the RKS, harmonized with LOD datasets and schemata as a real provider of interoperability that ensures a certain level of consistency, while preserving their levels of heterogeneity and diversity. Our approach of combining reason-able views and reference data, presents an optimal compromise for managing LOD at the present time, given that the state of the art of the alternative approaches does not meet the reasonability and precision criteria.

The RKS, the approach presented in the next section, is implemented, demonstrated and tested on an extended instance of FactForge (FactForge, 2011).

REFERENCE KNOWLEDGE STACK (RKS)

Achieving interoperability of data coming from dispersed and divergent sources with heterogeneous characteristics is central for making the data usable, optimizing their use and maximizing their value. "Making heterogeneous information interoperable—no matter the format or provenance—is the promise offered by semantic technologies and approaches. The premise of the Semantic Web and the semantic enterprise, respectively, is to provide the languages and methods by which this information can be represented, combined and made meaningful" (Bergman, 2011).

In our view, the means for realizing this vision is through reference data, consisting of interconnected ontologies with different degrees of generality and instance data, together forming a RKS.

Implementing this method will have to impact the LOD management in two aspects:

- The cost of accessing the data;
- The quality of accessing the data.

The importance of reference data for data management in the Web context can be explained by an analogy to forestry. Suppose data is wood and reference data represent beaten paths through the forest. Forests are dynamic and can be considered undetermined, at least to the extent that foresters do not know most of the particular trees so, even in areas they know well, they cannot be certain about the changes that can take place within several months. Forest paths are known reference points and communication facilities, which help with the navigation in the forest, its exploration and, overall, the access to the wood resources. In the same way reference data are well determined, relatively static and predictable data structures that can facilitate access to a diverse and dynamic set of the data as the web of linked data (Grinberg, Damova, & Kiryakov, 2011; Kiryakov, et al., 2011).

However, to access real volumes of wood foresters should, at some point, get off the beaten track and use methods and techniques to explore wild forest areas. Still, beaten paths help exploiting large forests by making it easier to explore them. Reference ontologies and more general reference knowledge structures have the potential to considerably lower the cost of using linked data as well as any dynamic and diverse data collection. Mastering these reference structures and thus ensuring uniformity in the interpretation of the LOD cloud data will pave the way for a next level

of interoperability—the exploration of techniques (statistical or symbolic methods) for dealing with unseen data without which the LOD management is unthinkable and, in a sense, pointless.

Developing the RKS with the methods described further on in this chapter provides a Golden Standard for managing the content on the Web (Bergman, 2011).

LOD and RKS

The concept of the RKS reifies the idea of reference data as an interoperability enabler for the web of data becoming a global giant graph.

The RKS includes upper-level ontologies with different degrees of generality—PROTON, UMBEL, and implicitly OpenCyc—and central datasets of LOD with general common sense knowledge—DBpedia, Freebase, and Geonames. The upper-level ontologies are interlinked together and with the schemata of the LOD datasets. Additionally, UMBEL is directly connected to the instance data of DBpedia and the LOD datasets are interlinked together at the instance level as explained previously in the chapter.

Figure 3 represents the interconnections between the different elements of the RKS.

The elements of RKS are:

- **PROTON** – an upper-level ontology, 542 entity classes and 183 properties, is mapped to UMBEL and separately to the schemata of DBpedia, Freebase and Geonames;
- **UMBEL** – 28,000 concepts extracted from OpenCyc and mapped to DBpedia instances and schema, as well as to PROTON;
- **OpenCyc** – the largest and most comprehensive hand-crafted knowledge base, including 1.6 million statements, which is part of the RKS indirectly via UMBEL;
- **DBpedia** – the RDF-ized version of Wikipedia, comprising the information from Wikipedia infoboxes, designed and developed to provide as full as possible

Figure 3. Reference knowledge stack

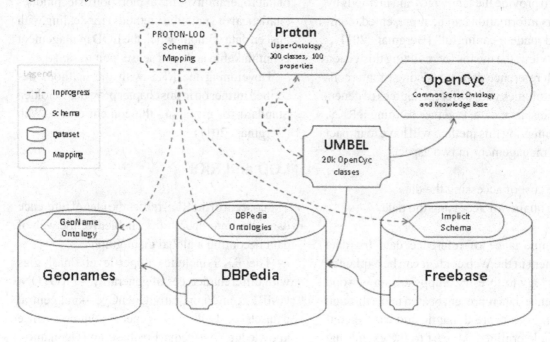

coverage of the factual knowledge that can be extracted from Wikipedia with a high level of precision. DBpedia describes more than 3.5 million things and covers 97 languages. 1.67 million things of DBpedia are classified in a consistent Ontology, including 364,000 persons, 462,000 places, and 99,000 music albums. The DBpedia knowledge base has over 672 million RDF triples out of which 286 million extracted from the English edition of Wikipedia and 386 million extracted from other language editions. DBpedia is interlinked with Geonames and Freebase at the instance level, and with PROTON and UMBEL at the schema level;

- **Freebase** (Freebase, 2011) – a large collaborative knowledge base of structured data from many sources like Wikipedia, Chemoz, NNDB, MusicBrainz and individually contributed data from its users. It has descriptions about over 20 million

topics, described with structured predicate names, which reflect a hidden class hierarchy and no defined ontology. Freebase has an overall of 19,632 predicates, which is constantly increasing. Freebase is interlinked with DBpedia at the instance level, and with PROTON;

- **Geonames** (Geonames, 2011) – a geographic database that covers 6 million of the most significant geographical features on Earth and contains over 8 million geographical names and consists in 7 million unique features whereof 2.6 million populated places and 2.8 million alternate names, integrating geographical data such as names of places in various languages, elevation, population and others from various sources. All lat/long coordinates are in WGS84 (World Geodetic System, 1984). Geonames is interlinked with DBpedia at the instance level and with PROTON at the schema level.

Table 1. Reference knowledge stack elements

Dataset	Size (approx.)	Schema-level Vocabulary	Instance-level vocabulary	Tractable formal semantics
PROTON	500+ concepts	+		+
UMBEL	27,917 classes	+		+
OpenCyc	2 million assertions	+	+	+
DBpedia	700 million assertions		+	
Freebase	500 million assertions		+	+
Geonames	100 million statements	+	+	+

The differences in the characteristics of RKS elements are shown in Table 1. The RKS elements are distinguished with respect to whether they have ontologies, e.g. schema-level vocabulary, instances, e.g. instance-level vocabulary, and allow for reasoning operations, e.g. consistency checking and tractable reasoning Note that not all components of the datasets are part of RKS. For example, DBpedia ontology is not included in the RKS. This is because (it will become clear later on in this chapter) DBpedia instances are directly accessible via the two upper-level ontologies PROTON and UMBEL. These linkages make the loading of DBpedia ontology actually unnecessary, as its instances will be directly accessible through UMBEL and PROTON, and the knowledge base will be efficiently managed without including statements, generated from inferences based on the DBpedia ontology. Freebase does not have a proper class hierarchy. Its classification model is represented in properties, which provide the basis for the tractable formal semantics applied in Freebase. Thus, most of the elements of the RKS have schema-level vocabularies and reliable formal semantics so they allow for consistency checking and tractable reasoning. The instance-level vocabularies ensure the linkages with the other datasets from LOD.

The harmonization between the ontologies of different size (PROTON and UMBEL) allows for an incremental use of the concepts from the more general ontologies to the ontologies with greater number of concepts, clustering the instances in the RKS in a finer grained way. PROTON and UMBEL have reliable formal semantics, which guarantees consistency of the explicit and implicit knowledge. And the consistency of exploring the interconnected datasets in LOD at the instance level is ensured by the linkage of UMBEL to the instances of DBpedia.

The following sections describe the elements of the RKS and the techniques and impacts of their integration in greater detail.

PROTON

PROTON was originally built with a basic subsumption hierarchy comprising about 250 classes and 100 properties, which provide coverage of most of the upper-level concepts necessary for semantic annotation, indexing, and retrieval. Its modular architecture allows for great flexibility of use, extension, integration and remodeling. PROTON is a modular, lightweight, upper-level ontology. It is domain independent and complies with standards in the field like DOLCE (DOLCE, 2011), Cyc (Cycorp, 2011), Dublin Core (Dublin Core, 2011). PROTON is encoded in OWL Lite, and contains a minimal set of custom entailment rules (axioms), which makes it tractable even at a web scale unlike the DOLCE and Cyc.

PROTON has three modules, superposed one to another. They are: (a) SYSTEM module, which contains a few meta-level primitives (6 classes -

`Entity, EntitySource, LexicalRe-source, Alias, systemPrimitive, transitiveOver` and 7 properties). It provides a sort of high-level system or meta-primitives, which are to be adopted by systems intending to use the PROTON ontology. This module cannot be changed or extended; (b) TOP module, which represents the highest, most general, conceptual level and consists of about 20 classes—`Abstract, Agent, ContactInformation, Document, Event, InformationResource, Location, Number, Object, Person, Product,` and `Role`. It defines the basic philosophically-reasoned distinctions between entity types: *Object*—existing entities, as agents, locations, vehicles; *Happening*—events and situations; *Abstract*—abstractions that are neither objects nor happenings, which are then further specialized by substantially real entity types of general importance like person, location, time, money, numbers etc.; (c) UPPER module, which has over 200 general classes of entities all sub-classes of the Top Ontology, and often appearing in multiple domains. Some upper module classes include branches of very specific entities and border at places with domain ontologies, for instance the Concepts Mountain, a specific type of Location and Resource Collection, a specific subclass of Information Resource.

Still, PROTON is a flexible, lightweight upper level all-purpose ontology, which is easy to adopt and extend, built with just a basic subsumption hierarchy and a few axioms, very easy to understand and interpret, and designed according to OntoClean principles. PROTON is widely used in knowledge intensive applications and platforms, such as KIM (KIM Platform, 2011) and GATE (GATE Platform, 2011).

The impacts on its structure and size, when integrated into the RKS and LOD, will be discussed in the Section **'Schema-Level Matching.'**

UMBEL

UMBEL, the Upper Mapping and Binding Exchange Layer (UMBEL 1.0), is a sub-set extraction of OpenCyc, providing the Cyc data in an RDF (Miller, 2004) ontology based on SKOS (Alistair & Bechhofer, 2011), OWL 2 (OWL 2, 2009) and RDFS (Brickley, et al., 2004). Its purpose is to relate Web content and data to a standard set of subject concepts and provide a fixed set of reference points in a global knowledge space. These subject concepts have defined relationships between them, and can act as binding or attachment points for any Web content or data. The actual goal of UMBEL is to provide a set of fixed references by which constituent content can be oriented and navigated. A central role of the UMBEL reference concepts is to provide contexts for relating information, based on OpenCyc.

UMBEL is fully OWL 2 compliant. It has originally 20,000 reference concepts, designed to be both classes (`owl:Class`) and instances of the class umbel: `RefConcept`, and may also sometimes be instances of other reference Concept classes. The UMBEL structure is lightweight and contains about 5-10% of the original size of Cyc, covering its most fundamental concepts, of a tractable set of reference nodes, which maintain 100% consistency with Cyc. All concepts in the UMBEL reference concept ontology are comprehensively organized into 33 SuperTypes, designed to be disjoint and to provide a higher-level of clustering and organization for more convenient use in user interfaces and for reasoning purposes. UMBEL as a reference ontology is not a knowledge base. In its schema it is a Tbox[2] in terms of Description Logic (Description Logic, 2011), establishing the structure used for governing the conceptual relationships in reference to external Web ontologies.

The UMBEL reference concept ontology is itself built upon the UMBEL vocabulary, which is designed to recognize that different sources of information have different contexts and different structures. By nature, these connections are not always exact, thus means for expressing the "approximateness" of relationships are essential. These approximate alignments can be oriented by means of UMBEL's 'Reference Concepts.' By design, these concepts act as fixed reference points broadly applicable as orienting nodes to any knowledge domain, all coherently structured and linked to one another. This lightweight UMBEL Reference Concept ontology is, in essence, a content graph of subject nodes, related to one another via broader-than and narrower-than relations. The reference concepts of the UMBEL ontology are not meant to model the world in all of its complexity and nuance. The UMBEL Vocabulary is itself a solid basis for constructing domain ontologies that can also act as reference ontologies within their domains. The UMBEL Vocabulary defines three "operational" classes: `RefConcept`, `SuperType`, and `Qualifier`; and 38 properties: `correspondsTo`, `isAbout`, `is RelatedTo`, `relatesToXXX` (31 variants), `isLike`, `hasMapping`, `hasCharacteristic`, and `isCharacteristicOf` which have operational role. In addition, UMBEL re-uses certain properties from external vocabularies. These classes and properties are used to instantiate the UMBEL Reference Concept ontology, and to link Reference Concepts to external ontology classes.

The languages used and the design of UMBEL are based on the open world approach. An open world assumption accepts that we never have all information and not having particular information does is not important. So, saying that a concept in an external ontology or information source "is about" a given reference concept in UMBEL does not define or limit what can be said about that external concept in other assertions.

UMBEL alone does not solve the interoperability problem. Rather, it is designed as a useful set of first steps in this direction. The internal UMBEL Reference Concepts may be related to external classes and individuals (instances and named entities) via a set of relational, equivalent, or alignment predicates. This is achieved in the RKS.

The impacts on UMBEL's original structure and size, when integrated into the RKS and LOD, will be discussed in Sections **'Schema-Level Matching** and **Instance-Level Matching.'**

OpenCyc

For the sake of self-sufficiency and consistency, in this section we briefly introduce Cyc (Cycorp, 2011) and its non-proprietary version OpenCyc (OpenCyc, 2011) as an implicit part of RKS. Cyc, developed by Cycorp since the 80s of the XX century, is a very large knowledge base, supplied with multi-contextual knowledge and inference engine. It is designed with the goal of providing the foundation of basic human-like 'common sense' knowledge, which can be used in intelligent, knowledge intense applications. Its main objective is to codify, in machine-usable form, millions of pieces of knowledge that comprise human common sense. Cyc, as the world's largest and most complete general knowledge base and common sense reasoning engine, generates deep level of understanding, which contributes to the flexibility of any application using it. It has developed and uses a special proprietary language to represent entities, relations and rules based on first order predicate logic. Cyc architectural components are:

- A knowledge base and inference engine;
- A natural language processing subsystem;
- A semantic integration bus.

The concepts covered in Cyc describe *individuals*, like concrete people and locations, *collections*, like ontological concepts, *truth functions*, like the Boolean operators, and *functions*, which produce new terms from already existing ones.

The Cyc technology and incorporated knowledge contains more than 155,000 concepts, hundreds of thousands of terms (concepts) and 2.5 million assertions, relating the terms to each other and forming an extensive ontology of human common sense. This ontology encodes subjective rules of thumb along with strictly logical statements. Its powerful inference capabilities rely on hundreds of pattern specific heuristic modules, as well as general, resolution-based theorem proving, to derive new conclusions (deduction) or introduce new hypotheses (abduction) from the assertions. Both forward and backward chaining are supported. It is able to provide complete explanations for its answers, including provenance information. Except for common sense knowledge, highly expert knowledge from the fields of chemistry, biology and the like, as well as linguistic (grammatical and lexical) knowledge complete the spectrum of Cyc's knowledge base. Its knowledge base capabilities can be deeply leveraged in areas like entity extraction, question answering, natural language processing, risk analysis, etc. Cyc structure has been tested and refined through many projects and applications with invested and estimated 1000 person years of engineering. It is a very popular and well-acknowledged resource with supporters in all areas of society. However, its scope is too large to easily comprehend and adopt for typical standard Web purposes. Its sophistication exceeds by far what is tractable for a lightweight reference structure.

OpenCyc is a version of Cyc, which contains the non-proprietary knowledge from Cyc that can be freely accessed and used. OpenCyc consists of millions assertions, facts, schemata and rules which allow to reason with the facts. OpenCyc has an upgrade path to the more capable ResearchCyc, full Cyc and the services of Cycorp, the producer of Cyc. It is published in the LOD cloud, and connected with several of LOD datasets, like DBpedia and Wordnet.

With these fundamental assets, OpenCyc, which is explicitly harmonized with UMBEL, is a natural implicit component of the RKS.

RKS and FactForge

FactForge (FactForge, 2011), the experimental setting of the RKS, is the largest and most heterogeneous body of factual general-purpose knowledge on which inference has been performed. It is a reason-able view, comprising a compound dataset of some of the most popular datasets of the LOD cloud, e.g datasets with general knowledge (DBpedia, Freebase, UMBEL, CIA World Factbook, MusicBrainz, New York Times, Open-Cyc), linguistic knowledge (Wordnet, Lingvoj), geographical knowledge (Geonames). It was designed with the following objectives:

- Consistency with respect to the formal semantics;
- Generality – no specific domain knowledge necessary to be able to comprehend most of the semantics;
- Heterogeneity – should include data from multiple data sources;
- Reasonability with respect to OWL 2 RL (OWL 2, 2009).

FactForge has an overall of 1.4 billion loaded statements, 2.2 billion stored statements and 10 billion retrievable statements. It is developed as an evaluation case in the European research project LarKC (Momchev, 2010) and is used as a testbed for different large scale reasoning experiments like WebPIE (Urbani, 2010). It is available as a free public service at http://factforge.net, offering the following access facilities: (a) incremental URI auto-suggest; (b) one-node-at-a-time exploration through Forest and tabulator linked data browsers; (c) RDF Search: retrieves a ranked list of URIs by keywords; (d) SPARQL end-point. FactForge provides efficient mechanisms to query data from multiple datasets and sources, considering their semantics.

OWLIM (Bishop, et al., 2011) semantic repository is used to load the data and "materialize" the facts that could be inferred from them with forward chaining. The inference during loading is performed with respect to a ruleset, derived from the so-called OWL Horst dialect, (OWL Horst Dialects, 2010), as only OWL Horst-like languages seem to be suitable for reasoning with data in the range of billions of statements.

The connectivity in FactForge is made via DBpedia. To ensure cleaner data, some modifications to DBpedia were made. For instance, the Yago module was removed to avoid incorrect classifications of entities and other faults causing wrong inference and generating plenty of incorrect statements. The category hierarchy of DBpedia has been cleaned up to remove cycles and lexical ambiguities of the category names, and to reduce the number of overgenerating transitive subsumption relations of `skos:broader` (Kiryakov, et al., 2009a, 2009b).

The RKS includes the following FactForge datasets—DBpedia, Freebase and Geonames, ensuring connectivity with the rest of the FactForge datasets via linkages at the instance- level.

The interconnectedness between the elements of the RKS is achieved by using semi-automatic and manual semantic matching methods. The adopted methods of schema-level and instance-level matching are described in the following sections.

RKS Schema-Level Matching

The schema-level matching for the RKS abides by several general principles:

- Extension of the upper-level concepts until an optimal coverage of the data is achieved with respect to the pre-defined scope of the upper-level ontology;
- Uni-directional mapping – making only the more general ontology referable from outside;

- Consistency – adopting the design principles of the upper-ontology in the process of mapping;
- 100% precision – hand-crafted rules and manual verification of automatically derived mappings;
- Consistency checking with reasoners.

The development of this approach is an iterative process of extension and modification.

The following sub-sections describe the mapping of PROTON to DBpedia, Geonames and Freebase, of PROTON to UMBEL, and of UMBEL to DBpedia.

Mapping PROTON to DBpedia, Geonames, and Freebase

Mapping PROTON to DBpedia[3], Geonames[4] and Freebase[5] involves matching ontologies and data structures, built according to different methods and design principles, e.g. data-driven ontologies and an upper-level ontology. Additionally, the ontologies of the FactForge datasets are also designed according to different methodologies. For example, the DBpedia and Geonames ontologies provide structure and semantics to a large amount of entities in a shallow structure, but nevertheless they are very different. The DBpedia ontology includes many ad hoc predicates, which appear in only one or just several statements reflecting the variety of knowledge it covers. It is shallow and counts 24 first level concepts with very different degree of generality, ranging from the philosophical concept of "Event" through "Person" and "Place" to very specific concepts like "Beverage", "Drug", "Protein", etc. Besides the ontology, DBpedia has a compendium of concepts and properties, gathered in a separate namespace – http://dbpedia.org/property. They pertain to ontological dimensions, for example, http://dbpedia.org/property/place, but are not modeled in the ontology. These concepts are used for instances and properties classification purposes and in some cases overlap with concepts and properties already available in DBpedia ontology. These additional concepts and properties are also considered in the mapping process as they give access to more data in DBpedia. The Geonames ontology has a concise conceptualization, organized in very few well-structured concepts and millions of instances. It also incorporates SKOS. Freebase does not have ontology, but a hidden class hierarchy, represented with predicates of the following structure: the leftmost word of the predicate name denotes the subject domain of the property; the middle word denotes a class, which is the domain of the property

denoted by the last rightmost word. For example, government.legislative_session.date_ended or celebrities.romantic_relationship.end_date.

These discrepancies in the source and target ontologies call for special matching methods.

For example, the differences in the design methods of the ontologies to be mapped show cases of structural differences and hidden relations. Figure 4 presents the difference in the conceptualisation of the professions in DBpedia and PROTON.

DBpedia describes the professions as a subclass of the class Person, e.g. refers to the profession with the professional person, whereas PROTON

Figure 4. Mapping of concepts in ontologies designed according to different principles (PROTON, DBpedia)

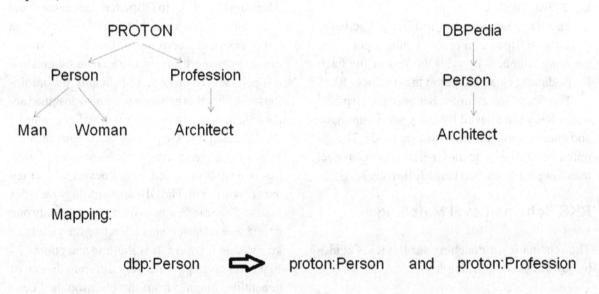

Mapping:

dbp:Person ⟹ proton:Person and proton:Profession

Box 1.

```
DBpedia:Architect rdfs:subClassOf [ rdf:type owl:Restriction ;
                          owl:onProperty proton:hasProfession ;
                          owl:hasValue proton:Architect ] .
```

separates the person from the profession he has, and links the two entities with the property `hasProfession` with `domain:Person` and `range:Profession`. This requires the mapping rule to be between a concept and an expression, see Box 1.

Besides using expressions in the mapping rules, the structural mismatches between the data-driven and the upper-level ontology trigger the need to generate new instances in the knowledge base to fill in the gaps in the diverging representations. For instance, Freebase conceptualises the ownership relation in two steps, as a relation between (a) the object and an act of owning, and (b) the act of owning and a given object, whereas PROTON has a direct predicate linking an owner to the owned object (cf. Figure 5).

This enrichment is specific to the OWLIM repository and takes place at the time of loading the knowledge base into the repository. It is enabled by adding inference rules for forward chaining to its standard owl-max rule set. An example of a rule that handles the discussed mismatch in the representation of the ownership relation is shown in Box 2.

It generates the additional fact a `<ptop:isOwnedBy>` c based on whether the combination of the facts of the premise is availabe.

The need of optimal data coverage described by the data-driven ontology drives the extension of the upper-level ontology. Thus, before drafting the mapping rules between single concepts, new concepts were introduced into PROTON. For example, Geonames has a concept Map, which refers to a webpage of a map. This concept does not exist in PROTON, whereas other types of documents like Report, Contract, etc. do exist. So, abiding by the design principles of completeness and balancing of the upper-ontology, the concept Map were introduced to PROTON. The extension of PROTON was guided by several design principles, e.g.

- Achieving full coverage of DBpedia ontology;
- Preserving the balance of a maximum of three to four levels of depth of the class hierarchy;
- Completing the conceptual domains of the class hierarchy, even if there are no

Figure 5. Conceptual difference involving situations and properties (PROTON, Freebase)

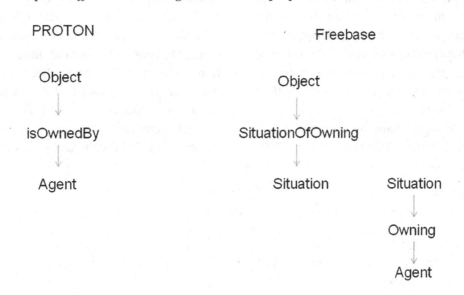

Box 2.

```
Id:owner
  a <fb:visual_art.artwork.owners> b
  b <fb:visual_art.artwork_owner_relationship.owner> c
  ----------------------------------------------------
  a <ptop:isOwnedBy> c
```

identified instances available for a newly introduced concept. For example, the existence of the concept `AirplaneModel` triggers the introduction of the concept `CarModel`, even if there are no specific instances of a `CarModel` in the RKS

To ensure the unidirectionality of the mappings, which guarantees data accessibility through the more general ontology first, all mapping rules between FactForge and PROTON embody subsumption relations, where the FactForge concepts are considered more specific than the PROTON ones, see Box 3.

The alignment of PROTON with DBpedia ontology, Geonames ontology and Freebase was hand crafted. This was deemed as the most suitable approach to finding the exact correspondences of the few upper-level concepts with 100% precision and capturing the hidden relationships and structural mismatches. The matching of the concepts and properties between DBpedia and PROTON, between Geonames and PROTON and between Freebase and PROTON was based on comparing the definitions of the concepts, their use, and their instances.

As a result of the mapping processes a new version of PROTON - PROTON 3.0 - (PRO-

TON3.0, 2011) has been created, which has 542 classes (an increase of about 40% with respect to its original version), 128 Object properties, and 55 Datatype properties. The mappings cover 203 mapped classes to DBpedia; 23 mapped properties to DBpedia; 6 mapped classes to Geonames; 14 mapped properties to Geonames; 382 mapped Geonames Codes; 9 mapped classes to Freebase; and 60 mapped properties to Freebase.

To check the consistency of PROTON and the mappings, they were loaded in TopBraidComposer (TopBraidComposer. Ontology Editor, 2011). This ontology editor loads succesfully only consistent ontologies.

UMBEL to PROTON Mapping: A Semi-Automatic Approach

The mapping between PROTON and UMBEL actualizes the idea of the RKS layered architecture. It takes place at the level of PROTON classes and UMBEL reference concepts ('RefConcepts'), which are connected with the subsumption relation `rdfs:subClassOf`. The linkage here is done from UMBEL to PROTON, where UMBEL is the more specific and PROTON - the more general reference structure, respecting the defined principle of unidirectionality in the schema-

Box 3.

```
FactForge:Concept rdfs:subClassOf PROTON:Concept .
FactForge:Property rdfs:subPropertyOf PROTON:Property .
```

level matching (cf. the beginning of Section **'Schema-Level Matching'**). The mapping shows PROTON to be a straight subset of UMBEL, e.g. all PROTON classes are directly mapped to corresponding UMBEL reference concepts. Hence all corresponding UMBEL reference concepts are referable via PROTON classes.

The mapping between PROTON and UMBEL is done semi-automatically using three categories of Web services:

- Finding Reference Concepts
  This Web service is used to find UMBEL reference concepts that match a search string. This is the primary tool for finding available reference concepts. Semantic vectors (Semantic Vectors, 2011) techniques are used to generate this first linkage between the two vocabularies, based on their labels ('prefLabels,' 'altLabels,' and definitions).
- Visualizing/Exploring Reference Concepts
  - ○ Reference Concept Report
    - ▪ This Web service is used to get basic information about a specific UMBEL reference concept. The information shown in the report is a definition of the reference concept and its semset[6] related to this concept. This semset is an aggregation of different labels with similar meaning that is used in practice to designate the concept.
  - ○ Reference Concept Detailed Report
    - ▪ This service provides detailed information about a specific UMBEL reference concept. The user interface is a special kind of service. It uses all existing UMBEL Web services to create a detailed report about a UMBEL reference concept and its relations to other UMBEL

reference concepts, external ontology classes, and existing named entities from different kinds of data sources.
  - ○ Reference Concepts Explorer
    - ▪ This service is a visualization interface that lets you browse the UMBEL graph of reference concept relationships. You can navigate from one node to another by clicking any of the circles. Each circle is an UMBEL reference concept or an external ontology class.

This service provides the tools to manually evaluate the mapping candidates, obtained from the automatic generation of mapping candidates, and to correct or complete the mappings until reaching full 100% coverage and 100% precision.

Finding the right mapping happens in the following way:

To find the right reference concept class <B> to link to a class <A>, it is necessary to determine the right relation that exists between class <A> and a given reference concept. There are three different relations:

a. Equivalence; `owl:equivalentClass`;
b. Sub-class of; `rdfs:subClassOf`;
c. Unrelated.

Not all relations have the same importance. The reference concept that shares the most important relation with the class <A> will be linked to it. To determine the relation that applies, the following procedure is used:

Do all individuals that belong to the reference concept class <B> also belong to the class <A>?

- If yes, do all individuals that belong to the class <A> also belong to the reference concept class <B>?

- ◦ If yes, then the two classes are equivalent
- ◦ If no, then the reference concept class <B> is a sub-class of class <A>
- If no, do all individuals of the class <A> belong to the reference concept class <B>?
  - ◦ If yes, then the class <A> is a sub-class of the reference concept class <B>
  - ◦ If no, is there a non-empty intersection between the class <A> and the reference concept class <B>?
    - ▪ If yes, then the class <A> is-about the reference concept class <B> given a certain confidence percentage value
    - ▪ If no, there is no relationship between the class <A> and the reference concept class <B>.

Additionally, the description of the class <A> and the reference concept class <B> are read to make sure that both classes share the same semantic meaning. Once the class matching between PROTON and UMBEL is done, e.g. the right reference concept for mapping class <B> to the class <A> is found, one instance for each PROTON class is created and merged with the UMBEL-PROTON ontology, and Pellet 2.2.2 reasoner (Pellet OWL 2 Reasoner for Java, 2011) is run to check if the ontology is consistent with the UMBEL to PROTON linkages. The consistency checking is enforced by the UMBEL SuperTypes disjointness constraints. This step is done to ensure that the UMBEL reference concept structure remains consistent after asserting that the class <A> is related, in some way, to the reference concept class <B>.

The analysis will differ, depending on the kind of relation that exists between class <A> and the reference concept class <B>.

This analysis is based on the OWL 2 DL description of external ontology (PROTON) classes and UMBEL reference concept classes. As we noted in the Section about UMBEL above, we can only conclude things according to what is known (or what is defined in these different ontologies).

UMBEL to DBpedia Ontology Mapping

The mappings between UMBEL and DBpedia are geared to allow any of the constituent ontologies of the RKS or their predicates to be used in conjunction with the other ontologies. UMBEL, at the level of reference concepts, is mapped to DBpedia vocabulary by hand. 272 DBpedia ontology classes are directly mapped to corresponding UMBEL reference concepts with a subsumption relation of `rdfs:subClassOf`, where DBpedia classes are defined as subclasses of UMBEL reference concepts.

Consequently, verification for consistency and satisfiability is done with the Pellet (Pellet OWL 2 Reasoner for Java, 2011) reasoner.

RKS Instance-Level Matching

Instance-level matching is presently the principal method for achieving interconnectedness between the datasets in the LOD cloud. When applied on a large scale, it causes fact explosion, which becomes challenging in real life settings and we need techniques to overcome it. For example, the reason-able view FactForge is built with a series of practical methods, which overcome many of the challenges in managing instance-level connectivity in the LOD cloud. These methods comprise optimizing the handling of the facts, generated by the predicate `owl:sameAs` (Kiryakov, et al., 2009b). They use a specific feature of the BigTRREE engine (Bishop, et al., 2011), implemented in BigOWLIM (OWLIM, 2011). In its indices, each set of equivalent URIs (equivalence class with respect to `owl:sameAs`) is presented by a *single super-node*. So, BigTRREE can still enumerate all statements that should be inferred through the equivalence, but it does not have to inflate its indices. This approach can be considered as a sort of partial materialization. However,

BigOWLIM takes special care to ensure that this trick does not hinder the ability to distinguish explicit from implicit statements. The optimisation allows OWLIM to efficiently handle large datasets, where `owl:sameAs` is extensively used. In the case of FactForge, this technique allows OWLIM to deal with more than 7 billion statements at the computational costs required for 860 million statements.

The next involvement of instances in the RKS is their linkage to upper-level ontologies classes.

Mapping UMBEL to DBpedia and Wikipedia

Given that the upper-level ontologies are to provide consistent reference points for navigating through the data in LOD, they have to be associated with real instances from its datasets. Currently the RKS includes direct linkages between DBpedia instances and UMBEL reference concepts, and between UMBEL referene concepts and Wikipedia pages. Wikipedia, upon which DBpedia is based, has more than a half million categories in the English version alone.

The mapping of UMBEL to DBpedia and Wikipedia consists of assigning UMBEL classes to DBpedia and Wikipedia instances. The mappings at schema-level between DBpedia and UMBEL have been used for that.

Three methods have been employed to link Wikipedia pages (instances) via the DBpedia[7] extraction to the UMBEL reference concept structure:

- In method one, the instances associated with the DBpedia ontology are inherited directly, based on their class mappings to the UMBEL reference concepts. These mappings also receive the rdf:type predicate. Some 659,527 unique pages were linked in this matter, resulting in a total of 876,125 `rdf:type` assignments;

- In method two, which uses Semantic Vectors (Semantic Vectors, 2011), applied to "clean" DBpedia categories, an association file to candidate UMBEL reference concepts with semantic vectors scores is created for every clean DBpedia category. These candidates are then checked and corrected manually. DBpedia instances associated with these categories are then mapped to the UMBEL structure and given a `relatesToXXX` predicate for the reference concepts associated, single ST (SuperType). Because multiple DBpedia instances can be related to different reference concepts, individual DBpedia pages may have been assigned multiple `relatesToXXX` predicates. (If the DBpedia page already had a rdf:type assignment, this would supersede the `relatesToXXX` predicates). With method two, 2,484 unique reference concepts participated in the linkage to 102,956 unique DBpedia pages. A total of 111,470 `relatesToXXX` predicates have been created, based on this method;

- In method three, the Wikipedia categories[8] have been deconstructed to discern their structural composition, largely based on suffix extensions. A script is used to relate by list these DBpedia categories to candidate UMBEL reference concepts. These lists are then presented to human experts for manual correction. Instances related to the assigned DBpedia category are then given the same `relatesToXXX` predicate that was associated with the related UMBEL reference concept. With method three, 1,668 unique reference concepts particated in the linkage to 1,808,782 unique DBpedia pages. A total of 2,947,553 `relatesToXXX` predicates were created, based on this method;

- Lastly, a fourth source, which is not really a method, adds 7,405 Wikipedia instances by virtue of hand-inspected OpenCyc to DBpedia page mappings within the current OpenCyc knowledge base.

All instance mappings are also related to one of 33 UMBEL SuperTypes, e.g. SuperClasses of reference concepts. As a result, the number of UMBEL reference concepts was expanded from 20,512 to 27,917 by 37%.

These are all fully integrated into the UMBEL ontology with one of 33 SuperTypes (ST) assigned.

Across all mappings, 3,527 UMBEL reference concepts are linked directly to Wikipedia (DBpedia). The result is that a total of 2,130,021 unique DBpedia pages are linked to this structure via nearly 4 million predicate relations (3,935,148). All of these pages are also characterized by one or more SuperTypes (STs).

Of these 2 million pages, 876,125 are assigned a specific SuperType via rdf:type; the remaining have a less certain relationship (`relates-ToXXX` predicate). Across all mappings, 60% of all UMBEL reference concepts (or 16,884) are now linked directly to Wikipedia via the new umbel:correspondsTo property. Across all these mappings, nearly 4 million predicate relations (3,935,148) link UMBEL to Wikipedia.

Three major changes to the UMBEL vocabulary and reference concept structure (ontology) are made as the result of this effort.

- The first major change has been to add 7,405 reference concepts to the core UMBEL structure. These additions aim to cover completely the general UMBEL structure in order to provide appropriate linkage points into the ontology. These additions were necessitated after analyzing existing OpenCyc to DBpedia linkages and missing linking concepts due to the DBpedia and GeoNames class mapping activities. This larger "core" UMBEL structure is now felt to be more adequate for ongoing reference

mappings to other external ontologies into the future;

- The second major change has been to add 31 new predicates to the UMBEL vocabulary to represent a linkage relationship to a SuperType. All these predicates have the form `relatesToXXX`, for instance `relatesToAbstraction`, `relatesToActivity`, `relatesToAnimal`, etc. The predicate indicates that the object instance has a relation to the SuperType, perhaps as a true class member or perhaps only as an attribute, but that the degree of this relationship cannot be resolved;
- The third major change has been to apply the UMBEL hasMapping predicate to all of the possible assignments, using a controlled vocabulary for characterizing the mapping assignment.

The criteria for deciding about adding of these close to 8 thousand concepts have been based on the twin interest to: a) have UMBEL provide a coherent ontology related to Wikipedia; b) have UMBEL RCs be a faithful subset of Cyc concepts.

Experiments

Implementing RKS, the mappings and verifying their effects requires placing them in a real use setting. This section outlines the performed experiments of loading and accessing LOD through the RKS in a new instance of FactForge in OWLIM, giving performance statistics and query designs.

Data Loading

The matching at the schema-level has very important impacts—both on the size of the RKS and on FactForge in general. The creation of a new instance of FactForge, including the mappings of PROTON to the FactForge datasets schemata described in the previous sections, results in the generation of many new implicit statements,

Table 2. Loading of PROTON to FactForge mappings into FactForge

Number of Statements	FactForge	FactForge with PROTON 2.0	Difference
Statements	1,782,541,506	2,630,453,334	847,911,828
Explicit Statements	1,143,317,531	1,942,349,578	799,032,047
Entities	354,635,159	404,798,593	50,163,434

derived from the inferencing through forward chaining and the full materialization after loading data into OWLIM. Including the mappings of UMBEL to DBpedia schema and DBpedia and Wikipedia instances into FactForge also gives a large number of additional implicit statements.

The loading of PROTON to FactForge mappings produces close to 850M additional statements (cf. Table 2); whereas the loading of UMBEL to FactForge produces about 37M new statements (cf. Table 3).

This difference in the generated implicit statements in the loading of PROTON and UMBEL mappings separately is due to the following reasons:

- PROTON has a relatively small class hierarchy, but also defines properties with domains and ranges, which imply inferences;
- UMBEL is designed as a class hierarchy with a large number of concepts aiming to present a Golden Standard for referencing content on the Web, which implies fewer inferences;
- UMBEL provides explicit mapping to DBpedia and Wikipedia instances, which also reduces the number of inferences;
- PROTON mapping approach includes new instance generation, and extends the

FactForge knowledge base at the time of loading when full materialization with forward chaining is performed to cope with the structural differences between the matched ontologies;
- PROTON mappings presently cover DBpedia, Geonames and Freebase schemata, whereas UMBEL mappings cover DBpedia schema only.

Data Access

Being able to obtain useful information from LOD by combining knowledge and facts from different datasets is one of the central goals of this initiative. MacManus in (MacManus, 2010) formulates one exemplar test for the Semantic Web. He introduces a conceptual query about cities around the world that have "Modigliani art works," and claims that the vision of the Semantic Web will be realized when an engine would be able to return a useful answer to it. To our knowledge FactForge is the only engine capable of passing this test as it provides with the infrastructure to retrieve the answer to this question, which can be found in LOD, where different facts about the artist, his artworks and the Museums or galleries that host them are placed in different datasets.

Table 3. Loading of UMBEL to FactForge mappings into FactForge

Number of Statements	FactForge	FactForge with UMBEL 1.0	Difference
Statements	1,749,085,942	1,785,722,627	36,636,685
Explicit Statements	1,356,586,824	1,387,718,322	31,131,498
Entities	382,074,688	387,579,810	5,505,122

Query 1.

```
PREFIX fb: <http://rdf.freebase.com/ns/>
PREFIX DBpedia: <http://DBpedia.org/resource/>
PREFIX dbp-prop: <http://DBpedia.org/property/>
PREFIX dbp-ont: <http://DBpedia.org/ontology/>
PREFIX umbel-sc: <http://umbel.org/umbel/sc/>
PREFIX rdf: <http://www.w3.org/1999/02/22-rdf-syntax-ns#>
PREFIX ot: <http://www.ontotext.com/>
SELECT DISTINCT ?painting_l ?owner_l ?city_fb_con ?city_db_loc ?city_db_cit
WHERE {
          ?p fb:visual_art.artwork.artist
                           DBpedia:Amedeo_Modigliani ;
             fb:visual_art.artwork.owners [
                fb:visual_art.artwork_owner_relationship.owner ?ow ] ;
                ot:preferredLabel ?painting_l.
          ?ow ot:preferredLabel ?owner_l .
          OPTIONAL { ?ow fb:location.location.containedby
                        [ ot:preferredLabel ?city_fb_con ] }
          OPTIONAL { ?ow dbp-prop:location ?loc.
                       ?loc rdf:type umbel-sc:City ;
                           ot:preferredLabel ?city_db_loc }
          OPTIONAL { ?ow dbp-ont:city [ ot:preferredLabel ?city_db_cit ] }
}
```

Figure 6. Results of the Modigliani test

SPARQL Query

Results for PREFIX fb: <http://rdf.fr... (12)   View as Exhibit   Download in JSON | SPARQL Results in XML | SPARQL Results in JSON

painting_l	owner_l	city_fb_con	city_db_loc	city_db_cit
Head@en	Museum of Modern Art	Manhattan		
Head@en	Museum of Modern Art	New York City		
Anna Zborowska@en	Museum of Modern Art	Manhattan		
Anna Zborowska@en	Museum of Modern Art	New York City		
Portrait of Diego Rivera@en	The São Paulo Museum of Art@en		Sao Paulo@en	
Portrait of Diego Rivera@en	The São Paulo Museum of Art@en		São Paulo	
Woman with a Necklace@en	School of the Art Institute of Chicago@en			Chicago
Portrait of a Woman@en	School of the Art Institute of Chicago@en			Chicago
Reclining Nude@en	Museum of Modern Art	Manhattan		
Reclining Nude@en	Museum of Modern Art	New York City		
Madam Pompadour@en	School of the Art Institute of Chicago@en			Chicago
Jeanne Hébuterne@en	Barnes Foundation@en	Philadelphia		

Query 2.

```
PREFIX DBpedia: <http://DBpedia.org/resource/>
PREFIX rdf: <http://www.w3.org/1999/02/22-rdf-syntax-ns#>
PREFIX ot: <http://www.ontotext.com/>
PREFIX ptop: <http://proton.semanticweb.org/protont#>
PREFIX p-ext: <http://proton.semanticweb.org/protonue#>
SELECT DISTINCT ?painting ?owner ?city
WHERE {
        ?p p-ext:author DBpedia:Amedeo_Modigliani ;
           p-ext:ownership [ ptop:isOwnedBy ?ow ] ;
         ot:preferredLabel ?painting .
        ?ow ot:preferredLabel ?owner .
      ?ow ptop:locatedIn [  rdf:type ploc:City ;
                            ot:preferredLabel ?city].

    }
```

The SPARQL (Prud'hommeaux, & Seaborne, 2008) query written for the standard version of FactForge[9] uses predicates from 5 datasets, and three OPTIONAL statements to cover the different predicates that would retrieve the locations of Modigliani paintings (see Query 1).

The results, shown in Figure 6, have the locations of the museums with Modigliani artwork, displayed in three columns corresponding to the three OPTIONAL location predicates from the SPARQL query.

The approach presented in this chapter provides evidence for an easier access to the data by allowing the formulation of simpler structured queries, where single predicates from the reference ontology refer to multiple predicates from different LOD schemata.

The SPARQL query given in Query 2[10], using PROTON predicates only, returns the same results as the FactForge standard SPARQL query, but is presented in a more intuitive and user friendly way with all locations placed in one single column.

Its practical advantages of using predicates from the reference layer are that

- One does not need to search through the vast majority of predicates defined in both DBpedia and Freebase or other datasets in FactForge or LOD;
- There is no need of multiple optional patterns because the most popular variations of "located in" relationships form Freebase and DBpedia are all mapped to a single PROTON predicate;
- The query is easier to define and understand.

This discussion shows that the advantages of having intermediary layers and a single access point to the LOD cloud are:

- Simpler queries;
- Leveraged query results.

Their role of providing consistency and reason-ability in navigating the data is to be further explored and proven experimentally in the future.

USE CASES

In what follows, three use cases will present the important advantages the RKS provides. These are: a) a real life application, Semantic Knowledge Base, developed for The National Archive (TNA, 2011) based on the idea of the RKS; b) an interface between external technologies such as the formal analysis of queries in natural language and a rich semantic knowledge base, represented by FactForge; c) a Golden Standard for testing advanced automated matching approaches

Semantic Knowledge Base for the National Archive

The methodology of the RKS presented in this chapter has been applied in the design of the semantic knowledge base of The National Archive. The access to knowledge from several structured sources (databases, XML files and file directories) and unstructured sources (archive documents), has been provided by a model integrating PROTON

with the Central Government Ontology (CGO, 2011). This was done by a Semantic Knowledge Base Ontology designed especially for the purpose and by building a reason-able view with all archive data, based on this model. This reason-able view contains close to 11,5 billion explicit and implicit statements with links to LOD data. Figure 7 shows the results from a query about the websites and roles of ministerial and non ministerial departments and the information from FactForge about them, where the query is formulated with Semantic Knowledge Base Ontology predicates only.

Natural Language Querying of a Triple Store via Reference Knowledge Stack

The RKS provides interoperability and consistency enabling knowledge intense applications. An evidence for this is another extension of the FactForge service allowing the formulation of queries in natural language, which get translated into SPARQL, and return results federated from the multiple datasets of FactForge (cf. Figure 8

Figure 7. Results from the semantic knowledge base of the national archive

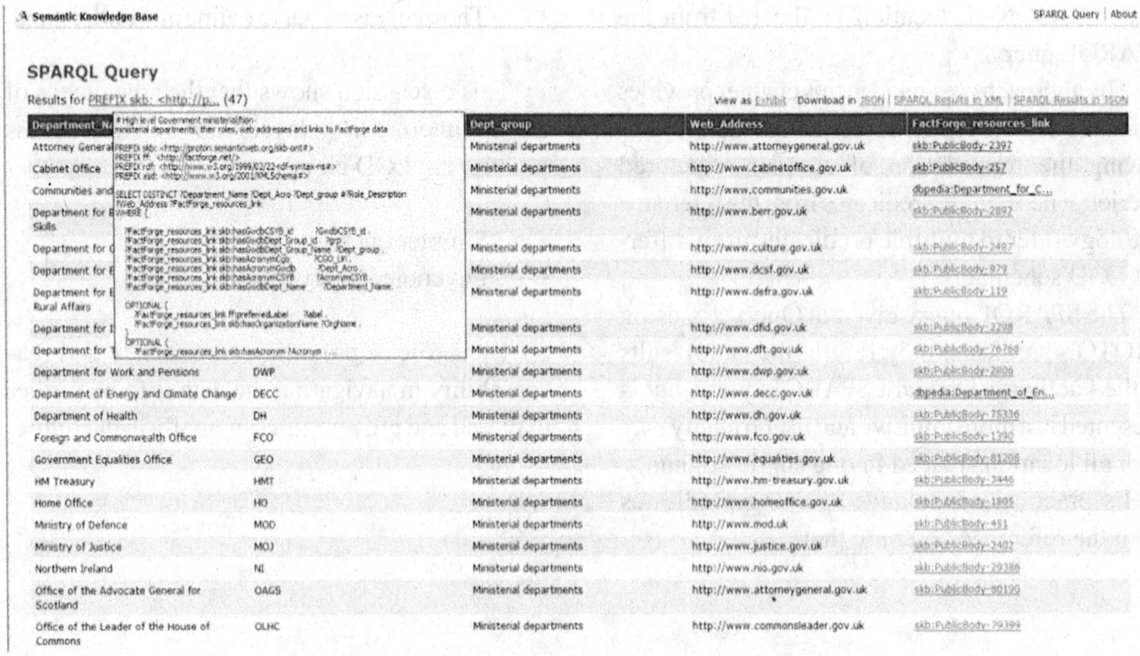

Figure 8. Query in natural language about organizations and their locations

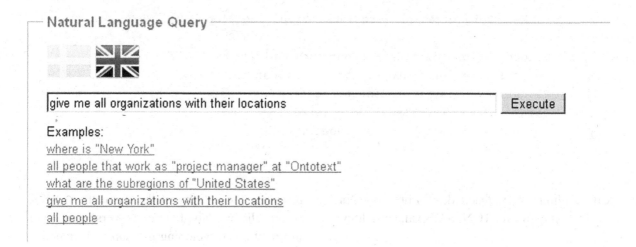

Figure 9. Results of a natural language query about organizations and their locations from FactForge

Natural Language Query
Results for SELECT DISTINCT ?organiza...
Download in JSON | SPARQL Results in XML | SPARQL Results in JSON

organization	organization_label	location	location_label
http://dbpedia.org/resource/Au...	Audi AG@en	http://dbpedia.org/resource/Zw...	Zwickau@en
http://dbpedia.org/resource/Au...	Audi@en	http://dbpedia.org/resource/Zw...	Zwickau@en
http://dbpedia.org/resource/Ap...	Apple Inc.@en	http://dbpedia.org/resource/Cu...	Cupertino, California@en
http://dbpedia.org/resource/AO...	AOL Inc.@en	http://dbpedia.org/resource/Vi...	Vienna, Virginia@en
http://dbpedia.org/resource/AO...	Aol@en	http://dbpedia.org/resource/Vi...	Vienna, Virginia@en
http://dbpedia.org/resource/AO...	AOL@en	http://dbpedia.org/resource/Vi...	Vienna, Virginia@en
http://dbpedia.org/resource/Ad...	Adobe Systems@en	http://dbpedia.org/resource/Mo...	Mountain View, California@en
http://dbpedia.org/resource/Cr...	Crandall University@en	http://dbpedia.org/resource/Mo...	Moncton@en
http://dbpedia.org/resource/Ar...	Arizona Cardinals@en	http://dbpedia.org/resource/Gl...	Glendale, Arizona@en
http://dbpedia.org/resource/Ar...	Arizona Cardinals@en	http://dbpedia.org/resource/Un...	University of Phoenix Stadium@en

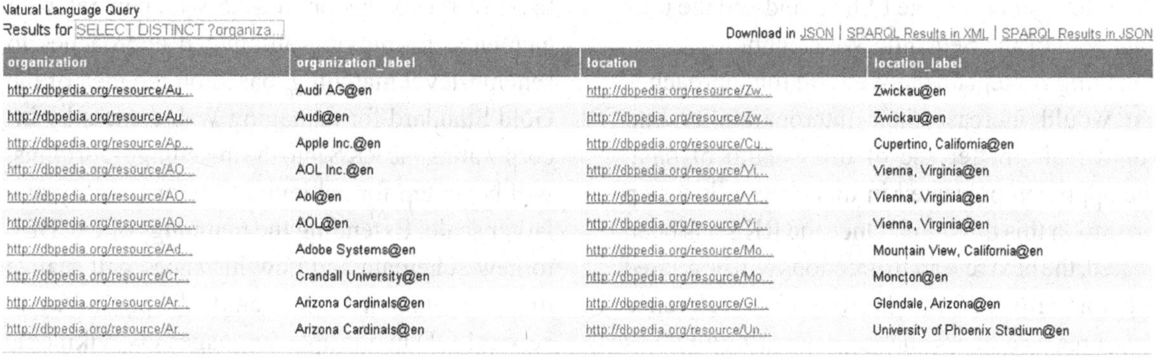

and Figure 9) (Mitankin & Ilchev, 2010; Damova, 2011).

This approach builds on RKS as the transformation of the formal natural language representation into SPARQL and makes use of PROTON predicates only (see the SPARQL query about organizations and their locations in Query 3).

Reference Ontologies: A Golden Standard for Automated Ontology Matching Approaches

Because of the methods applied to building the RKS the schema-level and instance-level mappings are of very high quality. That is why the RKS can play the role of a Golden Standard for automated ontology matching approaches. The PROTON to FactForge datasets mappings of the RKS have been preferred as an evaluation set for the BLOOMS+ system (Jain, et al., 2011), because it was created by an independent source for a real world use case by knowledge engineers through a systematic process, hence their high quality and coverage of a diverse set of ontologies. The evaluation results of BLOOMS+ showed precision rates higher than the state of the art of automated ontology matching systems tested at the last, 2010, annual Automated Ontology Matching

Query 3.

```
SELECT DISTINCT ?organization ?org_label ?location ?loc_label WHERE
{
        ?organization rdf:type protontop:Organization .
        ?organization protontop:locatedIn ?location .
        ?location rdf:type protontop:Location .
        ?organization rdfs:label ?org_label .
        ?location rdfs:label  ?loc_label .
}
```

Competitions. They reached 90% precision for the matching of PROTON to DBpedia ontology.

FUTURE RESEARCH DIRECTIONS

The heterogeneity of the LOD cloud and the ultimate goal of the Semantic Web technologies for managing content on the Web call for approaches that would increase their interoperability and would make better use of this wealth of data. The approach presented in this chapter is a step forward in this direction. Once the RKS has been created, the next research directions will be related to empirically validate the role of the reference structures as a backbone for navigating LOD as a global giant graph. This necessarily includes experiments with the two layered approach to data access both by human and computers, querying and then evaluating its impact, as a basis for semantic search and reasoning within LOD and for data analytics. It was pointed out that RKS creates pathways to ease the navigation of the LOD cloud, but what remains unanswered is how these pathways will match with the inherent diversity of the heterogeneous datasets of LOD. That is why a natural future research direction will be analyzing the diversity tolerance of RKS and discovers appropriate measures to help identifying diversity in LOD cloud. This could be done by identifying the boundaries between compatible or incompatible LOD clusters, and assessing the validity of the elements of RKS, seen as the overlap of various diverse sources of information. Developing measures of diversity, by defining similarity metrics between the reference data and the external data, giving rise to a quantitative evaluation of diversity is expected to allow the extension of RKS with new relevant elements. Employing automated approaches to schema-level matching, based on the idea of the Gold Standard for managing Web content by incorporating the RKS into the matching algorithms, will be a step for achieving interoperability at a larger scale. Extending the mappings of UMBEL to new schemata and new instances will realize the Gold Standard, and include the possibility to access LOD in multiple languages via Wikipedia and Wordnet. Developing methods for identifying unclean and inconsistent data throughout various datasets will contribute to improving the quality of the data in LOD. And finally, developing approaching to maintain the RKS in the context of dynamic modification of the LOD datasets that are part of it is a very important point for maintaining the relevance of the reference structures advances in this chapter.

CONCLUSION

LOD expand rapidly. The publishers of linked data on the Web increase, and publishing standards are being established and constantly improved. The fundamental issues of managing and making practical use of these vast amounts of heterogeneous data remain central for the success of the LOD initiative, and for the wide adoption of Semantic Web technologies in real world applications.

Part of the focus of this chapter was the role of interoperability in dealing with the challenges of LOD as the principal future form of web content. Another part was the design and creation of reference structures like RKS, aimed at being an essential reference backbone of LOD. Such reference structures consist of interconnected ontologies with different degrees of generality and inclusion of instance data from the central datasets of LOD. In the case of RKS, these ontologies are the reference ontologies PROTON and UMBEL, the FactForge ontologies DBpedia, Geonames and Freebase, and the instances from DBpedia. The introduction of PROTON and UMBEL and the mapping between them and the rest of the datasets in RKS is the main contribution of the chapter.

Our approach, following the general framework of creating instances of reason-able views of the data on the web, looks promising for solving the problem of navigating and accessing the large amounts of highly heterogeneous data available on the Web. The latter has been demonstrated by designing and building two reference ontologies—PROTON and UMBEL—and by integrating them into the biggest and most heterogeneous body of general knowledge on which inference has ever been performed—FactForge.

The result of the effort, presented in the chapter, is an innovative and efficient method for managing LOD, a reliable referential infrastructure, which enables the navigation throughout the web of data and reaches a very high level of interoperability between the datasets.

It was shown, that the reference structures we described can be succesfully used in the development of semi-automatic and fully automatic approaches to handle LOD. Such approaches will enable the easy adoption of linked data into new subject domains and will increase the extendability of the reference structures to new LOD datasets.

ACKNOWLEDGMENT

The authors would like to gratefully acknowledge the support of the FP7 EC projects LarKC FP7-ICT-215535, RENDER FP7-ICT-2009-5, Contract no.: 257790, and MOLTO FP7-ICT-247914 for the work presented in this chapter.

REFERENCES

Alistair, M., & Bechhofer, S. (2011). *SKOS.* Retrieved from http://www.w3.org/TR/skos-reference/skos.html.

Auer, S., Bizer, C., Kobilarov, G., Lehmann, J., Cyganiak, R., & Ives, Z. (2007). DBpedia: A nucleus for a web of open data. *Lecture Notes in Computer Science, 4825,* 722–735. doi:10.1007/978-3-540-76298-0_52

Bergman, M. K. (2010). *Bridging the gaps: Adaptive approaches to data interoperability.* Retrieved from http://www.dublincore.org/workshops/dc2010/DC-2010_20101022_Bergman_keynote.pdf.

Bergman, M. K. (2011). *Seeking a semantic web sweet spot.* Retrieved from http://www.mkbergman.com/946/seeking-a-semantic-web-sweet-spot.

Bergman, M. K., & Giasson, F. (2011). *UMBEL full specification.* Retrieved from http://www.umbel.org/specifications/full-specification.

Berners-Lee, T. (2006). *Design issues: Linked data.* Retrieved from http://www.w3.org/DesignIssues/LinkedData.html.

Bio2RDF. (2011). *Webpage*. Retrieved http://bio2rdf.org/.

Bing. (2011). *Bing Google Yahoo*. Retrieved from http://www.bing.com/community/site_blogs/b/search/archive/2011/06/01/bing-google-and-yahoo-unite-to-build-the-web-of-objects.aspx?form=MFEHPG&publ=TWITTER&crea=TEXT_MFEHPG_SM0602_cc0602_TW006_1x.

Bishop, B., Kiryakov, A., Ognyanoff, D., Peikov, I., Tashev, Z., & Velkov, R. (2011). OWLIM: A family of scalable semantic repositories. In P. Hitzler (Ed.), *Semantic Web Journal*. Retrieved from http://www.semantic-web-journal.net.

Bizer, C., Heath, T., & Berners-Lee, T. (2009). Linked data – The story so far. *International Journal on Semantic Web and Information Systems*, *5*(3). doi:10.4018/jswis.2009081901

Bouquet, P., Giunchiglia, F., van Harmelen, F., Serafini, L., & Stuckenschmidt, H. (2003). C-OWL: Contextualizing ontologies. In *Proceedings of ISWC, 2003*, 164–179.

Brickley, D., & Guha, R. V. (2004). *RDF vocabulary description language 1.0: RDF schema*. W3C Recommendation 10 February 2004. Retrieved from http://www.w3.org/TR/rdf-schema/.

Caracciolo, C., Euzenat, J., Hollink, L., Ichise, R., Isaac, A., & Malaisé, V. … Sváte, V. (2008). Results of the ontology alignment evaluation initiative 2008. In *Proceedings of the CEUR Workshop 431*. Karlsruhe, Germany: CEUR Press.

Choi, N., Song, I.-Y., & Han, H. (2006). A survey of ontology mapping. *SIGMOD Record*, *35*(3), 34–41. doi:10.1145/1168092.1168097

CIA. (2011). *The world factbook*. Retrieved from https://www.cia.gov/library/publications/the-world-factbook/.

Clarkparsia. (2011). *Pellet OWL 2 reasoner for Java*. Retrieved from http://clarkparsia.com/pellet.

CYC. (2011). *Cycorp: OpenCyc*. Retrieved from http://www.cyc.com/cyc/opencyc.

Damova, M. (2011). *D4.2 data models, alignment methodology, tools and documentation*. Retrieved from http://www.molto-project.eu/workplan/deliverables.

David, J., Guillet, F., & Briand, H. (2006). *Matching directories and OWL ontologies with AROMA*. Retrieved from http://exmo.inrialpes.fr/people/jdavid/publies/JDavid_CIKM_2006.pdf.

DBpedia. (2011). *Webpage*. Retrieved from http://DBpedia.org.

Description Logic. (2011). *Wikipedia entry*. Retrieved March 2011, from http://en.wikipedia.org/wiki/Description_logic.

Doan, A., Madhavan, J., Domingos, P., & Halevy, A. (2003). Learning to map between ontologies on the semantic web. *VLDB Journal*. Retrieved from http://pages.cs.wisc.edu/~anhai/papers/glue-vldbj.pdf.

DOLCE. (2011). *Webpage*. Retrieved from http://www.loa-cnr.it/DOLCE.html.

Dublin Core. (2011). *Webpage*. Retrieved from http://dublincore.org/documents/dces/.

El-Mekawy, M., & Östman, A. (2010). Mapping: An ontology engineering method for integrating building models in IFC and CITYGM. In *Proceedings of the 3rd ISDE Digital Earth Summit*. Nessebar, Bulgaria: ISDE Press.

Euzenat, J., Ferrara, A., Hollink, L., Isaac, A., Joslyn, C., & Malaisé, V. … Wang, S. (2009). Results of the ontology alignment evaluation initiative 2009. In *Proceedings of the 4th Ontology Matching Workshop at ISWC 2009*. Washington, DC: ISWC Press.

FactForge. (2011). *Webpage*. Retrieved from http://factforge.net, http://www.ontotext.com/factforge.

Freebase. (2011). *Webpage.* Retrieved from http://www.freebase.com/.

GATE. (2011). *Platform.* Retrieved from http://gate.ac.uk/.

Geonames. (2011). *Webpage.* Retrieved from http://www.geonames.org.

Google. (2011). *Semantic vectors.* Retrieved from http://code.google.com/p/semanticvectors/.

Grinberg, M., Damova, M., & Kiryakov, A. (2011). *D1.2.1: Initial data integration.* Sofia, Bulgaria: Project RENDER.

Guarino, N., & Welty, C. (2002). Evaluating Ontological Decisions with OntoClean. *Communications of the ACM, 45*(2), 61–65. doi:10.1145/503124.503150

Heath, T., & Bizer, C. (2011). Linked data: Evolving the web into a global data space. *Synthesis Lectures on the Semantic Web, 1*(1), 1–136. doi:10.2200/S00334ED1V01Y201102WBE001

Horst Dialects, O. W. L. (2010). *Webpage.* Retrieved from http://www.ontotext.com/inference/rdfs_rules_owl.html.

Jain, P., Hitzler, P., Sheth, A. P., Verma, K., & Yeh, P. Z. (2010). Ontology alignment for linked open data. In Y. P. P. Patel-Schneider (Ed.), *Proceedings of the 9th International Semantic Web Conference.* Shanghai, China: IEEE Press.

Jain, P., Hitzler, P., Yeh, P. Z., Verma, K., & Sheth, A. P. (2010). Linked data is merely more data. In Brickley, V. K. D. (Ed.), *Linked Data Meets Artificial Intelligence* (pp. 82–86). New York, NY: AAAI Press.

Jain, P., Yeh, P. Z., Verma, K., Vasquez, R. G., Damova, M., Hitzler, P., & Sheth, A. P. (2011). Contextual ontology alignment of LOD with an upper ontology: A case study with Proton. In G. Antoniou (Ed.), *Proceedings of 8th Extended Semantic Web Conference.* Heraklion, Crete: IEEE Press.

Jean-Mary, Y., & Kabuka, M. (2009). *ASMOV: Ontology alignment with semantic validation.* Retrieved from http://ebookbrowse.com/asmov-ontology-alignment-with-semantic-validation-pdf-d73258878.

KIM. (2011). *Platform.* Retrieved from http://www.ontotext.com/kim.

Kiryakov, A., Grinberg, M., Damova, M., & Russo, D. (2011). *D.D1.1.1: Initial collection of data.* Sofia, Bulgaria: Project RENDER.

Kiryakov, A., & Momtchev, V. (2009). *Two reason-able views to the web of linked data.* Paper presented at the Semantic Technology Conference. San Jose, CA.

Kiryakov, A., Ognyanoff, D., Velkov, R., Tashev, Z., & Peikov, I. (2009). LDSR: Materialized reason-able view to the web of linked data. In R. H. Patel-Schneider (Ed.), *Proceedings of OWLED 2009.* Chantilly, VA: OWED Press.

Kiryakov, A., Tashev, Z., Ognyanoff, D., Velkov, R., Momtchev, V., Balev, B., & Peikov, I. (2009). *D5.5.2: Validation goals and metrics for the LarKC platform.* Sofia, Bulgaria: Project RENDER.

Lambrix, P., & Tan, H. (2006). SAMBO-A system for aligning and merging biomedical ontologies. *Web Semantics, 4*(3).

Li, J., Tang, J., Li, Y., & Luo, Q. (2009). RiMOM: A dynamic multistrategy ontology alignment framework. *IEEE Transactions on Knowledge and Data Engineering, 21*(8), 1218–1232. doi:10.1109/TKDE.2008.202

Linked Data. (2011). *Linking open data.* Retrieved http://linkeddata.org/.

Linked Life Data. (2011). *Webpage.* Retrieved from http://linkedlifedata.com.

MacManus, R. (2010). *The Modigliani test: The semantic web's tipping point.* Retrieved April 2010, from http://www.readwriteweb.com/archives/the_modigliani_test_semantic_web_tipping_point.php.

Manola, F., & Miller, E. (2004). *RDF primer.* W3C Recommendation. Retrieved from http://www.w3.org/TR/rdf-primer/.

Masolo, C., Borgo, S., Gangemi, A., Guarino, N., & Oltramari, A. (2003). *Ontology library (final).* Retrieved from http://www.loa-cnr.it/Publications.html.

McGuinness, D., & van Harmelen, F. (2004). *Web ontology language overview.* W3C Recommendation. Retrieved from http://www.w3.org/TR/owl-features/.

Mitankin, P., & Ilchev, A. (2010). *D 4.1: Knowledge representation infrastucture.* Retrieved from http://www.molto-project.eu/workplan/deliverables.

Momchev, V., Assel, M., Cheptsov, A., Bishop, B., Bradesko, L., & Fuchs, C. … Tagni, G. (2010). *D5.5.3: Report on platform validation and recommendation for next version.* Retrieved from http://www.larkc.eu.

MusicBrainz. (2011). *Community music database.* Retrieved from http://musicbrainz.org.

New York Time. (2011). *Linked open data.* Retrieved from http://data.nytimes.com/.

Niles, I., & Pease, A. (2001). Towards a standard upper ontology. In E. C. Welty & B. Smith (Eds.), *Proceedings of the 2nd International Conference on Formal Ontology in Information Systems (FOIS-2001).* Ogunquit, ME: IEEE Press.

OAEI. (2011). *Webpage.* Retrieved from http://oaei.ontologymatching.org/.

OpenCyc. (2011). *Webpage.* Retrieved from http://www.cyc.com/opencyc.

OWL 2. (2009). *Webpage.* Retrieved from http://www.w3.org/TR/owl2-overview/.

OWLIM. (2011). *Webpage.* Retrieved from http://www.ontotext.com/owlim.

Princeton. (2011). *Wordnet.* Retrieved from http://wordnet.princeton.edu/.

PROTON 3.0. (2011). *PROTON 3.0 documentation.* Sofia, Bulgaria: Ontotext.

Prud'hommeaux, E., & Seaborne, A. (2008). *SPARQL query language for RDF.* W3C Recommendation 15 January 2008. Retrieved from http://www.w3.org/TR/rdf-sparql-query/.

Sabou, M., & Gracia, G. (2008). Spider: Bringing non-equivalence mappings to OAEI. In *Proceedings of the 3rd Ontology Matching Workshop (OM 2008), at 7th International Semantic Web Conference (ISWC 2008),* (pp. 199-205). Karlsruhe, Germany: CEUR-WS.

Shvaiko, P., & Euzenat, J. (2005). A survey of schema-based matching approaches. *Journal of Data Semantics, 4,* 146–171.

Shvaiko, P., & Euzenat, J. (2008). Ten challenges for ontology matching. In *Proceedings of ODBASE,* (pp. 1164-1182). ODBASE Press.

Siegel, N., Goolsbey, K., Kahlert, R., & Matthews, G. (2004). The Cyc® system: Notes on architecture. In *Proceedings of the AAAI Spring Symposium on Formalizing and Compiling Background Knowledge and Its Applications to Knowledge Representation and Question Answering,* (vol 3864), (pp. 44-49). AAAI Press.

Silva, N., & Rocha, J. (2003). MAFRA – An ontology mapping framework for the semantic web. In *Proceedings of the 6th International Conference on Business information Systems*. Colorado Springs, CO: UCCS.

Simple Knowledge Organization System. (2011). *Webpage*. Retrieved from http://www.w3.org/2004/02/skos/.

SKB. (2011). *Webpage*. Retrieved from http://skb.ontotext.com.

Stanford. (1998). *KIF*. Retrieved from http://logic.stanford.edu/kif/.

Stanford. (2009). *First order predicate logic*. Retrieved from http://plato.stanford.edu/entries/logic-classical/.

State of the LOD Cloud. (2011). *Webpage*. Retrieved from http://www4.wiwiss.fu-berlin.de/lodcloud/state.

Studer, R., Benjamin, V. R., & Fensel, D. (1998). Knowledge engineering: Principles and methods. *IEEE Transactions on Data and Knowledge Engineering, 25*(1-2), 161–199.

SUMO. (2011). *Webpage*. Retrieved from http://www.ontologyportal.org/.

SWEO. (2011). *Webpage*. Retrieved http://www.w3.org/2001/sw/sweo/.

Terziev, I., Kiryakov, A., & Manov, D. (2005). *D.1.8.1: Base upper-level ontology (BULO) guidance*. Deliverable of EU-IST Project IST – 2003 – 506826 SEKT. Retrieved from http://www.sekt-project.com.

TNA. (2011). *Webpage*. Retrieved from http://www.nationalarchives.gov.uk/.

TopBraidComposer. (2011). *Ontology editor*. Retrieved from http://www.topquadrant.com/products/TB_Composer.html.

UK Government. (2011). *CGO*. Retrieved from http://data.gov.uk.

UMBEL. (2011). *Webpage*. Retrieved from http://www.umbel.org/.

UMBEL 3.0. (2011). *Webpage*. Retrieved from http://umbel.org/content/finally-umbel-v-100.

Urbani, J., Kotoulas, S., Maassen, J., Drost, N., Seinstra, F., van Harmelen, F., & Bal, H. (2010). *WebPIE: A web-scale parallel inference engine*. Retrieved from http://www.few.vu.nl/~jui200/papers/ccgrid-scale10.pdf.

URI. (2011). *Wikipedia article*. Retrieved from http://en.wikipedia.org/wiki/Uniform_Resource_Identifier.

Wikipedia. (2011a). *Master data*. Retrieved from http://en.wikipedia.org/wiki/Master_data as of January 2011.

Wikipedia. (2011b). *Reference data*. Retrieved from http://en.wikipedia.org/wiki/Reference_data as of January 2011.

Withbrock, M. (2007). *Knowledge is more than data*. Retrieved http://www.cyc.com/cyc/technology/whitepapers_dir/Knowledge_is_more_than_Data.pdf.

Withbrock, M. (2007). *Knowledge is more than data*. Retrieved from http://www.cyc.com/cyc/technology/whitepapers_dir/Knowledge_is_more_than_Data.pdf.

Wolter, R., & Haselden, K. (2006). The what, why, and how of master data management. *Microsoft Corporation*. Retrieved from http://msdn.microsoft.com/en-us/library/bb190163.aspx.

World Geodetic System. (1984). *Webpage*. Retrieved from https://www1.nga.mil/PRODUCTSSERVICES/GEODESYGEOPHYSICS/WORLDGEODETICSYSTEM/Pages/default.aspx.

Zitgist. (2011). *Webpage*. Retrieved from http://www.zitgist.com/.

ADDITIONAL READING

BBC. (2010). *World cup 2010*. Retrieved from http://www.bbc.co.uk/worldcup.

Bishop, B., Kiryakov, A., Ognyanoff, D., Peikov, I., Tashev, Z., & Velkov, R. (2011). FactForge: A fast track to the web of data. *Semantic Web Journal*. Retrieved from http://www.semantic-web-journal. net/content/new-submission-factforge-fast-track-web-data.

Bizer, C., Lehmann, J., Kobilarov, G., Auer, S., Becker, C., & Cyganiak, R. (2009). DBpedia – A crystallization point for the web of data. *Journal of Web Semantics*, *7*, 154–165. doi:10.1016/j. websem.2009.07.002

Borst, P., Akkermans, H., & Top, J. (1997). Engineering ontologies. *International Journal of Human-Computer Studies*, *46*, 365–406. doi:10.1006/ijhc.1996.0096

Kiryakov, A., & Damova, M. (2011). Storing the semantic web. In *Semantic Web Handbook*. Heidelberg, Germany: Springer Verlag. doi:10.1007/978-3-540-92913-0_7

KEY TERMS AND DEFINITIONS

FactForge: A reason-able view to the web of data that allows users to find resources and facts based on the semantics of the data from the LOD cloud (http://factforge.net)

Instance-Level Matching: The process of determining the correspondences between instances of two data sources, datasets

Linked Open Data: A set of open datasets in RDF published on the Web with RDF links between data items from different data sources, produced as a result of a community project aiming to extend the Web with a data commons usable by computers.

Ontology Matching: The process of determining correspondences between concepts and relationships of two ontologies

OpenCyc: The open source version of the Cyc technology, the world's largest and most complete general knowledge base and commonsense reasoning engine

PROTON: A lightweight upper-level ontology developed by Ontotext, AD

Reason-Able View of the Web of Data: A practical approach for reasoning with the web of linked data. It is an assembly of independent datasets, which can be used as a single body of knowledge - *an integrated dataset* - with respect to reasoning and query evaluation.

Reference Knowledge Stack (RKS): A set of interlinked ontologies and instances, including PROTON, UMBEL, OpenCyc, DBpedia, Geonames, and Freebase, allowing for better management of LOD

Schema-Level Matching: Ontology matching

UMBEL: Upper Mapping and Binding Exchange Layer developed by Structured Dynamics

ENDNOTES

[1] LOD Cloud diagram as of September 2010, http://richard.cyganiak.de/2007/10/lod/.

[2] A Description Logic (DL) system is characterized by four fundamental aspects: the set of constructs used in concept and role expressions, the kind of assertions allowed in the TBox (assertions on concepts) and the ABox (assertions on individuals), and the inference mechanisms for reasoning on both the TBox and the ABox. (De Giacomo & Lenzerini, 1996)

[3] DBpedia version 3.6

4   Geonames version 2.2.1

5   The company Metaweb, developing Freebase, was acquired by Google in 2010.

6   *Semsets are semantically close terms or phrases synonymous or nearly so with the meanings of a* subject concept. Semsets are akin to WordNet synsets or Cyc aliases, but can also include more contemporary jargon or slang as may be drawn from Web tagging or folksonomies (Bergman et al., 2011).

7   DBpedia version 3.5.1

8   Wikipedia categories are used to group other pages and other subjects together. They are more than 500 000. http://simple.wikipedia.org/wiki/Wikipedia:Categories

9   This query can be run at http://factforge.net/sparql.

10   This query was run on an experimental local setting at Ontotext.

Section 3
Relevant Resources Supporting Ontology Development

Chapter 8
Aggregation and Maintenance of Multilingual Linked Data

Ernesto William De Luca
Berlin Institute of Technology, Germany

ABSTRACT

In this chapter, the author presents his approach to aggregating and maintaining Multilingual Linked Data. He describes Lexical Resources and Lexical Linked Data, presenting a hybridization that ports the largest lexical resource EuroWordNet to the Linked Open Data cloud, interlinking it with other lexical resources. Furthermore, he shows the LexiRes RDF/OWL tool that gives the possibility to navigate this lexical information, helping authors of already available lexical resources in deleting or restructuring concepts using automatic merging methods. The chapter is concluded by a discussion on personalizing information according to user preferences, filtering relevant information while taking into account the multilingual background of the user.

INTRODUCTION

With the advent of Linked Open Data (LOD) [1], more resources are interconnected and shared on the Web. The idea of Linked Open Data is to connect and share data, information, and knowledge following Semantic Web principals like URIs and RDF descriptions. While most Linked Data concentrates on linking facts, like music, movies, geo- or demographic information, we believe that one important task is to connect language resources in order to support the process of *Language Engineering*. We also believe that natural language processing plays an important role in order to achieve this goal. *Language Engineering* involves the development and application of software systems that perform tasks concerning the processing of human natural language (Cunningham, 1999). Different tools have been designed, constructed, and are used for tasks like translation, language

DOI: 10.4018/978-1-4666-0188-8.ch008

teaching, information extraction, and indexing. Other, more intangible "language engineering tools" are *language resources*. Language resources are essential components of language engineering, containing a wide range of linguistic information with different degrees of complexity. These linguistic resources are sets of language data and descriptions in machine readable form, used for building, improving, and evaluating natural language and speech systems or algorithms. Cole et al. (1997) give a brief overview about the various types of language resources, i.e. written and spoken language corpora, lexicons, and terminological databases.

Lexical Resources

In the following, we concentrate on lexical resources that provide linguistic information about words. This information can be represented in very diverse data structures, from simple lists to complex repositories with many types of linguistic information and relations attached to each entry, resulting in network-like structures. Lexical resources are used in Natural Language Processing, for example, to obtain descriptions and usage examples of different word senses. Different word senses refer to different concepts, and concepts can be distinguished from each other not only by their definitions or "glosses," but also by their specific relations to other concepts. Such disambiguating relations are intuitively used by humans. However, if we want to automate the process of distinguishing between word senses (word sense disambiguation), we have to use resources that provide appropriate knowledge, i.e. sufficient information about the usage context of a word. One of the most important resources available for this purpose is WordNet (Fellbaum, 1998) and its multilingual variants, including MultiWordNet (Pianta, et al., 2002) and EuroWordNet (Vossen, 1999).

Lexical Linked Data

Because the Web is evolving from a global information space of linked documents to one where both documents and data are linked, we agree that a set of best practices for publishing and connecting structured data on the Web is necessary and known as Linked Data. The Linked Open Data (LOD) project (Bizer, et al., 2009) is bootstrapping the Web of Data by converting it into RDF and publishing existing available "open datasets." In addition, LOD datasets often contain natural language texts, which are important to link and explore data not only in a broad LOD cloud vision, but also in localized applications within large organizations that make use of linked data (Baldassarre, et al., 2010; Nuzzolese, et al., 2011).

The combination of natural language processing and Semantic Web techniques has become important, in order to exploit lexical resources directly represented as linked data. One of the major examples is the WordNet RDF dataset (Schreiber, et al., 2006), which provides concepts (called synsets), each representing the sense of a set of synonymous words (Gangemi, et al., 2003). It has a low level of concept linking, because synsets are linked mostly by means of taxonomic relations, while LOD data is mostly linked by means of domain relations, such as parts of things, ways of participating in events or socially interacting, topics of documents, temporal and spatial references, etc. (Nuzzolese, et al., 2011).

An example of interlinking lexical resources like FrameNet[2] (Baker, et al., 1998) to the LOD Cloud is given in Gangemi and Presutti (2010). They create a LOD dataset that provides new possibilities to the lexical grounding of semantic knowledge and boosts the "lexical linked data" section of LOD by linking FrameNet to other LOD datasets such as WordNet RDF (Schreiber, et al., 2006).

Overview of the Chapter

In this chapter, we present our approach to aggregating and maintaining Multilingual Linked Data. After discussing Lexical Resources and Lexical Linked Data, we give an overview about WordNet and its different available representations. Afterwards, we address the hybridization research by porting the largest lexical resource EuroWordNet to the LOD cloud, interlinking it with other lexical resources. Then, we present the LexiRes RDF/OWL tool that gives the possibility of navigating lexical information and helping authors of already available lexical resources in deleting or restructuring concepts using automatic merging methods. The restructured information can be navigated and explored. Authors can decide if word senses are unambiguous and important enough to keep them in the hierarchy at the same place or if they express similar concepts and can be merged under the same (now, more general) meaning. All this lexical information is published as a dataset in the LOD cloud and linked to WordNet and other lexical datasets. In addition, at the end of the chapter, we describe how these resources can be used in combination with user modeling. We focus on the task of aggregating information from different user profiles in different Web applications containing data in different languages (based on the RDF/OWL-EuroWordNet representation). In this way, we can personalize retrieval results according to user preferences, filtering relevant information taking into account the multilingual background of the user. The chapter is concluded by a summary.

WORDNET

WordNet (Fellbaum, 1998; Miller, et al., 1990) is an electronic lexical database designed by use of psycholinguistic and computational theories of human lexical memory. It provides a list of word senses for each word, organized into synonym sets (synsets), each representing one constitutional lexicalized concept. Every synset is uniquely identified by an identifier (synsetId). It is unambiguous and carries exactly one meaning. Furthermore, different relations link these elements of synonym sets to semantically related terms (e.g. hyperonyms, hyponyms, etc.). All related terms are also represented as synset entries. These synsets also contain descriptions of nouns, verbs, adjectives, and adverbs. With this information we can describe the usage context of a word.

WordNet distinguishes two types of linguistic relations. The first type is represented by lexical relations (e.g. synonymy, antonymy, and polysemy) and the second by semantic relations (e.g. hyponymy and meronymy). Glosses (human descriptions) are often (about 70% of the time) associated to a synset (Ciravegna, et al., 1994). With WordNet 2.0, nominalizations—that link verbs and nouns pertaining to the same semantic class and domain links (based on an "ontology") that should support the disambiguation process—have been introduced. Figure 1 represents an example of the ontology hierarchy defined by WordNet (Miller, et al., 1990). This ontology hierarchy represents different meanings of a given word that are related to it (e.g. meaning 1, meaning 2, and meaning 3) having different linguistic relations (e.g. meaning 1 with hyponym 1.1 and hyperonym 1.1, hyperonym 1.2 and hyperonym 1.3). WordNet can be used for different applications, like word sense identification, information retrieval, and particularly for a variety of content-based tasks, such as semantic query expansion or conceptual indexing in order to improve the retrieval performance (Vintar, et al., 2003). It was first developed only for the English language. Then different versions were developed for several other languages, for example EuroWordNet (Vossen, 1999) for several European languages (Dutch, Italian, Spanish, German, French, Czech, and Estonian). Its structure is the same as the Princeton WordNet (Miller, et al., 1990) in terms of synsets with different semantic relations between them. Each individual WordNet represents a unique language-internal system of lexicalizations. Furthermore, the Inter-Lingual-Index (ILI) was introduced in order to connect the WordNets of the different languages. Thus, it is possible to access the concepts (Synsets) of a word sense in different languages.

Problems of the WordNet Hierarchy

In the following we briefly examine the main semantic limitations of WordNet (and its variants) and describe some problems that have to be solved for its better expressiveness:

- Some lexical links of WordNet should be interpreted using formal semantics in order to express "things in the world." Oltramari et al. (2002) revise the Top Level of WordNet (upper or general level), where the criteria of identity and unity are very general, in order to recognize the constraint violations occurring in it. The concepts of identity and unity are described in Oltramari, et al., 2002.

- The too fine-grained description of synsets is another limitation for its use in natural language processing. Therefore, a restructuring process of the synsets is needed (De Luca & Nürnberger, 2006a).

- Another critical point is given by the confusion between concepts and instances resulting in an "expressivity lack" (Gangemi, et al., 2001). For example, if we look for the hyponyms of "mountain" in older versions of WordNet, we will find the "Olympus mount" as a subsumed concept of the word treated as "volcano" and not as instance of it. Thus, we do not have a clear differentiation between abstract descriptions (concepts) and their instantiations

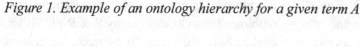

Figure 1. Example of an ontology hierarchy for a given term A

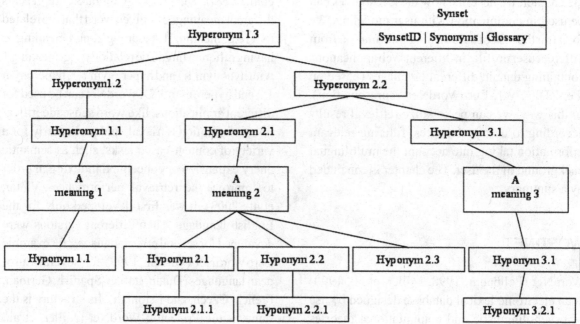

(instances). In the newer WordNet Version 3.0 "Olympus mount" has been changed in "Mount Olympus" and explained as instance of "mountain peak," but this problem has not been solved for all other cases. We also have the problem that we cannot use only concepts or only instances because there is no intended separation between them in WordNet.

- Motta et al. (1999) treat the important difference between endurance and perdurance of the entities that should be included in WordNet. Enduring and perduring entities are related to their behavior in time. Endurants are always entirely present at any time they are present. Perdurants are only partially present, in the sense that some of their proper parts (e.g., their previous phases) may be not present. However, these aspects of instances are not discussed in this article since they seem to be of less importance for the considered disambiguation problem.

When we concentrate on EuroWordNet, we can see that these problems persist, and other problems related to the Inter-Lingual-Index and to the language-dependent coverage of word senses come along. Further detailed discussions of these problems can be found in Gangemi et al. (2001), Oltramari et al. (2002), and Guarino & Welty (2004).

WordNet Related Work

Horák & Smrož (2004) developed VisDic for browsing and editing multilingual information taken from EuroWordNet. The tool supports users browsing static information by using only text blocks. Another Web interface for multilingual information browsing is presented in Ranieri et al. (2004). Here a parallel corpus annotated with MultiWordNet (Pianta, et al., 2002) can be browsed as well as the words with their related annotated word senses. However, the corpus is very restricted and all accessible information is static. This interface can be used only for a bilingual search in a closed domain. Other work dealing with the lexicography has shown that researchers in this area mostly deal with multilingual lexical resources or corpora only, without the possibility of merging similar word senses.

Given that the EuroWordNet format is defined by the EuroWordNet Database Editor Polaris that uses a proprietary specification, we decided to convert the EuroWordNet Database into a standardized OWL format in order to access it with standard OWL query tools. In this way we can also enrich this ontology with additional domain-specific ontologies (see Figure 2).

WORDNET IN XML AND RDF/OWL

The lexical database WordNet (WN) contains sets of word senses that are synonyms or near-synonyms of each other (synsets). We can also think of a synset as a concept and consider the word senses it contains as (largely interchangeable) linguistic expressions that can be used to refer to it (see Figure 3). Between synsets, semantic relations such as hyponymy (subsumption) and meronymy (part-whole-relation) are defined. For this reason, WordNet has also been called a lexical ontology. Although centered on the synset notion, WordNet also includes additional lexical relations,

Figure 2. Example of the set of nouns of "car" in WordNet 3.0

ex:car{car:1 auto:1 automobile:1 machine:6 motorcar:1}

Figure 3. OWL hierarchy of Princeton WordNet

```
Synset
        NounSynset
        VerbSynset
        AdjectiveSynset
                AdjectiveSatelliteSynset
        AdverbSynset

WordSense
        NounWordSense
        VerbWordSense
        AdjectiveWordSense
                AdjectiveSatelliteWordSense
        AdverbWordSense

Word
        Collocation
```

defined between individual word senses instead of synsets; antonymy (the relation between opposition pairs) is an example. EuroWordNet (EWN) (Vossen, 1999) is a multilingual lexical database built along the lines of the WordNet model. In addition to the central relations taken over from WordNet, EuroWordNet offers interlingual as well as further semantic relations. EWN data is distributed on CD-ROM in two formats: plain text and binary files. The binary data can be viewed with proprietary tools.

XML-Based Representations

The EuroWordNet data described above has been represented in a proprietary XML format. The XML entries were produced in the BalkaNet project and can be viewed and edited with different tools (VisDic [Horák & Smrož, 2004 and DEBVisDic [Horák, et al., 2006]). The work on VisDic was motivated by several factors; among others, distribution of the original tool for viewing and editing EWN data (Polaris) had long been discontinued, and a new platform was needed to work on BalkaNet. However, a different XML-based format for WordNet has been proposed by the Semantic Web community (van Assem, et al., 2006). Their RDF/OWL representation can be queried and processed by standard Semantic Web tools, thus facilitating the integration of WordNet data into Semantic Web applications.

OWL

Before describing how we converted EuroWordNet in OWL, we first give a brief introduction of the OWL definition. OWL (the Web Ontology Language) is a formal language used for describing Web ontologies. It is written in XML syntax and built using RDF Schemas, basing on a larger vocabulary and stronger syntax than RDF (Herman, et al., 2004). This enables an exact description of Web information and relationships between Web information. As a W3C recommendation OWL is seen as standard language for the implementation of the Semantic Web. It is subdivided into three sublanguages: OWL Lite, OWL DL, and OWL Full. OWL Lite is primarily used for creating classification hierarchies and simple constraints. The OWL DL sublanguage makes use of description logics, which form the formal logical foundation of OWL. In order to guarantee the representation in first order logic, various restrictions were inserted for the use of RDF-constructs (for example a class cannot be represented as an instance of another class). OWL Full consists of the same language constructs of OWL DL, but without their restrictions. Ontologies created with OWL can express predicate logic expressions of higher degree.

RDF/OWL Representation of WordNet

The WordNet Princeton (Fellbaum, 1998) has already been converted into an OWL format as described in (van Assem, et al., 2004) using the OWL-DL sublanguage. This representation in RDF/OWL is based on the WordNet data model shown in Figure 3. When we compare the original

Princeton WordNet synset (having only word senses) with the OWL representation, we can see that the RDF/OWL schema (in its full version) has three main classes: Synset, Word, and WordSense. The basic version contains only the Synset class.

The two classes—Synset and WordSense—have four subclasses, which are based on the distinction of lexical groups; these are Noun-Synset, VerbSynset, AdjectiveSynset (which has another subclass AdjectiveSatelliteSynset), and AdverbSynset. The Word class holds the subclass Collocation, which denotes terms that are composed of two or more words. In order to disambiguate the meanings of each instance of a synset, WordSense and Word have a unique URI, which can be used for retrieving words and word senses independently from the synsets. This property was not available in the original version of WordNet.

The URIs provide some information about the entity meaning and are built with patterns similar to: wn20instances: + synset- + lexical form- + type- + sense number.

For example if we want to retrieve the fourth word sense of the word "bank," we would get a URI like: "http://www.w3.org/2006/03/wn/wn20/instances/synset-bank-noun-4." The properties of the RDF schema are divided into three kinds of relations:

1. those that relate two synsets to each other (e.g. hyponymOf)
2. those that relate two word senses to each other (e.g. antonymOf)
3. and a set of properties that give information on entities (e.g. XML Schema data types like xsd:string as it is used in synsetId).

In order to avoid redundancy, only relations in one transitive direction (e.g. hyponymOf and not hyperonymOf) are listed, the others can be retrieved with the owl:inverseOf property implemented in the RDF Schema (see the Figures 6 and 7). Altogether there are 27 relations implemented in the RDF/OWL representation of WordNet. The instances of all classes and properties are separated in several data files, one for the synsets, one for the WordSenses and Words, and one for each relation. Although the RDF Schema is used to describe most class and property definitions, there are several OWL statements integrated in the schema to provide better semantic descriptions, like checking the correctness of the data or defining inverse relations. For these statements software has to support the OWL DL standard in order to store and query the data.

RDF/OWL EUROWORDNET

Because of the different problems related to WordNet and its variants as briefly discussed above, we decided to convert it into an RDF/OWL representation (see below), in order to enable the development of more flexible revision methods. In EuroWordNet, one synset contains all related word senses, synonyms and relations to other synsets, and to the Inter-Lingual-Index. This information had to be prepared for inclusion in the appropriate RDF Schema and reorganized for a new data representation. The decision to convert EuroWordNet was also based on the need to extend it (because not all meanings are covered) with other resources. Furthermore, since most domain-specific ontologies are represented in OWL and a WordNet monolingual RDF/OWL representation has already been implemented, a EuroWordNet conversion would add multilingual capabilities to these resources. Therefore, we converted EuroWordNet into an RDF/OWL representation based on the work presented in van Assem et al. (2004). Since EuroWordNet has several relations and a structure that are different from the Princeton WordNet, several steps were required to adapt the data to the RDF/OWL Schema of WordNet and to extend this RDF Schema with the new relations. We first analyzed the requirements for EuroWordNet and adapted the WordNet RDF Schema to a multilingual representation of EuroWordNet. Then, we converted the EuroWordNet relations into OWL properties and extended the ontology with two domain ontologies (De Luca, et al., 2007). In the following, we describe the steps of this conversion and the problems that arose in more detail.

Conversion of EuroWordNet in RDF/OWL

The steps required to convert EuroWordNet in RDF/OWL can be subdivided into:

- Analysis of the requirements for EuroWordNet
- Adaptation of The WordNet RDF-Schema to EuroWordNet
- Multilingualism
- OWL Property Conversion
- OWL Domain Extension

van Assem et al. (2004) distinguish Word and WordSense in their data model for two reasons. First of all, several relations are defined for word senses and synsets and WordNet uses this distinction in its database. Secondly, for the sake of ontological clarity, they assume that synsets include word senses, in order to partition the logical space of the lexicon (words as forms or meanings, and synsets as clusters of word senses by abstracting their distributional context). Agreeing with their model, we adapted their schema to convert EuroWordNet, applying these assumptions for a multilingual task. An example of an OWL-EuroWordNet synset is given in Figure 4. Here the word sense "bank" is shown within its synset (and synsetId), WordSense, Word, and synonyms (containsWordSense).

Analyzing the structures of EuroWordNet and of the OWL representation of WordNet, we could recognize that some relations are supported in both versions (see Figure 6). Since EuroWordNet contains relations and properties that are not supported in the WordNet OWL representation, we had to adapt the RDF-OWL Schema to our needs in order to cover these gaps.

Therefore, we created and stored new RDF structures, containing these new relations and thus extended the WordNet OWL implementation (see Figure 7). Some other properties that are covered in the WordNet OWL representation (e.g. the property tagCount used in the WordSense OWL declaration) are not available in EuroWordNet, so we could not consider them.

Because we also tried to avoid redundancy as discussed in van Assem et al. (2004), we decided to delete the relations in EuroWordNet that have an inverse form. We compared them updating their inverse relation property, where necessary (see the Figures 6 and 7). This means, if an instance of an inverse relation of a distinct instance is present, the instance can be deleted. If no inverse instance is available, the instance is added as an inverse relation instance. An example is the hyperonym-hyponym relation resulting in a simple hyponymOf relation. Here the hyponym relation was available in both representations but its name had to be changed from has_hyperonym EuroWordNet format to the hyponymOf OWL-WordNet format (see Figure 5).

Another point considered was that EuroWordNet contains different relations belonging to the same "upper relation description" (e.g. ROLE_AGENT, ROLE_INSTRUMENT, ROLE_LOCATION, etc. belonging to ROLE), because of their similar functionality. We decided in this case to merge them all into the same "Upper Relation" RDF file. A similar decision was made in the Princeton Conversion within the pertainsTo relation.

The complete mapping between EuroWordNet, OWL-WordNet, and OWL-EuroWordNet relations is given in Figure 6. The relations that are only available in EuroWordNet and have been

Figure 4. RDF/OWL-EuroWordNet synset example

```
<ewn20schema:NounSynset rdf:about="&ewn20instances;synset-bank-noun-1"
    rdfs:label="bank">
    <ewn20schema:synsetId>102690337</ewn20schema:synsetId>
</ewn20schema:NounSynset>
<ewn20schema:Word rdf:about="&ewn20instances;word-bank"
    ewn20schema:lexicalForm="bank"/>
<ewn20schema:NounWordSense rdf:about="&ewn20instances;wordsense-bank-noun-1"
    rdfs:label="bank">
    <ewn20schema:word rdf:resource="&ewn20instances;word-bank"/>
</ewn20schema:NounWordSense>
<rdf:Description rdf:about="&ewn20instances;synset-bank-noun-1">
    <ewn20schema:containsWordSense rdf:resource="&ewn20instances;wordsense-bank-noun-1"/>
    <ewn20schema:containsWordSense rdf:resource="&ewn20instances;wordsense-bank_building-noun-1"/>
</rdf:Description>
```

included as new RDF/OWL-EuroWordNet are shown in Figure 7.

Since EuroWordNet is a multilingual resource (and not a monolingual like WordNet), we had to create a unique set of files (containing the language-dependent synsets and relations) for every language. Every file of this set was additionally tagged with the name of the corresponding language (e.g. for English: eurowordnet-english-synset.rdf, eurowordnet-english-wordsensesand-words.rdf, eurowordnet-english-hyponymOf.rdf, etc.). We used the available EuroWordNet Inter-Lingual-Index that contains synsets, having the same identifier (synsetId) for all word meanings in all languages and an illustrative gloss. Because of the redundancy problem already described above, we decided to maintain only the gloss information included in the Inter-Lingual-Index deleting the word senses and synsetIds (already included in the English conversion). Therefore,

the gloss entries were extracted and stored in a separate RDF file. Depending on this decision, the synsets of all languages were connected to another through the same identifier (synsetId) describing the same concept in different languages, instead of the Inter-Lingual-Index entries.

INTERLINKING RDF/OWL-EUROWORDNET WITH OTHER LEXICAL RESOURCES

After the first conversion of EuroWordNet in an OWL representation (see De Luca et al., 2007), we decided to interlink different other lexical resources to this multilingual representation including metaphorical relations and multilingual concepts contained in lexical databases. The procedure is described in the following.

Figure 5. RDF/OWL-EuroWordNet hyponymOf example for the word "bank"

```
<rdf:Description rdf:about="&ewn20instances;synset-bank-noun-1">
    <ewn20schema:hyponymOf rdf:resource="&ewn20instances;synset-deposit-noun-1"/>
</rdf:Description>
```

Figure 6. EuroWordNet, RDF/OWL-EuroWordNet, and RDF/OWL WordNet relations. The crossed out relations have been removed, since they are inverse relations to the existing ones.

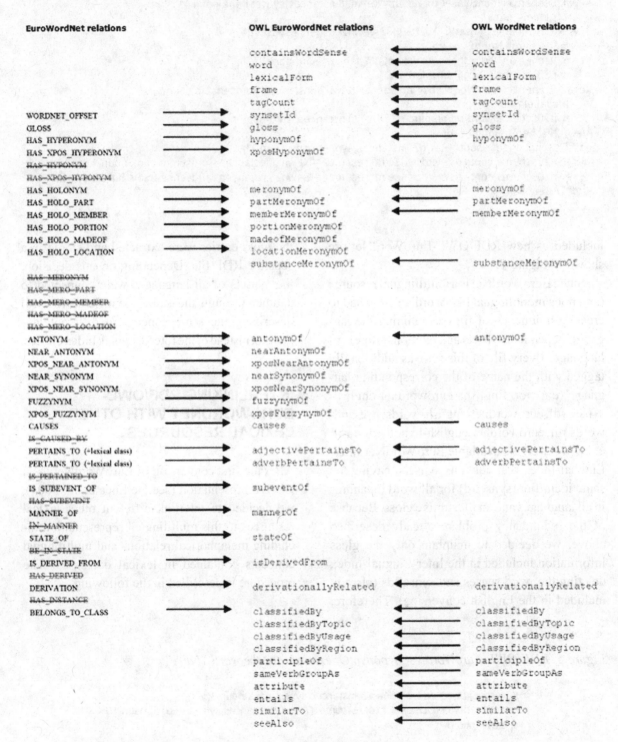

Figure 7. EuroWordNet and RDF/OWL-EuroWordNet relations missing in RDF/OWL WordNet. The crossed out relations have been removed, since they are inverse relations to the existing ones.

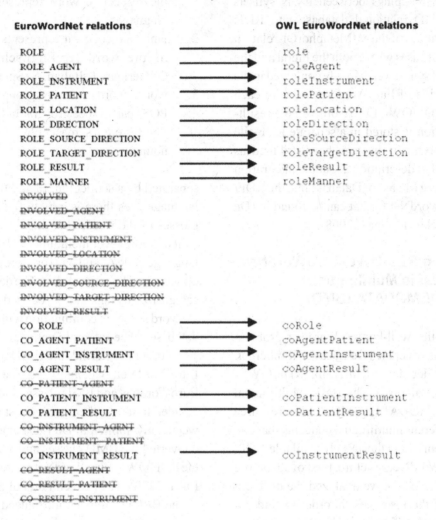

Interlinking RDF/OWL-EuroWordNet with the Hamburg Metaphor Database

The RDF/OWL-EuroWordNet representation has been interlinked with data included in the Hamburg Metaphor Database (HMD), a relational database of French and German corpus attestations containing metaphorical expressions (Lönneker-Rodman, 2008). In the HMD, each metaphor is manually analyzed and annotated at several levels. Among other lexical features, HMD provides references to EuroWordNet synsets. In addition, conceptual information is indicated in terms of domain labels from the Berkeley Master Metaphor List (Lakoff, et al., 1991). To provide an RDF/OWL representation of HMD data, we started by defining a new relation between the different synsets, the conceptual relation extMetaphorOf ("extension by metaphor of …"). This conceptual relation holds between a synset with a metaphorical meaning and a synset with a literal meaning of at least one of the contained word senses. The relation as such is defined by an RDF schema. We then populated the extMetaphorOf-relation by deriving 107 instances from the HMD data for French. This was done by converting the data concerning attested metaphorical mappings between EWN synsets from the HMD relational database into RDF. The 107 instances of the extMetaphorOf-relation thus represent cases where both the literal and the metaphorical synset were already contained in the original version of EuroWordNet. As with each relation in RDF/OWL EuroWordNet, the resulting information is stored in a separate RDF-file (extMetaphorOf.rdf) and can be distributed as such. A detailed description about the integration of the Hamburg Metaphor Database into the RDF/OWL-EuroWordNet format can be found in (De Luca&Lönneker-Rodman, 2008).

Interlinking RDF/OWL-EuroWordNet with the Basic Multilingual Lexicon MEMODATA (BMD)

Because of the well-known WordNet problem of conceptual coverage (De Luca & Nürnberger, 2006c), we decided to interlink RDF/OWL-EuroWordNet also with the Basic Multilingual Lexicon MEMODATA (BMD)[3]. This resource includes different multilingual concepts that can be used for enriching the already available RDF/OWL-EuroWordNet structure. First of all, before converting the BMD, we analyzed the different structures of the resources, in order to find out similarities and differences. The BMD contains words associated by the meaning in 5 languages: English, French, German, Italian, and Spanish. The lexical categories included are: nouns (5 * 18 000), verbs (5 * 8 000), adjectives (5 * 6 000) and adverbs (5 * 1 500). Sixteen Parts of Speech (POS) are distinguished and grammatical information is also contained. This resource is divided into five files, one for each language. Every file has different lines, each of them representing one word. Each line (e.g. 19223;E;Guyanese;s_masc_plur) includes:

1. id number - this number links the word to the respective word represented in other languages
2. language code - it represents the language of the word (E=Englisch, F=French, G=German, I=Italian, S=Spanish)
3. word - word or a word group
4. POS - part of speech or grammatical information (as e.g. "s_masc_plur" for male plural nouns).

separated by a semicolon. In addition to the five language files there is a meta file including the glosses of the words (but only in French), each sorted at line level including the ID number, the language code A, and one (or more) descriptions, all separated by a semicolon. The descriptions are categorized by tags and can be used to disambiguate word senses in combination with the complete database, "The Integral Dictionary"[4].

In order to interlink the BMD to RDF/OWL-EuroWordNet, we analyzed the RDF/OWL-EuroWordNet and BMD classes and relations and decided to merge them with the same procedure we already applied in De Luca et al. (2007). We converted the BMD classes and adapted them to the RDF/OWL-EuroWordNet classes (Laske & De Luca, 2010). The sixteen Parts of Speech (POS) of the BMD have been introduced as additional classes to WordSense and Synset. The properties that connect the main classes (containsWordSense and Word), the lexicalForm—the string representation of a word—and the synsetId have been extended: each synset contained in the BMD having several POS, have been split into more synsets with only one POS, like in WordNet. In order to be sure that each new synsets has a unique synsetId, we altered the synsetIds from a number into a complex string with the pattern:

%original synsetId in the BMD%-BMD-%part of speech%

In this way, two synsets belonging to the same source synsetId will differ in our extension by their Part of Speech (POS). Some new relations that exist in the BMD had to be added to the RDF/ OWL EuroWordNet representation.

For the grammatical POS information included in some BMD entries, we added a grammaticalForm as a relation from Word to xsd:string. Furthermore, the URIs of the Words had to be changed from *wn20instances: + word- + %label%* to *bmd20instances: + word- + %label% + (%grammatical form%).*

This avoided conflicts that a Word could have more than one grammatical form (e.g. transitive and intransitive form for a verb). Figure 8 shows the adaptation of the RDF/OWL BMD classes that give a more precise description of the Synsets (concepts) included in this resource. Here we extend the WordSense and Synset classes with the additional subclasses included in the RDF/ OWL BMD.

Figure 9 presents the comparison between the RDF/OWL-EuroWordNet and the RDF/OWL BMD relations. The crossed out relations have been removed, since they are inverse relations to the existing ones. The gloss relation has been extended (doing it more specific) due to the different glosses included in the BMD. The 'grammaticalForm' and the 'derivationallyRelated' relation of a word have been added to the already existing relations.

Finally, the interlinkage of BMD with RDF/ OWL EuroWordNet is useful for multilingual information retrieval or for expanding the coverage of the EuroWordNet synsets, as, e.g., the BMD glosses with different gloss types and the grammatical information available are used (Laske & De Luca, 2010).

THE LEXIRES RDF/OWL TOOL

The main idea of the LexiRes RDF/OWL Tool is to give authors the possibility to navigate the ontology hierarchy in order to re-structure it, by manual merging, adding or deleting word senses. The tool is implemented in Java and uses the Jena

Semantic Web Framework (McBride, et al., 2006) for querying and retrieving lexical data. It provides an RDF/OWL model in order to access and query the lexical resource. Using EuroWordNet for cross-language retrieval, we support the author in:

- Exploring the lexical resource ontology hierarchy
- Disambiguating the word senses of a query word
- Giving the translations of a query word in different languages
- Creating individual lexical collections
- Adding and deleting meanings
- Merging meanings
- Importing OWL ontologies

Figure 10 shows a screenshot of the LexiRes RDF/OWL editor. On the top left side, we can choose the source language and enter the query term. On the right side (under the "Show Relations" area), we can choose which collection we want to use and which linguistic relations are to be considered for visualization. Query translations can be enabled in the "Show Translations" area.

For example, looking for the word "bank," in the English language, the ontology engine retrieves 15 meanings. These meanings describe the different word senses. Every word sense is represented as a synset. The author can choose to "Show Properties" or "Hide Properties" with a left mouse click on a synset. Here all synset-related information is shown. The original RDF resource part of the synset can also be displayed by clicking on the right mouse button and choosing the "Show RDF Resource" option. The properties and the RDF code are then shown on the right-hand side under the "Details" box. After logging in, a user-specific lexical resource collection can be created. In our case, the collection contains a reference to the EuroWordNet lexical resource (as default). The author can add or remove meanings in order to enrich or restructure the hierarchy. It is also possible to query the adapted EuroWordNet

Figure 8. Comparison of the RDF/OWL-EuroWordNet and the new RDF/OWL BMD classes

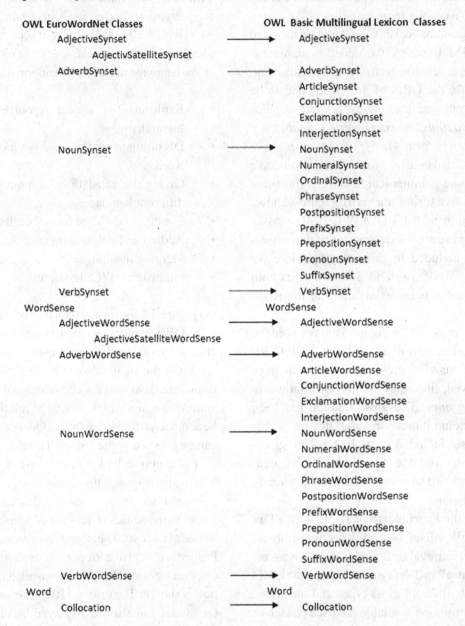

OWL EuroWordNet Classes	OWL Basic Multilingual Lexicon Classes
AdjectiveSynset	→ AdjectiveSynset
AdjectivSatelliteSynset	
AdverbSynset	→ AdverbSynset
	ArticleSynset
	ConjunctionSynset
	ExclamationSynset
	InterjectionSynset
NounSynset	→ NounSynset
	NumeralSynset
	OrdinalSynset
	PhraseSynset
	PostpositionSynset
	PrefixSynset
	PrepositionSynset
	PronounSynset
	SuffixSynset
VerbSynset	→ VerbSynset
WordSense	WordSense
AdjectiveWordSense	→ AdjectiveWordSense
AdjectiveSatelliteWordSense	
AdverbWordSense	→ AdverbWordSense
	ArticleWordSense
	ConjunctionWordSense
	ExclamationWordSense
	InterjectionWordSense
NounWordSense	→ NounWordSense
	NumeralWordSense
	OrdinalWordSense
	PhraseWordSense
	PostpositionWordSense
	PrefixWordSense
	PrepositionWordSense
	PronounWordSense
	SuffixWordSense
VerbWordSense	→ VerbWordSense
Word	Word
Collocation	→ Collocation

lexical resource. To create new meanings, the author has to integrate them into the hierarchy. This is achieved by specifying the most appropriate superordinate node. New words (and their related terms) can be entered in the "Create New Word Sense" dialog. The system searches for known meanings of these terms and suggests (to the author) a list of candidates with their synonyms, descriptions and generic terms. If any meaning matches the meaning of the query term in the hierarchical context, it can be selected and grouped under the superordinate node.

Alternatively, the author can generate a new meaning which is then added to the hierarchy (see Figure 11). External domain-specific ontologies can be merged into the collection using the

Figure 9. Comparison of the RDF/OWL-EuroWordNet and RDF/OWL BMD relations

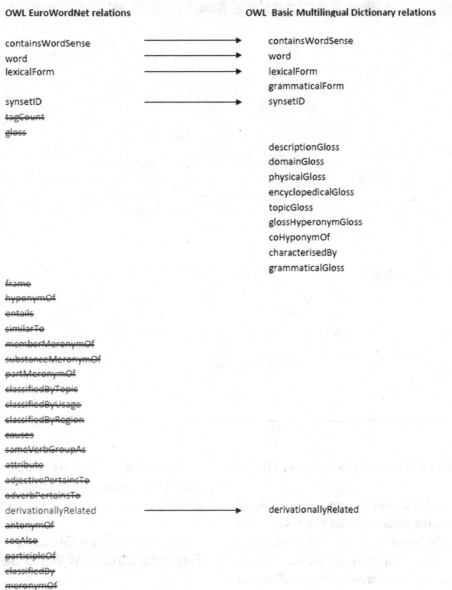

"Import Ontology" option. Then, the ontology can be uploaded and, if suitable, be added in the relation hierarchy. Further details are given in De Luca et al. (2007).

When a word sense is removed, the system updates the hierarchy by also removing the respective connections from the linguistic relations. In a graphical representation, this corresponds to deleting all adjacent edges along with the node. If a meaning is deleted, the resulting lack of connection between super- and subordinate words becomes a problem. Because semantic relations do not have to be transitive, the super- and subordinate nodes cannot always be directly con-

Figure 10. Example of the word "bank"—synset translations—in the LexiRes RDF/OWL editor

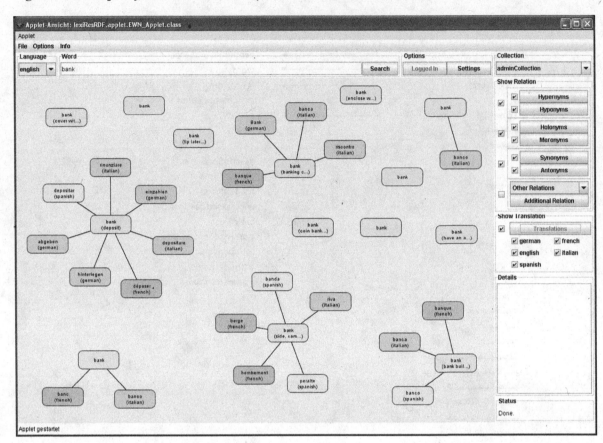

nected. Such situations have to be resolved by the author.

The tool also allows the manual merging of synsets when the author decides that two synsets belong to the same meaning and/or describe the same concept. For example, the two "bank" synsets under the superordinate "incline" synset in Figure 12 could be merged. Therefore, the author can pick a "source" synset in the hierarchy that should be merged to a "target" synset. The "Merge Word Sense To ..." menu shows all possible target meanings. The "source" meaning with all its relations is transferred to the "target" meaning. The synsets can be also automatically retrieved and translated in the different languages available in the ontology (see Figure 10). These can be set within the menu button language and can be shown—always synset-dependent—within

a simple click. We can notice that not all synsets have a translation, due to the lexical gaps or the missing entries in the lexical resource.

Fine and Coarse Grained Representation of Word Senses

The LexiRes RDF/OWL tool gives the possibility to manually merge synsets, when the authors decide that two synsets belong to the same meaning and/or describe the same concept. Authors working with LexiRes RDF/OWL tool can also use an automatically created list of candidate synsets that can be merged. This list can be created with the approaches discussed in De Luca & Nürnberger (2006a). The system proposes the list of changes and the user can select to accept all or check each proposal for merging manually. At the moment

Figure 11. Example of the word "bank"—create new word sense—in the LexiRes RDF/OWL editor

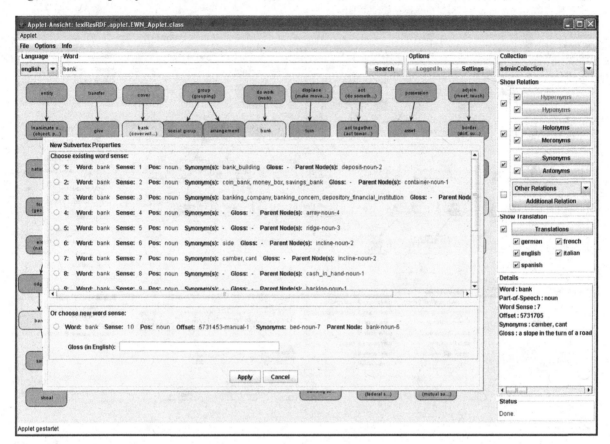

these merging methods are implemented outside the tool. The resulting list of possible merging synsets is first checked from the authors and then done manually. After having restructured the ontology hierarchy, a new set of synsets is created. This set is supposed to contain only word senses that are carrier of a distinctive meaning in the context of the considered application. This is a very important step for a use of lexical resources in information retrieval. The possibility to merge synsets in advance gives the advantage to categorize the retrieved documents disambiguating them with structured word senses that facilitate an automatic classification process (De Luca & Nürnberger, 2004). A detailed description of the evaluation of the automatic merging methods applied to the WordNet synsets in given in De Luca and Nürnberger (2006b).

MULTILINGUAL ONTOLOGY-BASED USER MODELING

After the description of the functionality of the LexiRes RDF/OWL Tool, we concentrate, in this section, on how to use the available resources (explained above) in combination with user modeling. In this example scenario, we focus on the task of aggregating information from different user profiles in different web applications of one user containing data in different languages. Today, people start to use more and more different web applications. They manage their bookmarks in social bookmarking systems, communicate with friends on Facebook[5] and use services like Twitter[6] to express personal opinions and interests. Thereby, they generate and distribute personal and social information like interests, preferences and goals

Figure 12. Example of the word "bank"—manual merging functions—in the LexiRes RDF/OWL editor

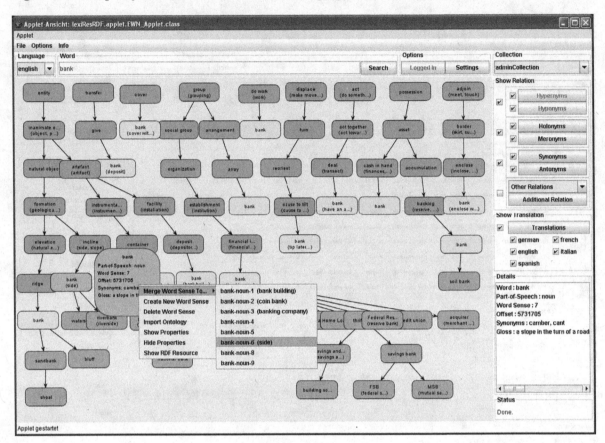

(Plumbaum, et al., 2009). This distributed and heterogeneous corpus of user information, stored in the User Model (UM) of each application, is a valuable source of knowledge for adaptive systems like information filtering services. These systems can utilize such knowledge for personalizing search results, recommend products or adapting the user interface to user preferences. Adaptive systems are highly needed, because the amount of information available on the Web is increasing constantly, requiring more and more effort to be adequately managed by the users. Therefore, these systems need more and more information about users interests, preferences, needs and goals and as precise as possible. However, this personal and social information stored in the distributed UMs usually exists in different languages (language

heterogeneity) due to the fact that we communicate with friends all over the world. Therefore, we recommend the integration of multilingual resources into the user model aggregation process to enable the aggregation of information in different languages which leads to better user models and thus to better adaptive systems.

The RDF/OWL EuroWordNet resource opens up new possibilities to overcome the problem of language heterogeneity in different user models and thus allows a better user model aggregation. Therefore, we propose here an ontology-based user modeling approach that combines mediator techniques to aggregate user models from different applications and utilize the RDF/OWL Euro-WordNet information to handle the multilingual information in the different models. Based on this idea, some requirements have to be fulfilled.

Requirement 1: Ontology-based profile aggregation. We need an approach to aggregate information that is both application independent and application overarching. This requires a solution that allows one to semantically define relations and coherences between different attributes of different UMs. The linked attributes must be easily accessible by applications such as recommender and information filtering systems. In addition, similarity must be expressed in these defined relations.

Requirement 2: Integrating semantic knowledge. A solution to handle the multilingual information for enriching user profiles is needed. Hence, methods that incorporate information from semantic data sources such as EuroWordNet and to aggregate complete profile information have to be developed.

Multilingual Ontology-Based Aggregation

For the aggregation of user models, the information in the different user models has to be linked to the multilingual information as we want to leverage this information and use it for a more precise and qualitatively better user modeling. We propose to utilize the knowledge available in RDF/OWL EuroWordNet (De Luca, et al., 2007). We treat these resources as a huge semantic profile that can be used to aggregate user models based on multilingual information.

Figure 13 describes the general idea. The goal is to create one big semantic user profile, containing all information from the three profiles of the user information, were the data is connected. The first step is to add the multilingual information to the data contained in the different user models. This gives us a first model where the same data is linked together through the multilingual information.

Integrating Semantic Knowledge

The second step is to add links between data that is not linked through the multilingual information. The target is to have a semantic user model were data is not only connected on a language level but also on a more semantic similarity level. The aggregation of information into semantic user models can be performed similarly to the approach described in Berkovsky et al. (2008), by using components that mediate between the different models and using recommendation frameworks that support semantic link prediction like Popescul&Ungar (2003). The combined user model should be stored in a commonly accepted ontology, like Heckmann et al. (2005) to be able to share the information with different applications. With such a semantic user model, overcoming language barriers, adaptive systems have more information about the user and can use this data to adapt better to the user preferences.

Enriching User Profiles with Semantic Data

In the following, we shortly present an example of enriching user profiles with semantic data (Plumbaum, et al., 2011). Our motivation is to cope with the cold start problem (Schein, et al., 2002) in a music recommendation scenario, when a user is searching for new music and wants to get new recommendations. Therefore, we believe that enriching the user profile with semantic encyclopedic knowledge can help in giving better recommendations, especially if the user profiles are small.

Studies about Wikipedia[7], as an example for online encyclopedias, proved that the quality and the accuracy of Wikipedia articles is on a high standard and hence a reliable information source (Huvila, 2010). Therefore, we follow the idea that semantic encyclopedic data is a good and "neutral" source for enriching user profiles with knowledge not influenced by subjective

Figure 13. Integrating semantic knowledge about multilingual dependencies with the information stored in the user models

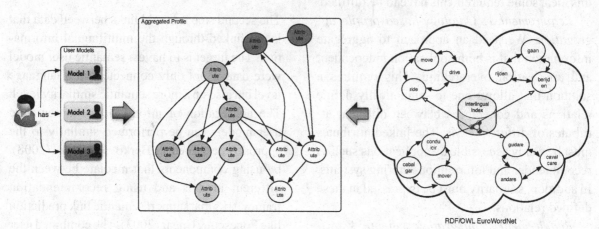

opinions or tastes. Enriching user profiles with items strongly related to the items already present in the user profile adds "similar concepts" for the existing entities. A similar concept means that we add information about an additional artist to the music profile of a user that is related to another artist already present in the user profile. This is done to increase the overlap of the enriched user profile with other profiles. Thus, it improves the similarity calculation, but does not change the taste of the user.

We evaluate our approach for a music recommendation scenario and we show that the enrichment works very well for users with an unusual music taste; in these scenarios the enriched profiles heighten the recommendation quality. In contrast, the enrichment is not helpful for users with large profiles or a popular music taste. In these cases the enrichment blurs the user profile and the therein specified user taste, because the Freebase data[8] contains general domain information, and for users with a common taste more or less universal knowledge is added. Adding the artist "Madonna" does not make sense for user profiles already containing a lot of pop artists; it only leads to more general profiles less tailored to the individual user preferences. Different strategies to overcome this problem are conceivable.

On the one hand, our approach needs to weigh the edge types in a more user centric way. A user may like an artist because of a certain song, but does not like the complete discography; or a user might like the artist because of the social engagement of that artist and not because of the music. Therefore, more context information about users is needed, enabling a context sensitive weighting of the information used for the profile enrichment. The increasing popularity of Social Semantic Web approaches and standards like FOAF[9] can be one important step in this direction. On the other hand, semantic datasets itself have to be enriched with more meta-information about the data. General quality and significance information, like prominence nodes and weighted relations, can improve semantic algorithms to better compute the importance of paths between nodes. An artist that made hundreds of bad albums may have a high number of links to, e.g., a genre node, but is not an important artist for this genre while another artist that produced only one or two albums defines a genre. In this case, a significant weight for the artists can improve the quality and performance of semantic algorithms.

The next step is to perform a live user evaluation asking them if the recommendation based on enriched profiles delivers better recommendations than the actual offline evaluations that hardly show the "real world" impact of such a user centric approach. Future steps are the evaluation of a focused enrichment, e.g. only using artist or genres information, based on the context of the user. Another direction is to implement a sophisticated weighting model (e.g. based on prominence, context, and user groups) as an overlay for the Freebase dataset, and to implement alternative network models (e.g. based on a low-rank approximation for the adjacency matrix of a relationship set [Kunegis & Lommatzsch, 2009]).

CONCLUSION

In this chapter we discussed the aggregation and maintenance of different Linked Open Data resources that can be managed through the LexiRes RDF/OWL tool, an editing and visualization tool we developed and adapted for handling multilingual resources (like EuroWordNet) with OWL ontology structures. Furthermore, we described the conversion of EuroWordNet in OWL and presented, based on this, the functionalities of the LexiRes RDF/OWL tool and the already implemented extensions available. In this work, we evaluated how appropriate EuroWordNet could be represented as OWL ontology and the interlinkage of existing available lexical resources (thesauri, dictionaries, ontologies, etc.) to the RDF/OWL EuroWordNet representation. The use of this OWL implementation and its performance has to be evaluated in more detail in order to be aware of its benefits and possibly recognize existing problems that could be solved by using this approach. In addition, we presented some ideas of how these resources can be used in combination with user modeling. We focused on the task of aggregating information from different user profiles in different Web applications of one user containing data in different languages (based on the presented RDF/OWL EuroWordNet representation).

REFERENCES

Baker, C. F., Fillmore, C. J., & Lowe, J. B. (1998). The Berkeley framenet project. In *Proceedings of the 17th International Conference on Computational Linguistics,* (pp. 86–90). Morristown, NJ: ACL Press.

Baldassarre, C., Daga, E., Gangemi, A., Gliozzo, A. M., Salvati, A., & Troiani, G. (2010). Semantic scout: Making sense of organizational knowledge. In *Proceedings of EKAW,* (pp. 272-286). EKAW Press.

Berkovsky, S., Kuflik, T., & Ricci, F. (2008). Mediation of user models for enhanced personalization in recommender systems. *User Modeling and User-Adapted Interaction, 18*(3), 245–286. doi:10.1007/s11257-007-9042-9

Bizer, C., Heath, T., & Berners-Lee, T. (2009). Linked data - The story so far. *International Journal on Semantic Web and Information Systems, 5*(3), 1–22. doi:10.4018/jswis.2009081901

Ciravegna, F., Magnini, B., Pianta, E., & Strapparava, C. (1994). *A project for the construction of an Italian lexical knowledge base in the framework of Wordnet.* Tech Report IRST 9406-15. Retrieved from http://www.irst.org.

Cole, R., Mariani, J., Uszkoreit, H., Zaenen, A., & Zue, V. (1997). *Survey of the state of the art in human language technology.* Pittsburgh, PA: Carnegie Mellon University.

Cunningham, H. (1999). A definition and short history of language engineering. *Natural Language Engineering, 5*(1), 1–16. doi:10.1017/S1351324999002144

De Luca, E. W., Eul, M., & Nürnberger, A. (2007). Converting EuroWordNet in OWL and extending it with domain ontologies. In *Proceedings of the Workshop on Lexical-Semantic and Ontological Resources in Conjunction With the GLDV Conference (GLDV 2007).* ACL Press.

De Luca, E. W., & Lönneker-Rodman, B. (2008). Integrating metaphor information into RDF/OWL EuroWordNet. In *Proceedings of the Sixth International Language Resources and Evaluation (LREC 2008)*. Marrakech, Morocco: ERLA Press.

De Luca, E. W., & Nürnberger, A. (2004). Improving ontology-based sense folder classification of document collections with clustering methods. In P. Joly, M. Detyniecki, & A. Nürnberger (Eds.), *Proceedings of the 2nd International Workshop on Adaptive Multimedia Retrieval (AMR 2004)*. ECAI Press.

De Luca, E. W., & Nürnberger, A. (2006a). Rebuilding lexical resources for information retrieval using sense folder detection and merging methods. In *Proceedings of the 5th International Conference on Language Resources and Evaluation (LREC 2006)*. Genova, Italy: LREC Press.

De Luca, E. W., & Nürnberger, A. (2006b). The use of lexical resources for sense folder disambiguation. In *Proceedings of the Workshop on Lexical Semantic Resources (DGFS 2006)*. Bielefeld, Germany: DGFS Press.

De Luca, E. W., & Nürnberger, A. (2006c). Using clustering methods to improve ontology-based query term disambiguation. *International Journal of Intelligent Systems*, *21*, 693–709. doi:10.1002/int.20155

Fellbaum, C. (1998). *Wordnet: An electronic lexical database*. Cambridge, MA: MIT Press.

Gangemi, A., Guarino, N., & Oltramari, A. (2001). Conceptual analysis of lexical taxonomies: The case of WordNet top-level. In *Proceedings of the International Conference on Formal Ontology in Information Systems*, (pp. 285–296). New York, NY: ACM Press.

Gangemi, A., Navigli, R., & Velardi, P. (2003). The OntoWordNet project: Extension and axiomatization of conceptual relations in WordNet. In Meersman, R., & Tari, Z. (Eds.), *Proceedings of On the Move to Meaningful Internet Systems (OTM2003)* (pp. 820–838). Catania, Italy: Springer-Verlag. doi:10.1007/978-3-540-39964-3_52

Gangemi, A., & Presutti, V. (2010). Towards a pattern science for the semantic web. *Semantic Web*, *1*(1-2), 61–68.

Guarino, N., & Welty, C. A. (2004). An overview of ontoclean. Retrieved from http://www.loa.istc.cnr.it/Papers/GuarinoWeltyOntoCleanv3.pdf.

Heckmann, D., Schwartz, T., Brandherm, B., Schmitz, M., & von Wilamowitz-Moellendorff, M. (2005). Gumo - The general user model ontology. *User Modeling*, *3538*, 428–432. doi:10.1007/11527886_58

Herman, I., Swick, R., & Brickley, D. (2004). *Resource description framework (RDF)*. Tech Report. Retrieved from http://www.w3c.org.

Horák, A., Pala, K., Rambousek, A., & Povolný, M. (2006). DEBVisDic - First version of new client-server Wordnet browsing and editing tool. In *Proceedings of the Third International Wordnet Conference (GWC 2006)*, (pp. 325-328). Seogwipo, Korea: GWC Press.

Horák, A., & Smrož, P. (2004). VisDic - Wordnet browsing and editing tool. In *Proceedings of the Second International Wordnet Conference (GWC2004)*. GWC Press.

Huvila, I. (2010). Where does the information come from? Information source use patterns in Wikipedia. *Information Research*, *15*(3).

Kunegis, J., & Lommatzsch, A. (2009). Learning spectral graph transformations for link prediction. In *Proceedings of the 26th Annual International Conference on Machine Learning*, (pp. 1–8). New York, NY: ACM.

Lakoff, G., Espenson, J., & Schwartz, A. (1991). Master metaphor list. *Tech Report*. Berkeley, CA: University of California Berkeley.

Laske, A., & De Luca, E. W. (2010). *Conversion of the basic multilingual dictionary into the RDF/ OWL format. Tech Report*. Magdeburg, Germany: Otto-von-Guericke University of Magdeburg.

Lönneker-Rodman, B. (2008). The Hamburg metaphor database project: Issues in resource creation. *Language Resources and Evaluation, 42*(3), 293–318. doi:10.1007/s10579-008-9073-9

McBride, B., Boothby, D., & Dollin, C. (2006). An introduction to RDF and the jena RDF API. Tech Report. Retrieved from http://www.hp.com.

Miller, G. A., Beckwith, R., Fellbaum, C., Gross, D., & Miller, K. (1990). Five papers on WordNet. *International Journal of Lexicology, 3*(4).

Motta, E., Shum, S. B., & Domingue, J. (1999). *Ontology-driven document enrichment: Principles and case studies*. Paper presented at the 12th Banff Knowledge Acquisition Workshop. Banff, Canada.

Nuzzolese, A., Gangemi, A., & Presutti, V. (2011). *Gathering lexical linked data and knowledge patterns from Framenet*. Paper presented at the Sixth International Conference on Knowledge Capture. Banff, Canada.

Oltramari, A., Gangemi, A., Guarino, N., & Masolo, C. (2002). Restructuring Wordnet's top-level: The Ontoclean approach. In *Proceedings of the Language Resources and Evaluation Conference, LREC2002*. ACL Press.

Pianta, E., Bentivogli, L., & Girardi, C. (2002). *Multiwordnet: Developing an aligned multilingual database*. Paper presented at the First International Conference on Global Wordnet. Mysore, India.

Plumbaum, T., Lommatzsch, A., Hennig, L., Luca, E. W. D., & Albayrak, S. (2011). *Improving recommendation quality using semantically enriched user profiles*. Paper submitted to the International Semantic Web Conference 2011 (ISWC2011). Bonn, Germany.

Plumbaum, T., Stelter, T., & Korth, A. (2009). Semantic web usage mining: Using semantics to understand user intentions. In *Proceedings of the 17th International Conference on User Modeling, Adaptation, and Personalization,* (pp. 391–396). Berlin, Germany: Springer-Verlag.

Popescu, A., & Ungar, L. H. (2003). Statistical relational learning for link prediction. In *Proceedings of the Workshop on Learning Statistical Models from Relational Data*. ACM.

Ranieri, M., Pianta, E., & Bentivogli, L. (2004). Browsing multilingual information with the MultiSemCor Web interface. In *Proceedings of the LREC 2004 Satellite Workshop on the Amazing Utility of Parallel and Comparable Corpora,* (pp. 38-41). Portugal: LREC Press.

Schein, A. I., Popescul, A., Ungar, L. H., & Pennock, D. M. (2002). Methods and metrics for cold-start recommendations. In *Proceedings of the 25th Annual International ACM Sigir Conference on Research and Development in Information Retrieval,* (pp. 253–260). New York, NY: ACM.

Schreiber, G., van Assem, M., & Gangemi, A. (2006). *RDF/OWL representation of WordNet*. Retrieved from http://www.w3.org/TR/2006/ WD-wordnet-rdf-20060619/.

van Assem, M., Gangemi, A., & Schreiber, G. (2004). *Wordnet in RDFS and OWL*. Retrieved from http://www.w3c.org.

van Assem, M., Gangemi, A., & Schreiber, G. (2006). *RDF/OWL representation of WordNet*. Retrieved from http://www.w3.org/2001/sw/ bestpractices/wnet/wn-conversion.html.

Vintar, S., Buitelaar, P., & Volk, M. (2003). Semantic relations in concept-based cross-language medical information retrieval. In *Proceedings of the ECML/PKDD Workshop on Adaptive Text Extraction and Mining*. Croatia: ECML Press.

Vossen, P. (1999). *EuroWordNet general document, version 3, final*. Retrieved from www.illc. uva.nl/EuroWordNet/docs/GeneralDocPS.zip.

ADDITIONAL READING

Enderton, H. B. (2002). *A mathematical introduction to logic* (2nd ed.). New York: Academic Press.

Gómez-Pérez, A., Fernández-López, M., & Corcho, O. (2004). *Ontological engineering*. Berlin, Germany: Springer Verlag.

Heath, T., & Bizer, C. (2011). *Linked data: Evolving the web into a global data space*. New York: Morgan & Claypool Publishers.

Hitzler, P., Krötzsch, M., & Rudolph, S. (2009). *Foundations of semantic web technologies*. New York: Chapman & Hall/CRC.

Lathauwer, L. D., Moor, B. D., & Vandewalle, J. (2000). A multilinear singular value decomposition. *Matrix Analysis and Applications*, *21*(4), 1253–1278. doi:10.1137/S0895479896305696

Mitchell, T. M. (1997). *Machine learning*. New York: McGraw-Hill.

Robinson, A., & Voronkov, A. (2001). *Handbook of automated reasoning* (*Vol. 1-2*). London: Elsevier.

Saul, L. K., Weinberger, K. Q., Sha, F., Ham, J., & Lee, D. D. (2006). Semisupervised learning. In Chapelle, O., Schölkop, B., & Zien, A. (Eds.), *Spectral Methods for Dimensionality Reduction*. Cambridge, MA: MIT Press.

Staab, S., & Studer, R. (Eds.). (2004). *Handbook on ontologies*. Berlin, Germany: Springer.

KEY TERMS AND DEFINITIONS

Language Engineering: Research field that involves the development and application of software systems that perform tasks concerning the processing of human natural language.

Language Resources: Essential components of language engineering, containing a wide range of linguistic information with different degrees of complexity. These linguistic resources are sets of language data and descriptions in machine readable form, used for building, improving or evaluating natural language and speech systems or algorithms.

Lexical Linked Data: Specific lexical resources that are interconnected to the Linked Open Data Cloud through lexical relations.

Lexical Resources: Specific language resources containing lexical information.

Linked Open Data (LOD): Different resources that are interconnected and shared on the Web. The idea of Linked Open Data is to connect and share data, information, or knowledge following Semantic Web principals like using URIs and RDF descriptions.

Machine Learning: A scientific discipline concerned with the design and development of algorithms that allow computers to evolve behaviours based on empirical data, such as from sensor data or databases

Ontology: A formal specification of a conceptualization of a domain of interest that specifies a set of constraints that declare what should necessarily hold in any possible world.

Semantic Web: Is the World Wide Web enhanced with Semantics yielding the "Web of Data" or "Linked Data" that enables machines to understand the semantics, or meaning of information on the World Wide Web.

ENDNOTES

1   http://linkeddata.org/
2   http://framenet.icsi.berkeley.edu/
3   http://catalog.elra.info/product_info.
    php?products_id=100
4   http://www.springerlink.com/
    content/4wc0lb70m57km7eu/
5   http://www.facebook.com/
6   http://twitter.com/
7   http://www.wikipedia.com
8   http://www.freebase.com/
9   http://www.foaf-project.org/

Chapter 9
Mining Multiword Terms from Wikipedia

Silvana Hartmann
Technische Universität Darmstadt, Germany

György Szarvas
Technische Universität Darmstadt, Germany & Research Group on Artificial Intelligence, Hungarian Academy of Sciences, Hungary

Iryna Gurevych
Technische Universität Darmstadt, Germany

ABSTRACT

The collection of the specialized vocabulary of a particular domain (terminology) is an important initial step of creating formalized domain knowledge representations (ontologies). Terminology Extraction (TE) aims at automating this process by collecting the relevant domain vocabulary from existing lexical resources or collections of domain texts. In this chapter, the authors address the extraction of multiword terminology, as multiword terms are very frequent in terminology but typically poorly represented in standard lexical resources. They present their method for mining multiword terminology from Wikipedia and the freely available terminology resource that they extracted using the presented method. Terminology extraction based on Wikipedia exploits the advantages of a huge multilingual, domain-transcending knowledge source and large scale structural information that can identify potential multiword units without the need for linguistic processing tools. Thus, while evaluated in English, the proposed method is basically applicable to all languages in Wikipedia.

INTRODUCTION

Automated ontology construction, or *ontology learning,* has received substantial research interest in recent years, as the manual development of formal knowledge models is labor-intensive and

DOI: 10.4018/978-1-4666-0188-8.ch009

cannot scale up to practical needs in the Semantic Web. *Terminology extraction*—i.e., the automated collection of domain terminology—is the first step towards computer-assisted ontology construction (Cimiano, 2006).

The *terminology of a domain* (referred to as *terms*) consists of a subset of general-language lexical units that have a domain-relevant meaning, and lexical units of the domain-specific sublanguage—i.e., technical terms. Accordingly, terminology extraction aims at finding domain-specific and general domain-relevant lexical units, where the particular domain is defined by the actual application. Figure 1 presents the continuum of domain specificity of lexical units, ranging from general-language units to specialized technical terms (Cabré, 1999). *Multiword expressions* are interpreted as lexical units which consist of several words and whose irregular semantic, syntactic, pragmatic or statistical properties justify their own entry in a natural-language lexicon (Sag, Baldwin, Bond, Copestake, & Flickinger, 2002). In this chapter, we will refer to domain-relevant multiword expressions as *multiword terms*.

Typically, the majority of domain-specific vocabulary consists of multiword terms (Nakagawa & Mori, 1998), which makes the extraction of multiword terminology an important problem on its own. In this chapter, we focus on the automatic extraction of multiword terminology, as multiword units (particularly domain-specific ones) are poorly represented in standard lexical resources like WordNet (Sag, et al., 2002). Since ontology construction might address any particular domain, or even domain-transcending areas such as e-learning, we aim at the extraction of a general-purpose multiword lexicon, which can later be filtered according to the particular application needs. We consider our resource to be a first step towards creating parameterized terminology resources, which allows flexible term selection for efficient ontology construction on the fly. A demand for such resources emerged as a consequence of advances in semi-automatic ontology construction and increasing employment of ontologies in semantically enhanced applications. In this context, Wikipedia is an ideal source for terminology extraction, due to its good coverage of a wide variety of domains in multiple languages and its encyclopedic style, placing an emphasis on specialized vocabulary, rather than expressions of linguistic interest, such as idioms.

The proposed flexible terminology resources require dynamic *domain adaptation*—i.e., the selection of terms for a particular application domain. Domain adaptation typically happens

Figure 1. Properties of terms: term size vs. degree of domain specialization

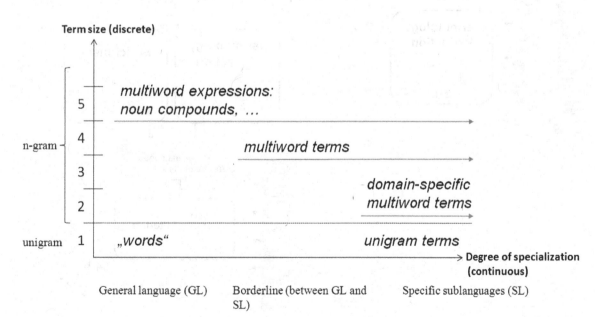

in the corpus collection stage of the terminology extraction cycle: for every new domain, a corpus of domain texts containing the domain-relevant terms is collected. Alternatively, we suggest performing domain adaptation as *domain filtering* on the Wikipedia-based terminology resource independent of the terminology extraction step. Our approach enables ad-hoc building of terminology resources for different domains and degrees of language specialization, and thus improves the lifecycle of terminology building: instead of running through the term extraction process—from corpus collection to term selection—for every new terminology resource, the term extraction process is run only once on Wikipedia. Then the term selection is performed on the Wikipedia-based resource for any domain. Figure 2 illustrates the

difference between conventional domain adaptation and enhanced domain adaptation on the Wikipedia-based resource. Although we do not perform the domain filtering ourselves in this work, we suggest ways how it can be done based on the information contained in our resource.

In this chapter, we present and evaluate the extraction process of our terminology resource and its enrichment with category and definition information from Wikipedia—information which can be used in the further ontology construction process. To the best of our knowledge, the present work is the first to evaluate Wikipedia as a source of multiword terms (other than named entities). Related work (Erdmann, Nakayama, Hara, & Nishio, 2008; Erdmann, Nakayama, Hara, & Nishio, 2009) exploits Wikipedia for *bilingual*

Figure 2. Difference between conventional and enhanced, Wikipedia-based domain adaptation of terminology resources

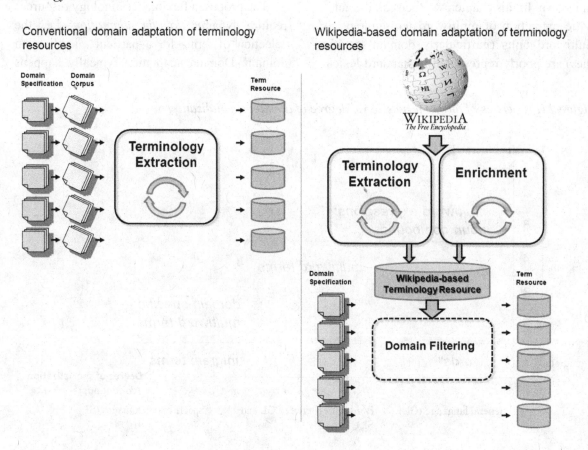

terminology extraction of unigram terms and multiword terms. They, however, evaluate their approach only on pairs of unigram terms, but not on the extracted multiword terms.

The proposed resource of multiword terms from Wikipedia is made publicly available to the research community; thus it can be evaluated in specific applications and serve as a base model for further development of flexible terminological resources for semi-automatic ontology construction.

Exploiting the unique characteristics of Wikipedia as a knowledge source offers the following advantages over terminology extraction from domain corpora:

- The approach is in general language-independent, since it does not rely on linguistic text analysis. Many previous approaches that extract terminology from domain-specific corpora use, for instance, Part-of-Speech (POS) patterns or syntactic parses. The absence of robust analysis tools for certain domains or languages might prohibit the application of such methods.
- Wikipedia provides high-quality multiword term candidates. Using Wikipedia as a source for the extraction of multiword terms, we rely on phrase boundaries explicitly marked by humans—i.e., we accept only those phrases as candidates which are explicitly highlighted by different typesetting (bold, italics) or wiki markup (links, link anchor texts, titles, headers). As a result, the extracted multiword term candidates are less noisy than those extracted from general texts with a knowledge-poor approach (e.g., n-grams).
- Wikipedia is a good source of domain-relevant terms: Wikipedia's broad coverage of various specialized domains and its quick evolution with respect to coverage of newly emerging scientific or technological areas makes it a uniquely well-suited resource for terminology extraction to sup-

port the construction of formal ontologies in new areas. Thus, Wikipedia is an attractive alternative to the collection of domain-specific texts for terminology extraction.

We note here that, even though the proposed method does not inherently rely on domain-specific texts or complex linguistic analysis, we can naturally exploit these when they are available: we might make use of domain-specific texts and/ or part-of-speech information to further filter the extracted candidate lists. Particularly in our study, we will make use of a part-of-speech tagger and a named entity tagger, as for English these tools are easy to obtain. Still, an important aspect of our method is that the use of such tools is not mandatory.

In the following sections, we first provide an overview of the state-of-the-art approaches to 1) term extraction—specifically, related work on term extraction for ontology construction, 2) multiword expression extraction, and 3) using knowledge extracted from Wikipedia in semi-automatic ontology construction. A particular focus is on extracting multiword terminology as opposed to unigram terms, also called *simple terms*. We also introduce Wikipedia and the various types of information contained therein.

In the main part of the chapter, we present our work on extracting multiword terminology from Wikipedia. Our analysis shows that over one million multiword term candidates consisting of two to four words can be extracted from the English version of Wikipedia using the method presented in the chapter. However, not all of the marked-up phrases are valid multiword terms; some of them are conventional natural language phrases, such as "list of countries." Therefore, the candidate phrases identified from Wikipedia are ranked by a statistical measure used in multiword expression mining which exploits corpus statistics of the multiword units and their constituent terms. Based on the ranking, the top-ranked phrases are selected as multiword terms. We describe the steps of this process ranging from candidate extraction and candidate ranking to the final filtering step separating named entities from multiword terms. The extracted multiword term resource is further augmented with definitions and category information from Wikipedia. For evaluation, a sample of the extracted multiword terms is evaluated by human raters. Additionally, we present a comparison of the resource to general-domain multiword terms represented in the Princeton WordNet (Fellbaum, 1998). The chapter closes with a discussion of future research directions and a summary of the presented work.

BACKGROUND

Terminology Extraction

Defining the terminology of a domain is a basic yet laborious task in ontology construction—particularly if performed manually by human experts. As a result, there is a high demand for automated solutions based on natural language processing to support this time consuming and costly process. In automated terminology extraction, domain-relevant terms are mined from text collections exploiting linguistic properties of terms, such as typical phrase structure patterns, their statistical distribution in corpora, or idiosyncratic properties in a particular domain (as with protein names in molecular biology).

The extracted terms serve as input to the later steps of the ontology construction process. The final composition of a vocabulary of terms depends on the type of ontology to be developed: task ontologies (e.g., travel booking as in Gómez-Pérez, Fernández-López, and Corcho, 2004) require a detailed description of events and general world knowledge, while formal domain ontologies often require highly specialized knowledge and scientific terminology. Scientific terminology is very productive—new terms are created continuously. Therefore, techniques for automatic terminology

extraction from texts, also called automatic term recognition, are required to efficiently create and maintain terminological resources.

Figure 3 introduces the architecture of the terminology extraction process. It starts with the collection of a corpus representing the target domain. From this corpus, term candidates are extracted and ranked according to their domain relevance. A subset of the ranked candidates is then selected to build the terminology resource. We describe each of these steps of the terminology extraction process in the following paragraphs.

Corpus creation. Corpora for terminology extraction are usually created from collections of domain-specific texts. Such collections can be obtained from edited publications—e.g., technical documentation (Aussenac-Gilles, Biébow, & Szulman, 2000)—or crawled from the web using targeted web search queries (Brunzel, 2008). The former approach yields high-quality texts, but access to large amounts of text might be problematic for certain specialized (or newly emerging) domains. The latter approach poses the problem of data quality management both on the surface

Figure 3. Terminology extraction architecture

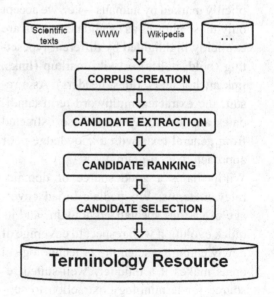

level (HTML cleaning, boilerplate removal, etc.) and on the content level (texts of low or questionable quality are common in the Web 2.0). These problems can be avoided by relying on high-quality, easily accessible, yet large-scale sources. Thus, the collaborative encyclopedia Wikipedia, which has proven to be of high quality with respect to text editing and information content (Giles, 2005), has been identified as an information source for corpus construction. Cui, Lu, Li, and Chen (2008), for instance, propose a method for automatically extracting domain corpora from Wikipedia.

Candidate extraction. Candidate extraction techniques using linguistic information exploit the fact that domain-specific terms are typically noun phrases. Conventional approaches extract noun phrases from automatically POS-tagged texts using manually defined regular expression patterns on POS tags.

For example, Frantzi, Ananiadou, and Mima (2000) use the patterns (Noun Noun+), (Adj* Noun+), and (((Adj|Noun)+|((Adj|Noun)*(Noun Prep)?)(Adj|Noun)*)Noun) to cover simple terms and noun compounds of variable length (e.g., "peptide," "signal peptide"), sequences of adjectives of variable size followed by at least one noun (e.g., "gross national product") and more complex terms comprised of sequences of adjectives, nouns and prepositions (e.g., "language acquisition in children"). The first pattern, retrieving only noun compounds, is more restrictive than the other patterns. This leads to higher precision, since noun compounds have a high likelihood of being domain terms, but lower recall, since terms containing adjectives and prepositions are not found. The patterns can be adapted to the requirements of specific domains regarding the *size* of term candidates—i.e., the number of words they contain, and their internal structure (for instance, whether they include other multiword terms).

If robust linguistic processing is not available, knowledge-poor approaches to term candidate extraction can be applied. The simplest one is to extract n-grams—i.e., continuous sequences of n words, from texts. This yields term candidates up to a pre-defined size n. Often stop words, such as function words like articles or auxiliary verbs, are filtered out before extracting the n-grams to restrict the size of the candidate set. Since this technique does not take the linguistic phrase structure into account, the mined term candidates are often noisy; they may, for instance, violate phrase structure constraints. Thus, this approach relies heavily on the subsequent candidate ranking step to identify high-quality terms. Moreover, the ranking of all n-grams up to a certain size of n might be computationally expensive.

To summarize, the linguistically informed approach requires more resources—namely, the availability of a POS tagger with robust performance in the target domain. The purely statistical approach can operate without it but consequently yields lower precision.

Another very different approach to candidate extraction is to exploit specific properties of a particular text source. While texts extracted from the web often pose difficulties for linguistic processing tools due to low text quality (which may be inherent to the texts or caused by removal of HTML markup), they contain structural information which can be used to identify term candidates: in light of this, Brunzel (2008) uses the XHTML markup in web texts to identify term candidates. XHTML tags, such as headers or emphasis tags, are used to identify suitable candidate sequences. Similarly, the MediaWiki markup in Wikipedia, highlighting Wikipedia article titles and link anchors, has been used to identify candidates for named entity recognition (Toral & Muñoz, 2006) and bilingual terminology extraction (Erdmann, et al., 2008). This approach exploits a higher degree of knowledge on phrase boundaries, since the marked-up sections are typically created by human editors. Still, the highlighted sections are not selected with terminology extraction in mind. This makes a ranking and filtering step necessary.

Candidate ranking and selection. Depending on the characteristics of the text collection and the candidate extraction method applied, a large number of term candidates are extracted that are subsequently ranked and filtered according to their domain-relevance. The final terminological resource is then selected from the ranked list. Either a predefined number of top-ranked terms are retained, or a cutoff value of the ranking function is determined, maximizing the accuracy on a predefined set of gold-standard terms.

The ranking process has to take into account two different characteristics of the term candidates. For simple terms, the property of *termhood*—i.e., whether the candidate represents a domain-specific concept—has to be measured. For multiword terms, the property of *unithood* has to be measured additionally. This property refers to the degree to which the words in a term are associated with each other to form a lexical unit (Kageura & Umino, 1996).

Valid lexical units (i.e., those with a high unithood value) are phrases that should obtain a separate entry in the lexicon ("gross national product"), while phrases that consist of an ad-hoc combination of terms and can be interpreted compositionally (such as "national product of the EU states") indicate a low unithood value. A large number of statistical methods based on the candidates' (and optionally, their constituents') frequency in a domain-specific corpus have been suggested for ranking. Some methods also consider the textual contexts of the terms in a corpus, or the distribution of the terms in another corpus from a different domain. Among the widely used methods are measures that model either the unithood, or the termhood of the candidates, and *hybrid methods* that try to combine both types of measures.

Figure 4 summarizes the most important term ranking approaches based on corpus statistics, grouped by whether they target termhood, unithood or both. Methods that measure unithood—also referred to as *statistical association measures*—are targeted to multiword terms and

cannot be applied to unigram terms. They evaluate either the strength of the association between the words in a multiword term candidate like Pointwise Mutual Information (PMI), or measure the significance of this association like χ^2 or Log-Likelihood Ratio (LLR) (Krenn & Evert, 2001). Some methods for the ranking of multiword terms can naturally deal with terms of varied length (see column n-grams in Figure 4), while a few of them are optimized for bigrams and have to be adapted to longer terms (Da Silva & Lopes, 1999). Termhood and hybrid methods, on the other hand, can be used to rank both unigram and multiword terms alike, and can naturally deal with terms of varied length (see column n-grams in Figure 4).

We further distinguish between ranking methods that use frequency information about the term only, and methods that also consider the textual context around the terms (column *Corpus Context* in Figure 4). Term frequency in a domain-specific corpus has also been used as a (baseline) ranking method. Frequency, however, is biased towards short terms, as unigrams have higher frequencies in a corpus than n-grams. Thus a size factor penalizing shorter term candidates is usually included in more sophisticated methods (such as the lexical cohesion measure in TermExtractor and Glossex—see Figure 4). In a similar manner, unithood methods and hybrid methods take into account the frequencies of both the term candidates and their constituent words. Tf-idf, a weighting scheme originally introduced in information retrieval (Salton, Wong, & Yang, 1975), relates the frequency of a term in a document to the number of documents the term occurs in (document frequency). The value is higher, if a term occurs frequently in a document, but only in few documents across the full corpus. Terms with a high tf-idf value are considered domain-relevant.

The C-value and NC-value (Frantzi & Ananiadou, 1999) also take contextual information into account. C-value considers a special form of contextual information: the occurrence of a term candidate c as part of a longer term e, called

Figure 4. Overview of statistical methods for term extraction

	Method	Type	n-grams	Corpus Context	Contrast Corpus	Formula
1	**Frequency**		1+	-	-	$f(c, D)$
2	**Tf–idf**	termhood	1+	-	-	$\text{tf–idf}(c) = f(c, D) \cdot \frac{|D|}{df(c)}$
3	**Weirdness**		1+	-	+	$W(c) = \frac{f(c,D)/t(D)}{f(c,C)/t(C)}$
4	**PMI**		2	-	-	$\text{PMI}(c = w_1 w_2) = \log \frac{P(c,D)}{P(w_1,D) \cdot P(w_2,D)}$
5	**Log-likelihood ratio**	unithood	2	-	-	$\text{LLR}(c) = -2 \sum_{ij} f(ij) \log \frac{f(ij)}{\hat{f}(ij)}$
6	**Pearson's χ^2**		2	-	-	$\chi^2(c) = \sum_{i,j} \frac{(f(ij) - \hat{f}(ij))^2}{f(ij)}$
7	**C-value**		1+	+	-	$C(c) = \begin{cases} \log_2 n \cdot f(c, D) & \text{- if } c \text{ is not nested} \\ \log_2 n \cdot \left(f(c, D) - \frac{1}{|N_c|} \sum_{e_i \in N_c} f(e_i, D)\right) & \text{- otherwise} \end{cases}$
8	**NC-value**	hybrid	1+	+	-	$\text{NC}(c) = 0.8 \cdot C(c) + 0.2 \cdot \sum_{m \in M} f(c, m, D) \cdot \omega(m, D)$
9	**Glossex**		1+	-	+	$\text{GL}(c) = \alpha \cdot \text{TD}(c) + \beta \cdot \text{TC}(c)$
10	**TermExtractor**		1+	-	+	$\text{TermExtractor}(c) = \alpha \cdot \text{DR}(c) + \beta \cdot \text{DC}(c) + \gamma \cdot \text{LC}(c)$

Domain Specificity: $\text{TD}(c) = \frac{1}{n} \cdot \sum_{w_i \in c} \log \frac{P(w_i, D)}{P(w_i, C)}$

Term Cohesion: $\text{TC}(c) = \frac{n \cdot f(c, D) \cdot \log(f(c, D))}{\sum_{w_i \in c} f(w_i, D)}$

Domain Relevance: $\text{DR}(c) = \frac{f(c, D)}{\max_j f(c, c_j \in C)}$

Domain Consensus: $\text{DC}(c) = -\sum_{d_i \in D} P(c, d_k) \log(P(c, d_k))$

Lexical Cohesion: $\text{LC}(c) = \text{TC}(c)$

Legend:
- Term candidate $c = w_1, \ldots, w_n, e$; number of words w in term c: $|c|$
- Domain corpus D, contrast corpus C; documents $d \in D, c \in C$; # of words in corpus X: $t(X)$
- Frequency of term c in X: $f(c, X)$; document frequency of term c in corpus X: $df(c, X)$
- Number of documents in corpus X: $|X|$
- Candidate term e contains term c (nestedness); $N_c = e_i, \ldots, e_n$ set of nested terms, $|N_c|$ = # of nested terms
- $M = m_1, \ldots, m_k$ set of "marker words"; $\omega(m, D)$: weight of marker word determined from D
- Frequency of c in X next to marker word m: $f(c, m, X)$
- Relative frequency of w in X: $P(w, X) = f(w, X)/t(X)$
- Parameters $\alpha, \beta, \gamma, \ldots$
- Contingency table: observed probabilities:

	w_2	$\not{w}_2$	
w_1	f_{11}	f_{12}	$f(w_2)$
$\not{w}_1$	f_{21}	f_{22}	$f(\not{w}_1)$
	$f(w_2)$	$f(\not{w}_2)$	

- In contingency table: $\hat{f}(ij)$ – expected frequency, under independence assumption: $\hat{f}(12) = (f(w_1)f(w_2))/N$

"nestedness." The enclosed occurrences f(e, D) are subtracted from the frequency of the term candidate, as they are not counted as evidence of the enclosed term. Thus the occurrence of "national product" nested in "gross national product" is not counted. Based on the observation that enclosed terms which occur in a large variety of contexts also occur independently, the number of different contexts the candidate appears in $|N_c|$ is used to normalize the subtracted number, as shown in Figure 4.

NC-value is a weighted sum of C-value and a "context information factor" (Frantzi & Ananiadou, 1999). The context information factor quantifies the assumption that there are specific words in a domain that frequently co-occur with domain-specific terms. These words are interpreted as markers of termhood. Frantzi and Ananiadou (1999) identify a set of these markers using a seed set of manually selected terms. The most frequent content words (nouns, verbs, or adjectives) occurring directly before or after the seed terms in a domain-specific corpus are selected as termhood markers. These markers receive a weight—$\omega(m, D)$ in Figure 4—based on the frequency they are found together with a term. The context information factor sums over the number of occurrences of the candidate next to the marker multiplied with the weight of the marker as shown in Figure 4.

Weirdness, TermExtractor, and Glossex use additional corpora besides those the candidates are extracted from. This is shown in column *Contrast Corpus* in Figure 4.

Weirdness (Ahmad, Gillam, & Tostevin, 1999) compares the relative term frequencies in the domain corpus to those in a general newswire corpus. Terms which have high weirdness are more closely related to the target domain.

Glossex (Kozakov, et al., 2004) incorporates a general-domain corpus as part of a domain specificity measure TC(c), which consists of the average log weirdness of a term's constituent words.

TermExtractor (Sclano & Velardi, 2007) is similar to Glossex, but uses a set of out-of-domain corpora, (i.e., domain-specific corpora from domains other than the target domain) to compute domain relevance DR(c) instead: this measure compares the frequency of a term candidate in the domain corpus to the highest frequency in the set of out-of-domain corpora.

Evaluation. To evaluate a particular term extraction method, the extracted terms are usually either compared to a terminological dictionary, or the top-ranked terms are manually annotated for domain relevance by a group of domain experts. Depending on the chosen evaluation strategy, precision (i.e., the proportion of correct terms in the list of extracted terms) and/or recall (i.e., the proportion of terms retrieved to the complete set of terms in the corpus) of the studied methods— and, of course, variants of these measures—can be estimated.

Both evaluation strategies have advantages and disadvantages: recall can only be measured with respect to an existing terminology resource, which is often not available in sufficient quality and size. This evaluation strategy, furthermore, does not consider that a term extraction method is able to extract previously unknown terms—exactly what it is required to do—and therefore may underestimate precision. Precision can be more reliably estimated by manually rating the extracted terms. As manual annotation is time consuming, typically only a subset of the extracted terms can be evaluated.

Comparison of term extraction techniques. Which method performs best in terminology extraction is essentially an open research question. Several works in the recent years compared different term extraction techniques on various domain corpora (Pazienza, Pennacchiotti, & Zanzotto, 2005; Korkontzelos, Klapaftis, & Manandhar, 2008; Zhang, Iria, Brewster, & Ciravegna, 2008). All these studies compare several popular methods of term extraction. They aim at identifying the best method based on an evaluation under the same conditions.

The term extraction methods compared include 1) frequency, C-value, NC-value, PMI, and significance of association measures (t-test, χ^2, LLR) (Korkontzelos, et al., 2008), 2) degree of association measures (mutual information), significance of association measures (t-test, LLR), frequency and C-value (Pazienza, et al., 2005), and 3) tf-idf, weirdness, C-Value, re-implementations of TermExtractor and Glossex (Zhang, et al., 2008). Note that the third set includes only those methods that can be applied to both simple and multiword terms, as Zhang et al. (2008) propose an integrated approach for both types of terms.

The studies mainly target the precision in their evaluation, since they typically evaluate the top-ranked terms (up to 300). Recall with respect to an existing terminology resource (term annotations in the PennBioIE and in the Genia corpus) is evaluated in Korkontzelos et al. (2008).

There is no general agreement on the preference of a particular term extraction algorithm. Evaluation results for the same method vary not only with the evaluation metric used, but also with the application domain and the corpus used for extraction.

Termhood methods and the methods measuring the significance of association are found to perform best on a corpus form the European Space Agency using expert judgments on terms (Pazienza, et al., 2005). Hybrid methods, together with termhood methods, performed best on corpora from the life science domain (Korkontzelos, et al., 2008); the PennBioIE corpus (Kulick, et al., 2004), which contains over 700,000 words; and the Genia corpus (Kim, Ohta, Tateisi, & Tsujii, 2003), which contains over 420,000 words.

Zhang et al. (2008) also evaluate term extraction on the Genia corpus and find that tf-idf performs well, but is outperformed by hybrid methods, particularly C-value, which performs best in their evaluation.

The evaluation by Zhang et al. (2008) explicitly contrasts different types of corpora: term extraction on the Genia corpus is compared to term extraction on a corpus of documents about animals extracted from Wikipedia and consisting of one million words. On the Wikipedia corpus a re-implementation of TermExtractor performs best. The difference in performance on the two corpora is explained with their different composition: C-value performs best on the Genia corpus, which contains a low proportion of unigram terms (reported 11%) and a large number of multiword terms. C-value performs worse on the Wikipedia corpus, which contains a large number of simple terms. Zhang et al. (2008) conclude that the composition of a domain corpus is an important factor in automated term recognition. Unfortunately, they do not present a separate evaluation of the performance on simple terms and multiword terms. Thus it is not clear whether the proposed integrated treatment of simple terms and multiword terms is of advantage.

While there is a lot of evidence in favor of C-value and hybrid methods, these are outperformed by a simple unithood based measure, namely LLR, in an evaluation on PennBioIE (Korkontzelos, et al., 2008).

To sum up, there is no general consensus on a single term extraction method, but there is a tendency to prefer hybrid methods such as C-value. The conclusion to be drawn, however, is that the optimal method is dependent on the particular setting: application domain, type of corpus and term type.

Pazienza et al. (2005) note another aspect of term extraction: they find that besides domain-specific terms, terms from other domains are also detected by the evaluated term extraction methods. This property of term extraction methods is also relevant for the domain independent term extraction setting in this work.

Figure 5. Multiword expression classification

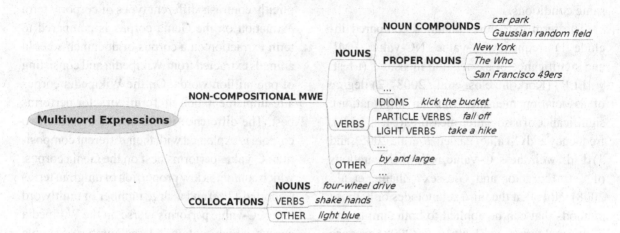

Multiword Expression Mining

Multiword term extraction is closely related to Multiword Expression (MWE) mining in computational corpus linguistics. Therefore, methods from MWE mining have been employed in terminology extraction, like the POS-pattern filtering and the statistical unithood methods introduced above. Multiword expression mining specifically targets unithood, as it aims at the creation of general-language lexicons. For this task, the crucial factor is whether a phrase forms a lexicalized multiword unit in a language; relevance to a particular domain is not required. Thus, a major difference between multiword terminology extraction and multiword expression mining is that general (newswire) corpora are used for mining multiword expressions as opposed to domain-specific corpora in terminology extraction.

Sag et al. (2002) define multiword expressions as "idiosyncratic units that cross word boundaries." Thus, multiword expressions include not only nominal expressions, but also other parts of speech, such as verbs, adjectives, and adverbial phrases. Multiword expressions are interpreted as lexical units, whose irregular semantic, syntactic, pragmatic, or statistical properties justify their own entry in a natural language lexicon. These properties include:

- Semantical non-compositionality: multiword expressions with irregular semantics are *semantically non-compositional*: the meaning of these expressions cannot be inferred from the meaning of their constituent words. Examples are idioms like "to kick the bucket," non-compositional verb-particle constructions like "to give up" or noun compounds like "hot dog."
- Syntactical irregularity: multiword expressions that contain co-ordinations of different parts-of-speech (e.g., a preposition and an adverb in "by and large") are syntactically irregular. Syntactically irregular multiword expressions are typically also semantically non-compositional.
- Statistical irregularity: some multiword expressions are semantically regular, but nevertheless perceived as a linguistic unit, for example "strong tea" or "four-wheel drive." They typically occur together and refer to a particular concept. Consequently, they are considered as institutionalized expressions and are also referred to as *collocations* (Evert & Krenn, 2001).

Figure 5 shows a classification of multiword expressions by part-of-speech and compositionality based on Sag et al. (2002). As multiword terms are multiword expressions, which are relevant to specific domains, all of the listed classes (in capital letters) may contain multiword terms. Some of these will be found only in domain-specific texts (multiword terms in specific sublanguages as in Figure 1), while others also occur in general-language texts (multiword terms placed between general language and specific sublanguages in Figure 1). Classes addressed in the present work in terminology extraction are printed in boldface in Figure 5.

Multiword expressions with different parts-of-speech—potentially divided into subtypes—are usually mined using techniques adapted to the given type/POS (Fazly & Stevenson, 2007). Therefore, various linguistic patterns for candidate identification using POS and syntactic information have been developed. For the identification of multiword expressions—similarly to term extraction—linguistic properties and frequency counts of the candidates and their constituents are taken into account. Additionally, syntactic fixedness and modifiability (Wermter & Hahn, 2005) are features used to distinguish between common natural language phrases and multiword expressions, since multiword expressions have been shown to occur in a narrower range of syntactic constructions and to withstand modifiability: while "kick the bucket" is acceptable, "kick the *big* bucket" is not when employing the idiomatic sense.

Typically, statistical methods measuring the strength of association between a multiword expression and its constituents are used to identify MWEs from corpora: these methods are similar to those for terminology extraction previously discussed. Another group of methods takes context information into account using distributional similarities of multiword expressions: first, context vectors describing the words surrounding the multiword expression candidates are derived from a corpus. Then, these representations are compared to those of their constituent words, using, for instance, the cosine metric, to identify how much the meaning of the multiword expression diverges from the meaning of the constituent words. These measures are used specifically to identify non-compositional multiword expressions such as idioms (Bannard, Baldwin, & Lascarides, 2003; Katz & Giesbrecht, 2006), but often suffer from data sparseness problems.

Another family of multiword expression mining methods exploits translational correspondences between multiword terms and single terms in different languages (Villada Moirón & Tiedemann, 2006): the English "traffic light" is typically translated as one word, "Ampel," in German. Translational correspondences of this kind can be used to identify multiword expressions in different languages using statistical methods. This method is successful in extracting multiword expressions, provided that large parallel corpora are at hand (which can be problematic for certain languages).

The current focus of multiword expression mining is the identification of the best statistical method for particular types of multiword expressions. As with the work in term extraction, different methods are compared: Pecina and Schlesinger (2006) evaluate over 80 statistical methods of MWE extraction on Czech collocations. They find that pointwise mutual information, Pearson's χ^2 test and a version of LLR perform equally well, and almost identically to the best method, which uses distributional semantics.

Additionally, they combine a large number of statistical association measures for multiword expression mining using machine learning techniques. They manage to improve evaluation results significantly from mean average precision of 66% for the best single measures to over 80%.

Within nominal MWEs, the current research is focused on certain types (e.g., noun compound identification (Tratz & Hovy, 2010)) and differentiating between semantically compositional and non-compositional multiword expressions (Korkontzelos & Manandhar, 2009).

Work on single statistical association measures also focuses on improving existing measures: Hoang, Kim, and Kan (2009) include penalization factors for statistical association measures—for instance, to alleviate the bias towards low-frequency terms by PMI; Bouma (2010) tries to avoid inappropriate independence assumptions for statistical association measures by incorporating models of dependence between terms.

Wikipedia as a Knowledge Source for Ontology Construction

In the last few years, Wikipedia, the most successful collaboratively edited encyclopedia, has received wide recognition as a collection of common-sense knowledge and as an information source for various knowledge-intensive technologies. Medelyan, Milne, Legg, and Witten (2009) give an overview of the various uses of Wikipedia and the types of information therein. Two of these are most relevant to this chapter: the taxonomic knowledge and the linguistic knowledge encoded in Wikipedia.

Wikipedia first gained popularity as an alternative to traditional encyclopedias. The quality of content and form has been scrutinized and found to match traditionally edited volumes like the *Encyclopedia Britannica* (Giles, 2005). Wikipedia has the additional advantages of being updated quickly and continuously: the English Wikipedia has reached more than 3.5 million entries in less than 10 years of existence.

Besides English, articles in a large number of languages are provided. They are linked to other languages at the article level. This turns Wikipedia to an interesting resource for multilingual applications and for the projection of language processing techniques from well-resourced to low-resourced languages.

The following information sources relevant for terminology extraction are contained in Wikipedia: *article titles*, the Wikipedia equivalent of encyclopedic headwords, are connected with *article texts*, which contain *definitions* of the titles and detailed descriptions of the article topic. *Links* between pages occur in the article texts. *Disambiguation pages* distinguish between different concepts entered under the same headword. *Redirect pages* introduce variants of an article title—including synonyms and closely related terms, and link to the corresponding article. Through the use of *categories*, articles are also organized in a taxonomy which adds hierarchical structure to the encyclopedia content, and organizes specialized entries under the corresponding, more general entries. Together with the articles and the internal links, the category hierarchy makes up a graph structure, in which concepts are connected by relations. This information can be exploited for relation extraction and ontological structure building.

Also relevant to relation extraction is the information contained in *infoboxes*. These are templates, which introduce attribute–value sets relevant to the topic of the article. Infoboxes are defined for articles belonging to certain categories, for instance locations, animal classes, or natural phenomena. The infobox on the page of a country (for instance, *Italy)* contains a field for the capital (*Rome)* and the currency (*euro*). Thus, semantic relations between concepts are introduced. Infoboxes have been used for tasks such as information extraction and ontology learning.

Wikipedia as a collection of common-sense knowledge backed up by extensive structural information is a good starting point for developing cross-domain and domain-specific ontologies on many subjects. Therefore, it has been exploited for various stages in the ontology construction process, from corpus and terminology extraction to ontology learning.

Corpora extracted from Wikipedia are relevant for terminology extraction, as they contain a large proportion of domain-specific terminology, as well as general-language terms and borderline cases (i.e., terms which occur in domain-specific contexts but also in general language). In evaluations for terminology extraction, they bear comparison with traditional domain-specific corpora (Zhang, et al., 2008; Bonin, Dell'Orletta, Venturi, & Montemagni, 2010). The Wikipedia corpus is either constructed based on a manual selection, using a *Wikiportal* (i.e., a collection of pages on a particular topic area) relevant to the application domain (Bonin, et al., 2010), or using a random selection of articles about animals (Zhang, et al., 2008).

Cui et al. (2008) introduce a more sophisticated approach to the extraction of domain-specific corpora from Wikipedia. Their approach exploits Wikipedia's category labels to extract domain-relevant articles for any given domain automatically. It automatically selects a set of articles relevant to a given root category using only the category information in Wikipedia. First, a so-called classification tree is developed from the root category. It contains the root category, its child categories and articles classified under the categories. The leaves of the tree, Wikipedia articles, are considered as candidates for the domain corpus. They are ranked by relevance to the root category node exploiting linking information between the nodes in the graph.

The next step in the ontology construction process, the extraction of terminology and entities from Wikipedia has been addressed in the context of automatic creation of bilingual dictionaries. Such approaches are usually dependent on parallel corpora, which are often unavailable in specialized domains. Therefore, Wikipedia with its inter-language links and broad coverage of technical domains is a valuable resource for such applications. Exploiting inter-language links appears to be a well-functioning baseline for bilingual terminology extraction, but information from redirect pages and link anchor text has been additionally used to increase the coverage (Erdmann, et al., 2008). Evaluating the extracted resource on a gold-standard dictionary, Erdmann et al. (2008) find that the Wikipedia-based approach compares well to the traditional approach using bilingual corpora, particularly with respect to recall and low-frequency items. Although they also extract multiword terms, Erdmann et al. (2008) evaluate only single words and do not consider multiword terms in their evaluation. They expect even better improvements using Wikipedia for the extraction of multiword terms compared to standard techniques and their Wikipedia baseline, but cannot prove this assumption.

Wikipedia has also been used for a task related to terminology extraction—namely recognition of named entities, which covers person names, location names and the like. Named Entities (NEs) are relevant to ontology construction, since they represent instances of ontological concepts. They are sometimes covered by terminology extraction, but, compared to ordinary terms, require special treatment: besides identifying word sequences as named entities, classification into NE types and disambiguation of NEs are required, as in the case of the person name "George Bush," which could refer to either the 41st or the 43rd president of the United States. The approach proposed by Cucerzan (2007), for instance, employs Wikipedia for the identification and disambiguation of named entities. First, a dictionary of named entities is created by collecting article titles and their spelling variants from redirects and link anchor texts. Disambiguation and classification information is then extracted from redirect pages, disambiguation pages, category tags, and using "list of *" entries in Wikipedia articles, where * represents a named entity category or a subtype (e.g., "list of countries"). Additionally, contexts of the extracted NEs are stored. Using this information, spelling variants of a NE are associated with a particular entity, and classification of this entity is performed. A new occurrence of a named entity can then be disambiguated by comparing its context with the Wikipedia article text of the candidate entities and the context information stored in the dictionary.

Wikipedia has also been subject to various ontology learning efforts, for instance the YAGO (Suchanek, Kasneci, & Weikum, 2007) and DBpedia (Auer, et al., 2007) projects. They aim at alleviating the coverage bottleneck of expert-built, handmade ontologies, like CYC (Lenat, 1995), and taxonomic resources, like WordNet (Fellbaum, 1998).

The examples introduced in this section show that Wikipedia contains a wealth of information relevant to ontology learning. Information in Wikipedia can be mined from article texts, infoboxes, and from structural elements, such as the internal link and category structures. All of these elements have been exploited for the semi-automatic construction of ontologies, either in the automatic creation of taxonomies and other structured resources, in the generation of terminological dictionaries and named entity gazetteers, or in the creation of domain-specific corpora. In the next section, we will present another application of Wikipedia as a knowledge source for ontology construction by introducing our work on extracting multiword terminology from Wikipedia.

MINING MULTIWORD TERMS FROM WIKIPEDIA

Motivation: Wikipedia as a Source of Multiword Terms

Wikipedia has been shown to be a valuable resource in ontology construction. In this work, we particularly focus on those properties of Wikipedia relevant for the extraction of multiword terms.

We assume that multiword terminology extraction needs to be treated differently from the extraction of unigram terms. This is backed up by previous work on term extraction techniques, such as the work by Zhang et al. (2008), who suggest an integrated approach for unigram and multiword terms, but find that some techniques work better than others, depending on the proportion of uni-

gram and multiword terms in the source corpora: they report that C-value—better equipped to deal with multiword terms, as it takes nestedness of terms into account – performs better on the Genia corpus (which contains a large proportion of multiword terms), than tf-idf, a measure that does not treat multiword terms different from unigram terms. Tf-idf in contrast performs better than C-value on a corpus with a large proportion of unigram terms. We conclude that optimal results could be achieved by extracting multiword terms and unigram terms separately, using appropriate methods for both.

We use Wikipedia as a knowledge source for the extraction of multiword terms for two reasons: first, it supplies human-generated markup which can be exploited for candidate extraction, and second, it is a valuable resource of domain-specific terminology and general world knowledge. With our approach, we extract domain-specific terms, but also multiword expressions found in general language. This is motivated by the fact that, as shown in Figure 1, the decision on the domain relevance of a term is not clear-cut. Wikipedia is expected to contain highly domain-specific multiword terminology, less specialized multiword terms relevant to various domains, and also general-language multiword expressions. Conventional methods of term extraction from domain-specific corpora often aim at excluding the third class: the tf-idf measure, for instance, penalizes terms, which occur in many documents in the corpus and are therefore considered less domain-specific; Bonin et al. (2010) use general-language corpora specifically to filter out general-language terms. There are, however, application scenarios, in which terms closer to general language cannot be neglected. One example is the creation of a medical knowledge base to be queried by lay persons: both specialized technical terminology and colloquial expressions referring to diseases or bodily functions are of relevance in such an application. Another application scenario which requires a term vocabulary covering various degrees of expertise and specificity is in the e-learning domain, where knowledge on various topics is presented to students of varying degrees of expertise. Moreover, the domain boundaries are more blurred for applications in e-learning than for many traditional applications of ontologies. Therefore, resources transcending traditional domains or study subjects are required. Being able to specify relevant domains on the fly, using only a seed list of domain terms or a domain corpus as input, is an additional asset of Wikipedia as an information source.

Summing up, domain relevance of a term greatly depends on the target domain and application. We therefore present a high-recall approach to extract a large domain-transcending resource of terms of varying domain-specificity from Wikipedia together with additional information, such as categories and definitions of terms that can be used to filter the terms with respect to specific domains and application scenarios. In the following sections we present the construction of the resource: term candidate identification, ranking and term selection, extraction of additional information and the evaluation of the extracted terms.

Candidate Extraction

We target the problem of phrase boundary identification for multiword term extraction by tapping into human knowledge encoded in Wikipedia markup: we rely on phrase boundaries explicitly marked by humans. These are word sequences marked by different typesetting (bold, italics), or wiki markup (link anchor texts, titles, headers). This is similar to work in automated term extraction from web texts which uses XHTML markup to identify phrase boundaries (Brunzel, 2008), and to work in bilingual terminology extraction which exploits Wikipedia's inter-language links to extract bilingual term pairs (Erdmann, et al., 2008; Erdmann, et al., 2009).

We extracted multiword term candidates from two data sources within the English Wikipedia using a Wikipedia dump from 2007 and the Java Wikipedia API (Zesch, Müller, & Gurevych, 2008) as a toolkit. The first data source is the set of Wikipedia *article titles*; the second source is the text of Wikipedia articles. We used article titles directly as term candidates, without further processing. From the article text, multiword term candidates were extracted using the following set of MediaWiki markup patterns,

- Anchor Text (Internal Links): [[target|**term_candidate**]]
- Section Headers:
  ===* **term_candidate** ===*
- Phrases in Boldface: '''**term_candidate**'''
- Phrases in Italics: ''**term_candidate**''

whereby **term_candidate** is defined as the sequence of two or more *words*, (sequences of characters, including numerals, hyphens, and apostrophes) separated by spaces.

Figure 6 lists the number of extracted term candidates by term size (i.e., the number of constituent words in a term) for Wikipedia titles. More than 40% of the over 3.3 million titles consist of two words, compared to 17.5% unigram titles. The multiword titles constitute 82.4% of the total, and those consisting of two to four words still represent 72.7% of all titles. Only 10% of the titles consist of terms longer than four words.

We restricted the size of term candidates extracted from the Wikipedia articles to two to four constituent words. We had several reasons for this filtering by term size: first, as the Wikipedia titles show, candidates consisting of two to four words were the majority of the extracted term candidates. Second, longer phrases, which were likely to occur in a larger proportion among the term candidates extracted from Wikipedia articles (marked by link anchor text, headers and special typesetting), contained full sentences or citations, which we did not target in our experiments. To ease the effort involved in further processing, we excluded these. A third reason for the size filtering

Figure 6. Term candidate statistics (Wikipedia titles)

# constituents	# terms	% of total
1	582,469	17.5
2	1,354,349	40.9
3	719,062	21.7
4	334,531	10.0
5	161,012	4.9
6	83,429	2.5
7	38,406	1.2
...	...	...
total	3,312,743	100.0
2+	2,730,274	82.5
5+	322,332	9.7
2–4	2,407,942	72.7

is that we aimed to alleviate the effects of term size on the statistical ranking.

The following filter was applied to all the extracted word sequences: multiword term candidates were not allowed to contain punctuation marks except for the following signs: '&%@-. Additionally, they were required to start with an alphanumeric character. We applied case folding, i.e., all candidates were lowercased, to avoid additional efforts of case normalization. This strategy made subsequent processing, such as the collection of term frequencies, easier.

Thus, we extracted more than 5 million multiword term candidates of size two to four. Of these, 1.6 million stem from titles and 4.3 million from markup in Wikipedia articles. The lower number of candidates from titles compared to the raw numbers in Figure 6 is due to the applied filters and lowercasing.

Note that this step did not require any linguistic information besides heuristics on term composition and word separation in English. Thus, our approach of term candidate extraction could easily be applied to other languages in Wikipedia.

Candidate Ranking

The quality of a term extraction process which relies only on Wikipedia-based filtering is quite high already—manual inspection of the extracted term candidates revealed a large number of domain-specific and general-language terms. We nevertheless apply a ranking step to filter out ungrammatical sequences ("amount of prize") and regular English phrases ("married couples"), because we expect them to receive a low score in the ranking.

Therefore, we combine our technique with statistical methods typically used for the extraction of multiword terms. Since we do not specifically focus on term extraction in a particular domain, but also include terms closer to general language, we apply a statistical association measure proven to be efficient for the extraction of multiword expressions from corpora, namely pointwise mutual information (Hoang, et al., 2009).

Pointwise Mutual Information (PMI) measures the strength of association between the constituent words of a multiword term candidate in a corpus by comparing the expected probabilities of the multiword term to the probabilities observed in the corpus. Expected probabilities are computed as products of the probabilities of the constituent words, assuming independence between the constituent words (see Figure 6). PMI is interpreted as follows: a high PMI value shows a strong association between the constituents of the candidate terms, and thus provides evidence, that they indeed constitute a multiword term.

The PMI measure is usually applied to bigram candidates. It needs to be adapted to appropriately deal with terms of longer size. Therefore, several options have been suggested (Da Silva & Lopes, 1999; Korkontzelos, et al., 2008): the standard application of the PMI measure compares the observed probabilities to the expected probabilities modeled as the product of the probabilities of the two constituent words w_1 and w_2 of a term:

$$PMI(w_1 w_2) = \log \frac{P(w_1 w_2)}{P(w_1)P(w_2)}$$

For term candidates consisting of three or more words ($c = w_1,\ldots,w_n$), there are several options to compute the expected probabilities of the multiword term. The easiest one is applying the approach for bigrams and calculating the expected probabilities as the product of the observed constituent probabilities under the assumption that the constituents of the n-gram are independent of each other:

$$PMI_{naive}(w_1,\ldots,w_n) = \log \frac{P(w_1,\ldots,w_n)}{\prod_{i=1}^{n} P(w_i)}$$

This assumption is criticized as being inadequate for bigrams (Bouma, 2010) and even more problematic for longer terms, since it does not take the phrase structure of multiword terms into account: 3-gram multiword terms are usually made up of a single word and a bigram ([Gaussian [random field]]), 4-gram multiword terms of two bigrams ([[finite dimensional] [vector space]]) or a 3-gram and an unigram ([[raster to vector] conversion]).

Da Silva and Lopes (1999) suggest a way of computing the expected probabilities for longer term candidates. It is called "fair dispersion normalization" and involves splitting longer n-grams into "pseudo-bigrams" using all possible split points and using the average of the probabilities as expected probabilities for the n-gram:

$$PMI_{naive}(w_1,\ldots,w_n) = \log \frac{P(w_1,\ldots,w_n)}{\prod_{i=1}^{n} P(w_i)}$$

For the multiword term candidate "Gaussian random field," the fair dispersion normalization would compute the average of the observed probabilities for the split [[Gaussian random] field] and [Gaussian [random field]].

A simpler variant, called "pessimistic split," uses the split with the highest observed likelihood (Korkontzelos, et al., 2008), in our example [Gaussian [random field]]:

$$PMI_{pess}(w_1,\ldots,w_n) = \\ \log \frac{P(w_1,\ldots,w_n)}{P(w_1,\ldots,w_i)P(w_{i+1},\ldots,w_n)}$$

Here, the split point i is determined as the one maximizing $P(w_1,\ldots,w_i)P(w_{i+1},\ldots,w_n)$. For this strategy, a comparatively high number of occurrences is required to receive a high PMI, so it leads to a conservative decision: if a candidate receives a high ranking using pessimistic split, it is very likely that the candidate actually is a collocation. In our evaluation, we compared both of those normalization strategies.

The collocation measure relies on corpus frequencies of the multiword expression candidates. Two benefits of using term candidates from Wikipedia are the good coverage of technical domains and neologisms. We use the Wikipedia text as a corpus for the candidate ranking, since we do not expect to find similar coverage on technical terms and neologisms in the newspaper corpora typically used for this task. Therefore, we extracted the counts for all extracted term candidates from Wikipedia texts. To collect the counts, we considered only the cleaned text without wiki markup. Additionally, we extracted counts for the subsequences of terms with more than two constituents. These were required to compute the normalized PMI scores for term candidates of size three and four.

We restrict minimum occurrences to accommodate the bias of PMI to prefer lower frequency items, as suggested by Pecina and Schlesinger (2006): only those candidates with at least six occurrences in the Wikipedia corpus were considered for ranking. Using a corpus as large as

Wikipedia, the slightly lower recall resulting from the frequency filtering is not an issue for us. Out of a total of 5.26 million multiword term candidates, a ranking was computed for 1,032,859. The size reduction is mainly due to the frequency cutoff. Besides, a few subsequences of terms were not found in the Wikipedia corpus because of errors in the automatic removal of wiki markup.

We found that term candidates with more than two constituents (i.e., 3-grams and 4-grams) receive both high and low positions in the ranking. This observation indicates that the applied normalization of the PMI measure works well: these longer terms are neither collectively favored nor disfavored. The fair dispersion and pessimistic split normalization provide very similar results (Spearman's rank order correlation between these measures being 0.996); therefore we proceeded with analysis and further processing based on the latter method.

Manual analysis of the ranking showed that the top ranks are mainly given to named entities, such as names from the scientific classification of plants and animals ("archaeocydippida hunsrueckiana," "suricata suricatta"). The lowest scores were given to ungrammatical phrases and misspellings ("would of"), or names and phrases that appear as such ("the who"). The middle ranks were occupied by multiword terms of varying compositionality ("swell box," "utility pole," "dog whistle," "aramaic speaker"), named entities ("cable guy," "milford railway station"), and specialized terminology ("sister clade").

To decide which candidates to admit to the final resource, we determined a cutoff value. Observed PMI scores range from −7.74 to 18.43. Since multiword term candidates have already been selected by human Wikipedia authors, either by marking up the candidate or specifying it as an article title, comparatively high quality can be expected in the resource. Therefore, we need only remove candidates with really low PMI scores from the full set. A score-over-rank plot of multiword term candidates (see Figure 7) suggests a cutoff at PMI=0. Therefore, all candidates with a score higher than 0 are selected for the multiword term resource. About 29,000 term candidates are thereby discarded; 1,003,508 remain.

Candidate Selection and Filtering

The set of selected candidates contains many different types of multiword terms: there is a large number of named entities as well as technical terms and general-language terms of varying compositionality (including non-compositional multiword expressions and collocations, see Figure 5). We performed automatic and manual analysis to classify the selected multiword terms and to get an estimate of the distribution of multiword term types in the resource.

During the extraction of term candidates, we tagged the Wikipedia text corpus with POS tags. A multiword term candidate was associated with the most frequently occurring POS sequence. The Stanford named entity tagger (Finkel, Grenager, & Manning, 2005) was used to assign general named entity tags (Person, Location and Organization) to occurrences of the term candidates. We use this information to divide the set of multiword terms into named entities and other terms. First, all multiword terms which have a corpus occurrence tagged as a named entity sequence are classified as named entities. Additionally, a particular sequence of POS tags was used to identify named entities missed by the Stanford NE tagger, such as film titles. The "proper noun" tag in the tag-set used refers to named entities and manual analysis showed that terms tagged as proper nouns are likely to be named entities. Therefore, terms which were tagged as a sequence of at least two proper nouns (NP, NPS), optionally modified by determiners (DT), adjectives (IN) and conjunctions (CC) and ending on a proper noun, identified with the pattern "(NP|NPS) ((CC|DT|IN|NP|NPS))*(NP|NPS)," were also classified as named entities. These are more than the half of the multiword term candidates surviving the PMI cutoff. We used linguistic

Figure 7. Score over rank plot (PMI ranking)

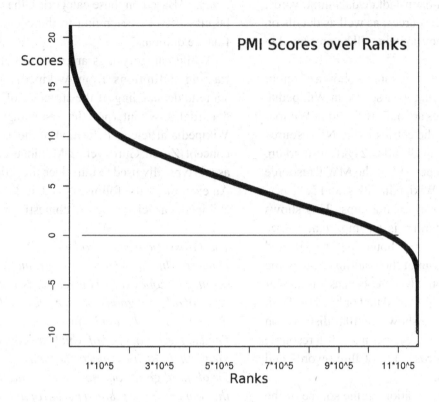

processing tools for POS tagging and named entity identification in our work. These could, however be replaced by language-independent approaches for named entity identification using structural information from Wikipedia, for instance using the technique suggested by Richman and Schone (2008) for multilingual named entity recognition in Wikipedia. Thus, our approach could easily be applied to languages other than English, for which language-dependent POS taggers and named entity recognizers are not available.

Multiword terms not classified as named entities were subject to additional filtering steps: they were filtered based on a set of heuristics in order to exclude what we call "Wikipediaisms"—expressions typical for Wikipedia which therefore receive a high score in the ranking. Examples include the phrase "external links" and multiword units of

the form "lists of X" (e.g., "lists of countries"). Additional filtering based on POS sequences was performed to exclude ungrammatical phrases, such as those starting with conjunctions or ending with definite or indefinite articles. Unlike previous work, we did not use a positive list of POS patterns for the extraction of multiword term candidates as this would exclude a wide range of multiword terms.

Properties of the Resource

The resource mined from Wikipedia contains more than 880,000 terms and consists of two parts: one part containing 528,536 named entities, and a second part containing 356,467 Multiword Terms (MWTs). We refer to the former as NE resource and the latter as MWT resource. Both resources are available for download in XML format at http://www.ukp.tu-darmstadt.de/data/multiwords. Properties of the resources, as well as details on the information they contain will be presented in this section.

The terms in the two resources show a different distribution regarding their source in Wikipedia. The Named entities are mainly found in Wikipedia titles: 76% of the entries in the NE resource originate from Wikipedia titles, 24% from markup, while (only) 45% percent of the MWT resource were mined from Wikipedia titles, and 55% percent come from various markups. This shows that Wikipedia markup is an important source of multiword terms and should not be neglected in favor of titles. Out of the markup terms in the MWT resource, roughly 55% occur as link anchor text and 45% as highlighted text or headers. Both parts of the resource show a similar distribution of term size. 73% of the terms in the full resource consist of two words, 21% of three words and 7% of four words.

Besides the information on the source of the term in Wikipedia, the resources provide POS and frequency information, and the PMI score.

In order to ease the integration of the Wikipedia-based multiword term resource into semi-automatic ontology construction, we augmented our resource with information from Wikipedia: we extracted definitions and category tags for those multiword terms in the MWT resource that can be associated with Wikipedia articles. Definition information and category information can be used to integrate terms into an existing ontology based on semantic similarity and to ease the establishment of relations between terms for a new ontology. Furthermore, the provided information can be used for adaptation of our domain-transcending resource to particular target domains—e.g., through the filtering for predefined categories.

Category tags added by Wikipedia editors are provided for each article and can be directly extracted for each article. The article on "gross domestic product" is tagged with the following categories: "*Index numbers*" and "*National accounts.*" Based on these categories, the term can be classified as belonging to the economy and finance domains.

While category tags are easy to obtain, extracting definitions from Wikipedia requires some understanding of the structure of Wikipedia articles. We interpret the first paragraph of a Wikipedia article as definition of the associated concept (Zesch, Gurevych, & Mühlhäuser, 2007), as it is typically used to introduce the article title. An example is the following text section for the Wikipedia article on "gross domestic product":

The Gross Domestic Product (GDP) or Gross Domestic Income (GDI), a basic measure of a country's economic performance, is the market value of all final goods and services made within the borders of a nation in a year. GDP can be defined in three ways, all of which are conceptually identical. First, it is equal to the total expenditures for all final goods and services produced within the country in a stipulated period of time (usually a 365-day year). Second, it is equal to the sum of the value added at every stage of production (the intermediate stages) by all the industries within a country, plus taxes less subsidies on products, in the period. Third, it is equal to the sum of the income generated by production in the country in the period - that is, compensation of employees, taxes on production and imports less subsidies, and gross operating surplus (or profits).

For some Wikipedia articles, the first section does not provide a textual definition, or only a very short text (less than 100 characters). In this case, we added the next section to the definition. In the resource, we highlight, when more than the first section was used to compile the definition.

Collecting category and definition information is straightforward for the 161,072 terms originating from Wikipedia titles. Additionally, the 195,395 terms from link anchor text can be associated with the target of the link. This allows us to associate

Box 1.

```
<mwe>
        <lemma> gross domestic product </lemma>
        <pos> JJ JJ NN </pos>
        <freq> 613 </freq>
        <pmi> 9.958813181942412 </pmi>
        <source> wiki_titles </source>
        <sense>
                <page_title> Gross domestic product </page_title>
                <category> Index numbers </category>
                <category> National accounts </category>
                <category> Gross Domestic Product</category>
                <category> All articles with unsourced statements </category>
                <definition_first_paragraph> The Gross Domestic Product (GDP)
or Gross Domestic Income (GDI), a basic measure of a country's economic per-
formance, is the market value of all final goods and services made within the
borders of a nation in a year.  GDP can be defined in three ways, all of which
are conceptually identical. First, it is equal to the total expenditures for
all final goods and services produced within the country in a stipulated pe-
riod of time (usually a 365-day year). Second, …
                </definition_first_paragraph>
        </sense>
</mwe>
```

link anchor texts with definitions and categories of their link targets, unless they link to overview pages such as "lists of X." Often, link anchors are associated with several targets, leading to different Wikipedia pages. These anchors can be considered ambiguous and receive several senses in our resource. Wikipedia titles can also be ambiguous, if they point to a disambiguation page.

The example entry for "gross domestic product" shows the information that our resource provides on the term in XML format. The term is associated with just one sense in Wikipedia, for which category information and a definition extracted from the first paragraph are available (see Box 1).

Summing up, we managed to enrich our MWT resource with over 240,000 definitions for multiword terms in the resource. We also extracted over 460,000 category tags. 148,793 of the multiword terms in the resource are tagged with an average 3 categories and provide a definition text.

Using the Resource for Ontology Construction

The enriched resource provides additional information which is typically not available when taking the standard approach of extracting terminology automatically from domain corpora. This information can be exploited in various tasks in the ontology construction process like 1) filtering (domain-specific terms can be extracted based on category information), 2) adding textual descriptions (definitions can serve as a starting point to provide concise descriptions in the ontology) or taxonomy construction (Wikipedia categories are useful for the hierarchical structuring of the terms). Furthermore, our resource is domain transcending, which we consider a great benefit for the development of new ontologies: instead of repeating the terminology extraction process for every new domain, the existing resource can be adapted to a particular domain using a domain filtering approach, which is less time and resource demanding.

Evaluation: Annotation Study and Comparison

In order to get a better estimate of the different types of multiword terms which constitute our resource, we performed an annotation study. The study was performed specifically to evaluate the MWT resource, as we are particularly interested in the quality of our resource for terminology extraction rather than named entities. We focused on the assessment of the unithood, rather than the termhood, of the extracted multiword terms. The reason for this is twofold: first, a high proportion of domain-relevant terms is to be expected in our resource due to Wikipedia's encyclopedic nature; second, as the resource is domain-independent – it is intended to cover a broad range of domains and terms of varying degrees of specialization – relevance with respect to a particular domain is not a good evaluation criterion in our case. Therefore, we relied on a classification frequently used for the evaluation of general-language multiword expressions. It classifies terms as being either

1. *non-compositional*, which covers phrases whose meaning cannot be completely inferred from the meaning of their parts and typically includes technical terminology,
2. *collocations*, which can be understood based on the composition of the constituent terms, but is lexicalized (and thus a useful candidate for ontology construction),
3. *regular phrases*, which is not considered lexicalized, or

4. *ungrammatical*.

Out of the 356,467 multiword terms in the MWT resource, we sampled 2500 randomly and had two human annotators annotate each term with one of these four classes. The annotators were additionally asked to mark terms which they considered named entities. This was done to identify named entities that slipped through the filtering step.

The annotators were equipped with a detailed annotation guide containing examples of the different classes and criteria and tests for identification. Furthermore, they were asked to perform a quick web search for each expression in order to get familiar with unknown terms and discover named entity usages of terms which would otherwise have been classified as regular phrases or as ungrammatical. (This frequently applies to film titles.)

To estimate the quality of the annotation, we measured the agreement between the annotators. For the binary NE classification ("NE" vs. "not NE"), we computed simple agreement: 0.87 of all rated terms receive the same rating in the NE-dimension. Terms identified unanimously as NE by the raters were not taken into account in the further agreement evaluation.

For the three termhood classes, we computed the κ-score value between the two annotators as suggested by Krippendorf (1980). The agreement score between the two annotators is $\kappa=0.42$ on the three-class rating ([1] vs [2] vs [3]). When considering only the binary classification into regular phrases [1] and valuable multiword terms (classes [2] and [3] together), agreement is $\kappa=0.48$.

This value is considered fair agreement according to the scale used by Landis and Koch (1977) and low agreement according to Krippendorf (1980). These results have to be interpreted in light of the difficulty of the rating task: the boundaries between the classes are often not clear cut and the raters cannot be expected to be familiar with all domains in Wikipedia. This means that low annotator agreement does not imply a low quality of the resource. Determining whether an expression is compositional is a difficult task, which is even more difficult in Wikipedia due to the large number of domain-specific terms. The fact that terms from Wikipedia are difficult to annotate suggests that they contain a high variety of technical terminology, which is desired for the construction of a terminological resource. Differing background knowledge of the annotators may lead to different annotations—for instance, when an annotator is familiar with a certain domain she may annotate a phrase as compositional, because the sense of the headword of the term is familiar, while the other annotator annotates the same phrase as non-compositional based on the more prominent prototypical meaning of the head word. One example is "gross national product" which can be understood as compositional by someone familiar with the financial domain and meanings of "gross" and "national product" in this domain. A person only familiar with more colloquial senses of "gross" (e.g., being bulky or disgusting) is more likely to classify "gross national product" as non-compositional. Another example is "plain dress," which can be understood compositionally as referring to an unadorned dress, while a person familiar with the lifestyle of the Amish will understand it to refer to their sumptuary rules, including particular modesty and conservative cut. The identification of named entities also relies on the familiarity of the annotators with geographical locations and company names, or the results that ranked top in the web search performed by the annotator.

In order to create a reliable annotation on the full set, the multiword terms on which the first two annotators disagreed were re-evaluated by the expert annotator who also designed the annotation guide. The third annotator agrees well with the two initial annotators, where the latter agree: the κ-score between the third rater and the first two raters is 0.69 on 3-class evaluation and 0.74 on binary evaluation. The score was computed based on a random sample of 150 terms from the set of terms on which the first two annotators agree. The fair agreement justifies using the expert rater's disambiguation of the terms on which the first two raters disagreed.

Terms which were rated as NE by both annotators were considered to be reliable NEs and therefore not re-evaluated by the expert rater. The unanimous initial ratings and the corrected annotations by the expert were used to compile a gold-standard annotation.

All together, 891 terms of the sample are classified as non-compositional, 505 as collocation, 881 as regular phrase, and 220 as NE. Three terms were identified as ungrammatical. The evaluation shows that the multiword term resource contains some noise, but still a large amount of valid terms. Figure 8 presents the percentage distribution on term classes in the evaluated set. Besides 8% named entities, which are also useful for ontology construction (albeit not the focus of our evaluation), the gold-standard set contains more than 55% valuable multiword terms (i.e., non-compositional multiword expressions and collocations). The same proportion can be expected in the full MWT resource. Moreover, terms which are neither classified as non-compositional or collocations, nor identified as a named entity cannot generally be considered noise from the point of view of offering a "multiword term resource," as manual evaluation on a sample of 200 terms showed that 75% of the regular phrases nevertheless represent domain concepts (e.g., "wheat field" in an agriculture setting). Thus, more than 81% (around 290,000) of the 356,467 multiword terms in our resource can be expected to be valuable terms.

Figure 8 compares the distribution of term types in the evaluated sample. The configuration of multiword term sources we used, Wikipedia markup and titles, is compared to the baseline of using titles only. Analyzing the gold-standard with respect to the source of the terms shows that the proportion of non-compositional multiword terms is higher when considering only the multiword terms stemming from Wikipedia titles: as shown

Figure 8. Distribution of term types in evaluated sample

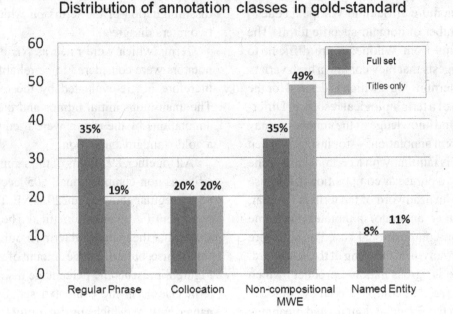

Distribution of annotation classes in gold-standard

in Figure 8, 49% of the 1146 title terms are non-compositional, but only 19% of them are regular phrases. Thus, the subset of terms in the resource stemming from titles, consisting of over 160,000 multiword terms, could be used for applications which require higher precision than recall. Splitting the markup terms further, into those originating from anchor text and other highlighting (headers and typesetting), would allow for a finer grained tuning of precision versus recall, as terms from anchor texts contain only 39% regular phrases, compared to over 50% for terms from headers and typesetting.

Focusing on precision however means a loss in recall: in the gold standard, 54% of the terms stem from titles and 46% of the terms from markup. In the whole MWT resource, multiword terms originating from Wikipedia markup, text highlighting and anchor text constitute more than the half, 55% of the resource. Not considering

these would reduce the size and coverage of the resource dramatically.

To further evaluate the Wikipedia-based resource, a comparison was performed with the multiword expressions contained in the Princeton WordNet (Fellbaum, 1998), an expert-built lexical semantic resource. WordNet contains a taxonomy of lexical entries. The basic structure is the *synset*, grouping all lexical entries considered synonymous to each other. Synsets are equipped with short definition glosses and inflectional information. Synsets are connected to each other via relations like hyponomy ("is-a") and antonymy, thus spanning a graph structure. WordNet has been widely used to compute similarities between words and to perform word sense disambiguation.

The comparison shows first of all that the multiword resource extracted from Wikipedia exceeds WordNet dramatically with respect to size, and second that a large proportion of the expressions in WordNet is covered by the Wikipedia-based resource. WordNet contains over 110,000 lexical entries on nouns, 68,000 of which are nominal multiword expressions. Of these, about 63,000 have the same size as the multiword terms in the Wikipedia-based resource—namely, two to four constituent terms. The Wikipedia-based resource covers over 70% of these 63,000 multiword expressions. This gives additional proof that a large number of high-quality terms are contained in the Wikipedia-based resource.

FUTURE RESEARCH DIRECTIONS

In this work, we specifically focused on the extraction of a multiword term resource and exploited properties of Wikipedia that are beneficial to this particular task. In future work, we plan to extract unigram terms as well, which would be a valuable extension to our Wikipedia-based resource of multiword terms. For the ranking of unigram terms extracted from Wikipedia, we will employ methods appropriate for unigram terms, focusing on termhood rather than unithood.

Another natural direction of future research is the implementation and evaluation of the domain filtering: we plan to evaluate our Wikipedia-based resource in the e-learning domain. Therefore, we will develop techniques to optimally select terms relevant to a particular domain (i.e., *domain filtering*) using category information and definitions from Wikipedia. We consider several options for domain filtering: the first is to select a seed set of categories relevant to the target domain and use it to extract relevant terms from the resource. Additionally, the category hierarchy can be exploited to expand the set of seed categories by their child categories, similar to the work by Cui et al. (2008).

The second option is to use a seed set of domain-relevant expressions as a domain filter: semantic similarity between the seed expressions and the information extracted from Wikipedia, especially definitions, but also categories, can be used to identify terms as relevant to the domain.

A collection of domain-specific texts can be alternatively used to filter the resource: terms from the resource occurring in the texts are likely to be domain relevant. This strategy requires the least effort, if a collection of relevant texts is available.

The implementation of the filtering method will allow us to further evaluate the resource quality with respect to particular application domains. In this context, an important aspect of terminology extraction for ontology construction is not only the domain relevance of the extracted terms, but also whether the domain is represented well by the terms in a resource (Zhang, Xia, Greenwood, & Iria, 2009). The former can be evaluated using precision, while the latter is related to recall: not only should the resource cover a large number of relevant terms, but *all relevant aspects* of the domain should be represented in the terminology resource. To evaluate this, a domain-specific text corpus can be applied: if there are documents in the corpus, which are not covered well by the resource—i.e., which do not contain any resource terms—or only terms generally relevant to the domain (as shown by high document frequency, the number of documents in a collection a term occurs in), the domain might not be covered adequately by the resource. Adequate domain coverage, however, is an essential feature of terminological resources, because omissions introduced in this foundational step of semi-automatic ontology construction are propagated throughout the construction process and affect the final quality of the ontology.

We furthermore plan 1) to evaluate our method for extracting multiword terms from Wikipedia on languages other than English, to prove the language independence of our approach, and 2) to evaluate statistical ranking methods besides PMI. Finally, we plan to make the software packages for language independent extraction of multiword terms from Wikipedia available for research purposes.

CONCLUSION

The efficient creation of high-quality terminological resources is a foundational step in semi-automatic ontology construction. In this chapter, we presented a method using the collaborative encyclopedia Wikipedia, which has received wide recognition as an information source of domain-specific and general world knowledge, for the creation of a domain-transcending multiword term resource. Wikipedia offers several advantages as a resource for term extraction: 1) high coverage of specialized domains, 2) quick evolution with respect to emerging research areas, 3) domain information in the form of a category hierarchy, and 4) its multilinguality and intra- as well as interlingual link structure. Moreover, Wikipedia offers structural elements (markup) supporting the task of phrase boundary detection, which is essential to multiword term extraction. Exploiting the markup for the extraction of term candidates, our method is basically language-independent, as it does not require language-specific processing tools. These tools can, however, be employed to further enhance the precision of the extraction process, for instance by applying POS-filters to term candidates and thus considering only grammatical phrases of a particular language.

Our method provides a set of over 500,000 NEs, including general categories like persons, locations, and NE types relevant to specific domains (film titles, chemical substances, etc.). Beyond that, we managed to extract over 350,000 multiword terms using our approach. For these, we additionally extracted category and definition information associated with the terms from Wikipedia and provide it as additional information as part of the resource. To evaluate the multiword part of the resource, a sample of terms was annotated for four linguistic classes of unithood by human raters. Focusing on unithood rather than termhood is motivated by the need of a domain independent evaluation of our domain transcending resource. Moreover, the extraction of a large proportion of domain-relevant terms is inherent to our method due to using Wikipedia as an information source. According to the evaluation, 55% of the terms in the sample are non-compositional multiword expressions and collocations, 35% regular phrases and 8% named entities (that could belong to the NE part of the resource, but were missed by our filters). While *regular phrases* are not considered lexicalized units in the annotation setting (i.e., they are neither semantically non-compositional nor institutionalized) manual analysis showed that over 75% of them nevertheless represent domain concepts (e.g., "wheat field" in an agriculture setting). This means that while the multiword term resource contains some noise it still holds a large amount (some 89%) of valid terms. The coverage of the resource also compares favorably to other dictionaries of multiword terms like WordNet. The entire resource, with all the information described here, is freely available at http://www.ukp.tudarmstadt.de/data/multiwords.

ACKNOWLEDGMENT

This work has been supported by the Emmy Noether Program of the German Research Foundation (DFG) under the grant No. GU 798/3-1 and by the Volkswagen Foundation as part of the Lichtenberg Professorship program under grant No. I/82806. We would like to thank the anonymous reviewers for their valuable comments and our colleagues at the Ubiquitous Knowledge Processing Lab for many fruitful discussions during the work on this chapter.

REFERENCES

Ahmad, K., Gillam, L., & Tostevin, L. (1999). University of Surrey participation in TREC-8: Weirdness indexing for logical document extrapolation and retrieval (WILDER). In *Proceedings of NIST Special Publication 500-246 the Eighth Text REtrieval Conference (TREC 8)*, (pp. 717–724). Retrieved from http://trec.nist.gov/pubs/trec8/papers/surrey2.pdf.

Auer, S., Bizer, C., Kobilarov, G., Lehmann, J., Cyganiak, R., & Ives, Z. (2007). Dbpedia: A nucleus for a web of open data. In Aberer, K. (Eds.), *The Semantic Web* (*Vol. 4825*, pp. 722–735). Lecture Notes in Computer Science Berlin, Germany: Springer. doi:10.1007/978-3-540-76298-0_52

Aussenac-Gilles, N., Biébow, B., & Szulman, S. (2000). Revisiting ontology design: A method based on corpus analysis. In Dieng, R., & Corby, O. (Eds.), *Knowledge Engineering and Knowledge Management Methods, Models, and Tools* (*Vol. 1937*, pp. 27–66). Lecture Notes in Computer Science Berlin, Germany: Springer. doi:10.1007/3-540-39967-4_13

Bannard, C., Baldwin, T., & Lascarides, A. (2003). A statistical approach to the semantics of verb-particles. In *Proceedings of the ACL 2003 Workshop on Multiword Expressions: Analysis, Acquisition and Treatment*, (pp. 65–72). Retrieved from http://www.aclweb.org/anthology/W03-1809.

Bonin, F., Dell'Orletta, F., Venturi, G., & Montemagni, S. (2010). Contrastive filtering of domain-specific multi-word terms from different types of corpora. In *Proceedings of the 2010 Workshop on Multiword Expressions: From Theory to Applications*, (pp. 77–80). Retrieved from http://www.aclweb.org/anthology/W10-3711.

Bouma, G. (2010). Collocation extraction beyond the independence assumption. In *Proceedings of the ACL 2010 Conference Short Papers*, (pp. 109–114). Retrieved from http://www.aclweb.org/anthology/P10-2020.

Brunzel, M. (2008). The XTREEM methods for ontology learning from web documents. In Buitelaar, P. (Eds.), *Ontology Learning and Population: Bridging the Gap Between Text and Knowledge* (pp. 3–28). Amsterdam, Netherlands: IOS Press.

Cabré, M. T. (1999). *Terminology: Theory, methods and applications*. Amsterdam, Netherlands: John Benjamins Publishing Company.

Cimiano, P. (2006). *Ontology learning and population from text: Algorithms, evaluation and application*. New York, NY: Springer.

Cucerzan, S. (2007). Large-scale named entity disambiguation based on Wikipedia data. In *Proceedings of the 2007 Joint Conference on Empirical Methods in Natural Language Processing and Computational Natural Language Learning*, (pp. 708–716). Retrieved from http://www.aclweb.org/anthology/D/D07/D07-1074.

Cui, G., Lu, Q., Li, W., & Chen, Y. (2008). Corpus exploitation from Wikipedia for ontology construction. In N. Calzolari, et al. (Eds.), *Proceedings of the 6th International Conference on Language Resources and Evaluation (LREC 2008)*, (pp. 2125–2132). Paris, France: ELRA. Retrieved from http://www.lrec-conf.org/proceedings/lrec2008/pdf/541_paper.pdf.

Da Silva, J. F., & Lopes, G. P. (1999). *A local maxima method and a fair dispersion normalization for extracting multi-word units from corpora*. Paper presented at the 6th Meeting on Mathematics of Language. Orlando, FL.

Erdmann, M., Nakayama, K., Hara, T., & Nishio, S. (2008). An approach for extracting bilingual terminology from Wikipedia. In Haritsa, J. R., Kotagiri, R., & Pudi, V. (Eds.), *DASFAA 2008* (*Vol. 4947*, pp. 380–392). Lecture Notes in Computer Science Berlin, Germany: Springer. doi:10.1007/978-3-540-78568-2_28

Erdmann, M., Nakayama, K., Hara, T., & Nishio, S. (2009). Improving the extraction of bilingual terminology from Wikipedia. *ACM Transactions on Multimedia Computing, Communications, and Applications*, *5*(4), 1–17. doi:10.1145/1596990.1596995

Evert, S., & Krenn, B. (2001). Methods for the qualitative evaluation of lexical association measures. In *Proceedings of 39th Annual Meeting of the Association for Computational Linguistics*, (pp. 188–195). Retrieved from http://www.aclweb.org/anthology/P01-1025.

Fazly, A., & Stevenson, S. (2007). Distinguishing subtypes of multiword expressions using linguistically-motivated statistical measures. In *Proceedings of the ACL 2007 Workshop on a Broader Perspective on Multiword Expressions*, (pp. 9–16). Retrieved from http://www.aclweb.org/anthology/W/W07/W07-1102.

Fellbaum, C. (1998). *WordNet: An electronic lexical database*. Cambridge, MA: MIT Press.

Finkel, J. R., Grenager, T., & Manning, C. (2005). Incorporating non-local information into information extraction systems by Gibbs sampling. In *Proceedings of the 43nd Annual Meeting of the Association for Computational Linguistics*, (pp. 363–370). Retrieved from http://www.aclweb.org/anthology/P/P05/P05-1045.pdf.

Frantzi, K., & Ananiadou, S. (1999). The C-value/NC-value domain independent method for multi-word term extraction. *Journal of Natural Language Processing*, *6*(3), 145–179.

Frantzi, K. T., Ananiadou, S., & Mima, H. (2000). Automatic recognition of multi-word terms: The C-value/NC-value method. *International Journal on Digital Libraries*, *3*(2), 115–130. doi:10.1007/s007999900023

Giles, J. (2005). Internet encyclopaedias go head to head. *Nature*, *138*(15), 900–901. doi:10.1038/438900a

Gómez-Pérez, A., Fernández-López, M., & Corcho, O. (2004). *Ontological engineering*. London, UK: Springer.

Hoang, H. H., Kim, S. N., & Kan, M.-Y. (2009). A re-examination of lexical association measures. In *Proceedings of the ACL 2009 Workshop on Multiword Expressions: Identification, Interpretation, Disambiguation and Applications*, (pp. 31–39). Retrieved from http://www.aclweb.org/anthology/W/W09/W09-290.

Kageura, K., & Umino, B. (1996). Methods of automatic term recognition: A review. *Terminology*, *3*(2), 259–289. doi:10.1075/term.3.2.03kag

Katz, G., & Giesbrecht, E. (2006). Automatic identification of non-compositional multi-word expressions using latent semantic analysis. In *Proceedings of the ACL 2006 Workshop on Multiword Expressions: Identifying and Exploiting Underlying Properties*, (pp. 12–19). Retrieved from http://www.aclweb.org/anthology/W/W06/W06-1203.

Kim, J.-D., Ohta, T., Tateisi, Y., & Tsujii, J. (2003). Genia corpus– Semantically annotated corpus for bio-textmining. *Bioinformatics (Oxford, England)*, *19*(1), 1180–1182. doi:10.1093/bioinformatics/btg1023

Korkontzelos, I., Klapaftis, I., & Manandhar, S. (2008). Reviewing and evaluating automatic term recognition techniques. In Ranta, A., & Nordström, B. (Eds.), *Lecture Notes in Artificial Intelligence: GoTAL 2008* (*Vol. 5221*, pp. 248–259). Berlin, Germany: Springer. doi:10.1007/978-3-540-85287-2_24

Korkontzelos, I., & Manandhar, S. (2009). Detecting compositionality in multi-word expressions. In *Proceedings of the ACL-IJCNLP 2009 Conference Short Papers*, (pp. 65–68). Retrieved from http://www.aclweb.org/anthology/P/P09/P09-2017.

Kozakov, L., Park, Y., Fin, T., Drissi, Y., Doganata, Y., & Cofino, T. (2004). Glossary extraction and utilization in the information search and delivery system for IBM technical support. *IBM Systems Journal, 43*(3), 546–563. doi:10.1147/sj.433.0546

Krenn, B., & Evert, S. (2001). Can we do better than frequency? A case study on extracting PP-verb collocations. In *Proceedings of the ACL Workshop on Collocations*, (pp. 39–46).

Krippendorf, K. (1980). *Content analysis*. London, UK: SAGE Publications.

Kulick, S., Bies, A., Liberman, M., Mandel, M., Mcdonald, R., & Palmer, M. … White, P. (2004). Integrated annotation for biomedical information extraction. In *Proceedings of the HLT-NAACL 2004 Workshop: BioLINK 2004, Linking Biological Literature, Ontologies and Databases,* (pp. 61–68). Retrieved from http://www.aclweb.org/anthology/W/W04/W04-3111.pdf.

Landis, J. R., & Koch, G. G. (1977). The measurement of observer agreement for categorical data. *Biometrics, 33*(1), 159–174. doi:10.2307/2529310

Lenat, D. B. (1995). CYC: A large-scale investment in knowledge infrastructure. *Communications of the ACM, 38*(11), 33–38. doi:10.1145/219717.219745

Medelyan, O., Milne, D., Legg, C., & Witten, I. H. (2009). Mining meaning from Wikipedia. *International Journal of Human-Computer Studies, 67*(9), 716–754. doi:10.1016/j.ijhcs.2009.05.004

Nakagawa, H., & Mori, T. (1998). Nested collocation and compound noun for term extraction. In *Proceedings of the First Workshop on Computational Terminology (Computerm 1998)*, (pp. 64–70).

Pazienza, M. T., Pennacchiotti, M., & Zanzotto, F. (2005). Terminology extraction: An analysis of linguistic and statistical approaches. In Sirmakessis, S. (Ed.), *Knowledge Mining Series: Studies in Fuzziness and Soft Computing* (pp. 255–279). Heidelberg, Germany: Springer. doi:10.1007/3-540-32394-5_20

Pecina, P., & Schlesinger, P. (2006). Combining association measures for collocation extraction. In *Proceedings of the COLING/ACL 2006 Main Conference Poster Sessions*, (pp. 651–658). Retrieved from http://www.aclweb.org/anthology/P/P06/P06-2084.

Richman, A. E., & Schone, P. (2008). Mining wiki resources for multilingual named entity recognition. In *Proceedings of ACL 2008: HLT*, (pp. 1–9). Retrieved from http://www.aclweb.org/anthology/P/P08/P08-1001.

Sag, I. A., Baldwin, T., Bond, F., Copestake, A., & Flickinger, D. (2002). Multiword expressions: A pain in the neck for NLP. In Gelbukh, A. (Ed.), *Computational Linguistics and Intelligent Text Processing* (pp. 189–206). Berlin, Germany: Springer. doi:10.1007/3-540-45715-1_1

Salton, G., Wong, A., & Yang, C. S. (1975). A vector space model for automatic indexing. *Communications of the ACM, 18*(11), 613–620. doi:10.1145/361219.361220

Sclano, F., & Velardi, P. (2007). *TermExtractor: A web application to learn the common terminology of interest groups and research communities.* Paper presented at TIA 2007. Sofia Antipolis, France.

Suchanek, F. M., Kasneci, G., & Weikum, G. (2007). Yago: A core of semantic knowledge. In *Proceedings of the 16th international World Wide Web conference (WWW 2007)*, (pp. 697–706). ACM. Retrieved from http://doi.acm.org/10.1145/1242572.1242667.

Toral, A., & Muñoz, R. (2006). A proposal to automatically build and maintain gazetteers for named entity recognition by using Wikipedia. In *Proceedings of the ACL 2006 Workshop on New Text: Wikis and Blogs and Other Dynamic Text Sources*, (pp. 56–61). Retrieved from http://www.aclweb.org/anthology/W/W06/W06-2809.pdf.

Tratz, S., & Hovy, E. (2010). A taxonomy, dataset, and classifier for automatic noun compound interpretation. In *Proceedings of the 48th Annual Meeting of the Association for Computational Linguistics*, (pp. 678–687). Retrieved from http://www.aclweb.org/anthology/P10-1070.

Villada Moirón, B., & Tiedemann, J. (2006). Identifying idiomatic expressions using automatic word-alignment. In *Proceedings of the EACL 2006 Workshop on Multiword Expressions in a Multilingual Context*, (pp. 33–40). Retrieved from http://www.aclweb.org/anthology/W/W06/W06-2405.pdf.

Wermter, J., & Hahn, U. (2005). Finding new terminology in very large corpora. In P. Clark & G. Schreiber (Eds.), *Proceedings of the 3rd International Conference on Knowledge Capture (K-CAP 2005)*, (pp. 137–144). Retrieved from http://doi.acm.org/10.1145/1088622.1088648.

Zesch, T., Gurevych, I., & Mühlhäuser, M. (2007). Analyzing and accessing Wikipedia as a lexical semantic resource. In Rehm, G., Witt, A., & Lemnitzer, L. (Eds.), *Data Structures for Linguistic Resources and Applications* (pp. 197–205). Tübingen, Germany: Gunter Narr.

Zesch, T., Müller, C., & Gurevych, I. (2008). Extracting lexical semantic knowledge from Wikipedia and Wiktionary. In N. Calzolari, et al. (Eds.), *Proceedings of the 6th International Conference on Language Resources and Evaluation (LREC 2008)*, (pp. 1646–1652). Paris, France: ELRA. Retrieved from http://www.lrec-conf.org/proceedings/lrec2008/pdf/420_paper.pdf.

Zhang, Z., Iria, J., Brewster, C., & Ciravegna, F. (2008). A comparative evaluation of term recognition algorithms. In N. Calzolari, et al. (Eds.), *Proceedings of the 6th International Conference on Language Resources and Evaluation (LREC 2008)*, (pp. 2208–2013). Paris, France: ELRA. Retrieved from http://www.lrec-conf.org/proceedings/lrec2008/pdf/538_paper.pdf.

Zhang, Z., Xia, L., Greenwood, M. A., & Iria, J. (2009). Too many mammals: Improving the diversity of automatically recognized terms. In *Proceedings of the International Conference on Recent Advances in Natural Language Processing 2009 (RANLP 2009)*, (pp. 490–495). Retrieved from http://www.aclweb.org/anthology/R09-1087.

ADDITIONAL READING

Artstein, R., & Poesio, M. (2008). Inter-coder agreement for computational linguistics. *Computational Linguistics*, *34*, 555–596. doi:10.1162/coli.07-034-R2

Baldwin, T., Bannard, C., Tanaka, T., & Widdows, D. (2003). An empirical model of multiword expression decomposability. In *Proceedings of the ACL-2003 Workshop on Multiword Expressions: Analysis, Acquisition and Treatment*, (pp. 89–96). Retrieved from http://www.aclweb.org/anthology/W03-1812.

Baldwin, T., & Kim, S. N. (2009). Multiword expressions. In Indurkhya, N., & Damerau, F. J. (Eds.), *Handbook of Natural Language Processing* (2nd ed., pp. 267–292). Boca Raton, FL: CRC Press.

Bunescu, R. C., & Pasca, M. (2006). Using encyclopedic knowledge for named entity disambiguation. In *Proceedings of the 11th Conference of the European Chapter of the Association for Computational Linguistics*, (pp. 9–16). Retrieved from http://www.aclweb.org/anthology/E/E06/E06-1002.pdf.

Calzolari, N., Fillmore, C., Grishman, R., Ide, N., Lenci, A., MacLeod, C., & Zampolli, A. (2002). Towards best practice for multiword expressions in computational lexicons. In M. G. Rodríguez & C. P. S. Araujo (Eds.), *Proceedings of the 3rd International Conference on Language Resources and Evaluation (LREC 2002)*, (pp. 1934–1940). Paris, France: ELRA.

Caseli, H., Villavicencio, A., Machado, A., & Finatto, M. J. (2009). Statistically-driven alignment-based multiword expression identification for technical domains. In *Proceedings of the ACL 2009 Workshop on Multiword Expressions: Identification, Interpretation, Disambiguation and Applications*, (pp. 1–8). Retrieved from http://www.aclweb.org/anthology/W/W09/W09-2901.

De Melo, G., & Weikum, G. (2010). Providing multilingual, multimodal answers to lexical database queries. In N. Calzolari, et al. (Eds.), *Proceedings of the 7th International Conference on Language Resources and Evaluation*, (pp. 348–355). Paris, France: ELRA. Retrieved from http://www.lrec-conf.org/proceedings/lrec2010/pdf/312_Paper.pdf.

Guarino, N. (1998). Formal ontology in information systems. In N. Guarino (Ed.), *1st International Conference on Formal Ontology in Information Systems (FOIS 1998)*, (pp. 3–15). Amsterdam, Netherlands: IOS Press.

Guarino, N., Oberle, D., & Staab, S. (2009). What is an ontology? In Staab, S., & Studer, R. (Eds.), *Handbook on Ontologies* (pp. 1–7). Berlin, Germany: Springer. doi:10.1007/978-3-540-92673-3_0

Gurevych, I., & Wolf, E. (2010). Expert-built and collaboratively constructed lexical semantic resources. *Language and Linguistics Compass*, *4*(11), 1074–1090. doi:10.1111/j.1749-818X.2010.00251.x

Justeson, J. S., & Katz, S. M. (1995). Technical terminology: Some linguistic properties and an algorithm for identification in text. *Natural Language Engineering*, *1*(1), 9–27. doi:10.1017/S1351324900000048

Kageura, K., Daille, B., Nakagawa, H., & Chien, L. F. (2004). Recent trends in computational terminology. *Terminology*, *10*(1), 1–21. doi:10.1075/term.10.1.02kag

Kazama, J., & Torisawa, K. (2008). Inducing gazetteers for named entity recognition by large-scale clustering of dependency relations. In *Proceedings of ACL-08: HLT*, (pp. 407–415). Retrieved from http://www.aclweb.org/anthology/P/P08/P08-1047.

Kim, S. N., & Kan, M.-Y. (2009). Re-examining automatic keyphrase extraction approaches in scientific articles. In *Proceedings of the Workshop on Multiword Expressions: Identification, Interpretation, Disambiguation and Applications*, (pp. 9–16). Retrieved from http://www.aclweb.org/anthology/W/W09/W09-2902.

Maedche, A., & Staab, S. (2004). Ontology learning. In Studer, R., & Staab, S. (Eds.), *Handbook of Information Systems* (pp. 173–190). Berlin, Germany: Springer.

Pecina, P. (2008): A machine learning approach to multiword expression extraction. In *Proceedings of Towards a Shared Task for Multiword Expressions (MWE 2008),* (pp. 54–57). Retrieved from http://www.lrec-conf.org/proceedings/lrec2008/workshops/W20_Proceedings.pdf.

Ramisch, C., Schreiner, P., Idiart, M., & Villavicencio, A. (2008). An evaluation of methods for the extraction of multiword expressions. In *Proceedings of Towards a Shared Task for Multiword Expressions (MWE 2008),* (pp. 50–53). Retrieved from http://www.lrec-conf.org/proceedings/lrec2008/workshops/W20_Proceedings.pdf.

Ruiz-Casado, M., Alfonseca, E., Okumura, M., & Castells, P. (2008). Information extraction and semantic annotation of Wikipedia. In Buitelaar, P. (Eds.), *Ontology Learning from Text: Methods, Evaluation and Applications* (pp. 91–106). Amsterdam, Netherlands: IOS Press.

Schone, P., & Jurafsky, D. (2001). Is knowledge-free induction of multiword unit dictionary headwords a solved problem? In *Proceedings of the 2001 Conference on Empirical Methods in Natural Language Processing,* (pp. 100–108). Retrieved from http://www.aclweb.org/anthology-new/w/w01/w01-0513.pdf.

Villavicencio, A., Bond, F., Korhonen, A., & McCarthy, D. (2005). Introduction to the special issue on multiword expressions: Having a crack at a hard nut. *Computer Speech & Language, 19*(4), 365–377. doi:10.1016/j.csl.2005.05.001

Zesch, T. (2010). What's the difference? Comparing expert-built and collaboratively-built lexical semantic resources. In N. Calzolari, P. Baroni, M. Monachini, & C. Soria (Eds.), *Proceedings of the 2nd European Language Resources and Technologies Forum Language Resources of the Future / the Future of Language Resources,* (pp. 91–92). Retrieved from http://www.flarenet.eu/sites/default/files/FLaReNet_Forum_2010_Proceedings.pdf.

KEY TERMS AND DEFINITIONS

Collocation: A collocation is a type of multiword expression. Collocations are semantically compositional, but are lexicalized terms due to being typically used as a unit to refer to a particular concept.

Multiword Expression: A lexical unit in general language consisting of more than one word. Multiword expressions receive their own entry in a natural language lexicon because of their irregular semantic, syntactic, pragmatic or statistical properties.

Multiword Term: A term consisting of more than one word.

Semantic Compositionality: Semantic compositionality is a property of multiword expressions. If the meaning of a multiword expression can be inferred from the meaning of its constituent words, the multiword expression is semantically compositional. If this is only partly or not at all possible, the multiword expression shows weak or strong non-compositionality.

Term: A lexical unit (a word or a phrase) representing a domain-relevant concept.

Termhood: Termhood refers to the degree of domain relevance of a lexical unit to a particular domain. Domain-specific terms have high termhood.

Unithood: Unithood refers to how strong the words in a phrase are associated with each other to form a lexical unit. Multiword expressions have high unithood.

Chapter 10
Exploiting Transitivity in Probabilistic Models for Ontology Learning

Francesca Fallucchi
University of Rome – Guglielmo Marconi, Italy

Fabio Massimo Zanzotto
University of Rome – Tor Vergata, Italy

ABSTRACT

Capturing word meaning is one of the challenges of Natural Language Processing (NLP). Formal models of meaning such as ontologies are knowledge repositories used in a variety of applications. To be effectively used, these ontologies have to be large or, at least, adapted to specific domains. This chapter's main goal is to practically contribute to the research on ontology learning models by covering different aspects of the task.

The authors propose probabilistic models for learning ontologies that expand existing ontologies taking into account both corpus-extracted evidence and the structure of the generated ontologies. The model exploits structural properties of target relations such as transitivity during learning. They then propose two extensions of the probabilistic models: a model for learning from a generic domain that can be exploited to extract new information in a specific domain and an incremental ontology learning system that puts human validations in the learning loop. This latter provides a graphical user interface and a human-computer interaction workflow supporting the incremental leaning loop.

INTRODUCTION

Gottfried Wilhelm Leibniz was convinced that human knowledge was like a *"bazaar"*: a place full of all sorts of goods without any order or inventory. As in a *"bazaar,"* searching a little piece of specific knowledge is a challenge that can last forever. Nowadays, we have powerful machines to process and collect data. These machines, combined with the human need of exchanging and sharing information, produced an incredibly large evolving collection of documents, partially shared with the World Wide Web. The Web is a

DOI: 10.4018/978-1-4666-0188-8.ch010

modern worldwide scale knowledge *"bazaar"* full of any sort of information where searching specific information is a titanic task.

Ontologies represent the Semantic Web's reply to the need of searching knowledge in the Web. These ontologies provide shared metadata vocabularies (Berners-Lee, Hendler, & Lassila, 2001). Data, documents, images, and information sources in general, described through these vocabularies, will be thus accessible as organized with explicit semantic references for humans as well as for machines. Yet, to be useful, ontologies should cover large part of human knowledge. Automatically learning these ontologies from document collections is the major challenge.

Models for automatically learning semantic networks of words from texts use both corpus-extracted evidences and existing language resources (Basili, Gliozzo, & Pennacchiotti, 2007). All these models rely on two hypotheses: *Distributional Hypothesis* (*DH*) (Harris, 1964) and *Lexico-Syntactic Patterns exploitation hypothesis* (LSP) (Robison, 1970). While these are powerful tools to extract relations among concepts using texts, models based on these hypotheses do not explicitly exploit structural properties of target relations when learning taxonomies or semantic networks of words. DH models intrinsically use structural properties of semantic networks of words such as transitivity, but these models cannot be applied for learning transitive semantic relations other than the generalization. LSP models are interesting because they can learn any kind of semantic relations. Yet, these models do not exploit structural properties of target relations when learning taxonomies or semantic networks of words. In general, structural properties of semantic networks of words, when relevant, are not used in machine learning models to better induce confidence values for extracted semantic relations. Even where transitivity is explicitly used (Snow, Jurafsky, & Ng, 2006), it is not directly exploited to model confidence values. It is only used in an iterative maximization process of the probability

of the entire semantic network. In this chapter, we propose a probabilistic approach that exploits LSP hypothesis and formally includes the exploitation of transitivity during learning.

Probabilistic models for learning semantic networks exploiting transitivity do not completely solve the problem of learning semantic networks. We have a second problem to tackle. When dealing with learning semantic networks of words from texts such as learning ontologies, we generally have *ontology-rich* domains with large structured domain knowledge repositories or large general corpora with large general structured knowledge repositories such as WordNet (Miller, 1995). Systems that automatically create, adapt, or extend existing semantic networks of words need a sufficiently large number of documents and existing structured knowledge to achieve reasonable performance. Thus, it is generally possible to extract good probabilistic models for *ontology-rich* domains or the general language. When building semantic networks for *ontology-poor* domains, we then need to rely on probabilistic models learnt out-of-domain or for the general language. If the target domain has not relevant pre-existing semantic networks of words to expand, we will not have enough data for training the initial model. In general, in learning methods the amount of out-of-domain data is larger than in-domain data. For this reason, in this chapter we present methods that, with a small effort for the adaptation to different specific knowledge domains, can exploit out-of-domain data for building in-domain models with bigger accuracy.

Finally, when learning semantic networks, we need to put human validations in the loop. Systems for creating or augmenting semantic networks of words using information extracted from texts need a manual validation for assessing the quality of semantic networks of words expansion. Yet, these systems do not use the manual validation for refining the information extraction model that proposes novel links in the networks. Manual validation can be efficiently exploited if used in an incremental model. In this chapter, we propose an incremental ontology learning system that puts final users in the learning loop providing an efficient way to interact with final users.

The rest of the Chapter is organized as follows. In Section **Methods for Ontology Learning** we give a survey of the main strategies and approaches, nowadays adopted, in learning semantic networks of words. In particular, we propose a review of the state-of-the-art and we point out the limits that can be overcome with our approaches. In Section **Transitivity in a Probabilistic Model** we introduce our probabilistic models to learn semantic networks of words that exploit structural properties of target relations in determining the probability of the word pairs to be in a particular relation. Then we present two extensions of our probabilistic model: a semantic networks learning method that can exploit models learned from a generic domain to extract new information in a specific domain, in Section **Generic Ontology Learners on Application domains**, and an incremental ontology learning system that puts final users in the learning loop and uses our probabilistic models to exploit transitive relations for inducing better extraction models, in Section **Probabilistic Ontology Learner in Semantic Turkey**. Finally, we draw some conclusions and we outline feature research directions.

METHODS FOR ONTOLOGY LEARNING

Automatically creating, adapting, or extending existing ontologies or semantic networks of words using domain texts is a very important and active area of research. Here, we report the state-of-the-art of learning semantic networks of words, which is the field where this chapter wants to give a contribution.

Ontology learning was originally started in (Maedche & Staab, 2001) but the fully automatic acquisition of knowledge by machines is still far from being realized. Ontology learning is not merely a rehash of existing ideas and techniques under a new name. Lexical acquisition, information extraction, knowledge base learning from texts, etc. are areas that contribute to the definition of this new problem. But, ontology learning is more than the sum of all these contributions. This new problem is inherently multidisciplinary due to its strong connection with philosophy, knowledge representation, database theories, formal logic, and natural language processing. Moreover, as ontologies are the basis for the Semantic Web, learning models have to work with massive and heterogeneous data and document collections.

In natural language processing and in many applications of the semantic web, semantic resources are ultimately exploited in text understanding systems as networks of words. Thus, learning semantic networks from text collections is possible. Here we focus on the learning of relations among concepts/words. In the following we analyze these techniques thoroughly, with particular reference to aspects and components that characterize them, limitations included. We focus on the three aspects the chapter deals with: a general introduction on semantic network learning methods to present the limitations with respect to the use of structural properties of target semantic relations; a general discussion of the problem of domain adaptation; and, finally, an analysis of the methods to include human validations in the learning loop.

Semantic Network Learning Methods

Models for automatically learning semantic networks of words from texts use both corpus-extracted evidences and existing language resources (Basili, Gliozzo, & Pennacchiotti, 2007). All these models rely on two hypotheses: *Distributional Hypothesis (DH)* (Harris, 1964) and *Lexico-Syntactic Patterns exploitation hypothesis* (LSP) (Robison, 1970). In this section we focus on how existing resources are used in the existing learning models and we note that these models do not explicitly exploit structural properties of target relations when learning taxonomies or semantic networks of words.

Distributional Hypothesis (*DH*) (Harris, 1964) models generally start learning from scratch. In (Cimiano, Hotho, & Staab, 2005), for example, lattices and related semantic networks are built from scratch. When prior knowledge is used in DH models (Pekar & Staab, 2002), the status of prior knowledge and of produced knowledge is extremely different. Inserting new words in semantic networks may be seen as a classification problem where target classes are nodes of existing hierarchies and the classification decision is taken over a pair of words, i.e. a word and its possible generalization. In this context, the classifier should decide if pairs belong or not to the semantic networks. Both existing and produced elements of the networks have the same nature, i.e., pairs of words. A distributional description of words is used to make the decision with respect to target classes. A new word and a word already existing in the network can be then treated differently, the first being represented with its distributional vector while the second being one of the final classes.

DH is widely used in many approaches in relation induction from texts. Relatedness confidences derived using the distributional hypothesis are transitive. If a word "*a*" is related to a word "*b*" and this latter is related to a word "*c*", we can somehow derive the confidence relations between the words "*a*" and "*c*". This can be derived from the formulation of the distributional hypothesis itself. Even when the distributional hypothesis is used to build hierarchies of words, structural properties of the semantic networks of words, such as transitivity and reflexivity are implicitly used. For example, DH is used in Cimiano, Hotho, and Staab (2005) for populating lattices (i.e. graphs of a particular class) of formal concepts. The idea of drawing semantic networks links using the inclusion of features derived exploiting the distributional hypothesis has been also used in

Geffet and Dagan (2005) where the *distributional inclusion hypothesis* is defined.

Lexico-Syntactic Patterns (LSP) (Robison, 1970) are instead generic ways to express a semantic relation in texts. LSP models have been applied for learning is-a relations, (Hearst, 1992; Snow, Jurafsky, & Ng, 2006), generic semantic relations between nouns (Pantel & Pennacchiotti, 2006; Szpektor, Tanev, Dagan, & Coppola, 2004), and specific relations between verbs (Chklovski & Pantel, 2004; Zanzotto & Pennacchiotti, 2006). But, LSP models do not directly exploit structural properties of semantic networks of words, i.e. these properties are not intrinsically inherited from the definition, as it differently happens for the distributional hypothesis. Semantic network learning models based on lexico-syntactic patterns present then three advantages with respect to DH models:

- These models can be used to learn any semantic relation: Hearst (1992), Morin (1999), Pantel and Pennacchiotti (2006), Chklovski and Pantel (2004), Ravichandran and Hovy (2002), Szpektor, Tanev, Dagan, and Coppola (2004), Zanzotto, Pennacchiotti, and Pazienza, 2006)
- These models coherently exploit existing taxonomies in the expansion phase: Snow, Jurafsky, and Ng (2006).
- The classification is binary, i.e., a word pair belongs or not to the taxonomy (Snow, Jurafsky, & Ng, 2006; Pantel & Pennacchiotti, 2006). In this way, a single classifier is associated to each treated relation.

Probabilistic LSP learning models (e.g., Snow, Jurafsky, and Ng [2006]) have further advantages. The first advantage is that modeling probability in the semantic network makes possible to take into accounts both corpus-extracted evidences and existing language resources during learning. This model is the only one using, even if only intrinsically, one of the properties of semantic networks (transitivity) to expand existing networks. Any corpus-based knowledge learning method augments existing knowledge repositories with new information extracted from texts. In this process, we have two big issues:

- We are mixing reliable with unreliable information
- As we are dealing with natural language, ambiguity affects every bit of discovered knowledge

Mixing reliable concepts, relations among concepts, and instances with semi-reliable extracted information is a big problem as final knowledge repositories cannot be considered reliable. Generally, extracted knowledge items are included in final resources if the related estimated confidence weights are above a threshold. Accuracy of added information is generally evaluated over a small randomly selected portion (e.g., Snow, Jurafsky, and Ng [2006], Pantel and Pennacchiotti [2006], and Lin and Pantel [2002]). Final knowledge repositories contain, then, two different kinds of information. The first kind is reliable and controlled. The second kind, i.e., the above threshold extracted information, is semi-reliable. Its accuracy is below 100% and it generally varies in different ranges of confidence weights. High confidence values guarantee high accuracy (e.g., Snow, Jurafsky, and Ng [2006]). Then, it is extremely important that corpus extracted knowledge items report the confidence weights that justifies the inclusion in the knowledge base. In this way, *consumers* of knowledge repositories can decide if information is "reliable enough" to be applied in their task. This is the first reason to include probability scores in knowledge repositories.

The second advantage is that stored probabilities enable the treatment of the ambiguity of natural language. For example, the word "*dog*" can be generalized to the word "*animal*" or to the word "*device*" according to which sense is

taken into account. A decision system working with words would benefit in accuracy from the knowledge of the probabilities of two different generalizations. The simple ordering of word senses in WordNet (Miller, 1995) (first sense heuristic) according to their frequencies is useful for open domain word sense dis-ambiguation models. Also the computation of prior sense probabilities within specific domains is useful for word sense dis-ambiguation processors (McCarthy, Koeling, Weeds, & Carroll, 2004).

We will select a probabilistic approach, among LSP semantic networks learning models, because in this way we can have the two described advantages.

Adapting Semantic Networks to New Domains

In learning methods the amount of *out-of-domain* data is generally larger than *in-domain* data. For this reason, we envis-age methods that, with a small effort for the adaptation to different specific knowledge domains, can exploit *out-of-domain* data for building *in-domain* models with bigger accuracy. We would like a model for learning semantic networks of words that can be used, with a small effort for the adaptation, in different specific knowledge domains.

One of the basic assumptions in machine learning and statistical learning is that learning data are enough representative of the environment where learned models will be applied. The statistical distribution of learning data is similar to the distribution of the data where the learned model is applied. In natural language processing tasks involving semantics, this assumption is extremely important. One of these semantic tasks is learning semantic networks of words from texts using lexico-syntactic pattern (LSP) based methods. LSP methods (Hearst, 1992; Snow, Jurafsky, & Ng, 2006; Pantel & Pennacchiotti, 2006) generally use existing ontological resources to extract learning examples. The learning examples are matched over collection of documents to derive lexico-syntactic patterns describing a semantic relation. These patterns are then used to expand the existing ontological resource by retrieving and selecting new examples. LSP semantic networks learning methods are generally used to expand existing domain ontologies using domain corpora or to expand generic lexical resources (e.g., WordNet [Miller, 1995]) using general corpora (Snow, Jurafsky, & Ng, 2006; Fallucchi & Zanzotto, 2009). In this way, the basic assumption of machine learning approaches is satisfied. Yet, the nature of the semantic networks learning task requires that models learned in a general or a specific domain may be applied in other domains for building or expanding poor initial semantic networks using domain corpora. In this case, the distribution of learning and application data is different. Learned LSP models are "domain-specific" and they being potentially related to the prose of a specific domain. These models are then accurate for the specific domain but may fail in other domains. For examples, if the target domain has not relevant pre-existing ontologies to expand, may be not enough data for training the initial model. In Snow, Jurafsky, and Ng (2006), all WordNet has been used as source of training examples. In this case, domain adaptation techniques must be adopted (Bacchiani, Roark, & Saraclar, 2004; Roark & Bacchiani, 2003; Chelba & Acero, 2006; Gao, 2009; Gildea, 2001).

Domain adaptation is a well-known problem in machine learning and statistical learning. The problem of domain adaptation arises in a large variety of applications: natural language processing (Chelba & Acero, 2006; Blitzer, McDonald, & Pereira, 2006), machine translation (Bertoldi & Federico, 2009), word sense dis-ambiguation (Chan & Ng, 2007), etc.

Different domain adaptation techniques are introduced in the context of specific applications and statistical learning methods. One of the possible ways of using the model adaptation is to adjust the model trained on the background domain to a different domain (the adaptation domain) modifying opportunely the parameters and/or the structure. The motivation of this approach is that usually the background domain has large amounts of training data while the adaptation domain has only small amounts of data. By analogy with Blitzer, McDonald, and Pereira (2006) we propose to learn common features, meaningful for both domains having different weights, where the weights are determined according to the occurrences in the respective corpus. We are confident that a model trained in the source domain using this common feature representation will generalize better the target domain.

Systems for creating or augmenting semantic networks of words using information extracted from texts foresee a manual validation for assessing the quality of semantic networks of words expansion. Yet, these systems do not use the manual validation for refining the information extraction model that proposes novel links in the networks. Manual validation can be efficiently exploited if used in an incremental model. We need an efficient way to interact with final users.

Incremental Ontology Learning

Exploiting the above (and also other) algorithms and techniques for inducing ontological structures from texts, different approaches have been devised, followed and applied regarding how to properly exploit the learned objects and how to translate them into real ontologies using dedicated editing tools. This is an aspect which is not trivially confined to importing induced data inside an existing (or empty) semantic network, but identifies iterative processes that could benefit from properly assessed interaction steps with the user, giving life to novel ways of interpreting semantic networks development.

One of the most notable examples of integration between semantic networks learning systems and ontology development frameworks is offered by Text-to-Onto (Maedche & Volz, 2001), an ontology learning module for the KAON tool suite, which discovers conceptual structures from different kind of sources (ranging from free texts to semi-structured information sources such as dictionaries, legacy ontologies and databases) using knowledge acquisition and machine learning techniques; OntoLT (Buitelaar, Olejnik, & Sintek, 2004) is a Protégé (Gennari, Musen, Fergerson, Grosso, Crubzy, & Eriksson, 2003) plug-in able to extract concepts (classes) and relations (Protégé slots or Protégé OWL properties) from linguistically annotated text collections. It provides mapping rules, defined by use of a precondition language, that allow for a mapping between extracted linguistic entities and classes/slots.

An outdated overview of this kind of integrated tools (which is part of a complete survey on ontology learning methods and techniques) can be found in the public Deliverable 1.5 (Gómez-Pérez & Manzano-Macho, 2003) of the OntoWeb project. A more recent example is offered by the Text2Onto (Cimiano & Volker, 2005) plug-in for the Neon toolkit (Haase, Lewen, Studer, Tran, d'Aquin, & Motta, 2008), a renewed version of Text-To-Onto with improvements featuring on-model independence (a *Probabilistic Ontology Model* is adopted as a replacement for any definite target ontology language), better user interaction and incremental learning.

Lastly, in Bagni, Cappella, Pazienza, Pennacchiotti, and Stellato (2007) the authors define a web browser extension based on the Semantic Turkey Knowledge Acquisition Framework (Griesi, Pazienza, & Stellato, 2007), offering two distinct learning modules: a relation extractor based on a light-weight and fast-to-perform version of algorithms for relation extraction defined in Pantel and Pennacchiotti (2006), and an ontology population module for harvesting data from html tables. Most of the above models defines supervised cyclic *develop and refine* processes controlled by domain experts. We propose to extend Semantic Turkey (ST) integrating ST with our novel probabilistic model to put final users in the learning loop with an efficient way to interact with final users.

In the rest of the chapter we propose solutions to some limits seen in this section. In particular we propose models to exploit structural properties of target relations such as transitivity during learning process. Then, we introduce two applications that use our probabilistic model: a model that can be used in different specific knowledge domains with a small effort for its adaptation and a model that allows to put final users in the learning loop for adapting the model.

TRANSITIVITY IN A PROBABILISTIC MODEL

Capturing word meaning is one of the challenges of natural language processing. Taxonomies and, in general, semantic networks of words (Miller, 1995) are often used as formal models of word meaning. In these networks, words are connected with other words by means of taxonomic and, in general, semantic relations. This is a way to capture part of the knowledge described in traditional dictionaries. For example, this informal definition of "*wheel*":

*a **wheel** is a circular frame turning about an axis ... used for supporting vehicles...*

contains a *taxonomic relation*, i.e., *the wheel is a circular frame*, and a sort of *part-of relation*, i.e., *the wheel is used for supporting vehicles*.

Transitivity is a well known property of some foundational semantic relations between words. Semantic networks are built over transitive semantic relations such as generalization, cotopy, meronymy, cause-effect, entailment, and so on. Knowing that "*dog*" is a "*mammal*" and "*mammal*" is a "*animal*," we can infer that "*dog*" is a "*animal*" or, knowing that "*snoring*" entails "*sleeping*" and "*sleeping*" entails "*resting*," we can state that "*snoring*" entails "*resting*." Yet, this property is generally not exploited in learning semantic relations from texts.

The semantic networks learning models do not explicitly exploit properties, such as transitivity, when learning taxonomies or networks of words. Transitivity, when relevant, is not used to better induce confidence values for extracted semantic relations. Even where transitivity is intrinsically used (Snow, Jurafsky, & Ng, 2006), it is not directly exploited to model confidence values, but it is used in an iterative maximization process of the probability of the entire semantic network. We transform this limitation into an opportunity. In particular we propose a novel probabilistic method for learning semantic networks of words that explicitly models transitivity for deriving confidence weights.

The rest of the section is organized as follows. We informally introduce our probabilistic model that explicitly used transitivity in semantic networks learning models. Then, we formalize the probabilistic definitions of concepts in an *induced* probabilistic model and we propose three different methods for modeling induced probabilities. Finally, we want to demonstrate that our *induced* models can effectively exploit transitivity when we replicate existing networks or we expand or build new semantic networks.

Probabilistic Definitions of Concepts in Semantic Networks Learning

When we consider semantic relations with structural properties as transitivity, including confidence weights in knowledge repositories is not a trivial problem. In methods such as Pantel and Pennacchiotti (2006), it seems to be possible to easily include some initial values in the final resource as these have been used for deciding whether or not the knowledge base should include a relation. Yet, when we need to combine these values in transitive relations, we need to be extremely careful on how these values have been estimated and computed. For example, if we discover from

corpus analysis that "*dog*" is a "*canine*" and we already know that "*canine*" is an "*animal*" (see Figure 1[a]), using transitivity we can derive the *induced* relation, i.e., *dog* is an *animal* (dashed arrow in Figure 1[a]). Yet, we cannot easily combine confidence weights if the nature of these weights is obscure. On the contrary if we discover from corpus analysis that "*dog*" is an "*animal*" and we already know that "*dog*" is "*canine*" (see Figure 1[b]), using the transitivity we can derive the *induced* relation, i.e., *canine* is an *animal* (dashed arrow in Figure 1[b]). Another example is shown in Figure 1(c). The solution generally proposed for combining confidence weights is neglecting its nature. The final relation between two words has the same confidence weight of reliable and controlled information.

Even in the probabilistic models (Snow, Jurafsky, & Ng, 2006), these reliable and unreliable information is mixed during the knowledge acquisition process. In these models, if "*canine*" is an "*animal*" (see Figure 1[a]) is in the original manually controlled network and "*dog*" is a "*canine*" has a high probability from the corpus observations, this latter is included in the knowledge base with the same degree of plausibility of "*canine*" is an "*animal*." Then, the induced relation "*dog*" is an "*animal*" has again the same degree of plausibility of manually controlled information. This represent a loss of information the uncertainty of the relation "*dog*" is an "*animal*" has been neglected.

Probabilistic Definitions for Concepts

Keeping and propagating uncertainty in transitive semantic networks is extremely important. We thus propose an *inductive semantic network learning model*, i.e., a probabilistic semantic network learning model based on lexico-syntactic patterns that exploits transitivity during learning and for determining combined confidence weights. Our model stems from the intuition that LSP learning

Figure 1. Examples of relations derived exploiting the transitivity

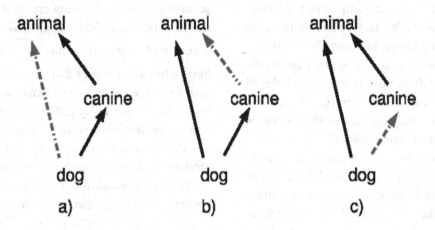

models contribute to *probabilistic definitions of target concepts* and that it is possible to combine these definitions to determine confidence weights derived from the transitive networks. Extracting evidence from corpora suggesting that "*dog*" is an "*animal*" contributes both to the definition of "*dog*" and to the definition of "*animal*." In the case of "*dog*," the relation between "*dog*" and "*animal*" contributes to the in tensional definition of "*dog*," it stating that "*dog*" is an "*animal*" with specific features. In the case of "*animal*," this relation contributes, in a wide sense, to the *extensional* definition[1] of "*animal*." It is like we are giving one of the possible instances[2] of the concept "*animal*." These formal *intensional* and *extensional* definitions are often used to derive the similarity among words or concepts. *Cotopy* (Maedche & Staab, 2002), a measure for determining similarity between concepts in two different semantic networks, uses exactly this information.

A *probabilistic definition* of a concept is an intensional definition associated with its *induced* probabilities. These probabilities are derived from the topology of the transitive semantic networks mixing existing knowledge and corpus estimated probabilities. In Figure 1 the solid arrow indicates relations derived from existing structured knowledge repositories and from corpus analysis while the dashed arrow type indicates probabilities induced from the structure of the network. We want to describe the probability of the dashed relations using the probabilities of the solid ones. We call *direct probabilities* the first type, and *induced probabilities* the second one.

Accord to Fallucchi and Zanzotto (2009), we define the *direct probabilities* as the direct events $R_{i,j} \in T$ where T is the semantic network. If Ri,j is in T, then "*i*" is in a R relation with "*j*" according to the semantic network T. For example, if R is the is-a relation, $R_{dog,animal} \in T$ describes that dog is an animal according to the semantic network T. The learning problem in the direct settings is to determine the probabilities:

$$P(R_{i,j} \in T|E)$$

Starting from the idea described above, we propose three models that derive *induced probabilistic definitions* from *direct probabilities*: the first exploits *intensional* definitions of concepts while the second exploits *extensional* definitions and the third exploits both *intensional* and *extensional* probabilistic definitions of concepts. We then define the three models respectively: the *intensional*, the *extensional* and the *mixed probabilistic inductive model*. To give an intuitive idea of our models, we can use the example in Figure 1.

The *intensional inductive model* exploits direct *intensional* definitions to derive an induced *intensional* definition. In Figure 1(a), we have as direct information the probabilities of the relations "*dog*" is a "*canine*" and "*canine*" is a "*animal*." From these two relations, we can derive the induced probability of the intensional definition of "*dog*" is a "*animal*." In this case we are exploiting and modeling the transitivity of the is-a relation.

The *extensional inductive model* uses the direct probabilities (solid arrows), to form *extensional* definitions of the concepts and, to compare the different *extensional* definitions for determining the final induced probability. In Figure 1(b), the relations "*dog*" is a "*animal*" and "*dog*" is a "*canine*" are used to form a very small part of the *extensional* definitions of, respectively, "*animal*" and "*canine*." The idea is that these *extensional* definitions can be used to determine the similarity of "*animal*" and "*canine*." Then, we can derive the induced probability of the relation "*dog*" is a "*animal*." Using the same intuition, the relations "*dog*" is a "*animal*" and "*canine*" is a "*animal*" contribute to the *extensional* definition of "*animal*" (see Figure 1[c]). Using all the other relations, we can derive also the induced probability of the relation "*dog*" is a "*canine*."

Inductive Probabilistic Model

In this section, we formalize the probabilistic definitions of concepts in an *induced* probabilistic model. We introduce three models for exploiting the probabilistic definitions of concepts within the *induced* probabilistic model. Without loss of generality, we focus the examples and the prose on semantic networks learning. Yet, these models can be adopted for any transitive semantic relation.

As in Pantel and Pennacchiotti (2006) and Snow, Jurafsky, and Ng (2006), we model the semantic networks learning problem as a binary classification task. Given a pair of words (i,j) and a vector of observed features $\overrightarrow{e_{i,j}}$, we want to build a binary classifier that determines if i is a j and gives the related confidence weight. As in Snow, Jurafsky, and Ng (2006), we see this problem in a probabilistic point of view as it gives the possibility to determine the *direct probabilistic model* as well as the *induced probabilistic model*.

We here propose a model to exploit transitivity within probabilistic semantic networks learners that use lexico-syntactic patterns. Using lexico-syntactic patterns on a corpus, we can extract pairs of words in a given relation along with their reliability. These pairs of words and their reliabilities are *directly* observed. For example (see Figure 2), given the hyperonymy relation, we *directly* derive the reliabilities of the pairs "*dog*" is a "*canine*" (0.8), "*canine*" is an "*animal*" (0.7), and "*dog*" is an "*animal*" (0.2) (solid arrows). If we now look at all these pairs as a whole, we can observe that these words form a semantic network where transitive property holds. Even if the *directly* observed reliability of the pair "*dog*" is an "*animal*" is low (0.2), transitivity of the network suggests that this reliability should be higher (0.648). We exactly want to exploit the transitive network to *induce* the reliability of the relation between "*dog*" and "*animal*" (dashed arrow) using all the reliabilities of the involved pairs *directly* observed from the corpus. We then use a probabilistic setting where this composition of confidence weights can be better controlled.

The example of Figure 2 we have the following *direct* probabilities (where *d*=dog, *a*=animal, and *c=canine*): $P\left(R_{d,a}|\vec{e}_{d,a}\right) = 0.2$, $P\left(R_{d,c}|\vec{e}_{d,c}\right) = 0.8$ and $P\left(R_{c,a}|\vec{e}_{c,a}\right) = 0.7$.

Figure 2. Example of relations derived exploiting transitivity

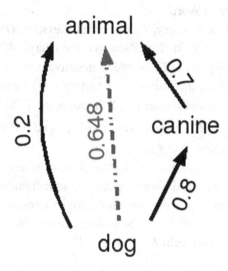

The *inductive probabilistic model* presents the main innovation of our approach to semantic networks learning. We want here to define an event space that models transitivity. We then introduce the events $\hat{R}_{i,j}$ and the related probability function:

$$P(\hat{R}_{i,j} \in T \mid E) \qquad (1)$$

This probability should capture the fact that a decision on the pair (i,j) also depends on the transitive relations activated by (i,j). Rarely these relations are activated by *existing semantic networks* links. Yet, this *induced* probability takes into account transitively related taxonomic links.

We examine different models to exploit the transitive property of the R relation and for each of these models we show that $P(\hat{R}_{i,j} \in T \mid E)$ can be rewritten in term of the involved $P(R_{h,k}|E)$.

For example, we can compute the *induced intensional* probability for the pair (*dog,animal*) in Figure 2. The *induced intensional* probability $P(\hat{R}_{d,a} \mid E)$ can be computed as the probability of the event $\hat{R}_{d,a} = R_{d,a} \bigcup (R_{d,c} \bigcap R_{c,a})$. This captures that the *induced* event $\hat{R}_{d,a}$ is active when $R_{d,a}$ happens or the joint event $R_{d,c} \bigcap R_{c,a}$ happens. Then, using the inclusion-exclusion property, the previous independence assumptions on the evidences E, and an independence assumption between $R_{i,j}$, we can compute $P(R_{d,a} \bigcup (R_{d,c} \bigcap R_{c,a}) \mid E)$ as presented in Exhibit 1.

We propose three different methods for modeling induced probabilities: *intensional*, *extensional*, and *mixed* model as described in Fallucchi and Zanzotto (2010). These three models exploit different definitions of the event $\hat{R}_{i,j} \in T$.

In the *intensional* model, the event $R_{i,j} \in T$ is represented as the event $R_{i,j} \in T$ and for any k all the alternative events $R_{i,k} \in T$ and $R_{k,j} \in T$. In the *extensional* model, the event $R_{i,j} \in T$ is represented as the event $R_{i,j} \in T$ and for any k all alternative events $R_{i,k} \in T$ and $R_{j,k} \in T$ and all the events $R_{k,j} \in T$ and $R_{k,i} \in T$. The *mixed* is a combination of the other two models.

Exhibit 1.

$$P(R_{d,a} \bigcup (R_{d,c} \bigcap R_{c,a}) \mid E) =$$
$$= P(R_{d,a} \mid E) + P(R_{d,c} \bigcap R_{c,a} \mid E) - P(R_{d,a} \bigcap R_{d,c} \bigcap R_{c,a} \mid E) =$$
$$= P(R_{d,a} \mid \vec{e}_{d,a}) + P(R_{d,c} \mid \vec{e}_{d,c}) P(R_{c,a} \mid \vec{e}_{c,a}) - P(R_{d,a} \mid \vec{e}_{d,a}) P(R_{d,c} \mid \vec{e}_{d,c}) P(R_{c,a} \mid \vec{e}_{c,a}) =$$
$$= 0.2 + 0.8 * 0.7 - 0.2 * 0.8 * 0.7 = 0.648$$

Experimental Evaluation

Here we want to demonstrate, with two sets of experiments, that our *induced* models can effectively exploit transitivity. The first experiment is a pilot experiment; the second experiment is a full experiment that differs from the pilot in the size of semantic networks and in target relations. For both sets of experiments we describe the experimental set up and we report the results.

The Pilot Experiment

In the *pilot experiment,* we replicate a small existing semantic network of works with few pair of words in is-a relation. To completely define the experiments we need to address some issues: how we defined the semantic networks to replicate, which corpus we have used to extract evidences for pairs of words, and which feature space and logit regressors we used. As corpus we used the *English Web as Corpus* (ukWaC) (Baroni, Berardini, Ferraresi, & Zanchetta, 2009).

The best way of determining how a semantic network of words learner is performing is to see if it can replicate an existing semantic network. As target semantic networks we selected a portion of WordNet[3] (Miller, 1995). Namely, we started from 44 concrete nouns divided in 3 classes: animal, artifact, and vegetable. For each word w, we selected the synset s_w that generalizes the class it belongs to. In this way we obtained a set S of synsets. We then expanded the set to S' adding the siblings (i.e., the coordinate terms) for each synset in S. The sets S' contains 265 coordinate terms plus the 44 original concrete nouns. For each element in S we collected the hypernyms, obtaining the set H of the hypernyms. We then removed from the set H the top classes (*entity*, *unit*, *object*, and *whole*), obtaining 77 hypernyms. For the purpose of the experiments we derived a taxonomy T from S and S' and a taxonomy $\bar{T}$ from the set of negative examples. The taxonomy

T is the portion of WordNet implied by $O = H \cup S'$, i.e., T contains all the $(s,h) \in O \times O$ that are in WordNet.

On the contrary, $\bar{T}$ contains all the $(s,h) \in O \times O$ that are not in WordNet. We then have 4596 positive pairs in T and 48354 negative pairs in $\bar{T}$. To obtain the training and testing sets, we randomly divided the set $T \cup \bar{T}$ in two parts, $T_{tr} \cup \bar{T}_{tr}$ and $T_{ts} \cup \bar{T}_{ts}$, respectively the 70% and 30% of the original $T \cup \bar{T}$.

We used a bag-of-n-gram feature space for implicitly modeling lexical-syntactic patterns. In learning process, we used a logistic regressor based on the Monroe-Penrose pseudo-inverse matrix (Fallucchi & Zanzotto, 2009).

Results

With the first set of experiments, we analyze the effectiveness of our *inductive* model with respect to the state-of-the-art. We evaluate the *iterative* probabilistic models (Snow, Jurafsky, & Ng, 2006), the *direct* probabilistic models (Fallucchi & Zanzotto, 2009), and the *induced* probabilistic models on their ability of sorting the pairs. We have two classes of methods. The *iterative* model adds some pairs at each step. The *direct* and the *inductive* probabilistic models, instead, produce a sorting of the pairs according to the probabilities.

We compared the two methods in the following way. For the *iterative* methods, we plot the curve that relates the accuracy to the number of added pairs. The accuracy is computed as the number of correctly added pairs with respect to the added pairs. On the contrary, for the probabilistic models we plot the accuracies with respect to the ranked pairs. For this set of experiments, we used k=100 for the pseudo-inverse matrix computation with SVD.

The results are reported in Figure 3. Firstly, we can observe that, after some initial steps, models that keep the probabilities are better than the model that makes a decision at each step.

Figure 3. Accuracy of the top-k ranked pairs for the iterative, direct, and inductive probabilistic learners

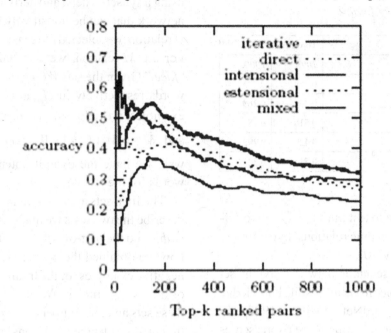

The *direct* model already outperforms the *iterative* model. The second observation is that the *inductive* (*extensional*, *intensional*, and *mixed*) models outperform the *direct* model. This shows that our way of encoding the transitivity is effective. Finally, among the *inductive* models, the *mixed* model exploits both the *intensional* and *extensional* probabilistic definitions of concepts, proves to be the best one.

The accuracies are reported in Table 1. The table reports the accuracies for the different probabilistic models for two different cuts of the sorted pair list. The second and the third columns report, respectively, the accuracies for 100 and for 1000 considered pairs. We used these two cuts to compute the statistical significance of the difference between the direct and the mixed model. To determine the statistical significance, we used the model described in (Yeh, 2000) as implemented in (Padó, 2006). We extended this latter for considering accuracies computed on sorted lists. According to these tests, the statistical significance is below 0.05.

The Full Experiment

Here, we want to demonstrate that our *induced* models can effectively exploit transitivity when increasing the size of the semantic network of both training and testing. Differently from the pilot experiment two target relations are considered: is-a and part-of relations. To carry out the experiments we then need: (1) a corpus for extracting evidences to derive probabilities; (2) a semantic network of words and a set of negative examples for the target relation; (3) the definition of the feature space; and, finally, (4) the definition of the logistic regressors.

As corpus we used the *English Web as Corpus* (ukWaC) (Baroni, Berardini, Ferraresi, & Zanchetta, 2009).

The semantic network of words will be used as source of training and testing examples. For each experiment we need: a training example set with positive pairs and negative pairs and a testing example set with positive pairs and negative pairs. The testing set *TS* should be a totally connected set for building the potential network

Table 1. Accuracy of the different models at top 100 and 1000 ranked pairs

	Top k-pairs	
Probabilistic Model	*100*	*1000*
iterative	0.350	0.225
direct	0.290	0.269
intentional	0.510	0.282
extensional	0.420	0.292
mixed	0.510	0.322

of words. We want to test our model for two different transitive semantic relations: hyperonymy (H) and meronymy (M).

We extract the semantic networks and the set of negative examples from an existing knowledge repository, i.e., WordNet[iii] (Miller, 1995). In WordNet, semantic relations R are expressed as pairs of synonymy sets (synset), i.e., $R = \{(S_1, S_2) \mid S_1 \text{ is in relation } R \text{ with } S_2\}$ where the synset S_1 and S_2 are the sets of words $S_1 = \{w_1^{(1)}, \ldots, w_n^{(1)}\}$ and $S_2 = \{w_1^{(2)}, \ldots, w_n^{(2)}\}$. The synset S_1 is in relation with the synset S_2 if S_1 is directly related with the synset S_2 or if it is reachable with the transitive property. We derive the semantic networks of words from the synset network.

Given one of the two target relations, we can derive the network of words R from the set R as follows:

$$R = \{(w_a, w_b) \mid (S_a, S_b) \in R, w_a \in S_a, w_b \in S_b)\}.$$

We then derived the semantic networks of words for hyperonymy H and for meronymy M. These networks consist of, respectively, 7879350 and 672571 as reported in Table 2.

The negative examples have been obtained as follows. Given the set of the words in WordNet W, the negative examples are respectively $\bar{H} = W \times W - H$ and $\bar{M} = W \times W - M$.

For generating the testing set, we selected a relevant and strictly connected sub portion of network of words. This portion has been obtained

using a synset as head and deriving the part of the network that can be transitively reached. For the H relation, we selected the sense 1 of "*vegetable.*" For the M relation, we selected the sense 1 of "*face.*" Given the sets $W(veg)$ and $W(face)$ of the words respectively in H_{ts} and M_{ts}, the negative examples are $\bar{H}_{ts} = W(veg) \times W(veg) - H_{ts}$, and $\bar{M}_{ts} = W(face) \times W(face) - M_{ts}$. In this way, we have the overall potential network of words for the testing.

The final sets are reported in Table 3. We here describe the two tests we made: the is-a with *vegetable* and the part-of with *face*. The table reports how we obtained the positive examples and the negative examples for the training and the testing of the two examples. We also report the size of these sets and the number of the pairs retrieved in the corpus under the conditions later on described.

We used a bag-of-n-gram feature space for implicitly modeling lexical-syntactic patterns.

We used two different logistic regressors: a logistic regressor based on the Monroe-Penrose pseudo-inverse matrix (Fallucchi & Zanzotto, 2009) and the support vector machines (Vapnik, 1995) as implemented in Joachims (1999).

Results

In the first set of experiments, we want to investigate how *induced* model behaves with respect to the *direct* model in the most common settings for semantic relation learning: enriching an existing semantic network without any additional information. We then have the existing network out of which we can derive positive examples but also some negative example. We obtained this setting, which we call *semi-supervised*, using the two proposed sets for the two transitive relations. We gave an initial probability of 0.99 to the positive examples and of 0.5 for the negative examples. These latter are then used as if no information is available. This is the natural setting in learning semantic networks that is used in many experi-

Table 2. Semantic networks used in the experiments

Test	Set	Description	Initial Size	Retrieved Pairs
is-a	TR_p	H/H_{ts}	1983197	212076
	TR_n	$\bar{H} / \bar{H}_{ts}$	5594387	315428
	TS_p	H_{ts}	506	150
	TS_n	$\bar{H}_{ts}$	80436	258
part-of	TR_p	M/M_{ts}	14333	8077
	TR_n	$\bar{H} / M_{ts}$	623616	318679
	TS_p	M_{ts}	408	101
	TS_n	$\bar{M}_{ts}$	34214	1713

ments (e.g., Pantel and Pennacchiotti [2006]). The results of these experiments for the is-a relation and the part-of relation are reported respectively in Table 3 and in Table 4. These tables report the *relative recall* of the different methods obtained using the first k ranked pairs. In line with Pantel and Pennacchiotti (2006), the *relative recall* RR is the ratio between the retrieved pairs with respect to the pairs that can be retrieved from the method, i.e., in our case the pairs that are retrieved in the corpus. In these tables, we report both the experiments with the pseudo-inverse matrix method (*PI*) and with SVM.

For each method, *direct, intentional*, and *extensional* we have the two columns representing the two methods for inducing the direct probabilities. For the is-a relation (Table 3), we report the

relative recall for the first 100, 200, and 300 first ranked pairs. For the part of relation (Table 4), we report the relative recall for 500 and 1000 first ranked pairs.

For the is-a relation (Table 3), experiments show that the best way to exploit the transitivity of the is-a relation is the *extensional* model. Only the *extensional* model outperforms the *direct* model. This is confirmed for both regression methods. We can also observe that the difference between the SVM and PI does not seem to be significant. For the part-of relation (Table 4), experiments confirm that the *extensional* model outperforms the *direct* model. Yet, the *intensional* model behaves better than in the case of the is-a relation.

To better explore our models, we then analyzed their behavior under ideal conditions. In

Table 3. Relative recall of is-a relation: case semi-supervised

	direct		intensional		extensional		mixed	
	PI	**SVM**	**PI**	**SVM**	**PI**	**SVM**	**PI**	**SVM**
100	30.67	30.00	4.00	4.00	37.33	35.33	24.00	24.00
200	56.67	49.33	27.33	27.33	60.67	61.33	45.33	43.33
300	74.67	74.67	64.00	64.00	81.33	78.67	64.67	66.00

Table 4. Relative recall of part-of relation: case semi-supervised

	direct		Intensional		extensional		mixed	
	PI	**SVM**	**PI**	**SVM**	**PI**	**SVM**	**PI**	**SVM**
500	28.71	28.71	32.67	32.67	33.66	33.66	34.66	33.64
1000	44.55	70.30	54.46	70.3	49.5	72.28	51.50	70.71

this setting, we have explicit negative cases. Yet, these conditions hardly represent the operational scenario where the models act. Generally, we have an existing semantic network that we want to expand and we have no knowledge about negative examples. We obtained this setting, which we call *supervised*, assigning an initial probability of 0.99 to positive examples and an initial probability of 0.01 to negative examples. The results of these experiments for the is-a and the part-of relations are reported respectively in Table 5 and in Table 6.

We report here the experiments for the Pseudo-Inverse method (PI). In the case of the is-a relation, we can observe that this setting increases the performance only when we consider 300 pairs with respect to the semi-supervised approach. The *extensional* model is still better than the *intensional* model. For the part-of, the increase in performance with respect to the semi-supervised approach is lower than the previous case. Some part-of pairs that have been considered negative examples are positive. Inheritance of the part-of is not considered in generating positive examples. Yet, even in this case, the *extensional* model outperforms the *intensional* model. For the part-of relation, both the *intensional* and the *extensional* models are suitable for exploiting transitivity.

GENERIC ONTOLOGY LEARNERS ON APPLICATION DOMAINS

Domain knowledge bases are extremely important in a variety of natural language processing applications but manually creating structured knowledge repositories is a very time consuming and expensive task. Semi-supervised learning of domain knowledge bases from texts is generally seen as the solution. This is a very attractive and rich research area that is full of challenges. Generally, the process for automatically creating, adapting, or extending existing knowledge bases relies on existing structured knowledge and domain corpora. In ontology learning models using Lexico-Syntactic Patterns (LSP) (Robison, 1970; Hearst, 1992; Pantel & Pennacchiotti, 2006), existing domain ontologies or structured knowledge bases give positive learning examples. These latter are exploited to learn lexico-syntactic patterns from domain corpora. Learnt LSPs are then used to extract and structure new knowledge from the domain corpora. For a successful application, these LSP methods for learning domain ontologies need large domain corpora and existing domain knowledge bases. LSP methods for learning ontologies from texts are good models only when we consider *ontology-rich* domains or

Table 5. Relative recall of is-a relation vegetable: case supervised

	direct	intensional	extensional	mixed
	PI	**PI**	**PI**	**PI**
100	28.00	2.67	37.33	21.333
200	56.67	27.33	60.67	45.333
300	80.67	66.00	82.67	64.667

Table 6. Relative recall of part-of relation face: case supervised

	direct	intensional	extensional	mixed
	PI	**PI**	**PI**	**PI**
500	26.73	28.71	28.71	28.70
1000	39.60	49.50	44.55	46.51

we do generic knowledge extraction. In this latter case, these methods can exploit large general corpora and large general structured knowledge repositories such as WordNet (Miller, 1995). There are only few domains with well-assessed existing structured knowledge bases where the problem is to expand these ontologies. On the contrary, the large number of applications domains has little or no existing structured knowledge. The big challenge is to successfully apply these methods in *ontology-poor* domains. One of the possible ways to address the above challenge is to build LSP models that learn lexico-syntactic patterns on generic and ontology rich domains and then apply these patterns on specific ontology poor domains. In line with Gao (2009), we respectively refer as the *background domains* and *application domains* to these two kinds of domains. Yet, in machine learning and in statistical learning data should be enough representative of the environment where learned models will be applied. The statistical distribution of learning data should be similar to the distribution of the data where the learn model is applied. In this application scenario, this assumption is inaccurate. *Background domain data*, also called out-of-domain data, used for learning lexico-syntactic patterns have generally a different distribution with respect to *application domain data*, also called in-domain data. Generally, out-of-domain data are more than in-domain data. We need to envis-age methods that exploit these data for building accurate in-domain models.

The rest of the section we present our model and then, we evaluate and assess the performance of our method on the target domain, i.e., Earth Observation Domain.

Learner Model: From Background to Application Domain

Can training data from one corpus be applied to learn another corpus? The basic idea is partly to answer this question because we want to define an ontology learning model that can be adapted to previously unseen distributions of data. This model is thought to exploit the information learned in a *background* domain for extracting information in an *adaptation* domain.

Our ontology learning method is based on the probabilistic formulation given in the previous section. We use this probabilistic setting to learn a model that takes into consideration corpus-extracted evidences over a list of training pairs. The initial feature space is built starting from the analysis of a generic corpus where we observe a list of training pairs of words that are in a target semantic relation. We can generate these pairs using general resources such as WordNet. These pairs are used to enable the probabilistic method to induce lexico-syntactic patterns for the model of the specific semantic relation (Hearst, 1992). The learned model can be used to estimate the probabilities of the new instances computing a new feature space using the corpus of the *adaptation* domain.

In the rest of this section, we will firstly describe the background ontology learning model and we will then illustrate the method that we will be adapted to the new domain.

Background Ontology Learner

In the probabilistic formulation, the task of learning ontologies from a corpus is seen as a maximum likelihood problem. The ontology is seen as a set O of assertions R over pairs $R_{i,j}$. In particular we will consider the *is-a* relation. In this case, if $R_{i,j}$ is in O, i is a concept and j is one of its generalizations. For example, $R_{dog,animal} \in O$ states that *dog* is an *animal* according to the ontology O.

The main probabilities are then: (1) the prior probability $P(R_{i,j} \in O)$ of an assertion $R_{i,j}$ to belong to the ontology O and (2) the posterior probability $P(R_{i,j} \in O \mid \vec{e}_{i,j})$ of an assertion $R_{i,j}$ to belong to the ontology O given a set of evidences $\vec{e}_{i,j}$ derived from the corpus. These evidences are derived from the contexts where the pair (i,j) is found in the corpus. The vector $\vec{e}_{i,j}$ is a feature vector associated to a pair (i,j). For example, a feature may describe how many times i and j are seen in patterns like "*i as j*" or "*i is a j*". But many other indicators exist of an Is-a relation between i and j (see Hearst [1992]). Given a set of evidences E over all the relevant word pairs, the probabilistic ontology learning task is defined as the problem of finding an ontology $\hat{O}$ that maximizes the probability of having the evidences of E, i.e.:

$$\hat{O} = \arg \max_{O} P(E \mid O)$$

In the original model (Snow, Jurafsky, & Ng, 2006; Fallucchi & Zanzotto, 2009), this maximization problem was solved by a local search.

In the present model at each step we maximize the ratio between the likelihood $P(E|O')$ and the likelihood $P(E|O)$ where $O'=O \cup N$ and N are the relations added at each step. As in Snow, Jurafsky, and Ng (2006) and Fallucchi and Zanzotto (2009) this ratio is called *odds*. It is calculated using the logistic regression and then solving a linear problem using the pseudo-inverse matrix model. The regression coefficients will be estimated as follows

$$\hat{\beta} = X_{C_B}^{+} l$$

where l is the logit vector and $X_{C_B}^{+}$ is the *Moore-Penrose pseudoinverse* (Penrose, 1955) matrix of the inverse evidence matrix $X_{C_B}^{+}$ obtained from a generic corpus C_B that includes a constant column of 1's, necessary to obtain the β_0 coefficients. The regressors represent the model that we learned from the training pairs using a generic corpus C_B that we will use to compute the probabilities of the testing pairs.

Estimator for Application Domain

In our task, instead of finding the ontology that maximizes the likelihood of having the evidences E, we calculate, given the regressors, the probabilities of the testing pairs step by step. The idea is that, given the domain based corpus C_A, for each testing pair we compute the vector space according to the features selected in the previous generic corpus feature space analysis. After the domain based corpus feature space analysis where we look for the testing pairs in C_A, we obtain a new feature space X_{C_A}. It is a matrix $n' \times m$ where n' is the number of the new instances found in the corpus C_A and m is the number of the features. We compute the logit of the new instances:

$$l' = \alpha X_{C_A} \beta \qquad (2)$$

where X_{C_A} is the inverse evidence matrix obtained from an *adaptation* domain corpus C_A that includes a constant column of 1's, necessary to obtain the β_0 coefficients. The parameter α is used to adapt the model by the β vector to the new domain.

From the definition of logit we can compute the probabilities of the new instances, i.e.:

$$p_i = \frac{\exp(l_i)}{1 + \exp(l_i)}$$

This latter can be used to build the know ledge base in the new domain.

Experimental Evaluation

We experimented with our model adaptation strategy using a generic domain as *background* domain and the Earth Observation Domain as specific domain. We took the is-a relation as the target relation. The target of the experiments is to understand whether or not our model adapt to specific domains. We then compare our system (Our-System) with respect to a system that uses only WordNet (WN-System). In this section, we firstly describe the general experimental set up. We then describe the quality of the target domain ontologies. Finally, we analyze the accuracy of our models with respect to the three different ontologies.

Experimental Setup

To completely define the experiments we have to define: both training and testing pairs, which corpus has been used to extract evidences for training pairs, which corpus to extract evidences for testing pairs, and which feature space we use for both corpora. To build the training pairs we generated all the pairs that were in hyperonym relation in WordNet[iii] (Miller, 1995) and we obtained about 2 millions of words.

Here, we firstly define the semantic networks used in the experiments. The network of words will be used as a source of training and testing examples. For each experiment we need: a training example set $TR=(TR_p, TR_n)$ with positive pairs and negative pairs TR_p, and a testing example set TS. To build TS we start from a given list of 63 terms that are relevant in Earth Observation Domain. Then we combine each term with the other terms and we generate 63×63 pairs. Furthermore, for each term w, we select all the synsets s_w in WordNet. In the case of a term with a synset in WordNet we generate the pairs combining w with all the hyperonyms for each synset. Otherwise, if w has compound words we look for our semantic head in WordNet. If we find the synsets, we generate the pairs combining with the hyperonyms of the semantic head of.

We extract the training example pairs from an existing knowledge repository: WordNet[iii] (Miller, 1995). Given hyperonymy as target relation, we can derive the network of words R from the set R as follows:

$$R = \left\{ (w_a, w_b) \mid (S_a, S_b) \in R,\ w_a \in S_a, w_b \in S_b \right\}.$$

We then build the set H that contains all pairs of words in WordNet that are in hyperonymy relation. Then $TR_p = H\text{-}TS$. Given the set of the words in WordNet W, the training negative example is $TR_n = W \times W - TR_p - TS$. We build TR_p, TR_n and TS without overlap. We searched for the pairs in in a corpus C_B (in particular the *English Web as Corpus* (ukWaC) [Baroni, Berardini, Ferraresi, & Zanchetta, 2009] has been used). This is a web extracted corpus of about 2700000 web pages containing more than 2 billion words. It contains documents of several different topics such as web, computers, education, public sphere, etc. It has been largely demonstrated that the web documents are good models for natural language (Lapata & Keller, 2004).

Using a web crawler, here we pick up a corpus related to Earth Observation Domain C_A, successively "cleaned," that contains about 8300 documents (115,6 MB). We use the bag-of-word feature space. Out of the $T \cup \bar{T}$, only those pairs that appeared at a distance of 3 tokens at most have been selected. Using these 3 tokens, we generate the *bag-of-word* feature space. The pairs in *TR* found in the ukWaC are 527348, while the pairs in *TS* found in it are 404. The two generated feature spaces have the same features that are 276670. The model to build ontologies in Earth Observation Domain has been generated by using the training pairs and the corpus ukWac.

Evaluating the Quality of Target Domain Specific Ontologies

We want to evaluate our approach in learning the bulk of the ontologies, i.e., the *is-a* relation in Earth Observation Domain between two pairs of words is a binary problem. We then asked three annotators (A_1, A_2, and A_3) to build three different ontologies: two of them are expert in the domain (A_1 and A_2), the third one is not (A_3). A_1, and A_2 have different levels of expertise: A_1 is a young expert in the domain and A_2 an older one. Each annotator made a binary classification of 641 pairs of words in Earth Observation Domain, i.e., the *TS* set introduced in the previous section.

We then wanted to judge the quality of the annotation procedure according to their inter annotation agreement. A simple measure of the quality of the agreement rate between two human annotators is the ratio between the number of items identically judged by two different annotators and the total number of items considered by the annotators. In Scott (1955), this measure is named **observed agreement** and it is defined as *the percentage of judgments on which the two analysts agree when coding the same data independently*. Accord to Artstein and Poesio (2008), we define the agreement value.

We can examine the issue of inter-annotator agreement by comparing the agreement rate of the human annotators. There are different methods for measuring the agreement among 3 annotators. When there are more than two annotators, some of them may agree and the rest dis-agrees on the

same item. In this case, the observed agreement can no longer be defined as the percentage of items getting agreement. To solve this problem, we can analyze two solutions: *pairwise agreement* and *multi-π agreement* both in (Fleiss, et al., 1971). In the section Pairwise agreement we will describe the inter-annotators agreement for each pair of annotators that has a personal distribution and we will show that this is similar to the distribution computed on both annotators of each pair. In the *multi-π agreement*, we examine the distribution of all the three annotators.

Pairwise Agreement

The pairwise agreement defines the agreement on a particular item as the proportion of agreed judgment pairs out of the total number of judgment pairs for that item (Fleiss, et al., 1971). We measure the inter-annotators agreement of the 3 pairs of annotators: $pair_1$ for the two annotators expert in the domain A_1 and A_2 ; $pair_2$ for one annotator expert in the domain A_1 and the other one not expert A_3; and, $pair_3$ for the second annotator expert in the domain A_2 and the other one not expert A_3.

Given the same data (641 or 404-annotations) with the same guidelines, we build the contingency tables for the 3 pairwise annotators (respectively Table 7 and Table 9). For each table we report the statistic of the two annotators. Then in Table 7(a) we summarize the inter-annotator agreement of the 3 pairwise agreements considering 641-annotators. For example, the observed agreement for this data is obtained summing up the cells of the table where the annotators assign the same judgment and dividing by the total number of annotations. For example, considering $pair_1$ (first row of the Table 8[a]), the two annotators label 47 occurrences as YES, and 490 as NO. The resulting observed agreement of $pair_1$ is $A_o = (47+490)/641 = 0.8377535$. As above mentioned, there are two different methods to compute the expected agreement. In the first method the expected agreement is governed by prior distributions that are unique for each annotator and it is computed looking the actual distribution. Then for $pair_1$ we have

$$A_e = 0.16848674 * 0.1404056 + 0.83151326 * 0.8595944 = 0.7384206$$

In the second method we get the same distribution for each annotator of the *pair*; then we have:

$$A_e = \left(\frac{90 + 108}{641 * 2}\right)^2 + \left(\frac{533 + 551}{641 * 2}\right)^2 = 0.7388149$$

Since the two A_e values are similar and the same occurs for the other pairs, we report only the expected agreement computed using the first method.

Finally, using both the observed and expected agreement, the possible agreement beyond change observed is

$$kappa = (0.83775350.7384206) / (1 - 0.7384206) = 0.3797428.$$

Analogously we compute kappa value for the other pair of annotators.

In the same way we compute Observed Agreement, we compute Expected Agreement and coefficient kappa for the pairwise agreement considering 404-annotations (Table 10). Summarizing only 641-annotations, the coefficient kappa is in the "fair" interval in accord to the scale proposed in Landis and Koch (1977). Most likely there is a fair agreement between annotators A_2 and A_3 because the first one is an older expert in the domain while the second one is not expert at all, so they have a different knowledge with respect to the specific Earth Observation Domain.

In all the other cases the pairwise agreement is better because the coefficient kappa belongs to the "moderate" interval. We are confident on the reliability of such annotations as the annotators agree on labeling the same pairs of words. This allows us to prove the validity of the annotation.

Multi-π Agreement

In a $multi - \pi$ agreement, the agreement of the annotators is considered as a whole. There is only one distribution for all the annotators, derived from the total proportions of categories assigned by each annotator.

When there are more than two annotators, the visualization of the data is a difficult task: a possible solution is in using the agreement table where each annotator is represented in a separate column.

The columns A_1, A_2 and A_3 of Table 11(a)Table 11(b) the label 1 or 0 assigned for each pair (first column) by the 3 annotators respectively in 641 or 404-annotations. For both tables we report in the columns YES and NO respectively the sum of 1s and 0s in A_1, A_2 and A_3. In Table 11(c) we report the observed and expected agreement and the relative kappa coefficient for both 641 and 404 annotations. The kappa value obtained from both annotations confirms the conclusions deduced with the pairwise agreement method that proved the validity of the annotations of the 3 annotators.

Result

In our experiments we investigated how the approach to compute a model using both a *background* domain and an existing network, can be positively used to learn the *is-a* relation in Earth Observation Domain. For the evaluation, we compare our learner model (*Our-System*) directly with currently existing hyperonym links in WordNet (*WN-System*) and we measure in both cases the performance to find correctly the testing pairs that are in is-a relation. In order to evaluate the performance of the two systems for the pairs in Earth Observation Domain we used the three dif-

Table 7. Contingency tables for pairwise annotator agreement for 641-annotations

		A₁		
		yes	no	
A₂	yes	47	61	108
	no	43	490	533
		90	551	641

(a) pair₁=(A₁,A₂)

		A₁		
		yes	no	
A₃	yes	76	83	159
	no	14	468	482
		90	551	641

(b) pair₂=(A₁,A₃)

		A₂		
		yes	no	
A₂	yes	72	87	159
	no	36	446	482
		180	553	641

(c) pair₃=(A₂,A₃)

Table 8. Pairwise agreement for 641-annotationsions

	Ao	Ae	Kappa
pair1=(A1,A2)	0.8377535	0.7384206	0.3797428
pair2=(A1,A3)	0.8486739	0.6811997	0.5253266
pair3=(A2,A3)	0.8081123	0.6670496	0.4236749

ferent ontologies produced by the three annotators. We will call these three target ontologies with the name of the annotator.

The results of the experiments are reported in Table 12(a) and in Table 12(b). In the first table we compute the recall, the precision and the f-measure of the *WN-System* against the 3 ontologies, while in the second table we compute the recall, the precision and the f-measure of the *Our-System*.

We can then draw some observations: First, *Our-System* behaves better than the *WN-System* on the ontologies produced by the expert annotators. The f-measure of both the expert annotators (and) is better for *Our-System* with respect to *WN-System*. On the contrary, for the last ontology () the *WN-System* has better performance than

our system. Then, our system is capturing knowledge of the specific domain as it is behaving better than the generic system with respect to domain experts. Second, in the case of the expert annotators, the recall of our system is higher than the recall of the WordNet based system. This confirms that the coverage of WordNet in the specific domain is low and only learning methods can be used to adapt the ontological information to the specific domain. On the contrary, for the non-domain expert, WordNet is good enough to cover domain knowledge. Results show that *Our-System* is a good learner method that can be positively used to learn the *is-a* relation in Earth Observation Domain.

Table 9. Contingency tables: pairwise annotator agreement for 404-annotations

		A_1		
		yes	no	
A_2	yes	40	61	108
	no	43	490	533
		90	551	641

(a) pair$_1$=(A$_1$,A$_2$)

		A_1		
		yes	no	
A_3	yes	76	83	159
	no	14	468	482
		90	551	641

(b) pair$_2$=(A$_1$,A$_3$)

		A_2		
		yes	no	
A_2	yes	72	87	159
	no	36	446	482
		180	553	641

(c) pair$_3$=(A$_2$,A$_3$)

PROBABILISTIC ONTOLOGY LEARNER IN SEMANTIC TURKEY

Ontologies and knowledge repositories are important components in Knowledge Representation (KR) and Natural Language Processing (NLP) applications. Yet, to be effectively used, ontologies and knowledge repositories have to be large or, at least, adapted to specific domains. Even huge knowledge repositories such as WordNet (Miller, 1995) are extremely poor when used in specific domains such as the medical domain (see Toumouth, Lehireche, Widdows, and Malki [2006]).

Automatically creating, adapting, or extending existing knowledge repositories using domain texts is a very important and active area. A large variety of methods have been proposed: ontology learning methods in KR (Medche, 2002; Cimi-ano, Hotho, & Staab, 2005; Navigli & Velardi, 2004) as well as knowledge harvesting methods in NLP (Hearst, 1992; Pantel & Pennacchiotti, 2006).These learning methods use variants of the distributional hypothesis or exploit some induced lexical-syntactic patterns (Robison, 1970). The task is generally seen as a classification (e.g., Pekar and Staab [2002] and Snow, Jarufsky, and Ng [2006]) or a clustering (e.g., Cimiano, Hotho, and Staab [2005]) problem. This allows the use of both machine learning and probabilistic models. But generally, automatic models for extracting ontological knowledge from texts do not have the performance needed to extend existing ontologies with a high degree of accuracy. As a consequence, the resulting automatically expanded ontologies can be completely useless. Generally, systems for augmenting ontologies extracting informa-

Table 10. Pairwise agreement for 404-annotations

	Ao	Ae	kappa
pair1=(A$_1$,A$_2$)	0.8341584	0.7023086	0.4429077
pair2=(A$_1$,A$_2$)	0.8415842	0.6291663	0.5728117
pair3=(A$_1$,A$_2$)	0.7896040	0.6322174	0.4279336

Table 11. Agreement table and multi-π agreement for 641 and 404 annotations

(a) Agreement table for 641-annotations					
pairs of words	A_1	A_2	A_3	Yes	NO
(agriculture,department)	0	0	0	0	3
(soil,earth)	1	1	1	3	0
(agriculture,business)	0	0	0	0	3
(wind,direction)	1	0	0	1	2
(climate,climate change)	0	0	0	0	3
(climate change,climate)	0	1	1	2	1
(climate change,activity)	1	0	1	2	1
(forest,terra firma)	1	1	1	3	0
...	...	...	...	...	...
TOTAL	90	108	159	357(0.19)	1566(0.81)
(b) Agreement table for 404-annotations					
pairs of words	A_1	A_2	A_3	Yes	NO
(forest,terra firma)	1	1	1	3	0
(wind,process)	0	0	0	0	3
(forest,object)	0	0	0	0	3
(cloud,state)	0	1	0	1	2
(soil,object)	0	1	1	2	1
(wind,breath)	0	0	0	0	3
(wind,act)	0	0	0	0	3
(topography,geography)	1	1	1	3	0
...	...	...	...	...	...
TOTAL	75	72	119	266(0.22)	946(0.78)
(c) Multi-π agreement respect to 641 and 404 annotations					
	Ao		Ae		kappa
641-annotations	0.83151		0.69764		0.44277
404-annotations	0.82382		0.65739		0.48577

tion from texts foresee a manual validation for assessing the quality of ontology expansion. Yet, these systems do not use the manual validation for refining the information extraction model that proposes novel ontological information. Here, the idea is to prefer methods that can use decisions of final users to incrementally refine the model for extracting ontological information from texts, i.e., each decision of final users is exploited in refining the parameters of the extraction model. Including these new examples as training for machines helps to augment the performances of the automatic extractor, as shown in Cimiano and Volker, 2005). In the following, we present the Semantic Turkey Ontology Learner (ST-OL) (Fallucchi, Scarpato, Stellato, & Zanzotto, 2009), an incremental ontology learning system that follows the above idea putting final users in the learning loop. Furthermore, this system uses the proposed probabilistic ontology learning model that exploits transitive relations for inducing better extraction models.

Table 12. Performance of both system with respect to 3 annotators

annotators	recall	precision	f-measure	annotators	recall	precision	f-measure
A_1	0,36	0.184932	0,244344	A_1	0,493333	0,253425	0,334842
A_2	0,305556	0,150685	0,201836	A_2	0,4305556	0,212329	0,284404
A_3	0,470588	0,383562	0,422642	A_3	0,4369748	0,356164	0,392453
(a) WN-System against the 3 annotators				*(b) Our-System against the 3 annotators*			

The chapter is organized as follows. We firstly present the ideas behind our new ontology learning system introducing the concept of incremental ontology learning. We then introduce ST-OL, the system that we have adopted following the above principles. Finally, we draw some conclusions.

Incremental Ontology Learning

To efficiently set-up an incremental model for ontology learning, we have to address two issues:

- We need an efficient way to interact with final users
- We need an incremental learning model

The rest of the section shows how we can address these issues using existing models and existing systems. We start from presenting the concept of incremental ontology learning. Then, we describe the used ontology editor and finally, we introduce the adopted ontology learning methodology.

The Concept

The incremental ontology learning process we want to model leverages on the positive interaction between an automatic model for *ontology learning* and the final users. We obtain this positive interaction using one additional component: an *ontology editor*. The overall process is organized in two phases: (1) the *initialization step* and (2) the *learning loop*. In the *initialization step*, the user selects the initial ontology and the corpus. The

system, then, uses these two elements to generate the first model for learning ontological information from documents. In the *learning loop*, the machine learning component extracts a ranked list of pairs (*candidate_concept,superconcept*) and the user selects, among the first k pairs, the correct ones to be added to the ontology. We then use these choices to generate both positive and negative training examples for the ontology learning component. Once the new ontology extraction model has been learnt (using the corpus, the updated ontology, and the growing *non-ontology*), the process restarts from the beginning of the loop.

Given a selected corpus C, the initial ontology O_0 and the generic ontology O_i at the iteration i, we can see the incremental learning process as the sequence of the resulting ontologies $O_0 \ldots O_n$. The *transition* function leverages on the ontology learning model M and on the interaction with the user, i.e., the user validation UV. This function can be represented as follows:

$$M_C(O_i, \overline{O}_i) = \widehat{O}_{i+1} \underset{\rightsquigarrow}{UV} (O_{i+1}, \overline{O}_{i+1})$$

(3)

where M_C is the model learnt from the corpus, O_i is the ontology at the i - th step and $\overline{O}_i$ are the negative choices of the users at the same step. This model gives as output a ranked list of possible updates of the ontology $\widehat{O}_{i+1}$. The UV on the first k possibilities produces the updated ontology and the updated *non-ontology* $\overline{O}_{i+1}$. At the initial step, the process has O_0 and $\overline{O}_0 = \varnothing$. The *ontology learner* produces the model $M_O(O_i, \overline{O}_i)$ building feature vectors representing the contexts of the corpus C where we can find pairs of pairs (*candidate_concept, superconcept*). These pairs are extracted from the ontology O_i and the *non-ontology* $\overline{O}_i$.

Semantic Turkey

Semantic Turkey is a Knowledge Management and Acquisition system developed by the Artificial Intelligence Group of the University of Rome, Tor Vergata. Semantic Turkey (ST, from now on) was initially developed as a web browser extension (it is currently implemented for the popular Web Browser Mozilla Firefox) for *Semantic Bookmarking* (Griesi, Pazienza, & Stellato, 2006), that is, the process of *eliciting* information from (Web) documents, to *acquire* new knowledge and *represent* it through representation standards, while *keeping reference* to its original information sources.

Semantic Bookmarks are different from their traditional cousins because they abandon the purely portative semantics of traditional links&folders bookmarking, and promote a new paradigm, aiming at "a clear separation between (acquired) knowledge data (the WHAT) and their associated information sources (the WHERE)." In practice, the user is able to select portions of text from web pages loaded from the browser, and to annotate them in an (user defined) ontology. A neat separation is maintained between the ontological resources created from the annotation, and the annotations themselves. In this way, the user can easily organize the knowledge (by establishing relationships between ontology objects, categorizing them, better defining them through attributes etc...), while keeping multiple bookmarks in a separated space, pointing to ontology resources and carrying with them all information related to the taken annotations (such as the page where the annotation has been taken, its title, the text which was referring to the created/referenced

ontology resource etc...). Easy-to-perform drag-and-drop operations were thought to optimize user interaction, concentrating the creation of both the ontological resources and their related annotations in a few mouse clicks.

ST has lately evolved (Griesi, Pazienza, & Stellato, 2007) into a complete Knowledge Management and Acquisition System based on Semantic Web technologies, introducing full support for ontology editing and improving functionalities for annotation and creation. ST has explored a new dimension without predecessors in the field of Ontology Development and Semantic Annotation, unique in the process of building new knowledge while exploring the Web. The new objective of ST has been thus reducing the impedance mismatch between domain experts and knowledge investigators on one side, and knowledge engineers on the other side, providing a unifying platform for acquiring, building up, reorganizing, and refining knowledge. The ontology learning module that we introduce here has been implemented and integrated upon the above exposed framework.

Probabilistic Ontology Learner

We use the proposed Probabilistic Ontology Learning (POL) to expand existing ontologies with new facts. In POL it is possible to take into consideration both corpus-extracted evidences and the structure of the generated ontology. In the probabilistic formulation (Snow, Jurafsky, & Ng, 2006), the task of learning ontologies from a corpus is seen as a maximum likelihood problem. The ontology is seen as a set O of assertions R over pairs. In particular we will consider the *is-a* relation. In this case, if it is in O, i is a concept and j is one of its generalizations (i.e., the direct or the indirect generalization). For example, describes that *dog* is an *animal* according to the ontology O.

The main probabilities are then: (1) the prior probability $P(R_{i,j} \in O)$ of an assertion $R_{i,j}$ to belong to the ontology O and (2) the posterior probability $P(R_{i,j} \in O \mid \vec{e}_{i,j})$ of an assertion $R_{i,j}$ to belong to the ontology O given a set of evidences $\vec{e}_{i,j}$ derived from the corpus. These evidences are derived from the contexts where the pair (i,j) is found in the corpus. The vector $\vec{e}_{i,j}$ is a feature vector associated with a pair (i,j). For example, a feature may describe how many times i and j are seen in patterns like "*i as j*" "*i is a j*". These, among many other features, are indicators of an *Is - a* relation between i and i (see Hearst [1992]).

Given a set of evidences over all the relevant word pairs, in Snow, Jurafsky, and Ng (2006) the probabilistic ontology learning task is defined as the problem of finding an ontology O that maximizes the probability of having the evidences E, i.e.:

$$O = arg^{max}_{O} \, P\big(E \mid O\big) \tag{4}$$

In the original model (Snow, Jurafsky, & Ng, 2006), this maximization problem is solved with a local search. In the incremental ontology learning model that we propose, this maximization function is solved using also the information coming from final users.

In the user-less model, what is maximized at each step is the ratio between the likelihood $P(E|O')$ and the likelihood $P(E|O)$ where $O'=O \bigcup N$ and N are the relations added at each step. This ratio is called multiplicative change $\Delta(N)$ and is defined as follows:

$$\Delta\big(N\big) = \frac{P\big(E \mid O'\big)}{P\big(E \mid O\big)}$$

It is also possible to demonstrate that

$$\Delta\big(R_{i,j}\big) = k \cdot \frac{P(R_{i,j} \in O \mid \vec{e}_{i,j})}{1 - P(R_{i,j} \in O \mid \vec{e}_{i,j})} = k \cdot odds(R_{i,j})$$

where k is a constant (see Snow, Jurafsky, and Ng [2006]) that will be neglected in the maximization process.

We calculate the *odds* using the logistic regression. The regression coefficients can be estimated using the Monroe-Penrose pseudo-inverse matrix (Fallucchi & Zanzotto, 2009).

$$\hat{\beta} = \mathbf{X}^{+}\mathbf{1} \tag{5}$$

where β is an approximation of the regression coefficients vector, X^{+} is the inverse evidence matrix, and l the logit vector.

In our user-oriented incremental ontology learning model we propose to include final users in the loop. In our task we do not find the ontology that maximizes the likelihood of having the evidences E. We calculate the probabilities step by step. Then we present an ordered set of choices to final users that make the final decision on what to use in the next iteration. The order set is obtained using the logit function as it is equivalent to the order given by the probabilities. For this reason, in the following we will operate directly on the logit rather than on the probabilities. It is possible to calculate the logit vector at the *i-th* iteration:

$$XX^{+}l_i = \hat{l}_{i+1} \xrightarrow{UV} l_{i+1} \tag{6}$$

At each iteration, we calculate the logit vector using the logit vector of the previous iteration. The logit vector is then changed in the User Validation (*UV*). When the user accepts a new relation its probability is set to 0.99. On the contrary, when the user discards a relation its probability is set to 0.01. The matrix XX^{+} is constant for each iteration. In particular, we have found a matrix XX^{+} that is the constant model M_C of equation (1). The matrix depends only on the corpus C and not on the initial ontology. The logit vector l represents both the current ontology O_i and the negative ontology $\bar{O}_i$ as it includes the logit of both probabilities (0.99 and 0.01).

Semantic Turkey-Ontology Learner (ST-OL)

The model described in the previous section has been implemented and integrated in a Semantic Turkey extension called ST Ontology Learner (ST-OL). ST-OL provides a graphical user interface and a human-computer interaction work-flow supporting the incremental learning loop of our learning theory. If the user has loaded an ontology in ST, he can to improve it by adding new classes and new instances using ST-OL. The interaction process is achieved through the following steps:

- An *initialization phase* where the user selects the initial ontology and the bunch of documents where the new knowledge is extracted;
- An *iterative phase* where the user launches the learning and validates the proposals of ST-OL

Thus, starting from the initial ontology *O* and a bunch of documents *C*, the user has the possibility of using an incremental ontology learning model.

For the *initialization phase*, the User Interface (UI) of ST-OL allows users to select the initial set of documents *C* (corpus), and to send both the ontology *O* and the corpus *C* to the learning module. To start this stage of the process, the user selects *"Initialize POL"* on the ST-OL panel (see Figure 4). The probabilistic ontology learner analyzes the corpus, finds the contexts for each ontological pair, computes the first extraction model, and, finally, proposes the pairs that are in is-a relation. This first analysis is the most expensive, because devoted to computing the matrix XX^+. Yet, this computation is done only once in the iterative process.

Once this initialization finishes, the *iterative phase* starts. ST-OL enables the button labeled *"Proposed Ontology."* The effect of this button is to show the initial ontology extended with the pairs proposed by POL. Figure 4 shows an example of an enriched initial ontology.

The main goal of ST-OL is draw the attention to the good added information. The user has the possibility of selecting the pairs he wants to add among the proposed pairs. To drive the attention towards the good pairs, we use different brightness of red for the different probabilities. More intense tonalities of red represent higher probabilities.

In order to focus, if possible, only on good pairs, ST-OL shows only pairs above a threshold of probabilities. For example, in Figure 4 the relation (i.e., the pair) between "truck" and "container" is more probable than the relation between "spreader" and "container." Then different red tones are used. At this point, the user can accept or reject the information. After acceptance, the new information is stored in the ST ontological repository and can be browsed as usual through the ontology panel on the Firefox sidebar. Figure 5 shows what happened when the user accepted two proposed pairs: "mango" as instance of "fruit" and "pepper" as subclass of "vegetable."

In the incremental model the above activity enables to build an upgraded probability vector. When the user accepts a new pair, ST-OL updates its probability to 0.99. When the user discards the pair, its probability is set to 0.01. These new values are used for the next iteration of the leaning process. After some manual evaluation, the user can decide to update the proposed ontology. Given the probabilistic ontology learning model, this new evaluation is just a simple multiplication between the existing matrix XX^+ and the new vector. To force the recompilation, the user can use the *"Proposed Ontology"* button.

CONCLUSION AND FUTURE RESEARCH DIRECTIONS

Describing word meaning is one of the most interesting challenges of natural language processing, as texts cannot be "understood" without a clear

Figure 4. Initial ontology extended with the pairs proposed by the POL system

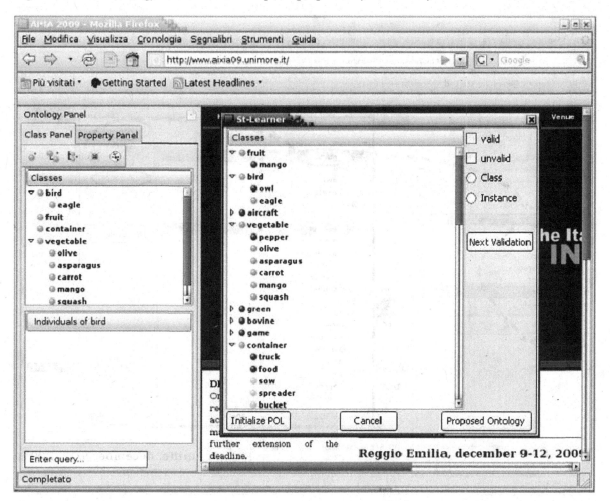

and formal model of their basic components. Semantic networks of words are often used as formal models of word meaning, but, to be useful for final NLP applications, these networks should large enough to cover words used in the final domain of the applications. It is nearly impossible to manually obtain a wide coverage for these semantic networks. Automatically learning these semantic networks from domain corpora is then the preferred solution. Models for automatically expanding semantic networks of words from texts use corpus-extracted evidences to determine whether or not new pairs of words are in a given semantic relation and, then, have to be included in existing knowledge repositories. These decision

systems are trained observing how pairs of words in a given semantic relation behave in document collections. This information is used to induce a model that is then applied to novel word pairs. This chapter has explored this important area of research giving important contributions and advancing state-of-art models.

First, we observed that structural properties of semantic networks of words, when relevant, are not used in machine learning models to better induce relevant features to determine confidence values for extracting semantic relations. Semantic relation learning models based on the distributional hypothesis, for example, use the structural properties of semantic networks of words such as

Figure 5. Manual validation of new resources added to the ontology

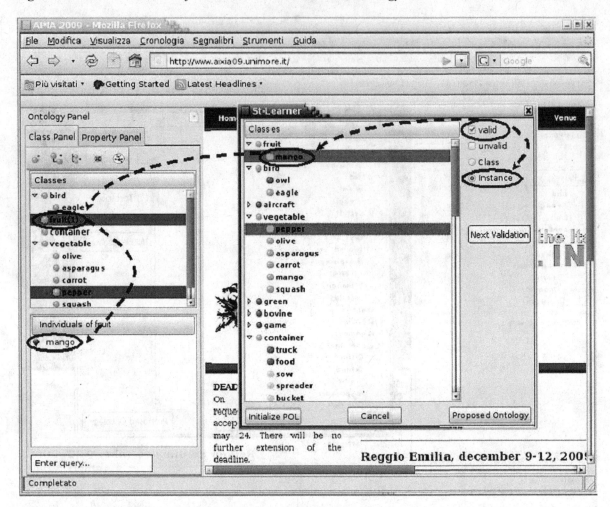

transitivity only intrinsically, but they cannot be applied for learning transitive semantic relations other than the generalizations. Even where transitivity is explicitly used, it is not directly exploited to model confidence values. On the contrary, LSP models can learn any kind of semantic relations, but they do not explicitly exploit the structural properties of target relations when learning taxonomies or semantic networks of words. We have demonstrated that keeping the probability within the final knowledge base is extremely important for the performances of the learning method as it gives the possibility to better use structural properties of target relations such as transitivity.

Our probabilistic model is suitable for exploiting the structural properties of semantic relations in learning semantic networks.

Second, we observed that systems that automatically create, adapt, or extend existing semantic networks of words need a sufficiently large number of documents and existing structured knowledge to achieve reasonable performance. If the target domain has not relevant pre-existing semantic networks of words, we will not have enough data for training the initial model. Obtaining manually structured knowledge repositories in specific domains is a very time consuming and expensive task. We have shown that our learning method, that exploits the models learned from a generic domain, is helpful in discovering the relation between two words in a specific domain. Our learning model exploits training data for building in-domain models with more accuracy and little effort for the adaptation to specific knowledge domains.

Finally, we studied models to include the manual validation for assessing the quality of semantic networks of word expansion within systems for creating or augmenting the semantic networks of words. ST-OL provides a graphical user interface and a human-computer interaction work-flow supporting the incremental learning loop of our probabilistic learning models. This system efficiently interacts with final users exploiting an incremental model that in learning loop includes final users. The probabilistic model is integrated in a Knowledge Management and Acquisition platform Semantic Turkey. Thus, ST-OL has proven to be the right environment for embodying this kind of process, providing the crossroads between users, Web, and knowledge.

In the future, a natural improvement is the analysis of different and more informative feature spaces such as those based on syntactic models. We believe this will boost the performances of our model. We have here shown that the model can be applied to different transitive relations (i.e., is-a and part-of). Yet, we need to explore different transitive semantic relations, e.g., cause-effect and entailment, and we plan to extend the model to consider other structural properties of semantic networks.

REFERENCES

Artstein, R., & Poesio, M. (2008). Inter-coder agreement for computational linguistics. *Journal of Computational Linguistics, 34*(4).

Bacchiani, M., Roark, B., & Saraclar, M. (2004). Language model adaptation with MAP estimation and the perceptron algorithm. In D. M. Susan, & S. Roukos (Eds.), *Proceedings of HLT-NAACL: Short Papers,* (p. 21-24). Association for Computational Linguistics.

Bagni, D., Cappella, M., Pazienza, M. T., Pennacchiotti, M., & Stellato, A. (2007). Harvesting relational and structured knowledge for ontology building in the WPro architecture. In R. Basili, & M. T. Pazienza (Eds.), *Proceedings of the 10th Congress of the Italian Association for Artificial Intelligence on AI*IA 2007: Artificial Intelligence and Human-Oriented Computing,* (pp. 157-169). Springer.

Baroni, M., Berardini, S., Ferraresi, A., & Zanchetta, E. (2009). The wacky wide web: A collection of very large linguistically processed web-crawled corpora. *Language Resources and Evaluation, 43,* 209–226. doi:10.1007/s10579-009-9081-4

Basili, R., Gliozzo, A., & Pennacchiotti, M. (2007). Harvesting ontologies from open domain corpora: A dynamic approach. In *Proceedings of Recent Advances on Natural Language Processing.* Borovets, Bulgaria: ACL Press.

Berners-Lee, T., Hendler, J., & Lassila, O. (2001). The semantic web. *Scientific American, 284*(5), 34–43. doi:10.1038/scientificamerican0501-34

Bertoldi, N., & Federico, M. (2009). Domain adaptation for statistical machine translation with monolingual resources. In *Proceedings of the Fourth Workshop on Statistical Machine Translation,* (pp. 182-189). Association for Computational Linguistics.

Blitzer, J., McDonald, R., & Pereira, F. (2006). Domain adaptation with structural correspondence learning. In *Proceedings of the 2006 Conference on Empirical Methods in Natural Language Processing.* Association for Computational Linguistics.

Buitelaar, P., Olejnik, D., & Sintek, M. (2004). A protégé plug-in for ontology extraction from text based on linguistic analysis. In *Proceedings of the 1st European Semantic Web Symposium (ESWS)*. ESWS Press.

Carletta, J. (1996). Assessing agreement on classification tasks: The kappa statistic. *Computational Linguistics, 22*(2), 249–254.

Chan, Y. S., & Ng, H. T. (2007). Domain adaptation with active learning for word sense disambiguation. In *Proceedings of the 45th Annual Meeting of the Association of Computational Linguistics,* (pp. 49-56). Association for Computational Linguistics.

Chelba, C., & Acero, A. (2006). Adaptation of maximum entropy capitalizer: Little data can help a lot. *Computer Speech & Language, 20*(4), 382–399. doi:10.1016/j.csl.2005.05.005

Chklovski, T., & Pantel, P. (2004). VerbOCEAN: Mining the web for fine-grained semantic verb relations. In *Proceedings of EMNLP 2004*. Association for Computational Linguistics.

Cimiano, P., Hotho, A., & Staab, S. (2005). Learning concept hierarchies from text corpora using formal concept analysis. *Journal of Artificial Intelligence Research, 24*, 305–339.

Cimiano, P., & Volker, J. (2005). Text2Onto - A framework for ontology learning and data-driven change discovery. In A. Montoyo, R. Munoz, & E. Metais (Eds.), *Proceedings of the 10th International Conference on Applications of Natural Language to Information Systems (NLDB),* (pp. 227-238). Springer.

Cohen, J. (1960). A coefficient of agreement for nominal scales. *Psychological Bulletin, 20*, 37–46.

Fallucchi, F., Scarpato, N., Stellato, A., & Zanzotto, F. M. (2009). Probabilistic ontology learner in semantic turkey. In *Proceedings of the XIth International Conference of the Italian Association for Artificial Intelligence Reggio Emilia on Emergent Perspectives in Artificial Intelligence,* (pp. 294-303). Springer-Verlag.

Fallucchi, F., & Zanzotto, F. M. (2009). SVD feature selection for probabilistic taxonomy learning. In *Proceedings of the Workshop on Geometrical Models of Natural Language Semantics,* (pp. 66-73). Association for Computational Linguistics.

Fallucchi, F., & Zanzotto, F. M. (2010). Inductive probabilistic taxonomy learning using singular value decomposition. *Journal of Natural Language Engineering*.

Fleiss, J. (1971). Measuring nominal scale agreement among many raters. *Psychological Bulletin, 76*(5), 378–382. doi:10.1037/h0031619

Gao, J. (2009). Model adaptation via model interpolation and boosting for web search observations of markov chains. *IEEE Transactions on Speech and Audio Processing, 2*, 291–298.

Geffet, M., & Dagan, I. (2005). The distributional inclusion hypotheses and lexical entailment. In *Proceedings of The 43rd Annual Meeting of the Association for Computational Linguistics,* (p. 107-114). Association for Computational Linguistics.

Gennari, J., Musen, M., Fergerson, R., Grosso, W., Crubzy, M., & Eriksson, H. (2003). The evolution of Protégé-2000: An environment for knowledge-based systems development. *International Journal of Human-Computer Studies, 58*(1), 89–123. doi:10.1016/S1071-5819(02)00127-1

Gildea, D. (2001). Corpus variation and parser performance. In *Proceedings of Conference on Empirical Methods in Natural Language Processing EMNLP*. EMNLP Press.

Gómez-Pérez, A., & Manzano-Macho, D. (2003). *Deliverable 1.5: A survey of ontology learning methods and techniques*. Retrieved from http://www.sti-innsbruck.at/fileadmin/documents/deliverables/Ontoweb/D1.5.pdf.

Griesi, D., Pazienza, M. T., & Stellato, A. (2006). Gobbleing over the web with semantic turkey. In *Proceedings of SWAP 2006*. SWAP Press.

Griesi, D., Pazienza, M. T., & Stellato, A. (2007). Semantic turkey - A semantic bookmarking tool (system description). In E. Franconi, M. Kifer, & W. May (Eds.), *The Semantic Web: Research and Applications*, (pp. 779-788). Springer.

Haase, P., Lewen, H., Studer, R., Tran, D. T., d'Aquin, M., & Motta, E. (2008). *The neon ontology engineering toolkit*. Retrieved from http://neon-toolkit.org/wiki/Main_Page.

Harris, Z. (1964). Distributional structure. In Katz, J. J., & Fodor, J. A. (Eds.), *The Philosophy of Linguistics*. Oxford, UK: Oxford University Press.

Hearst, M. A. (1992). Automatic acquisition of hyponyms from large text corpora. In *Proceedings of the 14th Conference on Computational Linguistics*. ACL Press.

Joachims, T. (1999). Making large-scale SVM learning practical. In Schölkopf, B., Burges, C., & Smola, A. (Eds.), *Advances in Kernel Methods - Support Vector Learning*. Cambridge, MA: MIT Press.

Landis, J. R., & Koch, G. G. (1977). The measurement of observer agreement for categorical data. *Biometrics, 33*(1), 159–174. doi:10.2307/2529310

Lapata, M., & Keller, F. (2004). The web as a baseline: Evaluating the performance of unsupervised web-based models for a range of NLP tasks. In *Proceedings of HLT-NAACL 2004*. NAACL Press.

Lin, D., & Pantel, P. (2002). Concept discovery from text. In *Proceedings of the 19th International Conference on Computational Linguistics*. ICCL Press.

Maedche, A., & Staab, S. (2001). Ontology learning for the semantic web. *IEEE Intelligent Systems, 16*(2), 72–79. doi:10.1109/5254.920602

Maedche, A., & Staab, S. (2002). Measuring similarity between ontologies. In *Proceedings of the 13th International Conference on Knowledge Engineering and Knowledge Management: Ontologies and the Semantic Web*. Springer-Verlag.

Maedche, A., & Volz, R. (2001). The ontology extraction maintenance framework text-to-onto. In *Proceedings of the ICDM Workshop on Integrating Data Mining and Knowledge Management*. ICDM Press.

McCarthy, D., Koeling, R., Weeds, J., & Carroll, J. (2004). Finding predominant word senses in untagged text. In *Proceedings of the 42nd Annual Meeting on Association for Computational Linguistics*. Association for Computational Linguistics.

Medche, A. (2002). *Ontology learning for the semantic web (Vol. 665)*. Berlin, Germany: Kluwer International.

Miller, G. A. (1995). WordNet: A lexical database for English. *Communications of the ACM, 38*(11), 39–41. doi:10.1145/219717.219748

Morin, E. (1999). *Extraction de liens sèmantiques entre termes à partir de corpus de textes techniques*. Nantes, France: Univesitè de Nantes.

Navigli, R., & Velardi, P. (2004). Learning domain ontologies from document warehouses and dedicated web sites. *Computational Linguistics, 30*(2), 151–179. doi:10.1162/089120104323093276

Padó, S. (2006). *User's guide to SIGF: Significance testing by approximate randomisation.* Retrieved from http://www.nlpado.de/~sebastian/sigf.html.

Pantel, P., & Pennacchiotti, M. (2006). Espresso: Leveraging generic patterns for automatically harvesting semantic relations. In *Proceedings of the 21st International Conference on Computational Linguistics and the 44th Annual Meeting of the Association for Computational Linguistics.* Association for Computational Linguistics.

Pekar, V., & Staab, S. (2002). Taxonomy learning: Factoring the structure of a taxonomy into a semantic classification decision. In *Proceedings of the Nineteenth Conference on Computational Linguistics,* (vol 2), (pp. 786-792). ACL Press.

Penrose, R. (1955). A generalized inverse for matrices. In *Proceedings of the Cambridge Philosophical Society,* (p. 51). Cambridge, UK: Cambridge University Press.

Ravichandran, D., & Hovy, E. (2002). Learning surface text patterns for a question answering system. In: *Proceedings of the 40th Annual Meeting on Association for Computational Linguistics.* ACL Press.

Roark, B., & Bacchiani, M. (2003). Supervised and unsupervised PCFG adaptation to novel domains. In *Proceedings of the 2003 Conference of the North American Chapter of the Association for Computational Linguistics on Human Language Technology,* (vol 1), (pp. 126-133). Association for Computational Linguistics.

Robison, H. R. (1970). Computer-detectable semantic structures. *Information Storage and Retrieval, 6*(3), 273–288. doi:10.1016/0020-0271(70)90002-1

Scott, W. A. (1955). Reliability of content analysis: The case of nominal scale coding. *Public Opinion Quarterly, 19*(3), 321–325. doi:10.1086/266577

Snow, R., Jurafsky, D., & Ng, A. Y. (2006). Semantic taxonomy induction from heterogenous evidence. In *Proceedings of the 21st International Conference on Computational Linguistics and the 44th Annual Meeting of the Association for Computational Linguistics,* (pp. 801-808). ACL Press.

Szpektor, I., Tanev, H., Dagan, I., & Coppola, B. (2004). Scaling web-based acquisition of entailment relations. In *Proceedings of EMNLP 2004.* EMNLP Press.

Toumouth, A., Lehireche, A., Widdows, D., & Malki, M. (2006). Adapting WordNet to the medical domain using lexicosyntactic patterns in the ohsumed corpus. In *Proceedings of IEEE International Conference on Computer Systems and Applications,* (pp. 1029-1036). IEEE Computer Society.

Vapnik, V. (1995). *The nature of statistical learning theory.* Berlin, Germany: Springer.

Yeh, A. (2000). More accurate tests for the statistical significance of result differences. In *Proceedings of the 18th Conference on Computational linguistics,* (vol 2), (pp. 947-953). Association for Computational Linguistics.

Yoshida, K., Tsuruoka, Y., Miyao, Y., & Tsujii, J. I. (2007). Ambiguous part-of-speech tagging for improving accuracy and domain portability of syntactic parsers. In *Proceedings of the Twentieth International Joint Conference on Artificial Intelligence,* (pp. 1783-1788). IEEE Press.

Zanzotto, F. M., Pennacchiotti, M., & Pazienza, M. T. (2006). Discovering asymmetric entailment relations between verbs using selectional preferences. In *Proceedings of the 21st International Conference on Computational Linguistics and 44th Annual Meeting of the Association for Computational Linguistics,* (pp. 849-856). Association for Computational Linguistics.

KEY TERMS AND DEFINITIONS

Incremental Learning: Is a type of learning model where the learner updates its model with new information.

Logistic Regression: Is a generalized linear model used for binomial regression

Ontology Learning: Is a type of learning model where the learner (semi-)automatically extract relevant concepts and relations from a given corpus to create or to extend an ontology.

Probabilistic Model: Is a type of learning model where the learner store probabilities or confidence weights in the model.

Pseudoinverse: Is a generalization of the inverse matrix.

Semantic Turkey: Is a platform for Semantic Bookmarking and Ontology Development.

SVD: Method for dimentionality reduction.

Transitivity: Relationship between three elements. If the relationship holds between the first and second elements and between the second and third elements, it necessarily holds between the first and third elements.

ENDNOTES

1. The extensional definition of a concept is the enumeration of all its instances.
2. Considering *"dog"* as instance of *"animal"* is not completely correct as *dog* can be a concept in the structured knowledge repository. Yet, it is useful to describe the difference between *intensional* and *extensional* definitions.
3. We used the version 3.0 of WordNet

Compilation of References

Ahmad, K., Gillam, L., & Tostevin, L. (1999). University of Surrey participation in TREC-8: Weirdness indexing for logical document extrapolation and retrieval (WILDER). In *Proceedings of NIST Special Publication 500-246 the Eighth Text REtrieval Conference (TREC 8)*, (pp. 717–724). Retrieved from http://trec.nist.gov/pubs/trec8/papers/surrey2.pdf.

Alfonseca, E., & Manandhar, S. (2002). Extending a lexical ontology by a combination of distributional semantics signatures. *Lecture Notes in Computer Science, 2473*, 1–7. doi:10.1007/3-540-45810-7_1

Alistair, M., & Bechhofer, S. (2011). *SKOS*. Retrieved from http://www.w3.org/TR/skos-reference/skos.html.

Almeida, M. B. (2009). A proposal to evaluate ontology content. *Applied Ontology, 4*(3-4), 245–265.

Almuhareb, A., & Poesio, M. (2004). Attribute-based and value-based clustering: An evaluation. In [Barcelona, Spain.]. *Proceedings of EMNLP, 2004*, 158–165.

Alshawi, H. (1987). Processing dictionary definitions with phrasal pattern hierarchies. In *Computational Linguistics* (*Vol. 13*, pp. 195–202). Cambridge, MA: MIT Press.

Alshawi, H. (1989). Analysing the dictionary definitions. In *Computational Lexicography for Natural Language Processing* (pp. 153–169). New York, NY: Longman.

Amsler, R. (1981). A taxonomy for English nouns and verbs. In *Proceedings of the 19th Annual Meeting of the Association for Computational Linguistics,* (pp. 133-138). Stanford, CA: ACL Press.

An, Y., Borgida, A., & Mylopoulos, J. (2005). Constructing complex semantic mappings between XML data and ontologies. In Y. Gil, E. Motta, V. R. Benjamins, & M. A. Musen (Eds.), *Proceedings of ISWC 2005*, (vol 3729), (pp. 6–20). Berlin, Germany: Springer.

Antoniou, G., & van Harmelen, F. (2004). Ontology engineering. In *A Semantic Web Primer* (pp. 205–222). Cambridge, MA: Massachusetts Institute of Technology Press.

Artstein, R., & Poesio, M. (2008). Inter-coder agreement for computational linguistics. *Computational Linguistics, 34*(4), 555–596. doi:10.1162/coli.07-034-R2

Atkins, B. T. S., & Rundell, M. (2008). *The Oxford guide to practical lexicography*. Oxford, UK: Oxford University Press.

Auer, S., Bizer, C., Kobilarov, G., Lehmann, J., Cyganiak, R., & Ives, Z. (2007). Dbpedia: A nucleus for a web of open data. In Aberer, K. (Eds.), *The Semantic Web* (*Vol. 4825*, pp. 722–735). Lecture Notes in Computer Science Berlin, Germany: Springer. doi:10.1007/978-3-540-76298-0_52

Aumueller, D. Do. H., Massmann, S., & Rahm, E. (2005). Schema and ontology matching with COMA++. In *Proceedings of International Conference on Management of Data 2005*, (pp. 906-908). Baltimore, MD: ACM Press.

Aussenac-Gilles, N., Biébow, B., & Szulman, S. (2000). Revisiting ontology design: A method based on corpus analysis. In Dieng, R., & Corby, O. (Eds.), *Knowledge Engineering and Knowledge Management Methods, Models, and Tools* (*Vol. 1937*, pp. 27–66). Lecture Notes in Computer Science Berlin, Germany: Springer. doi:10.1007/3-540-39967-4_13

Aussenac-Gilles, N., Despres, S., & Szulman, S. (2008). The TERMINAE method and platform for ontology engineering from texts. In Buitelaar, P., & Cimiano, P. (Eds.), *Bridging the Gap between Text and Knowledge* (pp. 199–223). Amsterdam, The Netherlands: IOS Press.

Aussenac-Gilles, N., & Jacques, M.-P. (2008). Terminology. *Pattern-Based Approaches to Semantic Relations, 14*(1), 45–73.

Baader, F., Calvanese, D., McGuinness, D. L., Nardi, D., & Patel-Schneider, P. F. (2003). *The description logic handbook: Theory, implementation, applications.* Cambridge, UK: Cambridge University Press.

Baccar Ben Amar, F. Khemakhem. A., Gargouri. B., Haddar. K., & Ben Hamadou, A. (2008). LMF standardized model for the editorial electronic dictionaries of Arabic. In *Proceeding of Natural Language Processing and Cognitive Science Workshop*, (pp. 64-73). Barcelona, Spain: NLPCSW Press.

Baccar Ben Amar, F., Gargouri, B., & Ben Hamadou, A. (2010). Towards generation of domain ontology from LMF standardized dictionaries. In *Proceedings of the 22nd International Conference on Software Engineering and Knowledge Engineering,* (pp. 515-520). Redwood City, CA: IEEE Press.

Bacchiani, M., Roark, B., & Saraclar, M. (2004). Language model adaptation with MAP estimation and the perceptron algorithm. In D. M. Susan, & S. Roukos (Eds.), *Proceedings of HLT-NAACL: Short Papers,* (p. 21-24). Association for Computational Linguistics.

Bagni, D., Cappella, M., Pazienza, M. T., Pennacchiotti, M., & Stellato, A. (2007). Harvesting relational and structured knowledge for ontology building in the WPro architecture. In R. Basili, & M. T. Pazienza (Eds.), *Proceedings of the 10th Congress of the Italian Association for Artificial Intelligence on AI*IA 2007: Artificial Intelligence and Human-Oriented Computing,* (pp. 157-169). Springer.

Baker, C. F., Fillmore, C. J., & Lowe, J. B. (1998). The Berkeley framenet project. In *Proceedings of the 17th International Conference on Computational Linguistics,* (pp. 86–90). Morristown, NJ: ACL Press.

Baldassarre, C., Daga, E., Gangemi, A., Gliozzo, A. M., Salvati, A., & Troiani, G. (2010). Semantic scout: Making sense of organizational knowledge. In *Proceedings of EKAW,* (pp. 272-286). EKAW Press.

Banko, M., Cafarella, M. J., Soderland, S., Broadhead, M., & Etzioni, O. (2007). Open information extraction from the web. In *Proceedings of the 20th International Joint Conference on Artificial Intelligence,* (pp. 2670–2676). IEEE Press.

Bannard, C., Baldwin, T., & Lascarides, A. (2003). A statistical approach to the semantics of verb-particles. In *Proceedings of the ACL 2003 Workshop on Multiword Expressions: Analysis, Acquisition and Treatment,* (pp. 65–72). Retrieved from http://www.aclweb.org/anthology/W03-1809.

Baroni, M., Berardini, S., Ferraresi, A., & Zanchetta, E. (2009). The wacky wide web: A collection of very large linguistically processed web-crawled corpora. *Language Resources and Evaluation, 43,* 209–226. doi:10.1007/s10579-009-9081-4

Basili, R., Vindigni, M., & Zanzotto, F. (2003). *Integrating ontological and linguistic knowledge for conceptual information extraction.* Paper presented at the IEEE/WIC International Conference on Web Intelligence. Washington, DC.

Basili, R., Gliozzo, A., & Pennacchiotti, M. (2007). Harvesting ontologies from open domain corpora: A dynamic approach. In *Proceedings of Recent Advances on Natural Language Processing.* Borovets, Bulgaria: ACL Press.

Basili, R., Moschitti, A., Pazienza, M. T., & Zanzotto, F. (2003). Personalizing web publishing via information extraction. *IEEE Intelligent Systems and Their Applications, 18*(1), 62–70. doi:10.1109/MIS.2003.1179195

Beckett, D., & Berners-Lee, T. (2008). *Turtle - Terse RDF triple language.* W3C Team Submission, 14 January 2008. Retrieved from http://www.w3c.org.

Bedini, I. (2010). *Deriving ontologies automatically from XML schemas applied to the B2B domain.* Doctoral dissertation. University of Versailles. Retrieved April 15, 2011 from http://bivan.free.fr/Janus/Docs/PhD_Report_IvanBedini.pdf.

Beneventano, D. (Ed.). (2008). *Semantic and ontology language specification*. STASIS Project Deliverable 2.3.2, Version 10.

Benzécri, J. P. (1990). Programs for linguistic statistics based on merge sort of text files. In *Les Cahiers de l'Analyse des Données* (*Vol. XIV*). Paris, France: Dounod.

Benzécri, J.-P. (1976). *L'analyse des donnes*. Paris, France: Dounod.

Bergman, M. K. (2010). *Bridging the gaps: Adaptive approaches to data interoperability*. Retrieved from http://www.dublincore.org/workshops/dc2010/DC-2010_20101022_Bergman_keynote.pdf.

Bergman, M. K. (2011). *Seeking a semantic web sweet spot*. [Blog post]. Retrieved from http://www.mkbergman.com/946/seeking-a-semantic-web-sweet-spot.

Bergman, M. K., & Giasson, F. (2011). *UMBEL full specification*. Retrieved from http://www.umbel.org/specifications/full-specification.

Berkovsky, S., Kuflik, T., & Ricci, F. (2008). Mediation of user models for enhanced personalization in recommender systems. *User Modeling and User-Adapted Interaction*, *18*(3), 245–286. doi:10.1007/s11257-007-9042-9

Berland, M., & Charniak, E. (1999), Finding parts in very large corpora. In *Proceedings of the 37th Meeting of the Association for Computational Linguistics*, (pp. 57-64). ACL Press.

Berners-Lee, T. (2006). *Design issues: Linked data*. Retrieved from http://www.w3.org/DesignIssues/LinkedData.html.

Berners-Lee, T., Hall, W., Hendler, J., Shadbolt, N., & Weitzner, D. J. (2006). Creating a science of the web. *Science*, *313*(5788), 769–771. doi:10.1126/science.1126902

Berners-Lee, T., Hendler, J. A., & Lassila, O. (2001). The semantic web: A new form of web content that is meaningful to computers will unleash a revolution of new possibilities. *Scientific American*, *279*(5), 34–43. doi:10.1038/scientificamerican0501-34

Bertoldi, N., & Federico, M. (2009). Domain adaptation for statistical machine translation with monolingual resources. In *Proceedings of the Fourth Workshop on Statistical Machine Translation*, (pp. 182-189). Association for Computational Linguistics.

Bikel, D., Miller, S., Schwartz, R., & Weischedel, R. (1997). Nymble: A high-performance learning name finder. In *Proceedings of the Fifth Conference on Applied Natural Language Processing*, (pp. 194-201). San Francisco, CA: Morgan Kaufmann.

Bing. (2011). *Bing Google Yahoo*. Retrieved from http://www.bing.com/community/site_blogs/b/search/archive/2011/06/01/bing-google-and-yahoo-unite-to-build-the-web-of-objects.aspx?form=MFEHPG&publ=TWITTER&crea=TEXT_MFEHPG_SM0602_cc0602_TW006_1x.

Bio2RDF. (2011). *Webpage*. Retrieved http://bio2rdf.org/.

Biron, P. V., & Malhotra, A. (2004). *XML schema part 2: Datatypes* (2nd ed). W3C Recommendation 28 October 2004. Retrieved from http://www.w3c.org.

Bischof, S., Lopes, N., & Polleres, A. (2011). Improve efficiency of mapping data between XML and RDF with XSPARQL. In *Proceedings of the The Fifth International Conference on Web Reasoning and Rule Systems*. Springer.

Bishop, B., Kiryakov, A., Ognyanoff, D., Peikov, I., Tashev, Z., & Velkov, R. (2011). OWLIM: A family of scalable semantic repositories. In P. Hitzler (Ed.), *Semantic Web Journal*. Retrieved from http://www.semantic-web-journal.net.

Bizer, C., Heath, T., & Berners-Lee, T. (2009). Linked data - The story so far. *International Journal on Semantic Web and Information Systems*, *5*(3), 1–22. doi:10.4018/jswis.2009081901

Bizer, C., Lehmann, J., Kobilarov, G., Auer, S., Becker, C., Cyganiak, R., & Hellmann, S. (2009). DBpedia—A crystallization point for the web of data. *Journal of Web Semantics*, *7*(3), 154–165. doi:10.1016/j.websem.2009.07.002

Blitzer, J., McDonald, R., & Pereira, F. (2006). Domain adaptation with structural correspondence learning. In *Proceedings of the 2006 Conference on Empirical Methods in Natural Language Processing*. Association for Computational Linguistics.

Compilation of References

Bohring, H., & Auer, S. (2005). *Mapping XML to OWL ontologies*. Leipzig, Germnay: Leipziger Informatik-Tage.

Bonin, F., Dell'Orletta, F., Venturi, G., & Montemagni, S. (2010). Contrastive filtering of domain-specific multiword terms from different types of corpora. In *Proceedings of the 2010 Workshop on Multiword Expressions: From Theory to Applications*, (pp. 77–80). Retrieved from http://www.aclweb.org/anthology/W10-3711.

Bouma, G. (2010). Collocation extraction beyond the independence assumption. In *Proceedings of the ACL 2010 Conference Short Papers*, (pp. 109–114). Retrieved from http://www.aclweb.org/anthology/P10-2020.

Bouquet, P., Stoermer, H., & Bazzanella, B. (2008). An entity naming system for the semantic web. In *Proceedings of the 5th European Semantic Web Conference (ESWC 2008)*. Springer Verlag.

Bouquet, P., Giunchiglia, F., van Harmelen, F., Serafini, L., & Stuckenschmidt, H. (2003). C-OWL: Contextualizing ontologies. In [IEEE Press.]. *Proceedings of ISWC, 2003*, 164–179.

Brank, J., Grobelnik, M., & Mladenic, D. (2005), A survey of ontology evaluation techniques. In *Proceedings of the Conference on Data Mining and Data Warehouses (SiKDD 2005)*. IEEE Press.

Bray, T., Paoli, J., Sperberg-McQueen, C. M., Maler, E., & Yergeau, F. (2008). *Extensible markup language (XML) 1.0* (5th ed). W3C Recommendation 26 November 2008. Retrieved from http://www.w3c.org.

Brewster, C., Alani, H., Dasmahapatra, S., & Wilk, Y. (2004). Data driven ontology evaluation. In *Proceedings of the International Conference on Language Resources and Evaluation*, (pp.164-168). Lisbon, Portugal: ACL Press.

Brickley, D., & Guha, R. V. (2004). *RDF vocabulary description language 1.0: RDF schema*. W3C Recommendation 10 February 2004. Retrieved from http://www.w3.org/TR/rdf-schema/.

Brunzel, M. (2008). The XTREEM methods for ontology learning from web documents. In Buitelaar, P. (Eds.), *Ontology Learning and Population: Bridging the Gap Between Text and Knowledge* (pp. 3–28). Amsterdam, Netherlands: IOS Press.

Buitelaar, P., Cimiano, P., Haase, P., & Sintek, M. (2009). Towards linguistically grounded ontologies. In *Proceedings of the 6th Extended Semantic Web Conference*, (pp. 111-125). Heraklion, Greece: ACM Press.

Buitelaar, P., Cimiano, P., Racioppa, S., & Siegel, M. (2006). Ontology-based information extraction with soba. In *Proceedings of the International Conference on Language Resources and Evaluation*, (pp. 2321–2324). ACM Press.

Buitelaar, P., Declerck, T., Frank, A., Racioppa, S., Kiesel, M., Sintek, M., et al. (2006). *LingInfo: Design and applications of a model for the integration of linguistic information in ontologies*. Paper presented at OntoLex06. Genoa, Italy.

Buitelaar, P., Olejnik, D., & Sintek, M. (2004). A protégé plug-in for ontology extraction from text based on linguistic analysis. In *Proceedings of the 1st European Semantic Web Symposium (ESWS)*. Heraklion, Greece: ESWS Press.

Buitelaar, P., Cimiano, P., Frank, A., Hartung, M., & Racioppa, S. (2008). Ontology-based information extraction and integration from heterogeneous data sources. *International Journal of Human-Computer Studies, 66*(11), 759–788. doi:10.1016/j.ijhcs.2008.07.007

Buyko, E., Chiarcos, C., & Pareja Lora, A. (2008). Ontology-based interface specifications for an NLP pipeline architecture. In *Proceedings of the 6th International Conference on Language Resources and Evaluation*. Marrakech, Morocco: LREC Press.

Cabré, M. T. (1999). *Terminology: Theory, methods and applications*. Amsterdam, Netherlands: John Benjamins Publishing Company.

Calzolari, N. (1984). Detecting patterns in a lexical data base. In *Proceedings of the 22nd Annual Meeting on Association for Computational Linguistics*, (pp. 170-173). Morristown, NJ: ACL Press.

Calzolari, N. (1984). Detecting patterns in a lexical database. In *Proceedings of the 10th International Conference on Computational Linguistics*, (pp. 170-173). Stroudsburg, PA: ACL Press.

Caraballo, S. (1999). Automatic construction of a hypernym-labeled noun hierarchy from text. In *Proceedings of the 37th Annual Meeting of the Association for Computational Linguistics,* (pp. 120-126). Morristown, NJ: Association for Computational Linguistics.

Caraballo, S., & Charniak, E. (1998). New figures of merit for best-first probabilistic chart parsing. *Computational Linguistics, 24,* 275–298.

Caracciolo, C., Euzenat, J., Hollink, L., Ichise, R., Isaac, A., & Malaisé, V. … Sváte, V. (2008). Results of the ontology alignment evaluation initiative 2008. In *Proceedings of the CEUR Workshop 431.* Karlsruhe, Germany: CEUR Press.

Carletta, J. (1996). Assessing agreement on classification tasks: The kappa statistic. *Computational Linguistics, 22*(2), 249–254.

Carpenter, B. (1992). *The logic of typed feature structures: Cambridge tracts in theoretical computer science (Vol. 32).* Cambridge, UK: Cambridge University Press. doi:10.1017/CBO9780511530098

Castano, S., Peraldi, I., Ferrara, A., Karkaletsis, V., Kaya, A., & Moller, R. (2009). Multimedia interpretation for dynamic ontology evolution. *Journal of Logic and Computation, 19*(5), 859–897. doi:10.1093/logcom/exn049

Cerbah, F., & Daille, B. (2007). A service oriented architecture for adaptable terminology acquisition. In Kedad, Z., Lammari, N., Métais, E., Meziane, F., & Rezgui, Y. (Eds.), *Natural Language Processing and Information Systems (Vol. 4592,* pp. 420–426). Berlin, Germany: Springer. doi:10.1007/978-3-540-73351-5_40

Chaâben-Kammoun, N., Hadrichn Belguith, L., & Ben Hamadou, A. (2010). *The MORPH2 new version: A robust morphological analyzer for Arabic texts.* Paper presented at JADT 2010. Rome, Italy.

Chan, Y. S., & Ng, H. T. (2007). Domain adaptation with active learning for word sense dis-ambiguation. In *Proceedings of the 45th Annual Meeting of the Association of Computational Linguistics,* (pp. 49-56). Association for Computational Linguistics.

Chaudhri, V. K., Farquhar, A., Fikes, R., Karp, P., & Rice, J. P. (1998). OKBC: A programmatic foundation for knowledge base interoperability. In *Proceedings of the Fifteenth National Conference on Artificial Intelligence (AAAI-98),* (pp. 600-607). Cambridge, MA: MIT Press.

Chelba, C., & Acero, A. (2006). Adaptation of maximum entropy capitalizer: Little data can help a lot. *Computer Speech & Language, 20*(4), 382–399. doi:10.1016/j.csl.2005.05.005

Chinchor, N., Hirschman, L., & Lewis, D. D. (2002). Evaluating message understanding systems: An analysis of the third message understanding conference. *Computational Linguistics, 19,* 409–449.

Chklovski, T., & Pantel, P. (2004). VerbOCEAN: Mining the web for fine-grained semantic verb relations. In *Proceedings of EMNLP 2004.* Association for Computational Linguistics.

Chodorow, M. S., Byrd, R. J., & Heidorn, G. E. (1985). Extracting semantic hierarchies from a large on-line dictionary. In *Proceedings of the 23rd annual meeting on Association for Computational Linguistics,* (pp. 299-304). Morristown, NJ: ACL Press.

Choi, N., Song, I.-Y., & Han, H. (2006). A survey of ontology mapping. *SIGMOD Record, 35*(3), 34–41. doi:10.1145/1168092.1168097

Chrisment, C., Haemmerlé, O., Hernandez, N., & Mothe, J. (2008). Méthodologie de transformation d'un thesaurus en une ontologie de domaine. *Revue d'Intelligence Artificielle, 22*(1), 7–37. doi:10.3166/ria.22.7-37

CIA. (2011). *The world factbook.* Retrieved from https://www.cia.gov/library/publications/the-world-factbook/.

Cimiano, P., & Völker, J. (2005). Text2Onto - A framework for ontology learning and data-driven change discovery. In *Proceedings of the 10th International Conference on Applications of Natural Language to Information Systems,* (pp. 227-238). Alicante, Spain: NLIS Press.

Cimiano, P., & Wenderoth, J. (2007). Automatic acquisition of ranked qualia structures from the Web. In *Proceedings of the 45th Annual Meeting of the Association of Computational Linguistics,* (pp. 888-895). Prague, Czech Republic: ACL Press.

Cimiano, P., Haase, P., Herold, M., Mantel, M., & Buitelaar, P. (2007). LexOnto: A model for ontology lexicons for ontology-based NLP. In *Proceedings of the OntoLex07 Workshop*. ISWC Press.

Cimiano, P., Handschuh, S., & Staab, S. (2004). Towards the self-annotating web. In *Proceedings of the 13th World Wide Web Conference*, (pp. 462-471). New York, NY: ACM.

Cimiano, P., Ladwig, G., & Staab, S. (2005). Gimme the context: Context driven automatic semantic annotation with C-Pankow. In *Proceedings of the 14th International Conference on World Wide Web*, (pp. 332–341). IEEE Press.

Cimiano, P. (2006). *Ontology learning and population from text: Algorithms, evaluation and application*. New York, NY: Springer.

Cimiano, P., Hotho, A., & Staab, S. (2005). Learning concept hierarchies from text corpora using formal concept analysis. *Journal of Artificial Intelligence Research, 24*, 305–339.

Ciravegna, F., Dingli, A., & Petrelli, D. (2002). Document annotation via adaptive information extraction. In *Proceedings of the 25th Annual International ACM SIGIR Conference on Research and Development in Information Retrieval*. ACM Press.

Ciravegna, F., Magnini, B., Pianta, E., & Strapparava, C. (1994). *A project for the construction of an Italian lexical knowledge base in the framework of Wordnet*. Tech Report IRST 9406-15. Retrieved from http://www.irst.org.

Ciravegna, F., & Lavelli, A. (2003). Learning Pinocchio: Adaptive information extraction for real world applications. *Natural Language Engineering, 1*(1), 1–21.

Clarkparsia. (2011). *Pellet OWL 2 reasoner for Java*. Retrieved from http://clarkparsia.com/pellet.

Cohen, J. (1960). A coefficient of agreement for nominal scales. *Psychological Bulletin, 20*, 37–46.

Cole, R., Mariani, J., Uszkoreit, H., Zaenen, A., & Zue, V. (1997). *Survey of the state of the art in human language technology*. Pittsburgh, PA: Carnegie Mellon University.

Craven, M., DiPasquo, D., Freitag, D., McCallum, A., Mitchell, T., Nigam, K., & Slattery, S. (2000). Learning to construct knowledge bases from the world wide web. *Artificial Intelligence, 118*, 69–113. doi:10.1016/S0004-3702(00)00004-7

Cucerzan, S. (2007). Large-scale named entity disambiguation based on Wikipedia data. In *Proceedings of the 2007 Joint Conference on Empirical Methods in Natural Language Processing and Computational Natural Language Learning*, (pp. 708–716). Retrieved from http://www.aclweb.org/anthology/D/D07/D07-1074.

Cui, G., Lu, Q., Li, W., & Chen, Y. (2008). Corpus exploitation from Wikipedia for ontology construction. In N. Calzolari, et al. (Eds.), *Proceedings of the 6th International Conference on Language Resources and Evaluation (LREC 2008)*, (pp. 2125–2132). Paris, France: ELRA. Retrieved from http://www.lrec-conf.org/proceedings/lrec2008/pdf/541_paper.pdf.

Cunningham, H. (1999). A definition and short history of language engineering. *Natural Language Engineering, 5*(1), 1–16. doi:10.1017/S1351324999002144

Cunningham, H. (2002). GATE: A general architecture for text engineering. *Computers and the Humanities, 36*, 223–254. doi:10.1023/A:1014348124664

CYC. (2011). *Cycorp: OpenCyc*. Retrieved from http://www.cyc.com/cyc/opencyc.

Da Silva, J. F., & Lopes, G. P. (1999). *A local maxima method and a fair dispersion normalization for extracting multi-word units from corpora*. Paper presented at the 6th Meeting on Mathematics of Language. Orlando, FL.

Damova, M. (2011). *D4.2 data models, alignment methodology, tools and documentation*. Retrieved from http://www.molto-project.eu/workplan/deliverables.

DARPA. (1995). Defense advanced research project agency. In *Proceedings of the 6th Message Understanding Conference*. DARPA Press.

DARPA. (1998). Defense advanced research project agency. In *Proceedings of the 7th Message Understanding Conference*. DARPA Press.

David, J., Guillet, F., & Briand, H. (2006). *Matching directories and OWL ontologies with AROMA*. Retrieved from http://exmo.inrialpes.fr/people/jdavid/publies/JDavid_CIKM_2006.pdf.

DBpedia. (2011). *Webpage*. Retrieved from http://DBpedia.org.

De Luca, E. W., & Lönneker-Rodman, B. (2008). Integrating metaphor information into RDF/OWL EuroWordNet. In *Proceedings of the Sixth International Language Resources and Evaluation (LREC 2008)*. Marrakech, Morocco: ERLA Press.

De Luca, E. W., & Nürnberger, A. (2004). Improving ontology-based sense folder classification of document collections with clustering methods. In P. Joly, M. Detyniecki, & A. Nürnberger (Eds.), *Proceedings of the 2nd International Workshop on Adaptive Multimedia Retrieval (AMR 2004)*. ECAI Press.

De Luca, E. W., & Nürnberger, A. (2006a). Rebuilding lexical resources for information retrieval using sense folder detection and merging methods. In *Proceedings of the 5th International Conference on Language Resources and Evaluation (LREC 2006)*. Genova, Italy: LREC Press.

De Luca, E. W., & Nürnberger, A. (2006b). The use of lexical resources for sense folder disambiguation. In *Proceedings of the Workshop on Lexical Semantic Resources (DGFS 2006)*. Bielefeld, Germany: DGFS Press.

De Luca, E. W., Eul, M., & Nürnberger, A. (2007). Converting EuroWordNet in OWL and extending it with domain ontologies. In *Proceedings of the Workshop on Lexical-Semantic and Ontological Resources in Conjunction With the GLDV Conference (GLDV 2007)*. ACL Press.

De Luca, E. W., & Nürnberger, A. (2006c). Using clustering methods to improve ontology-based query term disambiguation. *International Journal of Intelligent Systems*, *21*, 693–709. doi:10.1002/int.20155

Dean, M., & Schreiber, G. (2004). *OWL web ontology language reference*. W3C recommendation. Retrieved from http://www.w3c.org.

Dellschaft, K., & Staab, S. (2008). Strategies for the evaluation of ontology learning. In *Bridging the Gap between Text and Knowledge*. Amsterdam: IOS Press.

Description Logic. (2011). *Wikipedia entry*. Retrieved March 2011, from http://en.wikipedia.org/wiki/Description_logic.

Doan, A., Madhavan, J., Domingos, P., & Halevy, A. (2003). Learning to map between ontologies on the semantic web. *VLDB Journal*. Retrieved from http://pages.cs.wisc.edu/~anhai/papers/glue-vldbj.pdf.

Dodinet, G. (2005). *Exploiting maven in eclipse*. Retrieved from http://www.ibm.com/developerworks/.

Dolan, W., Vanderwende, L., & Richardson, S. (1993). Automatically deriving structured knowledge bases from online dictionaries. In *Proceedings of the Pacific Association for Computational Linguistics*, (pp. 5-14). ACL Press.

DOLCE. (2011). *Webpage*. Retrieved from http://www.loa-cnr.it/DOLCE.html.

Dublin Core. (2011). *Webpage*. Retrieved from http://dublincore.org/documents/dces/.

Echarte, F., Astrain, J., Córdoba, A., & Villadangos, J. (2007). *Ontology of folksonomy: A new modeling method*. Paper presented at the Semantic Authoring, Annotation and Knowledge Markup Workshop. Whistler, Canada.

El Sayed, A., Hacid, H., & Zighed, D. (2008). A new framework for taxonomy discovery from text. In *Proceedings of the 12th Pacific-Asia conference on Advances in Knowledge Discovery and Data Mining*, (pp. 985-991). Berlin, Germany: Springer-Verlag.

El-Mekawy, M., & Östman, A. (2010). Mapping: An ontology engineering method for integrating building models in IFC and CITYGM. In *Proceedings of the 3rd ISDE Digital Earth Summit*. Nessebar, Bulgaria: ISDE Press.

Erdmann, M., Nakayama, K., Hara, T., & Nishio, S. (2008). An approach for extracting bilingual terminology from Wikipedia. In Haritsa, J. R., Kotagiri, R., & Pudi, V. (Eds.), *DASFAA 2008* (*Vol. 4947*, pp. 380–392). Lecture Notes in Computer Science Berlin, Germany: Springer. doi:10.1007/978-3-540-78568-2_28

Erdmann, M., Nakayama, K., Hara, T., & Nishio, S. (2009). Improving the extraction of bilingual terminology from Wikipedia. *ACM Transactions on Multimedia Computing, Communications, and Applications*, *5*(4), 1–17. doi:10.1145/1596990.1596995

Espinosa, S., Kaya, A., Melzer, S., & Moller, R. (2008). On ontology based abduction for text interpretation. In *Proceedings of 9th International Conference on Intelligent Text Processing and Computational Linguistics (CICLing 2008)*, (pp. 194-205). Springer.

Etzioni, O., Cafarella, M., Downey, D., Kok, S., Popescu, A., & Shaked, T. ... Yates, A. (2004). Web-scale information extraction in knowitall: Preliminary results. In *Proceedings of the 13th International Conference on World Wide Web*, (pp. 100-110). New York, NY: ACM.

Etzioni, O., Kok, S., Soderland, S., Cagarella, M., Popescu, A. M., & Weld, D. S. (2005). Unsupervised named-entity extraction from the web: An experimental Study. *Artificial Intelligence, 165*, 91–134. doi:10.1016/j.artint.2005.03.001

Euzenat, J., Ferrara, A., Hollink, L., Isaac, A., Joslyn, C., & Malaisé, V. ... Wang, S. (2009). Results of the ontology alignment evaluation initiative 2009. In *Proceedings of the 4th Ontology Matching Workshop at ISWC 2009*. Washington, DC: ISWC Press.

Evert, S., & Krenn, B. (2001). Methods for the qualitative evaluation of lexical association measures. In *Proceedings of 39th Annual Meeting of the Association for Computational Linguistics*, (pp. 188–195). Retrieved from http://www.aclweb.org/anthology/P01-1025.

FactForge. (2011). *Webpage.* Retrieved from http://factforge.net, http://www.ontotext.com/factforge.

Fallside, D. C., & Walmsley, P. (2004). *XML schema part 0: Primer* (2nd ed). W3C Recommendation 28 October 2004. Retrieved from http://www.w3c.org.

Fallucchi, F., & Zanzotto, F. M. (2009). SVD feature selection for probabilistic taxonomy learning. In *Proceedings of the Workshop on Geometrical Models of Natural Language Semantics,* (pp. 66-73). Association for Computational Linguistics.

Fallucchi, F., & Zanzotto, F. M. (2010). Inductive probabilistic taxonomy learning using singular value decomposition. *Journal of Natural Language Engineering.*

Fallucchi, F., Scarpato, N., Stellato, A., & Zanzotto, F. M. (2009). Probabilistic ontology learner in semantic turkey. In *Proceedings of the XIth International Conference of the Italian Association for Artificial Intelligence Reggio Emilia on Emergent Perspectives in Artificial Intelligence,* (pp. 294-303). Springer-Verlag.

Faure, D., & Nédellec, C. (1998). A corpus-based conceptual clustering method for verb frames and ontology. In *Proceedings of the LREC Workshop on Adapting Lexical and Corpus Resources to Sublanguages and Applications,* (5-12). Granada, Spain: Springer.

Faure, D., & Poibeau, T. (2000). First experiments of using semantic knowledge learned by ASIUM for information extraction task using INTEX. In *Proceedings of the ECAI Workshop on Ontology Learning*. ECAI Press.

Fazly, A., & Stevenson, S. (2007). Distinguishing subtypes of multiword expressions using linguistically-motivated statistical measures. In *Proceedings of the ACL 2007 Workshop on a Broader Perspective on Multiword Expressions,* (pp. 9–16). ACL Press. Retrieved from http://www.aclweb.org/anthology/W/W07/W07-1102.

Fellbaum, C. (1998). *WordNet: An electronic lexical database.* Cambridge, MA: MIT Press.

Ferdinand, M., Zirpins, C., & Trastour, D. (2004). Lifting XML schema to OWL. In *Proceedings of Web Engineering, 4th International Conference, ICWE 2004,* (pp. 354-358). Munich, Germany: Springer.

Ferrucci, D. (2009). Unstructured information management architecture (UIMA) version 1.0. In A. Lally, K. Verspoor, & E. Nyberg (Eds.), *OASIS Standard*. Retrieved from http://www.oasis-open.org/.

Ferrucci, D., & Lally, A. (2004). Uima: An architectural approach to unstructured information processing in the corporate research environment. *Natural Language Engineering, 10*(3-4), 327–348. doi:10.1017/S1351324904003523

Finkel, J. R., Grenager, T., & Manning, C. (2005). Incorporating non-local information into information extraction systems by Gibbs sampling. In *Proceedings of the 43nd Annual Meeting of the Association for Computational Linguistics*, (pp. 363–370). ACL Press. Retrieved from http://www.aclweb.org/anthology/P/P05/P05-1045.pdf.

Finkelstein, L., Gabrilovich, E., Matias, Y., Rivlin, E., Solan, Z., Wolfman, G., & Ruppin, E. (2002). Placing search in context: The concept revisited. *ACM Transactions on Information Systems*, *20*(1), 116–131. doi:10.1145/503104.503110

Fiorelli, M., Pazienza, M. T., Petruzza, S., Stellato, A., & Turbati, A. (2010). *Computer-aided ontology development: An integrated environment*. Paper presented at New Challenges for NLP Frameworks 2010. La Valletta, Malta.

Firth, J. R. (1957). A synopsis of linguistic theory 1930-55. In *Studies in Linguistic Analysis 1952-59* (pp. 1–32). Oxford, UK: Blackwell.

Fleiss, J. (1971). Measuring nominal scale agreement among many raters. *Psychological Bulletin*, *76*(5), 378–382. doi:10.1037/h0031619

Fleiss, J. L. (1971). Measuring nominal scale agreement among many raters. *Psychological Bulletin*, *76*(5), 378–381. doi:10.1037/h0031619

Francopoulo, G., & George, M. (2008). *Language resource management - Lexical markup framework (LMF). Technical Report, ISO/TC 37/SC 4 N453 (N330 Rev. 16)*. Washington, DC: US Government Press.

Frantzi, K. T., Ananiadou, S., & Mima, H. (2000). Automatic recognition of multi-word terms: The C-value/NC-value method. *International Journal on Digital Libraries*, *3*(2), 115–130. doi:10.1007/s007999900023

Frantzi, K., & Ananjadou, S. (1999). The C-value/NC-value domain independent method for multi-word term extraction. *Journal of Natural Language Processing*, *6*(3), 145–179.

Freebase. (2011). *Webpage*. Retrieved from http://www.freebase.com/.

Gabrilovich, E., & Markovitch, S. (2007). Computing semantic relatedness using Wikipedia-based explicit semantic analysis. In *Proceedings of the 20th International Joint Conference on Artificial Intelligence*, (pp. 1606–1611). IEEE Press.

Gangemi, A., Catenacci, C., Ciaramita, M., & Lehmann, J. (2006). *Qood grid: A metaontology-based framework for ontology evaluation and selection*. Paper presented at the 4th International Workshop on Evaluation of Ontologies for the Web (EON 2006) at the 15th International World Wide Web Conference. Edinburgh, UK.

Gangemi, A., Guarino, N., & Oltramari, A. (2001). Conceptual analysis of lexical taxonomies: The case of WordNet top-level. In *Proceedings of the International Conference on Formal Ontology in Information Systems*, (pp. 285–296). New York, NY: ACM Press.

Gangemi, A., Navigli, R., & Velardi, P. (2003). The OntoWordNet project: Extension and axiomatization of conceptual relations in WordNet. In Meersman, R., & Tari, Z. (Eds.), *Proceedings of On the Move to Meaningful Internet Systems (OTM2003)* (pp. 820–838). Catania, Italy: Springer-Verlag. doi:10.1007/978-3-540-39964-3_52

Gangemi, A., Navigli, R., & Velardi, P. (2003). The OntoWordNet project: Extension and axiomatization of conceptual relations in WordNet. In Meersman, R., Tari, Z., & Schmidt, D. C. (Eds.), *On the Move to Meaningful Internet Systems* (pp. 820–838). Berlin, Germany: Springer. doi:10.1007/978-3-540-39964-3_52

Gangemi, A., & Presutti, V. (2010). Towards a pattern science for the semantic web. *Semantic Web*, *1*(1-2), 61–68.

Gao, J. (2009). Model adaptation via model interpolation and boosting for web search observations of markov chains. *IEEE Transactions on Speech and Audio Processing*, *2*, 291–298.

García, R. (2006). *A semantic web approach to digital rights management*. Doctoral Dissertation. University of Versailles. Retrieved June 23rd, 2011, from http://rhizomik.net/html/~roberto/thesis/.

GATE. (2011). *Platform*. Retrieved from http://gate.ac.uk/.

Geffet, M., & Dagan, I. (2005). The distributional inclusion hypotheses and lexical entailment. In *Proceedings of The 43rd Annual Meeting of the Association for Computational Linguistics*, (p. 107-114). Association for Computational Linguistics.

Gennari, J., Musen, M., Fergerson, R., Grosso, W., Crubézy, M., & Eriksson, H. (2003). The evolution of Protégé-2000: An environment for knowledge-based systems development. *International Journal of Human-Computer Studies, 58*(1), 89–123. doi:10.1016/S1071-5819(02)00127-1

Geonames. (2011). *Webpage*. Retrieved from http://www.geonames.org.

Gildea, D. (2001). Corpus variation and parser performance. In *Proceedings of Conference on Empirical Methods in Natural Language Processing EMNLP.* EMNLP Press.

Giles, J. (2005). Internet encyclopaedias go head to head. *Nature, 138*(15), 900–901. doi:10.1038/438900a

Giles, J. (2005). Internet encyclopaedias go head to head. *Nature, 438*(7070), 900–901. doi:10.1038/438900a

Gómez-Pérez, A. (1999). Evaluation of taxonomic knowledge on ontologies and knowledge-based systems. In *Proceedings of the North American Workshop on Knowledge Acquisition, Modeling, and Management.* KAW Press.

Gómez-Pérez, A., & Manzano-Macho, D. (2003). *Deliverable 1.5: A survey of ontology learning methods and techniques.* Retrieved from http://www.sti-innsbruck.at/fileadmin/documents/deliverables/Ontoweb/D1.5.pdf.

Gomez-Perez, A. (1994). *Some ideas and examples to evaluate ontologies.* Palo Alto, CA: Stanford University Press.

Gómez-Pérez, A. (2004). Ontology evaluation. In Staab, S., & Studer, R. (Eds.), *Handbook on Ontologies in Information Systems* (1st ed., pp. 251–274). Berlin, Germany: Springer.

Gómez-Pérez, A., Fernández-López, M., & Corcho, O. (2004). *Ontological engineering.* London, UK: Springer.

Google. (2011). *Semantic vectors.* Retrieved from http://code.google.com/p/semanticvectors/.

Gospodnetic, O., & Hatcher, E. (2005). *Lucene in action.* Greenwich, CT: Manning.

Grefenstette, G. (1994). *Explorations in automatic thesaurus construction.* Berlin, Germany: Kluwer.

Griesi, D., Pazienza, M. T., & Stellato, A. (2006). Gobbleing over the web with semantic turkey. In *Proceedings of SWAP 2006.* SWAP Press.

Griesi, D., Pazienza, M. T., & Stellato, A. (2007). Semantic turkey - A semantic bookmarking tool (system description). In E. Franconi, M. Kifer, & W. May (Eds.), *The Semantic Web: Research and Applications,* (pp. 779-788). Springer.

Griesi, D., Pazienza, M., & Stellato, A. (2007). Semantic turkey - A *Semantic Bookmarking tool: System description. Lecture Notes in Computer Science, 4519,* 779–788. doi:10.1007/978-3-540-72667-8_56

Grinberg, M., Damova, M., & Kiryakov, A. (2011). *D1.2.1: Initial data integration.* Sofia, Bulgaria: Project RENDER.

Gruber, T. (2007). Ontology of folksonomy: A mash-up of apples and oranges. *International Journal on Semantic Web and Information Systems, 3*(1), 1–11. doi:10.4018/jswis.2007010101

Guarino, N., & Welty, C. A. (2004). An overview of ontoclean. Retrieved from http://www.loa.istc.cnr.it/Papers/GuarinoWeltyOntoCleanv3.pdf.

Guarino, N. (1998). Formal ontology in information systems. In Guarino, N. (Ed.), *Formal Ontology in Information Systems* (pp. 3–15). Amsterdam, The Netherlands: IOS Press.

Guarino, N., Oberle, D., & Staab, S. (2009). What is an ontology? In Staab, S., & Studer, R. (Eds.), *Handbook on Ontologies* (pp. 1–7). Berlin, Germany: Springer. doi:10.1007/978-3-540-92673-3_0

Guarino, N., & Welty, C. (2002). Evaluating Ontological Decisions with OntoClean. *Communications of the ACM, 45*(2), 61–65. doi:10.1145/503124.503150

Gumwon, H. (2005). Relation extraction using support vector machine. In *Proceedings of the 2nd International Joint Conference on Natural Language Processing,* (pp. 366–377). IEEE Press.

Haase, P., Lewen, H., Studer, R., Tran, D. T., d'Aquin, M., & Motta, E. (2008). *The neon ontology engineering toolkit.* Retrieved from http://neon-toolkit.org/wiki/Main_Page.

Hahn, U., Romacker, M., & Schulz, S. (2002). Creating knowledge repositories from biomedical repots: Medsyndikate text mining system. In *Proceedings of the PSB*, (pp. 338–349). PSB Press.

Hajič, J., Smrž, O., Buckwalter, T., & Jin, H. (2005). Feature-based tagger of approximations of functional Arabic morphology. In Civit, M. A. M. M., & Kübler, S. (Eds.), *Proceedings of Treebanks and Linguistic Theories (TLT)* (pp. 53–64). Barcelona, Spain: TLT Press.

Harman, D. (1992). The DARPA TIPSTER project. *SIGIR Forum*, *26*(2), 26–28. doi:10.1145/146565.146567

Harris, Z. (1964). Distributional structure. In Katz, J. J., & Fodor, J. A. (Eds.), *The Philosophy of Linguistics*. Oxford, UK: Oxford University Press.

Harris, Z. (1968). *Mathematical structures of language*. New York: Wiley.

Hearst, M. (1992). Automatic acquisition of hyponyms from large text corpora. In *Proceedings of the 14th International Conference on Computational Linguistics*, (pp. 539-545). ACL Press.

Hearst, M., & Schütze, H. (1996). *Customizing a lexicon to better suit a computational task*. Paper presented at the ACL SIGLEX Workshop on Lexical Acquisition. Columbus, OH.

Heath, T., & Bizer, C. (2011). Linked data: Evolving the web into a global data space. *Synthesis Lectures on the Semantic Web*, *1*(1), 1–136. doi:10.2200/S00334ED1V01Y201102WBE001

Heckmann, D., Schwartz, T., Brandherm, B., Schmitz, M., & von Wilamowitz-Moellendorff, M. (2005). Gumo - The general user model ontology. *User Modeling*, *3538*, 428–432. doi:10.1007/11527886_58

Herman, I., Swick, R., & Brickley, D. (2004). *Resource description framework (RDF)*. Tech Report. Retrieved from http://www.w3c.org.

Hirst, G. (1995). Near-synonymy and the structure of lexical knowledge. In *Proceedings of the AAAI Spring Symposium Representation and Acquisition of Lexical Knowledge: Polysemy, Ambiguity, and Generativity*, (pp. 51–56). Menlo Park, CA: The AAAI Press.

Hirst, G. (2004). Ontology and the lexicon. In Staab, S., & Studer, R. (Eds.), *Handbook on Ontologies and Information Systems*. Berlin, Germany: Springer.

Hitzler, P., Krötzsch, M., Parsia, B., Patel-Schneider, P. F., & Rudolph, S. (2009). *OWL 2 web ontology language primer*. W3C Recommendation 27 October 2009. Retrieved from http://www.w3c.org.

Hoang, H. H., Kim, S. N., & Kan, M.-Y. (2009). A re-examination of lexical association measures. In *Proceedings of the ACL 2009 Workshop on Multiword Expressions: Identification, Interpretation, Disambiguation and Applications*, (pp. 31–39). Retrieved from http://www.aclweb.org/anthology/W/W09/W09-290.

Hobbs, J. R., Stickel, M., Appelt, D., & Martin, P. (1990). *Interpretation as abduction. Technical Note 499*. SRI International.

Horák, A., & Smrož, P. (2004). VisDic - Wordnet browsing and editing tool. In *Proceedings of the Second International Wordnet Conference (GWC2004)*. GWC Press.

Horák, A., Pala, K., Rambousek, A., & Povolný, M. (2006). DEBVisDic - First version of new client-server Wordnet browsing and editing tool. In *Proceedings of the Third International Wordnet Conference (GWC 2006)*, (pp. 325-328). Seogwipo, Korea: GWC Press.

Horridge, M., & Bechhofer, S. (2009). *The OWL API: A Java API for working with OWL 2 ontologies*. Paper presented at OWLED 2009, 6th OWL Experienced and Directions Workshop. Chantilly, VA.

Horst Dialects, O. W. L. (2010). *Webpage*. Retrieved from http://www.ontotext.com/inference/rdfs_rules_owl.html.

Huvila, I. (2010). Where does the information come from? Information source use patterns in Wikipedia. *Information Research*, *15*(3).

ISO 24613 (2008). *Lexical markup framework (LMF) revision 16*. ISO FDIS 24613:2008. Washington, DC: US Government Press.

Jain, P., Hitzler, P., Sheth, A. P., Verma, K., & Yeh, P. Z. (2010). Ontology alignment for linked open data. In Y. P. P. Patel-Schneider (Ed.), *Proceedings of the 9th International Semantic Web Conference*. Shanghai, China: IEEE Press.

Jain, P., Yeh, P. Z., Verma, K., Vasquez, R. G., Damova, M., Hitzler, P., & Sheth, A. P. (2011). Contextual ontology alignment of LOD with an upper ontology: A case study with Proton. In G. Antoniou (Ed.), *Proceedings of 8th Extended Semantic Web Conference*. Heraklion, Crete: IEEE Press.

Jain, P., Hitzler, P., Yeh, P. Z., Verma, K., & Sheth, A. P. (2010). Linked data is merely more data. In Brickley, V. K. D. (Ed.), *Linked Data Meets Artificial Intelligence* (pp. 82–86). New York, NY: AAAI Press.

Jannink, J., & Wiederhold, G. (1999). Ontology maintenance with an algebraic methodology: A case study. In *Proceedings of AAAI Workshop on Ontology Management*. AAAI Press.

Jannink, J. (1999). Thesaurus entry extraction from an online dictionary. In *Proceedings of Fusion 1999*. ACL Press.

Jean-Mary, Y., & Kabuka, M. (2009). *ASMOV: Ontology alignment with semantic validation*. Retrieved from http://ebookbrowse.com/asmov-ontology-alignment-with-semantic-validation-pdf-d73258878.

Jiang, J., & Zhai, C. (2007). A systematic exploration of the feature space for relation extraction. In *Proceedings of the North American Chapter of the Association for Computational Linguistics-Human Language Technologies Conference*. ACLHLT Press.

Joachims, T. (1999). Making large-scale SVM learning practical. In Schölkopf, B., Burges, C., & Smola, A. (Eds.), *Advances in Kernel Methods - Support Vector Learning*. Cambridge, MA: MIT Press.

Kageura, K., & Umino, B. (1996). Methods of automatic term recognition: A review. *Terminology, 3*(2), 259–289. doi:10.1075/term.3.2.03kag

Karkaletsis, V., Spyropoulos, C., Grover, C., Pazienza, M., Coch, J., & Souflis, D. (2004). A platform for cross-lingual, domain and user adaptive web information extraction. In *Proceedings of the European Conference in Artificial Intelligence*, (pp. 725–729). EAI Press.

Karkaletsis, V., Farmakiotou, D., Androutsopoulos, I., Koutsiasa, J., Paliouras, G., & Spyropoulos, C. D. (2000). *Information extraction from Greek texts in the MITOS information management system*. *NCSR Technical Report*. Athens, Greece: NCSR.

Katz, G., & Giesbrecht, E. (2006). Automatic identification of non-compositional multi-word expressions using latent semantic analysis. In *Proceedings of the ACL 2006 Workshop on Multiword Expressions: Identifying and Exploiting Underlying Properties*, (pp. 12–19). Retrieved from http://www.aclweb.org/anthology/W/W06/W06-1203.

Kietz, J. U., Maedche, A., & Volz, R. (2000). A method for semi-automatic ontology acquisition from a corporate intranet. In *Proceedings of Workshop Ontologies and Text*. KAW Press.

Kilgarriff, A., & Grefenstette, G. (2003). Introduction to the special issue on the web as corpus. *Computational Linguistics, 29*(3), 333–347. doi:10.1162/089120103322711569

KIM. (2011). *Platform*. Retrieved from http://www.ontotext.com/kim.

Kim, J.-D., Ohta, T., Tateisi, Y., & Tsujii, J. (2003). Genia corpus– Semantically annotated corpus for bio-textmining. *Bioinformatics (Oxford, England), 19*(1), 1180–1182. doi:10.1093/bioinformatics/btg1023

Kiryakov, A., & Momtchev, V. (2009). *Two reason-able views to the web of linked data*. Paper presented at the Semantic Technology Conference. San Jose, CA.

Kiryakov, A., Ognyanoff, D., Velkov, R., Tashev, Z., & Peikov, I. (2009). LDSR: Materialized reason-able view to the web of linked data. In R. H. Patel-Schneider (Ed.), *Proceedings of OWLED 2009*. Chantilly, VA: OWED Press.

Kiryakov, A., Grinberg, M., Damova, M., & Russo, D. (2011). *D.D1.1.1: Initial collection of data*. Sofia, Bulgaria: Project RENDER.

Kiryakov, A., Tashev, Z., Ognyanoff, D., Velkov, R., Momtchev, V., Balev, B., & Peikov, I. (2009). *D5.5.2: Validation goals and metrics for the LarKC platform*. Sofia, Bulgaria: Project RENDER.

Klein, M. C. A., Broekstra, J., Fensel, D., Van Harmelen, F., & Horrocks, I. (2003). Ontologies and schema languages on the Web. In *Spinning the Semantic Web* (pp. 95–139). Cambridge, MA: MIT Press.

Klinger, R., & Tomanek, K. (2007). *Classical probabilistic models and conditional random fields*. Technical Report TR07-2-013. Dortmund, Germany: Dortmund University of Technology.

Korkontzelos, I., & Manandhar, S. (2009). Detecting compositionality in multi-word expressions. In *Proceedings of the ACL-IJCNLP 2009 Conference Short Papers*, (pp. 65–68). Retrieved from http://www.aclweb.org/anthology/P/P09/P09-2017.

Korkontzelos, I., Klapaftis, I., & Manandhar, S. (2008). Reviewing and evaluating automatic term recognition techniques. In Ranta, A., & Nordström, B. (Eds.), *Lecture Notes in Artificial Intelligence: GoTAL 2008 (Vol. 5221*, pp. 248–259). Berlin, Germany: Springer. doi:10.1007/978-3-540-85287-2_24

Kozakov, L., Park, Y., Fin, T., Drissi, Y., Doganata, Y., & Cofino, T. (2004). Glossary extraction and utilization in the information search and delivery system for IBM technical support. *IBM Systems Journal, 43*(3), 546–563. doi:10.1147/sj.433.0546

Krenn, B., & Evert, S. (2001). Can we do better than frequency? A case study on extracting PP-verb collocations. In *Proceedings of the ACL Workshop on Collocations*, (pp. 39–46). ACL Press.

Krippendorff, K. (1980). *Content analysis: An introduction to its methodology*. Thousand Oaks, CA: Sage Publications.

Krizhanovsky, A., & Lin, F. (2009). Related terms search based on WordNet / Wiktionary and its application in ontology matching. In *Proceedings of the 11th Russian Conference on Digital Libraries*, (pp. 363–369). RCDL Press.

Kulick, S., Bies, A., Liberman, M., Mandel, M., Mcdonald, R., & Palmer, M. … White, P. (2004). Integrated annotation for biomedical information extraction. In *Proceedings of the HLT-NAACL 2004 Workshop: BioLINK 2004, Linking Biological Literature, Ontologies and Databases*, (pp. 61–68). ACL Press. Retrieved from http://www.aclweb.org/anthology/W/W04/W04-3111.pdf.

Kunegis, J., & Lommatzsch, A. (2009). Learning spectral graph transformations for link prediction. In *Proceedings of the 26th Annual International Conference on Machine Learning*, (pp. 1–8). New York, NY: ACM.

Kurematsu, M., Iwade, T., Nakaya, N., & Yamaguchi, T. (2004). DODDLE II: A domain ontology development environment using a MRD and text corpus. *IEICE(E). E (Norwalk, Conn.), 87-D*(4), 908–916.

Kurmas, Z. (2010). *Zawilinski: A library for studying grammar in Wiktionary*. Paper presented at the 6th International Symposium on Wikis and Open Collaboration. Gdańsk, Poland.

Lafferty, J., McCallum, A., & Pereira, F. (2001). Conditional random fields: Probabilistic models for segmenting and labeling sequence data. In *Proceedings of the 18th International Conference on Machine Learning*, (pp. 282–289). IEEE Press.

Lakoff, G., Espenson, J., & Schwartz, A. (1991). Master metaphor list. *Tech Report*. Berkeley, CA: University of California Berkeley.

Lambrix, P., & Tan, H. (2006). SAMBO-A system for aligning and merging biomedical ontologies. *Web Semantics, 4*(3).

Landis, J. R., & Koch, G. G. (1977). The measurement of observer agreement for categorical data. *Biometrics, 33*(1), 159–174. doi:10.2307/2529310

Lapata, M., & Keller, F. (2004). The web as a baseline: Evaluating the performance of unsupervised web-based models for a range of NLP tasks. In *Proceedings of HLT-NAACL 2004*. NAACL Press.

Laske, A., & De Luca, E. W. (2010). *Conversion of the basic multilingual dictionary into the RDF/OWL format. Tech Report*. Magdeburg, Germany: Otto-von-Guericke University of Magdeburg.

Lehnert, W. C., Fisher, D., Riloff, E., & Williams, R. (1991). Description of the CIRCUS system as used for MUC-3. In *Proceedings of the Third Message Understanding Conference*. Boston, MA: Morgan Kaufmann.

Lenat, D. B. (1995). CYC: A large-scale investment in knowledge infrastructure. *Communications of the ACM, 38*(11), 33–38. doi:10.1145/219717.219745

Li, S., Lu, Q., & Li, W. (2005). Experiments of ontology construction with formal concept analysis. In *Proceedings of the OntoLex Workshop IJCNLP*, (pp. 67–75). Korea: IJCNLP Press.

Li, J., Tang, J., Li, Y., & Luo, Q. (2009). RiMOM: A dynamic multistrategy ontology alignment framework. *IEEE Transactions on Knowledge and Data Engineering, 21*(8), 1218–1232. doi:10.1109/TKDE.2008.202

Lin, D., & Pantel, P. (2002). Concept discovery from text. In *Proceedings of the 19th International Conference on Computational Linguistics.* ICCL Press.

Linked Data. (2011). *Linking open data.* Retrieved http://linkeddata.org/.

Linked Life Data. (2011). *Webpage.* Retrieved from http://linkedlifedata.com.

Lönneker-Rodman, B. (2008). The Hamburg metaphor database project: Issues in resource creation. *Language Resources and Evaluation, 42*(3), 293–318. doi:10.1007/s10579-008-9073-9

Lonsdale, D., Embley, D., Ding, D., Xu, L., & Hepp, M. (2010). Reusing ontologies and language components for ontology generation. *Journal of Data & Knowledge Engineering, 69*(4), 318–330. doi:10.1016/j.datak.2009.08.003

MacManus, R. (2010). *The Modigliani test: The semantic web's tipping point.* Retrieved April 2010, from http://www.readwriteweb.com/archives/the_modigliani_test_semantic_web_tipping_point.php.

Maedche, A., & Staab, A. (2002). Measuring similarity between ontologies. In *Proceedings of the European Conference on Knowledge Acquisition and Management,* (vol 2473), (pp. 251-263). Berlin, Germany: Springer.

Maedche, A., & Staab, S. (2002). Measuring similarity between ontologies. In *Proceedings of the 13th International Conference on Knowledge Engineering and Knowledge Management: Ontologies and the Semantic Web.* Springer-Verlag.

Maedche, A., & Volz, R. (2001). The ontology extraction maintenance framework text-to-onto. In *Proceedings of the ICDM Workshop on Integrating Data Mining and Knowledge Management.* ICDM Press.

Maedche, A., Neumann, G., & Staab, S. (2002). Bootstrapping an ontology-based information extraction system. In Szczepaniak, P. S., Segovia, J., Kacprzyk, J., & Zadeh, L. A. (Eds.), *Intelligent Exploration of the Web Series - Studies in Fuzziness and Soft Computing.* Berlin, Germany: Physica.

Maedche, A., Pekar, V., & Staab, S. (2003). *On discovering taxonomic relations from the web. Technical Report.* Karlsruhe, Germany: University of Karlsruhe.

Maedche, A., & Staab, S. (2001). Ontology learning for the semantic web. *IEEE Intelligent Systems, 16*(2), 72–79. doi:10.1109/5254.920602

Maedche, A., & Staab, S. (2001). Ontology learning for the semantic web. *IEEE Journal on Intelligent Systems, 16*(2), 72–79. doi:10.1109/5254.920602

Maedche, A., & Staab, S. (2004). Ontology learning. In *Handbook on Ontologies* (pp. 173–189). Berlin, Germany: Springer.

Manola, F., & Miller, E. (2004). *RDF primer.* W3C Recommendation. Retrieved from http://www.w3.org/TR/rdf-primer/.

Markert, K., Modjeska, N., & Nissim, M. (2003). Using the web for nominal anaphora resolution. In *Proceedings of the EACL Workshop on the Computational Treatment of Anaphora,* (pp. 39-46). EACL Press.

Martin, P. (2003). Correction and extension of WordNet 1.7. In *Conceptual Structures for Knowledge Creation and Communication: 11th International Conference on Conceptual Structures,* (pp. 160–173). Berlin, Germany: Springer.

Masolo, C., Borgo, S., Gangemi, A., Guarino, N., & Oltramari, A. (2003). *Ontology library (final).* Retrieved from http://www.loa-cnr.it/Publications.html.

Maynard, D., Li, Y., & Peters, W. (2008). NLP techniques for term extraction and ontology population. In Buitelaar, P., & Cimiano, P. (Eds.), *Ontology Learning and Population: Bridging the Gap between Text and Knowledge* (pp. 107–127). Amsterdam: IOS Press.

McBride, B., Boothby, D., & Dollin, C. (2006). An introduction to RDF and the jena RDF API. Tech Report. Retrieved from http://www.hp.com.

McCallum, A., & Li, W. (2003). Early results for named entity recognition with conditional random fields, feature induction and web-enhanced lexicons. In *Proceedings of the 7th Conference on Natural Language Learning at HLT-NAACL,* (pp. 188–191). NAACL Press.

McCarthy, D., Koeling, R., Weeds, J., & Carroll, J. (2004). Finding predominant word senses in untagged text. In *Proceedings of the 42nd Annual Meeting on Association for Computational Linguistics.* Association for Computational Linguistics.

McGuinness, D., & van Harmelen, F. (2004). *Web ontology language overview*. W3C Recommendation. Retrieved from http://www.w3.org/TR/owl-features/.

Medche, A. (2002). *Ontology learning for the semantic web* (*Vol. 665*). Berlin, Germany: Kluwer International.

Medelyan, O., Milne, D., Legg, C., & Witten, I. H. (2009). Mining meaning from Wikipedia. *International Journal of Human-Computer Studies, 67*(9), 716–754. doi:10.1016/j.ijhcs.2009.05.004

Meyer, C. M., & Gurevych, I. (2010a). Worth its weight in gold or yet another resource – A comparative study of Wiktionary, OpenThesaurus and GermaNet. In A. Gelbukh (Ed.), *Computational Linguistics and Intelligent Text Processing: 11th International Conference,* (pp. 38–49). Berlin, Germany: Springer.

Meyer, C. M., & Gurevych, I. (2010b). *How Web communities analyze human language: Word senses in Wiktionary*. Paper presented at the Second Web Science Conference. Raleigh, NC.

Mezghanni Hammami, S., Hadrich Belguith, L., & Ben Hamadou, A. (2009). Anaphora resolution: Corpora annotation with coreferential links. *International Arab Journal of Information Technology, 6*(5), 481–489.

Michiels, A., Mullenders, J., & Noël, J. (1980). Exploiting a large data base by Longman. In *Proceedings of the 8th Conference on Computational linguistics,* (pp. 374-382). Morristown, NJ: ACL Press.

Mika, P. (2007). Ontologies are us: A unified model of social networks and semantics. *Web Semantics: Science. Services and Agents on the World Wide Web, 5*(1), 5–15. doi:10.1016/j.websem.2006.11.002

Mikheev, A., Grover, C., & Moens, A. (1998). *Description of the LTG system used for MUC-7*. Retrieved from http://muc.saic.com/proceedings/muc_7_toc.html.

Miller, G. (1995). Wordnet: A lexical database for English. *Communications of the ACM, 38*, 9–41. doi:10.1145/219717.219748

Miller, G. A. (1995). WordNet: A lexical database for English. *Communications of the ACM, 38*(11), 39–41. doi:10.1145/219717.219748

Miller, G. A., Beckwith, R., Fellbaum, C., Gross, D., & Miller, K. (1990). Five papers on WordNet. *International Journal of Lexicology, 3*(4).

Mitankin, P., & Ilchev, A. (2010). *D 4.1: Knowledge representation infrastucture*. Retrieved from http://www.molto-project.eu/workplan/deliverables.

Momchev, V., Assel, M., Cheptsov, A., Bishop, B., Bradesko, L., & Fuchs, C. ... Tagni, G. (2010). *D5.5.3: Report on platform validation and recommendation for next version*. Retrieved from http://www.larkc.eu.

Morin, E. (1999). *Extraction de liens sèmantiques entre termes à partir de corpus de textes techniques*. Nantes, France: Univesitè de Nantes.

Motik, B., Grau, B. C., Horrocks, I., Wu, Z., Fokoue, A., & Lutz, C. (2009). *OWL 2 Web ontology language profiles*. W3C Recommendation 27 October 2009. Retrieved from http://www.w3c.org.

Motta, E., Shum, S. B., & Domingue, J. (1999). *Ontology-driven document enrichment: Principles and case studies*. Paper presented at the 12th Banff Knowledge Acquisition Workshop. Banff, Canada.

Murtagh, F. (2005). *Correspondence analysis and data coding with Java and R*. New York: Chapman & Hall.

Murtagh, F. (2007). *Ontology from hierarchical structure in text. Technical Report*. London, UK: University of London Egham.

MusicBrainz. (2011). *Community music database*. Retrieved from http://musicbrainz.org.

Nakagawa, H., & Mori, T. (1998). Nested collocation and compound noun for term extraction. In *Proceedings of the First Workshop on Computational Terminology (Computerm 1998),* (pp. 64–70). ACL Press.

Navigli, R., & Velardi, P. (2004). Learning domain ontologies from document warehouses and dedicated web sites. *Computational Linguistics, 30*(2), 151–179. doi:10.1162/089120104323093276

Navigli, R., Velardi, P., & Gangemi, A. (2003). Ontology learning and its application to automated terminology translation. *IEEE Intelligent Systems, 18*, 22–31. doi:10.1109/MIS.2003.1179190

Nedellec, C., & Nazarenko, A. (2006). *Ontologies and information extraction*. Retrieved from http://arxiv.org/abs/cs/0609137.

New York Time. (2011). *Linked open data*. Retrieved from http://data.nytimes.com/.

Nichols, E., Bond, F., & Flickinger, D. (2005). Robust ontology acquisition from machine-readable dictionaries. In *Proceedings of the International Joint Conference on Artificial Intelligence IJCAI-2005*, (pp. 1111–1116). Edinburgh, UK: IEEE Press.

Niles, I., & Pease, A. (2001). Towards a standard upper ontology. In E. C. Welty & B. Smith (Eds.), *Proceedings of the 2nd International Conference on Formal Ontology in Information Systems (FOIS-2001)*. Ogunquit, ME: IEEE Press.

Nuzzolese, A., Gangemi, A., & Presutti, V. (2011). *Gathering lexical linked data and knowledge patterns from Framenet*. Paper presented at the Sixth International Conference on Knowledge Capture. Banff, Canada.

OAEI. (2011). *Webpage*. Retrieved from http://oaei.ontologymatching.org/.

Oltramari, A., Gangemi, A., Guarino, N., & Masolo, C. (2002). Restructuring Wordnet's top-level: The Ontoclean approach. In *Proceedings of the Language Resources and Evaluation Conference, LREC2002*. ACL Press.

OpenCyc. (2011). *Webpage*. Retrieved from http://www.cyc.com/opencyc.

OWL 2. (2009). *Webpage*. Retrieved from http://www.w3.org/TR/owl2-overview/.

OWLIM. (2011). *Webpage*. Retrieved from http://www.ontotext.com/owlim.

Padó, S. (2006). *User's guide to SIGF: Significance testing by approximate randomisation*. Retrieved from http://www.nlpado.de/~sebastian/sigf.html.

Pantel, P., & Pennacchiotti, M. (2006). Espresso: Leveraging generic patterns for automatically harvesting semantic relations. In *Proceedings of the 21st International Conference on Computational Linguistics and the 44th Annual Meeting of the Association for Computational Linguistics*. Association for Computational Linguistics.

Pantel, P., & Pennacchiotti, M. (2008). Automatically harvesting and ontologizing semantic relations. In Buitelaar, P., & Cimiano, P. (Eds.), *Ontology Learning and Population: Bridging the Gap between Text and Knowledge* (pp. 171–198). Amsterdam: IOS Press.

Pasca, M. (2004). Acquisition of categorized named entities for web search. In *Proceedings of the 13th ACM International Conference on Information and Knowledge Management*, (pp. 137-145). New York, NY: ACM.

Passonneau, R. J. (2006). Measuring agreement on set-valued items (MASI) for semantic and pragmatic annotation. In *Proceedings of the Fifth International Conference on Language Resources and Evaluation*, (pp. 831–836). ACL Press.

Pazienza, M. T., Sguera, S., & Stellato, A. (2007). Let's talk about our "being": A linguistic-based ontology framework for coordinating agents. In R. Ferrario & L. Prévot (Eds.), *Applied Ontology, 2*(3-4), 305-332.

Pazienza, M. T., Stellato, A., & Turbati, A. (2008). Linguistic watermark 3.0: An RDF framework and a software library for bridging language and ontologies in the semantic web. In *Proceedings of the 5th Workshop on Semantic Web Applications and Perspectives*. Rome, Italy: IEEE Press.

Pazienza, M., Scarpato, N., Stellato, A., & Turbati, A. (2008). Din din! The (semantic) turkey is served! *Semantic Web Applications and Perspectives*. Retrieved from http://art.uniroma2.it/publications/docs/2008_SWAP2008_The%20(Semantic)%20Turkey%20is%20served.pdf.

Pazienza, M., Stellato, A., & Turbati, A. (2008). *Linguistic watermark 3.0: An RDF framework and a software library for bridging language and ontologies in the semantic web*. Paper presented at the Semantic Web Applications and Perspectives, 5th Italian Semantic Web Workshop (SWAP2008). Rome, Italy.

Pazienza, M. T., Pennacchiotti, M., & Zanzotto, F. (2005). Terminology extraction: An analysis of linguistic and statistical approaches. In Sirmakessis, S. (Ed.), *Knowledge Mining Series: Studies in Fuzziness and Soft Computing* (pp. 255–279). Heidelberg, Germany: Springer. doi:10.1007/3-540-32394-5_20

Pazienza, M. T., Stellato, A., & Turbati, A. (2010). A suite of semantic web tools supporting development of multilingual ontologies. In Armano, G., de Gemmis, M., Semeraro, G., & Vargiu, E. (Eds.), *Intelligent Information Access*. Berlin, Germany: Springer-Verlag. doi:10.1007/978-3-642-14000-6_6

Pecina, P., & Schlesinger, P. (2006). Combining association measures for collocation extraction. In *Proceedings of the COLING/ACL 2006 Main Conference Poster Sessions*, (pp. 651–658). ACL Press. Retrieved from http://www.aclweb.org/anthology/P/P06/P06-2084.

Pekar, V., & Staab, S. (2002). Taxonomy learning: Factoring the structure of a taxonomy into a semantic classification decision. In *Proceedings of the Nineteenth Conference on Computational Linguistics*, (vol 2), (pp. 786-792). ACL Press.

Penrose, R. (1955). A generalized inverse for matrices. In *Proceedings of the Cambridge Philosophical Society*, (p. 51). Cambridge, UK: Cambridge University Press.

Petasis, G., Karkaletsis, V., Paliouras, G., Androutsopoulos, I., & Spyropoulos, C. D. (2002). Ellogon: A new text engineering platform. In *Proceedings of the 3rd International Conference on Language Resources and Evaluation (LREC 2002)*, (vol 1), (pp. 72-78). Canary Islands, Spain: LREC Press.

Petasis, G., Karkaletsis, V., Paliouras, G., Krithara, A., & Zavitsanos, E. (2011). Ontology population and enrichment: State of the art. In Paliouras, G., Spyropoulos, C., & Tsatsaronis, G. (Eds.), *Knowledge-Driven Multimedia Information Extraction and Ontology Evolution*. Berlin, Germany: Springer Verlag. doi:10.1007/978-3-642-20795-2_6

Peter, H., Sack, H., & Beckstein, C. (2006). *SMARTIN-DEXER – Amalgamating ontologies and lexical resources for document indexing*. Paper presented at the Workshop on Interfacing Ontologies and Lexical Resources for Semantic Web Technologies (OntoLex2006). Genoa, Italy.

Peters, W., Montiel-Ponsoda, E., Aguado de Cea, G., & Gómez-Pérez, A. (2007). Localizing ontologies in OWL. In *Proceedings of the OntoLex07 Workshop*. ISWC Press.

Pianta, E., Bentivogli, L., & Girardi, C. (2002). *Multiwordnet: Developing an aligned multilingual database*. Paper presented at the First International Conference on Global Wordnet. Mysore, India.

Plumbaum, T., Lommatzsch, A., Hennig, L., Luca, E. W. D., & Albayrak, S. (2011). *Improving recommendation quality using semantically enriched user profiles*. Paper submitted to the International Semantic Web Conference 2011 (ISWC2011). Bonn, Germany.

Plumbaum, T., Stelter, T., & Korth, A. (2009). Semantic web usage mining: Using semantics to understand user intentions. In *Proceedings of the 17th International Conference on User Modeling, Adaptation, and Personalization*, (pp. 391–396). Berlin, Germany: Springer-Verlag.

Polleres, A., Krennwallner, T., Lopes, N., Kopecký, J., & Decker, S. (2009). *XSPARQL language specification*. W3C Member Submission, January 2009. Retrieved from http://www.w3c.org.

Ponzetto, S. P., & Strube, M. (2007). Deriving a large-scale taxonomy from Wikipedia, In *Proceedings of the Twenty-Second AAAI Conference on Artificial Intelligence*, (pp. 1440–1445). Menlo Park, CA: AAAI Press.

Popescu, A., & Ungar, L. H. (2003). Statistical relational learning for link prediction. In *Proceedings of the Workshop on Learning Statistical Models from Relational Data*. ACM.

Porzel, R., & Malaka, R. (2004). A task-based approach for ontology evaluation. In *Proceedings of ECAI 2004 Workshop on Ontology Learning and Population*, (pp. 7-12). ECAI Press.

Prévot, L., Borgo, S., & Oltramari, A. (2005). Interfacing ontologies and lexical resources. In *Proceedings of the IJCNLP 2005 Workshop Ontologies and Lexical Resources*, (pp. 91–102). IJCNLP Press.

Princeton. (2011). *Wordnet*. Retrieved from http://wordnet.princeton.edu/.

PROTON 3.0. (2011). *PROTON 3.0 documentation*. Sofia, Bulgaria: Ontotext.

Prud'hommeaux, E., & Seaborne, A. (2008). *SPARQL query language for RDF*. W3C Recommendation 15 January 2008. Retrieved from http://www.w3.org/TR/rdf-sparql-query/.

Rabiner, L. R. (1989). A tutorial on hidden Markov models and selected applications in speech recognition. *Proceedings of the IEEE, 77*(2), 257–286. doi:10.1109/5.18626

Ranieri, M., Pianta, E., & Bentivogli, L. (2004). Browsing multilingual information with the MultiSemCor Web interface. In *Proceedings of the LREC 2004 Satellite Workshop on the Amazing Utility of Parallel and Comparable Corpora,* (pp. 38-41). Portugal: LREC Press.

Ravichandran, D., & Hovy, E. (2002). Learning surface text patterns for a question answering system. In: *Proceedings of the 40th Annual Meeting on Association for Computational Linguistics.* ACL Press.

Reed, S. L., & Lenat, D. B. (2002). Mapping ontologies into Cyc. In *Proceedings of the AAAI 2002 Workshop Ontologies and the Semantic Web,* (pp. 1–6). AAAI Press.

Reinberger, M.-L., & Spyns, P. (2004). Discovering knowledge in texts for the learning of dogma-inspired ontologies. In P. Buitelaar, S. Handschuh, & B. Magnini (Eds.), *Proceedings of the ECAI Workshop on Ontology Learning and Population,* (pp. 19-24). ECAI Press.

Richman, A. E., & Schone, P. (2008). Mining wiki resources for multilingual named entity recognition. In *Proceedings of ACL 2008: HLT,* (pp. 1–9). ACL Press. Retrieved from http://www.aclweb.org/anthology/P/P08/P08-1001.

Rigau, G., Rodríguez, H., & Agirre, E. (1998). Building accurate semantic taxonomies from monolingual MRDs. In *Proceedings of the 17ᵗʰ International Conference on Computational Linguistics and 36ᵗʰ Annual Meeting of the Association for Computational Linguistics COLING-ACL 1998.* Montreal, Canada: ACL Press.

Ritter, A., Soderl, S., & Etzioni, O. (2009). What is this, anyway: Automatic hypernym discovery. In *Proceedings of the AAAI 2009 Spring Symposium on Learning,* (pp. 88-93). AAAI Press.

Roark, B., & Bacchiani, M. (2003). Supervised and unsupervised PCFG adaptation to novel domains. In *Proceedings of the 2003 Conference of the North American Chapter of the Association for Computational Linguistics on Human Language Technology,* (vol 1), (pp. 126-133). Association for Computational Linguistics.

Robison, H. R. (1970). Computer-detectable semantic structures. *Information Storage and Retrieval, 6*(3), 273–288. doi:10.1016/0020-0271(70)90002-1

Rodrigues, T., Rosa, P., & Cardoso, J. (2008). Moving from syntactic to semantic organizations using jxml2owl. *Computers in Industry, 59*(8), 808–819. doi:10.1016/j.compind.2008.06.002

Rosendfeld, B., Feldman, R., & Fresko, M. (2005). Teg-a hybrid approach to information extraction. *Knowledge and Information Systems, 9*(1), 1–18.

Russell, S., & Norvig, P. (2010). *Artificial intelligence: A modern approach.* Upper Saddle River, NJ: Prentice Hall.

Sabou, M., & Gracia, G. (2008). Spider: Bringing non-equivalence mappings to OAEI. In *Proceedings of the 3rd Ontology Matching Workshop (OM 2008), at 7th International Semantic Web Conference (ISWC 2008),* (pp. 199-205). Karlsruhe, Germany: CEUR-WS.

Sag, I. A., Baldwin, T., Bond, F., Copestake, A., & Flickinger, D. (2002). Multiword expressions: A pain in the neck for NLP. In Gelbukh, A. (Ed.), *Computational Linguistics and Intelligent Text Processing* (pp. 189–206). Berlin, Germany: Springer. doi:10.1007/3-540-45715-1_1

Sajous, F., Navarro, E., Gaume, B., Prévot, L., & Chudy, Y. (2010). Semi-automatic endogenous enrichment of collaboratively constructed lexical resources: Piggybacking onto Wiktionary. In H. Loftsson, E. Rögnvaldsson, & S. Helgadóttir (Eds.), *Advances in Natural Language Processing: Proceedings of the 7th International Conference on NLP,* (pp. 332–344). Berlin, Germany: Springer.

Salton, G., Wong, A., & Yang, C. S. (1975). A vector space model for automatic indexing. *Communications of the ACM, 18*(11), 613–620. doi:10.1145/361219.361220

Schein, A. I., Popescul, A., Ungar, L. H., & Pennock, D. M. (2002). Methods and metrics for cold-start recommendations. In *Proceedings of the 25ᵗʰ Annual International ACM Sigir Conference on Research and Development in Information Retrieval,* (pp. 253–260). New York, NY: ACM.

Schmid, H. (1994). Probabilistic part-of-speech tagging using decision trees. In *Proceedings of International Conference on New Methods in Language Processing,* (pp. 44–49). ICLP Press.

Schreiber, G., van Assem, M., & Gangemi, A. (2006). *RDF/OWL representation of WordNet*. Retrieved from http://www.w3.org/TR/2006/WD-wordnet-rdf-20060619/.

Schutze, H. (1993). Word space. *Advances in Neural Information Processing Systems, 5*, 895–902.

Sclano, F., & Velardi, P. (2007). *TermExtractor: A web application to learn the common terminology of interest groups and research communities*. Paper presented at TIA 2007. Sofia Antipolis, France.

Scott, W. A. (1955). Reliability of content analysis: The case of nominal scale coding. *Public Opinion Quarterly, 19*(3), 321–325. doi:10.1086/266577

Settles, B. (2004). Biomedical named entity recognition using conditional random fields and rich feature sets. In *Proceedings of the International Joint Workshop on Natural Language Processing in Biomedicine and its Applications*, (pp. 104-107). IEEE Press.

Sha, F., & Pereira, F. (2003). Shallow parsing with conditional random fields. In *Proceedings of HLT-NAACL*, (pp. 134–141). NAACL Press.

Shamsfar, M., & Barforoush, A. A. (2002). An introduction to HASTI: An ontology learning system. In *Proceedings of 6th Conference on Artificial Intelligence and Soft Computing*. IEEE Press.

Shvaiko, P., & Euzenat, J. (2008). Ten challenges for ontology matching. In *Proceedings of ODBASE*, (pp. 1164-1182). ODBASE Press.

Shvaiko, P., & Euzenat, J. (2005). A survey of schema-based matching approaches. *Journal of Data Semantics, 4*, 146–171.

Siegel, N., Goolsbey, K., Kahlert, R., & Matthews, G. (2004). The Cyc® system: Notes on architecture. In *Proceedings of the AAAI Spring Symposium on Formalizing and Compiling Background Knowledge and Its Applications to Knowledge Representation and Question Answering*, (vol 3864), (pp. 44-49). AAAI Press.

Silva, N., & Rocha, J. (2003). MAFRA – An ontology mapping framework for the semantic web. In *Proceedings of the 6th International Conference on Business information Systems*. Colorado Springs, CO: UCCS.

Simple Knowledge Organization System. (2011). *Webpage*. Retrieved from http://www.w3.org/2004/02/skos/.

Singh, P. (2002). The public acquisition of commonsense knowledge. In *Proceedings of AAAI Spring Symposium on Acquiring (and Using) Linguistic (and World) Knowledge for Information Access*, (pp. 47–52). Menlo Park, CA: The AAAI Press.

Sirin, E., Parsia, B., Grau, B., Kalyanpur, A., & Katz, Y. (2007). Pellet: A practical OWL DL reasoner. *Journal of Web Semantics, 5*(2), 51–53. doi:10.1016/j.websem.2007.03.004

SKB. (2011). *Webpage*. Retrieved from http://skb.ontotext.com.

Snow, R., Jurafsky, D., & Ng, A. Y. (2006). Semantic taxonomy induction from heterogenous evidence. In *Proceedings of the 21st International Conference on Computational Linguistics and the 44th Annual Meeting of the Association for Computational Linguistics*, (pp. 801-808). ACL Press.

Soderland, S. (1997). *Learning text analysis rules for domain-specific natural language processing*. PhD Thesis. Amherst, MA: University of Massachusetts.

Soergel, D., Lauser, B., Liang, A., Fisseha, F., Keizer, J., & Katz, S. (2004). Reengineering thesauri for new applications: The AGROVOC example. *Journal of Digital Information, 4*(4).

Stanford. (1998). *KIF*. Retrieved from http://logic.stanford.edu/kif/.

Stanford. (2009). *First order predicate logic*. Retrieved from http://plato.stanford.edu/entries/logic-classical/.

State of the LOD Cloud. (2011). *Webpage*. Retrieved from http://www4.wiwiss.fu-berlin.de/lodcloud/state.

Studer, R., Benjamin, V. R., & Fensel, D. (1998). Knowledge engineering: Principles and methods. *IEEE Transactions on Data and Knowledge Engineering, 25*(1-2), 161–199.

Suchanek, F. (2009). *Automated construction and growth of a large ontology*. Unpublished Doctoral Dissertation. Saarbrücken, Germany: Saarland University.

Suchanek, F. M., Kasneci, G., & Weikum, G. (2007). Yago: A core of semantic knowledge. In *Proceedings of the 16th international World Wide Web conference (WWW 2007)*, (pp. 697–706). ACM. Retrieved from http://doi.acm.org/10.1145/1242572.1242667.

Suchanek, F., Kasneci, G., & Weikum, G. (2008). YAGO – A large ontology from Wikipedia and WordNet. *Web Semantics: Science. Services and Agents on the World Wide Web, 6*(3), 203–217. doi:10.1016/j.websem.2008.06.001

SUMO. (2011). *Webpage.* Retrieved from http://www.ontologyportal.org/.

Surowiecki, J. (2005). *The wisdom of crowds.* New York, NY: Anchor Books.

SWEO. (2011). *Webpage.* Retrieved http://www.w3.org/2001/sw/sweo/.

Szpektor, I., Tanev, H., Dagan, I., & Coppola, B. (2004). Scaling web-based acquisition of entailment relations. In *Proceedings of EMNLP 2004.* EMNLP Press.

Terziev, I., Kiryakov, A., & Manov, D. (2005). *D.1.8.1: Base upper-level ontology (BULO) guidance.* Deliverable of EU-IST Project IST – 2003 – 506826 SEKT. Retrieved from http://www.sekt-project.com.

Thompson, H. S., Beech, D., Maloney, M., & Mendelsohn, N. (2004). *XML schema part 1: Structures* (2nd ed). W3C Recommendation 28 October 2004. Retrieved from http://www.w3c.org.

TNA. (2011). *Webpage.* Retrieved from http://www.nationalarchives.gov.uk/.

Tomanek, K., Wermter, J., & Hahn, U. (2007). Sentence and token splitting based on conditional random fields. In *Proceedings of the 10th Conference of the Pacific Association for Computational Linguistics*, (pp. 49–57). PACL Press.

TopBraidComposer. (2011). *Ontology editor.* Retrieved from http://www.topquadrant.com/products/TB_Composer.html.

Toral, A., & Muñoz, R. (2006). A proposal to automatically build and maintain gazetteers for named entity recognition by using Wikipedia. In *Proceedings of the ACL 2006 Workshop on New Text: Wikis and Blogs and Other Dynamic Text Sources*, (pp. 56–61). ACL Press. Retrieved from http://www.aclweb.org/anthology/W/W06/W06-2809.pdf.

Toumouth, A., Lehireche, A., Widdows, D., & Malki, M. (2006). Adapting WordNet to the medical domain using lexicosyntactic patterns in the ohsumed corpus. In *Proceedings of IEEE International Conference on Computer Systems and Applications*, (pp. 1029-1036). IEEE Computer Society.

Tratz, S., & Hovy, E. (2010). A taxonomy, dataset, and classifier for automatic noun compound interpretation. In *Proceedings of the 48th Annual Meeting of the Association for Computational Linguistics*, (pp. 678–687). Retrieved from http://www.aclweb.org/anthology/P10-1070.

UK Government. (2011). *CGO.* Retrieved from http://data.gov.uk.

UMBEL 3.0. (2011). *Webpage.* Retrieved from http://umbel.org/content/finally-umbel-v-100.

UMBEL. (2011). *Webpage.* Retrieved from http://www.umbel.org/.

Urbani, J., Kotoulas, S., Maassen, J., Drost, N., Seinstra, F., van Harmelen, F., & Bal, H. (2010). *WebPIE: A web-scale parallel inference engine.* Retrieved from http://www.few.vu.nl/~jui200/papers/ccgrid-scale10.pdf.

URI. (2011). *Wikipedia article.* Retrieved from http://en.wikipedia.org/wiki/Uniform_Resource_Identifier.

van Assem, M., Gangemi, A., & Schreiber, G. (2004). *Wordnet in RDFS and OWL.* Retrieved from http://www.w3c.org.

van Assem, M., Gangemi, A., & Schreiber, G. (2006). *RDF/OWL representation of WordNet.* Retrieved from http://www.w3.org/2001/sw/bestpractices/wnet/wn-conversion.html.

Vapnik, V. (1995). *The nature of statistical learning theory.* Berlin, Germany: Springer.

Vaquero, A., Sáenz, F., & Álvarez, F. J. (2007). A review of common problems in linguistic resources and a new way to represent ontological relationships. *Electronic Journal of Argentine Society for Informatics and Operations Research, 7*(1), 1–11.

Velardi, P., Navigli, R., Cucchiarelli, A., & Neri, F. (2005). Evaluation of ontolearn: A methodology for automatic population of domain ontologie. In *Ontology Learning from Text: Methods, Applications and Evaluation.* IOS Press.

Villada Moirón, B., & Tiedemann, J. (2006). Identifying idiomatic expressions using automatic word-alignment. In *Proceedings of the EACL 2006 Workshop on Multiword Expressions in a Multilingual Context,* (pp. 33–40). Retrieved from http://www.aclweb.org/anthology/W/W06/W06-2405.pdf.

Vintar, S., Buitelaar, P., & Volk, M. (2003). Semantic relations in concept-based cross-language medical information retrieval. In *Proceedings of the ECML/PKDD Workshop on Adaptive Text Extraction and Mining.* Croatia: ECML Press.

Vossen, P. (1999). *EuroWordNet general document, version 3, final.* Retrieved from www.illc.uva.nl/EuroWordNet/docs/GeneralDocPS.zip.

Vossen, P. (1998). Introduction to EuroWordNet. *Computers and the Humanities, 32*(2–3), 73–89. doi:10.1023/A:1001175424222

W3C. (2004). *OWL web ontology language.* Retrieved from http://www.w3.org/TR/owl-features/.

W3C. (2009). *SKOS simple knowledge organization system reference.* Retrieved from http://www.w3.org.

Wang, T., Bontcheva, K., Li, Y., & Cunningham, H. (2005). *Ontology-based information extraction (obie) v 2.* Berlin, Germany: Semantically Enabled Knowledge Technologies.

Wermter, J., & Hahn, U. (2005). Finding new terminology in very large corpora. In P. Clark & G. Schreiber (Eds.), *Proceedings of the 3rd International Conference on Knowledge Capture (K-CAP 2005),* (pp.137–144). Retrieved from http://doi.acm.org/10.1145/1088622.1088648.

Widdows, D., & Dorow, B. (2002). A graph model for unsupervised lexical acquisition. In *Proceedings of the 19th International Conference on Computational Linguistics,* (pp. 1093-1099). Taipei, Taiwan: ACL Press.

Wikipedia. (2011a). *Master data.* Retrieved from http://en.wikipedia.org/wiki/Master_data as of January 2011.

Wikipedia. (2011b). *Reference data.* Retrieved from http://en.wikipedia.org/wiki/Reference_data as of January 2011.

Wilkinson, M., Vandervalk, B., & McCarthy, L. (2009). SADI semantic web services - Cause you can't always get what you want! In *Proceedings of the IEEE International Workshop on Semantic Web Services in Practice,* (pp 13-18). Singapore: IEEE Press.

Withbrock, M. (2007). *Knowledge is more than data.* Retrieved from http://www.cyc.com/cyc/technology/whitepapers_dir/Knowledge_is_more_than_Data.pdf.

Witte, R., & Gitzinger, T. (2009). Semantic assistants -- User-centric natural language processing services for desktop clients. In *Proceedings of the 3rd Asian Semantic Web Conference (ASWC 2008),* (vol 5367), (pp. 360-374). Bangkok, Thailand: Springer.

Witte, R., & Papadakis, N. (2009). *Semantic assistants: SOA for text mining.* Paper presented at the CASCON 2009 Technical Showcase. Markham, Canada.

Wolter, R., & Haselden, K. (2006). The what, why, and how of master data management. *Microsoft Corporation.* Retrieved from http://msdn.microsoft.com/en-us/library/bb190163.aspx.

World Geodetic System. (1984). *Webpage.* Retrieved from https://www1.nga.mil/PRODUCTSSERVICES/GEODESYGEOPHYSICS/WORLDGEODETICSYSTEM/Pages/default.aspx.

Yamaguchi, T. (1999). Constructing domain ontologies based on concept drift analysis. In *Proceedings of IJCAI 1999 Workshop on Ontologies and Problem-Solving Methods: Lessons Learned and Future Trends.* Stockholm, Sweden: ACL Press.

Yeh, A. (2000). More accurate tests for the statistical significance of result differences. In *Proceedings of the 18th Conference on Computational linguistics,* (vol 2), (pp. 947-953). Association for Computational Linguistics.

Yoshida, K., Tsuruoka, Y., Miyao, Y., & Tsujii, J. I. (2007). Ambiguous part-of-speech tagging for improving accuracy and domain portability of syntactic parsers. In *Proceedings of the Twentieth International Joint Conference on Artificial Intelligence,* (pp. 1783-1788). IEEE Press.

Zanzotto, F. M., Pennacchiotti, M., & Pazienza, M. T. (2006). Discovering asymmetric entailment relations between verbs using selectional preferences. In *Proceedings of the 21st International Conference on Computational Linguistics and 44th Annual Meeting of the Association for Computational Linguistics,* (pp. 849-856). Association for Computational Linguistics.

Zesch, T., Müller, C., & Gurevych, I. (2008a). Extracting lexical semantic knowledge from Wikipedia and Wiktionary. In *Proceedings of the 6th International Conference on Language Resources and Evaluation,* (pp. 1646–1652). ACL Press.

Zesch, T., Müller, C., & Gurevych, I. (2008b). Using Wiktionary for computing semantic relatedness. In *Proceedings of the Twenty-Third AAAI Conference on Artificial Intelligence,* (pp. 861–867). AAAI Press.

Zesch, T., Gurevych, I., & Mühlhäuser, M. (2007). Analyzing and accessing Wikipedia as a lexical semantic resource. In Rehm, G., Witt, A., & Lemnitzer, L. (Eds.), *Data Structures for Linguistic Resources and Applications* (pp. 197–205). Tübingen, Germany: Gunter Narr.

Zhang, Z., Iria, J., Brewster, C., & Ciravegna, F. (2008). A comparative evaluation of term recognition algorithms. In N. Calzolari, et al. (Eds.), *Proceedings of the 6th International Conference on Language Resources and Evaluation (LREC 2008),* (pp. 2208–2013). Paris, France: ELRA. Retrieved from http://www.lrec-conf.org/proceedings/lrec2008/pdf/538_paper.pdf.

Zhang, Z., Xia, L., Greenwood, M. A., & Iria, J. (2009). Too many mammals: Improving the diversity of automatically recognized terms. In *Proceedings of the International Conference on Recent Advances in Natural Language Processing 2009 (RANLP 2009),* (pp. 490–495). Retrieved from http://www.aclweb.org/anthology/R09-1087.

Zhou, G., Su, J., Zhang, J., & Zhang, M. (2005). Exploring various knowledge in relation extraction. In *Proceedings of the 43rd Annual Meeting on Association for Computational Linguistics,* (pp. 427–434). ACL Press.

Zhou, G., & Zhang, M. (2007). Extracting relation information from text documents by exploring various types of knowledge. *Information Processing & Management, 43*(4), 969–982. doi:10.1016/j.ipm.2006.09.012

Zitgist. (2011). *Webpage.* Retrieved from http://www.zitgist.com/.

About the Contributors

Maria Teresa Pazienza is currently full Professor of Artificial Intelligence at the Engineering Faculty of the University of Roma "Tor Vergata," where she founded dedicated curricula on AI both at degree and doctoral levels. She coordinates research and development activities on Artificial Intelligence, Knowledge Representation and Management, and Natural Language Processing at the Department of Enterprise Engineering, where she founded the ART Laboratory in 1988 (http://art.uniroma2.it/). Her areas of expertise include education, research, system development, and user applications of AI technologies (natural language processing, information extraction, conceptual knowledge engineering, applied ontologies, knowledge-based systems, linguistic resources production, linguistic agents, semantic Web). She is author/co-author of more than 150 scientific publications. Professor Pazienza cooperates with several research groups, international institutions, and companies for NLP research and application programs. In the context of European consortia/projects, she has been (and currently is) responsible for the activities carried out at the University of Roma "Tor Vergata." She is reviewer and evaluator for the European Community, for the Danish Council for Strategic Research, for the Science Foundation Ireland, for Chile Superior Council of the National Fund for Scientific and Technological Development, and for the Italian Ministry of University. In 2010 she received the IBM Faculty Award. She is on the editorial board of a few international journals (*Journal of Terminology*, *Cognitive Processing*, and *Applied Ontology*), in the scientific committee of CERTIA (academic consortium for cognitive science and applied AI technologies), and participates in the scientific committees of several international conferences on AI. Professor Pazienza is director of the Unit of Roma Tor Vergata University for CINI Consortium, and is in the Steering Committee of ESA (European Space Agency), ESRIN, and Roma Tor Vergata University Convention.

Armando Stellato obtained a PhD in Computer Science at the University of Rome, Tor Vergata, with a thesis on "Alignment and Mediation of Distributed Information Sources in the Semantic Web" and is working, since 2005, as a Research Associate at the ART Research group of the University of Tor Vergata. He is author of more than 50 publications in conferences and journals in the fields of Semantic Web, Natural Language Processing, and other related fields and has been in the program committee of many academic events. Currently his main interests cover Architecture Design for Knowledge-Based Systems, Management of Knowledge Elicitation Processes, and Onto-Linguistic Interfaces. He is also consultant at the Food and Agriculture Organization (FAO) of the United Nations as a Semantic Architect, and he is working on all aspects (vocabulary design, publication on Linked Open Data, evolution of FAO software for collaborative RDF management known as VocBench) related to the maintenance and publication of FAO RDF vocabularies and resources such as AGROVOC, Biotech, and Journal Authority Data.

* * *

Feten Baccar Ben Amar received an Engineering degree in Computer Science in 2006 from the National Engineering School of Sfax University, Tunisia, and a Master degree in Computer Sciences in 2008 from the Faculty of Economic Sciences and Management of Sfax University, Tunisia. Since 2009, she has been preparing her PhD in Computer Sciences, and is a member of the Multimédia Information Systems and Advanced Computing (MIRACL) Laboratory of Sfax University, Tunisia. Her research is focused on ontology building from LMF-standardized dictionaries especially in the case of Arabic language.

Ivan Bedini is a Member of the Technical Staff at Bell Labs Research in Ireland. He holds a PhD in Computer Science from the University of Versailles. Before Bell Labs he was a Research Engineer at Orange Labs in France, where he held various research, standardization, and technical project management roles. Since 2000, he has contributed to several projects related to Workflow and BPM (Business Process Management) as developer, consultant, and technical project manager. In 2004, he specialised in B2B (Business to Business) and became a member of the UN/CEFACT Information Content Management Group and member of OASIS an ebXML Registry/Repository Committee. Since 2007 his interests focus on knowledge engineering, information extraction, semantic technologies, and he has actively contributed to research and innovation projects related to semantic data representation and applications.

Michael K. Bergman is the CEO and co-founder of Structured Dynamics LLC, a provider of software and professional services for the semantic Web, and co-editor of the lightweight UMBEL reference concept ontology. He is author of the popular *AI3: Adaptive Innovation* blog (http://mkbergman.com). For the past twenty years, Mike has been an independent consultant, a Web scientist, and an entrepreneur. Mike was CEO of Zitgist LLC, SD's predecessor company, and for six years the co-founder, CTO, and chairman of BrightPlanet Corporation, a deep Web search firm. Prior software companies include VisualMetrics Corporation, a data warehousing firm with an emphasis on large-scale Internet databases and bioinformatics, and TheWebTools Company, a pioneer in metasearch tools. Mike is an acknowledged expert in federated search, information theory, document content, and semi-structured data. He was a magna cum laude graduate of Pomona College in botany and a doctoral candidate at Duke University in population genetics.

Aidan Boran is a Member of the Technical Staff in Bell Labs Research since 2004. He received his PhD from the Trinity College of Dublin. He has more than twenty years of experience in Telco domain and Network administration. In 2004 he started to work in semantic technologies domain and information integration. He is currently working on the application of semantic Web technologies to enable simple access to Telco data and is co-founder of the Semantic Data Access program at Bell Labs Research. Prior to Bell Labs, he was Technical Manager at Lucent Technology Network Management Development division.

Mariana Damova is a Knowledge Management Expert at Ontotext AD, where she specializes in ontology engineering and linked data management. She has degrees in Classical Studies from Sofia University, Multilingual Engineering from Sorbonne-Paris 13, and a PhD in Linguistics from the University of Stuttgart. Mariana is also a Lecturer at the New Bulgarian University. She has contributed to several unique systems such as morphological knowledge base and a large-scale computational dictionary (Morpho-Assistant, Bulgaria), machine translation (VerbMobil, Germany), natural language understanding and dialogue (Virtual Customer Service Representative, Canada), information extraction and retrieval (DioWeb, Canada), and recently semantic technologies projects. Mariana was the Chief Linguistic Officer at Delphes Technologies International and an Associate Director of Speech Recognition Technologies at Bell Canada. She regularly reviews books and articles for acmreviews.com and has authored publications in linguistics and semantic technologies.

Ernesto William De Luca is Head of the Competence Center for Information Retrieval and Machine Learning at the DAI-Lab, Berlin Institute of Technology, Germany. His research areas include Semantic Web technologies, Recommender Systems, and Information Retrieval. He has authored more than 50 papers in national and international conferences, books, and journals in these fields. He has organized a large number of workshops and served as programme committee member at top level conferences.

Davide Eynard is a Post Doctoral Researcher at University of Lugano, Switzerland, and Politecnico di Milano, Italy. He earned a MS in Computer Engineering in 2005 and a PhD in Computer Science in 2009 at Politecnico di Milano. His current research is mainly focused on participative systems (such as wikis, folksonomies, and annotation systems) and Semantic Web technologies, following two different approaches: on the one hand, using semantics in social systems, with the aim of making them better while incentivising user participation; on the other hand, studying the possibility of extracting knowledge from unstructured or semi-structured user generated contents.

Francesca Fallucchi is currently a Researcher at University of Rome Guglielmo Marconi. She is a PhD in Computer Science and Engineering at the University of Rome Tor Vergata. The title of her thesis is "Exploiting Transitivity in Probabilistic Models for Ontology Learning," and she is working, since 2006, as a Researcher at the ART Research group of the University of Tor Vergata. She is the author of publications in conferences and journals in the fields of Semantic Web, Natural Language Processing, and related fields. Currently her main interests cover probabilistic taxonomy learning, ontology learning, and ontology engineering. She is also researching in dialogue systems for cultural heritage and education support. She has a collaboration through the ART Research Group with the international organization European Space Agency (ESA) as a Researcher and as a Software Designer and Developer.

Bilel Gargouri received his PhD in Computer Sciences in 2000 from the Faculty of Economic Sciences and Management of Sfax University, Tunisia. He is currently an Associate Professor in the Department of Computer Science at the Faculty of Economic Sciences and Management of Sfax, Tunisia. He is a member of the MIRACL Laboratory of Sfax University, Tunisia. His research is mainly focused on electronic dictionaries management and natural language processing, especially for Arabic language.

Frédérick Giasson is a Computer Scientist, a Software Developer, and an Entrepreneur. He is the CTO and Co-Founder of Structured Dynamics LLC, a thought leader and innovator helping to catalyze the semantic enterprise using the Semantic Web and open source technologies that they develop. He co-founded Zitgist LLC in 2006 and was its Chief Technology Officer until 2008. He is the Creator or Co-Creator of multiple projects such as: structWSF, conStruct, Semantic Components, OSF, Citizen DAN, irON, UMBEL, the Music Ontology, the Bibliographic Ontology, and many projects from Zitgist such as the Zitgist DataViewer and Ping the Semantic Web.

Maurice Grinberg is an Associate Professor in Cognitive Science and Physics at the New Bulgarian University and a Project Manager at Ontotext AD. He is also a Director of the HiLab Usability Lab at the Central and East European Center for Cognitive Science at NBU. His interests include cognitive modeling, cognitive technologies for the semantic Web, conceptual change, clustering of large datasets, etc. He is the author of a number of publications in the field of fundamental and applied cognitive science and physics. He has also been the Principal Investigator in several FP6 and FP7 European projects, among which are MindRaces, Rascalli, LarKC, and Render. He is a member of the II European Network for the Advancement of Artificial Cognitive Systems, Interaction, and Robotics, EuCogII.

Iryna Gurevych is full Professor in the Computer Science Department of the Technische Universität (TU) Darmstadt in Germany. She holds an endowed Lichtenberg-Chair "Ubiquitous Knowledge Processing" of the Volkswagen Foundation with a focus in Natural Language Processing (NLP) and analyzing unstructured text data on the Web. Iryna Gurevych has founded and coordinates the interdisciplinary research initiative "Web Research" (WeRC) at the TU Darmstadt. Iryna's research primarily concerns approaches that utilize the collective intelligence on the Web, such as collaboratively constructed semantic resources, to enhance the performance of NLP techniques. These techniques include opinion mining, paraphrase recognition, question answering, summarization, and collaborative acquisition of lexical semantic knowledge. She has authored and co-authored papers in major journals and conferences in Natural Language Processing and Computational Linguistics. Iryna Gurevych has recently organized two workshops on "Collaboratively Constructed Semantic Resources" (ACL-IJCNLP 2009 and COLING 2010) and is Co-Editor of the Special Issue of the *Language Resources and Evaluation Journal* on this topic.

Abdelmajid Ben Hamadou received his PhD in Computer Sciences from the Orsay University of Paris, France, in 1979 and his "Doctorat d'Etat" in Computer Sciences from University of Tunis, in 1993. Currently he is a full Professor at the Higher Institute of Computer Sciences and Multimedia, Sfax, Tunisia, and he is also the Director of the research laboratory MIRACL. He has published 20 papers in refereed journals and lecture notes and about 100 papers in conference proceedings. His research areas include software engineering, object oriented software development, and natural language processing.

Silvana Hartmann is a Research Associate at the Ubiquitous Knowledge Processing (UKP) Lab at the Technische Universität Darmstadt in Germany. Her research primarily concerns mining lexical semantic knowledge from collaborative and expert-built lexical semantic resources and utilizing this information to enhance the performance of question answering systems based on social media content. Her research interests include mining and interpretation of multiword expressions, the acquisition of semantic role information, and their application in various fields, such as question answering and digital humanities. Silvana holds a degree in Computational Linguistics ("Diplom Linguistik") from Universität Stuttgart, Germany, where she previously worked on developing discriminative language models for query re-ranking in recall-driven query expansion.

Elias Iosif received the Diploma and the MS degrees from the Department of Electronic and Computer Engineering, Technical University of Crete, Greece, in 2005 and 2007, respectively. Since 2007, he is a Research Assistant and a PhD student at the Department of Electronic and Computer Engineering,

Technical University of Crete, Greece. He is a member of the Cyprus Scientific and Technical Chamber since 2005 and IEEE Student Member since 2008. His research interests include Natural Language Processing, Computational Linguistics, and Web Mining.

Vangelis Karkaletsis has substantial experience in the field of Language and Knowledge Engineering, applied to content analysis, data fusion from multimedia content, ontology engineering, and personalization. He has been involved in several national and international RTD projects. He was the coordinator of the DG-SANCO project MedIEQ, technical manager of the SIAP project QUATRO Plus, and coordinator of the national project OntoSum. He is the Technical Manager of the EC-funded project NOMAD on opinion mining and argument extraction from social media. He is Research Director at NCSRD and head of the Software and Knowledge Engineering Lab. He was the Local Chair of the 12th Conference of the European Chapter of the Association for Computational Linguistics (EACL-09), held in Athens, and Co-Chair of the 6th Hellenic Conference on Artificial Intelligence (SETN-2010).

Atanas Kiryakov obtained his M.Sc. degree in CS from the Sofia University, Bulgaria, in 1995, with a thesis on Knowledge Representation (KR). His research interests include KR, ontologies, lexical semantics, reasoning, information extraction, information retrieval. He is the author of more than 20 refereed publications and book chapters and is involved in the program committees of most of the international scientific events in the area of the Semantic Web. In 2000, Atanas Kiryakov founded Ontotext lab, which became Ontotext AD in 2008. This Bulgarian company is now a leading developer of core semantic technology with representatives in many countries around the world. Since 2000, Kiryakov has been a member of the board of Sirma Group. In 2005, he also became a member of the board of Innovantage, a vertical search engine providing business intelligence for the recruitment market in the UK.

Fabio Marfia is a Computer Engineer graduated at Politecnico di Milano in 2010. His research mainly deals with ontology learning from text and the application of data mining techniques on semantic annotations. He is currently working as an information technology consultant for the business intelligence company Simbologica S.R.L. (Milano, Italy).

Christopher J. Matheus is a Member of the Technical Staff at Bell Labs Research in Ireland, where he leads the Semantic Data Access effort in exploring ways of applying semantic technologies to simplify the access to and processing of distributed heterogeneous data sources and services. He received his Ph.D. from the University of Illinois at Urbana-Champaign in 1989 in the area of machine learning. He has more than twenty-five years of R&D experience in the areas of Semantic Web technologies, artificial intelligence, interactive Web applications, machine learning, knowledge discovery and technology management. Prior to joining Bell Labs in 2010, Dr. Matheus was the Chief Technology Officer at VIStology, a Boston R&D firm specializing in the application of semantic technologies to problems in the area of information fusion and situation awareness. Earlier in his career, he did research at Oak Ridge National Laboratories and spent ten years at GTE Laboratories (now Verizon Technologies) specializing in the areas of artificial intelligence and interactive Internet technologies. Dr. Matheus has more than 70 technical publications, was both a University Fellow and a Cognitive Science/AI Fellow at UIUC, is a recipient of the Leslie Warner Technical Achievement Award, and is a former Thomas J. Watson Fellow.

Matteo Matteucci is an Assistant Professor at the Politecnico di Milano. In 1999 he earned a Laurea degree in Computer Engineering at Politecnico di Milano; in 2002, he earned a Master of Science in Knowledge Discovery and Data Mining at Carnegie Mellon University (Pittsburgh, PA), and in 2003, a PhD in Computer Engineering and Automation at the Politecnico di Milano. He is working in both Robotics and Machine Learning, mainly applying, in a practical way, techniques for adaptation and learning to autonomous robotics systems. He has applied learning methods to different industrial and academic applications. Bayesian approaches to model adaptation and learning, development of models from biological signals, adaptive color modeling, augmented and alternative language models for user support systems, adaptive models for traffic prediction optimization and modeling are just few examples of his activity in complex system modeling.

Christian M. Meyer is a Research Associate at the Ubiquitous Knowledge Processing (UKP) Lab at the Technische Universität Darmstadt in Germany. His research primarily concerns mining lexical semantic knowledge from Wikipedia and Wiktionary and aligning lexical resources and sense inventories at the level of word senses. He has been the main author of multiple long papers accepted at peer-reviewed NLP conferences, including major conferences such as IJCNLP. Recently, he has been a reviewer at the CICLing 2011 conference. He holds a M.Sc. in Computer Science from the Technische Universität Darmstadt, Germany, where he previously worked on automatic question answering using collaboratively created knowledge resources.

Benjamin Nguyen is alumni from the Ecole Normale Supérieure de Cachan, and received his PhD from University of Paris XI in 2003. He has been Associate Professor at the University of Versailles St. Quentin (France) since 2004, and previously Associate Director of the Computer Science Department of the University of Versailles St. Quentin. He is member of the PRiSM Laboratory (UMR 8133 CNRS) since 2004 and the INRIA Secured and Mobile Information Systems (SMIS) team since 2010. His current interests concern two main areas: a) the Web: its social aspects, in particular the problem of privacy in the management of personal information or business information; and b) the management of semi-structured information (XML/XQuery). He is Invited Expert in the W3C XML Query WG.

Peter F. Patel-Schneider is a Member of the Technical Staff in Bell Labs Research. He received his Ph. D. from the University of Toronto in 1987. Peter was a member of the AI Principles Research Department at AT&T Bell Laboratories from 1988 to 1995, and went to AT&T Labs – Research when AT&T split up. In August 1997 he rejoined Bell Labs. Peter's research interests centre on the properties and use of Description Logics, particularly in the W3C OWL Web Ontology Language. Peter has designed and implemented large sections of CLASSIC, a description logic-based knowledge representation system. He designed and implemented DLP, a heavily-optimized prover for expressive description logics and propositional modal logics. He has performed extensive empirical evaluation of DLP and other provers for description logics and propositional modal logics. He developed much of OWL, and its predecessor, DAML+OIL.

Georgios Petasis has extensive experience in language technology and, in particular, shallow information extraction techniques. Having performed basic and applied research for the last 15 years, he has published work in the areas of named-entity recognition, information extraction, ontology learning, linguistic resources, speech synthesis, natural language infrastructures, grammatical inference and machine learning. He is the author of the Ellogon language engineering platform and the eg-GRIDS+ grammatical inference algorithm. Finally, he has been involved in more than ten European and national research projects.

Kiril Simov is an Associate Professor at the Institute of Information and Communication Technologies (IICT), Bulgarian Academy of Sciences, and an Ontology Consultant at Ontotext AD. His interests include computational linguistics, formal grammars, lexical semantics, knowledge representation, and semantic technology. Kiril Simov is the author of numerous publications in the area of NLP, language resources, ontology developments, and applications. He was the principal researcher in three successful German-Bulgarian projects and several FP6 and FP7 European projects: LT4eL, AsIsKnown, LTfLL, and EuroMatrixPlus. He is also the Bulgarian coordinator for the infrastructural EU project CLARIN. He was a member of the standing committee of the international Head-Driven Phrase Structure Grammar Society (2002-2009) and a member of the board of the European chapter of Association for Computational Linguistics (2007-2010).

György Szarvas is a Senior Researcher at the Computer Science Department of the Technische Universität (TU) Darmstadt in Germany. He holds a PhD in Computer Science from the University of Szeged, Hungary. György's research interests include natural language processing, and in particular the application of machine learning techniques to linguistic problems (such as detection and processing of modalities in text, named entity recognition, multiword expression mining, classification of semantic relations, recognition of paraphrases) to improve information extraction from text documents. He authored and co-authored more than 30 peer-reviewed publications in the area of natural language processing, and among other activities, co-organized the CoNLL 2010 Shared Task: Learning to Detect Hedges and their Scope in Natural Language Texts.

Andrea Turbati is a PhD student at the University of Rome, Tor Vergata, where he also obtained his MSc degree in Computer Science and Engineering in 2008. His main interests are knowledge representation and ontology engineering. Currently he is working on the definition and implementation of an architecture and framework for ontology development and population based on the elicitation of unstructured text annotated using the UIMA architecture. For the last 3 years, he's been contributing to the courses of "Knowledge and Data Management" and "Artificial Intelligence" at the Engineering Faculty of the University of Rome, Tor Vergata. Since 2011, he has been part of the Program Committee of the Semantic Technology and Knowledge Engineering Conference (STAKE).

Fabio Massimo Zanzotto is an Associate Professor at the Faculty of Humanities University of Rome, Tor Vergata. His main interests are on applying machine learning models on natural language processing syntactic and semantic tasks. In recent years, he has been particularly active in the area of textual entailment recognition. He proposed novel models and systems to learn textual entailment recognizers from labeled and unlabeled data. He is also focused on modular and lexicalized approaches to syntactic parsing and to shallow models for semantic analysis. He participated in many national and international projects, where natural language processing has been one of the core technologies. He is the author of more than 90 publications on international conferences, workshops, and journals.

Index

X

XML Schema Component 104
XML Schema (XSD) 80

Y

YAGO 137-138, 157, 179, 240, 256